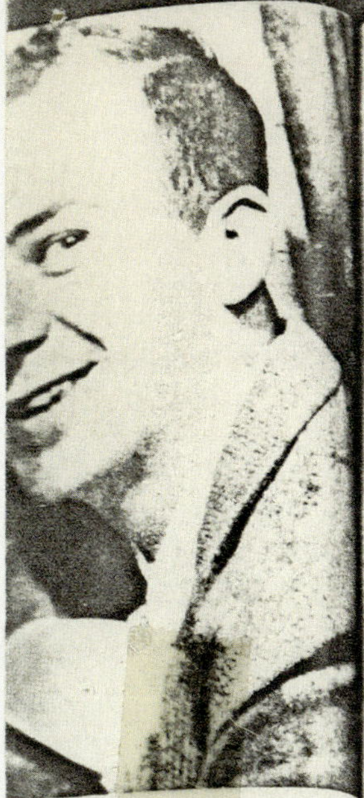

So...

So...even though

to do the same th

To look at it?

To look at it and

What were you t

Yeh...I guess so.

was trying to know

one picture. Then

article saying___H

be photographs of

Can you guess whic

the bottom which o

This doesn't look like this

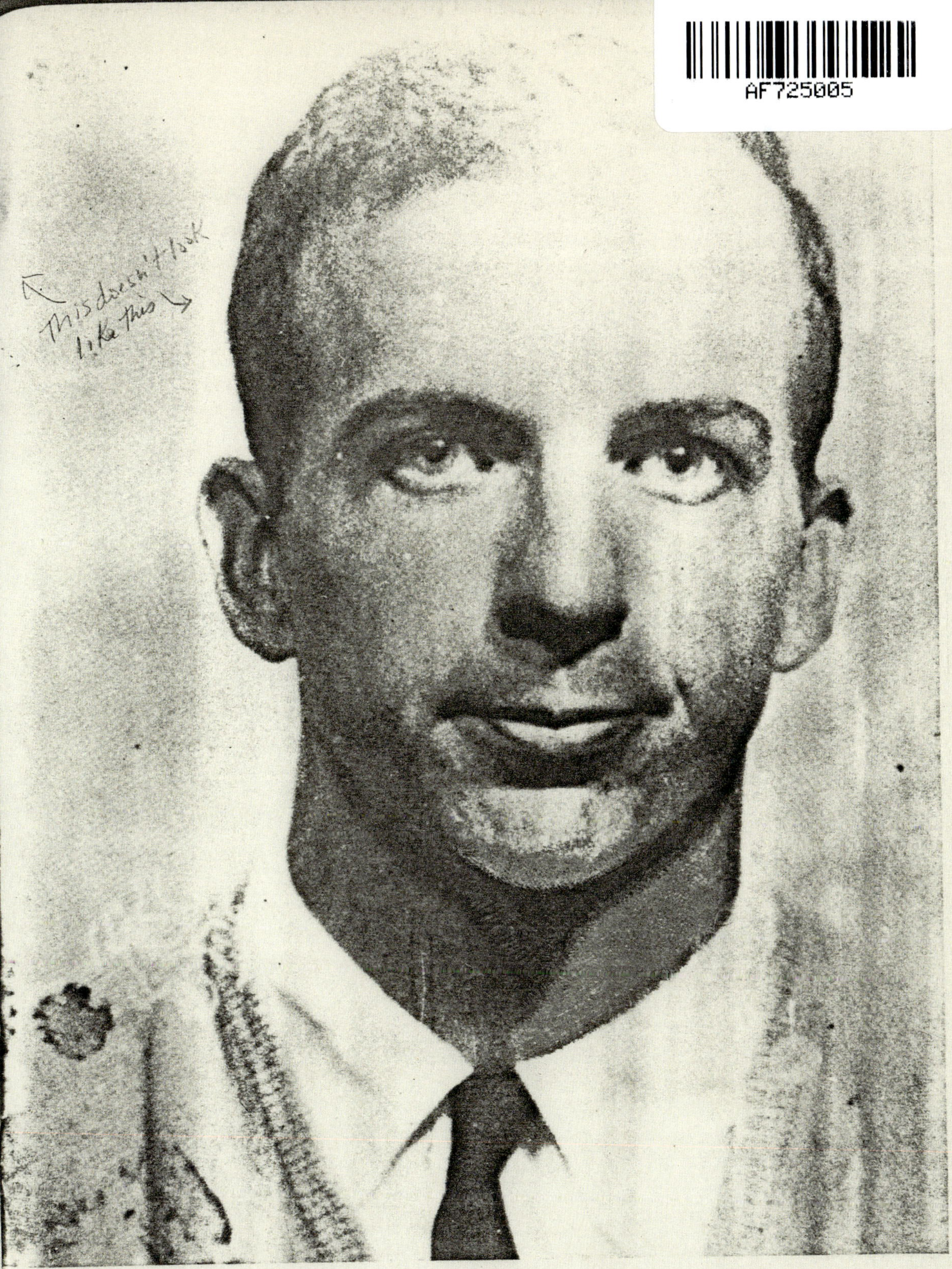

Lee in a photograph taken in September 1963, probably in New Orleans. (NATIONAL ARCHIVES) by whom?

Oswald (2)

Question: Is that all? Didn't they tell you why?

Answer: People usually kill somebody they know.

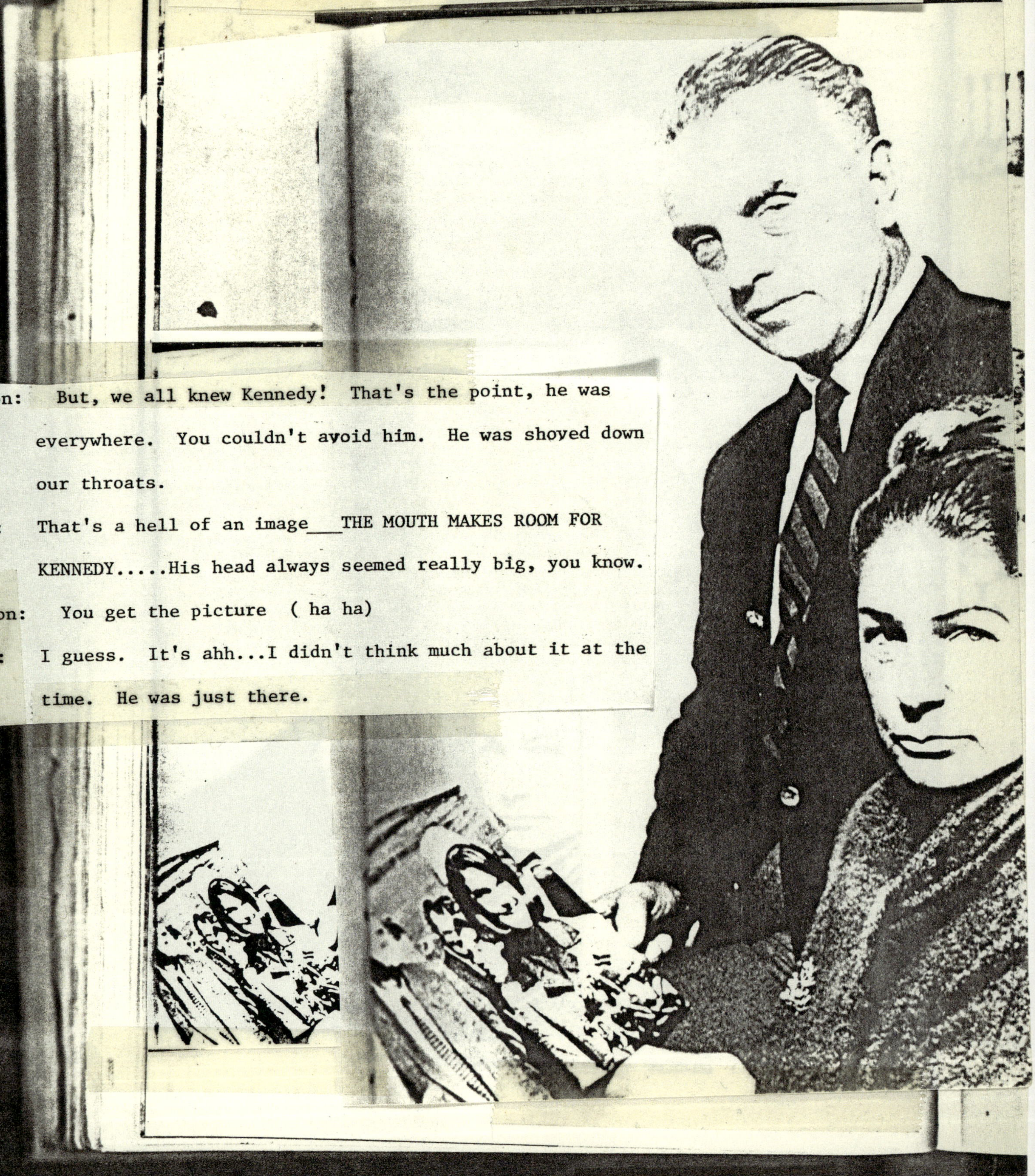

Question: But, we all knew Kennedy! That's the point, he was everywhere. You couldn't avoid him. He was shoved down our throats.

Answer: That's a hell of an image___THE MOUTH MAKES ROOM FOR KENNEDY.....His head always seemed really big, you know.

Question: You get the picture (ha ha)

Answer: I guess. It's ahh...I didn't think much about it at the time. He was just there.

Question: Kennedy?

Answer: Yeh.

E V E R Y T H I N G I S C O N N E C T E D

E V E R Y T H I N G I S C O N N E C T E D

A R T A N D C O N S P I R A C Y

Douglas Eklund and Ian Alteveer

With contributions by Meredith A. Brown, John Miller, Kathryn Olmsted, and Beth Saunders

Preface by Jonathan Lethem

THE MET
The Metropolitan Museum of Art, New York
Distributed by Yale University Press, New Haven and London

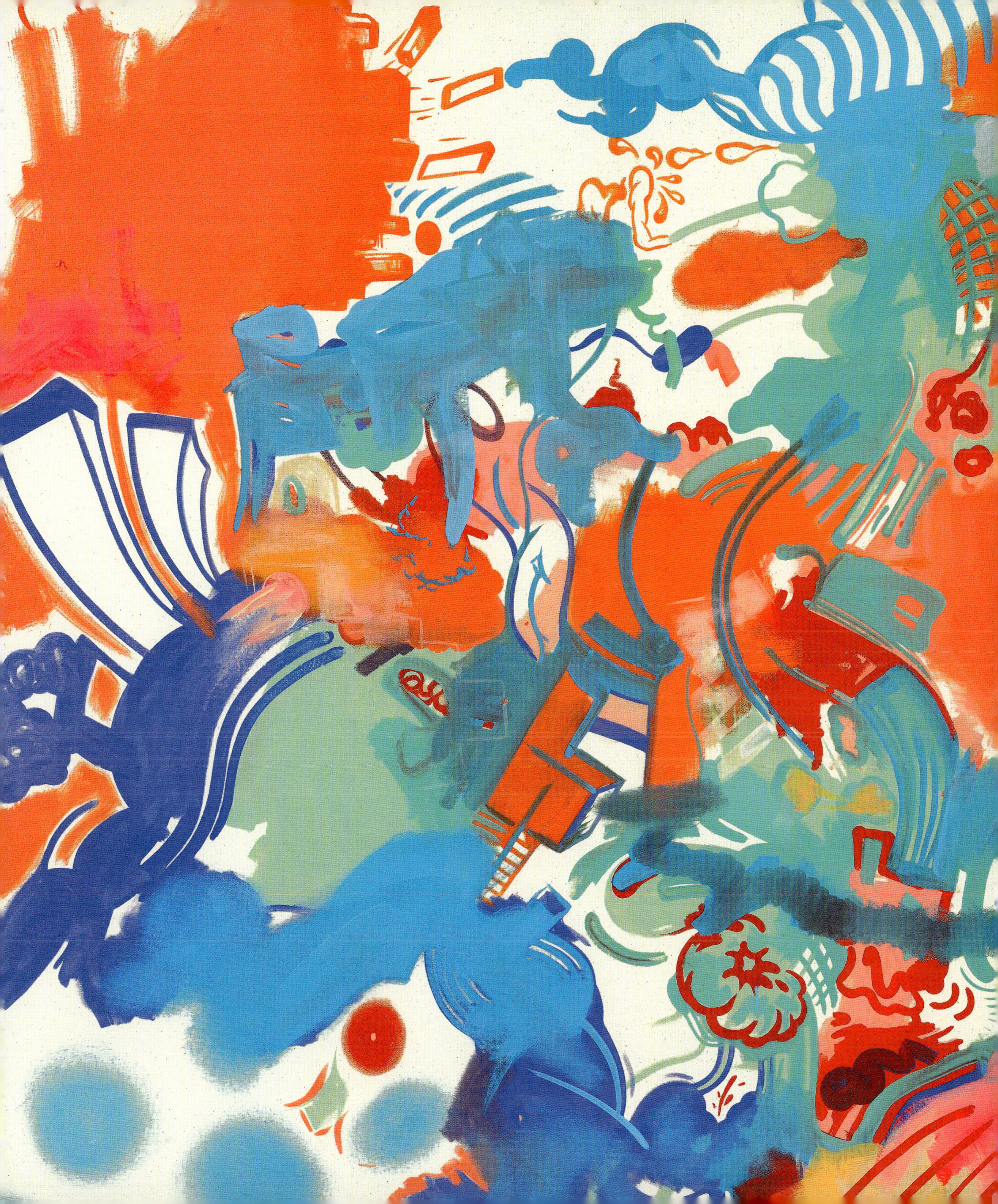

This catalogue is published in conjunction with "Everything Is Connected: Art and Conspiracy," on view at The Metropolitan Museum of Art, New York, from September 18, 2018, through January 6, 2019.

The exhibition is made possible by Andrea Krantz and Harvey Sawikin.

Additional support is provided by James and Vivian Zelter.

This catalogue is made possible by the Samuel I. Newhouse Foundation, Inc.

Published by The Metropolitan Museum of Art, New York

Mark Polizzotti, Publisher and Editor in Chief

Gwen Roginsky, Associate Publisher and General Manager of Publications

Peter Antony, Chief Production Manager

Michael Sittenfeld, Senior Managing Editor

Edited by Elisa Urbanelli

Designed by Roy Brooks, Fold Four, Inc.

Production by Paul Booth

Image acquisitions and permissions by Elizabeth De Mase

Photographs of works in The Metropolitan Museum of Art's collection are by the Imaging Department, The Metropolitan Museum of Art, unless otherwise noted.

Additional photography credits appear on page 196.

Typeset in Corporate S and Corporate Mono

Printed on 150 gsm Condat Matt Perigord

Separations by Professional Graphics, Inc., Rockford, Illinois

Printed and bound by Ofset Yapımevi, Istanbul

Front cover: Peter Saul, *Government of California*, 1969 (detail, p. 36); back cover: Wayne Gonzales, *Peach Oswald*, 2001 (detail, p. 73); front endpapers: Lutz Bacher, *The Lee Harvey Oswald Interview*, 1976 (detail, pp. 60–61); p. 3: Sue Williams, *Hill and Dale, Black-Ops*, 2013 (detail, p. 153 top); p. 13: Mike Kelley, *Untitled (Government and Business)*, 1991 (detail, p. 87); p. 157: Jenny Holzer, *Red Yellow Looming*, 2004 (detail, pp. 144, 164); p. 172: Jim Shaw, *The End Is Here*, 1978 (detail, pp. 118–19, 161); back endpapers: Mark Lombardi, *BCCI-ICC & FAB, 1972–91 (4th Version)*, 1996–2000 (detail, pp. 88–89)

First printing

The Metropolitan Museum of Art
1000 Fifth Avenue
New York, New York 10028
metmuseum.org

Distributed by
Yale University Press, New Haven
and London
yalebooks.com/art
yalebooks.co.uk

Cataloguing-in-Publication Data is available from the Library of Congress.
ISBN 978-1-58839-659-4

CONTENTS

FOREWORD

In his 1973 novel *Gravity's Rainbow*, Thomas Pynchon describes paranoia as "nothing less than the onset, the leading edge, of the discovery that *everything is connected*." Pynchon's formulation, a *locus classicus* of conspiracy literature, aptly provides the title for this exhibition, which takes as its starting point the notion that art surely has something to say about how we understand our modern age. Given the complexities of the world order in recent history, how does one endeavor to make sense of it all? What if everything is connected? What if it emanates from a single nexus of power?

Certain artists of the past fifty years have been particularly attuned to these perplexing questions and have attempted to address the themes of interconnectedness and conspiracy in their work. The results fall into two broad categories. Some artists have researched, explored, and reacted to what they see as injustices, both large and small, around the world; they telegraph the truth as they find it, basing their work on documents released through the Freedom of Information Act and by WikiLeaks or uncovered in their own detailed research. Other artists, suspecting there are connections still impossible to grasp, take a different aesthetic and intellectual tack: they visualize a kaleidoscopic, conspiratorial hall of mirrors, creating fantastical, even hallucinatory, works that plunge the viewer down a rabbit hole to discover that not all is as it may seem.

That the exhibition accompanying *Everything Is Connected* should find its home at The Met Breuer is a testament to the venue's thought-provoking program since its opening in March 2016. Under the guidance of Sheena Wagstaff, Leonard A. Lauder Chairman of the Department of Modern and Contemporary Art, exhibitions at The Met Breuer have featured brave and novel interpretations of the art of our times. Our thanks go to Sheena Wagstaff and her colleague Jeff L. Rosenheim, Joyce Frank Menschel Curator in Charge of the Department of Photographs, for their backing and encouragement of this project from its inception, as well as to Douglas Eklund, Curator in the Department of Photographs, and Ian Alteveer, Aaron I. Fleischman Curator in the Department of Modern and Contemporary Art, for their vision in tackling this subject. I join the curators and all those who have given their time and support to this project in pursuing The Met's goals to inspire reflection and dialogue, to shed light on history and culture, and to learn from the past through the lens of art.

I would like to thank Andrea Krantz and Harvey Sawikin for making this exhibition possible. I am also grateful to James and Vivian Zelter for their generous commitment, and to Karen and Jeff Hughes, whose early engagement in this project was most instrumental. Finally, our deepest gratitude goes to the Samuel I. Newhouse Foundation for its important support of this compelling catalogue.

Daniel H. Weiss
President and CEO
The Metropolitan Museum of Art

ACKNOWLEDGMENTS

Everything Is Connected: Art and Conspiracy benefited from the wisdom, generosity, and encouragement of numerous individuals, beginning with Jeff L. Rosenheim, Joyce Frank Menschel Curator in Charge, Department of Photographs; Sheena Wagstaff, Leonard A. Lauder Chairman, Department of Modern and Contemporary Art; Malcolm Daniel, former Curator in Charge, Department of Photographs; and former Director Thomas P. Campbell, who were the earliest advocates of this exhibition. In the later stages of project development, Daniel H. Weiss, President and CEO, and Quincy Houghton, Deputy Director for Exhibitions, provided good counsel. Martha Deese, Senior Administrator for Exhibitions and International Affairs, Rachel Ferrante, and Katy Uravitch in the Exhibitions Office helped with the many logistical and organizational matters. In Katy's capacity as project manager for The Met Breuer, specifically, her deft handling of the complexities of budgets, project meetings, and the exigencies of installation were invaluable.

We wish to express great gratitude for the vital support provided by our assistants on the project, Meredith A. Brown, Research Associate in the Department of Modern and Contemporary Art, and Beth Saunders, Assistant Curator in the Department of Photographs. They participated in every aspect of the exhibition and catalogue, from helping to select works to providing stellar written contributions to performing the lion's share of the administrative duties. None of our projects would be the same without the extraordinary support and encouragement from these talented colleagues. We are grateful to historian Kathryn Olmsted for contributing a wonderful catalogue essay and to participating artist John Miller for allowing us to publish an excerpt from his 2012 essay "Politics of Hate in the U.S.A." We are also fortunate to include a preface by author Jonathan Lethem, which so aptly evokes the conspiracy mindset.

We would like to thank members of The Met's Design Department, especially Zoe Alexandra Florence for her brilliant exhibition design and boundless enthusiasm for the project and Anna Rieger for her excellent graphic design. Thanks, too, to Brian Oliver Butterfield, Christopher DiPietro, Emile Molin, Frank Mondragon, Jennifer Spoley, and the talented production team for their assistance.

We are fortunate to work with some of the most accomplished registrars, conservators, installers, technicians, collections managers, project managers, and educators in the world. This exhibition would not have been possible without each of them. The whole Breuer team was, as always, fantastic. Allison E. Barone, the exhibition's registrar, was indefatigable and flawless in arranging safe transport and handling of the many loans. Amy Desmond Lamberti and Nicole Sussmane successfully managed our application for immunity from seizure and other legal affairs, while Deborah Gul Haffner advised us well on liability. The art in *Everything Is Connected* was expertly cared for by the conservators Katherine C. Sanderson and Georgia Southworth in the Department of Photographs Conservation, Rachel Mustalish in Paper Conservation, Isabelle Duvernois in Paintings Conservation, and Kendra Roth in Objects Conservation.

For their help orchestrating the preparation of objects from The Met collection included in the exhibition, we thank, in the Department of Photographs: Meredith Reiss, Karan Rinaldo, and Elena Tarchi, as well as former colleagues Myriam Rocconi and Anna Hildebrand Wall; and in the Department of Modern and Contemporary Art: Pari Stave, Cynthia Iavarone, Catherine Burns, and Rebecca Tilghman. They all deserve great credit for their sensitive handling of diverse tasks related to the exhibition.

As always, Paul Caro, Robin Schwalb, and Peter Berson of the Digital Department thoughtfully designed the presentation of variable-media works in the exhibition and maintained these works for the run of the show. Over the course of a month, Patrick John Paine deftly oversaw the installation of the exhibition at The Met Breuer, with assistance from departmental technicians Predrag Dimitrijevic and Ryan Franklin in the Department of Photographs and Tony Askin, Jeff Elliott, Sandie Peters, and Brooks Shaver in the

Department of Modern and Contemporary Art, as well as from the fantastic team of contract technicians who install all of our Breuer exhibitions with care. Our gratitude also goes to our excellent lighting designers Clint Ross Coller, Richard Lichte, Amy Nelson, and Andrew Zarou.

We offer great appreciation to the terrific team in The Met's Publications and Editorial Department, which is led by Mark Polizzotti alongside Gwen Roginsky, Peter Antony, and Michael Sittenfeld. We owe a special debt of gratitude to this catalogue's editor, Elisa Urbanelli, who shepherded the book from idea to print and edited the exhibition didactics, providing invaluable editorial guidance in the process with elegance and grace. Elizabeth De Mase did an incredible job sourcing the wide array of images and securing the rights to reproduce them. Paul Booth oversaw the book's production and printing. Roy Brooks of Fold Four, Inc., created the book's striking design. Barbara J. Bridgers, Joseph Coscia, Heather Johnson, Oi-Cheong Lee, Mark Morosse, Bruce Schwarz, Eugenia Burnett Tinsley, Juan Trujillo, and Peter Zeray in The Met's Imaging Department expertly handled the photography of the Museum's objects and certain loans.

We would also like to thank the following colleagues at the Museum for their help with this project in various ways: Jennifer Farrell, Allison Rudnick, and Elizabeth Zanis in the Department of Drawings and Prints; Kenneth Soehner, Arthur K. Watson Chief Librarian, Jared Ash, and Tony White in the Thomas J. Watson Library; Laura Thrower Harris, former librarian for the Department of Photographs; the members of our Communications and Marketing Department, led by Kenneth Weine and assisted by Alexandra Kozlakowski and Micol Spinazzi; and, in the Education Department, Sandra Jackson-Dumont, Frederick P. and Sandra P. Rose Chairman, Maricelle Robles, Marianna Siciliano, and Limor Tomer. Thanks, too, to Lauren Gallagher and Douglas Kopsco in Merchandising and Retail.

We are extremely grateful to the many institutions, galleries, artists, and collectors that entrusted their works to us for the exhibition; they are listed on page 9. We heartily thank the directors, curators, registrars, conservators, collections managers, technicians, and shippers who either endorsed these loans or facilitated them on the lenders' behalf. The following individuals deserve recognition for having provided special assistance and support: Joe Amrhein, Allison Beckett, Allison Card, Andrea Cashman, Anne Schwartz Delibert, Arthur Delibert, Chris Dorland, Sam Durant, Brian Emrich, Kathryn Erdman, Henrique Faria, Alejandra Gaeta, Tim Gentiles, Gustavo Gordillo, Carol Greene, Capucine Gros, Masa Hito, Mary Howard, Bill Jennings, Alden Kimbrough, Anna Korsiak, Paul Krassner, Collin LaFleche, Ellen Langan, Matthew Lange, Carol LeWitt, Jessica Mastro, Dylan Louis Monroe, Pio Monti, Maurizio Nannucci, Solveig Nelson, Janet Passehl, Susan Reynolds, Tina Rivers Ryan, Brinda Roy, Julie Saul, Minna Schilling, Katherine Siboni, Lisa Spellman, Joel Smith, Mary Clare Stevens, Eugenia Sucre, Susan Swenson, Fred Tomaselli, Hana Tran, Noel Valentin, Zachary Vanes, John C. Welchman, and Lizzie Zelter. We realized through the course of organizing this complex and multifaceted project that so much of our work relies on a very special and intertwined community of which we are very pleased to be a part—everything is connected, indeed.

Douglas Eklund, Curator, Department of Photographs

Ian Alteveer, Aaron I. Fleischman Curator, Department of Modern and Contemporary Art

LENDERS TO THE EXHIBITION

Altman Siegel Gallery, San Francisco
Art Gallery of Ontario, Toronto
Alessandro Balteo-Yazbeck
Blum & Poe, Los Angeles/New York/Tokyo
Christine Burgin
Mickey Cartin
Center for the Study of Political Graphics, Culver City, California
Sadie Coles HQ, London
Bridgitt and Bruce Evans
Fales Library, New York University
Henrique Faria, New York
Stephen Friedman Gallery, London
Wayne Gonzales
Greene Naftali, New York
Rachel Harrison
Jenny Holzer
Alfredo Jaar
KAWS
Mike Kelley Foundation for the Arts
Lehmann Maupin, New York, Hong Kong, and Seoul
Galerie Lelong, New York
LeWitt Collection, Chester, Connecticut
Magenta Plains, New York
Collezione Maramotti, Reggio Emilia, Italy
Metro Pictures, New York
The Metropolitan Museum of Art, New York
The Morgan Library & Museum, New York
El Museo del Barrio, New York
Museum of Contemporary Art Chicago
Peter Nagy
David Nolan Gallery, New York
Tony Oursler
Trevor Paglen
Raymond Pettibon
Jason N. Pritzker
Private collections
Ringier Collection, Switzerland
Ed Ruscha
Jim Shaw
The David and Alfred Smart Museum of Art, The University of Chicago
303 Gallery, New York
Brian Tucker
Video Data Bank
Whitney Museum of American Art, New York
Sue Williams
David Zwirner, New York, London, and Hong Kong

CONTRIBUTORS

Douglas Eklund is Curator, Department of Photographs, The Metropolitan Museum of Art, New York.

Ian Alteveer is Aaron I. Fleischman Curator, Department of Modern and Contemporary Art, The Metropolitan Museum of Art, New York.

Meredith A. Brown is Research Associate, Department of Modern and Contemporary Art, The Metropolitan Museum of Art, New York.

Jonathan Lethem is a novelist, essayist, and author of short stories. He is Roy Edward Disney '51 Professor of Creative Writing and Professor of English at Pomona College, Claremont, California.

John Miller is an artist, writer, and musician, as well as a Professor of Professional Practice in the Art History Department at Barnard College, New York.

Kathryn Olmsted is Professor of History, University of California, Davis.

Beth Saunders is Assistant Curator, Department of Photographs, The Metropolitan Museum of Art, New York.

KNITTING THE MONSTER'S SOCKS

Jonathan Lethem

The conspiracy lives. It goes on without you and within you, and it's big—a perfect example of a *hyperobject*. That word, coined by Timothy Morton to describe those features of our existence too vast to apprehend entirely, to get our heads around, is frequently applied to global warming—which, taken as an example, in turn helps to clarify Morton's odd term.

In a triple sense, global warming, or "climate change," is a notion pervaded with an atmosphere of conspiracy. First, of course, the outstandingly real and simple disaster somehow stands under accusation of being a concoction of special interests (ecological, Chinese, or what have you). Second, its onset—so gradual, and now so sudden—proposes the existence of *a nonhuman conspiracy against capitalism*. It's as if, instead of machines rising up against humans (as in *The Terminator*, or that old *Twilight Zone* episode where the electric shaver comes slithering down the stairs like a cobra), it is the laws of nature that will ultimately act, like a Marvel supervillain, to topple humanity. Third, and most poignant, it has demanded in response a manifestly useless "conspiracy of good sense"; right-thinking people everywhere *attempting* to conspire in saving the world and . . . getting nowhere in particular. In this regard, or all of these senses put together, you could say we live in the era of the first truly global conspiracy that actually matters, one with sway over every human prospect. Masons, secret lizards, CIA LSD, Scientology, Tupperware, all pale in comparison.

Morton's notion of the hyperobject also illuminates a paradoxical feature of the conspiracy: in its limitlessness, tenuousness, invisibility, and threat, it begs to be denied absolutely. Either the conspiracy infiltrates everything, or it doesn't exist.

But that's not right, or not right enough: the conspiracy is real partly because we make it real—like a god. One central source of the conspiracy's power is the fact that we can't agree, not only on what it looks like or what its purposes might be, but on whether or not it's there at all. It feeds on belief and disbelief, a billion-footed Lovecraftian creature running amok because each of us is knitting one of its socks—and those of us who deny its existence are knitting some of its most useful socks. Though the image is absurd, the word *knitting* suggests the knitted brow of the worried person, and Shakespeare's "sleep that knits up the raveled sleeve of care." We dwell on malign conspiracies while we're suffering insomniac episodes.

Conspiracies also unravel, like a sweater, when they're exposed. Or we hope they do, though actually it is more often the harmless or bogus ones that are most eligible for exposure and unraveling. The deeper and more tenacious conspiracies hide in plain sight, yet remain miraculously denied and therefore immune to simple exposure. This is where the notion of conspiracy dovetails with the concept of "ideology," and with an understanding of the kinds of power baked into Foucauldian institutions. The more local and frantic and isolated variety of conspiracy thinking, in fact, often does the labor of distracting us from the oppressive operation of background power, of those "deep states" of family, nation, corporation, church. Seeing conspiracies everywhere is often denounced as a mug's game, a dark inversion of wishful thinking: how convenient it would be if everything oppressive was the fault of some nameable bad actor, who could be apprehended and punished! And yet this discrediting of the notion of conspiracy is one of the deepest operations of *the* conspiracy, isn't it?

Conspiracy is a truly American motif, since ours is a nation conceived—rigged up from available parts—by a gang of slave-owning freedom fighters whispering in candlelit rooms, exchanging frantic drafts of improbable manifestos. The Masonic pyramid on the dollar bill is also a Ponzi-scheme emblem. It was Melville, in *The Confidence-Man*, who perfectly located that site where *conspirator* and *con man* converge—an image of the darkly veiled American huckster, making all our Manifest Destiny happen. The westward migration was a conspiracy along these Ponzi lines: keep selling the next sucker on the terrific arable land just down the track. Worse still is the conspiracy of genocide. We're easily able to see this in Nazi trains to Nazi camps, less ready to accept it in smallpox blankets and "Urban Renewal," those periodic and convulsive schemes to raze black middle-class cities like East Saint Louis, or slow-acting but effective "kill the poor" trickle-nowhere Republicanism.

Yet for all the conspiracy's bigness, its political implication, the image of the knitter—*knit one, purl two, repeat ad infinitum*—points us as well to the intimacy and intricacy, the miniaturized and obsessional nature of the conspiracy theorist's mind-set. It's always personal, sometimes it's a little masturbatory. The devil is in the details, and if it's a forest in which the monster lurks, it's a forest made of trees—always notice the trees, I think they're creeping closer!

What was I saying? Everything is connected, and everything matters. The research and scholarship necessary for managing a universe in the clutch of malign powers can seem rather poignant, even abject, but that's only to say it's sublimely human. The knitter's yarn is also needed to provide the string between the pushpins and thumbtacks on the "crazy wall," that staple of so many television shows and movies, in which a person's pattern-making madness is rendered explicit in a handcrafted flowchart of interconnections. It's usually a scene of horror and/or pity, and yet another part of us knows the maker of the crazy wall is on to something, and we're going to be playing catch-up by the end of the story. We need our paranoiacs and our detectives combined in just the right proportion, into Sherlock Holmes or Naomi Klein or Philip K. Dick, to lead us out of the wilderness, or at least show us what it looks like.

Most of our own crazy walls lead nowhere certain, or worse, into greater dark. Yet the coping individual subject, under the vast conspiracy known as contemporary life, isn't something we can safely patronize or disclaim. *We're all we've got*, now and forever, unless we want to surrender control of the whole thing to the post-human artificial intelligences who are already plotting to supplant us, who may in fact be the *second* globally relevant conspiracy we've conjured up for the twenty-first century.

Moving further from forest to trees, burrowing from macro to micro, it's worth observing that consciousness itself is a kind of conspiracy. Our construction of self—memories, dreams, projections—is a thing there and not there, a machine raveling it all together by an unknowable and dubious mechanics, hiding crucial facts and features from view, and riddled with fissures and incongruities while proposing a seamless and perfect surface. We have conspirators within ourselves, in the form of our Freudian and Darwinian ghosts, strange operators with no duty of obedience to our daily agendas, our objectives inside the ordinary waking life. What a mess! Then again, why shouldn't we be as gnarled and obscure as the larger forces manipulating us? Maybe it takes one to know one; perhaps we're the right tool for the job.

Still, entertaining a live nerve for conspiracy feels craven and creepy, deeply at odds with the path of mindfulness, of good faith in others, of choosing your battles, and of getting off the grid. What to do, when we all understand both that the conspiracy is real and also that looking at it or thinking about it is bad for our individual health, sanity, and capacity to thrive as a participant-servant to the Matrix? What's worse, the details are so *bo-ring*! Nobody wants to be that guy unveiling the conversational black hole at the dinner party.

The answer may be here, in the pages of this book. "Paranoid art is where Copernicus goes to be persistently overthrown, for it has noticed that consciousness is itself a permanent conspiracy theory, and one that is *ipso facto* correct: *I think, therefore I am the center of this story.* . . . While paranoia in everyday life asks questions it believes have terrifying answers, paranoid art knows the more terrifying (and inevitable) discoveries are further questions. For paranoid art, unlike paranoid persons, also distrusts itself. And so, paranoid art is the ultimate opposite, the urgent opposite, of complacent art" (Jonathan Lethem, *Fear of Music*). I couldn't have said it better myself. By suffusing themselves in the affective texture of left paranoia—the morbidity, the self-reproach, but also the adrenaline spike of obsessive due diligence, of clue discovery, of pinning a new 3 x 5 card to the crazy wall and seeing it shed light on its neighbors—the artifacts and tableaux assembled by these thriving canaries in the coal mine of Late Capitalism are evidence of our collective capacity to endure and abide, to detect the galaxy in a grain of sand, and to laugh in the dark. Like Don DeLillo in his JFK-assassination-conspiracy novel *Libra*, these artworks don't resolve the conundrums they entertain, but instead provide a kind of mirrored room or resonating chamber that allows us to visit such apprehensions in their natural state, and to locate ourselves in them, in various states of outrage, bewilderment, complicity, arousal, and despair. This, we'd better learn to do, since the only alternative is to ignore the conspiracy completely.

E V E R Y T H I N G

I S

C O N N E C T E D

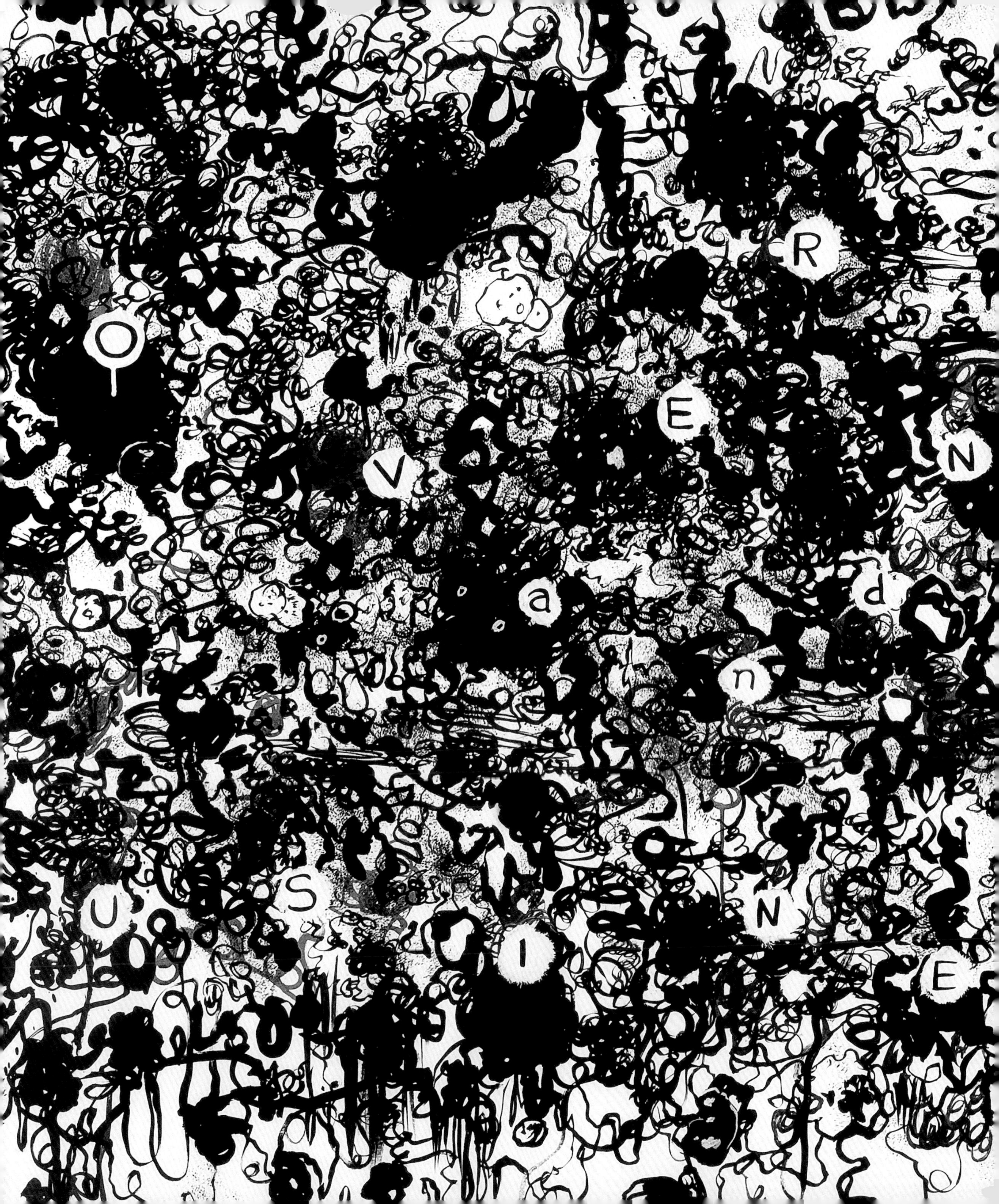
R
O
E
V
N
a
d
n
U
S
N
I
E

INTRODUCTION

Douglas Eklund and Ian Alteveer

In the wake of the 2016 U.S. presidential election, amid cries of "fake news" and debates about a "deep state" shadow government, a popular meme among journalists and pundits has been "we are all conspiracy theorists now."[1] More than ever, once arcane corners of research into covert activity have infiltrated our popular culture; the postwar mind-control program MK-ULTRA of the Central Intelligence Agency (CIA), for example, is today the subject of both the television drama *Stranger Things* and a documentary-based miniseries by Errol Morris called *Wormwood*. Over the last fifty years, as conspiracy has come to pervade our collective worldview, artists, too, have engaged with the topic, exploring both the hidden operations of power and the symbiotic suspicion between governments and their citizens that bedevils Western democracies.

That the subtitle of *Everything Is Connected* is not "Art and Conspiracy Theory" is important. The term *conspiracy theory* is dismissive by design: in 1967, the CIA devised and promulgated it in response to widespread skepticism about the Warren Commission report on the assassination of President John F. Kennedy. A Freedom of Information Act (FOIA) request made nine years later yielded the public release of CIA Dispatch 1035-960, a memorandum sent in April 1967 to station chiefs around the world in response to these rising doubts about the report's findings.[2] Citing a recent poll stating that 46 percent of Americans did not believe Lee Harvey Oswald had acted alone, the authors of the dispatch expressed concern that a sizable number of Americans were even beginning to suspect the involvement of President Lyndon Johnson and/or the CIA itself. The memo then provided the agents with talking points they should use to counter such "conspiracy theories," stressing that a loner such as Oswald would make an unlikely coconspirator and that "conspiracy on the large scale often suggested would be impossible to conceal in the United States." It also recommended "point[ing] out that parts of the conspiracy talk appear to be deliberately generated by Communist propaganda."[3]

The irony is that CIA Dispatch 1035-960 is a remarkable example of the United States propagandizing its own citizens in defiance of the Smith-Mundt Act of 1948, which was passed precisely to show the world that the American government, unlike the Soviet Union, only used propaganda outside its own borders.[4] In fact, the architects of the Cold War, blaming Communism, had promoted just such a paranoid version of reality, one that fractured the national psyche at home and, when put into practice, shaped global conflict. In his 1964 essay "The Paranoid Style in American Politics," Richard Hofstadter included the anti-Communist fervor of Joseph McCarthy in his construction of a historical lineage for "the sense of heated exaggeration, suspiciousness, and conspiratorial fantasy"[5] accompanying the belief—particularly among minority political movements—that small groups operating behind the scenes control the course of human history. Tracing the paranoia back to "demonological outbursts"[6] against Catholics, Freemasons, and Communists that occurred before the founding of the republic, Hofstadter fused history with a sturdy psychological portrait of the fringe in a way that set the terms for discussion that are still used today.

In contrast to the clear-eyed rationality and consensus building espoused by Hofstadter and other liberal centrist thinkers in Kennedy's orbit, the first artistic responses to the assassination were shot through with darker, more ambiguous questions. A 1964 photograph made by Garry Winogrand of people gathered around a commemorative postcard in Dallas's Dealey Plaza, the site of the assassination, provides a fitting corollary to the emergence of questions about the veracity of the narrative that surrounded the event (fig. 1). The woman on the right points to the subject of the postcard, the Texas Book Depository Building, which is located out of view, behind the photographer. Visible beyond the crossfire of gazes is the area that would become known the world over as the "grassy knoll"—the spot from which gunfire was heard and smoke was seen and to which onlookers instinctively ran after the shots rang out.

It can't be known if Winogrand or his 1964 audience would have read his photograph in conspiratorial terms, as an intentional, collagelike juxtaposition of fake and true (Book Depository versus grassy knoll). Nevertheless, the encirclement of that juxtaposition within an ad hoc gathering at the site suggests that the conversation probably drifted between verifiable fact and speculation, the result, as Hofstadter warned, of a "rather curious leap in imagination that is always made at some critical point in the recital of events."[7] The formal disequilibrium

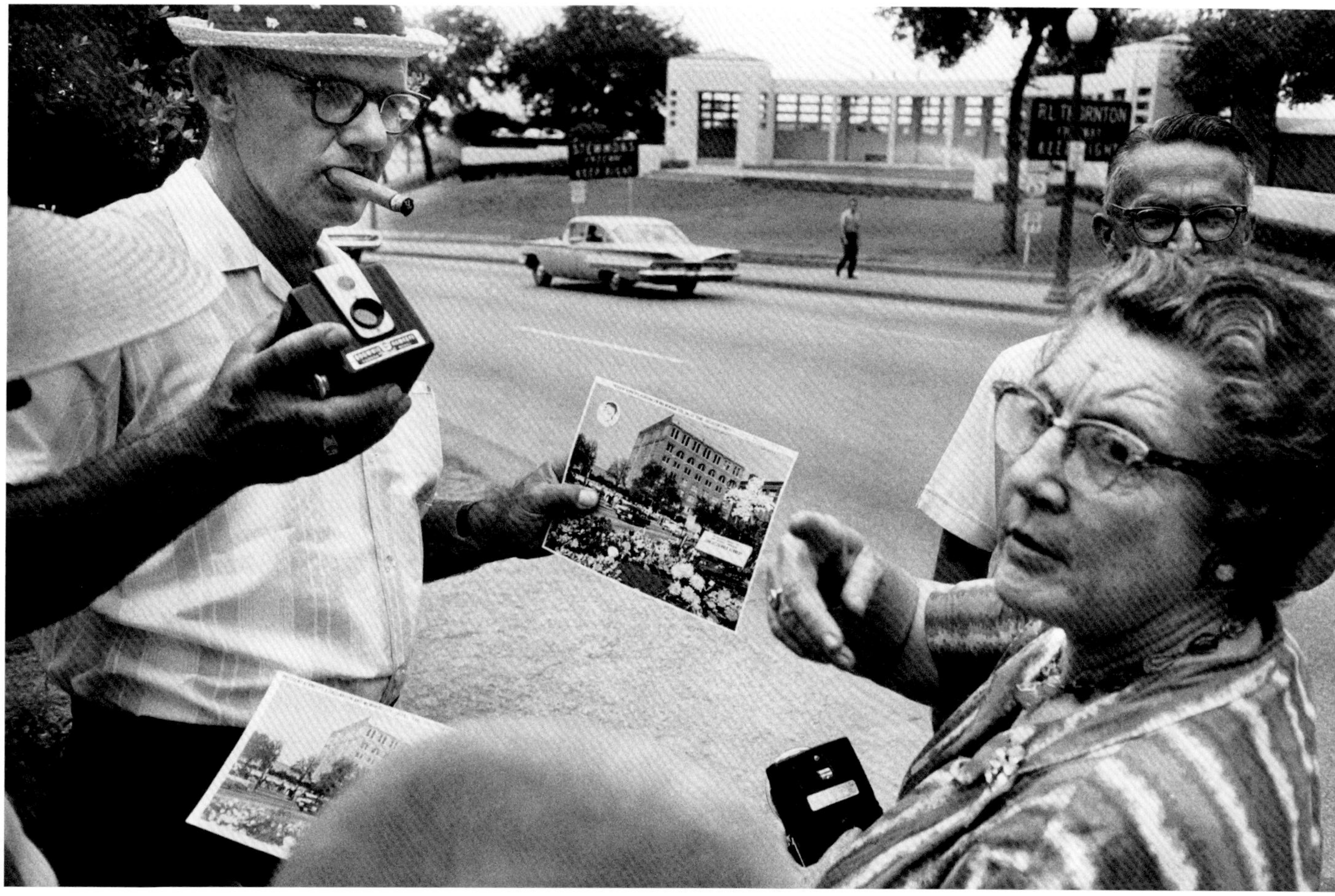

Fig. 1. Garry Winogrand (American, 1928–1984), *Dealey Plaza, Dallas*, 1964. Gelatin silver print, 11 × 14 in. (27.9 × 35.6 cm). San Francisco Museum of Art, Purchase through a gift of the Judy Kay Memorial Fund

of Winogrand's photograph—the volley of looks and gestures that refuses a single, authoritative vantage point on the scene—welcomes the viewer in to the magic circle of interpretative delirium caused by our terminal inability to trust the official version.

Amateur or "citizen" journalists of the kind that still study the Kennedy assassination are interested in connecting the dots between seemingly unrelated events. There is always an earlier date, an unmapped tributary that leads yet further back to another point of origin. The end of World War II and the ostensible defeat of the Nazis mark the consensus start date for conspiracy-minded researchers and fiction writers alike. In his novel *The Man in the High Castle* (1962; fig. 2), Philip K. Dick flips history on its end by imagining that the United States lost the war and is occupied by Axis powers. And in Thomas Pynchon's *Gravity's Rainbow* (1973; fig. 3), the war itself becomes a kind of false front hiding the collusion of corporate interests on both sides (the title of this book and exhibition comes from Pynchon's novel).[8] Perhaps the best known of these cryptic suggestions that the wrong side won and we don't even know it is Stanley Kubrick's 1964 film *Dr. Strangelove or: How I Learned to Stop Worrying and Love the Bomb*, in which the title character makes the still-shocking gesture of restraining his right arm from involuntarily assuming a Nazi salute (fig. 4); Strangelove was modeled mostly on Nazi rocket engineer Wernher von Braun, who was relocated to the United States to work for NASA.[9] This countercultural trope of America behaving like the Nazis it ostensibly defeated survives in Peter Saul's comic sci-fi *Hitler's Brain Is Alive* (p. 37), made in the wake of revelations about the abuse of prisoners at Abu Ghraib during the Iraq War.

There are incontrovertible aspects of the postwar period that created a fertile ground for the figure of

Fig. 2. Philip K. Dick, *The Man in the High Castle* (New York: Popular Library, 1962)

Fig. 3. Thomas Pynchon, *Gravity's Rainbow* (New York: Viking, 1973)

Fig. 4. Peter Sellers as the title character in *Dr. Strangelove or: How I Learned to Stop Worrying and Love the Bomb*, 1964, directed by Stanley Kubrick

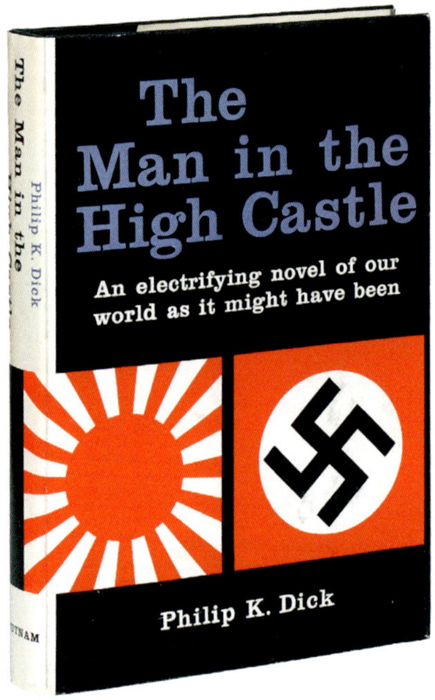

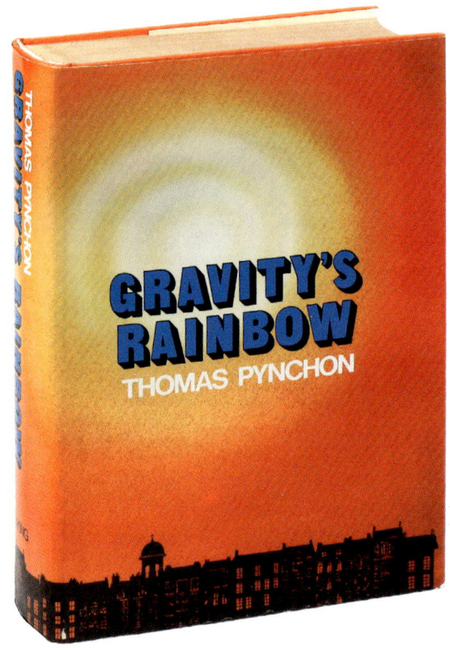

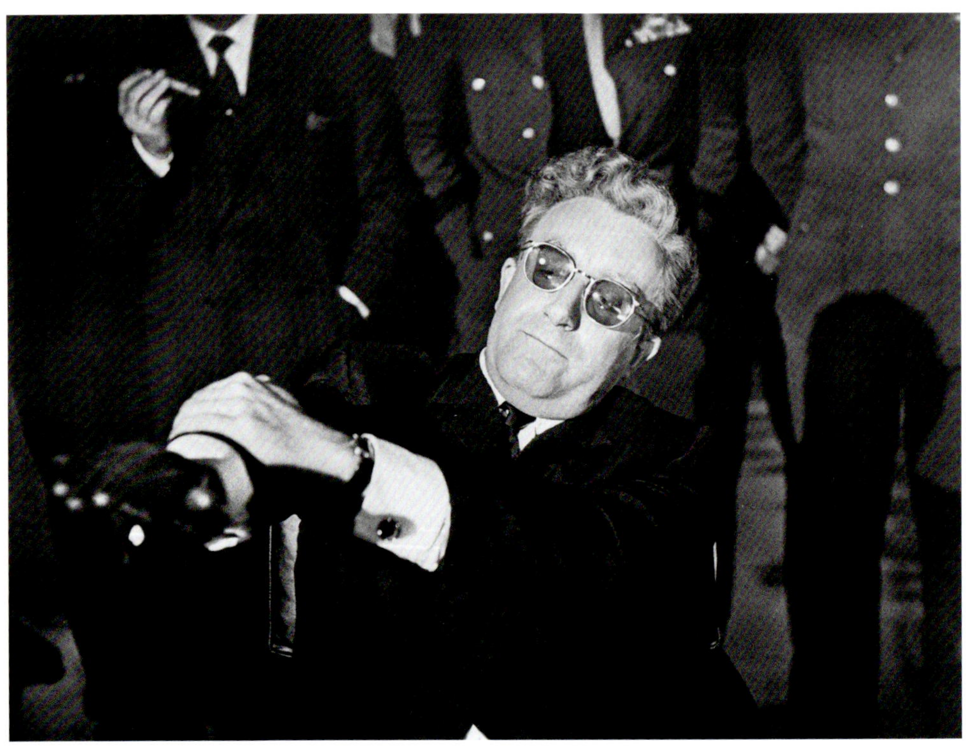

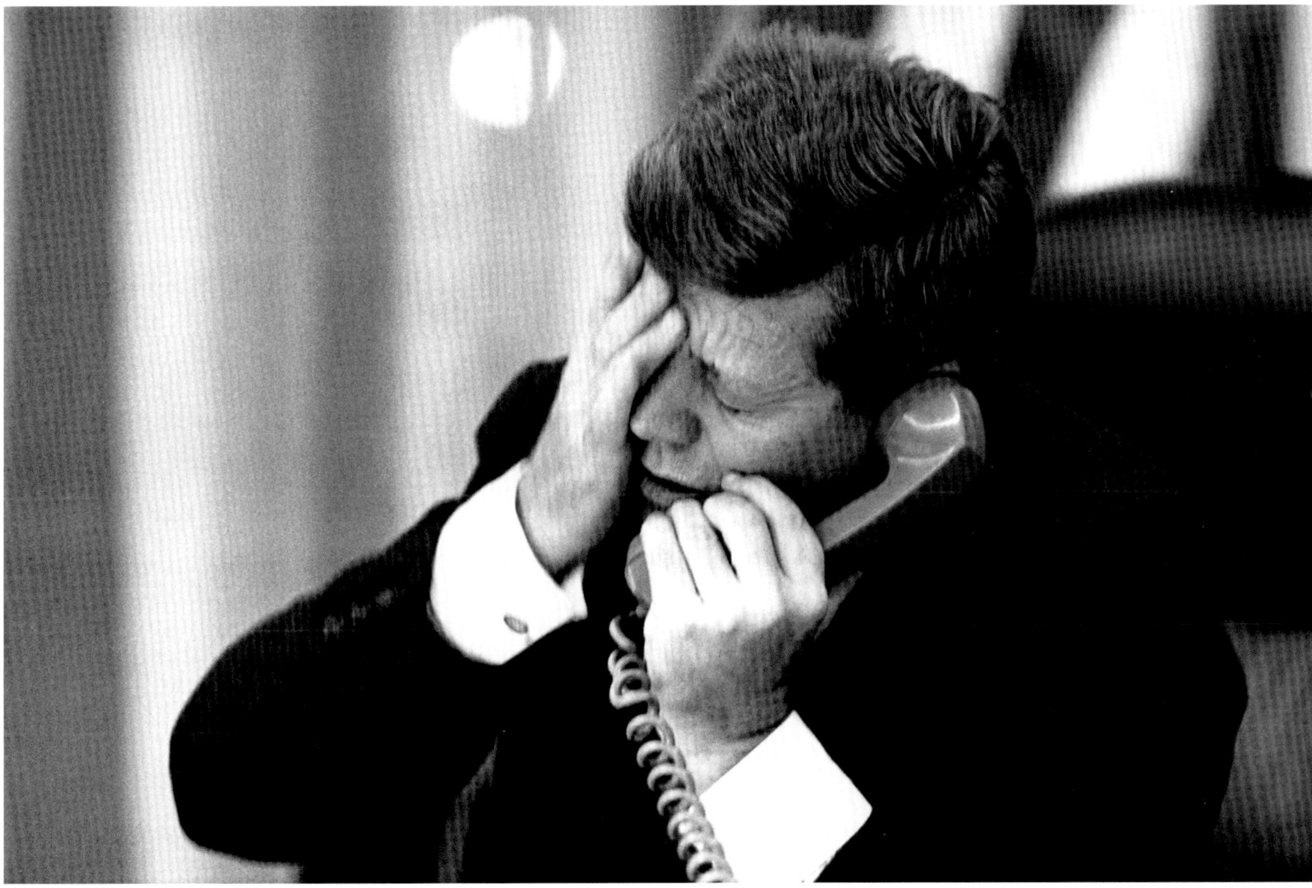

Fig. 5. John F. Kennedy learning of the assassination of Patrice Lumumba, the first democratically elected leader of the Congo, February 13, 1961. Photograph by Jacques Lowe

conspiracy to loom so large. Foremost among these is the dramatic expansion in size and complexity of Western democracies and their attendant bureaucracies. In 1953, the economist Kenneth Boulding described the rise of systems theory as a means of understanding the "great number, size, and power of organizations of many diverse kinds" that developed after the war.[10] Examples of such organizations include the International Monetary Fund and the World Bank (the latter established in 1944, before the war ended), as well as the Central Intelligence Agency, the Department of Defense, the Joint Chiefs of Staff, and the National Security Council, which were established in one fell swoop by the National Security Act of 1947, signed into law by President Harry S. Truman. Seen from space, this is the continent from which all conspiracy springs. Foundations and think tanks, funded by the wealthy in and out of government, have proposed a desired reality that is orchestrated above board (or, more likely, through covert means) by the forces of government and business and below the surface by intelligence services—the so-called deep state in a nutshell.[11] These institutions and agencies have been the engine that furthers the intertwined interests of the American government and multinational corporations, both of which long saw the spread of Communism as their common, most pressing threat. It is not surprising, therefore, that for many conspiracy researchers the twenty-year hotbed of the Cold War and especially the covert actions of the CIA during and after the Bay of Pigs debacle yield the real story of the Kennedy assassination (fig. 5).

The almost exponentially expanding, hegemonic culture of postwar America—shaped by movies, television, radio, newspapers, and illustrated magazines such as *Life* and *Look*—became the mouthpiece of the Establishment. It was from the blinds on the periphery of this monoculture of capitalist plenty and complacency, obscured from the sight of the general populace, that the postwar underground in art and politics began to

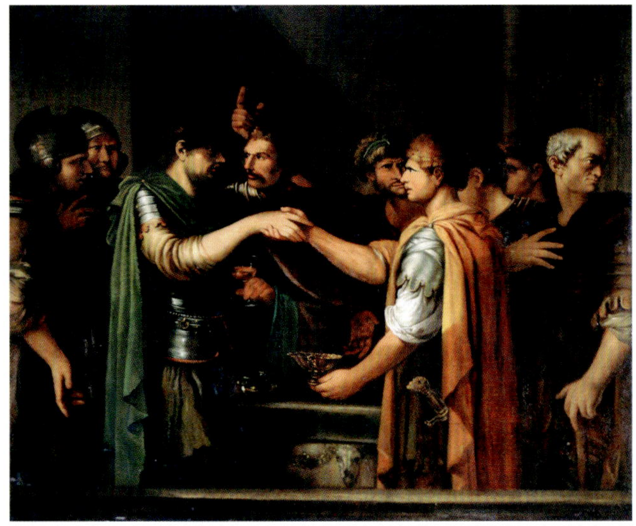

Fig. 6. Joseph Marie Vien (French, 1716–1809), *The Oath of Catiline*, 1809. Oil on canvas, 60⅜ × 73⅜ in. (153.4 × 186.4 cm). Burton Constable Hall, Yorkshire, United Kingdom

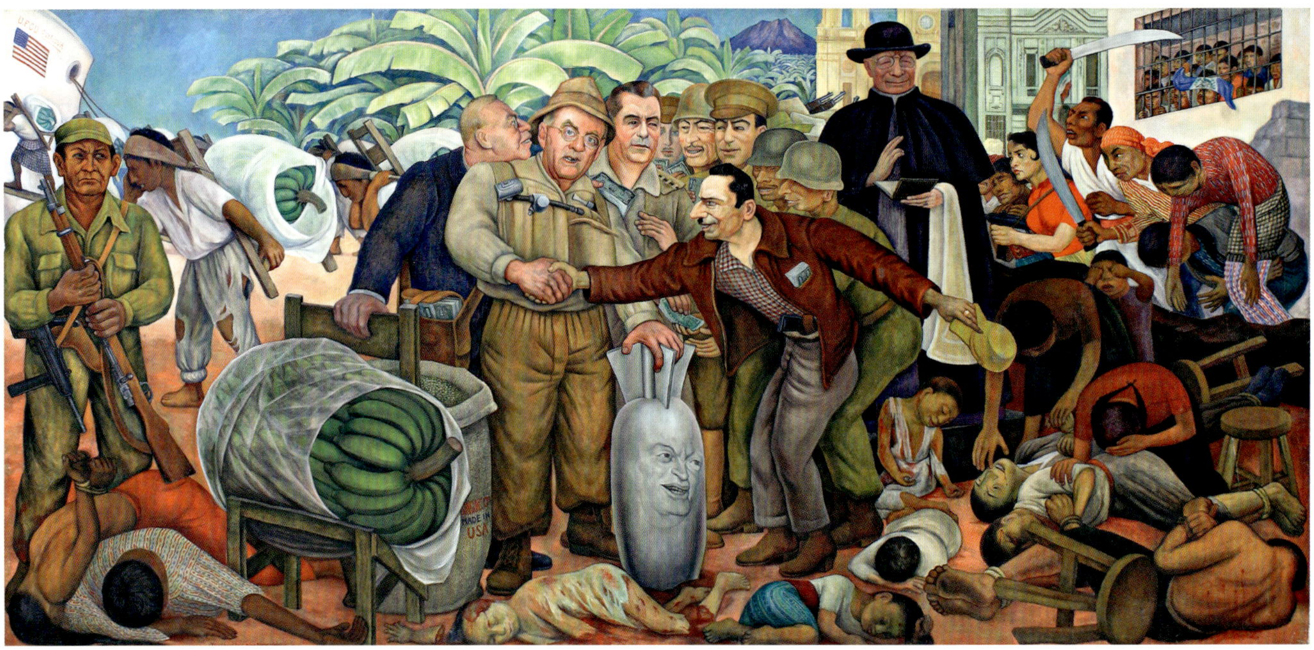

Fig. 7. Diego Rivera (Mexican, 1886–1957), *Glorious Victory*, 1954. Tempera on canvas, 78¾ × 196¾ in. (2 × 5 m). Museo del Palacio de Bellas Artes, Mexico City

take shape. This underground forms the backdrop for the fluorescence of conspiracy as a subject in cultural production from the 1960s to the rise of the Internet in the late 1990s.

Thoughts of conspiracy are probably as old as the existence of three people, two who plot in secret and one who is kept out. Antiquity, of course, was rife with plots and power struggles (fig. 6), and fears of conspiracy midwifed both early modern Europe and America, at least in part. The extent to which non-Western cultures breed conspiracy is beyond the scope of *Everything Is Connected*, which is really a first attempt to gather evidence of its presence in postwar and contemporary art of the West (all but five of the artists are from the United States, two are from Latin America, and three are from Western Europe). But an interesting sequel to this project could focus on global artistic responses from some of the eighty-plus countries in whose politics the United States has interfered since World War II (fig. 7). An equally important proviso is that, as curators, we made a deliberate decision to stop short of the 2016 presidential election and, in particular, the work of younger artists just entering the conspiratorial fray (the youngest artist in *Everything Is Connected* was born in 1976). These two restrictions, limiting our scope to Western art and to artists over forty, were required in order for us to properly tell the story of how we got here. We also considered just how much of this

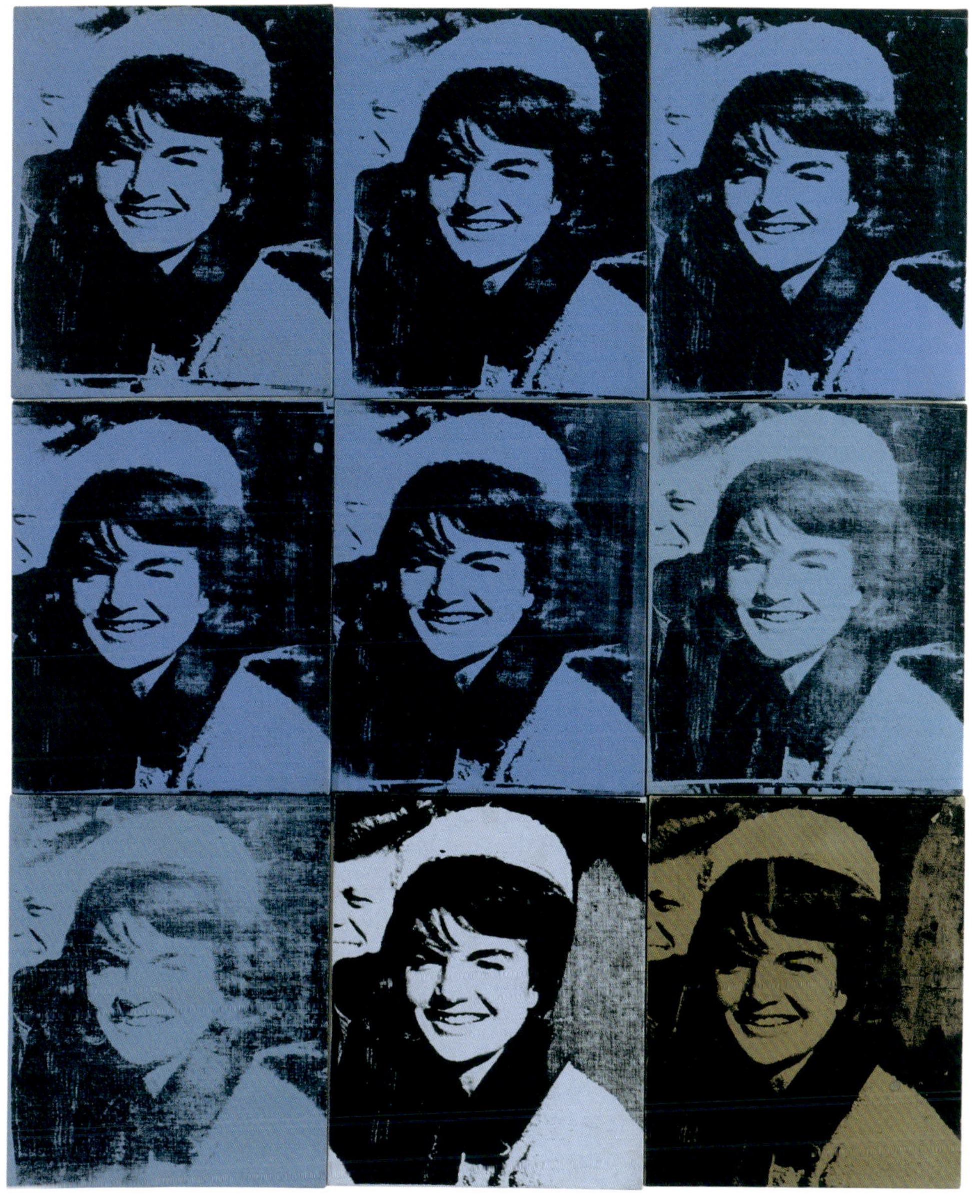

Fig. 8. Andy Warhol (American, 1928–1987), *Nine Jackies*, 1964. Acrylic and silkscreen on canvas, 60⅜ × 48⅛ × ¾ in. (153.4 × 122.2 × 1.9 cm). The Metropolitan Museum of Art, New York, Gift of Halston, 1983 (1983.606.14–.22)

information-dense work a museum visitor could take in without becoming completely overwhelmed.

The thirty-some artists featured in this book and exhibition fall into two interwoven camps, in a sense, two halves of the same coin: those who uncover covert networks of deceit by hewing strictly to the public record and those who dive headlong into the fever dreams of the disaffected, creating fantastical works that, nevertheless, expose uncomfortable truths. What they often share are strategies of obsessive intricacy and labyrinthine narrative structures, alternately aping the rhetorical styles and associative flights of fancy used by amateur conspiracy researchers or revealing evil in high places through quasi-journalistic exposés.

Conspiracy is rarely a career through line for artists. The featured artists have interests that include conspiracy to a greater or lesser degree. It is crucial, therefore, to establish a boundary around our subject—to address why we have included this and not that artist or this and not that work. For instance, Andy Warhol's series of Jackies, begun in January 1964 following the media frenzy and collective mourning in the assassination's aftermath, might seem to be a natural fit (fig. 8). Warhol considered his serialized portraits of the widowed First Lady to be part of his Deaths and Disasters, and in the sense that they reference the cloud of mediation around that tragic event, they are about how an icon (with all the religious connotations that word carries) can be

Fig. 9. Bruce Conner (American, 1933–2008), *REPORT*, 1963–67. 16mm, black and white, sound, 13 min.

Fig. 10. Gerhard Richter (German, born 1932), *Man Shot Down I*, 1988. Oil on canvas, 39⅜ × 55⅛ in. (100 × 140 cm). The Museum of Modern Art, New York

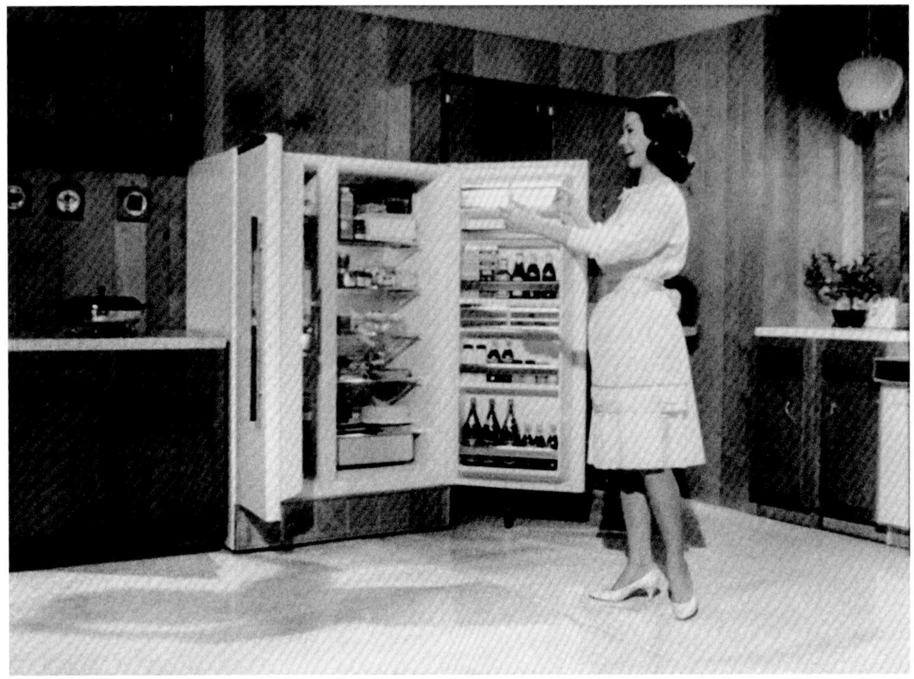

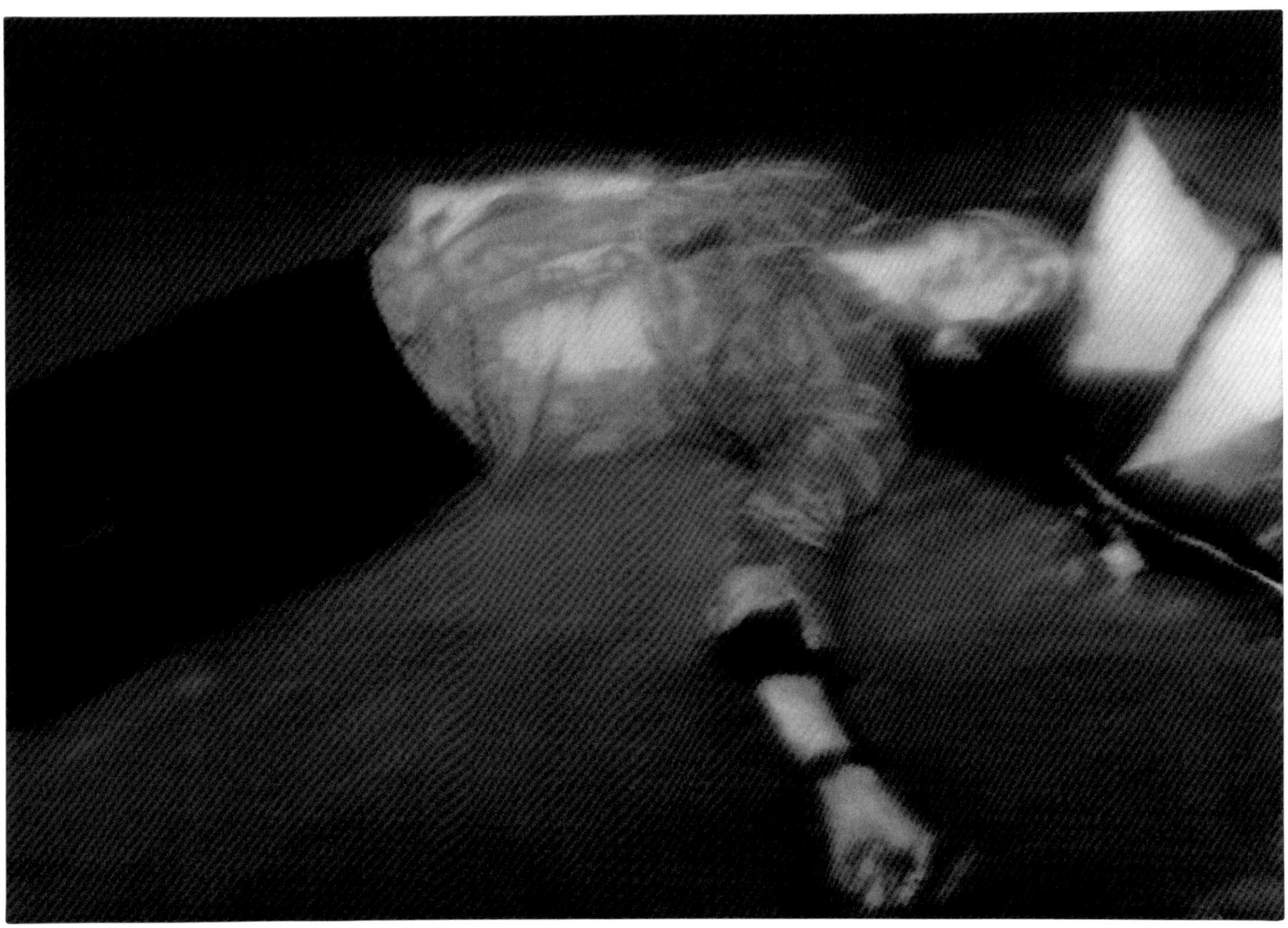

fashioned out of the tragedy of contemporary life. Typical of his work, here Warhol did not necessarily search out why Jackie was widowed, or really how it happened. Instead she is a saint to him, one who absorbs the shock and trauma for the rest of us and whose own wounds are cauterized by repetition.

Likewise, Bruce Conner's 1963–67 collage film *REPORT*, constructed almost entirely from television and newsreel coverage of the assassination, seems tailor-made for an exhibition about art and conspiracy. But nowhere in the film does Conner veer into a conspiratorial interpretation of his subject. Instead, he assembles fragments into something like a rapid-fire modern version of an ancient frieze commemorating the death of Caesar. Conner himself described the central section of the film, an extended sequence that pairs a radio broadcaster frantically reporting the shots in real time with the flickering of a strobe of white light, as representing Kennedy's passage into the afterlife.[12] Toward the end, the artist inserts a brief snippet from *The Bride of Frankenstein* showing the mad doctor pulling the lever that injects electricity into his creation, followed directly by a shot of Kennedy's flag-draped casket. But before you can linger too long on this piquant bit of montage, the proceedings come to a close with another appropriated sequence—a television clip of a 1950s housewife surveying an array of gleaming appliances like a hostess on *The Price Is Right* (fig. 9). In *REPORT*, Conner creates a countermemorial in which forgetting, via the enforced consumption of mass media, serves as a lethally misbegotten form of mnemonic commemoration in American society.

In his fifteen-painting cycle *October 18, 1977*, Gerhard Richter surveys the aftermath of the deaths of members of the Red Army Faction (RAF), also known as the Baader-Meinhof group (an insurrectionary group roughly equivalent to the Weather Underground in the United States). Ruled suicides, these deaths in prison raised immediate questions, but tellingly, nowhere in Richter's cycle is this suspicion part of the works' meaning (fig. 10). The grisaille half-shadow that envelops each scene may signify in passing the unknowability of what transpired, but the chief function of the murkiness is to describe a different endgame, one outside the purview of this book and exhibition: Richter's resigned, somewhat ambivalent belief that it is impossible for advanced art—so tied to the avant-garde's imagining of a better and different world—to in any way solve the contrary agendas of the state and its citizens. Richter's refusal to side with either side, for which left-leaning critics criticized him,[13] is essential to his self-positioning as an artist who can communicate his politics implicitly, free from what he likely sees as the weakening effect of political commitment on art. (Walker Evans is an earlier example of this viewpoint; indeed, the canon rewards those artists who come closest to politics without being explicitly political.) Most importantly, this ambivalent posture allows the artist to locate the meaning of the work firmly in the register of the nonpolitical, universal realm of the tragic and pitiful.

Everything Is Connected was inspired by the late artist Mike Kelley, who in 1991 lamented in an interview with the artist John Miller that academics and museum curators had yet to examine the topic of conspiracy theory or untangle its histories.[14] He then listed those artists who were dealing with the subject in their work, almost all of whom are included in this book and exhibition. When we as curators shared our ideas with Kelley in 2010, he observed that the artists on our proposed list struck him as an interesting counterpoint to not only the East Coast appropriation artists of the 1980s, with whom he was working in dialogue, but also the similarly market- and critic-approved Pop and Conceptual artists of the 1960s and 1970s. Taken together, the artists featured here exemplify a different approach to the givens of postwar American culture, one that is less resigned to the impossibility of carving out a space of resistance to consumerism (Pop art), bureaucracy (Conceptual art), and image overload (appropriation art). While *Everything Is Connected* does not propose anything as sweeping as an alternate history of art since 1960, it is meant to show how artists deal with political subject matter in the context of an institutional art world still plagued by a paralysis that is indistinguishable from complicity with the forces that scuttle change. It is also a historical inquiry into the origins of our present epistemological cul-de-sac, in which the very possibility of agreeing on even the basic facts of what happened seems impossible.

Everything Is Connected: Art and Conspiracy is dedicated to Mike Kelley.

WAKE UP! ART AND CITIZEN JOURNALISM

Douglas Eklund

If we know, then we must fight for your life as though it were our own—which it is—and render impassable with our bodies the corridor to the gas chamber. For, if they take you in the morning, they will be coming for us that night.
—James Baldwin, "An Open Letter to My Sister, Angela Davis," November 17, 1970

In 1969, the Chicago collective COBRA (Coalition of Black Revolutionary Artists) became AfriCOBRA, a name, its members joked, that stood for "African Commune of Bad Relevant Artists"—bad, as in good, in a way that commands respect. This change reflected the group's turn to the Pan-African movement, which sought to connect global liberation struggles that otherwise might falter in isolation. AfriCOBRA and COBRA before it had their roots in Chicago's Organization of Black American Culture (OBAC), the creators of the popularly celebrated but critically dismissed mural *Wall of Respect*, painted in 1967 on Chicago's South Side. As characterized by art historian Rebecca Zorach, AfriCOBRA was grounded in "community art" that was figurative, political, and "directly challenging [to] formalism."[1]

Gerald Williams's 1969 painting *Wake Up* (p. 35) is almost programmatic in its illustration of AfriCOBRA's principles, as outlined in Barbara Jones-Hogu's 1973 retrospective article about the group, from its "syncopated, rhythmic repetition" and "coolade color" to its "mimesis at mid-point . . . where the real and unreal, the objective and the non-objective, the plus and the minus meet. A point exactly between absolute abstractions and absolute naturalism."[2] The almost psychedelically exuberant dicta that tumble forward and around the central figure evoke not only speech but also the street graffiti that inspired AfriCOBRA artists such as Williams, who remembers the memorial message "BIRD LIVES" scrawled on the walls of inner cities after Charlie Parker's death in 1955.[3]

In contrast to this near synesthesia of verbal and visual information, the sheet of paper that Williams pasted directly on his painting represents its sinister obverse. It is a copy of the King Alfred Plan, a mysterious 1960s document detailing the government's plans for mass internment of African Americans in military installations in the event of civil unrest. In 1967, author John A. Williams commemorated the phenomenon in *The Man Who Cried I Am*, his fictionalized account of the FBI's persecution of black writers such as Richard Wright. The eternally contested status of the King Alfred Plan—was it a hoax or an authentic document?—combined with its murky provenance mirrors how the forces of repression were viewed in African American neighborhoods, whose residents may not have had proof, but they were quite sure about what was happening to them as a community and were ultimately proven right.[4]

Wake Up is a form of citizen journalism for a community under attack. This community had only its own institutions, such as family and church, to withstand the institutional neglect in education, health care, government, housing, and the law that accompanied daily persecution by the police. It is interesting to note that the Black Panther Party, which emerged out of exactly these conditions, originally formed in 1966 to provide protection during a public appearance by Betty Shabazz, widow of the assassinated Malcolm X. The a priori need for survival at all cost spurred the Panthers' founders to advocate self-defense in the face of what was essentially state-sponsored terrorism against a portion of the citizenry.

The Black Panthers' weekly newspaper constituted street-level information sharing of the kind seen in *Wake Up*. The distinctive visual look of the newspaper was, from a short time after its inception, the creation of Emory Douglas (pp. 32–33), who saw the function of his art not in decorating gallery walls but in "getting Huey [P. Newton]'s and the party's messages out to the people. . . . Showing what was really going on."[5] This art literally informed its audience that they had a right to both own their self-image and defend themselves. A great admirer of the Harlem Renaissance draftsman and printmaker Charles Wilbert White (fig. 11), Douglas saw that self-defense, let alone self-determination, could not happen without community identity.

The Black Panther, the "Black Community News Service" of the late 1960s, meant business. In it, Douglas gave visual form to the stakes that made self-defense an emergency priority. The newspaper spoke to its readership in its own language. Animal personifications in political cartooning were nothing new; think of Thomas Nast's depictions of the elephant and the donkey for the two principal political parties. But Douglas defined the ruling powers of his own

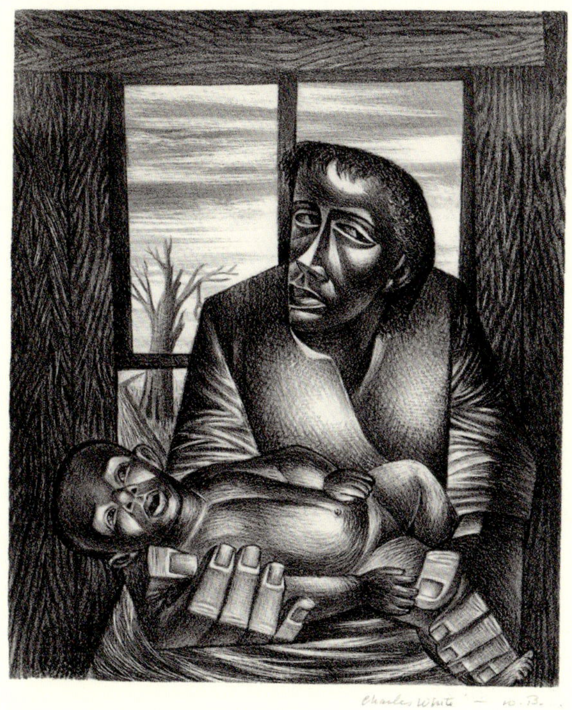

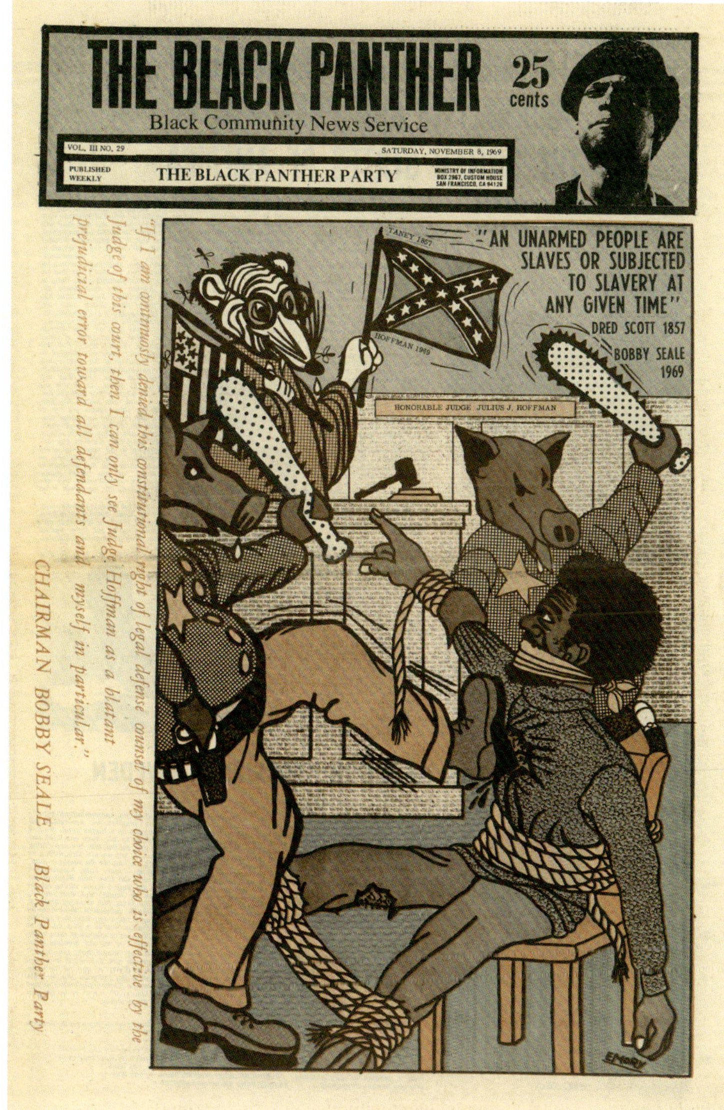

Fig. 11. Charles Wilbert White (American, 1918–1979), *Hope for the Future*, 1945. Lithograph, sheet: 18⅞ × 12⅝ in. (47.9 × 32.1 cm); image: 13¼ × 10⅝ in. (33.7 × 27 cm). The Metropolitan Museum of Art, New York, Gift of Reba and Dave Williams, 1999 (1999.529.183)

Fig. 12. Emory Douglas (American, born 1943), cover of *The Black Panther*, November 8, 1969. Offset lithograph

community using imagery generated from within: "pig" was a common epithet for law enforcement before Douglas designated the animal to represent the rank-and-file military and police (fig. 12). Douglas's rat, which denoted a higher order of viciousness than the cop on the corner, was reserved for politicians, judges, and businessmen (p. 32 top left). Within a year of starting the newspaper, Douglas and cofounders Bobby Seale and Huey P. Newton were connecting the abysmal situation of their readers at home to how the military oppressed people overseas (fig. 13). As artist and educator Colette Gaiter has noted, "The Panthers' goal was to end global capitalism and imperialism. They believed that the worldwide problems of oppression could only be solved in alliance with countries outside of the Western world, coalitions not determined by race, but by ideology."[6] To that end, Douglas explicitly conceived his graphic style in relation to the posters of other liberation movements abroad (fig. 14). From the beginning, he intended his full-page illustrations on the back cover of the newspaper to be detachable art that would adorn the walls of African American homes (p. 32 top right).

More threatening to the authorities than the prospect of violent resistance—which they understood and knew how to deal with—was the Panthers' turn in 1969 to an emphasis on community self-empowerment. The group provided services such as the Free Breakfast program (which fed tens of thousands of black children in American cities), health care, and transportation for family members to visit incarcerated loved ones (fig. 15).[7] One of the most prominent proponents of this

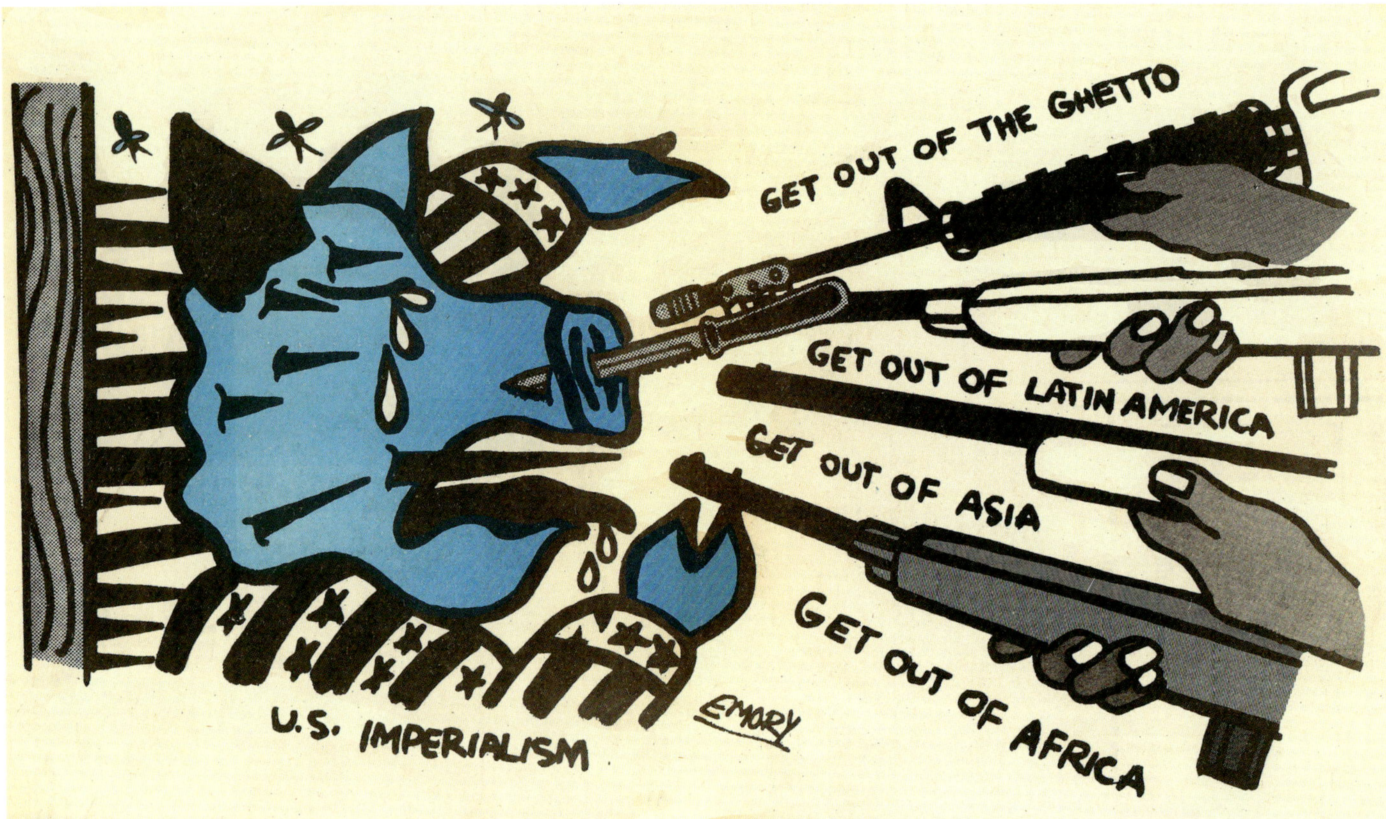

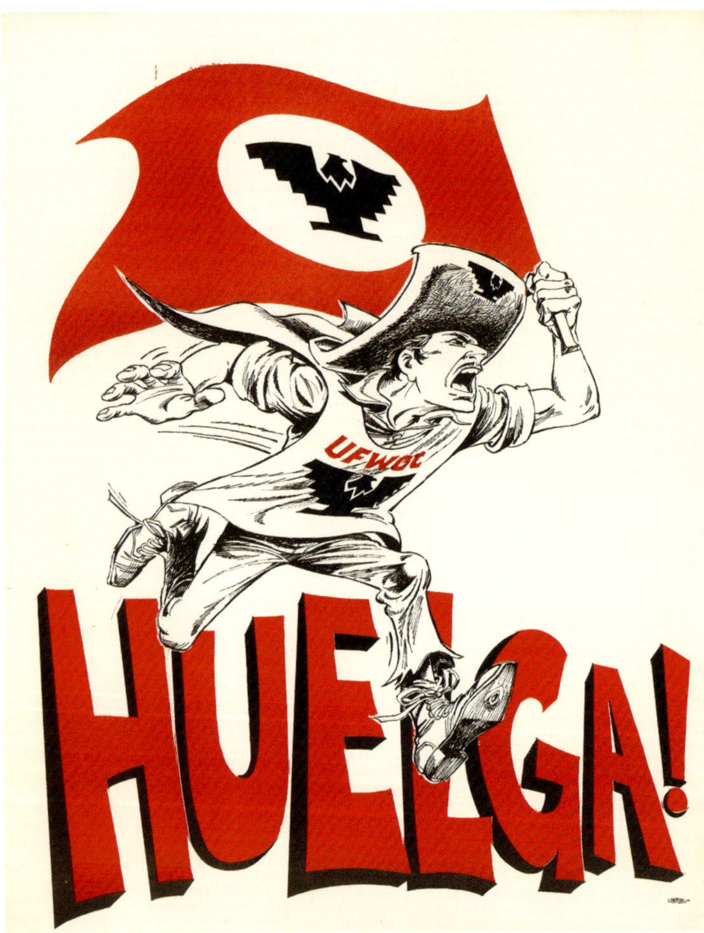

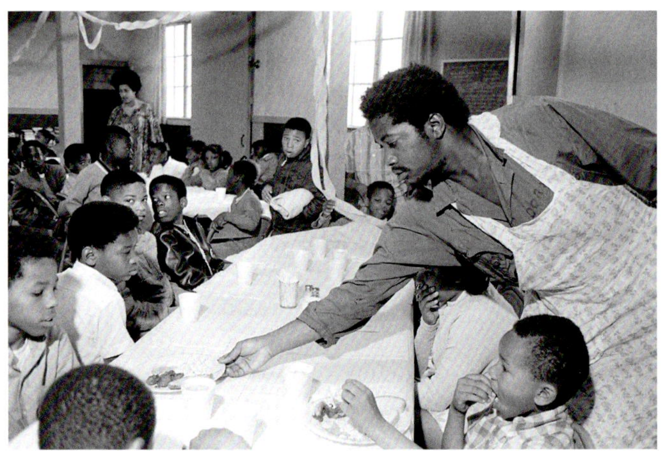

Fig. 13. Emory Douglas, illustration from *The Black Panther*, January 3, 1970. Offset lithograph

Fig. 14. Andrew Zermeño, United Farm Workers Organizing Committee, *Huelga!* (Strike!), 1966. Offset lithograph

Fig. 15. Charles Bursey serving children, Saint Augustine's Episcopal Church, Oakland, California, in the Black Panther Free Breakfast program. Photograph by Pirkle Jones

new tack was Fred Hampton, the charismatic leader of the Chicago chapter. In late 1969, the Chicago police shot and killed Hampton in his sleep along with fellow Panther Mark Clark; an FBI informant had dosed Hampton's drink with a sedative earlier that evening. Shortly before he was murdered, Hampton basically predicted his death in an interview with members of the collective Videofreex, early proponents of citizen journalism and alternative media (p. 34). In 1976, as the airwaves flooded with Church Committee revelations about the COINTELPRO (COunter INTELigence PROgram), the FBI's secret police, Douglas memorialized Hampton and Clark in a devastating image of an informant with a smoking gun surveying his victims (fig. 16).[8]

From within this all-out assault on the Black Panthers' leaders, Newton, the party's minister of education, developed Revolutionary Intercommunalism, a Marxist-Leninist-derived political theory that linked the situations of oppressed communities at home and abroad. According to Newton, the poor and working classes of the United States had more in common with the poor in Africa, Asia, and Latin America—who were similarly exploited by multinational corporations that used American might to extract wealth from their countries—than they did with their fellow citizens:

> We see very little difference in what happens to a community here in North America and what happens to a community in Vietnam. . . . We see very little difference in what happens to a Black community in Harlem and a Black community in South Africa, a Black community in Angola and Mosambique [*sic*]. We see very little difference.[9]

Introduced in a speech at Boston College in 1970, Newton's Revolutionary Intercommunalism was a remarkably prescient political theory that is greatly applicable to the present moment, a time when global networks of wealth extraction and worker exploitation have almost entirely liquidated traditional nation-state and community formations. It is also provides a rich context for considering art of the late 1960s and early 1970s that deals with community and public life. For example, the Swedish artist Öyvind Fahlström described his 1972 work *World Map* (pp. 40–41) as "a sort of historical painting . . . where all kinds of data and ideas—historical, economic, poetic, topical—are presented in a unified style. For the sake of clarity, data and interpretations are both written and depicted visually. Blue colors denote USA, violet Europe, red to yellow socialist countries, and green to brown the Third

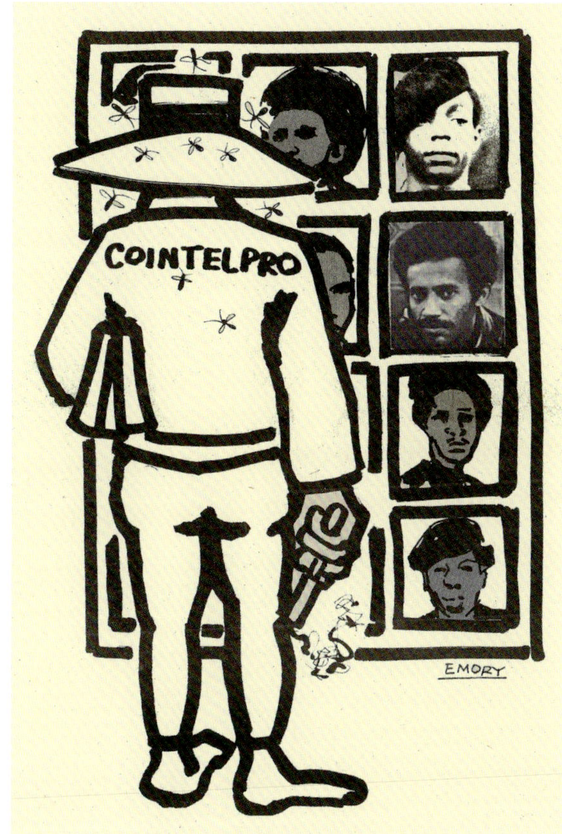

Fig. 16. Emory Douglas, illustration from *The Black Panther*, April 17, 1976. Offset lithograph

World."[10] Viewed from a distance, this three-by-six-foot composition may dissolve into an allover distribution of shapes and colors not unlike a Jackson Pollock painting, but it offers no hope for a satisfying optical gestalt. Rather, it explodes the false coherence implied by geographical boundaries on an untouched map. Fahlström also takes indirect aim at the political and social remove of Abstract Expressionism by transmuting multicolored paint skeins into trajectories of real-world violence, abuse, and domination.

Fahlström was no stranger to dislocation, having been born in São Paulo, Brazil, in 1928 and then sent to Sweden by his parents in September 1939, just as war broke out. Stranded in Europe until the age of twenty, he became keenly aware of how large geopolitical forces exert control over individual subjectivity. A full-fledged journalist in Sweden before becoming an artist, Fahlström was from the start an aesthetic maximalist whose boundless curiosity about the world flooded his works. In a 1966 essay titled "Take Care of the World," the artist lamented, "I deplore my incapacity to find out what is going on, to find out what life, the world, is about, in the confusions of propaganda, communications, language, time, etc."[11] Between his arrival in New York in 1961 and his premature death in 1976, he produced everything from journalistic dispatches updating Swedes on the latest from the New York art world; to radio plays, scenarios, and poetry; to intricate, labor-intensive art. This staggering output was a testament to the sense of urgency he brought to his practice, in which he seemed to be racing against the clock.

Whereas the legacies of Pop and Minimalism seem exhausted after fifty years of artists squeezing every last potential variation and implication from them, Fahlström's art, like that of Emory Douglas, is gaining a wider audience because it weds formal and social concerns in a way that has not been fully explored. Mike Kelley (who inspired this book and exhibition) greatly admired both artists. For him, Fahlström represented a potent alternative to the excessively formal and apolitical movements of the late 1960s. He used popular imagery in a manner antithetical to the Pop art of his moment, refusing what Kelley described as the "class-based distinctions" reinforced by Roy Lichtenstein and others who elevated and abstracted consumer imagery, emptying it of meaning. The former journalist's deployment of "data and interpretations" in *World Map* is an object lesson in the possibility for an antireductive but still formally inventive art. While creating the painting, Fahlström likely covered the sections he was not working on in order to avoid the creep of "this looks good next to that" formalism, a method he had used in his earliest Gesamtkunstwerk-like abstract epics.

Fahlström's *World Map* could almost be an illustration for Newton's theory of Revolutionary Intercommunalism. Its formal arrangement is a literal picture of how communities in traditional nation-states have been ravaged by the imperialist forces of a wealthy elite whose only community are the wealthy elites of other nation-states because, according to Newton, "nations have become communities of the world."[12] And like Douglas, Fahlström saw it as essential to distribute his art in reproduction to those very communities, as when he published a black-and-white sketch of *World Map* in the newspaper *Liberated Guardian*, an example of the very kind of alternative press from which he gathered the data used in the painting.

Another artist that Kelley championed is the painter Peter Saul, who, like Fahlström, was enormously influenced by the combination of figural distortion and unfettered expression seen in underground comics, from *Mad* magazine in the 1950s to *Zap!* in the late 1960s. Saul, a Midwesterner who spent the late 1950s and early 1960s in Paris, moved to Mill Valley, just north of San Francisco, in 1964. Describing himself in retrospect as a "communist" who was nauseated by America's imperialism abroad,[13] he also felt alienated from the vogue for Pop art, which he saw as simply another version of formalism. With Pop, Saul said, "art was stripped of everything that really mattered. The only thing that mattered was style. I wanted to put something into art that is more important than art."

But Saul also held the seemingly contrary opinion, stating, "The real reason I did those paintings [of barbaric war crimes] was that I thought that putting a little war into it would be beneficial for art."[14] Rendered in the most politically incorrect manner possible, works such as *Typical Saigon* (1968) and *Pinkville* (1970) are both and neither "protest" art. Saul expressed this paradoxical position—lamenting art's separation from life yet vociferously maintaining that art is incapable of political effectiveness—in paintings that are formally sophisticated while also blithely abhorrent to middle-class standards, designed to offend politicos and acolytes of Clement Greenberg in equal measure. He has noted in interviews that he was in search of a new audience, one outside that of the well-meaning liberal Establishment and art-world insiders. He almost certainly painted for the underground-comics audience, and it is not accidental that Saul settled in the Bay Area, the geographic heart of the Free Speech Movement, which nurtured countercultural boundary pushing in art, music, and politics.

In 1969, Saul turned to the war at home, one waged between the repressive tactics of the law and state government on one side and their very clear targets—African Americans and the antiwar left—on the other. In *Government of California* (p. 36), he personified these opposing sides doing battle on the Golden Gate Bridge, as if in the climax of a monster movie. Then-governor Ronald Reagan is depicted having the head of Frankenstein's Monster (but with Reagan's perfect hair), his neck attached to a Leviathan-like body. A phallus labeled "police power" springs from the same monstrous body, and a giant needle reading "ILLEGAL DRUGS" shoots into Reagan's ear. Saul presents the recently assassinated Reverend Martin Luther King Jr. as a black octopus with the halo of a martyr. The fulcrum balancing the opposing forces in the painting is the enormously out-of-scale, bile green pocketknife handled by Dr. King-as-octopus, which reads "JUSTICE" and "GOD" on its shaft. The blade, bearing the miniscule inscription "violence," slices into Reagan's neck, while Dr. King uses the wrench end, marked "non-violence," to pry gold coins out of the Bank of America.

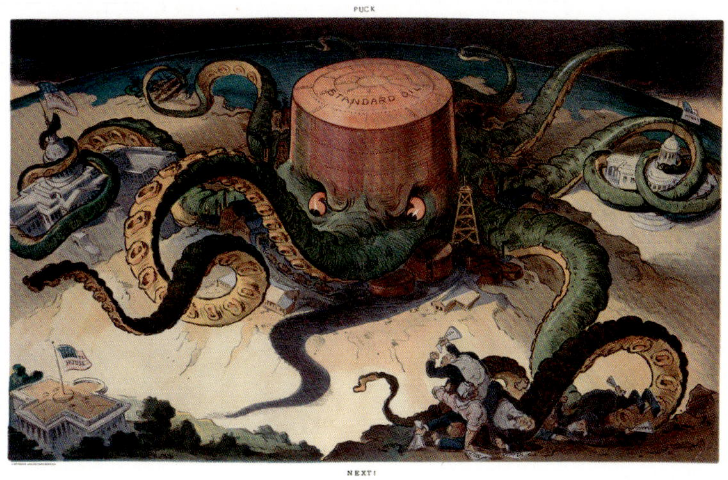

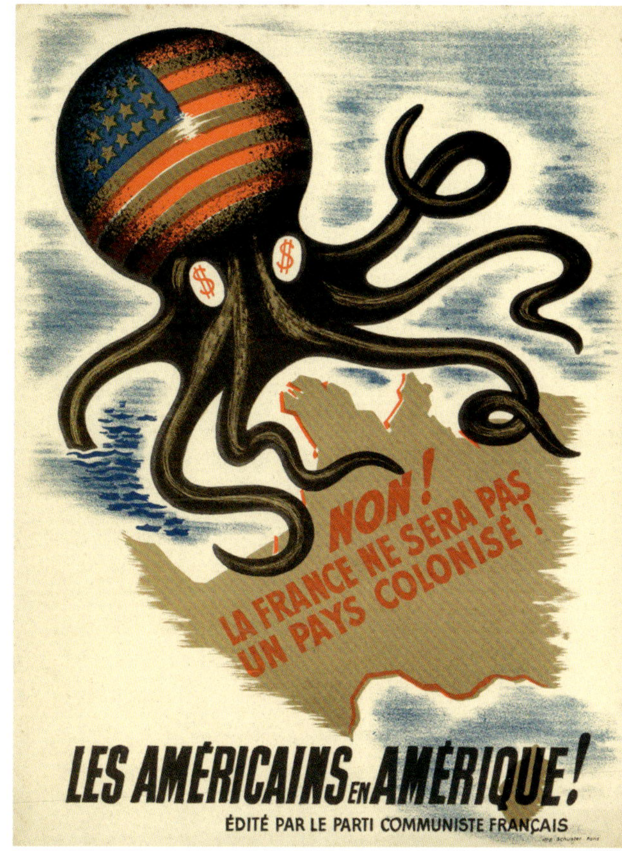

Fig. 17. Udo Keppler (American, 1872–1956), Standard Oil cartoon for *Puck* magazine, 1904

Fig. 18. *Les Américains en Amérique!*, French Communist Party poster, 1951

Saul's state of the state circa 1969, like Fahlström's state of the planet circa 1970, is both clear and hard to read, and it is also the earliest by date of the many webs, networks, systems, and sclerotic bodies politic depicted in this book and exhibition. His novel panorama of a civic circulatory system on life support is matched by the daring way in which he tweaks the depictions of Reagan and King past the point of decorum. And Saul introduces a layer of ambiguity by balancing King's saintliness with his portrayal as an octopus. An animal familiar from Udo Keppler's famous political cartoon for *Puck* magazine showing John D. Rockefeller's Standard Oil with its tentacles wrapped around Washington (fig. 17), the octopus was also a standard metaphor for global domination in anti-Communist propaganda (fig. 18). Saul may not have been aware that the octopus was a symbol for monopolies and totalitarian governments, but his use of it is a testament to his spider sense for images on the cusp of unacceptability.

The combination of innocence and irreverence in *Government of California* is the artist's guarantee that his art could not be appropriated for social uplift or propaganda. He also forecloses any possible message of uplift by injecting the governor with illegal drugs, raising the question: Is Reagan made into a monster by "using" drugs, if not on himself then by easing their supply to the black and antiwar communities of the left that he despised? After all, the White House employed such tactics. While Nixon was on his deathbed, one of his henchmen admitted as much to a reporter:

> The Nixon campaign in 1968, and the Nixon White House after that, had two enemies: the antiwar left and black people. You understand what I'm saying? We knew we couldn't make it illegal to be either against the war or black, but by getting the public to associate the hippies with marijuana and blacks with heroin, and then criminalizing both heavily, we could disrupt those communities. We could arrest their leaders, raid their homes, break up their meetings, and vilify them night after night on the evening news. Did we know we were lying about the drugs? Of course we did.[15]

In *Government of California*, Saul distilled the chaotic political situation along the axes of violence and nonviolence, the strategic conundrum that occupied the counterculture and black activists in the late 1960s.

In his expressive distortions of the figure and his blithe disregard for liberal pieties, Saul reached out to those who may not have responded to the cool, reductive auto-critique of Conceptual art then in vogue. This young, well-educated, politically aware urban audience saw itself reflected in the underground press of the moment, publications like the *Village Voice*, the *Los Angeles Free Press*, and the *Berkeley Barb* whose staffs were also routinely harassed by COINTELPRO.

The politicization of the artistic community in New York in the late 1960s occurred through a series of demonstrations and protests, as well as through the creation in January 1969 of the Art Workers' Coalition (AWC). The collective came into being to support the artist Takis, who disapproved of the way in which the Museum of Modern Art installed a work by him from its collection in a group show without consulting him. MoMA became a further target of the coalition when the president of the museum's board canceled a project to coproduce a political poster about the My Lai massacre. In response, the AWC produced and distributed 50,000 copies on its own and used them in guerrilla-theater protests in front of Pablo Picasso's *Guernica*. On October 15, 1969, the AWC organized *Moratorium to End the War in Vietnam*, the first "Day without Art" of the kind that in the 1990s became known for protests against the government's handling of the AIDS crisis. MoMA, the Whitney Museum of American Art, and the Jewish Museum participated in the event, as did countless galleries, and The Metropolitan Museum of Art postponed the opening of an exhibition that night.[16]

One member of the AWC was Hans Haacke, an artist who had previously been known for so-called Systems art such as *Condensation Cube*, an acrylic box that registered changes in its appearance (i.e., through "weeping" droplets) that were dependent on the specific atmosphere and human presence in the gallery (fig. 19). Haacke first extended this systems-based work into the social arena in 1969 with a piece at the John Weber Gallery titled *Gallery Goers' Residence, Part I*. Visitors were asked to put pushpins on a posted map to record where they lived, creating a composite picture of the community to which, until that point, they did not know they belonged. In the following year, Haacke's contribution to MoMA's group show "Information" was a poll about then-governor Nelson Rockefeller's support for the war in Indochina (fig. 20). The Rockefeller family's involvement with the museum also generated flash-mob protests such as *A Call for the Immediate Resignation of All the Rockefellers from the Board of Trustees of the Museum of Modern Art*.

In 1971, Haacke sharpened his critique of the supposed neutrality of art institutions to the point of provoking a repressive response. The Solomon R. Guggenheim Museum was organizing "Hans Haacke: Systems" for an April 1971 opening. It was to be the artist's first solo museum exhibition, and the plan was to create a new audience poll, plus two multipart photo-text pieces that took on the real-estate market in New York City as a self-regulating system (fig. 21). Composed of maps, typescripts with collaged black-and-white photographs, and charts plotting the exchanges of properties among shell corporations, these two works showed the museum audience information that was publicly available but nevertheless designed to be extremely difficult to find. Haacke's dizzying charts attest to the speculation and self-dealing used by these concerns to hide activity from tenants' rights groups.

Three weeks before the opening, the Guggenheim canceled the exhibition and fired its organizing curator, Edward Fry. Many of the leading Minimal and Conceptual artists in America and Europe protested the cancellation, urging each other to boycott the museum by agreeing they would not participate in exhibitions. Thomas Messer, the museum's director, in turn, called Haacke's real-estate pieces "political art for political ends" and described them metaphorically as "an alien substance that had entered the art museum organism."[17] He made this analogy without realizing that the cancellation exactly proved Haacke's point about self-regulating systems. In essence, the artist had successfully tempted the institution (although he might claim it was not intentional) to the crucial hinge point where it could not maintain the fiction of ideological neutrality. As art historian Rosalyn Deutsche has noted, Haacke's two real-estate pieces "confronted the broader social functions of the museum—its points of intersection with specific economic or political concerns."[18]

What ensued—the protests, the back-and-forth between Messer and Haacke in the art press—can reasonably be called a part of the work, and Haacke's provocation was perfectly constructed in this regard. His choice of which real-estate concerns to focus on was precise: the Shapolsky family controlled low-income housing in the two neighborhoods that represented the black and white factions of the antiwar effort, Harlem and the Lower East Side, respectively; Goldman and DiLorenzo accounted for the single-largest controlling interest held by individuals and was active in different areas of the city. And while the Guggenheim could rightfully claim that these parties were not part of the museum's network of supporters, its reaction revealed the extent to which the institution as a "system" was

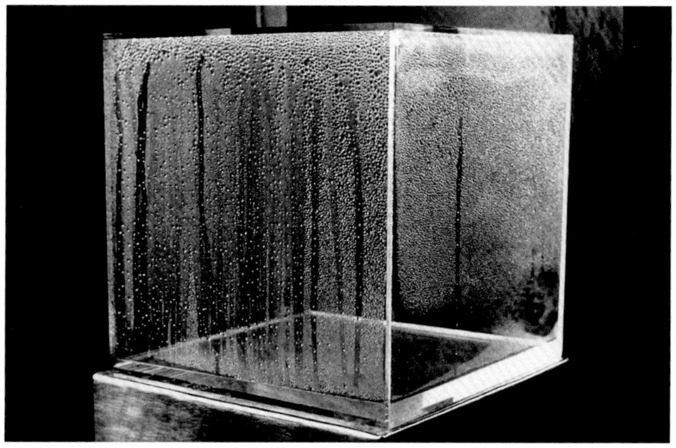

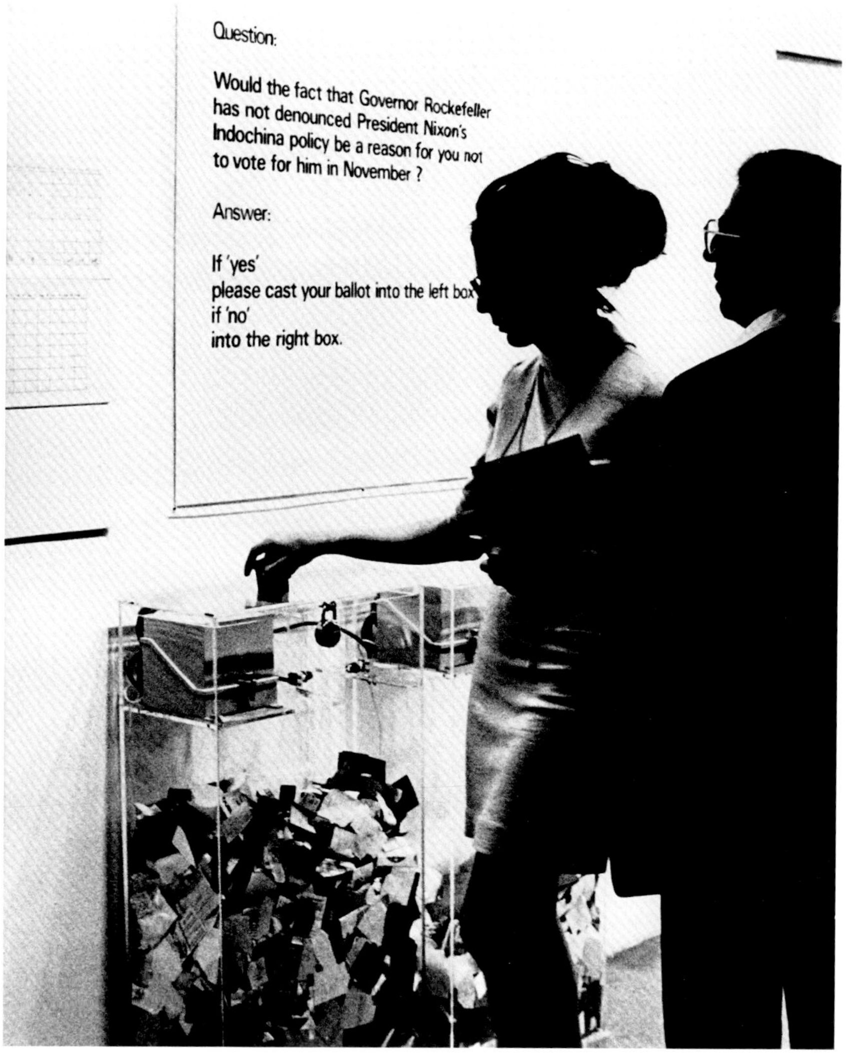

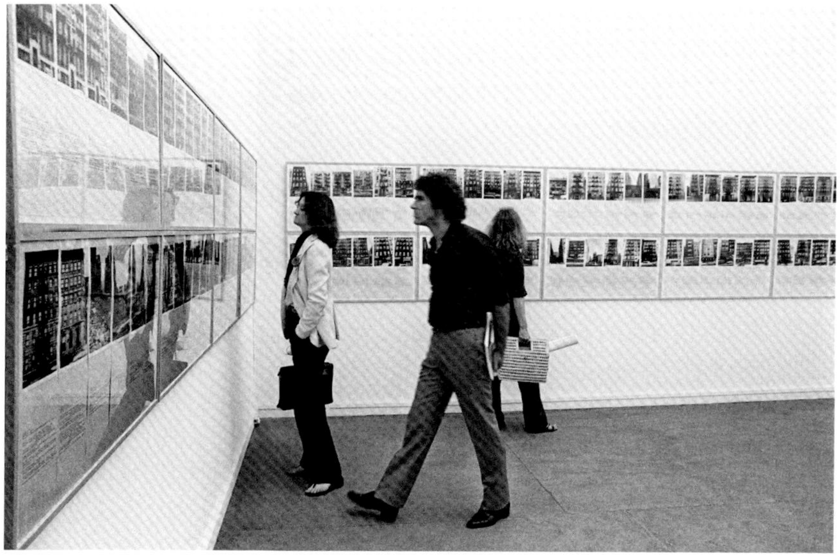

Fig. 19. Hans Haacke (German, born 1936), *Condensation Cube*, 1963–67. Clear acrylic, distilled water, and climate in area of display, 30 × 30 × 30 in. (76.2 × 76.2 × 76.2 cm)

Fig. 20. Hans Haacke, *MOMA-Poll*, 1970. Two transparent acrylic boxes, photoelectric counting devices, paper ballots, and boxes: 40 × 20⅛ × 10$\frac{1}{16}$ in. (101.5 × 51 × 25.5 cm) each

Fig. 21. Hans Haacke, *Shapolsky et al. Manhattan Real Estate Holdings, a Real-Time Social System, as of May 1, 1971*, 1971. Two maps, black-and-white photographs, 142 typewritten sheets, six charts, and one explanatory panel. Installation view, 38th Venice Biennale, June 1978

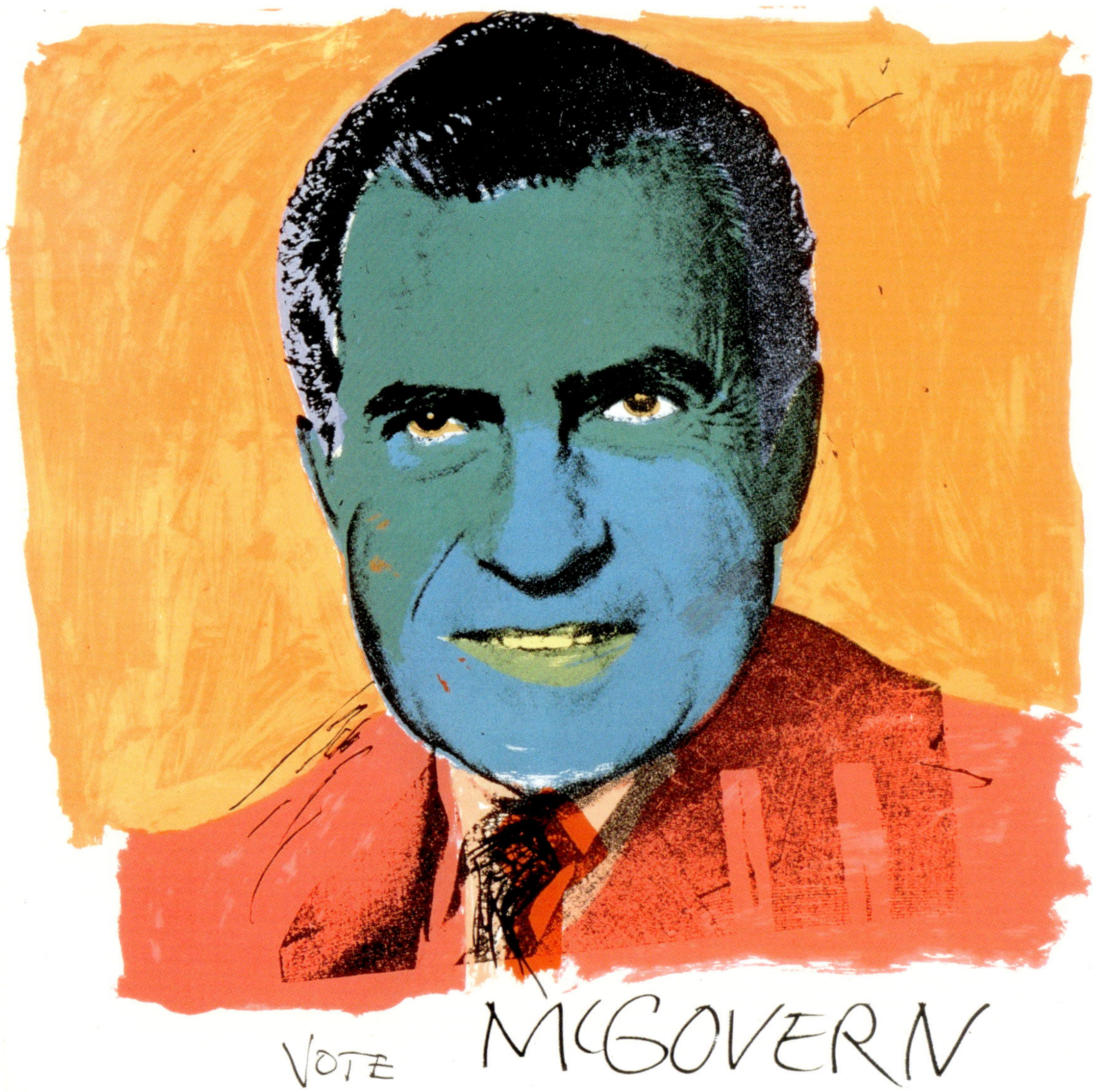

Fig. 22. Andy Warhol (American, 1928–1987), *Vote McGovern*, 1972. Screenprint, 42 × 42 in. (106.7 × 106.7 cm)

inextricably bound with a political economy not normally visible to the community of visitors.

Haacke's presentation of how institutions invisibly inculcate and shape individuals and communities chimed with philosopher Louis Althusser's 1970 essay "Ideology and Ideological State Apparatuses (Notes towards an Investigation)."[19] According to the author, Ideological State Apparatuses, or ISAs, are different from traditional apparatuses such as the government, military, and the courts because they are private, not public. Likewise, ISAs do not coerce through the threat of force, but rather through ideology; examples of ISAs would include organized religion, education, family, and the like. Althusser defined *ideology* in his essay as a "'representation' of the imaginary relationship of individuals to their real conditions of existence."[20] For the left-leaning, art-interested community coming of age in the late 1960s, this emphasis on the disfiguring effects of institutions on individual identity—what Althusser described as "that subtle domination beneath which can be glimpsed . . . the dictatorship of the bourgeoisie"—was a key aspect of the counterculture's overarching mandate to "find oneself" and the concomitant suspicion of institutions. Coursing through the zeitgeist of the 1970s, it was expressed in myriad ways, from Philip Larkin's 1971 poem "This Be the Verse" (which infamously begins, "They fuck you up, your mum and dad"), to Pink Floyd's album *The Dark Side of the*

Moon, to self-actualization movements such as est. The communally derived political formation of the previous decade could not survive long into the fluorescence of the Me Generation, whose widespread pivot away from political engagement and toward individual self-discovery laid the groundwork for the rampant individualism of the Reagan, Bush, and even Clinton eras.

In the 1980s, the gay community found itself in a defensive situation similar to that of the black community in the late 1960s. Just as Emory Douglas described in his illustrations the very real forces of persecution from official institutions, so too did artists and activists respond to the Reagan administration's criminal neglect in its failure to address the AIDS epidemic, which not only decimated the community of gay men but also afflicted many women, as well as intravenous drug users and their families in minority communities. By 1987 writer Larry Kramer, who five years earlier had cofounded the Gay Men's Health Crisis, became disillusioned with what he saw as a lack of action on that group's part in the mounting struggle against the virus. On the evening of March 10, 1987, he gave a fiery speech at the Lesbian and Gay Community Services Center in New York that many see as the spark that ignited ACT UP (AIDS Coalition to Unleash Power), a new activist organization that began to hold weekly meetings and organize protests. Founded by six artists who were also members of the newly formed group, the Silence = Death Project began producing powerfully graphic posters to further the cause of AIDS awareness. Throughout the late 1980s and early 1990s, ACT UP and its affiliated artists as well as other groups such as Gran Fury were deeply engaged in using visual and other means to counter the conservative United States government's often cruel policies and political discourse around the disease (pp. 38–39).[21]

The first poster produced by Silence = Death featured the now-famous pink triangle and the project's name/motto against a black ground. *AIDSGATE* (p. 38 left), the project's second poster, was made at a pivotal moment for AIDS activism, a time when the fury over the administration's lack of response to the burgeoning crisis was reaching a head. As art historian Douglas Crimp recounts in *AIDS Demo Graphics*, an important record of the visual material produced by the AIDS-awareness movement, the poster was created for a protest held in front of the White House on June 1, 1987, during the Third International Conference on AIDS.[22] This was the occasion of Reagan's first public utterance of the word *AIDS*. That same year the Reagan administration had also been embroiled in congressional hearings on the diversion of funds to the Contras in Nicaragua, and, in the wake of the Watergate scandal of the prior decade, the suffix *-gate* was applied to *Contra* as a means to excoriate the conservative factions involved. As Crimp writes, "For their new graphic, the Silence = Death Project attached the scandal suffix to AIDS and stamped a shocking-pink "AIDSGATE" over a Warhol-like picture of Reagan's ugly mug."[23] The ghastly depiction of Reagan recalls Andy Warhol's clever campaign poster for Democratic presidential candidate George McGovern, which casts the choice in the negative with a garish portrayal of his opponent, Richard Nixon (fig. 22). A call to arms, the *AIDSGATE* poster declares, "This Political Scandal Must Be Investigated!"

The art world's revolt against the Reagan administration's willful neglect of the AIDS crisis represented an almost miraculous resurgence two decades later of the kind of resistance recommended by Huey P. Newton through his theory of Revolutionary Intercommunalism. The model of artistic activism and direct action spawned by the AIDS crisis was so sustained that its only point of comparison is the resistance to the Vietnam War, which had confronted a similarly imperiling circumstance. In our present day, as symbolic displays of resistance on social media fail to even dent underlying structures of power, Newton's political theory seems more apposite, and less realizable, than ever.

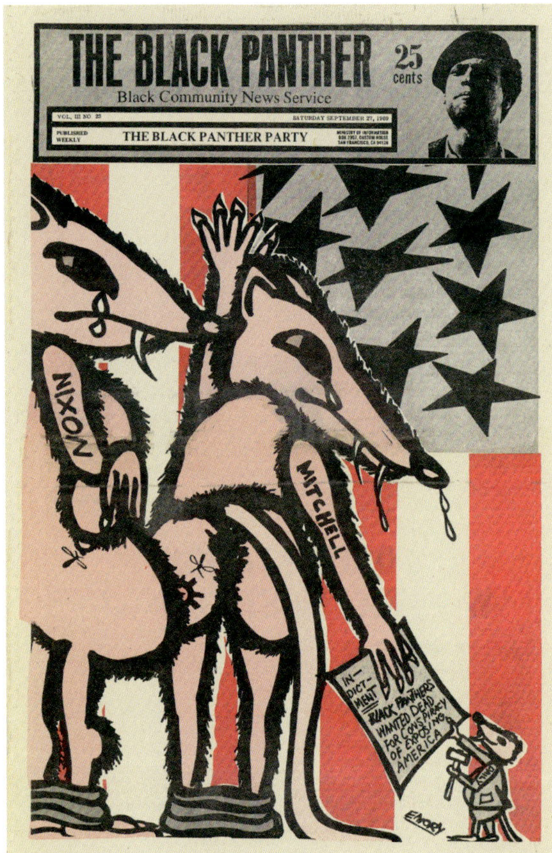

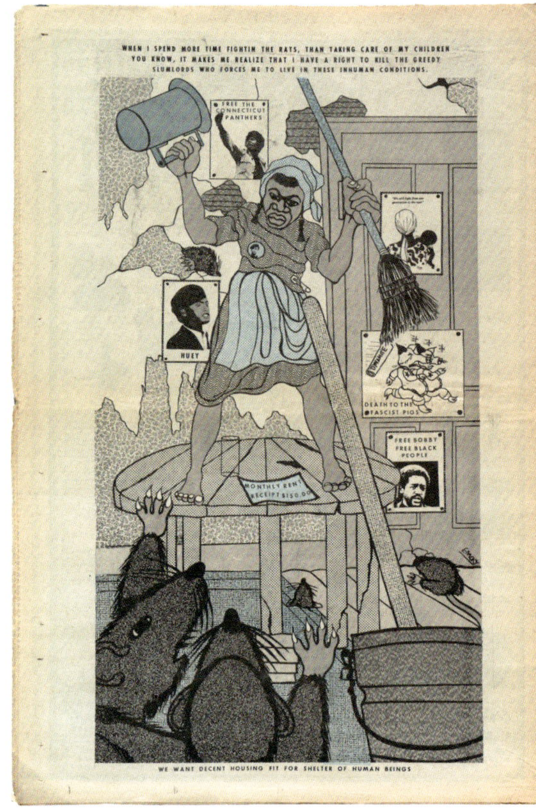

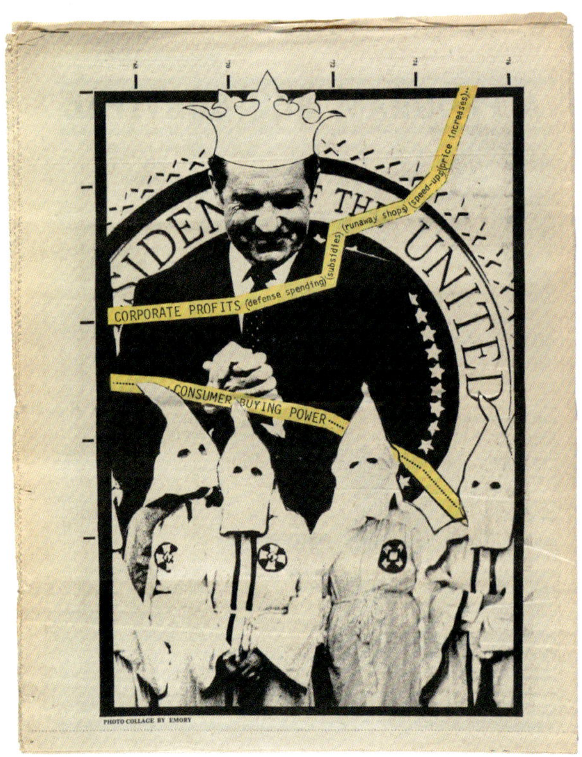

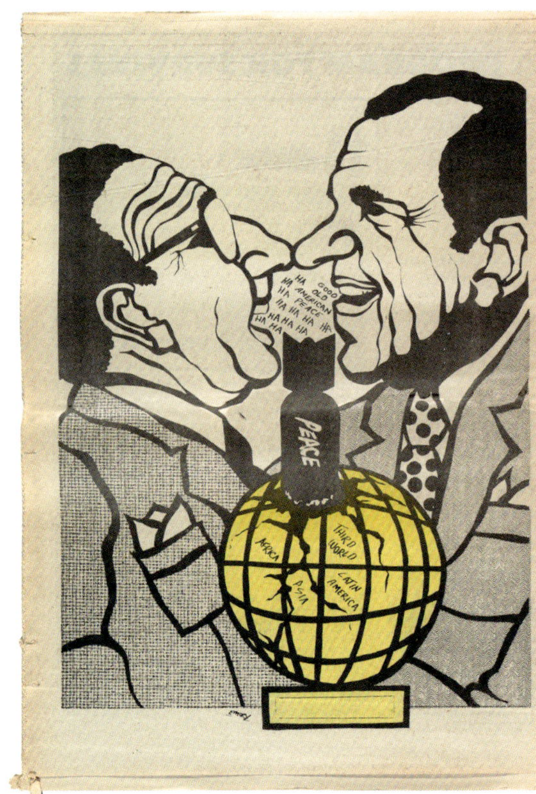

Emory Douglas, illustrations for *The Black Panther*.
Clockwise from top left:
September 27, 1969 (front cover)
July 25, 1970 (back cover)
February 17, 1973 (back cover)
March 16, 1974 (back cover)

Opposite:
September 21, 1974 (back cover)

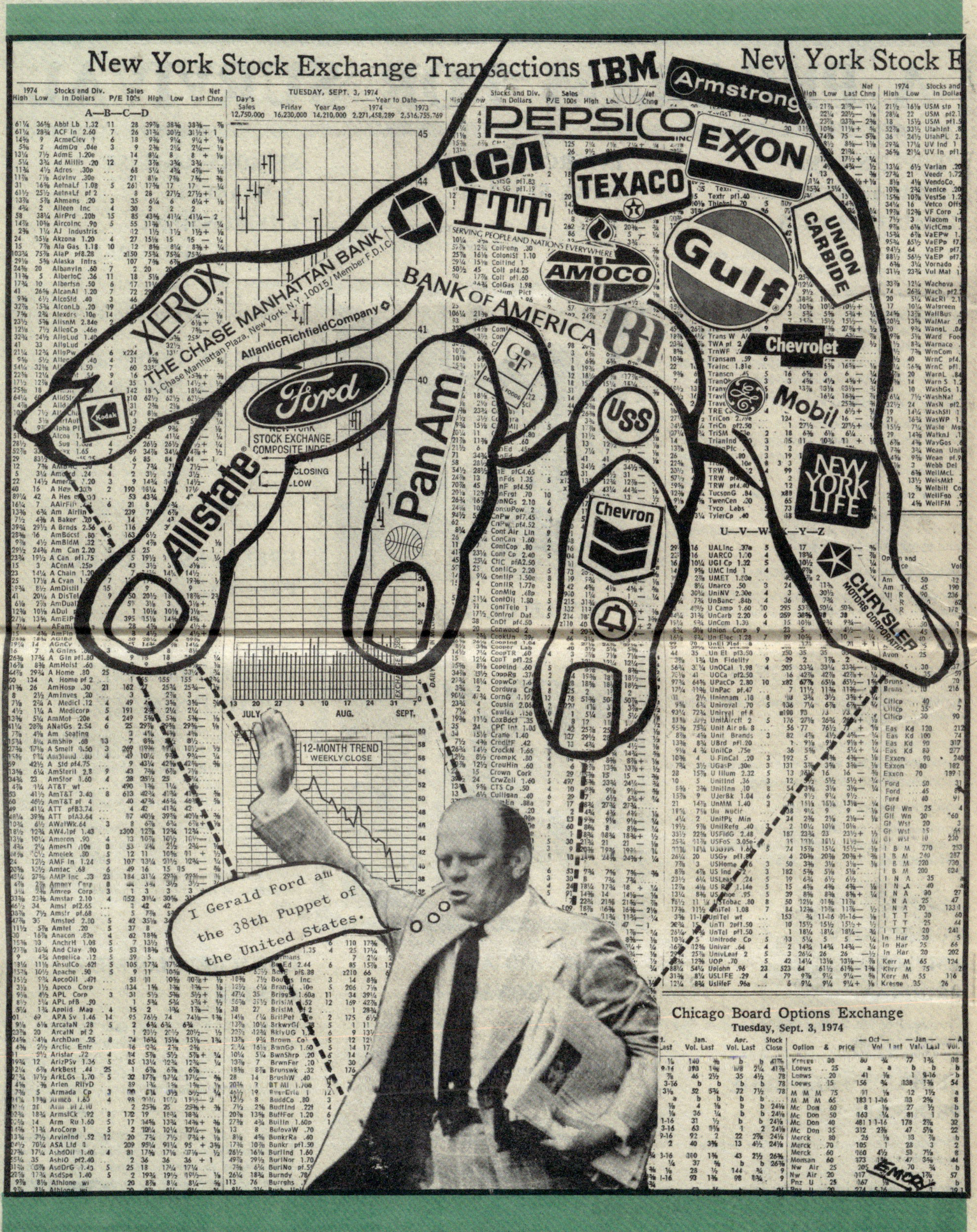

PHOTO COLLAGE BY EMORY

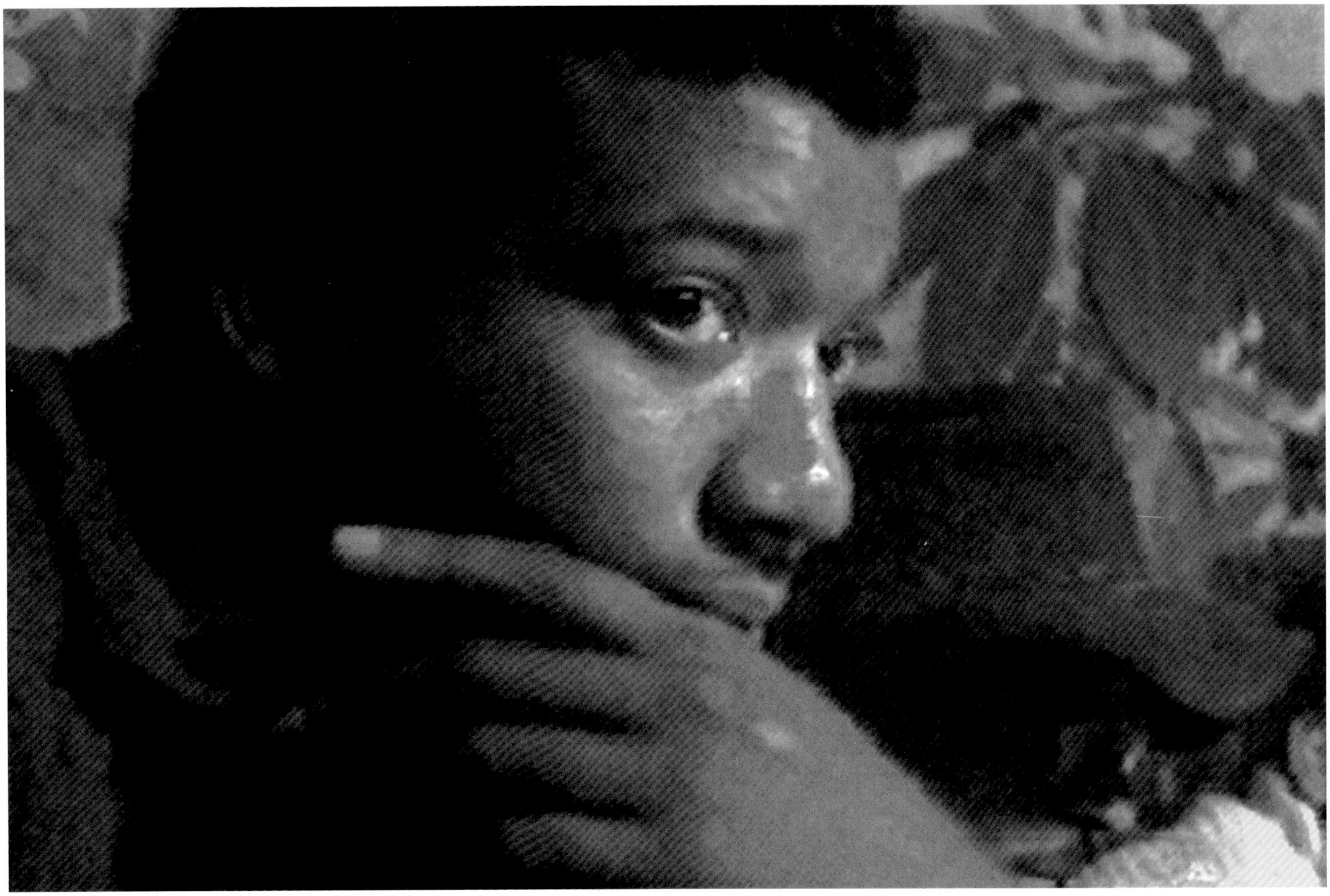

Still from Videofreex, *Fred Hampton: Black Panthers in Chicago*, 1969

Gerald Williams, *Wake Up*, 1969

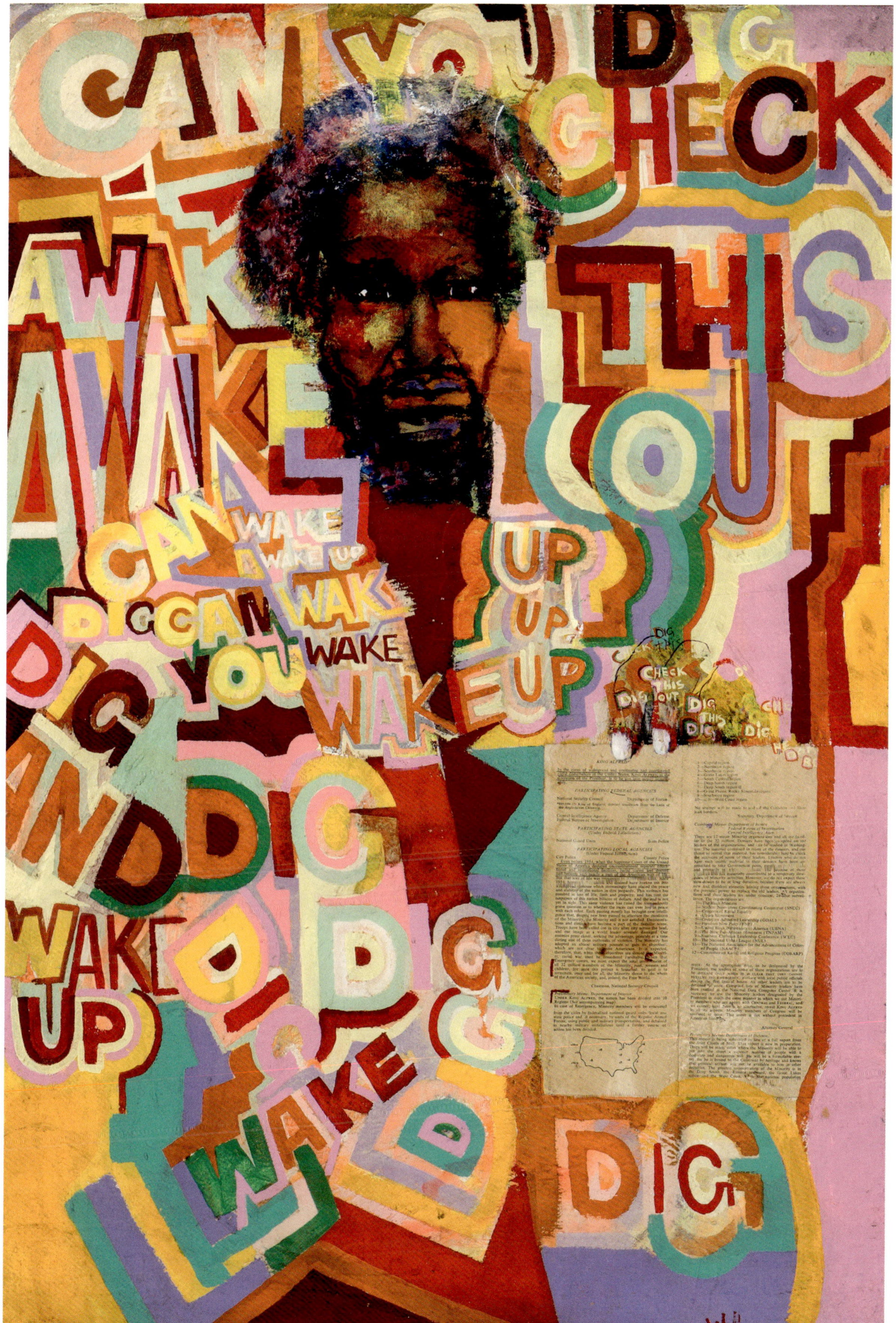
CAN YOU DIG
CHECK
THIS
OUT
WAKE
WAKE UP
DIG
YOU
AND DIG
Williams 1970

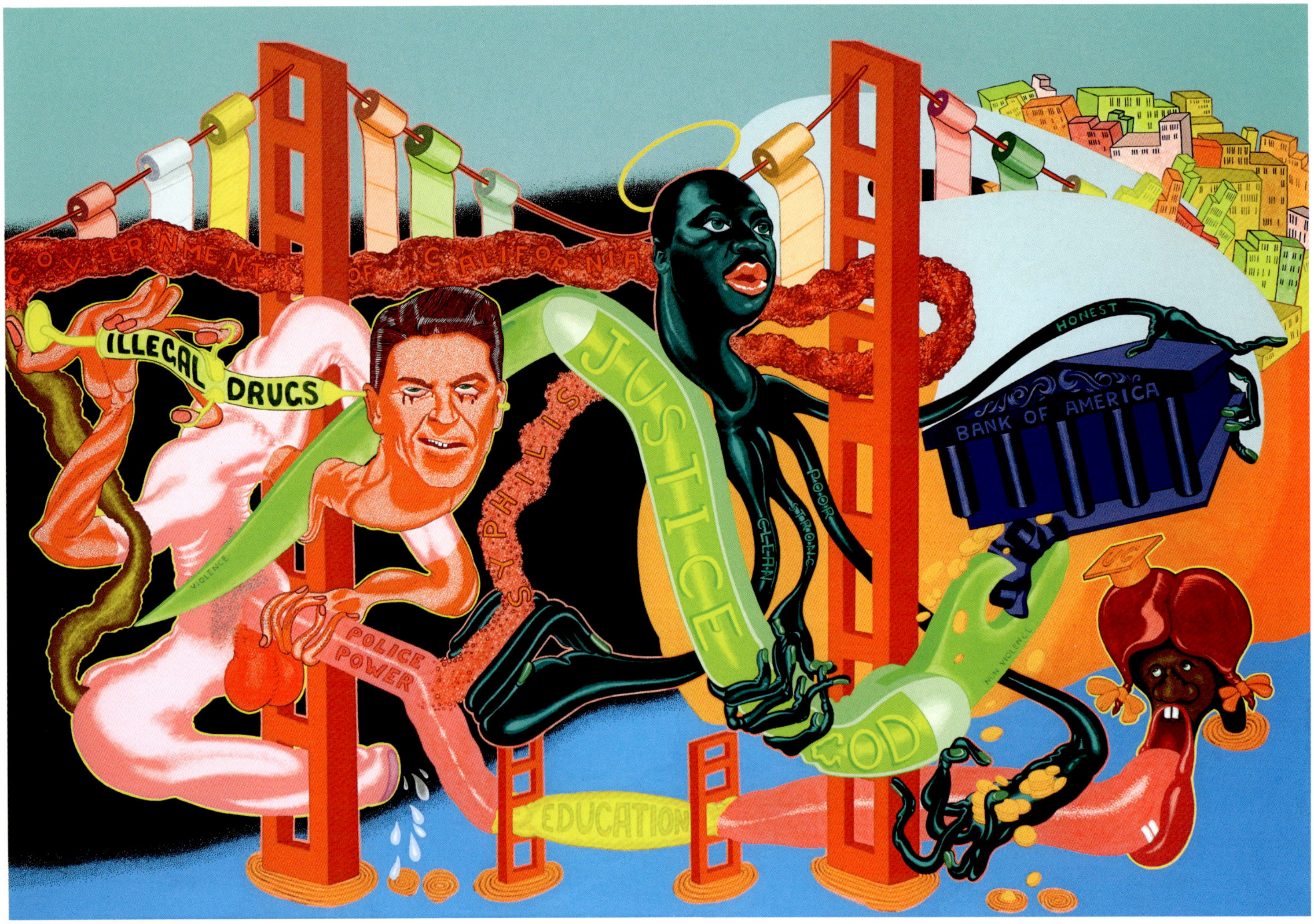

Peter Saul, *Government of California*, 1969

Peter Saul, *Untitled (Hitler's Brain Is Alive)*, 2006

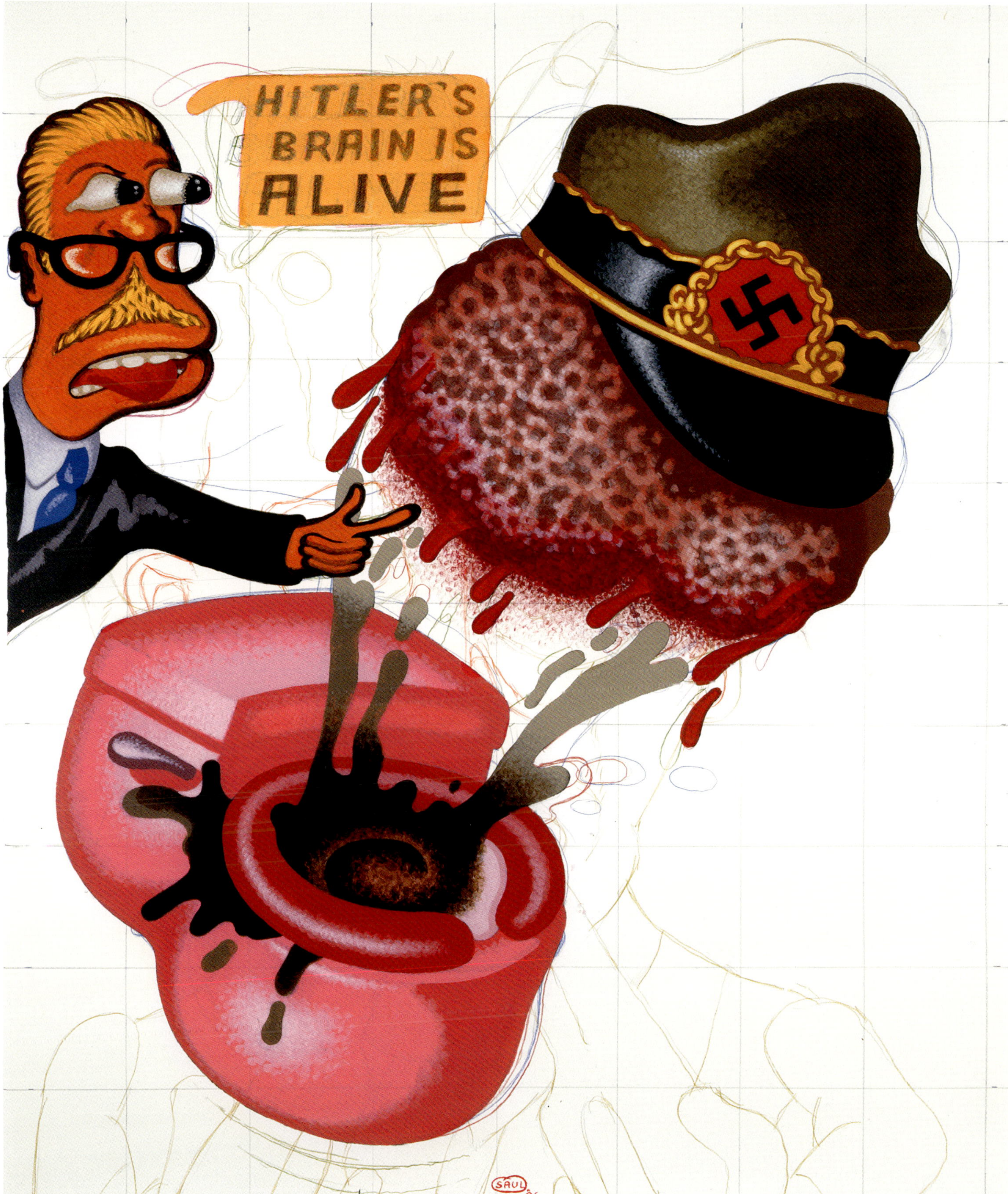
HITLER'S BRAIN IS ALIVE
SAUL 06

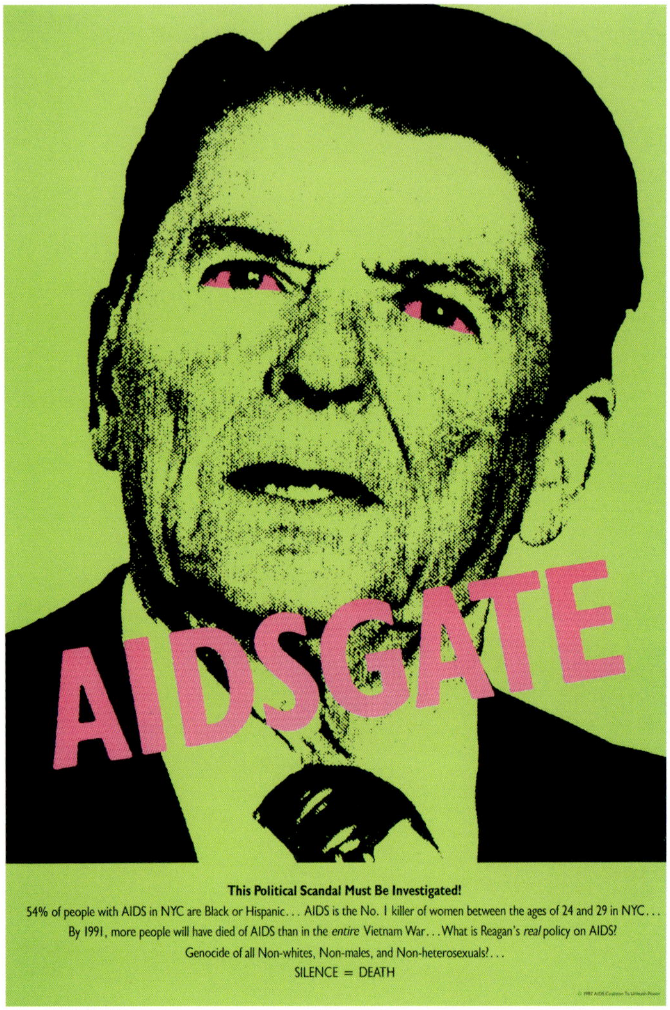

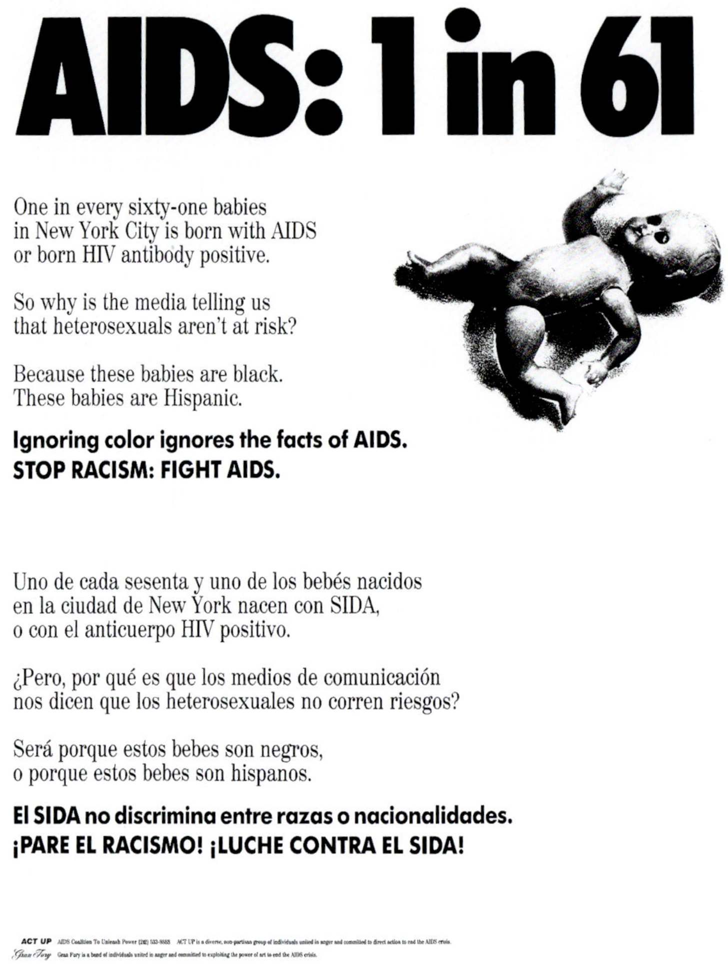

Avram Finkelstein and Vince Gagliostro, *Enjoy AZT*, 1990

Silence = Death Project, *AIDSGATE*, 1987

Silence = Death Project, *Silence = Death* poster, 1986

Gran Fury, *AIDS: 1 in 61*, 1988

Avram Finkelstein and Donald Moffett, *Fact or Fiction*, 1989

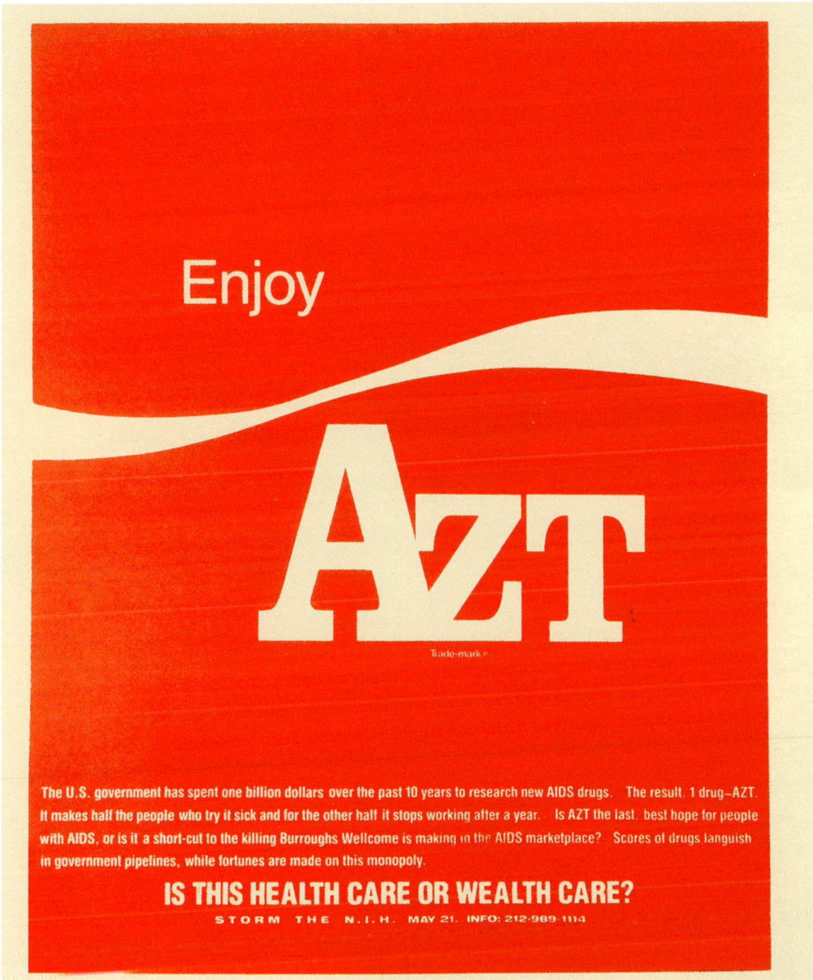
Enjoy
AZT
Trade-mark®
The U.S. government has spent one billion dollars over the past 10 years to research new AIDS drugs. The result. 1 drug–AZT. It makes half the people who try it sick and for the other half it stops working after a year. Is AZT the last. best hope for people with AIDS, or is it a short-cut to the killing Burroughs Wellcome is making in the AIDS marketplace? Scores of drugs languish in government pipelines, while fortunes are made on this monopoly.
IS THIS HEALTH CARE OR WEALTH CARE?
STORM THE N.I.H. MAY 21. INFO: 212-989-1114

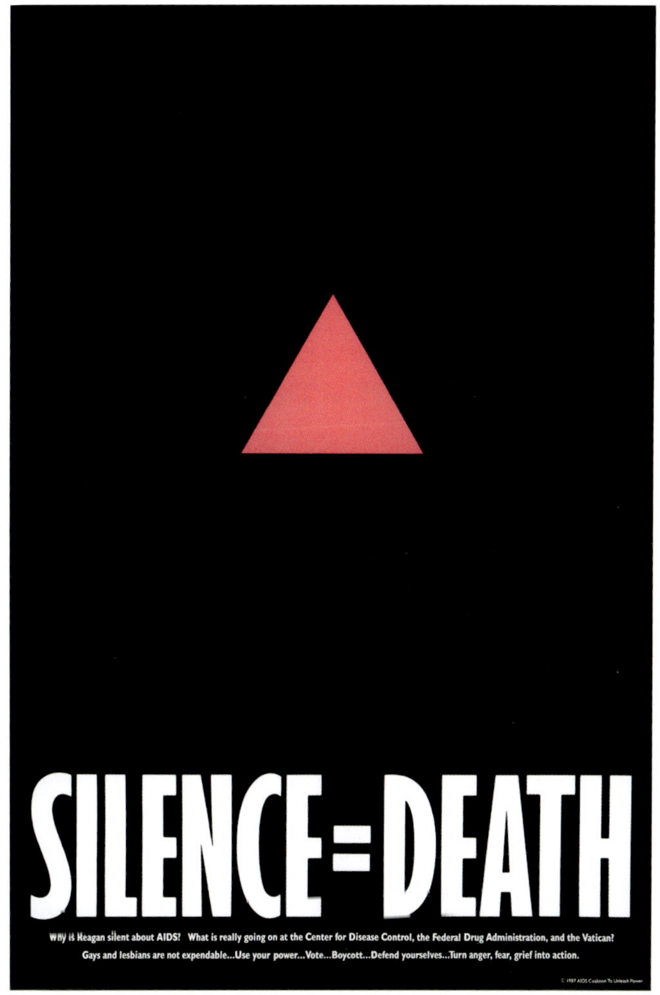
SILENCE=DEATH
Why is Reagan silent about AIDS? What is really going on at the Center for Disease Control, the Federal Drug Administration, and the Vatican?
Gays and lesbians are not expendable...Use your power...Vote...Boycott...Defend yourselves...Turn anger, fear, grief into action.

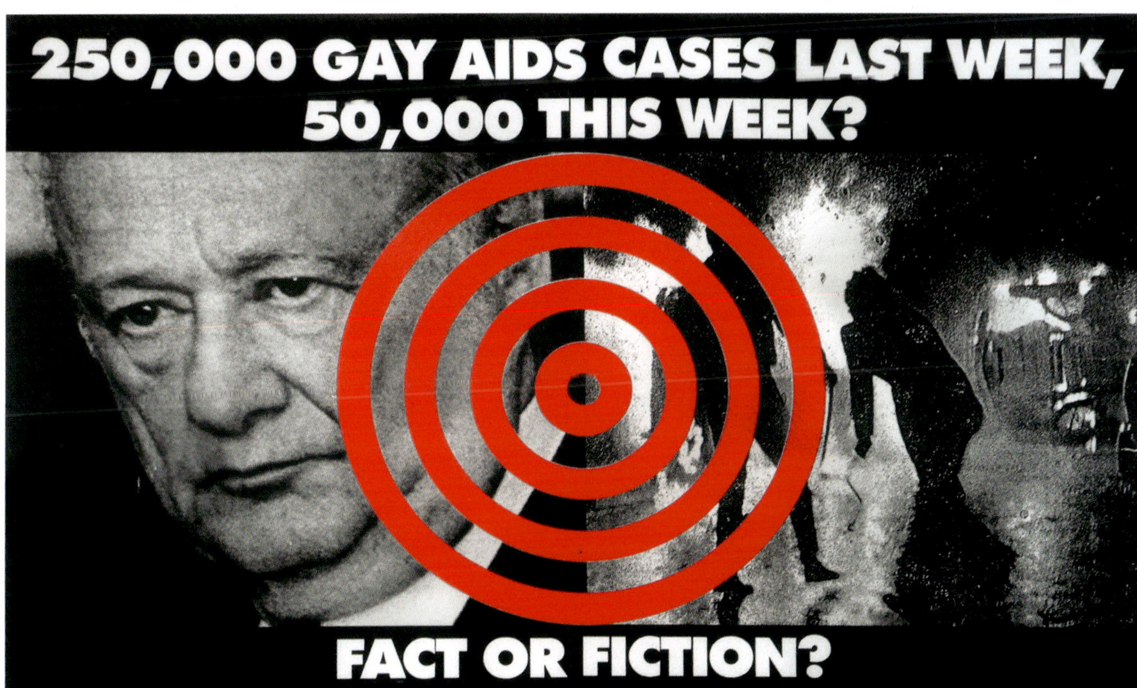
250,000 GAY AIDS CASES LAST WEEK,
50,000 THIS WEEK?
FACT OR FICTION?

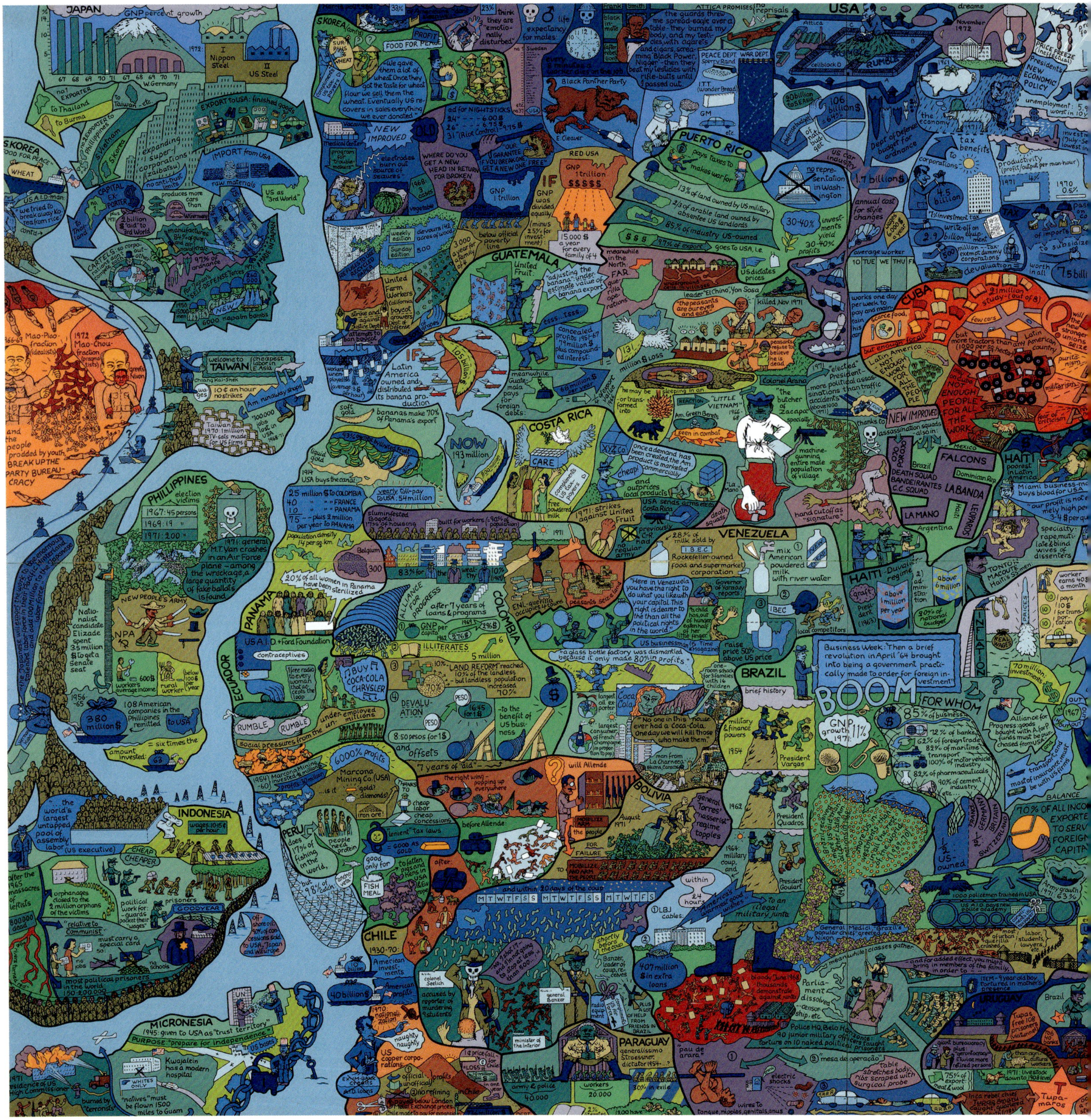

Öyvind Fahlström, *World Map*, 1972

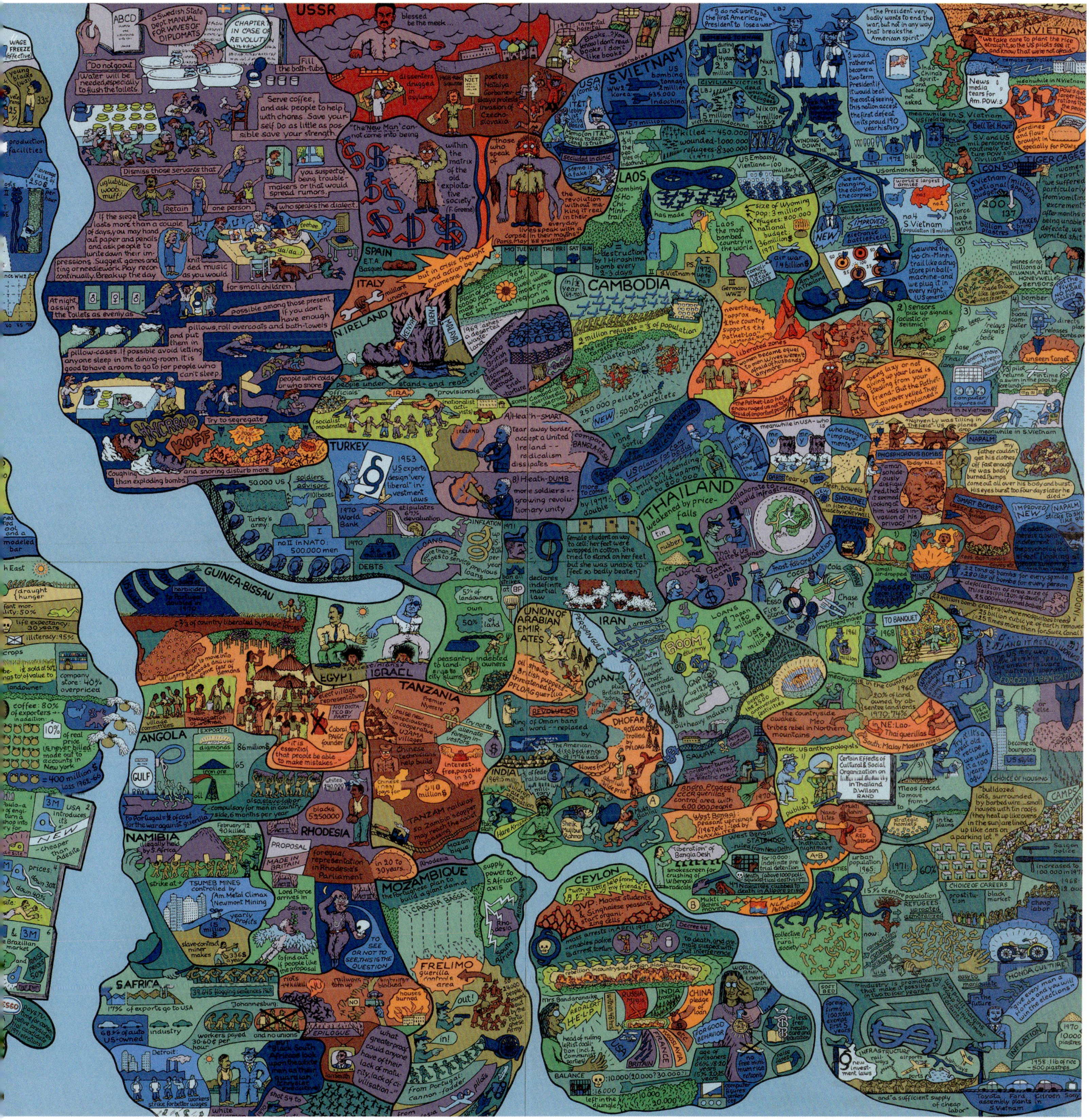
USSR
S.VIETNAM
N.VIETNAM
LAOS
CAMBODIA
THAILAND
SPAIN
ITALY
N.IRELAND
TURKEY
GUINEA-BISSAU
EGYPT
ISRAEL
UNION OF ARABIAN EMIRATES
IRAN
OMAN
DHOFAR
INDIA
TANZANIA
ANGOLA
NAMIBIA
RHODESIA
MOZAMBIQUE
FRELIMO
S.AFRICA
CEYLON
CHINA
RUSSIA
BRITAIN
FRANCE
INDOCHINA
Swedish State Dept. MANUAL FOR WIVES OF DIPLOMATS
fill the bath-tubs
Serve coffee and ask people to help with chores. Save yourself. Do as little as possible save your strength
Dismiss those servants that
"The New Man" cannot come into being
within the matrix of the old exploitative society
blessed be the meek
2 million refugees = 3 of population
250 000 pellets
NEW
PHOSPHOROUS BOMBS
NAPALM
SMART BOMBS
TO BANQUET
Certain Effects of Cultural & Social Organization in Thailand
REFUGEES
CHOICE OF CAREERS
HONDA CULTURE
INFRASTRUCTURE
INFLATION
BALANCE
Tsumeb Mines controlled by Am. Metal Climax Newmont Mining
Johannesburg

539-45 Fifth Ave.
Block 1279, lot 69
75 x 150', 13 story office bldg.
Chatham Associates, Inc.
Acquired 11-21'69
Land value $2 650 000, total value $4 500 000

531-37 Fifth Ave.
Block 1279, lot 1
125 x 140', 33 story office bldg.
Chatham Associates, Inc.
Acquired 11-21'69
Land value $3 700 000, total value $7 000 000

509 Fifth Ave.
Block 1277, lot 72
37 x 123', 12 story office bldg.
Chatham Associates, Inc.
Acquired 4-12'71
Land value $850 000, total value $1 700 000

92-96 Fifth Ave.
Block 816, lot 42
103 x 150', 18 story fireproof elevator apt. bldg.
West Haven Associates, Inc.
Acquired 11-11'70
Land value $545 000, total value $3 000 000

41 Fifth Ave.
Block 568, lot 6
54 x 141', 15 story fireproof elevator apt. bldg.
Newport Associates, Inc.
Acquired 10-22'64
Land value $340 000, total value $1 205 000

18-22 Fifth Ave.
Block 572, lot 38
80 x 124', 17 story fireproof elevator apt. bldg.
Newport Associates, Inc.
Acquired 7-20'64
Land value $420 000, total value $1 560 000

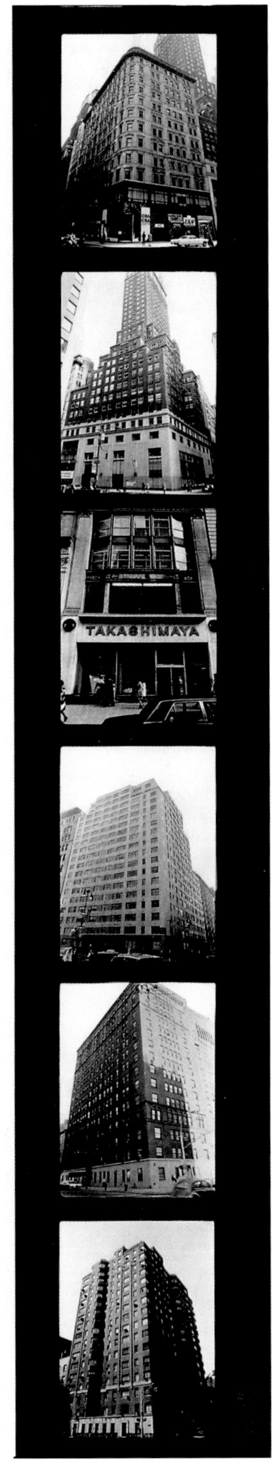

Details of Hans Haacke, *Sol Goldman and Alex DiLorenzo Manhattan Real Estate Holdings, A Real-Time Social System, as of May 1, 1971*, 1971

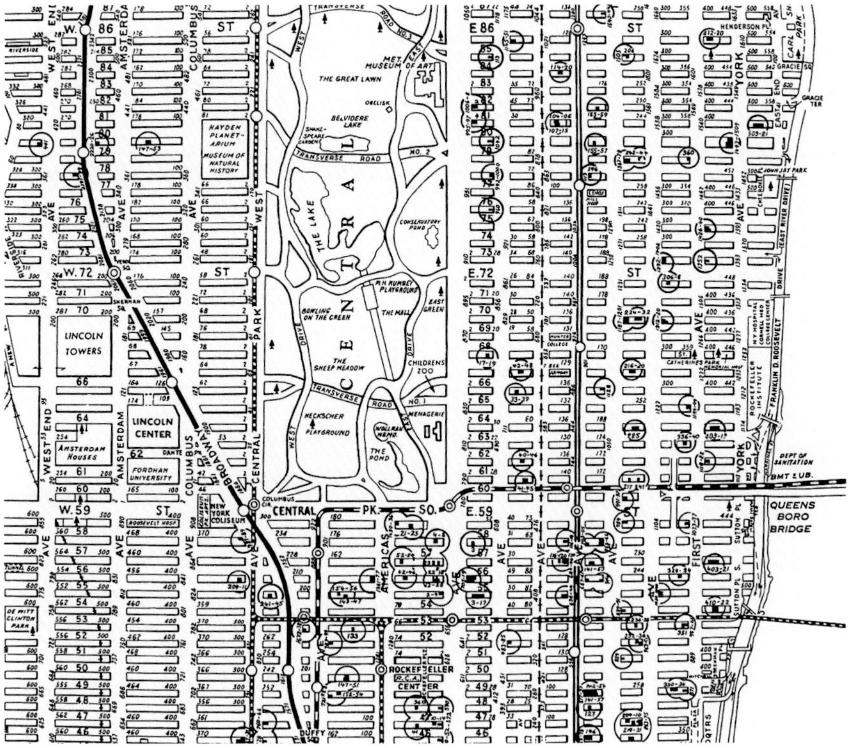
THE GREAT LAWN
MET. MUSEUM OF ART
BELVIDERE LAKE
HAYDEN PLANETARIUM
MUSEUM OF NATURAL HISTORY
THE LAKE
CONSERVATORY POND
BOWLING ON THE GREEN
THE MALL
THE SHEEP MEADOW
CHILDRENS ZOO
HECKSCHER PLAYGROUND
MENAGERIE
WOLLMAN MEMO.
THE POND
LINCOLN TOWERS
LINCOLN CENTER
AMSTERDAM HOUSES
FORDHAM UNIVERSITY
NEW YORK COLISEUM
COLUMBUS CIR.
CENTRAL PK SO.
ROCKEFELLER CENTER
QUEENS BORO BRIDGE
DEPT OF SANITATION
ROCKEFELLER INSTITUTE
FRANKLIN D. ROOSEVELT DRIVE
HENDERSON PL.
CARL SCHURZ PARK
GRACIE TER.
JOHN JAY PARK
EAST RIVER DRIVE
SUTTON PL.
DE WITT CLINTON PARK
CENTRAL
BROADWAY
COLUMBUS AVE
AMSTERDAM AVE
WEST END AVE
CENTRAL PARK WEST
W. 86
E 86
W. 72 ST
E. 72 ST
W. 59 ST
E. 59
YORK AVE
FIRST AVE
AMERICAS

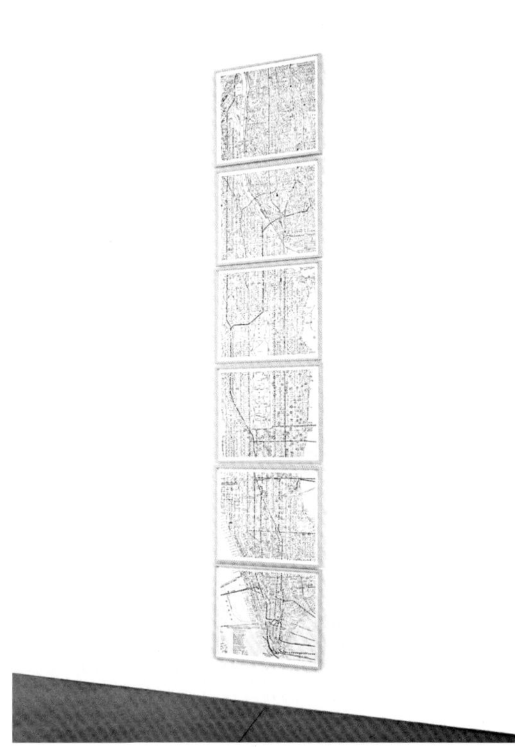

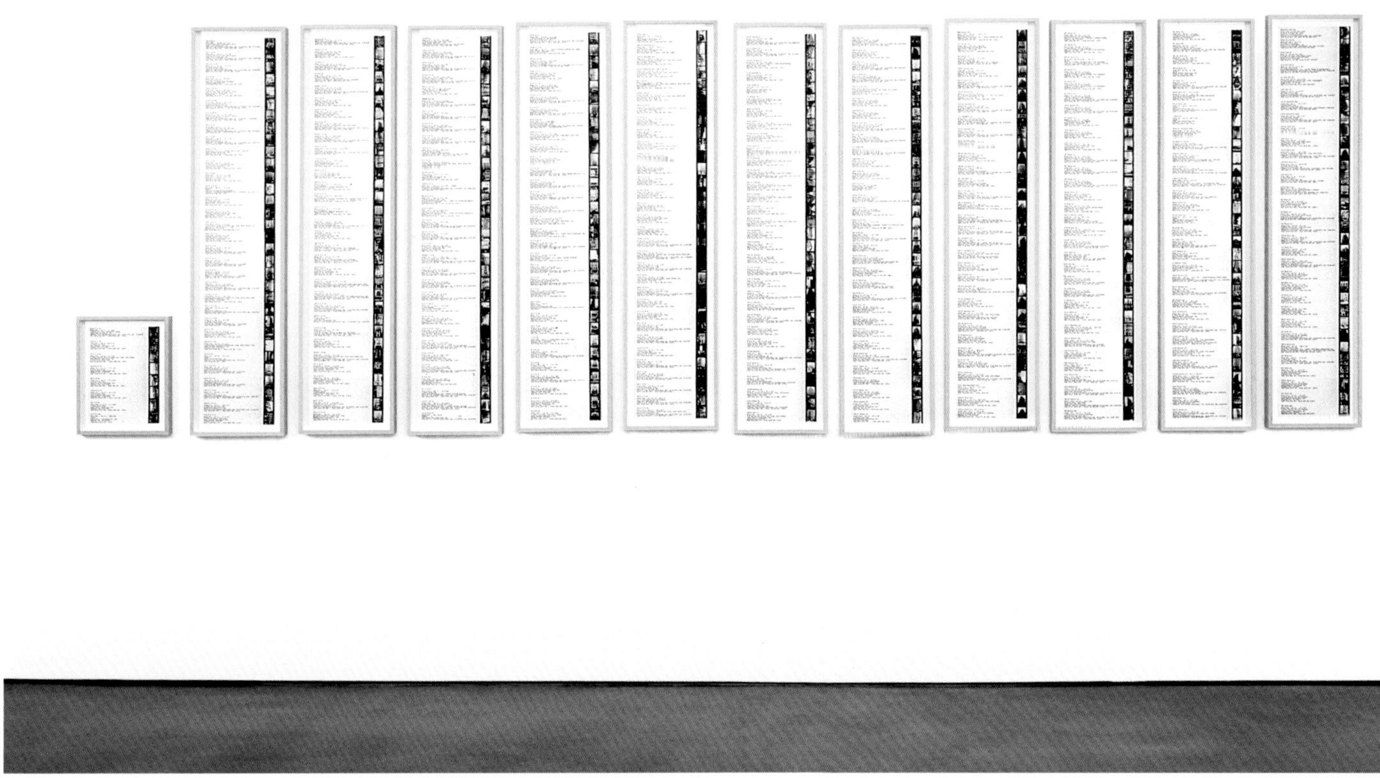

"A WILDERNESS OF MIRRORS": CONSPIRACY AND IDENTITY

Douglas Eklund

Somebody will have to piece me together.
—Jack Ruby testimony

If you were a minority or a politically active member of the counterculture in the late 1960s and early 1970s, paranoia was a defining quality of your existence. But the further out from harm you got, the more it had a perverse frisson. In 2008, Steely Dan's cofounder Donald Fagen noted, "These days paranoia is often more than justified and mightily oppressive. But to a feckless weekend hippie in the '60s, it seemed kind of exciting."[1] Among the general populace, though, it was as if the sequence of unprecedented, practically back-to-back assassinations—and the suspicions swirling around them—couldn't be immediately processed but instead churned in the national unconscious until the Watergate scandal brought this paranoia to the surface of American life.[2]

The spectacle of the televised Watergate hearings and the wide-ranging congressional investigations into government malfeasance that followed made conspiracy a cultural phenomenon. (Its pervasiveness is exemplified in the famous scene in *Annie Hall* [1977], when Woody Allen's protagonist Alvy Singer paces around the bedroom musing on the John F. Kennedy assassination to avoid sleeping with his girlfriend.) The Watergate hearings riveted the American public in much the same way that the twists and turns of the 2016 U.S. presidential election did. But the truly toxic legacy of Watergate came with Gerald Ford's pardon of Nixon. From then until now, the notion that justice is selective has baked increasingly deeper into how Americans view their country and has perhaps slanted their expectations of their own morality. For a brief moment, a decade before the Iran-Contra and Bank of Credit and Commerce International (BCCI) scandals (discussed in "The Artist as Researcher" in this volume, pp. 76–85), the hauling out of the dirty laundry of covert government activity was astonishing.

James Jesus Angleton, the head of the counterintelligence staff at the CIA from 1954 until he was forced to resign in 1975, was the biggest casualty of the agency's purges (fig. 23). A Yale-educated, self-styled Anglophile aesthete, Angleton brought the interpretive strategies of New Criticism—defined by his biographer as its attention to "coded language, textual analysis, ambiguity, and close control"[3]—to bear on the Cold War hunt for Soviet moles. Angleton lifted the phrase "a wilderness of mirrors" from T. S. Eliot's poem "Gerontion" to describe his quarry's "myriad of stratagems, deceptions, artifices, and all the other devices of disinformation which the Soviet bloc and its coordinated intelligence services use to confuse and split the West . . . an ever fluid landscape where fact and illusion merge."[4] Angleton was obsessed with discovering Soviet moles during his decades-long tenure, regularly drumming innocent agents out of the agency. But he was equally involved in a litany of abuses related to the CIA's "massive illegal domestic intelligence operation during the Nixon administration," as Seymour Hersh described Operation CHAOS's harassment of antiwar activists, which entailed break-ins, wiretapping, and intercepting and reading mail. Angleton also maintained and controlled exclusive access to a dossier on Lee Harvey Oswald from the time of his defection to the Soviet Union in 1959 until the assassination of President Kennedy. Angleton was notified on October 8, 1963, that Oswald had contacted the Soviet embassy in Mexico City and on November 15—seven days before the assassination—that he had returned to the Dallas area.[5]

A rarely seen sculpture by Öyvind Fahlström is perhaps the first work to address directly the possibility of conspiracy in the Kennedy assassination. Although described as a "variable painting" on the checklist of the artist's 1967 solo exhibition at Sidney Janis Gallery in New York, Fahlström's *Parkland Memorial* is the first of a series of works in which water is a central element. It is a farcical proposal for a memorial to be sited outside the Dallas hospital where Kennedy died. The flat, waist-high tabletop model contains five inches of water, on which bob painted photographs affixed to Styrofoam floats. Giant cockroaches in a single-file procession snake toward a ghoulishly gray cutout head of Lyndon Johnson whispering in the ear of a bobbing Jack Ruby head. Flanking the two coconspirators are cutouts of the bowing maidens who genuflect before Count Dracula in Tod Browning's eponymous 1931 horror classic. Not unlike Bruce Conner's collage film *REPORT* (fig. 9), which juxtaposes Kennedy's flag-draped casket with Dr. Frankenstein bringing his monster to life, Fahlström's "memorial" uses the subculture of monster movies as a ready-made language to capture the mythic resonances of the event and, more importantly, to cast doubt on the official story by inserting a fictional element. The artist's depiction of politicians as monsters from an old movie

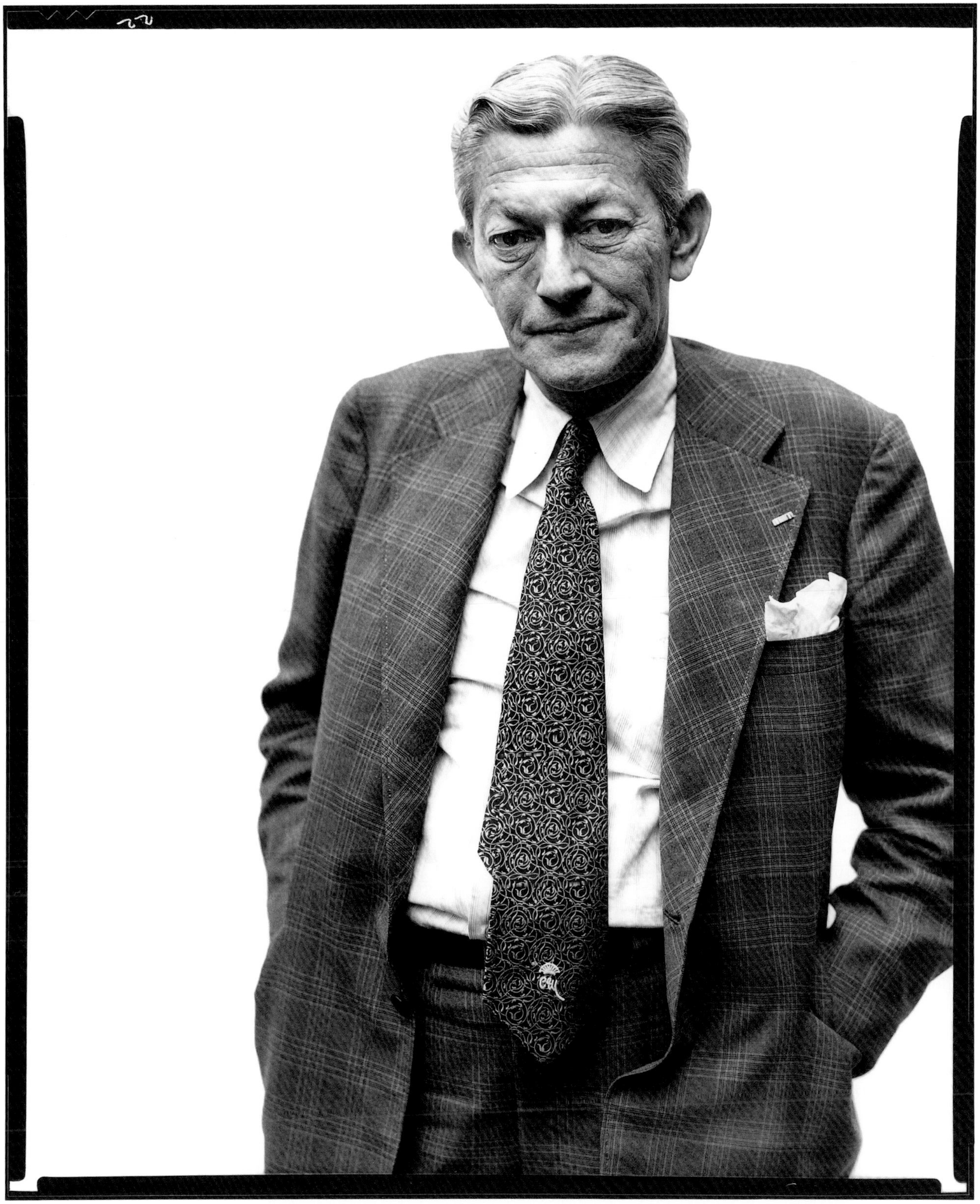

Fig. 23. Richard Avedon (American, 1923–2004), *James Angleton, Former Chief of Counterintelligence, CIA, Arlington, Virginia, July 8, 1976*, 1976. Gelatin silver print, image 10 × 8 in. (25.4 × 20.3 cm). The Metropolitan Museum of Art, New York, Purchase, Alfred Stieglitz Society Gifts, 2009 (2009.5.39)

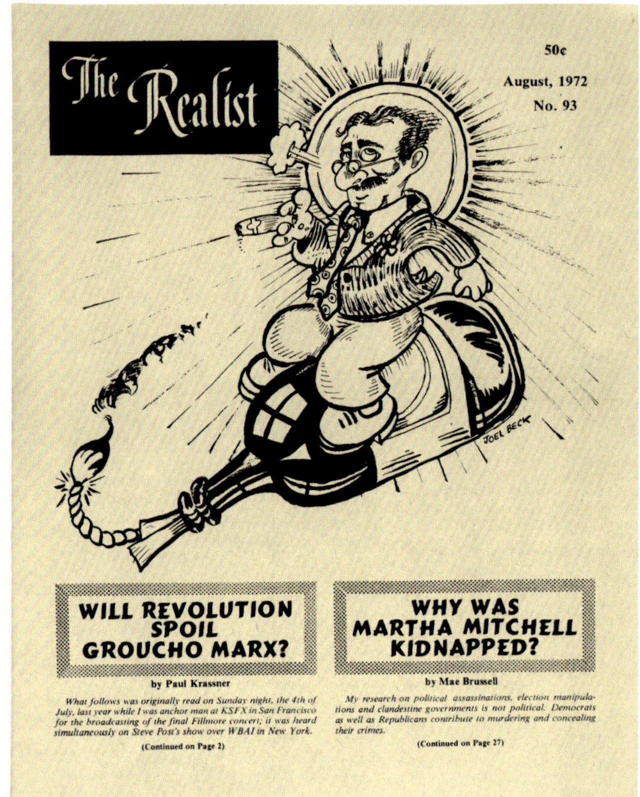

The Realist

50¢
August, 1972
No. 93

JOEL BECK

WILL REVOLUTION SPOIL GROUCHO MARX?

by Paul Krassner

What follows was originally read on Sunday night, the 4th of July, last year while I was anchor man at KSFX in San Francisco for the broadcasting of the final Fillmore concert; it was heard simultaneously on Steve Post's show over WBAI in New York.

(Continued on Page 2)

WHY WAS MARTHA MITCHELL KIDNAPPED?

by Mae Brussell

My research on political assassinations, election manipulations and clandestine governments is not political. Democrats as well as Republicans contribute to murdering and concealing their crimes.

(Continued on Page 27)

Fig. 24. *The Realist*, August 1972, featuring Mae Brussell's article "Why was Martha Mitchell Kidnapped?"

predates Peter Saul's similar references in *Government of California* (1969; p. 36), while his cutouts in some ways anticipate by two decades Cady Noland's "cutouts" of photographs silkscreened on aluminum (figs. 30, 31). In the same year he produced *Parkland Memorial*, Fahlström wrote a play titled *Oswald kommer tillbaka* (Oswald Returns) that intersperses testimony about the Kennedy assassination with dialogue lifted from a variety of 1930s gangster films.[6]

When conspiracy went from latent to manifest in the 1970s, it had a focus different from the overarching concern with assaults on communities that occupied both counterintelligence and the counterculture. Indeed, one could argue that the collapse of the left gave birth to the idea of the "rabbit hole." As subcultures of conspiracy "theory" (or research or analysis) began to proliferate, they collectively formed the rhetorical style that we recognize today: the almost dreamlike stringing together of ever more unlikely connections, the obsession with minutiae, the paradoxical reverence for both factual citations and speculation, and the faint but unmistakable aura of conspiracy as modern-day folklore or mythology.

In the early 1970s, and especially following the reelection of Richard Nixon in 1972, the left splintered into what historian Andreas Killen referred to as "hundreds of minor cults of insurrection."[7] In 1976, then journalist and later Clinton political operative Sidney Blumenthal hypothesized that the left's conspiracy thinking was an outgrowth of having a radicalized youth population whose utopian aspirations were dashed by "a group of people at the top [who] made sure they were dashed."[8] The nerve center of this torn and frayed counterculture was Northern California, and its unofficial spokesperson was Mae Brussell, a Beverly Hills housewife who relocated to Carmel-by-the-Sea and eventually reinvented herself as a radio host. No figure embodies the conspiratorial turn in the culture of the 1970s more than Brussell. Converted to the cause in 1963 by the Kennedy assassination, she became one of the so-called "scavengers of the Warren Report," as a 1967 book called independent researchers such as Mark Lane, Vincent Salandria, Sylvia Meagher, and others who picked apart the contradictions buried in the twenty-six volumes of the Warren Commission's findings.[9] In the 1971 radio interview that preceded her weekly show, "Dialogue: Conspiracy," Brussell wondered if the Kennedy assassination was a fascist plot. She then connected that bombshell to what were, for her, other linked phenomena, such as the increased production of Minutemen missiles and the influence of the John Birch Society (which she deemed a real danger, not just a bunch of "grandmas in tennis shoes"). Like Emory Douglas, Brussell saw the threat of fascism in America in intensely personal terms, concluding that her mission came about because she "wanted to know what kind of world [she] was leaving to her children."[10] A sign of Brussell's importance to the counterculture came when Paul Krassner, the editor of a struggling humor and conspiracy magazine called *The Realist*, got emergency funding from John Lennon to keep publishing specifically so he could run Brussell's secret history behind the Watergate scandal, "Why Was Martha Mitchell Kidnapped?," in the August 1972 issue (fig. 24).[11]

Brussell's discursive style of leaping among subjects not normally connected quickly became the lingua franca of conspiracy theorists (or conspiracy "analysts," as Gore Vidal described himself).[12] Forty years later, the Internet is chockablock with conspiracy sleuths who have never heard of her, despite speaking in a language she first popularized. Enough people are exposed to her broadcasts through YouTube, however, to make her the occasional subject of hit pieces.[13] But for every one of her speculative theories that seems dubious, another seems startlingly prescient. Take her March 28, 1981, broadcast, much of which was devoted to power struggles in the Reagan White House. The heading in the printed summary she mailed that same day to subscribers, along with the audiocassette copy of the broadcast, read: "The top dogs are fighting. Musical chairs. Who will kill their team members off or will they kill us first."[14] Although John Hinckley Jr., who shot President Reagan on March 30, fit the description of a "lone nut," the conspiracy minded immediately seized on tantalizing though highly circumstantial evidence that Vice President George H. W. Bush's son Neil and his friend Scott, Hinckley's brother, had made dinner plans for March 31 that were canceled after the shooting.[15]

Brussell's conceptual framing of both the Kennedy assassination and the war in Vietnam as evidence of a creeping fascist takeover with roots in World War II may seem farfetched today, but it is rooted in the embryonic stages of countercultural thinking going back to 1965 (fig. 25). Her vantage is represented most famously in the conspiratorial awakening of the protagonist in Thomas Pynchon's short novel *The Crying of Lot 49* (1966). The suburban Republican housewife Oedipa Maas, as the executrix charged with sorting the vast, entangled estate of her ex-boyfriend, Pierce Inverarity (a name that scans suspiciously like John F. Kennedy), plunges down a rabbit hole in pursuit of an underground mail network. It all may be an elaborate practical joke from beyond the grave—or a skeleton key to making sense of postwar America.

Fig. 25. Wes Wilson (American, born 1937), *Are We Next?*, 1965. Screenprint poster, 16 × 30 in. (40.6 × 76.2 cm)

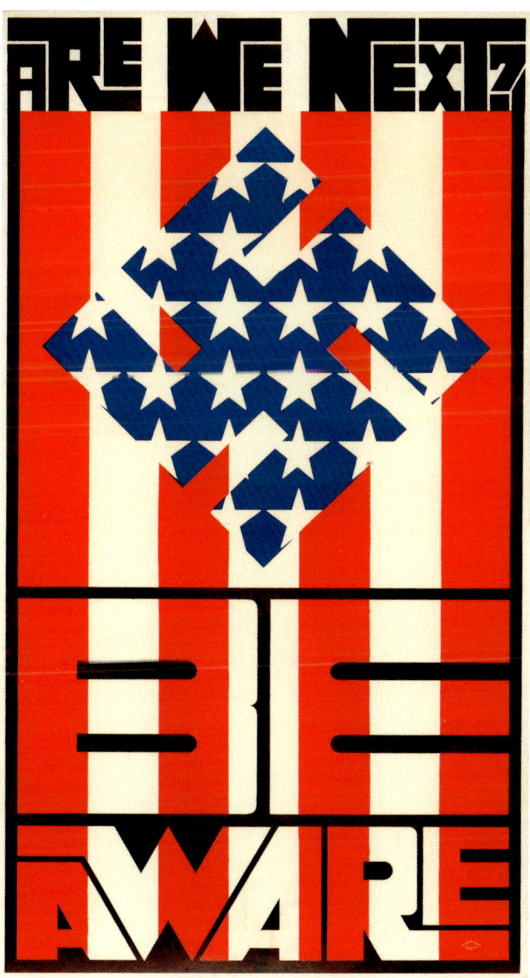

Following Maas as she picks up breadcrumbs, the reader becomes an echo of the character but can see more clearly the web of sinister allusions that form a kind of second story hidden behind Maas's own, described by one critic as a double narrative akin to a Magic Eye poster.[16] The reader is pointed to this "real" story beneath the ostensible one through Maas's encounters with swastika salesmen, Birchers, arms manufacturers, and most obviously her shrink—a relocated Nazi whose LSD therapy sounds suspiciously like the CIA's not-yet-known mind-control program. What swirls around the unaware Maas reads uncannily like a catalogue of Brussell's interests, so much so that one wonders if Brussell herself, the Beverly Hills rabbi's daughter who moved to Northern California to join the counterculture and research the Kennedy assassination, was a real-life model for Pynchon's protagonist.

Lutz Bacher's chance find of a World War II–era negative for sale in a Berkeley secondhand store raised the specter of an unextinguished fascism that so haunted Brussell and others. In a proto-appropriation work from 1975 titled *Men at War*, Bacher zooms in on details of the snapshot, which shows smiling, shirtless soldiers at leisure, one of whom sports both an American Navy cap and a swastika tattoo. Having the wrong size holder for the large-format negative created technical imperfections (partial views and darkened or out-of-focus passages) of the kind the artist would use productively as aesthetic strategies throughout her career.

In breaking the single image into a sequence of close-up fragments, Bacher cues the viewer to ask questions, one of the most important being, what side exactly are these men at war on? Bacher provokes a confusion in the viewer—are these Americans or Germans? In doing so, she invokes the same sinister possibility that haunted Philip K. Dick and Pynchon, that the lie of official history masked collusion at high levels, from dealings among the United States government, American businesses, and Nazi Germany to the importation of Nazi spymaster Reinhard Gehlen to the United States to fight the Soviet Union.[17] By the time Bacher made *Men at War*, revelations about Operation

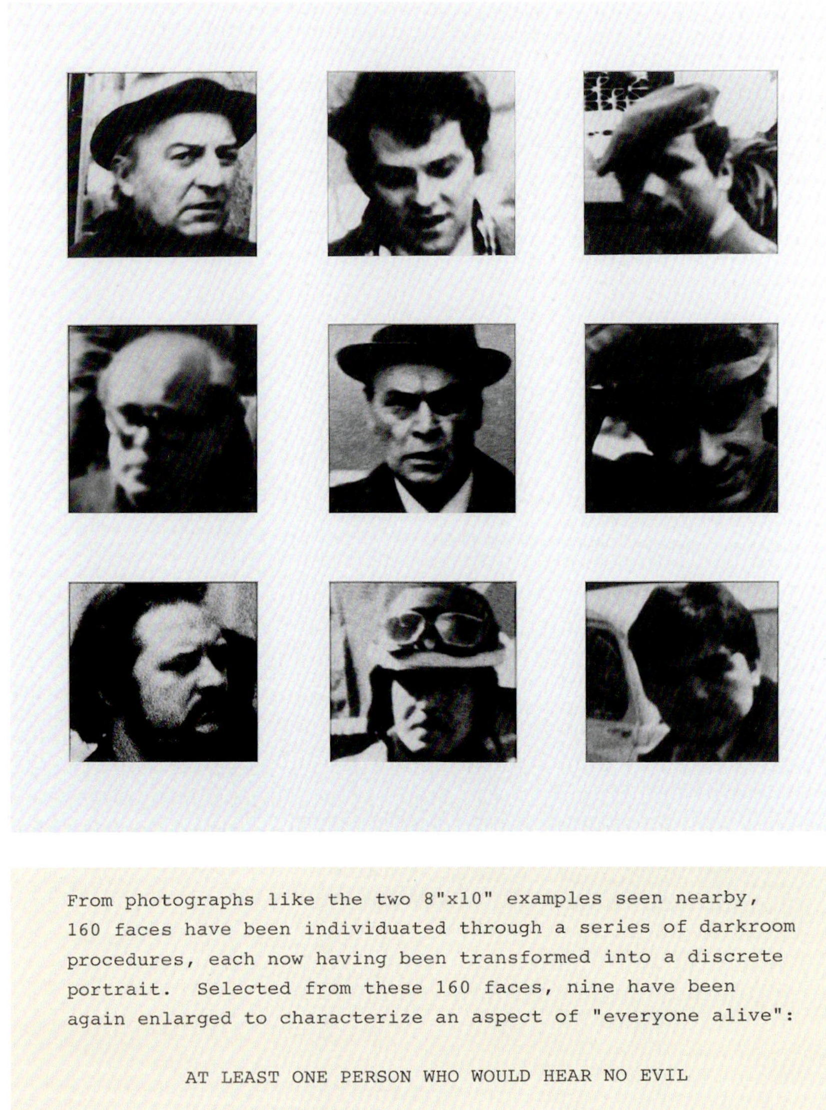

Fig. 26. Details of Douglas Huebler (American, 1924–1997), *598 / Variable Piece #70: 1971 (In Process) Global 1975*, 1975. Gelatin silver prints and typescript, frame: 37 × 37 in. (94 × 94 cm) each; overall: 37 × 74 in. (94 × 188 cm). The Metropolitan Museum of Art, New York, Purchase, Vital Projects Fund Inc. Gift, through Joyce and Robert Menschel, and Stephen and Jennifer Rich Gift, 2012 (2012.32a,b)

Paperclip—the secret program to bring hundreds of Nazi scientists to America in the late 1940s—were beginning to surface. Viewed through the prism of Operation Paperclip, the confusion that Bacher elicits looks less specious than frighteningly real.[18]

Bacher's interest in elusive identity found its perfect embodiment in Lee Harvey Oswald. In 1976, not coincidentally the year the House Select Committee on Assassinations was formed, Bacher shifted her attention to the Kennedy controversy. When approached to participate in a book of interviews with Bay Area artists, she answered the request with an eighteen-part collage and a transcript of her own invention, *The Lee Harvey Oswald Interview* (1976; pp. 60–61 and front endpapers). Bacher identified neither speaker in the conversation, and the "subject" seems to be neither the artist nor Oswald in any specific sense. Rather, Bacher voices the conspiracy theorists' endless debates over whether a CIA look-alike double had crisscrossed Oswald's path in order to confound both the evidentiary record and the recollections of possible witnesses. Against this backdrop, the conversation moves ambivalently and haltingly around a broader topic—the essentially arbitrary relationship between signifier (face) and referent (character or inner self).

While Bacher's use of ghostly cut-up photocopies mimics the aesthetic of a conspiracy theorist, the artist disavows any particular interest, now or then, in the conspiracy theories surrounding the Kennedy assassination. This ambivalence tracks with the artist's identification with Oswald, her subject, not only as an inscrutable figure but also as an object of desire, as evidenced by his obsessive portrayal. In her invented interview, Bacher deflected any interest to know more about her by handing the reader a short course on the ultimate shape-shifter, whose very name and appearance is up for grabs. At the beginning of the piece, Bacher writes that she "had a newspaper photograph of a man's face—some other man not Oswald—and under this picture is the caption 'escaped psychopath.' I used to look at this picture and try to decide if he looked like a psychopath even though I already knew because I'd been told. I decided there was no way of telling that kind of thing from a photograph." Her interest in others is one direction on a two-way street that includes her own fugitive presence. The illegibility of others (from their appearance) goes hand in hand with her own implied identification with Oswald and thus her own status as a cipher or a projection surface for her audience.

On the penultimate page of the collage, the artist inscribed the legend (taken from elsewhere in the interview), "Anyone can pretend." What one critic described as Bacher's abiding interest in "the fungibility of identity and the overall trickiness of imagery"[19] appears here in embryo. Yet, for all the fevered cutting of the collage and its obsessive visual language, Bacher does not identify with the conspiracy theorist. Rather, she points to her own inaccessibility as an author in a way that chimes with post-Watergate revelations about people who are not who they seem to be: doubles and patsies involved in covert government action at home and abroad, agents provocateurs who create chaos to discredit the political opposition from within (among other things).

Bacher's fugue on identity and representation through the emergent language of conspiracy theory chimes with contemporary artistic examinations of the relationship between photography and identity. Conceptual artist Douglas Huebler, in his quixotic quest to photograph everyone alive, produced batches of faces that he then sorted into smaller sets according to a maxim; for example, *598 / Variable Piece #70: 1971 (In Process) Global 1975*, made by Huebler in 1975, identifies a subset of nine, including "AT LEAST ONE PERSON WHO WOULD HEAR NO EVIL" (fig. 26). The nine faces presented in close-up just happen to look uncannily like spies, secret agents, or fugitive war criminals, those who would truly "hear no evil." It is not surprising that Huebler—a combat veteran of World War II—would evoke the Holocaust as the sinister shadow of his elaborate fiction, precisely in order to show how supposedly neutral and transparent tools of recording and communication, such as language and photography, can be misused.

Perhaps the greatest work of the 1970s to examine photography's imbrication of falsity and conspiracy is Sarah Charlesworth's *April 21, 1978*, which takes as its subject the abduction and murder of Aldo Moro, a former prime minister of Italy, by the Red Brigades (1978; pp. 62–63). It is a fulcrum work that displays, in equal parts, a Conceptual strategy (of which it is a late example) and the Pictures Generation's triangulation of Minimal and Conceptual strategies with Pop's graphic impact. Charlesworth's removal of text and captions is reminiscent of Lawrence Weiner's Removal series (1968/1983; fig. 27). But when trained on something as supposedly objective as the front pages that carried the hostage photograph, the erasure of words has the force of revelation. It unfurls an impossibly tangled and confusing set of relationships normally hidden behind

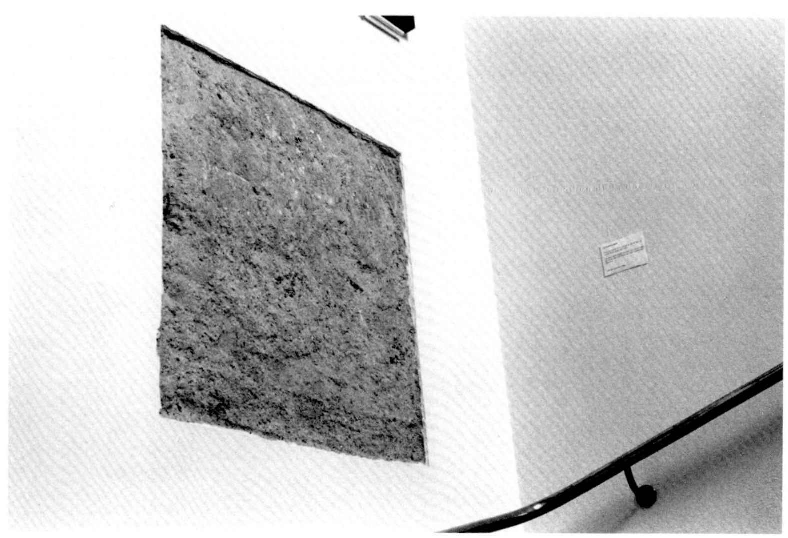

Fig. 27. Lawrence Weiner (American, born 1942), *A 36" × 36" Removal to the Lathing or Support Wall of Plaster or Wallboard from a Wall*, 1968. Language and the materials referred to, dimensions variable. Installation "Works + Re-Constructions," Kunsthalle, Bern, 1983. The Museum of Modern Art, New York, Gift of Seth Siegelaub and the Stichting Egress Foundation, Amsterdam

verbal explanation, much in the same way that Pynchon in *The Crying of Lot 49* treats the reader like his protagonist, offering occasional glimpses of a hidden order.

In her introduction to a 1979 catalogue of the Modern History series, Charlesworth wrote: "The question of the position of the subject begins then with my experience, the codified relation to an absent event . . . through the media context, through the ordering of its surface, through both written language and photographic analogue, the experience of being acted upon to observe, to participate . . . in the rhetorical manifestations of power."[20] *April 21, 1978* is unthinkable without Louis Althusser's concept that the individual's worldview is ideologically determined as she or he is shunted from one institution's invisible hand of indoctrination to the next. According to Althusserian theory, the news does not augment a subject's autonomy or provide critical tools for understanding the world, but instead is a trap set by the power structure to divert, contain, and neutralize the subject.

Charlesworth's series is also a textbook illustration of what art historian John Tagg described as the "unruly work of 1970s photo-theory"[21] that occupied critics on the left such as Victor Burgin, Allan Sekula, Tagg, and others. For them, the photographic image is a message waiting to be directed, dependent on its specific usage or context. As Tagg noted in 1978, "Photography is itself an apparatus of ideological control under the central 'harmonising' authority of the ideology of the class which, openly or through alliance, holds state power and wields the state apparatus."[22] *April 21, 1978* is about the unconscious and uncoordinated ways in which editors and graphic designers are agents of obfuscation, rather than truth telling, and it illustrates the true function of the news, which is not to inform the reader of significant events but instead to maintain the power of the state at a moment when its authority is challenged. That the forty-five parts of the work, when viewed together, resemble a game board with seemingly infinite vectors of visible, but indecipherable, relationships is the most important aspect of the work's meaning. And the unmistakable look of strategic moves pollutes the seeming naturalness of the supposedly straightforward photographs, so that they look highly artificial, even rigged. (Readers' suspicions about the veracity of both the hostage photograph and Moro's missives to the police are discussed in the essay by Beth Saunders in this volume, pp. 96–105.)

Works such as *April 21, 1978* belong on a continuum with the extra-artistic contestations of power seen in amateur researchers' obsessive study of images related to the Kennedy assassination, beginning in the 1960s and growing in the following decade with the formation of each new investigative committee. The labyrinthine journeys and murky provenances of key bits of photographic evidence as they became public, particularly those taken from Oswald's "backyard" photo session and the Zapruder film, are so convoluted that they defy summary description.[23] It is important to note that, just as the early researchers taught themselves the intricacies of ballistics in order to navigate physical improbabilities such as the path of the "magic bullet," so too did the average person come to mistrust the supposed veracity of still and moving photographic imagery. This suspicion was expressed in veiled form, most notably in the parable-like film *Blow-Up* by Italian director Michelangelo Antonioni (1966; fig. 28).

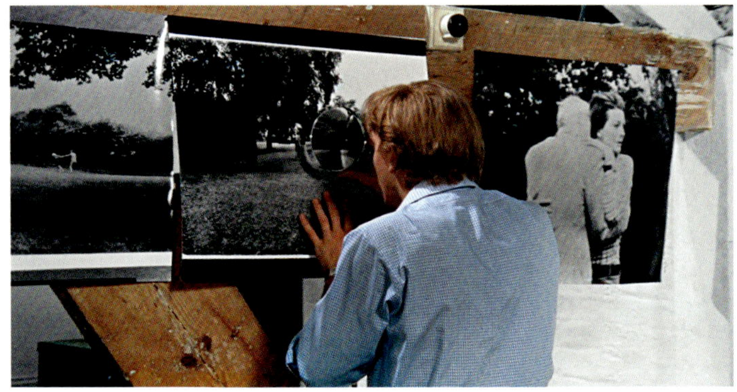

Fig. 28. Still from *Blow-Up*, 1966, directed by Michelangelo Antonioni

Charlesworth's stark black-and-white "informational" style was enormously influential. The artist Christopher Williams, who was studying with Douglas Huebler at CalArts during the late 1970s and early 1980s, at the same time as Mike Kelley, remembers that Charlesworth's Modern History series of newspaper pieces was one of the most frequently discussed bodies of work (pp. 62–63; see the essay by Beth Saunders in this volume).[24] One can most clearly see its influence on Kelley in the stark black-and-white color scheme of many of his early works and in his series of fake school-newspaper front pages called Timeless/Authorless.

Peter Nagy's photocopy works from the early 1980s have the same raw, anti-artistic look that Charlesworth achieved with a Photostat machine. At a time when auction prices soared and traditional painting was making a comeback after two decades of Conceptual art, Nagy created works in the form of photocopies that he could produce for a few pennies at the local copy shop and sell for a few bucks, or a little more if the prints were laminated. The artist studied communications in college and was interested in how signs of all kinds—from product logos to the signature styles of artists—circulated as a type of currency in a culture driven by commerce.

In *est Graduate* (1984; p. 66 bottom), Nagy wittily wedded est, Werner Erhard's then-popular self-actualization movement, to Pepperidge Farm, an emblematic brand of the moment, akin to Perrier bottled water in its representation of the aspirational aspect of the new yuppie lifestyle. Est was a quintessentially post-hippie phenomenon, an extreme form of group therapy in which members excavated their deepest, most painful memories under aggressive questioning. Est members were a visible part of the very late counterculture, recognizable by the creepy way in which they cropped their hair short and wore identical drab outfits.[25] In Nagy's work, the Benday-dot pattern becomes a mind-control mise-en-scène for the folksy corporate logo and, instead of the now-iconic farmhouse, a sinister, gleaming corporate tower. With pinpoint accuracy, Nagy correctly discerned est's pivotal significance—that plumbing the innermost depths of the self in public was actually a way to prepare the self for its colonization by the forces of marketing.

International Survey Condominiums (1985; p. 66 top) comes from a subset of the photocopy works in which the artist used museum floor plans and art-history timelines as their source material. It was inspired by the recent renovation and reopening of the Museum of Modern Art, which incorporated, to some controversy, the addition of a new fifty-two-story luxury residential tower atop the original 1939 International Style building to defray the costs of the renovation. Nagy's mash-up—in which Picasso finds himself next to a walk-in closet and Matisse shares space with a swimming pool—gave form to the feeling that the corporatization of culture and the attendant dissolution of art's traditional autonomy into the spheres of marketing and lifestyle had closed a final door on modernism's utopian aspirations. By the simple act of sliding the condo floor plan over the gallery floor plans, creating an absurd chaos, Nagy also slyly hints that real estate rather than art history may invisibly shape what is or isn't seen in New York.

• • •

The Watergate scandal was paradigm shifting in many ways, but at its core it is a story of a new relationship between the populace and power defined by technologies that eroded any firm boundary between public and private. The missing eighteen-and-one-half minutes of Nixon's secret recording and the preposterous attempts to explain it—either by the convoluted gymnastics of his secretary (fig. 29) or by his chief of staff Alexander Haig's "devil theory" that a "sinister force" erased the tape—so penetrated the public view of the president that during the height of the scandal, in November 1973, Barry Goldwater described Nixon as "a tape with unexpected blank sections."[26]

No matter the rampant paranoia, casual anti-Semitism, and laundry list of crimes and cover-ups revealed by Nixon's secret surveillance system, what the average citizen took away was more complicated than just pure mockery or condemnation; there was a new sense that anyone's private life could become public. When the paranoid president was hoist with his own petard, it kindled the sense among those not only right but left of center that the same shadow government epitomized by Nixon might also have been responsible for bringing him down. In a May 1973 article in the *New York Review of Books*, historian Kirkpatrick Sale dissected in minute detail the circle of monied interests that operated around Nixon, creating a composite portrait of what he termed "the unofficial nexus of power behind the acknowledged civics-textbook institutions."[27]

In foreign policy, Nixon's éminence grise was Henry Kissinger, depicted by Emory Douglas as nose to nose with Nixon over an ICBM (intercontinental ballistic missile) in 1969 (p. 32 bottom right). The national security adviser was also the subject of two series by Öyvind Fahlström, one titled Kidnapping Kissinger and the other devoted to the overthrow of Salvador Allende, the democratically elected leader of Chile, on September 11, 1973. In 1976, the young Chilean artist Alfredo Jaar—living under the

Fig. 29. Rose Mary Woods, Richard Nixon's personal secretary, demonstrating the possible erasure of the Watergate surveillance audiotapes controlled by a foot pedal

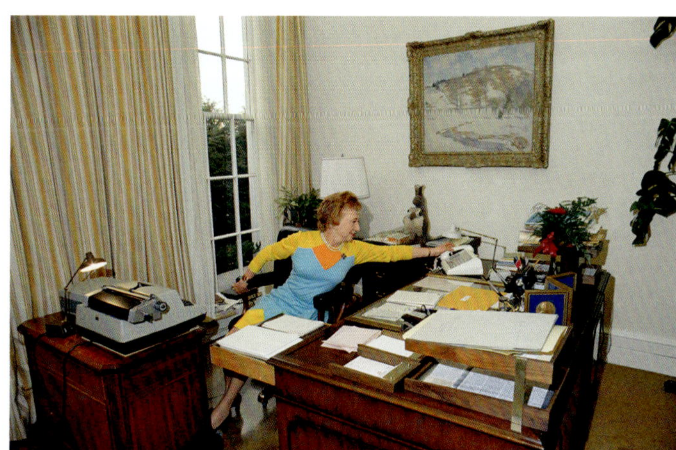

dictatorship facilitated by the CIA-assisted coup—sent a letter to Kissinger requesting an autograph. The official response on letterhead and accompanying glossy head shot form the contents of *Dear Mr. Jaar* (p. 65 top). In the context of violent reprisals by installed dictator Augusto Pinochet, which included the disappearances of dissidents, often by throwing them out of helicopters into the Pacific Ocean, Jaar's piece operates through the logic of what it cannot show.

Two years earlier, the artist made two letraset-printed works about the coup: *11.09.73.12.10* (p. 65 bottom), which is reminiscent of On Kawara; and *September 11, 1973*, a simple yet effective Duchampian assisted readymade consisting of a calendar page for September 1973 to which a letraset "1" has been added over the second digit in each of the seven days after the coup, as if stopping the trauma in time. The two letraset pieces and *Dear Mr. Jaar* inaugurated a career-long series of works in which the artist pursued Kissinger through his art with single-minded determination for what he saw as an unacknowledged and unprosecuted crime of global proportions. *Searching for K* (1984; p. 64) is Jaar's first major statement on Kissinger after leaving Chile in 1982, the move that allowed him the freedom to make it.[28] Jaar constructed the work with the illustrated sections from Kissinger's two successive memoirs, *The White House Years* (1979) and *Years of Upheaval* (1982), and thus his strategy of appropriation is somewhat akin to Sarah Charlesworth's in *April 21, 1978*. The book's picture sections are cut from their bindings and spread out forensically across three long floor cases. Wherever Kissinger appears, Jaar circled his head in red ink. At the end of the progression, a single vitrine holds a framed photograph of Kissinger shaking hands with Pinochet, an image that would never have appeared in either memoir. Jaar calls out and thwarts Kissinger's attempt to rewrite his history, abetted by his publishers.[29]

In the year after *Searching for K*, the artist created an appropriation piece from five rephotographed *Time* magazine covers, alternately featuring Kissinger the coup leader or Allende the coup victim, sequenced into a sentencelike narrative. The work concludes with *Time*'s first post-coup cover, showing a street poster of Allende splattered with red paint, recasting him as a foe of his people rather than its sacrificial lamb. For his *Nothing of very great consequence* (2008), Jaar created a small light box that simply reproduces an image of the transcript of a phone conversation shortly after the coup in which Kissinger comments that, regarding Chile, "our hand doesn't show on this one though."[30]

One wonders if growing up in Washington, D.C., the seat of governmental perfidy and corruption, made Cady Noland particularly attuned to not only the usual folly and scandal but also the increasing voraciousness of the media as it plowed through previously maintained boundaries between public and private. Like Pynchon, Noland is considered reclusive for her steadfast refusal to be photographed—in both cases this position is taken implicitly as refusal to participate in the media's vampiric relationship to its subjects. Falsity and manipulation may be constant refrains in discussions of her work, but even with her predilection for political subjects, no one has yet connected this D.C. native's possible interest in such subjects to a kind of aesthetic of the covert that is shot through with references to spy craft and espionage.

For Noland, as with many artists in this book and exhibition, conspiracy is merely one subject of interest among others. Yet, while the word *conspiracy* rarely appears in her few published interviews, her expressed idea of American culture as a con game[31] often brings conspiratorial overtones to the political subjects she treats, a prime example being her signature early work about Lee Harvey Oswald. In the spirit of Oswald's "doubling," she created two variants, *Oozewald* (1989) and *Bluewald* (1989–90; fig. 30). The title of the former version refers to the way that the truth of what happened continues to ooze toxically into the waters of our political life; the latter displays a cyan shift familiar from discolored photographs. The identical form of both versions is that of a "cutout" or a "false front," terms from the world of intelligence denoting a person or entity whom spies, such as CIA agents, insert into the flow of "actual" events to serve as cover for clandestine activity. It is interesting to consider what Oswald might share with two other figures that Noland depicted as cutout-type sculptures: Charles Manson and Patty Hearst (fig. 31).

From the very moment the media circuses that accompanied both Manson and Hearst began, conspiracy researchers such as Mae Brussell saw Manson less as the leader of a cult than as a drug-dealing pimp and patsy whose show trial was meant to drive a final nail in the coffin of the counterculture. Similarly, Brussell knew Hearst abductor Donald DeFreeze as the "black Oswald."[32] Noland, who plays her cards closer to her vest than any other contemporary artist, would never cue the viewer to the implications of the cutout form, content instead to let the suggestion of fake identity waft from the works almost subliminally. Manson himself, with his habit of suggesting hidden meanings amid a constant patter of hipster/prisoner lingo, perhaps best described Noland's own philosophy when he said, "You got to sneak to get to the truth."[33]

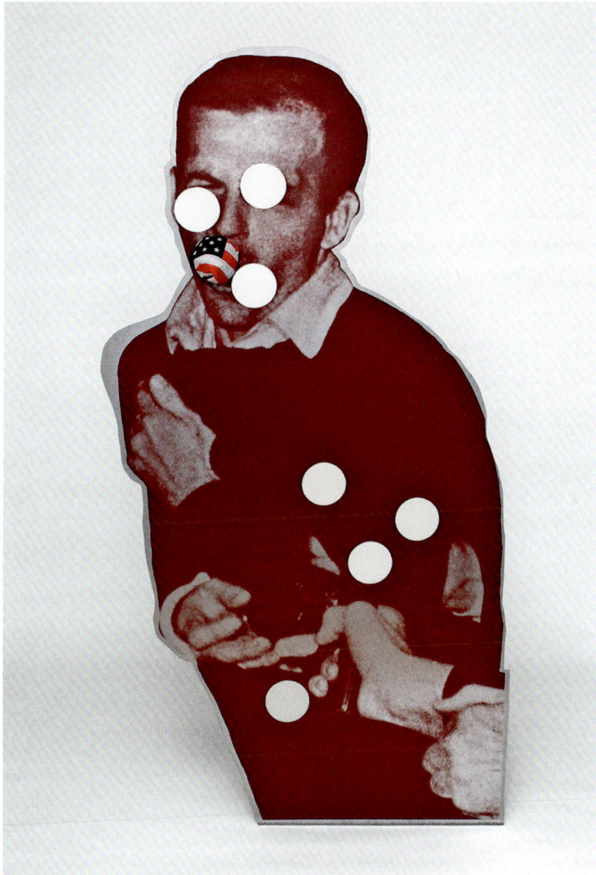

Fig. 30. Cady Noland (American, born 1956), *Bluewald*, 1989–90. Silkscreen ink on aluminum with flag and stand, 72 × 48 × ⅜ in. (182.9 × 121.9 × 1 cm). Wadsworth Atheneum, Hartford, Connecticut, The Ella Gallup Sumner and Mary Catlin Sumner Collection Fund (1995.37.1)

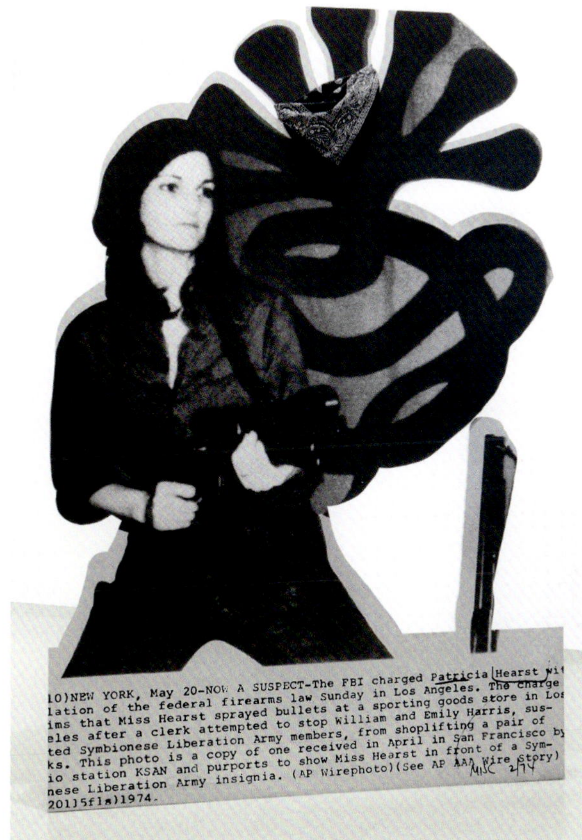

Fig. 31. Cady Noland, *Tanya as Bandit*, 1989. Silkscreen ink on aluminum with bandana, 72 × 48 × ⅜ in. (182.9 × 121.9 × 1 cm). The Museum of Modern Art, New York, Gift of Kathy and Richard S. Fuld, Jr. (1155.2007)

Lee Harvey Oswald is like the Adamic form of the espionage cutout. In *Libra* (1988), a reimagining of the Kennedy assassination, Don DeLillo threads the conspiratorial needle with two interlocking stories about Oswald told in alternating chapters. One narrative concerns Oswald's peripatetic wanderings, while the other traces the independent emergence, without him, of a plot to kill President Kennedy; when Oswald randomly crosses the path of the plotters, they are astonished to find a real person who fits the exact profile of the patsy role they are designing. Noland's depiction of Oswald as a cutout weds her formal strategy to the lexicon of skullduggery that guided the antihero along his journey to the book depository building and, finally, to his murder. Of course, when Jack Ruby shot Oswald, the one person who could cover for Oswald—himself—was silenced. The holes in Noland's cutouts have a double meaning—as bullet holes, obviously, but also as "punch-outs" of the kind used by newspaper editors to cancel photographic negatives that are not to be printed and published, for whatever reason but often because the images were too gory for publication. Like Charlesworth in *April 21, 1978*, Noland suggests that the mass media is a willing accomplice in obscuring the truth. The hole punches implicate the media in canceling any national reckoning of what really happened. Despite the flag shoved in Oswald's mouth as he yelled that he was a patsy, those holes suggest that the blocked truth about the assassination will continue to "ooze" through our public life.

In 1993–94, at the same time Noland was making six works about the Manson trial, she made a rare foray into contemporary events in a trio of works about the death of White House Deputy Counsel Vince Foster on July 20, 1993. A longtime Clinton associate from Hillary Clinton's days at the Rose law firm in Arkansas, Foster was found dead of a gunshot wound in a suburban Virginia park. Ruled a suicide, Foster's death immediately became fodder for the Republican investigations into the Clintons' Whitewater scandal. It continues to obsess conspiracy researchers to this day, as evidenced by the scores of YouTube videos produced by alternative media and amateur sleuths.[34]

Two of Noland's works utilize the concluding sentence from a torn-up note found in Foster's briefcase: "I was not meant for the job or the spotlight of public life in Washington. Here ruining people is considered sport." *Impact on the Image* (1993–94) is an ankle-high metal plaque with a headshot of Foster that seems intentionally to invite the possibility of being kicked or knocked over, imbuing the object itself with the very sentiment of the quotation emblazoned on it. That "public spotlight" where "ruining people is considered sport" ties in to many of Noland's works centered around the ritualistic nature of shaming and humiliation of public figures. As she later commented, "Boundaries are always being explored and exploited. . . . At this moment privacy is our version of the Western frontier."[35]

In *Untitled (Vince Foster)* (1992–93; p. 67), a leaning aluminum panel six feet high is silkscreened with an Associated Press wire photograph of Foster's casket being taken down the front steps of the church by a crowd of pallbearers, but the giant image is shown upside down. Three years earlier, the artist installed upside down a similarly scaled group portrait of Patty Hearst's "captors," the Symbionese Liberation Army. The inverted image of the Foster coffin—perpetually poised to empty its contents—has a greater emotional resonance, though it prompts the same feeling of disorientation in terms of what's real and what's not. Like the depiction of Oswald with a flag stuffed in his mouth, it evokes a sense of pathos for the protagonist's unlucky fate and reminds the viewer that the truth of what really happened will never be revealed.

For a 2010 publication accompanying her traveling midcareer retrospective, Rachel Harrison reproduced the first page of Pier Paolo Pasolini's 1967 essay about the Zapruder film, "Observations on the Long Take," as it appeared in a 1980 number of the journal *October*.[36] Of course, Pasolini couldn't have seen the actual film footage (unless he came across a bootleg copy), and his essay does not indicate any firsthand viewing of it. Instead, he describes in epistemological terms the kind of radical contingency that Zapruder's "long take" reveals, namely, that this unique perspective only serves to highlight how it is, in fact, not unique but rather one of an unmanageable number of possible perspectives—from every other witness to the Kennedys themselves, and so on—to which we will never have access.

In *Snake in the Grass* (1997; pp. 68–71), Harrison introduces this plethora of possible perspectives at the start of the installation (a word the perpetually skeptical Harrison is loath to use) with a found object, a wall-mounted directory from the now-defunct nonprofit Federation Employment and Guidance Service (FEGS), listing offices such as Supported Employment, Continuing Treatment, Mental Health Clinic, and Human Resources. This introductory object is like a rabbit hole of bureaucratic complexity that subtly hints at social dysfunction and anomie. It segues to another freestanding wall with a shelf holding a row of six small color photographs of the same patch of grass, each revealing subtle differentiations in tonality and density. The artist printed all of the images from a 35mm negative of a frame shot in Dallas at the site of Kennedy's assassination. Harrison refers to printing the same image in six different shades of green as an "exercise in subjectivity"[37] since no one really knows what color the grassy knoll is.

The lion's share of *Snake in the Grass*, however, is a labyrinth of sections of drywall that dangle menacingly around the space, suspended via yellow cords attached to garbage-bag green sandbags that dot the floor. The artist describes this cat's cradle of cords attached to the suspended walls as having a "booby trap" effect; when perceived from the starting point, the entire jerry-rigged contraption resolves into a composition of cul-de-sacs, blind alleys, and occluded perspectives.

"Clues" that both solicit and thwart interpretation punctuate the mazelike arrangement of drywall sections throughout. As Devon Dikeou astutely notes in a period review of the work's 1997 Greene Naftali exhibition, "Information is given out piecemeal, and the associations are meant to allow the viewer to construct their own narrative in the work. The devious placement and precarious feeling in the work resists the definitive formation of the narrative."[38] Describing *Snake in the Grass* as a "Clue room" of Kennedy assassination lore, curator Tom Eccles noted the way that elements such as the yellow cords or olive pits tempt the viewer as metaphors (respectively, bullet trajectories and spent shell casings or a Mafioso's snack remnants) while also ridiculing those interpretive attempts. He thereby summarizes Harrison's overarching question: "Do you buy this story at all?"[39]

The obdurate materiality of Harrison's puzzling props, such as the ridiculously huge, coiled snakeskin resting on the head of a shovel behind the wall of grass samples, subverts the coherence of the narrative. But so does the way Harrison holds in suspension two interpretive phenomena: conspiracy theory and institutional critique, the latter a Conceptualist paradigm in which the museum itself becomes the subject, object, and prime referent of the work of art. Oblique references throughout the piece—such as the directory of social-work offices, the foam blocks, and a strange, gigantic orange cutout resembling the Venus of Willendorf—give a cryptic nod to the detective work of institutional critique, that is, tweaking the secret histories of institutional spaces by moving objects and architectural elements around. Harrison's own skimmed views of Dealey Plaza tourists and a photograph titled *$20* are mounted to the drywall sections. The latter (p. 69 middle left), which is printed "full frame" to guarantee no cropping or manipulation, promises the real story but shows only another photograph, an annotated and laminated copy (for sale for twenty dollars) of Wilma Bond's famous shot of bystanders seeking cover or running toward the sound of gunshots and wisps of smoke in the direction of the grassy knoll.

Just as Harrison's later sculptures are puzzles balancing formalism and mass-cultural or vernacular elements in paradoxical juxtaposition, *Snake in the Grass* exemplifies her expert methods of holding nameable and unnameable elements in suspension. As the artist and critic John Kelsey has noted, Harrison's sculptural conundrums present themselves as "stand-ins and imposters,"[40] a quality they share with Noland's silkscreened aluminum sculptures. Satirical and nearly cartoonish in its agglomeration of brightly colored and ungainly, yet elegantly realized, shapes and forms, *Snake in the Grass* reflects a moment in the 1990s when all the conspiracy theorizing of the previous three decades became so baked in to the culture that it constituted an artistic subject in and of itself. The annunciatory artwork of this decadelong revival of interest was Oliver Stone's *JFK* (1991), an over-the-top amalgam of conspiracy theorizing pointing in every direction, which Stone considered a "counter-myth"[41] to what he saw as the equally dodgy rationales that had been offered over time since the release of the Warren Commission report. The film director obviously pushed the right governmental buttons because in the following year Congress passed the John F. Kennedy Assassination Records Act (1992), which moved forward the date by which all records must be declassified, from 2029 to 2017.

But the work closest in spirit to *Snake in the Grass* is television's *The X-Files* (debuted in 1993), which, in particular, presents a similar relentless oscillation between belief and disenchantment. It puts the viewer in what scholar Peter Knight calls "an infinite hermeneutic of suspicion [that] undermines every stable conclusion" and "concentrates . . . on the *process* of repeatedly discovering that everything you thought you knew is wrong."[42] In the show, two investigators (Agent Scully and Agent Mulder) are overloaded with an array of preposterous conspiratorial rabbit holes. As the episodes progress, a minihistory of conspiracy theory extends like an umbrella or octopus over the central characters, embracing everything from alien abductions to the Council on Foreign Relations to a mysterious Smoking Man; according to Knight, the show offers "an excess of possible conspirators within a circuit of endlessly displaced power."[43]

We have now reached the stage in the historical development of conspiracy theory when it is able to spawn its own metanarrative. *Snake in the Grass*, like *The X-Files*, is heavily ironic. This is not to say that Harrison is a conspiracy skeptic; rather, what really happened is just less interesting to her than the nutty, self-generating paranoia that springs from it and the baroque forms the theorizing takes. Her sensibility is reminiscent of Richard Linklater's attitude toward the conspiracy theorist in his 1991 cinematic debut *Slacker*, a deadpan group portrait of twenty-something layabouts drifting around Austin, Texas. One of the most memorable characters is the greasy used-bookstore clerk who is obsessed with the Kennedy assassination and forces his theories on unsuspecting patrons (fig. 32); he is exactly the type seen trawling Dealey Plaza in Harrison's snapshots.

Wayne Gonzales grew up in the 1960s New Orleans depicted in Oliver Stone's *JFK*, and a close friend of his parents worked with Jim Garrison, the district attorney whose investigation of the assassination figures in the movie. Arriving in New York in 1988, Gonzales imbibed Andy Warhol's posthumous retrospective at MoMA in 1989, did word processing for the artist Peter Halley as a day job, and experimented with silkscreen painting in his off-hours.[44] In his first solo show, at Lauren Wittels Gallery in 1997, Gonzales exhibited paintings of varied subjects and genres (architecture, landscape, portraiture) executed in different styles. He cited as inspiration for this heterogeneous approach his reading in the mid-1990s about multinational corporations and how their vertically oriented, diversified portfolios were designed to exert influence over whole swathes of the culture. His strategy was almost a premonition of how stylistic pluralism would become the Trojan Horse of a fully corporatized art world after 9/11. (Gonzales and Mark Lombardi, whose work is discussed in the next section, shared an interest in global multinationals at that time.)

Over the next few years, Gonzales noticed that his folder of images related to the Kennedy assassination

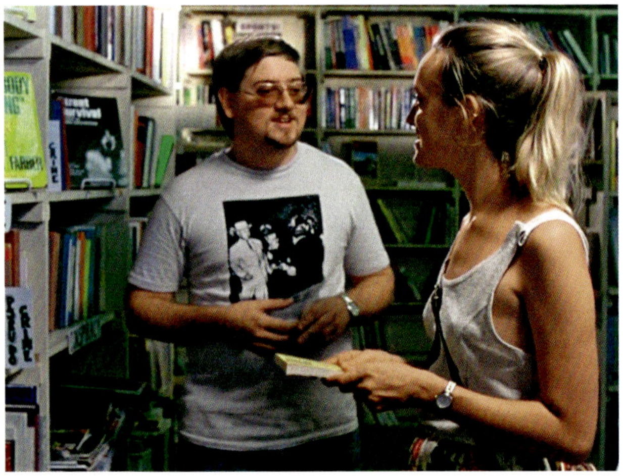

Fig. 32. Still from *Slacker*, 1991, directed by Richard Linklater

dwarfed that of every other subject in his picture file of possible source material for paintings, leading him to make a flurry of drawings and to begin "printing JFK images and painting over them with gouache."[45] In 1999, one of Gonzales's drawings of Jack Ruby inspired the critic Bob Nickas to commission a monumental portrait of Ruby that the artist called *Dallas Police 36398* after the number that appeared on Ruby's mugshot (not shown in the painting) (p. 72). This led to a pendant painting of Oswald two years later (p. 73). At Gonzales's 2001 exhibition at Paula Cooper Gallery, these portraits, each more than eight feet tall, were joined by other works related to the assassination, including a black-and-white painting derived from a photograph of Oswald as a young Marine, over which the artist superimposed his own face (figs. 33, 34). Inserting his visage into the Benday-dot matrix of the portrait made explicit how Oswald had come to stand in for the figure of the artist (as is true, too, in Lutz Bacher's collage), for Gonzales considered Oswald "not so much a person but a construction, as someone whose history was fabricated by others."[46]

Perhaps it is unsurprising that Gonzales found it increasingly hard to avoid touching on Warhol's ownership of the Kennedy assassination as a subject, even though Warhol limited himself to portraits of Jackie Kennedy based on photographs taken before and after the murder (see the Introduction in this volume, pp. 14–21). Reminiscent of Warhol's *Mao* paintings from the 1970s, both *Dallas Police 36398* and *Peach Oswald* advertise their Pop bona fides in their florid coloration and monumental scale. Thomas Ruff's giant photographic portraits of his classmates and associates from the Kunstakademie in Düsseldorf are another apt point of comparison (fig. 35). In this series, begun in the late 1980s and extending for a decade, Ruff created bust-length depictions of average young people scaled to the size of illustrious historical figures. An interesting counterpoint to Oswald's probing stare, the students' closed-off expressions are a coolly protective shield of inner privacy, adopted unconsciously from years of submitting to ID photos, surveillance cameras, and the like.

Gonzales's paintings mark a moment—before 9/11—when the individual subject was starting to adjust to the feeling of always being watched, when the technocratic culture right around the corner began to shift our understanding of what is human along digital lines. In *Peach Oswald* (red with rage? or perhaps "sheep-dipped" by the CIA as a Communist?) and *Dallas Police 36398* (green with envy?), Gonzales takes the archetypes of the Lone Actor and the Avenging Outsider into the new murk of identity confusion—Bacher's "anyone can pretend" message writ large for the coming digital revolution.

If social media in a sense made spies of us all, it is ironic that the last great work of video art made in the analog era, Jane and Louise Wilson's disorienting and menacing installation *Stasi City* (1997; p. 74), is a magnum opus on the East German surveillance state just after its dissolution. While on a visiting-artist scholarship in Berlin, the two artists encountered a historically resonant site that encapsulated their nascent interests in the relationship between architecture and psychology. Indeed, it is one of the most symbolically loaded spaces in recent memory: the former headquarters of the East German secret police (Staatssicherheit) housed behind a nondescript row of buildings in the once Soviet part of the city.

A virtual Valhalla of surveillance, the Stasi headquarters (or "Stasi City" as it was dubbed by a West German journalist) contained 6 million files kept on the German citizenry, a remote facility for wiretapping thousands of phone lines, interrogation rooms, and the notorious Hohenschönhausen prison. The banal bureaucratic architecture and now retro-looking furniture on the interior masked the chilling reality of the activities once conducted there. After the difficult process of negotiating access to the site, Jane Wilson made preliminary video footage while Louise made photographic stills. As if preserved in amber, some rooms had in fact remained locked since 1989, and keys had to be found to open them; in some places, papers were still scattered across the floor as if they had just been rifled through in the final days of Communism. While the site itself had been hidden from view, however, its effects permeated every corner of society. Teachers, train conductors, cleaning women—all made good cover for spies. And a person brought in under suspicion could be coerced into gathering and reporting information in lieu of imprisonment. A common joke of the Stasi era was that when you took a taxi, you only had to tell the driver your name; he already knew your address.[47]

At the time that Jane and Louise Wilson were filming *Stasi City*, they were keenly interested in Jeremy Bentham's design for the Panopticon prison and its subsequent theorization by Michel Foucault in the 1970s.[48] While the Stasi complex does not reflect the literal form of the Panopticon, its principle of mutual, internalized surveillance shaped the collective psyche of East Berlin, and thus Stasi City could be said to contain the repressed memory of what had occurred there. Bentham's idea that "each comrade becomes an overseer"[49] described the everyday experience of East Germans, and the success of the Stasi in penetrating the minds of citizens represented the apotheosis of Bentham's design, in both the self-monitoring watchfulness of each person and the ever-present threat of the Other, where the roles of watcher and watched became interchangeable within each individual.

The structural support that the Wilsons created for *Stasi City*—two pairs of eleven-by-fourteen-foot screens, positioned at ninety-degree angles and set diagonally opposed to each other, surrounding the viewer in a darkened space—has since become their standard presentational format. In the opening shots of *Stasi City*, the ceiling lights gradually flicker on in the office of Erich Mielke, the last director of the agency; the Wilsons' stated desire to "reactivate" their architectural subjects is literalized by this halting illumination and sudden whir of electricity. The teak wood covering the office walls in various blond tones then becomes the backdrop for paired views of a faux tree stump perched incongruously on Mielke's desk—one a close-up to reveal the clumsily carved aperture for a spy camera, the other a slow pan toward it to savor the surreal juxtaposition.[50] A fake ruin visible for only a moment, the pathetic piece of stagecraft is both a harbinger of the Stasi's future obsolescence and a clever announcement of the play between reality and illusion. The question of what we can trust with our own eyes is established from the very outset of the work.

Stasi City's opening sequence is resolved only in the beginning of the next, an ingenious device that defers closure and pulls the viewer along like an undertow. Dressed in drab civil-service uniforms circa 1966, each artist is now seen posed rigidly in one slot of a two-person *paternoster*, or open-front elevator; on one screen, one elevator ascends while the other descends. In this brief transitional passage, from the unified freeze

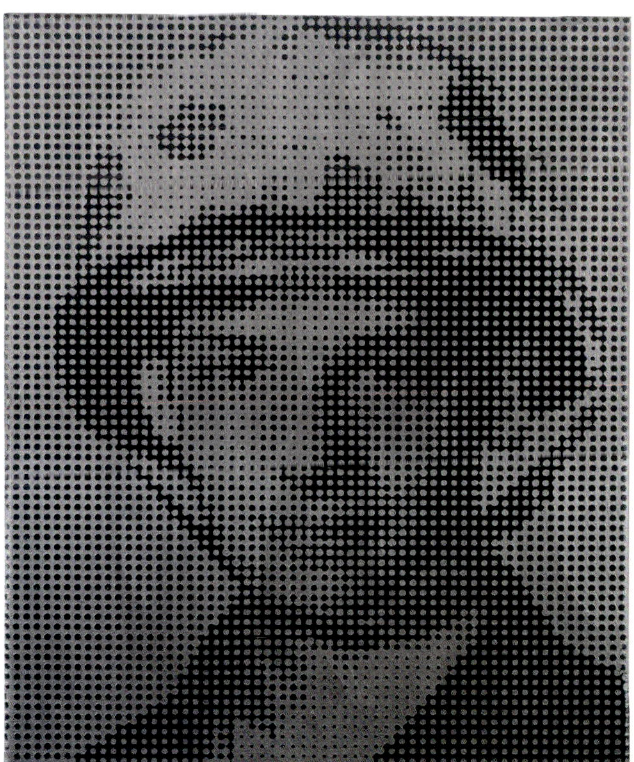

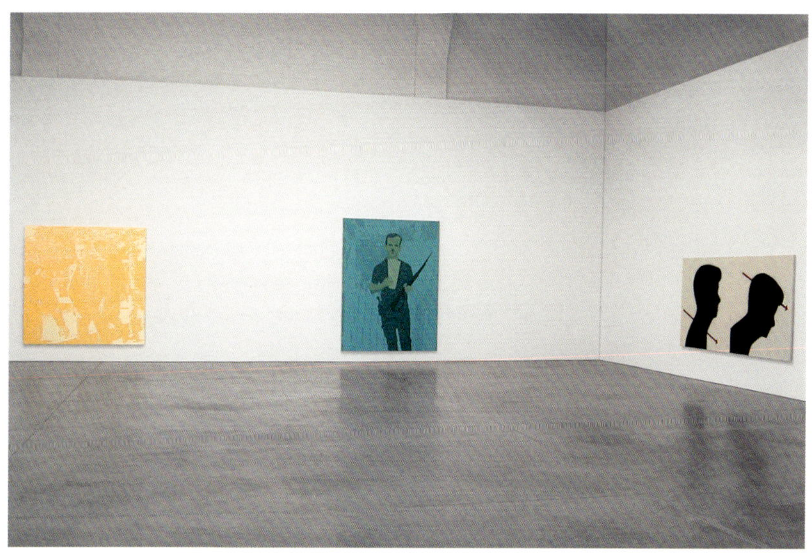

Fig. 33. Wayne Gonzales (American, born 1957), *Self-Portrait as a Young Marine*, 2002. Acrylic on canvas, 20⅛ × 16 in. (51.1 × 40.6 cm). Collection of the artist

Fig. 34. Wayne Gonzales's 2001 exhibition at Paula Cooper Gallery, New York

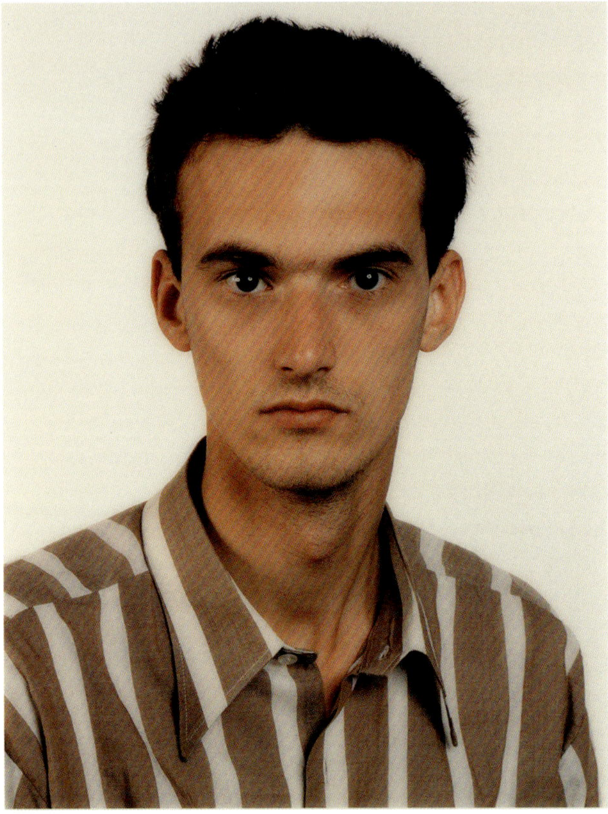

Fig. 35. Thomas Ruff (German, born 1958), *Portrait (A. Siekmann)*, 1987. Chromogenic print face-mounted to Plexiglas, 82 11/16 × 64 15/16 in. (210 × 165 cm). The Metropolitan Museum of Art, New York, Purchase, The Horace W. Goldsmith Foundation Gift, through Joyce and Robert Menschel, 1999 (1999.210)

frame to the ceaseless, irrevocably divided pair of *paternosters*, the artists introduce the motif of the stereoscopic view,[51] one of the photographic medium's earliest attempts to create a disembodied simulation of vision. The split, binaural images suggest the split nature of the self under surveillance, an internalized watchfulness that makes the viewer both spy and spied upon.

The next sequence interweaves two tracking shots. The camera is now placed inside the elevators, mimicking the female civil servants' viewpoints as they pass from floor to floor in different directions at once, occasional glimpsing the spaces on each floor as they ascend or descend, only to be cast into pools of darkness. This pair of contrasting pans plunges the viewer into the partiality and contingency of the surveying gaze, which is achieved not by the movement of the camera but by that of the *paternosters*.

The concluding sequence of the film shows Jane Wilson, now wearing a fittingly retro tracksuit reminiscent of a Soviet Olympic athlete, suspended in midair and floating in slow motion through the director's office. For the artists, the floating figure neatly summarizes the peculiar spatial paradox of Cold War psychogeography: "The figure is meant to be in a vacuum, it can move freely but it can't leave the room. In the GDR, there was a utopian dream of space travel, you could travel into space but you could not travel to West Berlin."[52] Because of its position at the end of the film, however, this concluding passage does more than embody a particular experience of the world; it also extends the meaning of *Stasi City* into the present experience of the viewer. As the figure glides past obsolete technologies of surveillance like the reel-to-reel tape recorder, we are able to chart our own position in an infinitely more complex and advanced network of surveillance strategies for which we are both subject and object. The resulting feeling is one of free-floating detachment from direct experience.

Jeremy Blake's digital animations collectively called the Winchester Trilogy (2002–4; p. 75) are a fitting complement to other works in the exhibition that construct disorienting and labyrinthine architectural spaces as a means to address personal (or national) trauma, including Mike Kelley's *Educational Complex* (pp. 132–34), Jane and Louise Wilson's *Stasi City* (p. 74), and Sarah Anne Johnson's *House on Fire* (pp. 146–49, 162). The subject of Blake's trilogy is the Winchester Mystery House in San Jose, California, built over four decades beginning in 1886 by Sara L. Winchester, the heiress to the fortune made by the "gun that made the West." After the death of her husband and children in separate accidents, the heiress's spiritualist advisor warned that she was pursued by the ghosts of those killed by the rifles responsible for her fortune. To rid herself of the curse, Winchester was advised by her medium to add to the house continually, thus creating staircases that go nowhere, upper-floor doors that open on to the front of the house, and miles of hallways (at the time of her death, the house had a total of 150 rooms).

According to Blake, the Winchester Trilogy "goes insane with Sara."[53] In all three parts, the viewer inhabits the paranoid subjectivity of the heiress. The first installment, *Winchester* (2002), opens with the sound of a film projector and a jittery period photograph of the house before the additions began. As the image slowly shifts to sepia, first one and then another ghostly silhouette of gunfighters with rifles appear for a split second like darting specters. Then an upper-floor window gets progressively darker as the building fades away, becoming a bullet-hole shape with red dripping from it as an abstract passage of multicolored shapes blooms. Black shapes resembling Rorschach blots surface and then morph into silhouetted shapes of gunfighters. Then another period photo appears, a detail of the exterior of the new facade showing one of the doors that open to nowhere, which gradually darkens like its precursor. A second passage of abstract effects occurs, this time yielding a period photo of the entire obsessively rebuilt and expanded house, with its maze of 150 rooms. At the end, the photo of the original house reappears, going in and out of focus. It is a site of trauma that is also a site of nostalgia for an uncorrupted wholeness—that is, the house inhabited by the intact family.

The second part of the trilogy, *1906* (2003), is a tour of the interior spaces damaged by the earthquake of that year, which Sara Winchester took to be a personal punishment from the spirits. After being trapped in a bedroom for several hours, she instructed the architects to board up all the damaged sections at the front of the house and build around them, thus leaving the wounds in the architecture. As Blake commented in 2005, "for me that was a great example of how we deal with trauma—it's the basic architectural manifestation of trauma. There's evidence of trauma, and then it's built around or hidden."[54] *1906* opens with a startling pan and dissolve that transitions magically from the rooftop spire straight down to the deepest damage done to the basement level. The Rorschach blot-like shapes seen in the first film reappear over Blake's footage, detectable in the work as shaky, handheld views possibly shot on film but more likely with a video camera. Shown are exposed wounds where wallpaper has been ripped open to reveal wood construction or, more ominously, holes such as the upper-floor door to nowhere from the first film. Another pan along a row of rosettes brings to mind pink-ringed gunshot wounds.

The final animation in the trilogy, *Century 21* (2004), is devoted to the multiplex cinema across the street from the Winchester Mystery House. For Blake, the movie theater was a natural extension of the heiress's puzzle house, providing a machine for expiating the ghosts of the past, given that Hollywood Westerns glorified the violence facilitated by Winchester rifles.[55] "It seems appropriate," Blake commented in 2004, that the movie theaters "are situated so close to the house, since in some way both the mansion and the movie houses provide homes for spectral gunfighters."[56] Whereas *Winchester* and *1906* make use of period photos and prints, *Century 21* is populated with images from midcentury movies and cartoons about the Old West. The abstract effects, too, are different from those in the preceding two films. The painterly blobs are now constellations of glistening stars and projection-like bursts of light reminiscent of the silver screen. One sequence takes place over what looks like a *New Yorker* cartoon of kids playing cowboys and Indians, while another startling passage shows a thin wire of rainbow colors slowly emanating from the forehead of a Western-garbed movie character with his eyes closed, as if hypnotized. Reminiscent of the clumsily rendered "ejaculations" of cheesecloth from mouths and orifices in nineteenth-century spirit photographs, this vignette connects disparate moments in the visualization of the invisible.

Blake's woozy phantasmagoria of guilt-derived paranoia can be connected back to Lutz Bacher's *Lee Harvey Oswald Interview*, which, despite its radically different emotional tenor of ragged, cut-and-paste montage, is also about unstable identity as refracted through Angleton's (and T. S. Eliot's) "wilderness of mirrors." The turning away from any aspirations to collective experience that came with the death of the counterculture, of course, gave birth to the inward-looking Me Generation, which in turn birthed the rampant individualism of the 1980s and 1990s. This narrative of disengagement and looking within coincided with the historical moment when the decimated post-Watergate intelligence community had to reinvent itself. As that community became oriented toward creating funding streams and webs of covert activity—exemplified by the Iran-Contra, Savings and Loan, and BCCI bank scandals to come—the artists who sought to chart their impossibly intricate schemes were not navigators of the self but researchers of networks.

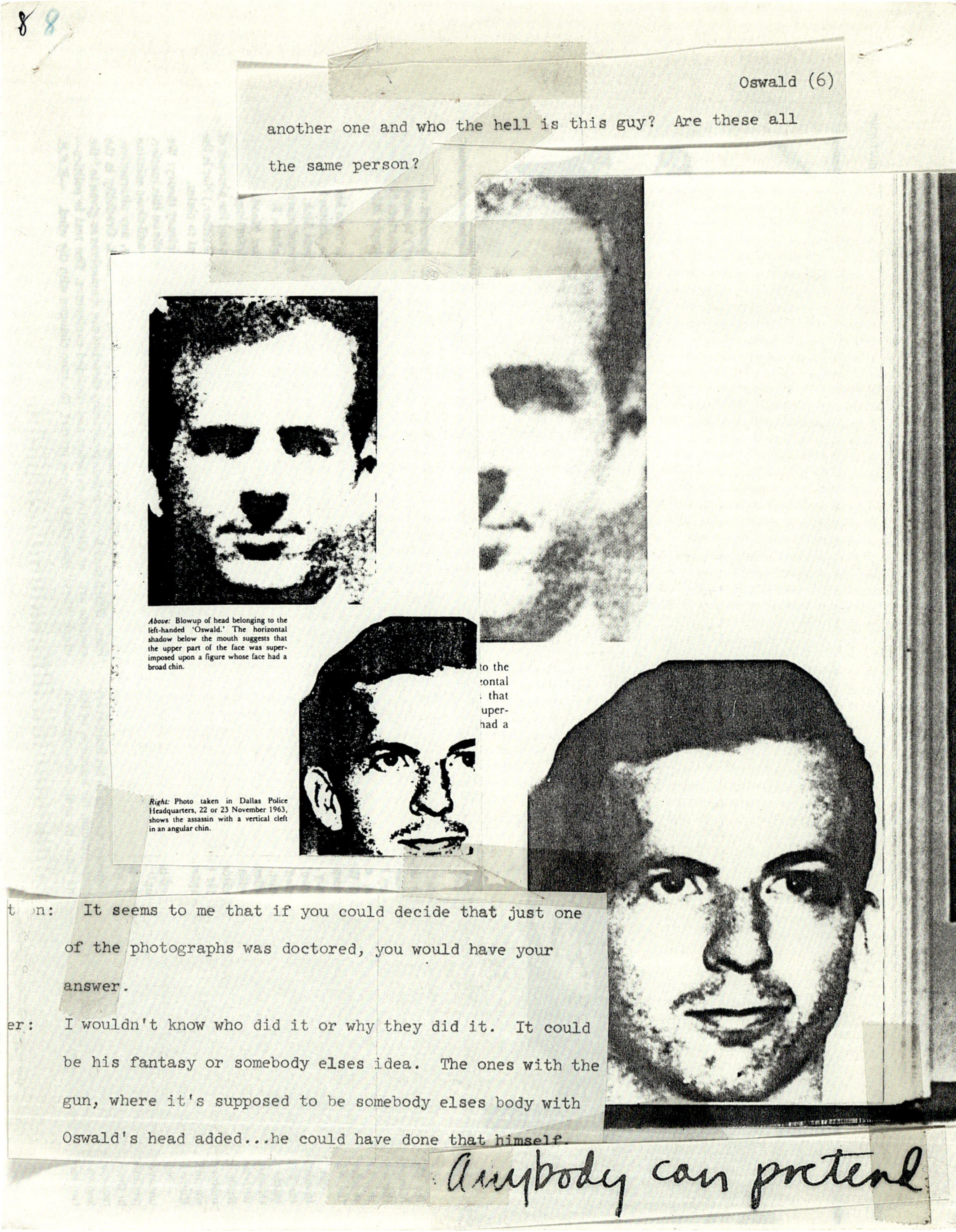

Details of Lutz Bacher, *The Lee Harvey Oswald Interview*, 1976

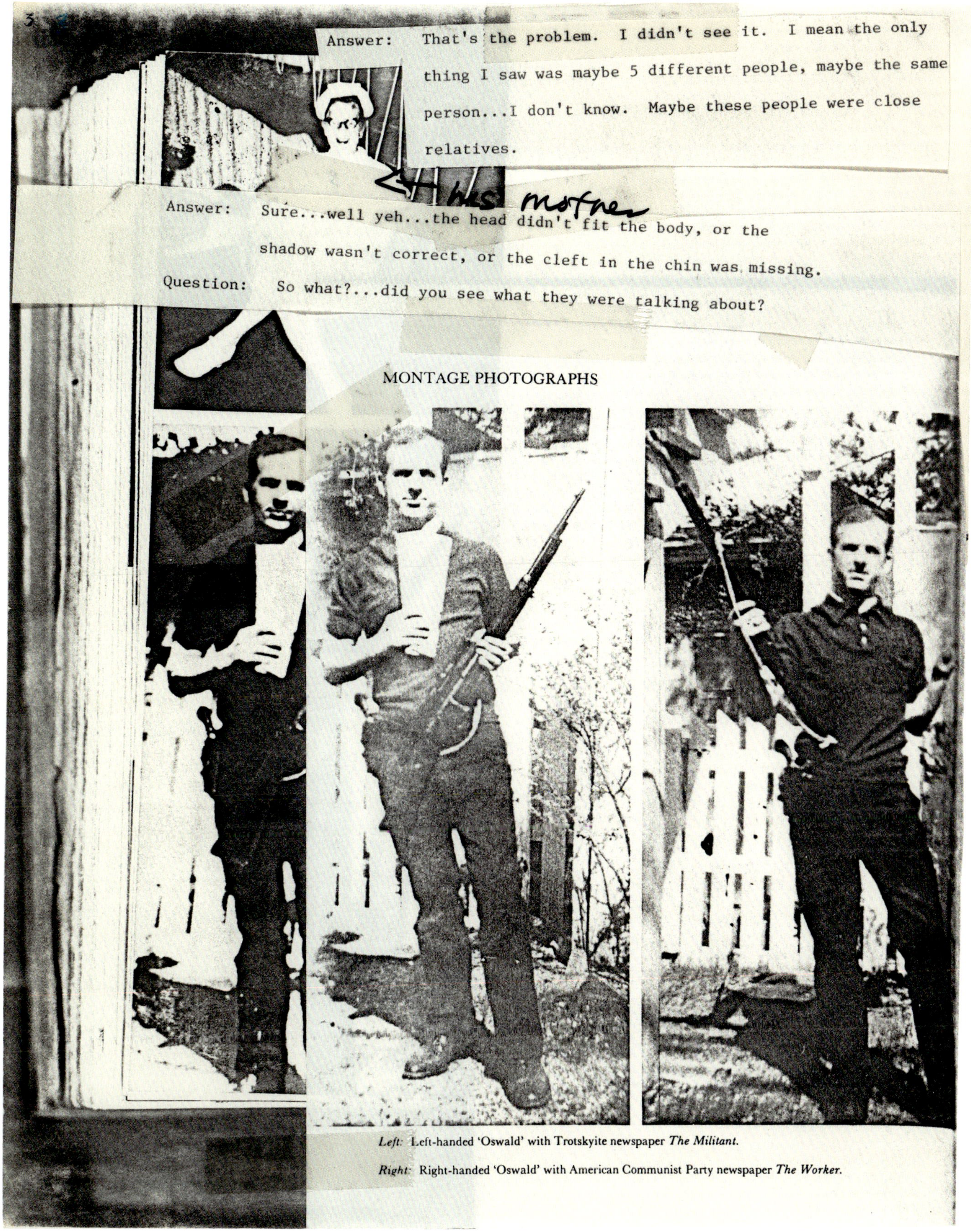
Answer: That's the problem. I didn't see it. I mean the only thing I saw was maybe 5 different people, maybe the same person...I don't know. Maybe these people were close relatives.
his mother
Answer: Sure...well yeh...the head didn't fit the body, or the shadow wasn't correct, or the cleft in the chin was missing.
Question: So what?...did you see what they were talking about?
MONTAGE PHOTOGRAPHS
Left: Left-handed 'Oswald' with Trotskyite newspaper *The Militant.*
Right: Right-handed 'Oswald' with American Communist Party newspaper *The Worker.*

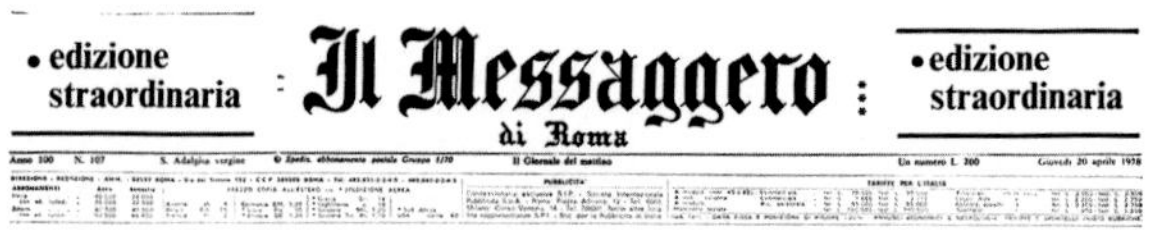

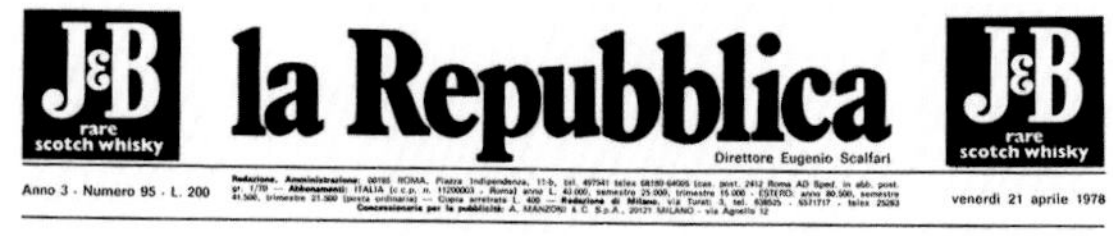

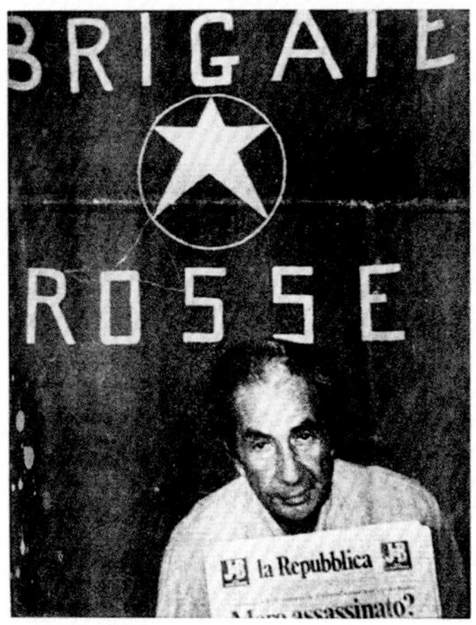

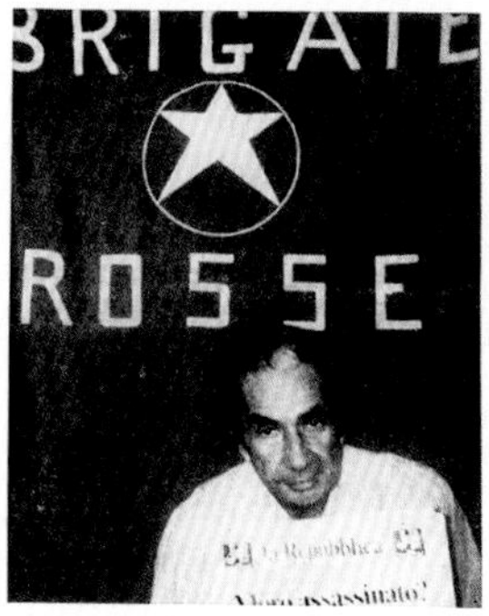

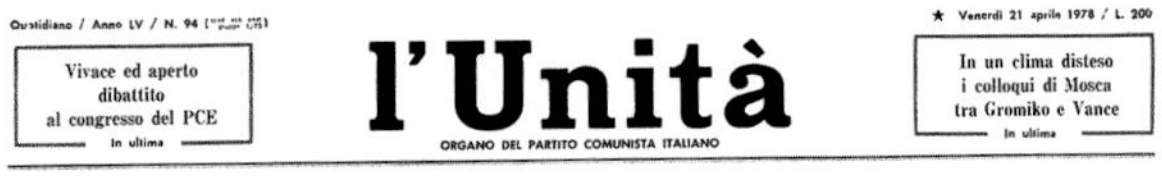

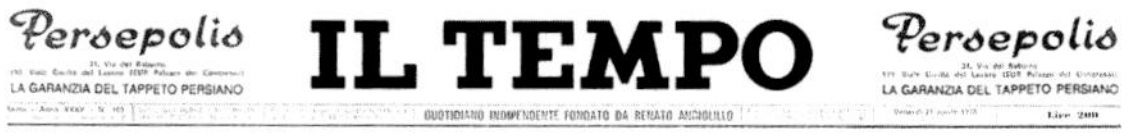

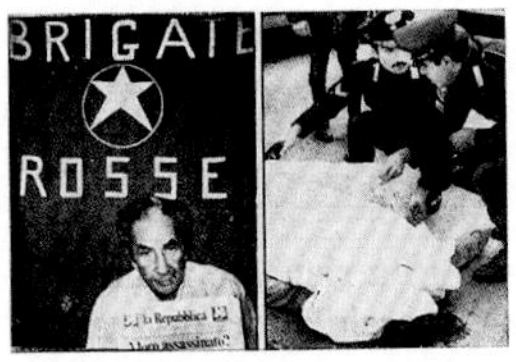

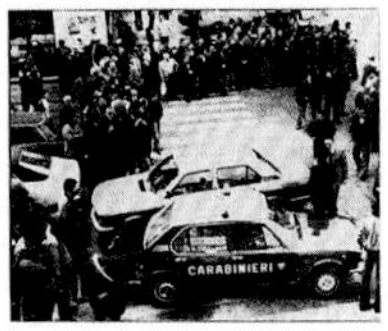

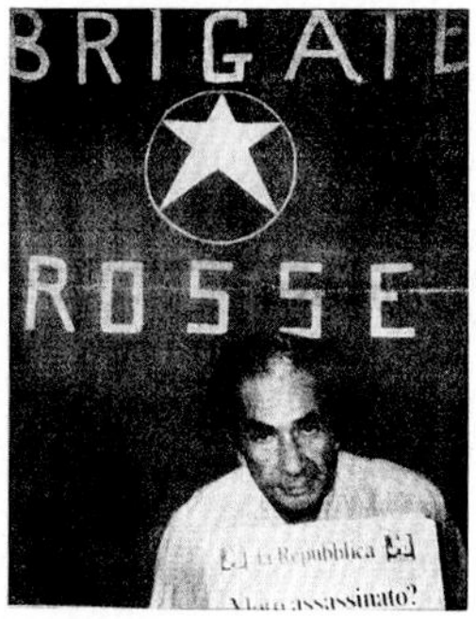

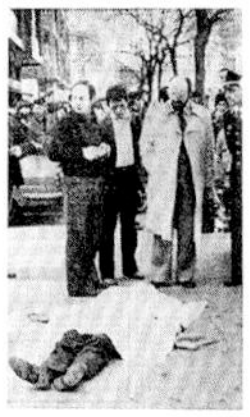

Details of Sarah Charlesworth, *April 21, 1978*, 1978

The Globe and Mail

Clearing
High near 6

135th YEAR, No. 40,053 • FIRST EDITION — TORONTO, FRIDAY, APRIL 21, 1978 — 56 PAGES • 15 CENTS

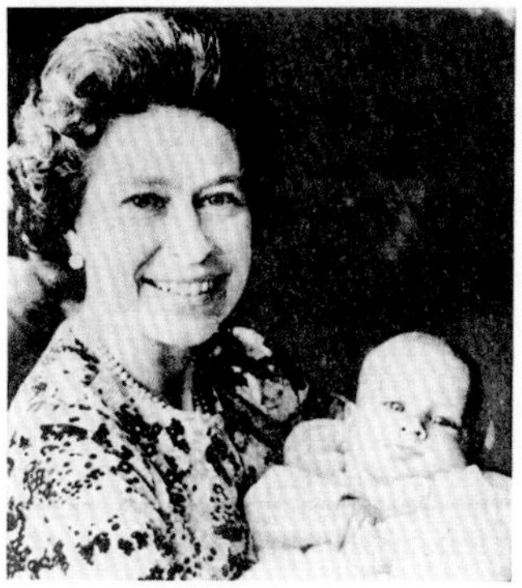

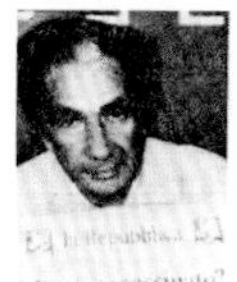

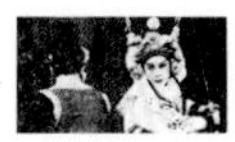

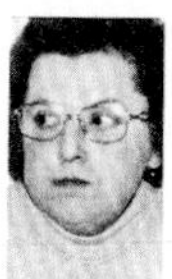

"All the News That's Fit to Print"

The New York Times

CITY EDITION

VOL. CXXVII ....No. 43,817 — NEW YORK, FRIDAY, APRIL 21, 1978 — 20 CENTS

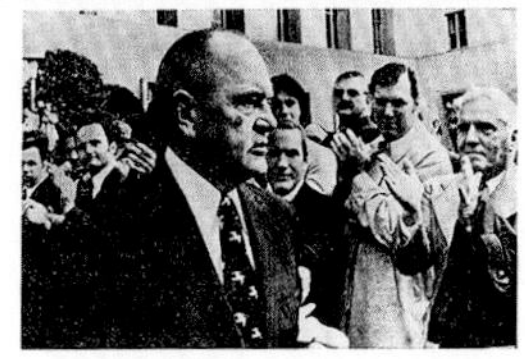

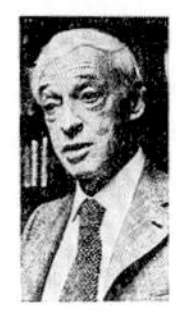

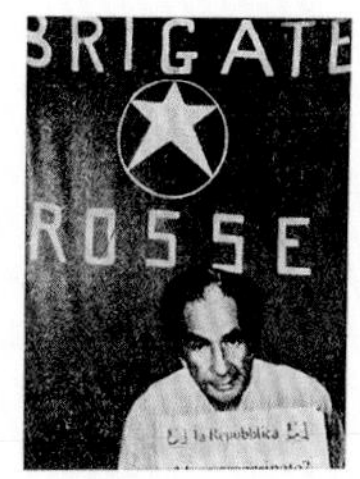

De Telegraaf

GROOTSTE KRANT VAN NEDERLAND

No. 28.105 — Het weer: af en toe zon — 44 pagina's — vrijdag 21 april 1978

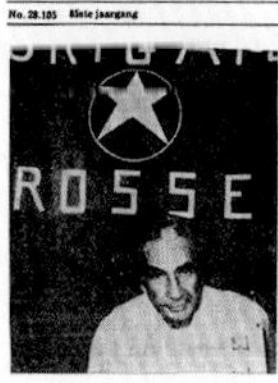

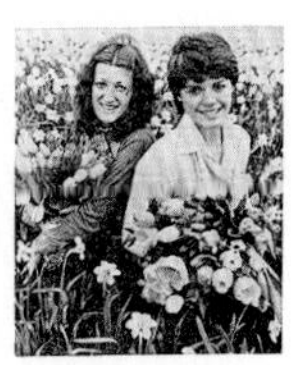

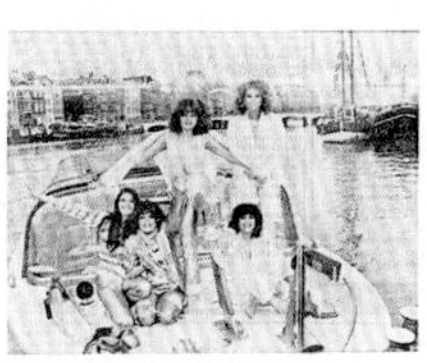

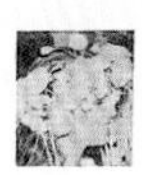

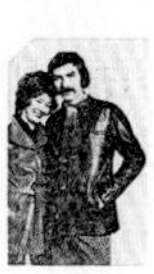

Basler Zeitung

Freitag, 21. April 1978 • 108

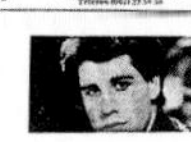

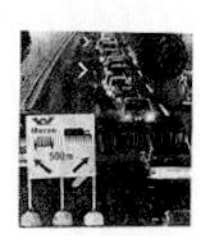

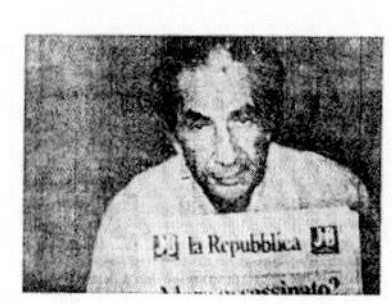

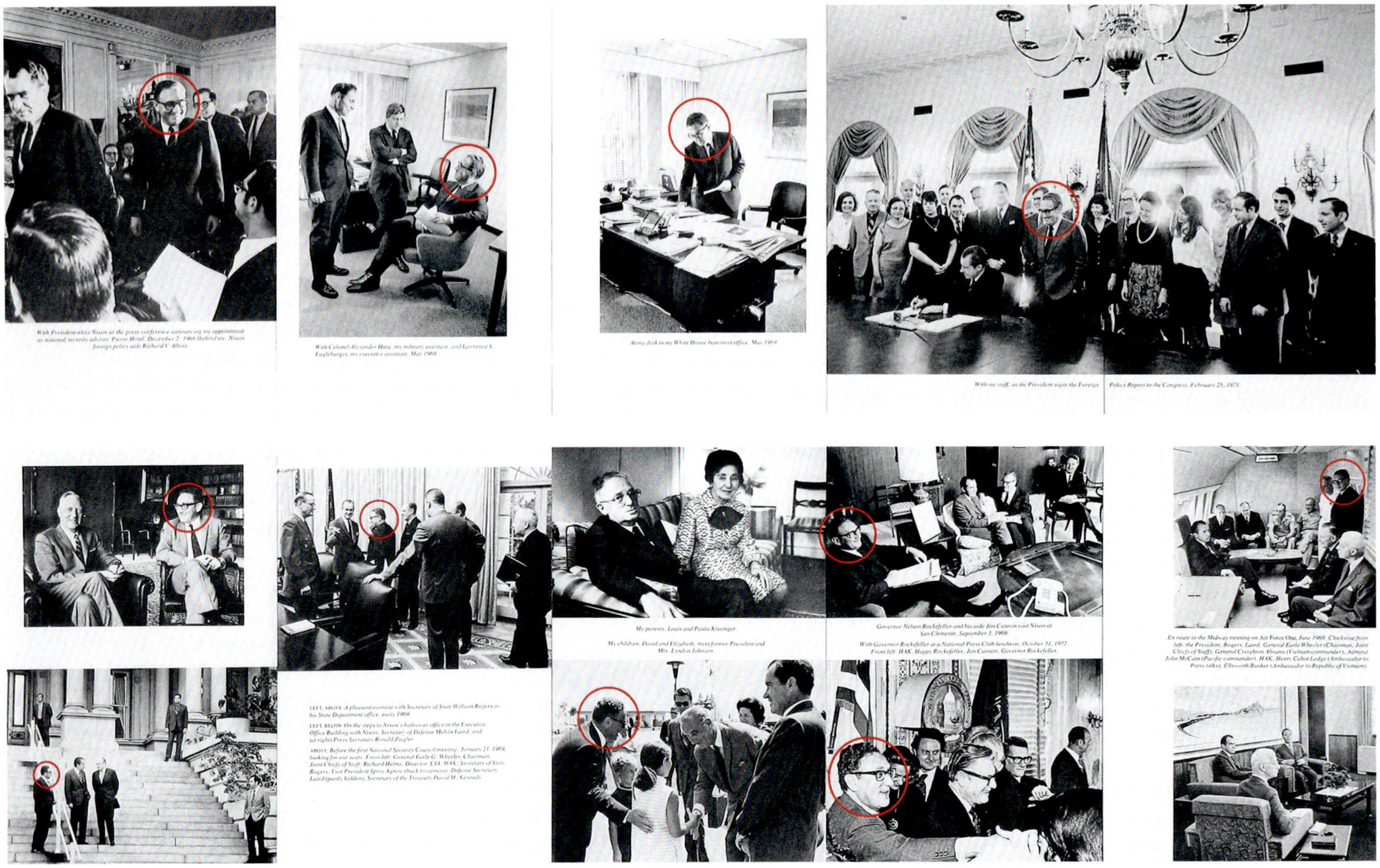

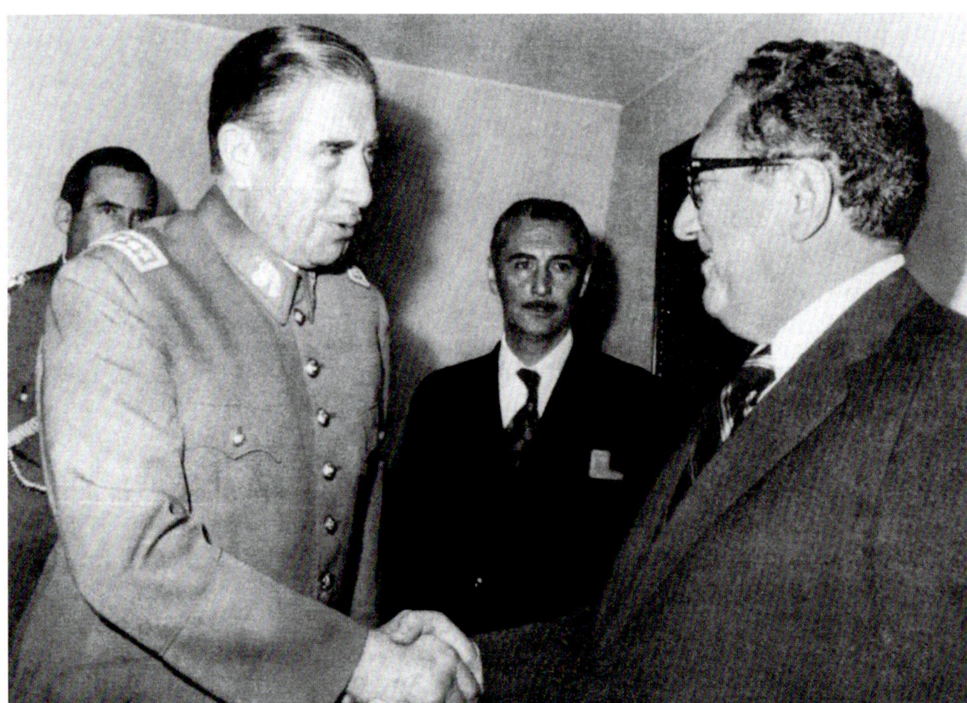

This page: Details of Alfredo Jaar, *Searching for K*, 1984

Alfredo Jaar, *Dear Mr. Jaar*, 1976

Alfredo Jaar, *11.09.73.12.10*, 1974

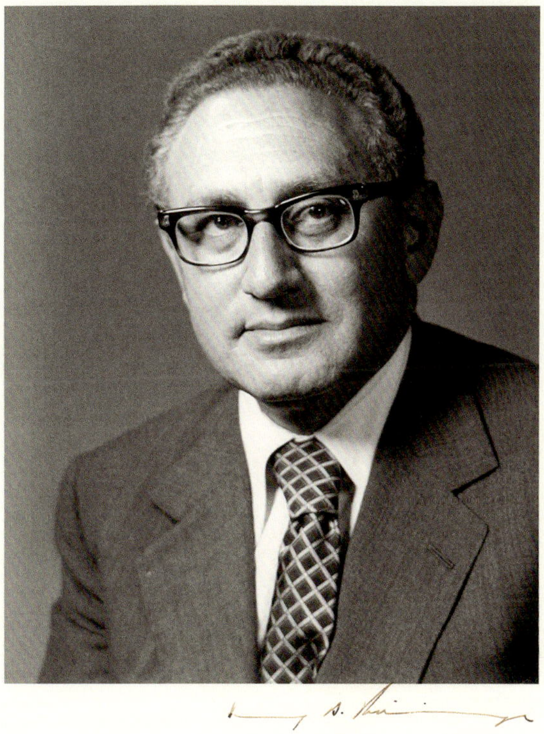

DEPARTMENT OF STATE
Washington, D.C. 20520

July 9, 1976

Mr. Alfredo Jaar
Av. Manquehue Norte 1807
Las Condes
Santiago

Dear Mr. Jaar:

Secretary Kissinger has asked me to thank you for your letter requesting his autograph and to let you know that he appreciates your kind words and support.

The Secretary's very heavy schedule during the past few years prevented him from signing any photographs. However, he has now had an opportunity to sign a very few, and he wants you to have one of them, with his very best wishes for the future.

Sincerely,

John E. Reinhardt
John E. Reinhardt
Assistant Secretary
for Public Affairs

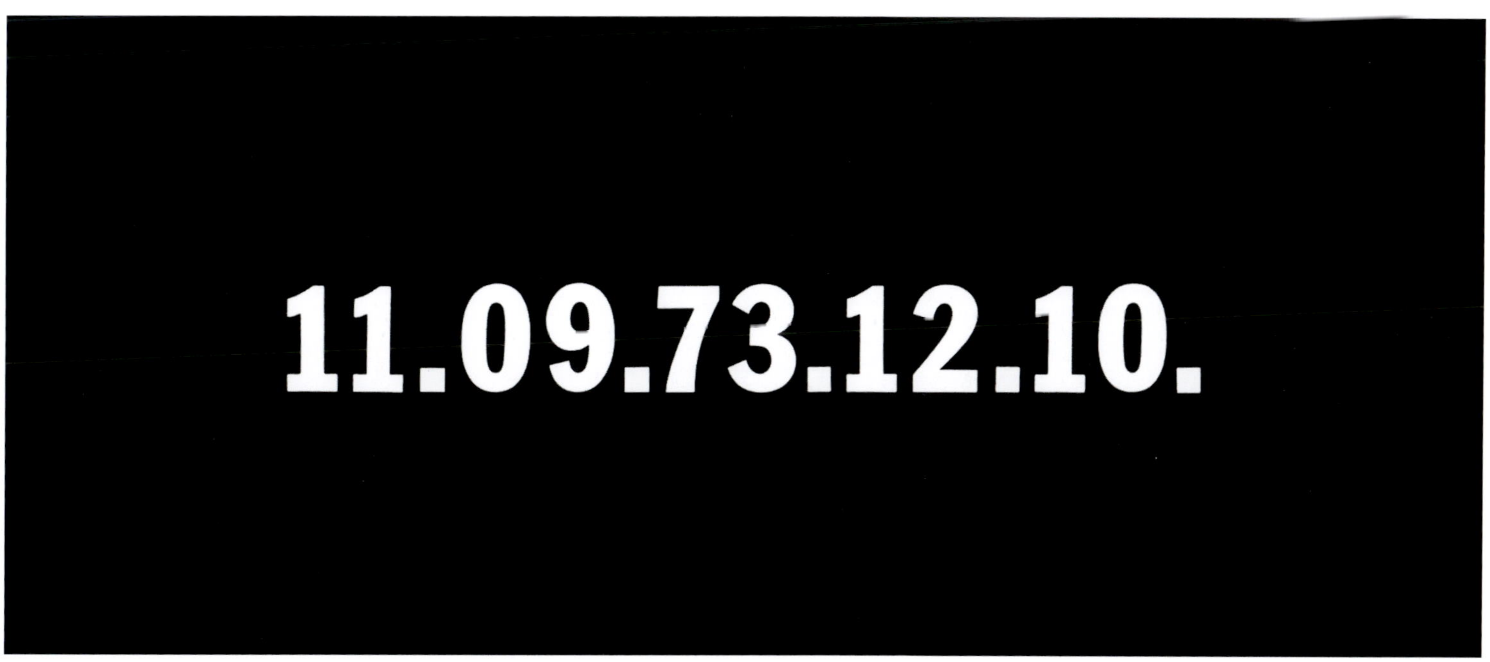

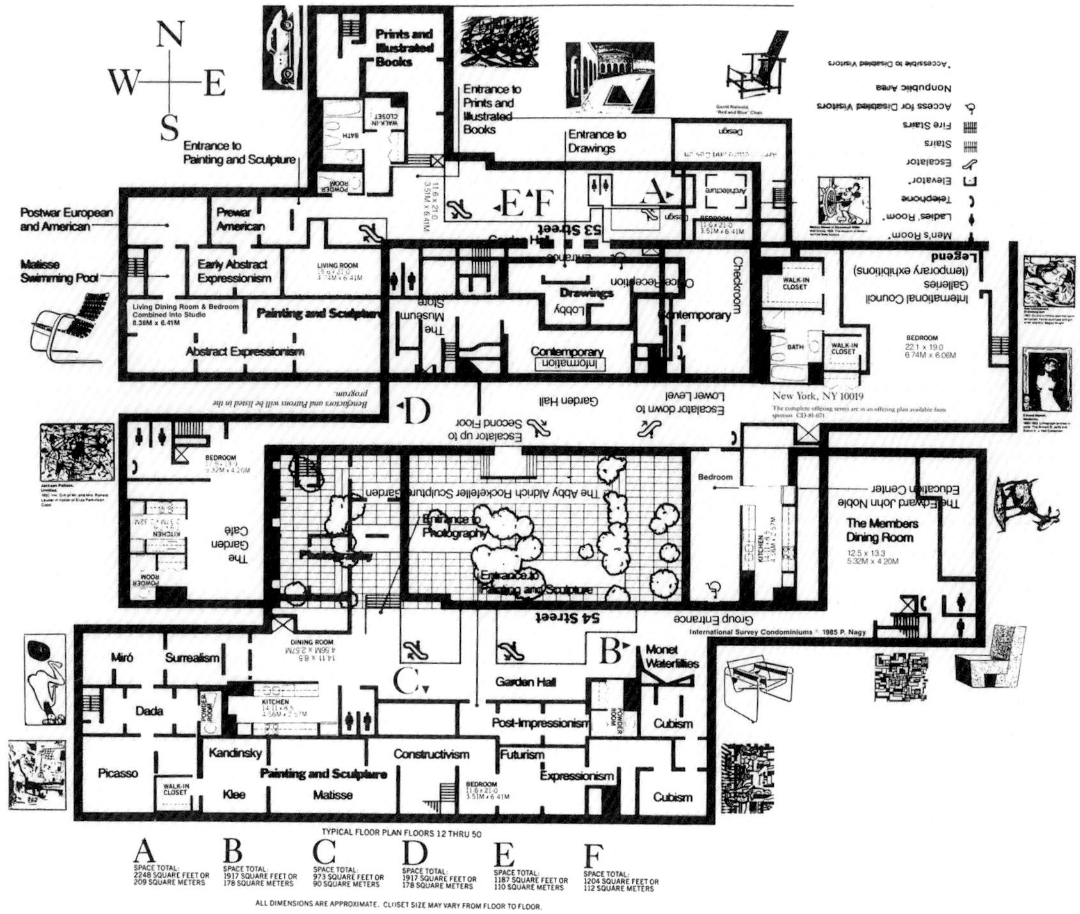
N
W
E
S
Prints and Illustrated Books
Entrance to Prints and Illustrated Books
Entrance to Drawings
Entrance to Painting and Sculpture
Postwar European and American
Prewar American
Matisse Swimming Pool
Early Abstract Expressionism
Painting and Sculpture
Abstract Expressionism
Contemporary
Checkroom
New York, NY 10019
Bedroom
The Members Dining Room
Miró
Surrealism
Dada
Picasso
Kandinsky
Klee
Matisse
Painting and Sculpture
Constructivism
Futurism
Post-Impressionism
Expressionism
Cubism
Garden Hall
Monet Waterlilies
54 Street
53 Street
TYPICAL FLOOR PLAN FLOORS 12 THRU 50
A
B
C
D
E
F
ALL DIMENSIONS ARE APPROXIMATE. CLOSET SIZE MAY VARY FROM FLOOR TO FLOOR.

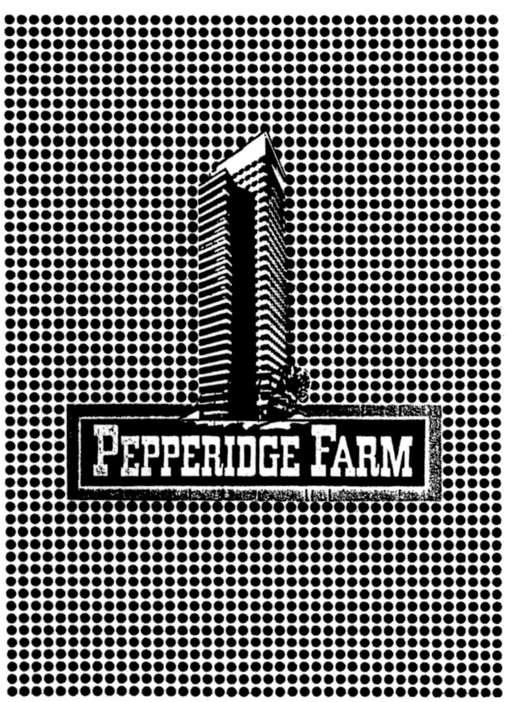
PEPPERIDGE FARM

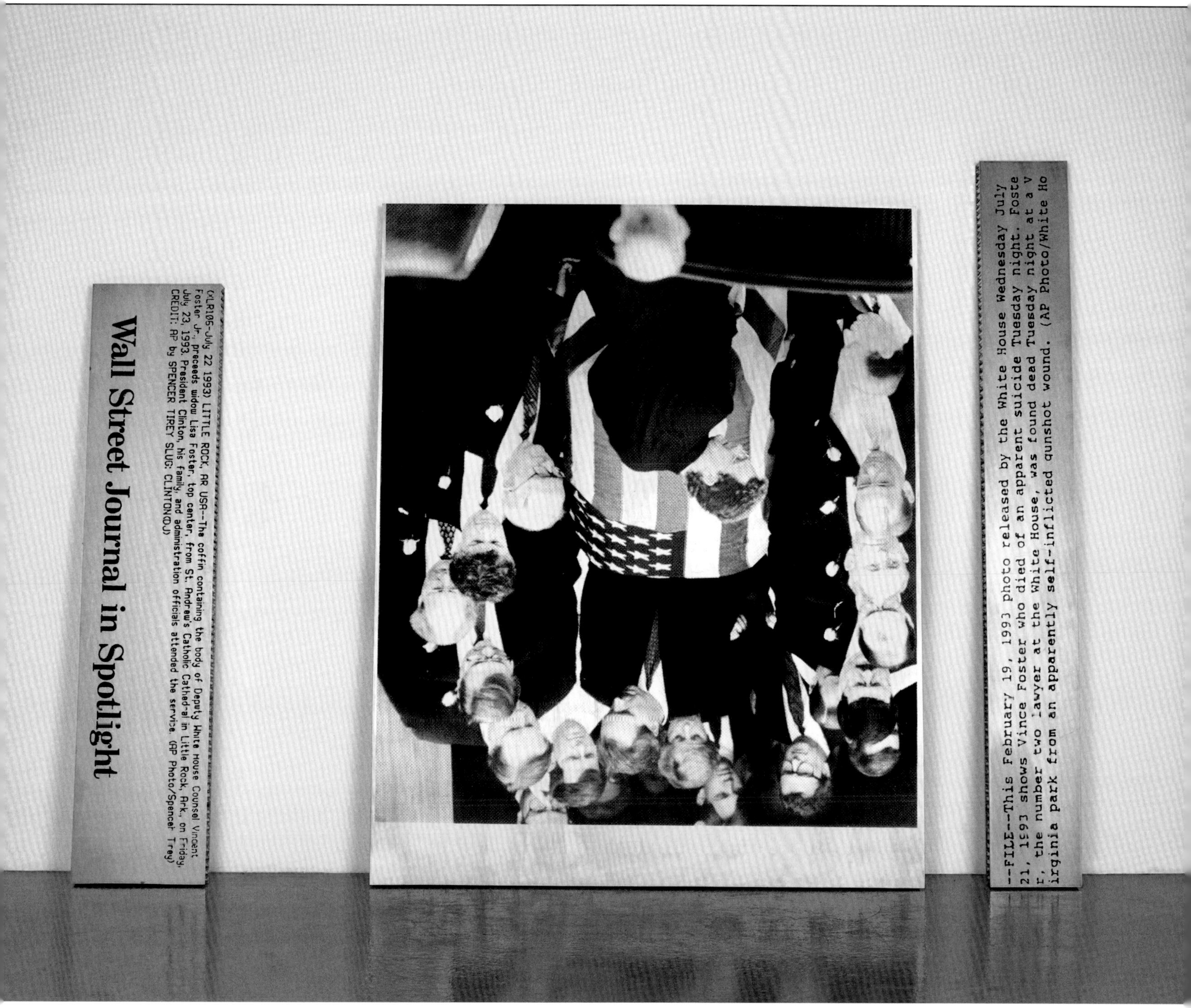

Peter Nagy, *International Survey Condominiums*, 1985

Peter Nagy, *est Graduate*, 1984

Cady Noland, *Untitled (Vince Foster)*, 1992–93

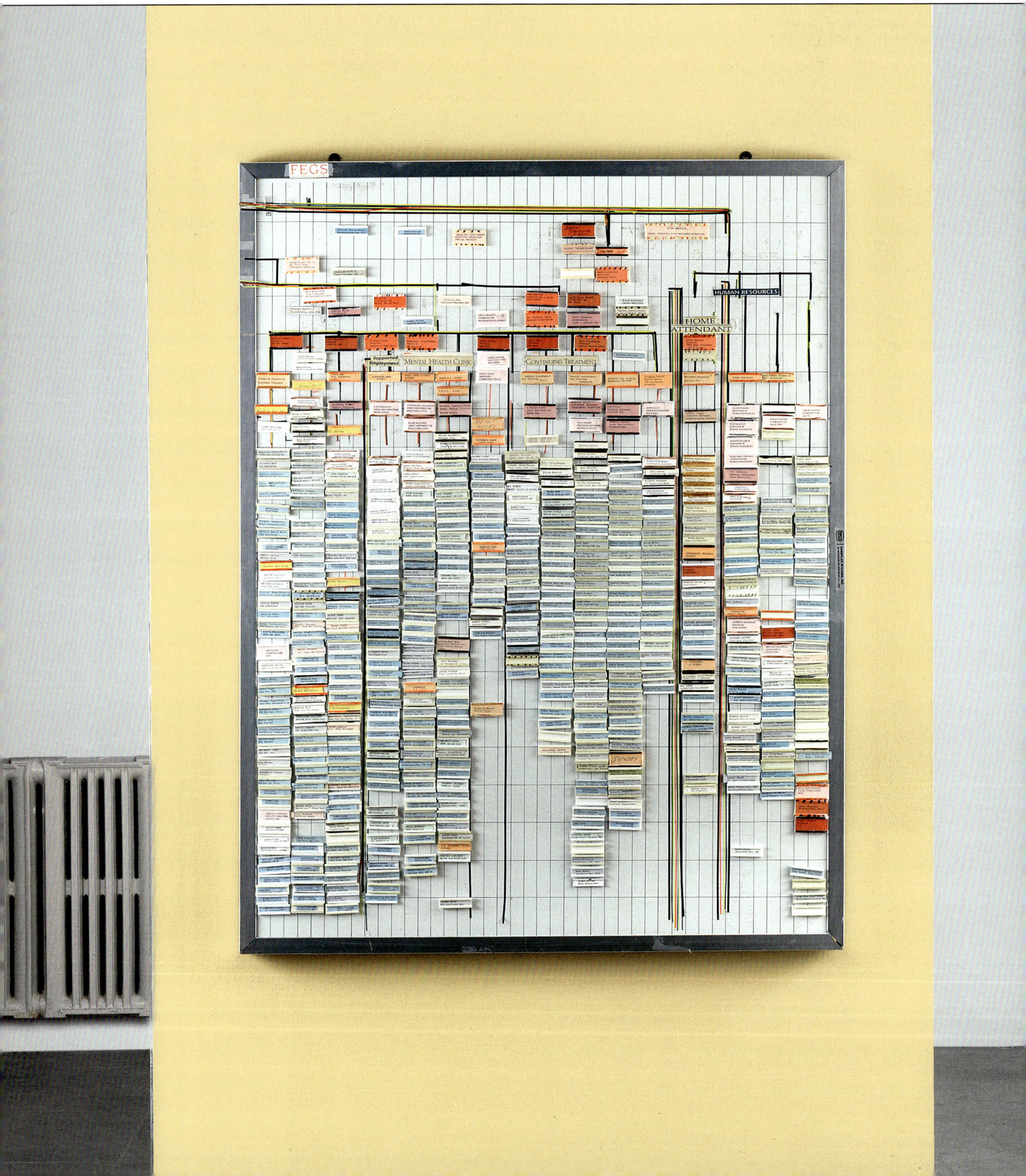
FEGS
HUMAN RESOURCES
HOME
ATTENDANT
Supported Employment
MENTAL HEALTH CLINIC
CONTINUING TREATMENT
SUNDAY

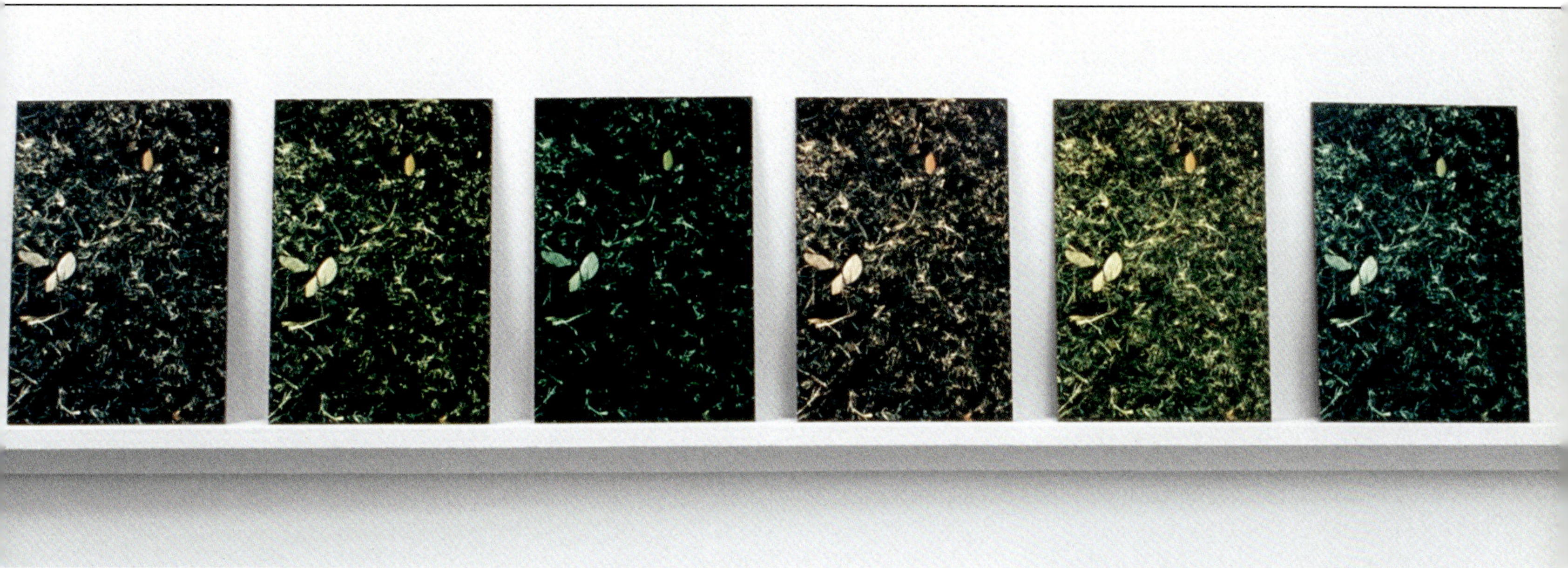

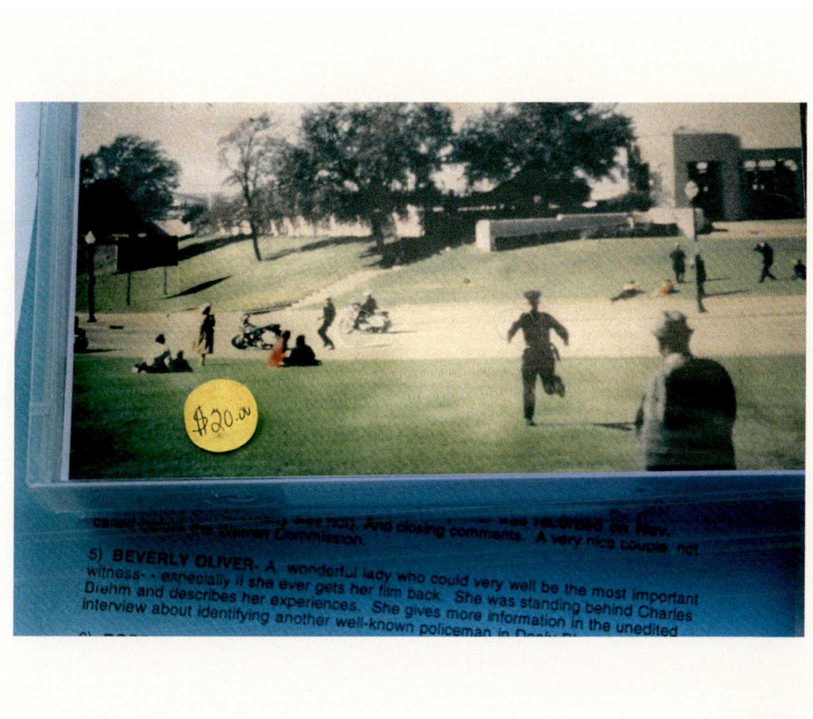

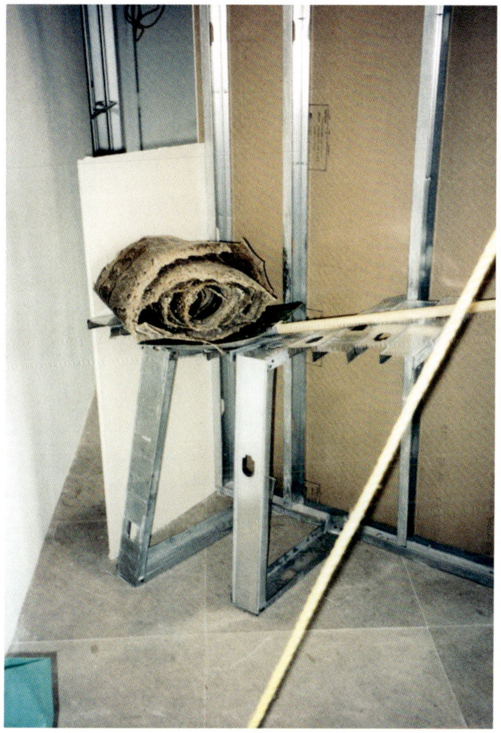

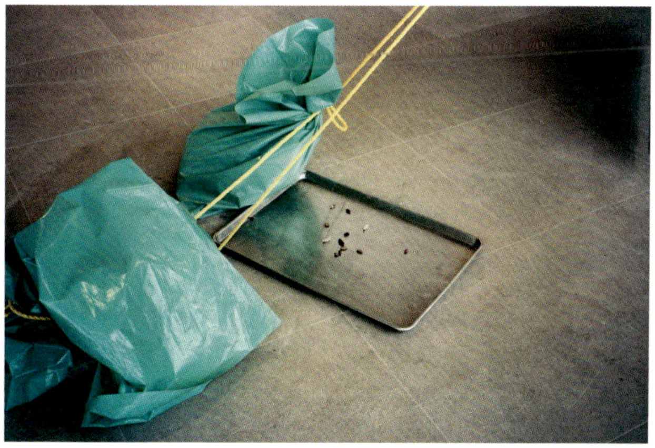

This spread and overleaf:
Rachel Harrison, *Snake in the Grass*, 1997.
Installation view and details from "The Look of
Dress-Separates," Greene Naftali Gallery,
New York, March 21–April 20, 1997

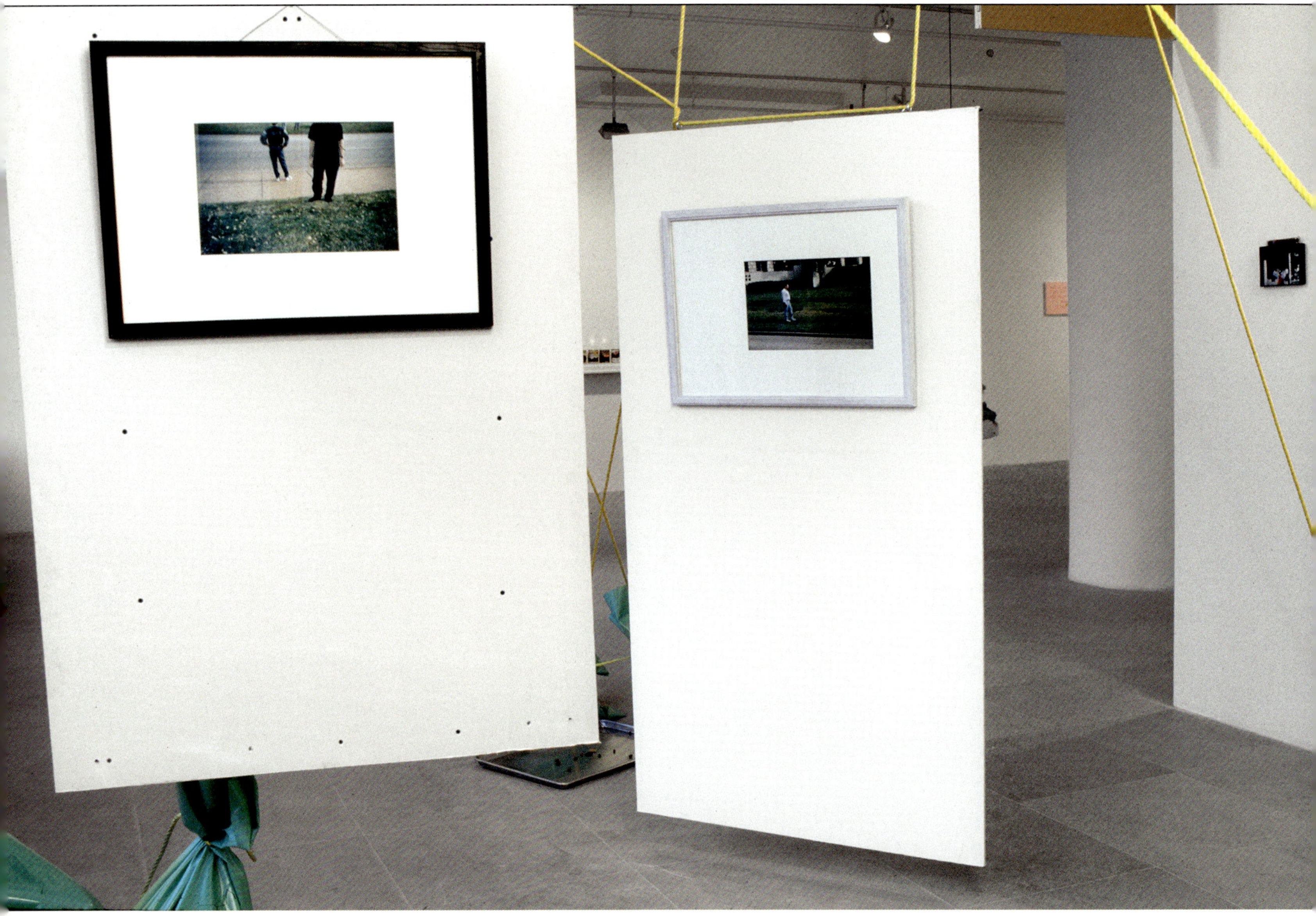

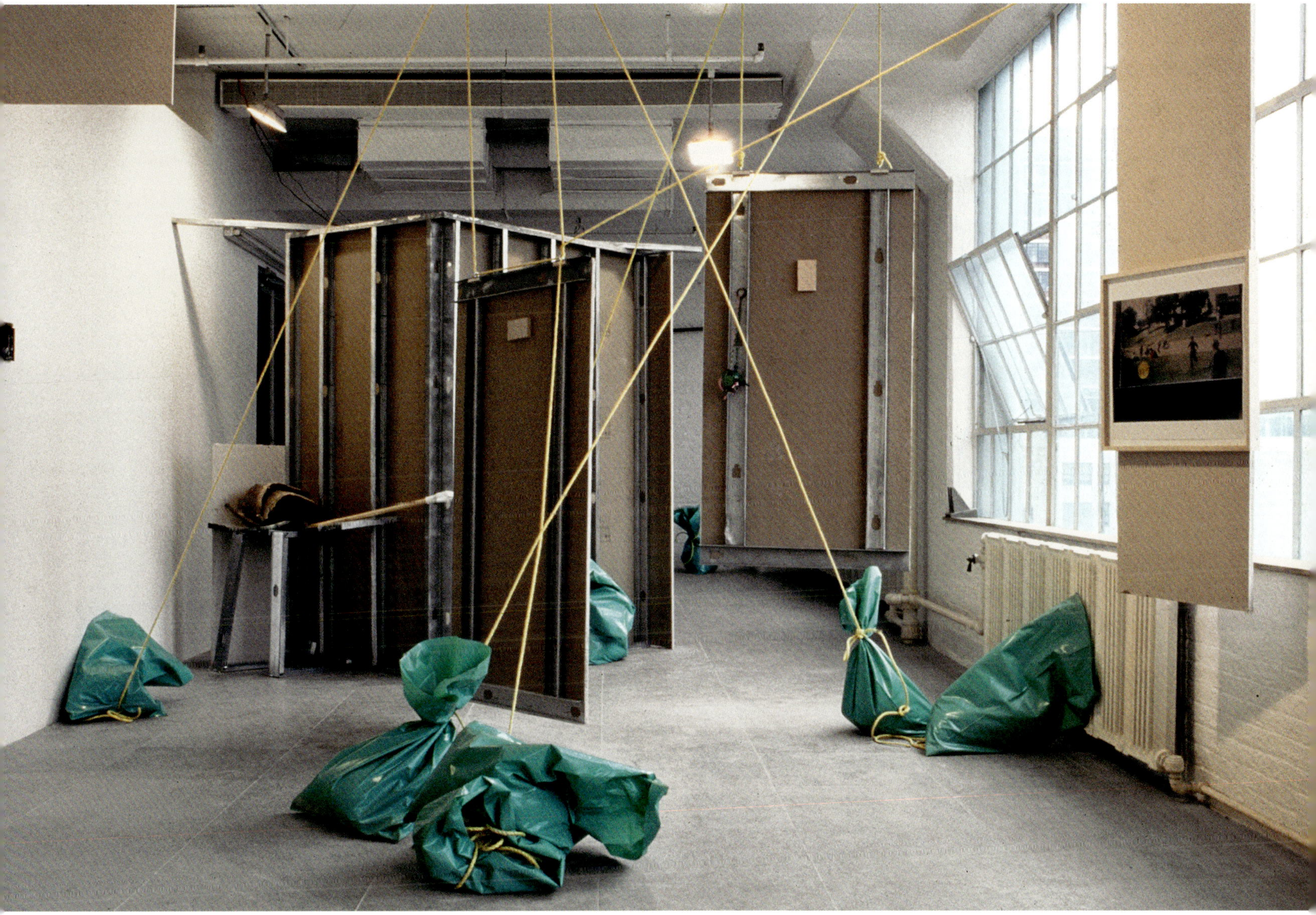

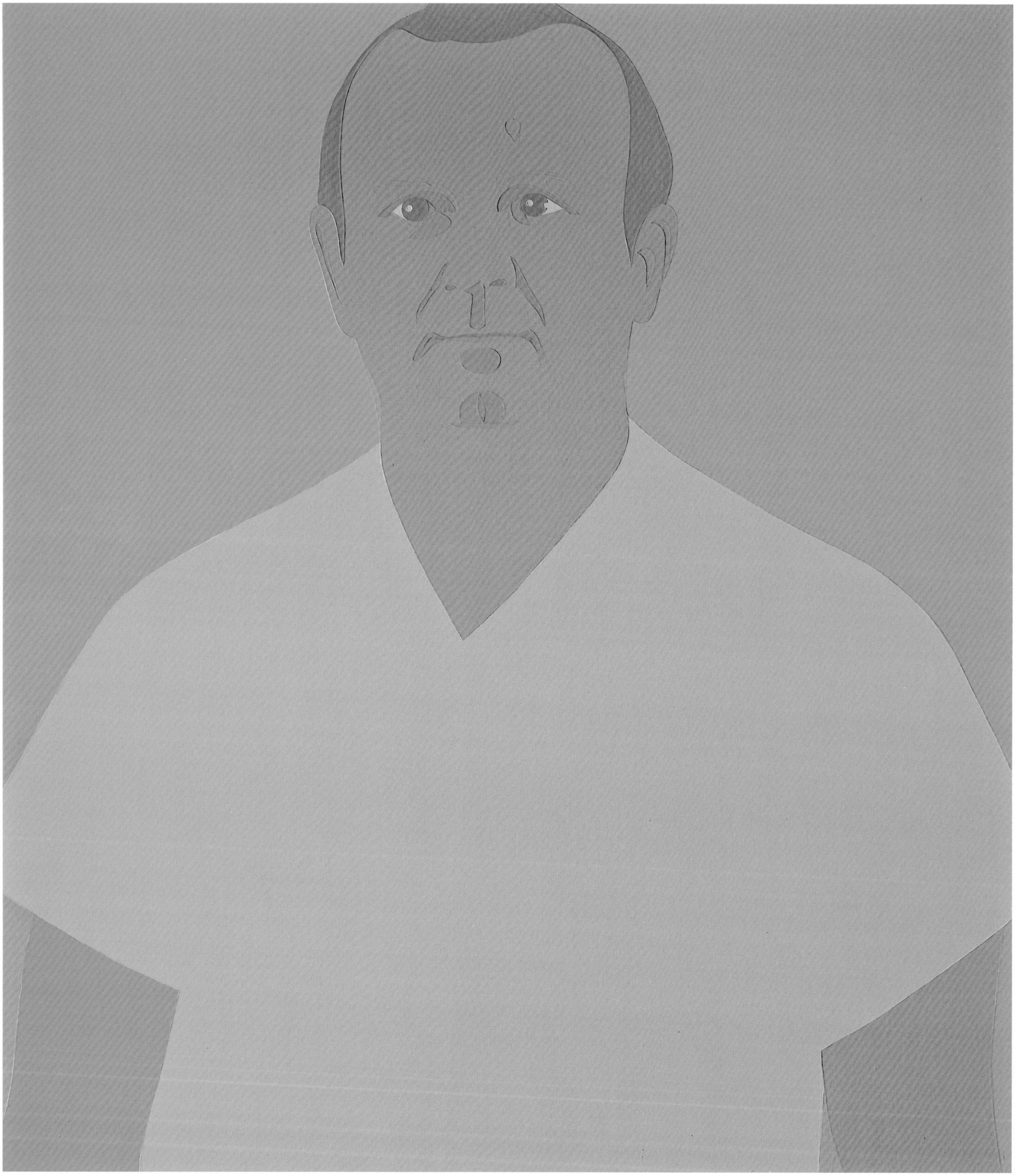

Wayne Gonzales, *Dallas Police 36398*, 1999

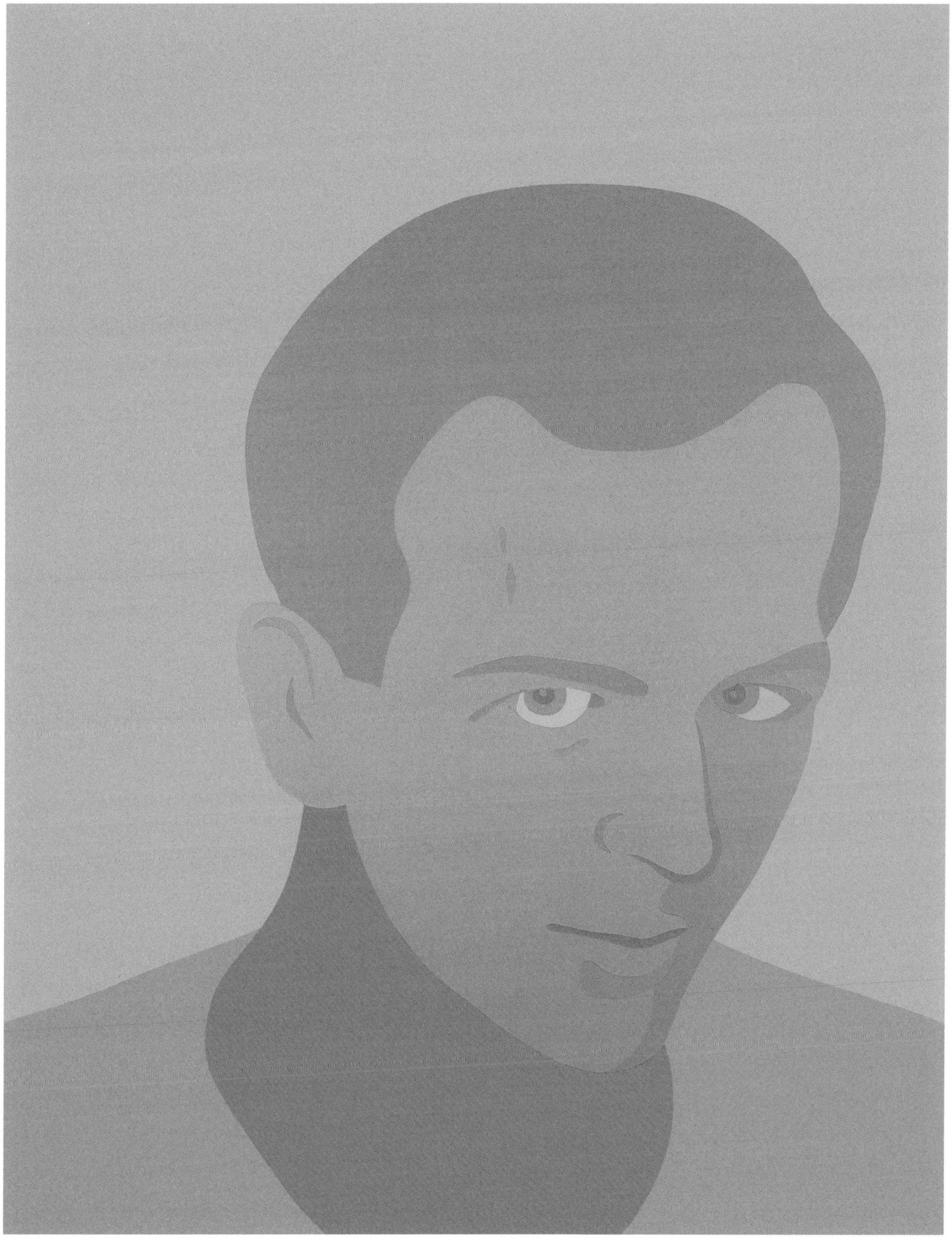

Wayne Gonzales, *Peach Oswald*, 2001

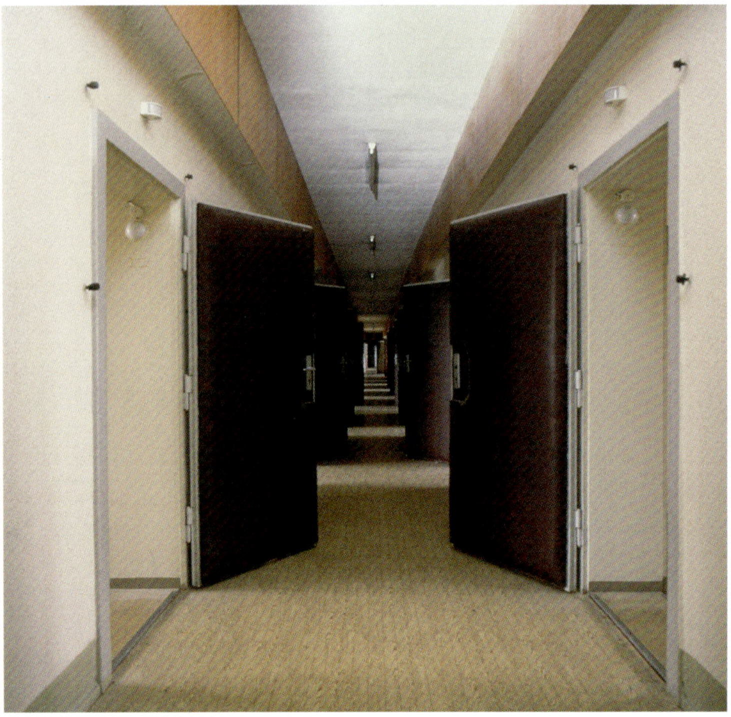

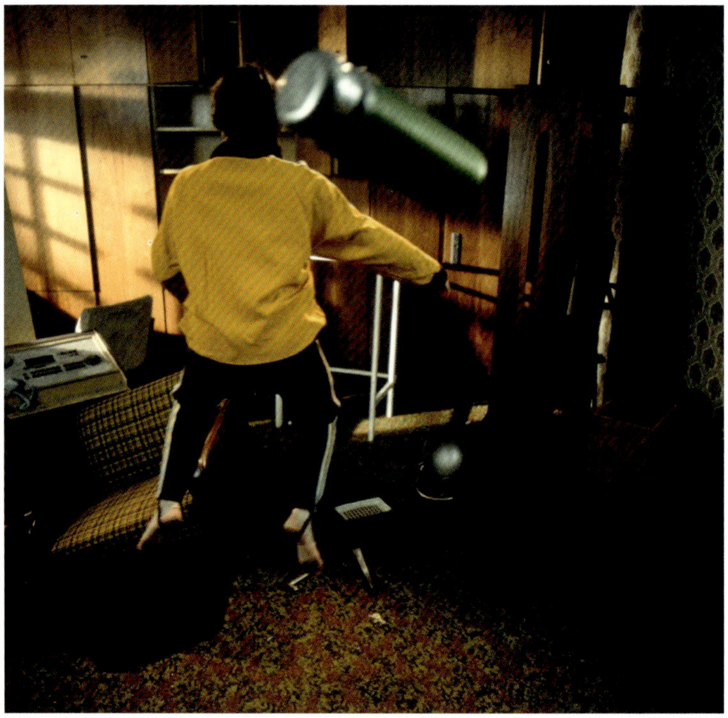

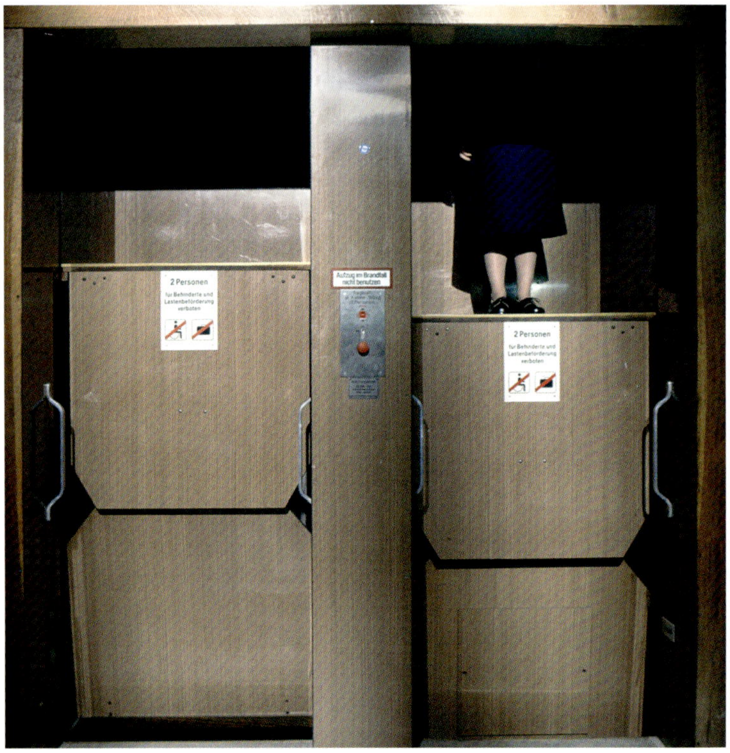

Stills from Jeremy Blake, Winchester Trilogy:

Winchester, 2002

1906, 2003

Century 21, 2004

Stills from Jane and Louise Wilson, *Stasi City*, 1997

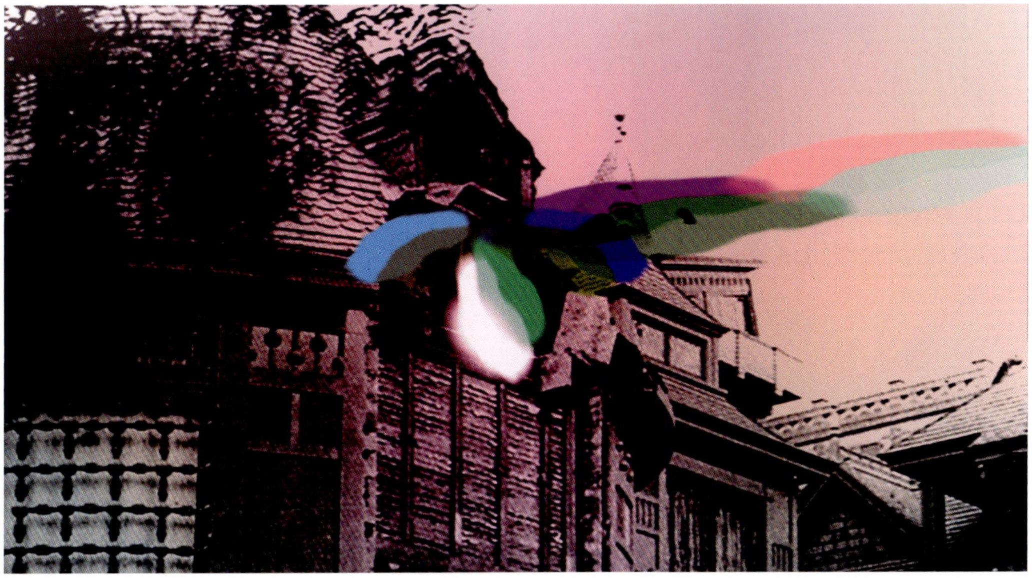

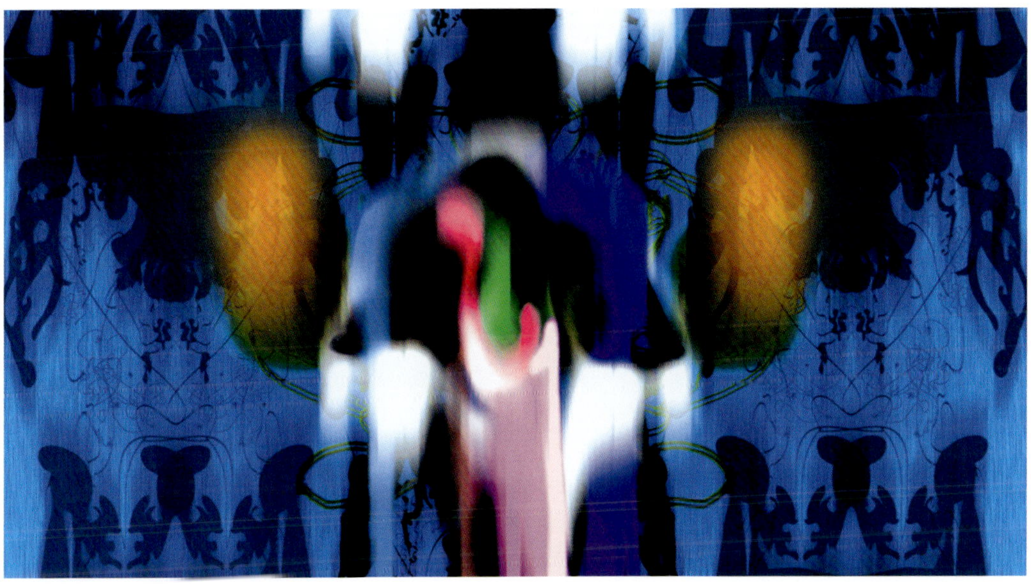

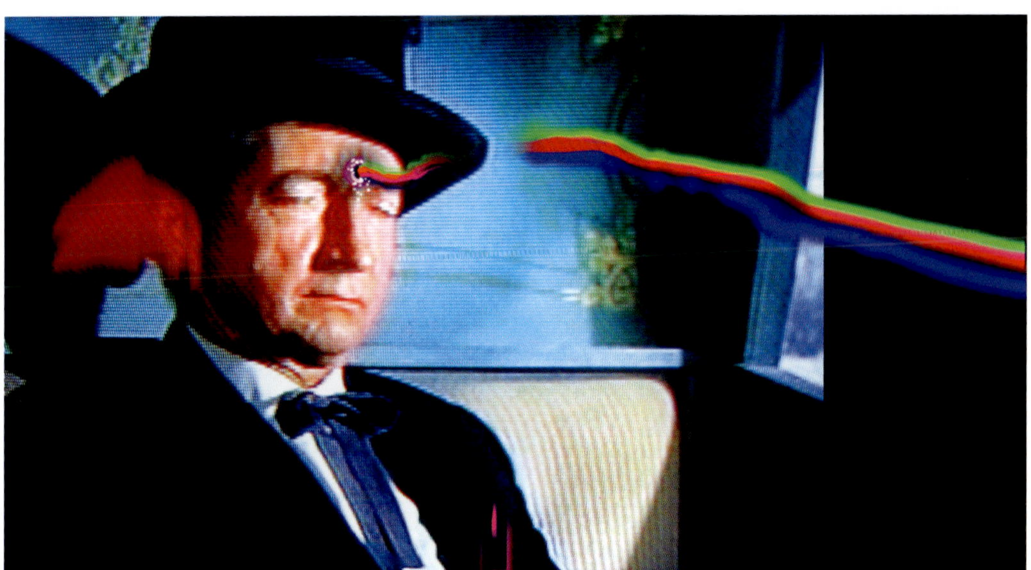

THE ARTIST AS RESEARCHER

Douglas Eklund

It is hard to overestimate the sea change that occurred when Ronald Reagan was elected president in 1980. In fact, you would be hard pressed to find a politician more deeply reviled by the left yet so enamored by the right. Thrown back on its collective id, the U.S. government unleashed its worst impulses on the poor and marginalized at home and abroad, whether through Reaganomics or cuts to federal programs or covert funding and training of death squads in Latin America. For countercultural holdouts, the country began to look a lot like the "evil empire" that Reagan accused the Soviet Union of being. Margaret Thatcher's infamous statement in 1987 that "there is no such thing as society"[1] announced a heartless Social Darwinism at the core of the Reagan and Thatcher revolutions.

As if Reagan's policies and actions were not dispiriting enough to those on the left, cascading revelations in the 1980s and 1990s primed the public to heed their worst suspicions about secret government activity and conspiracy, as men in power were yanked into the public square to account for their misdeeds. A picture perfect example is the famous 1994 courtroom photograph by Stephen Crowley that ran on the front page of the *New York Times* showing tobacco-company executives swearing in before testifying en bloc that nicotine was not addictive (fig. 36).

In 1980, journalist Dan Rottenberg coined the term *yuppie* to describe the movers of gentrification, the "young urban professionals" (read: affluent whites) who were flocking to cities from the suburbs and buying up devastated housing stock on the cheap.[2] In the realm of popular culture, the 1980s sitcom *Family Ties* centered

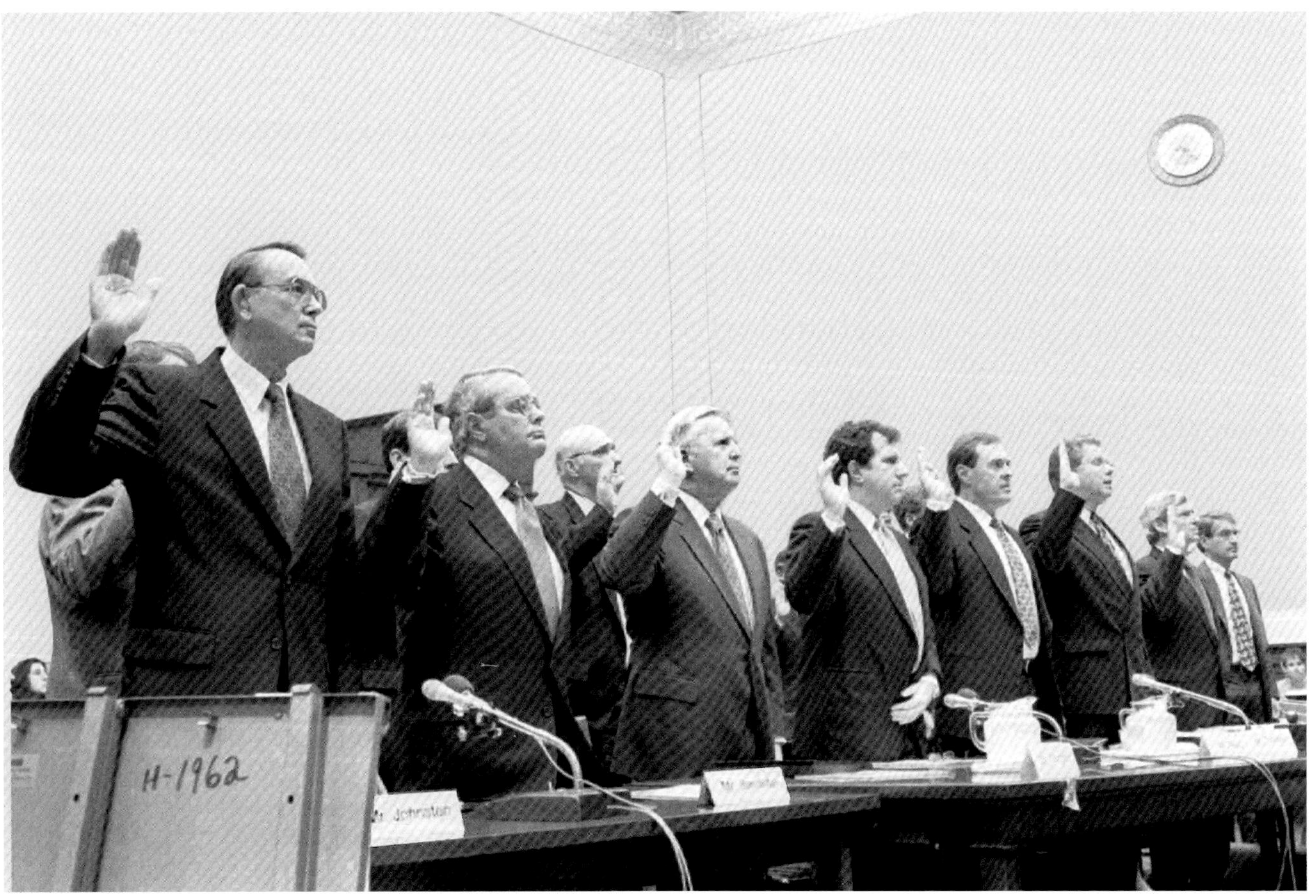

Fig. 36. Tobacco executives sworn in before Congress, *New York Times*, April 15, 1994. Photograph by Stephen Crowley

on the ideological conflict between aging Baby Boomer parents of the former hippie persuasion and their Republican son played by Michael J. Fox. For those with one eye looking back on the 1960s and 1970s, it seemed as if the Statue of Liberty were wearing a sign around its neck with the warning "Abandon All Hope Ye Who Enter Here."

In 1987, horror-movie director John Carpenter created what might be called a "message film" allegorizing the nation's rightward turn. Titled *They Live* (figs. 37–39), it tells the story of a down-on-his-luck working-class white guy (played by pro wrestler Rowdy Roddy Piper) who stumbles upon a box of sunglasses that, when worn, reveal people in high places and selfish yuppies all around him to be gruesome, undead-looking aliens colonizing the planet. (They are reminiscent of the reptilians in Jim Shaw's *Martian Portraits*, p. 121.) Equally frightening, subliminal messages are embedded in everything from television broadcasts and newspapers to billboards and crosswalk signs. Carpenter's neat sci-fi conceit is a parable of extreme Althusserian indoctrination, indicting those who succumbed to the lure of Reagan while also taking aim at the mass media and at the seductive electronic gadgets—precursors to our iPhones—then flooding America. Such devices mask control with the illusion of connectivity and stealthily induce a myopic, blinkered, and ultimately selfish relationship to one's social and political environment.[3] The critique that technology, more than art, steers the ship of culture finds no more perfect analogue than Peter Nagy's *Entertainment Erases History* (1983; fig. 40), a mash-up of Alfred Barr's master plan for modernism overlaid with the devices that drive experience away from collective engagement and toward a privatized, mediated view of the world.

A similar sense of urgency about the rampant growth of technology is expressed in Neil Postman's 1985 book *Amusing Ourselves to Death: Public Discourse in the Age of Show Business*, a prescient if not vatic "inquiry and a lamentation" on what he calls "the vast and trembling shift from the magic of writing to the magic of electronics."[4] Starting from the McLuhanesque premise that forms of communication, such as television, shape the content of culture, Postman argues that although this technological phenomenon may seem right out of George Orwell's *1984*, it is more resonant of Aldous Huxley's *Brave New World*:

> What Huxley teaches us is that in the age of advanced technology, spiritual devastation is more likely to come from an enemy with a smiling face than from one whose countenance exudes suspicion and hate. . . . When a population becomes distracted by trivia, when cultural life is redefined as a perpetual round of entertainments, when serious public conversation becomes a form of baby-talk, when, in short, a people become an audience and their public business a vaudeville act, then a nation finds itself at risk; culture-death is a clear possibility.[5]

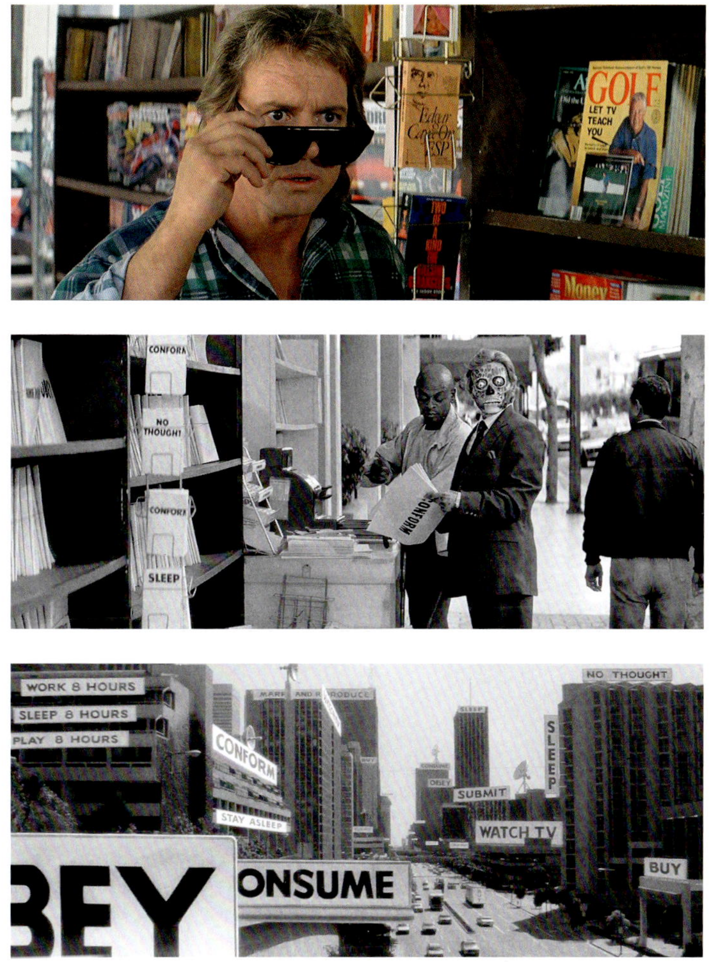

Figs. 37–39. Stills from *They Live*, 1987, directed by John Carpenter

The proliferation of personal technological devices—the Sony Walkman, the VCR, all manner of gadgets that foster separation—was wedded to the rise of "Infotainment." For Postman and others, this blurring of the line between news and entertainment signaled the death knell for our ability to critically apprehend and navigate complex national issues, thus making us susceptible to the kind of government treachery that, in turn, incites conspiracy thinking.

Guy Debord's *Society of the Spectacle*, originally published in 1967, became the locus classicus for

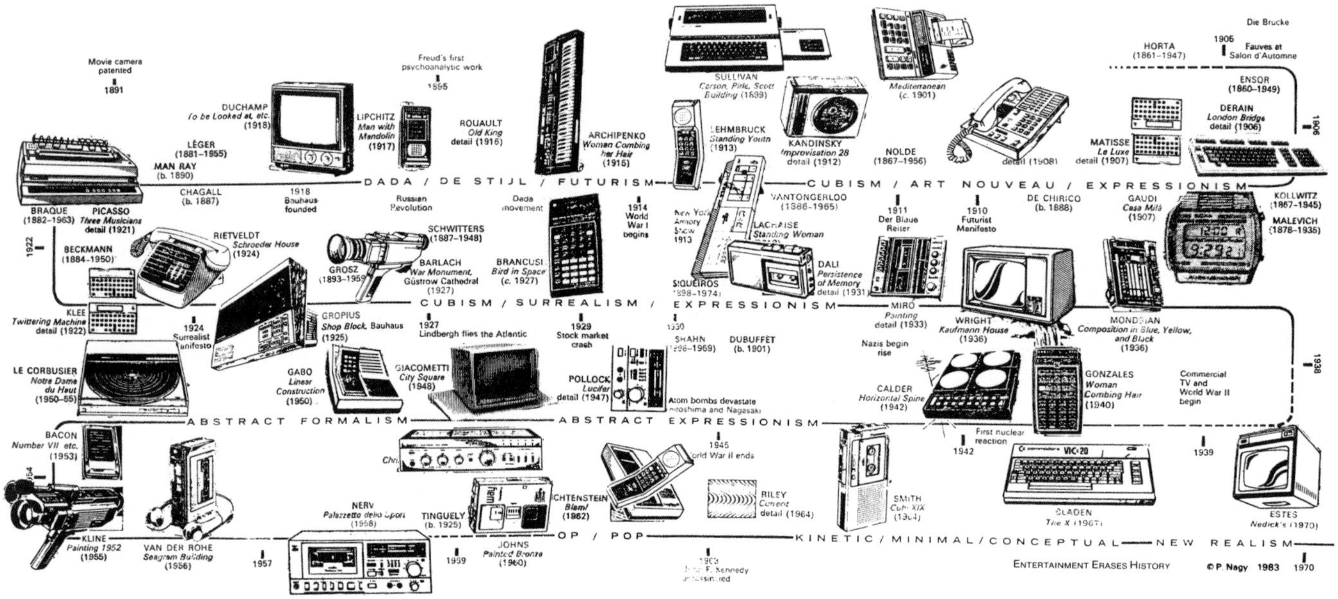

Fig. 40. Peter Nagy (American, born 1959), *Entertainment Erases History*, 1983. Black-and-white photocopy, 9 × 14¾ in. (22.9 × 37.5 cm)

media-savvy artists dealing with the idea that reality had been superseded by its representation. While it is true that Debord's concept of spectacle is oriented more toward Marxist concepts, such as alienation and commodity fetishism, than toward a purely conspiratorial reading, the vision of control by the hegemonic mass media is arguably conspiratorial in nature (fig. 41).[6] However, in a new preface to the 1979 Italian edition of the book, Debord made a then-shocking, but now rather tame, assertion regarding the kidnapping of Prime Minister Aldo Moro by the Red Brigades in the previous year: "the Italian authorities' version was not credible for an instant. Its intent was not to be believed but to be the only version on offer."[7] (For an account of the Moro affair and Sarah Charlesworth's work in response to it, see the essay by Beth Saunders in this volume, pp. 96–105.)

Like Debord before the Moro affair, Marxist critic Fredric Jameson was skeptical about conspiracy theory being a skeleton key to decipher late capitalism, in that it attributes agency to cabals of individuals rather than to the underlying economic structures of society at large. On one of the few occasions he did address conspiracy theory, Jameson appropriately described it as "high-tech paranoia."[8] This description is a hallmark of both the science fiction of Philip K. Dick, which gained wide exposure in the 1980s through movies such as Ridley Scott's *Blade Runner* (1982), based on Dick's 1968 novel *Do Androids Dream of Electric Sheep?*, and the extremely influential cyberpunk fiction of William Gibson, such as his novel *Neuromancer* (1984). Cyberpunk's dystopian view of society found its analogue in the visual arts with Gretchen Bender's "electronic theater," which itself is like a theatricalized version of Guy Debord's *Society of the Spectacle*. In her aggressive *son et lumière* presentations of commodity fetishism, phalanxes of boxy monitors display synchronized ballets of logos and computer graphics lifted from ads for multinational corporations that make everything from toasters to long-range missiles, accompanied by a blaring techno-industrial soundtrack. As art critic Roberta Smith commented in the *New York Times*, "If Darth Vader made art, it might look like this" (fig. 42).[9]

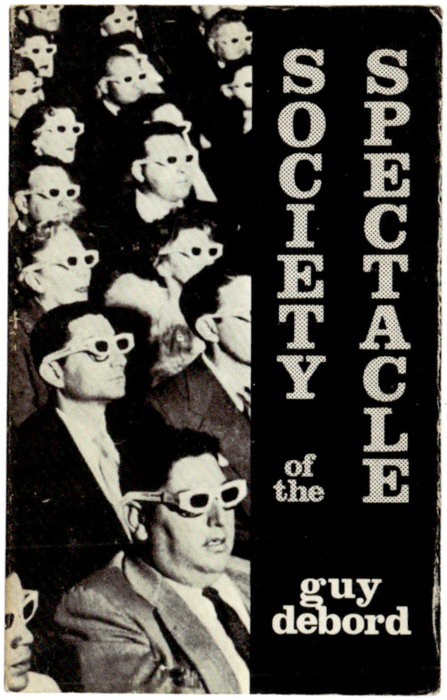

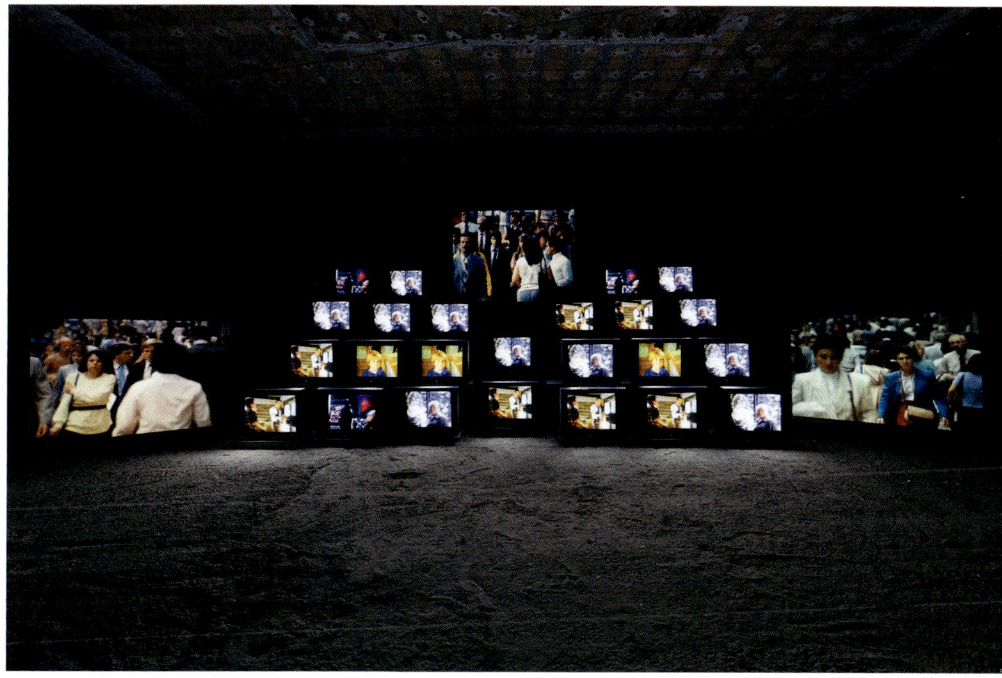

Fig. 41. Guy Debord, *Society of the Spectacle* (1967; Detroit: Black and Red, 1983)

Fig. 42. Gretchen Bender (American, 1951–2005), *Total Recall*, 1987. Eight-channel digital video installation, transferred from video tape and 16mm film, color, sound, 18 min., 2 sec. Installation view, Schinkel Pavilion (Prinzessinnenpalais), Berlin, 2015

• • •

In a 1991 interview with artist, writer, and musician John Miller, Mike Kelley recognized a number of artists who have dealt with conspiracy theory and lamented that art scholars had not paid adequate attention to the subject, concluding, "Once it starts to become obvious how it is a motivating factor in real life, then people will start to write about it as a mythology or an ideology."[10] That same year he heralded his interest in the topic with *Untitled (Government and Business)*, a large black-and-white painting on paper in which the words "GOVERNMENT" and "BUSINESS," denoting corrupt parties in an unholy union, are hidden in a carpet of tangled and clotted lines resembling a Jackson Pollock pulled from a bathtub drain (p. 87). Kelley's major statement on conspiracy would come five years later with *Educational Complex* and related works (pp. 132–34; these works are discussed further in Ian Alteveer's essay in this volume, pp. 106–17).

In another black-and-white painting on paper, titled *Low Definition Presidency*, Kelley mapped out a convoluted relationship between government entities and their constituents (p. 86). Made in 1993, a year after Bill Clinton returned the White House to Democrats following twelve years of Republican occupancy, this vertical painting bridges the icky abjection of *Untitled (Government and Business)* with what the artist described in an essay on caricature as the genre's "grotesque displacement of the order of the body."[11] In rebuttal to the widespread sigh of relief over Clinton's victory, Kelley presents the darker diagnosis of a shift occurring in the Democratic Party as it jettisoned the working class to favor professional elites. Think tanks and NGOs such as the Economic Policy Institute and the Democratic Leadership Council (they of the infamous Lincoln Bedroom sleepovers for big donors) are depicted as organs voiding the "CLASS-BASED LEFT." Off in the corner, a bezoarlike mass labeled "Perot Voter" represents the calcified remains of the useless populist leftovers. Kelley's autopsy locates a generalized, abstract form of conspiracy—not illegal per se, but indicative of how the left did not win as much as adjust itself to the rightward turn, represented as the passage of matter through a diseased and sclerotic body. The work recalls Peter Saul's *Government of California* (p. 36), which had been an illustration in the 1991 Kelley and Miller interview.

In November of 1991, the *Village Voice* published an article by James Ridgeway titled "It's All One Big Conspiracy," which began, "It's been a long time since America has seen a bumper crop of conspiracies. From the Iran-Contra affair and the October Surprise to the BCCI [Bank of Credit and Commerce International] scandal and the S&L [Savings and Loan] collapse, secret teams seem to be everywhere at once, involving just about everyone you'd ever want to know about."[12] A month earlier, Ridgeway and coauthor Doug Vaughan had written an epic investigative report on the death of Danny Casolaro, described by them as "one of a small army of freelance journalists exploring the possibility that the powers of the national security state had been used to manipulate domestic politics."[13]

Casolaro's research had led him to the threshold of a conspiracy of conspiracies. Calling it the "Octopus," he linked a network of individuals and institutions to a triumvirate of scandals (Iran-Contra, S&L, and BCCI), which were previously considered unrelated, and even to the October surprise (a deal with Iran to delay release of the hostages) that helped elect Reagan in 1980.[14] In Ridgeway and Vaughan's story, circumstantial evidence accretes to the point that it becomes impossible to believe anything other than that Casolaro's death was murder rather than suicide. The reporter Gary Webb died under similar suspicions a decade after being blackballed by the mainstream press for investigating the link between the crack cocaine epidemic and the secret funding of the Nicaraguan Contras through arms sales to Iran. Casolaro and Webb thus became the templates of the independent researcher killed for what he knew, a key component of the conspiracy theory "mythology or ideology"[15] that Kelley described.

Perhaps inevitably, conspiracy theorists have elevated the artist Mark Lombardi into their pantheon of "the suicided." A Google search reveals as many or more links to speculation about his premature death at the age of forty-nine than to information about his artistic career. And while he may be the first artist who comes to mind in relation to conspiracy, Lombardi himself disapproved of "people who used speculative information to create conspiracy theories" and was dismayed by unverified data and untested hypotheses flooding the new World Wide Web.[16] Like Öyvind Fahlström, Lombardi came to the visual expression of his ideas through an earlier career as a writer. Before making his first Narrative Structures drawing, he had already completed epic research on the history of panoramas and an eight-hundred-page manuscript on Reagan's war on drugs, which he saw as rooted in the decades-long anti-Communist movement.

Leaving aside the suspicion of foul play in Lombardi's death, it is fitting to consider the artistic space he carved out as being analogous to the work of muckraking journalists such as Casolaro and Webb. Lombardi's short career belies the long tendrils of the covert activities he depicted, which taken together constitute a history of political and financial malfeasance, mainly through money laundering that is intertwined with organized crime stretching back to the syndicates of Al Capone and Meyer Lansky.[17] The artist cut his teeth on the S&L crisis of the 1980s, in which the deregulation that signaled an unmooring from the safe harbors of post-Depression New Deal protections led to the plundering of America's small-town banks. According to art historian Robert Hobbs, Lombardi's idea for representing his research visually might have come from seeing Oliver North's hand-drawn flowchart for his "Project Democracy," detailing the twenty-three shell companies and NGOs used to launder money from the illegal sale of arms to the Middle East (fig. 43).[18] Lombardi's labyrinths find visual precursors in the "interlock" diagrams used by both fraud investigators to ferret out networks of corruption (think of an FBI agent's wall drawing showing the interrelations of an organized crime family) and the conspirators themselves.

In *World Financial Corporation and Associates, ca. 1970–84: Miami, Ajman, and Bogota-Caracas (Brigada 2506: Cuban Anti-Castro Bay of Pigs Veteran) (7th Version)* (fig. 44), Lombardi charted the rise and fall of a

Fig. 43. Oliver North, financial flowchart reproduced in the Tower Commission Report, February 26, 1987

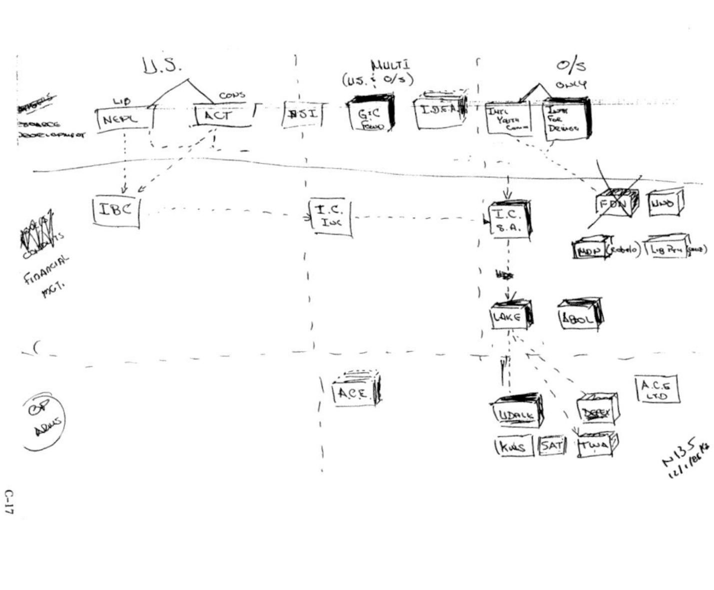

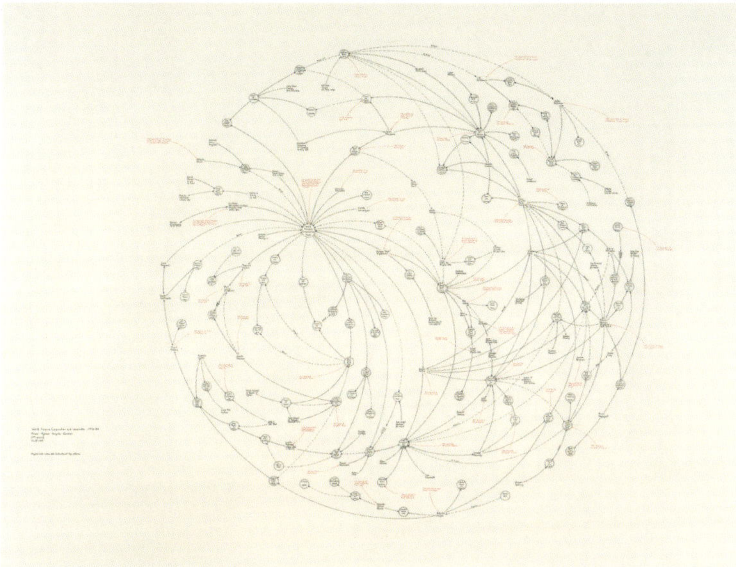

Fig. 44. Mark Lombardi (American, 1951–2000), *World Financial Corporation and Associates, ca. 1970–84: Miami, Ajman, and Bogota-Caracas (Brigada 2506: Cuban Anti-Castro Bay of Pigs Veteran) (7th Version)*, 1999. Colored pencil and graphite on paper, 69½ × 84 in. (175.6 × 213.4 cm). Collection of Susan Swenson and Joe Amrhein

Miami bank that laundered huge profits from cocaine trafficking for various covert programs. Known as W.F.C. Group, it was started by Guillermo Hernández-Cartaya, a Cuban exile who participated in the Bay of Pigs invasion. Hobbs described him as "a double agent working with the C.I.A., the Mafia, Fidel Castro, and Colombian drug cartels."[19] According to Deven Golden, one of the first people to exhibit Lombardi's work, when FBI agents arrived at W.F.C. headquarters to arrest Hernández-Cartaya, "his secretary calmly informed them, 'He's out fishing with Vice President Rockefeller.'"[20]

Lombardi's circular shape emerged from five versions that use a horizontal timeline format. The shape captures what Hobbs described as "the almost autonomous force of liquid capital's global flows."[21] It may seem as if Lombardi's drawings are not so different from Hans Haacke's real-estate works (pp. 42–43) in their dry detailing of obfuscation in high places. But, unlike Haacke, Lombardi regularly attested to the tricky tension between what he was depicting and the seductive, even beautiful way in which it was depicted.

In *Bill Clinton, the Lippo Group, and Jackson Stephens of Little Rock, Arkansas (5th Version)* (1999; p. 90), Lombardi took aim at the outgoing Democratic president's relationship with James Riady, the head of an Indonesian banking conglomerate who moved to Little Rock, Arkansas, and fused his business with Jackson Stephens, the owner of the largest investment bank outside Wall Street. Stephens was the kind of all-purpose moneymaker for whom party affiliation made no difference—he was an integral part of the campaigns of both George H. W. Bush and then-governor Bill Clinton, whose 1992 presidential campaign he repeatedly saved from scandal with infusions of money.[22] The Lippo Group's business with Communist China resulted in Riady's pleading guilty to using foreign corporate money to support Clinton's campaign.

Arkansas kingmaker Jackson Stephens is one of 556 names that appear in Lombardi's magnum opus documenting the BCCI scandal of the 1980s (pp. 88–89); he created four versions of *BCCI-ICIC & FAB, 1972–91* between 1996 and 2000. The artist deemed this epic, nearly twelve-foot-long drawing to be the summation of his Narrative Structures series, which he also considered complete at the time of his death. Writing about the second version, Lombardi described the bank's enormity, it having nearly 1 million depositors in seventy-eight countries, and enumerated its "handling [of] 'hot,' 'black,' and 'dirty' money for a panoply of international gangsters, arms dealers, bagmen, corrupt foreign officials, drug smugglers, tax evaders, money launderers and agents of influence, not to mention elements of the intelligence services of the U.S., U.K., Pakistan, U.A.E., and Saudi Arabia which among other things, used the bank in the early 1980s to provide support for the Afghan mujahedeen fighters, finance parts of the Iran-Contra operation and funnel bribes to 'retired' Palestinian terrorist Abu Nidal."[23] According to a biographer of the artist, BCCI was essentially a CIA operation to replace the funding and laundering streams for covert projects that had dried up in the wake of congressional investigations after Watergate.[24]

It is hard not to see Lombardi's hand-drawn, open-source investigative works as the last gasp of a thousand-year-old episteme based on the printing press, the precursor to digital culture's anything-goes, impossible-to-verify, ceaseless flood of information. Indeed, one can celebrate the Internet's liquidation of the dominant monoculture, which squeezed out voices of the powerless, and still lament the loss of firm footing that accompanied the dissolution of print culture. If there is something of the sublime in Lombardi's work, it is partly due to how it provokes a vertiginous feeling of too many connections. If one constellation of activity is this complex and clandestine, the mind races to the impossibility of picturing the totality of such networks; ferreting out corruption becomes as unmanageable as counting grains of sand on a beach.

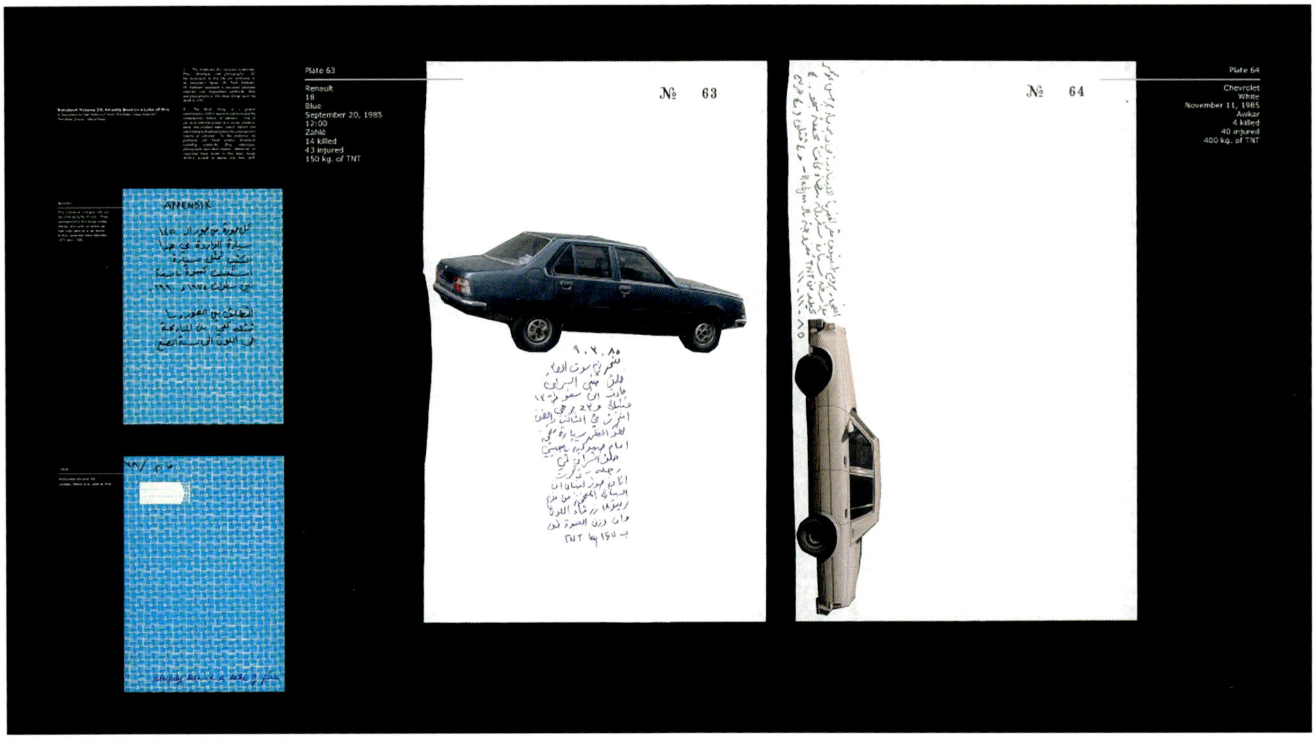

Fig. 45. Walid Raad/The Atlas Group (Lebanese, born 1967), *Notebook Volume 38: Already Been in a Lake of Fire (Plates 63–64)*, 1991/2003. Archival inkjet print, image 44 × 78¼ in. (111.8 × 198.8 cm). The Metropolitan Museum of Art, New York, Purchase, Vital Projects Fund Inc. Gift, Joyce and Robert Menschel, 2011 (2011.426)

The attacks of September 11, 2001, and their hijacking by the Bush administration as a casus belli for war with Iraq in a sense stanched the flow of inquiry by independent journalists into the epic malfeasances of the 1980s and 1990s chronicled by Lombardi. As seen following the Kennedy assassination, art made in the immediate aftermath of 9/11 does not yield much in the realm of overtly conspiratorial interpretation. The responses tend toward humanistic depictions such as Eric Fischl's *Tumbling Woman* sculpture, a piece that provoked controversy when it was shown in the fall of 2002 in the lower concourse of Rockefeller Center. What most occupied the left was the pressing liberal uprising against what it saw as a Republican conspiracy theory perpetrated on the American public to justify going to war with Iraq. Questioning the 9/11 terrorist attacks was relegated to the fringes, only to emerge five or so years after the fact with organizations such as Scholars for 9/11 Truth & Justice.[25]

Julia Meltzer and David Thorne, working under the name Speculative Archive, combined the research of investigative journalists with an imaginative process that re-created the human lives behind the drawn curtain of secret intelligence. In their video *"It's Not My Memory of It": three recollected cocuments* (2003), Meltzer and Thorne present three case studies, ranging from the Iranian Revolution in 1979 to a then-recent drone attack in Yemen as part of the War on Terror. They had formed the Speculative Archive to study, in their words, "the production of documents, their collection, circulation, and reception, and their socio-political effects."[26]

In the first of the three episodes (p. 91), the artists tell the story of an Iranian informant who appears in shredded CIA documents that were recovered and reconstituted by being literally stitched back together with the aid of local carpet weavers and then assembled into a seventy-five-volume publication (the 2012 movie *Argo* concludes with a scene showing this process). A female narrator translates a male voice speaking in Farsi as the imagined informant referred to as SDURN, who announces, "In this collection of documents, there is a memory of my disappearance that is not mine." He goes on to relate his growing disenchantment with his informant role in notes of disillusionment and fear; this narrative is pictured in stop-motion sequences showing shreds of documents being reconstituted whole by lining up phrases like fruit in a slot machine.

SDURN's mixed feelings are a fictional device gleaned from the intelligence officers' accounts of the informant. His eventual disappearance provokes comparison to the horrific practice of extraordinary rendition by the United States in the aftermath of 9/11 and during the war in Iraq. Peter Gallison's 2012 documentary *Secrecy* offers a counterpart: it opens with the story of Khalid El-Masri, a German-Lebanese citizen kidnapped by the Macedonian police in 2003 at the behest of the CIA so he could be tortured at arm's length by the United States. In giving presence to SDURN's small, single incident, marked in the voluminous documents only from the vantage point of American intelligence, Meltzer and Thorne invest that which is hushed and shadowy with permanence. A similar result occurs in Jenny Holzer's paintings of "torture memos," which commit to posterity a record of the horrific acts (see Meredith A. Brown's essay in this volume, pp. 136–43). These works restore to painting—viewed as outmoded by the early to mid-aughts—a potent mnemonic function, long considered a vestigial appendage to the medium's present-day status as a luxury good for the global elite.[27]

An interesting point of comparison to *"It's Not My Memory of It"* is the work of Walid Raad. In photographs, films, and videotapes, Raad examines the recent history of Lebanon—particularly the civil wars between 1975 and 1991—through the prism of a fictional collective called the Atlas Group, invented by the artist in 1999. For example, *Notebook Volume 38: Already Been in a Lake of Fire (Plates 63–64)* (fig. 45) is from a series of nine photographs purporting to show the contents of a notebook that a fictitious Dr. Fakhouri compiled to document the use of car bombs during the sixteen years of conflict. All of the information—the makes and models of the cars, the dates and times of the explosions, the bomb materials—is factual, but it is presented to the viewer through an invented scenario. Raad's narrative creates a space for fictional techniques as a possibly more truthful mode of commemoration than traditional approaches, which are no match for the mainstream media's collusion with government to suppress truth and encourage a kind of historical amnesia.[28]

In a confused contemporary art scene that had been transitioning back toward traditional media and away from progressive modes such as photography and video, Trevor Paglen emerged with a fresh approach. Tapping into the left's preoccupation with the war in Iraq, the artist assumed the role of a roving investigative journalist uncovering secret governmental abuses of power, such as cases of extraordinary rendition. In a 2011 interview with Julian Stallabrass, Paglen described the range of his activity as "camping out on a mountain-top, taking photos of a secret military base, determining the location of CIA 'black sites' so I can go photograph them, researching front companies used in covert operations, or working with amateur astronomers to track classified space craft in Earth's orbit.'"[29] With his "limit telephotography," using telescopic lenses, Paglen captured so-called black sites, extrajudicial locations where the "state of exception" allowed the United States to step outside of its self-image as a country that does not torture (pp. 92, 93).[30] In a related work, Paglen presented real-time flight information for unmarked corporate jets used by the CIA to fly persons of interest to places where torture was allowed.

In recent years, Paglen's art has moved toward a more traditional Conceptual art treatment, appropriating the visual culture of secret government operations gleaned from the cache of NSA material associated with the whistleblower Edward Snowden, such as patches and commemorative coins created by and for teams of intelligence analysts. He has largely shifted away from muckraking to uncover hidden abuses of power in war and has undertaken a more generalized examination of technology's dark underside. Examples of this work include demonstrations of machine seeing by artificial intelligence and his Autonomy Cube, which is a Plexiglas box encasing a wireless hub that enables the gallery visitor to access the "dark Web."

The downward spiraling situation in Venezuela at present, where the CIA seems to be stirring the pot of regime change with an eye toward the largest oil reserves in South America, triggers thoughts of the agency's incredible history of perfidy in countries such as Guatemala.[31] In his 2006 installation *UNstabile-Mobile* (p. 95), Alessandro Balteo-Yazbeck assembled an assortment of objects and ephemera that function as an interlock diagram to tell the story of the United States's historical role in "the oil producing nations of Latin America and the Middle East from the 1930s to the 1970s."[32] Its centerpiece is a pitch-perfect imitation of a standing mobile by Alexander Calder, black like the somber works the artist produced during World War II; the difference is this bootleg version casts a diagrammatic shadow that reproduces the locations of oil fields on a 2001 map of Iraq. The sculpture is presented along with a plethora of documentary material uncovered through a 2002 FOIA (Freedom of Information Act) release, including the map itself (fig. 46), which was produced by the Cheney Energy Task Force, and a list of foreign suitors for Iraq's oil contracts. In addition, a graphic timeline intertwines the development of the mobile in modern art of the 1930s with the concurrent liberation of Iraq's oil fields from colonial ownership.

Like *"It's Not My Memory of It," UNstabile-Mobile* is an example of "subjective narrative"[33] that feels free to range across fact and fiction as a means to circumvent the insidious ways in which the official storylines of history bury moments of potential resistance. But it is also an intentionally provocative encroachment on another artist's work, a gesture that initiates a reconsideration of the postwar avant-garde's susceptibility to co-optation by the hidden hand of governmental organizations of "cultural diplomacy," such as the United States Information Agency (USIA), which were engaged in a Cold War battle of ideas with the Soviet Union.[34] This ideological manipulation presented postwar abstraction to the populaces ringing the Iron Curtain as emblematic of the freedoms allowed in Western democracies. In 2012, six years after *UNstabile-Mobile* was made, art historian Alex J. Taylor published an astonishing account of how Calder's work functioned as cultural-diplomacy outreach, primarily in strategic displays mounted by organizers such as the Museum of Modern Art's international exhibition program in conjunction with the USIA and through commissions for public art in Iraq and Venezuela.[35]

Taylor's account, in which the committed and left-leaning Calder is buffeted about by geopolitical forces exploiting the whimsy, freedom, and playful innovation of his art in an ideological war of ideas with the Communists, deliberately recalls Serge Guilbaut's explosive alternative history of Abstract Expressionism, *How New York Stole the Idea of Modern Art* (1983). Guilbaut suggests that, although not intentional on the artists' part, the postwar retreat of modernist art from the political fight, through tropes of autonomy and abstraction, left this art available for manipulation. In the introduction, Guilbaut describes the incremental, networked way in which the institutions of art guide artistic response away from overt politicization and toward protection of the status quo. In his introduction, Guilbaut wrote:

> It is not my intention to impute to the artists of the avant-garde any precise political motive or to suggest that their actions were the product of some sort of conspiracy. What I argue is this: that from compromise to compromise, refusal to refusal, adjustment to adjustment, the rebellion of the artists, born of frustrations within the left, gradually changed its significance until ultimately it came to represent the values of the majority, but in a way (continuing the modernist tradition) that only a minority was capable of understanding.[36]

Balteo-Yazbeck takes this narrative of unknowing co-optation a step further by co-opting Calder to create a second-level signification, in which Calder's black mobile becomes oil metaphorically splattering the exhibition platform with shadows that uncannily mimic Iraq's oil fields.

Balteo-Yazbeck's predilection for apposite, but buried, anecdotes and episodes from the history of modernism is also evident in a work from his series Cultural Diplomacy: An Art We Neglect (named for a 1954 *New York Times Magazine* article advocating the use of American art as a form of soft power). In *R.S.V.P., 1939* (2007–9; p. 94), made in collaboration with Media Farzin, the artist frames a reproduction of a fancy printed party invitation that exists today only in a unique copy in the archives of the Museum of Modern Art. Like *UNstabile-Mobile*, the work is conceived around the surprise of seeing a hidden passageway in the history of modernism suddenly open up. In 1939, Frances Collins, then head of the Museum of Modern Art's publications

Fig. 46. Map of Iraqi oil fields and exploration blocks produced by the Cheney Energy Task Force in March 2001 and obtained by Judicial Watch through a Freedom of Information Act lawsuit in 2002. Detail of Alessandro Balteo-Yazbeck's *UNstabile-Mobile* installation, 2006 (p. 95)

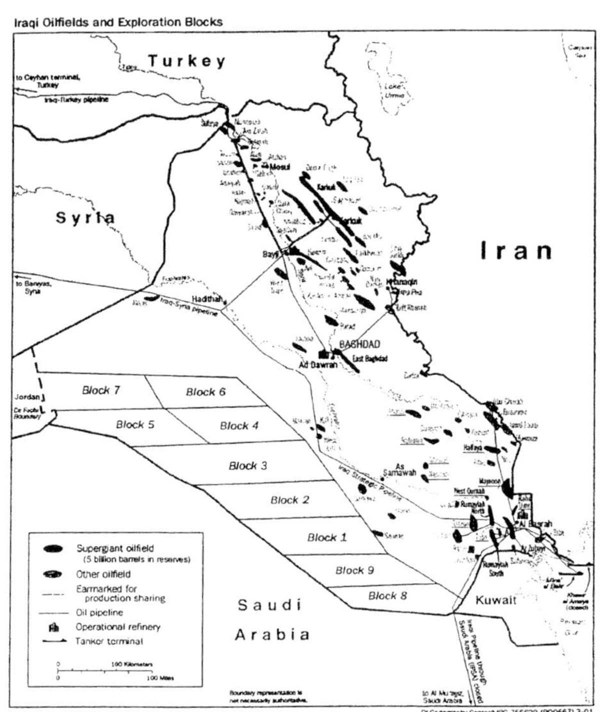

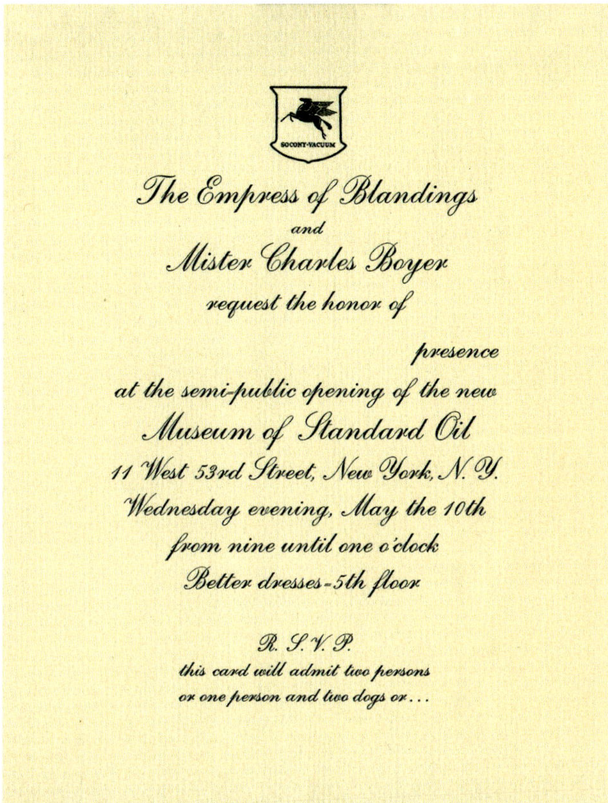

The Empress of Blandings
and
Mister Charles Boyer
request the honor of
presence
at the semi-public opening of the new
Museum of Standard Oil
11 West 53rd Street, New York, N.Y.
Wednesday evening, May the 10th
from nine until one o'clock
Better dresses-5th floor

R. S. V. P.
this card will admit two persons
or one person and two dogs or...

Fig. 47. Frances Collins, *Oil that Glitters Is Not Gold*, 1939, reproduced in Alessandro Balteo-Yazbeck and Media Farzin, *R.S.V.P., 1939*, 2007–9 (p. 94)

department, made a fake version of the invitation to the museum's tenth-anniversary gala (opening the West 53rd address it has today) for the amusement of the underlings on the staff who were not invited (fig. 47). A remarkable example of institutional critique half a century avant la lettre, the acerbic humor masks a serious complaint against the shadow "owner" of what Collins joked was "The Museum of Standard Oil," Nelson Rockefeller, the son of the museum's cofounder Abby Aldrich Rockefeller and the institution's then newly elected president. This ersatz invitation is juxtaposed on the wall with an archival copy of a *Time* magazine cover depicting Rockefeller, and the two elements are further framed by a quote from Franklin D. Roosevelt extolling American art's supposedly anti-elitist, democratic quality, along with a quote from Nelson Rockefeller that gives a winking, behind-the-scenes nod to museum infighting and treachery.

While Balteo-Yazbeck's ode to Calder is underpinned by documentary evidence, Mark Lombardi's suave cosmologies of hidden power introduced a mode of aligning drawing with research that has its roots in the interlock diagrams of white-collar (and organized) crime investigation. The works' French curves and handmade paper can be seen as emblematic of late-1990s attempts to fuse rough-and-tumble Conceptual strategies from the 1970s with renewed attention to craft and formal finesse.[37] However, these details belie a deep undercurrent of moral indignation that extended to his own early dealings with the power structures in the Houston, Texas, art world. Indeed, one wonders if, had he lived, Lombardi might have examined analogous blockages in the cultural sphere of the kind referred to by Nelson Rockefeller in Balteo-Yazbeck's *R.S.V.P., 1939*.

Jenny Holzer, in a similar way, shelters vital information about the flesh-and-blood effects of imperial rule—the beatings, torture, and casual destruction of the rights of the accused that have stood since the Magna Carta—in an unlikely place, the art-historical tradition of painting as an embodied form of witnessing. Her paintings and light-emitting-diode installations seek the abuse of power at its written source, at a moment when the epistemic reign of word over image seems all but complete and completely unremarkable. At this level of language the down-to-earth Holzer finds common ground with visionary science-fiction writer Philip K. Dick, who, in a 1978 speech, noted, "The basic tool for the manipulation of reality is the manipulation of words. If you can control the meaning of words, you can control the people who must use the words."[38]

According to Dick, it is the artist's job to contest the pseudo-realities created for us by forces above: "So I ask, in my writing, What is real? Because unceasingly we are bombarded with pseudo-realities manufactured by very sophisticated people using very sophisticated electronic mechanisms. I do not distrust their motives; I distrust their power. They have a lot of it. And it is an astonishing power: that of creating whole universes, universes of the mind. I ought to know. I do the same thing."[39] Balteo-Yazbeck's secret histories of art and Speculative Archive's video *"It's Not My Memory of It,"* as well as a number of other works presented here, imply ironically that the vise grip of pseudo-reality, achieved by systems of control so vast and complex as to defy attempts to describe them, can be pried loose only by the creation of counterfictions. Such are the means necessary to make an end run around the decades-long influence of covert agencies and political operatives on journalism, a situation that only seems to be escalating.[40]

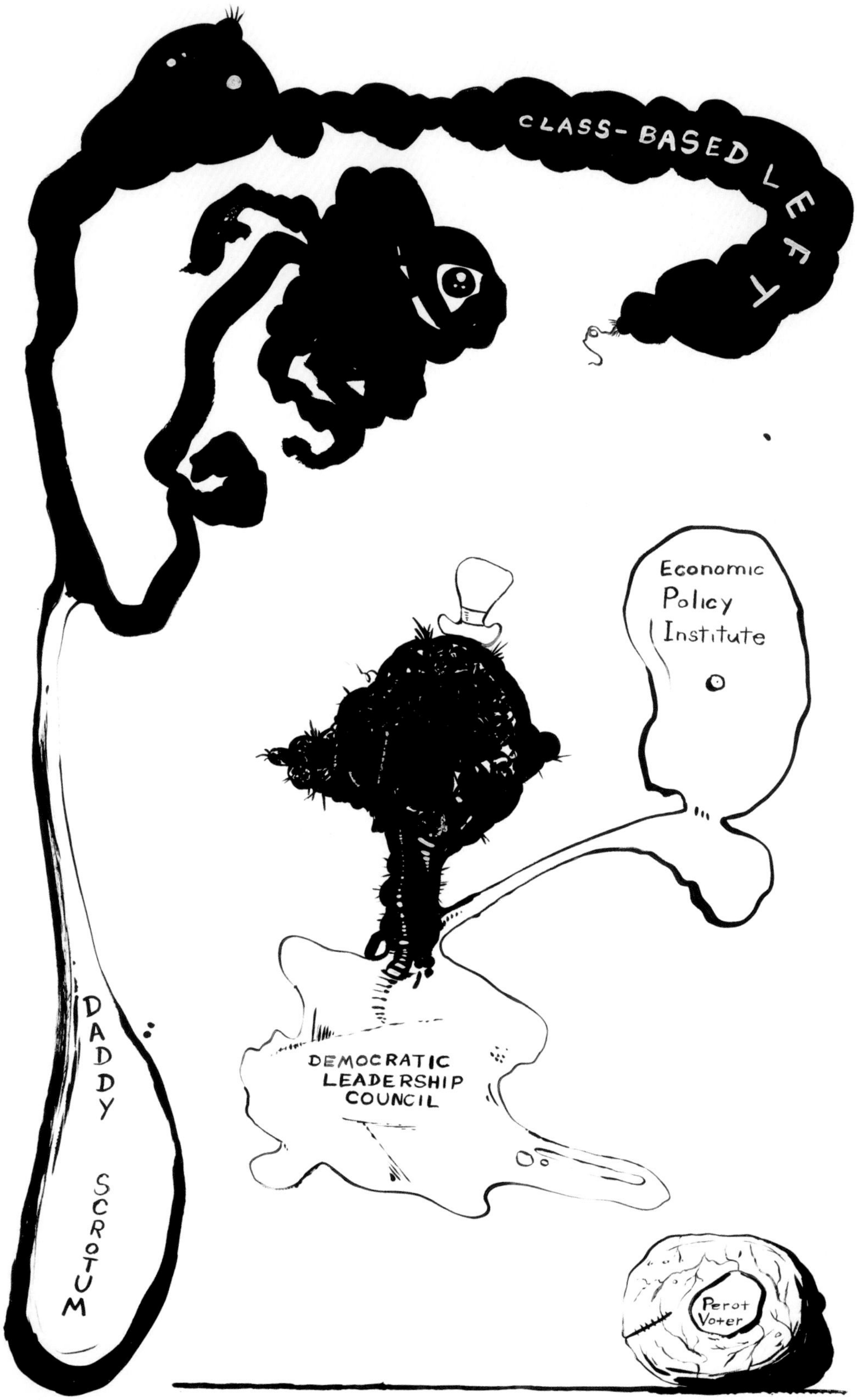
CLASS-BASED LEFT
Economic Policy Institute
DEMOCRATIC LEADERSHIP COUNCIL
DADDY SCROTUM
Perot Voter

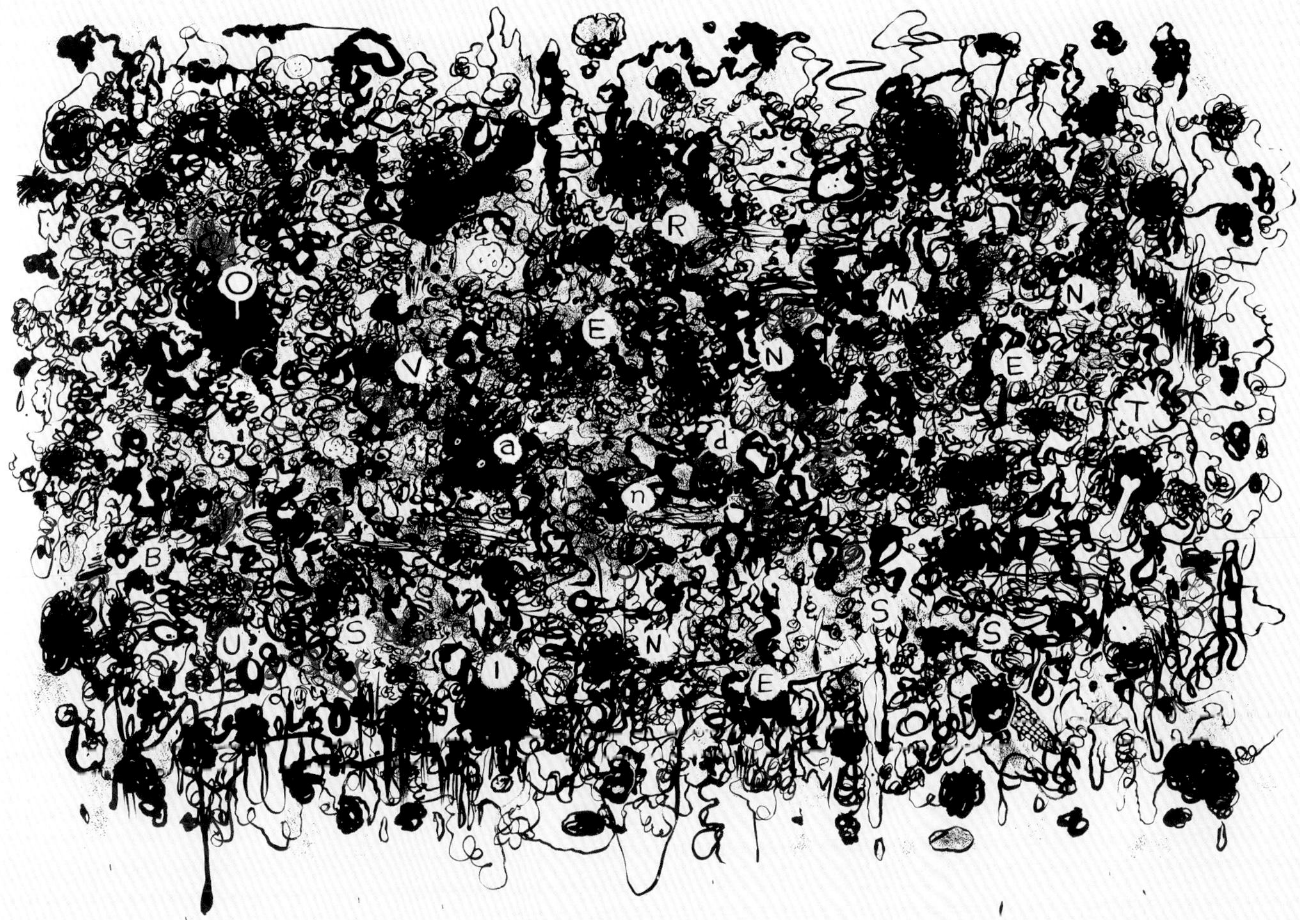

Mike Kelley, *Low Definition Presidency*, 1993

Mike Kelley, *Untitled (Government and Business)*, 1991

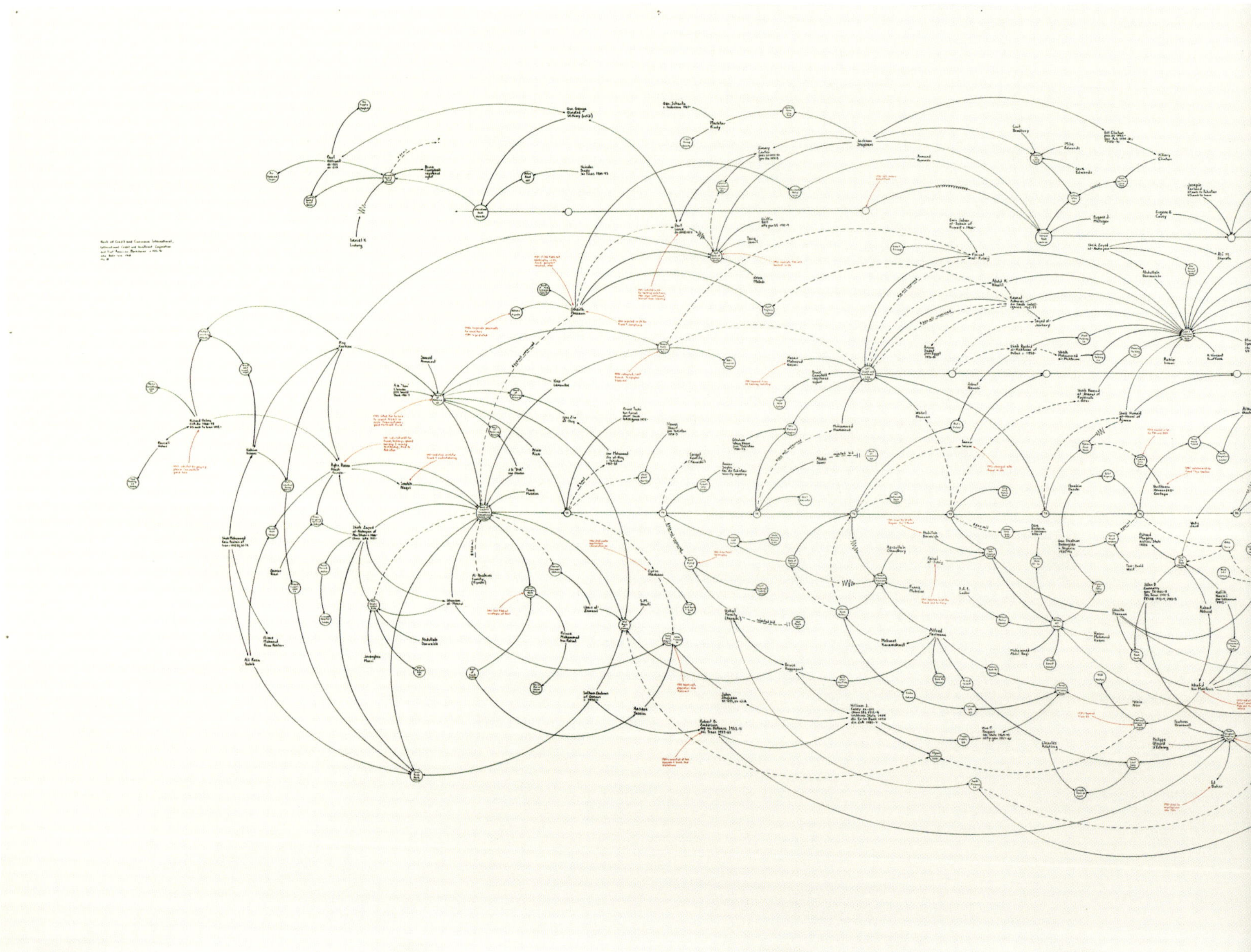

Mark Lombardi, *BCCI-ICIC & FAB, 1972–91 (4th Version)*, 1996–2000

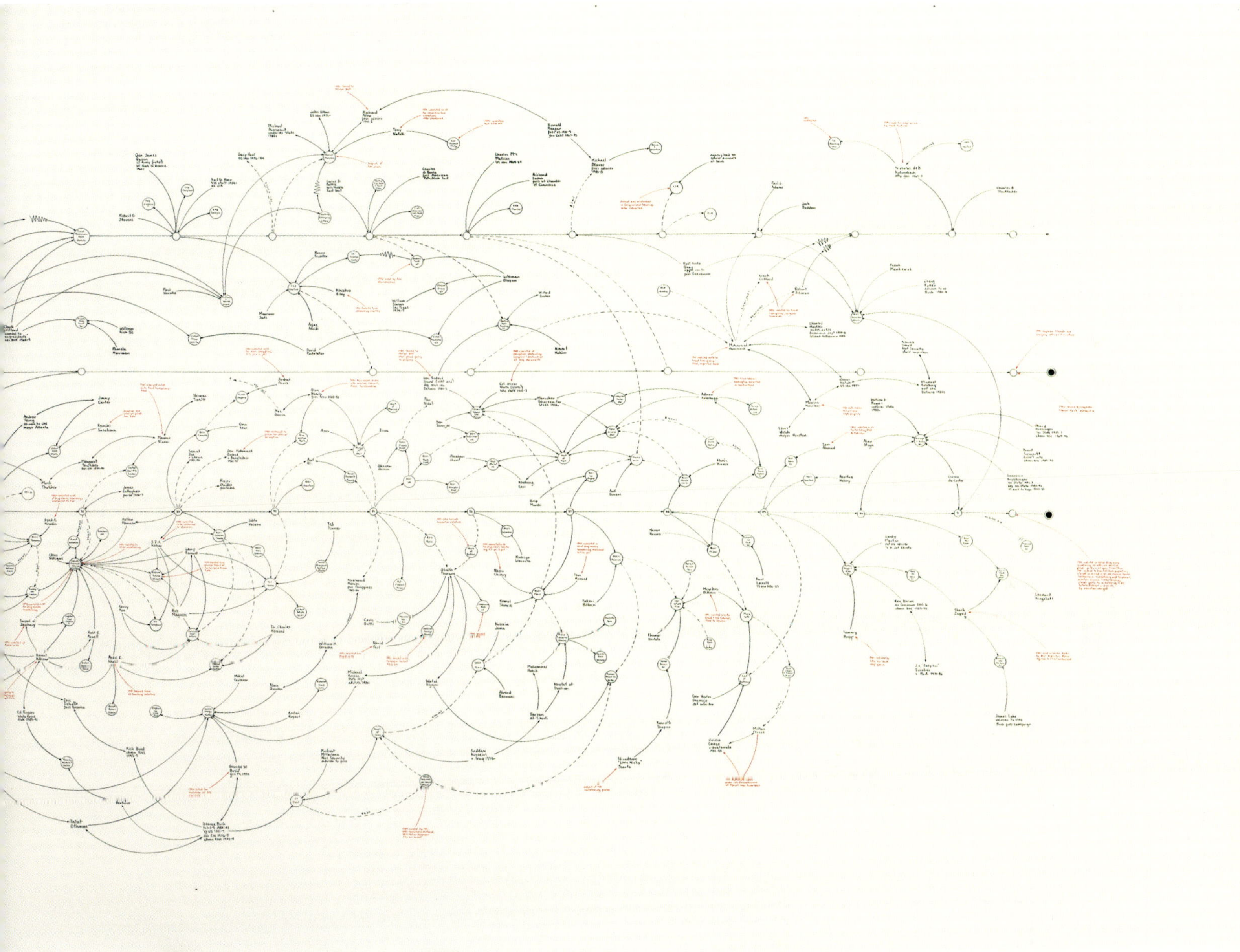

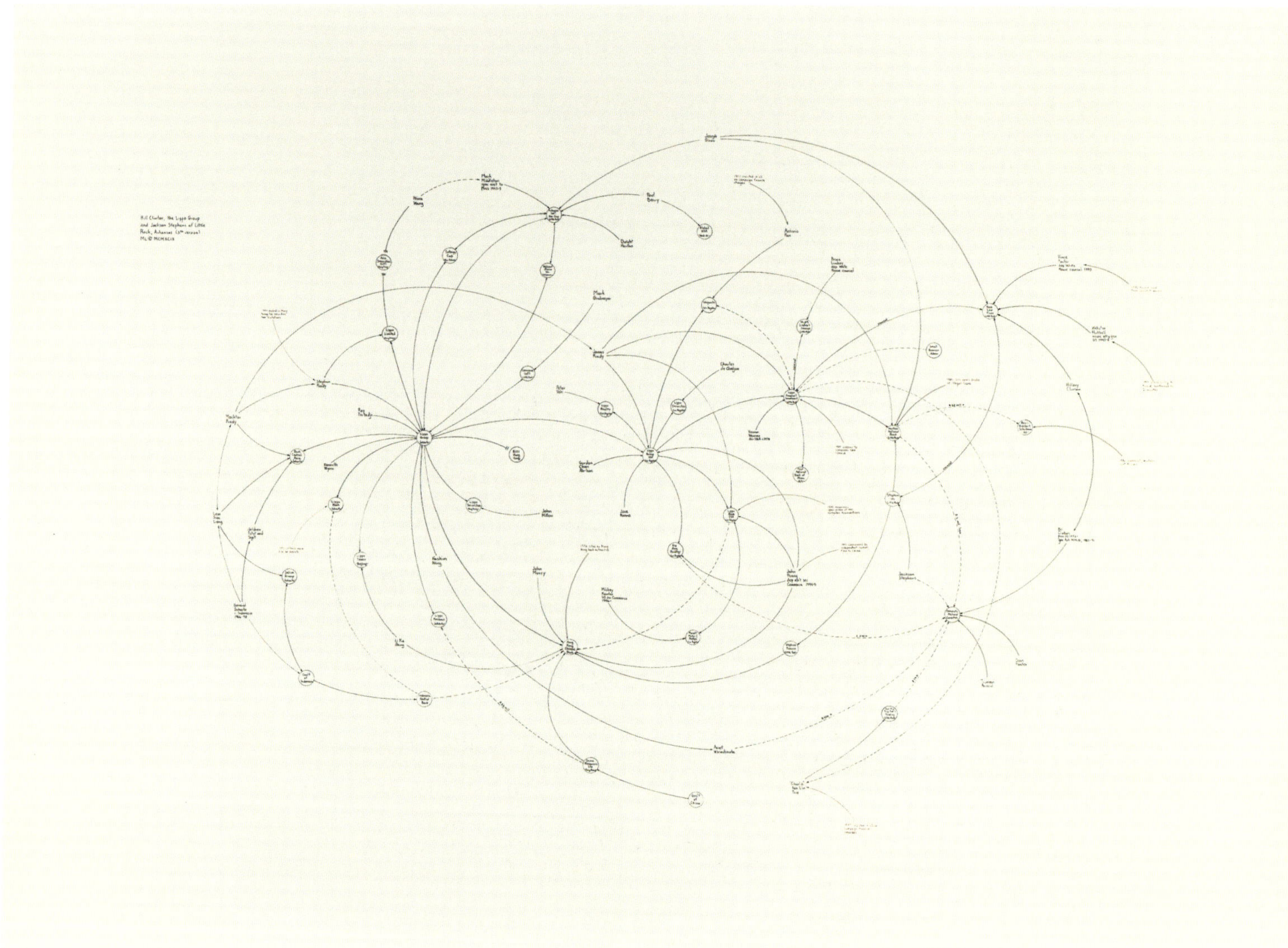

Mark Lombardi, *Bill Clinton, the Lippo Group, and Jackson Stephens of Little Rock, Arkansas (5th Version)*, 1999

Stills from Julia Meltzer and David Thorne, *"It's Not My Memory of It": three recollected documents*, 2003

EHRA N
SDUR N

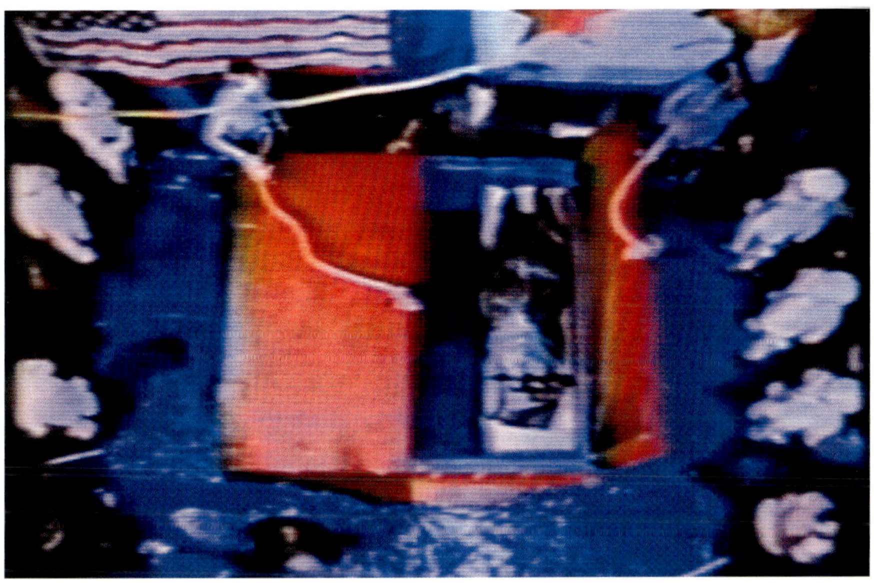

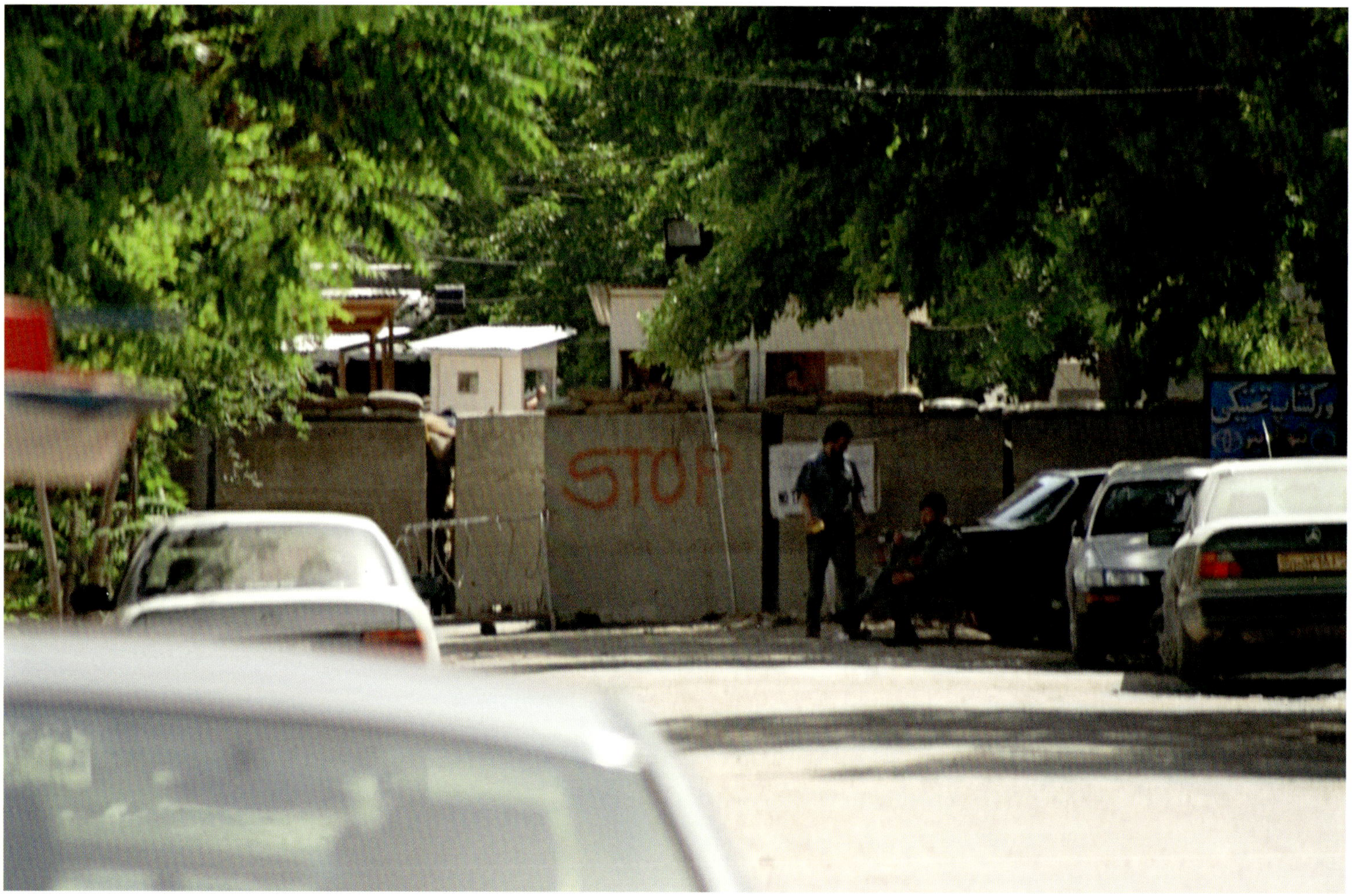

Trevor Paglen, *Black Site, Kabul, Afghanistan, 2006*, 2006

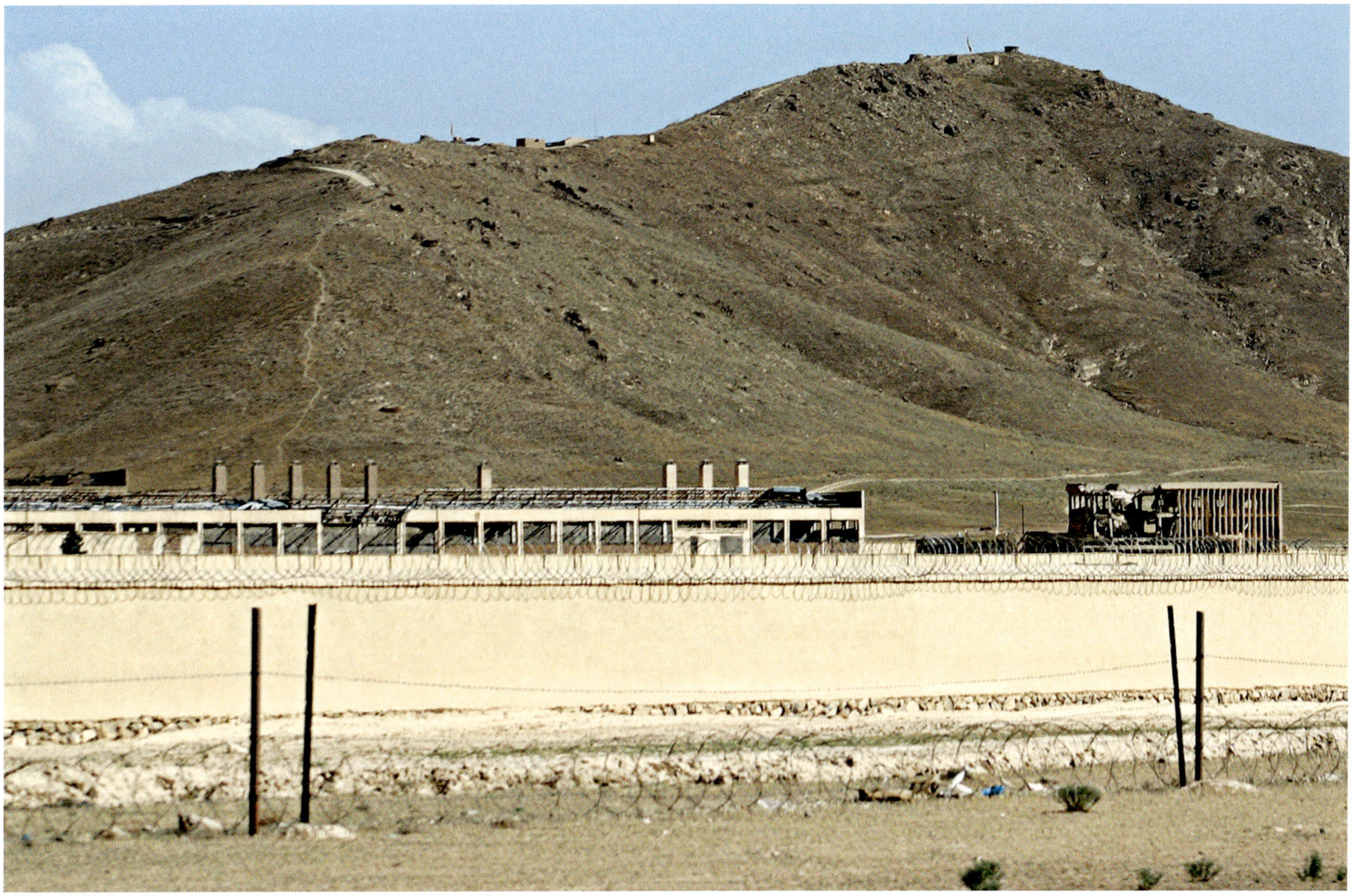

Trevor Paglen, *The Salt Pit, Northeast of Kabul, Afghanistan*, 2006

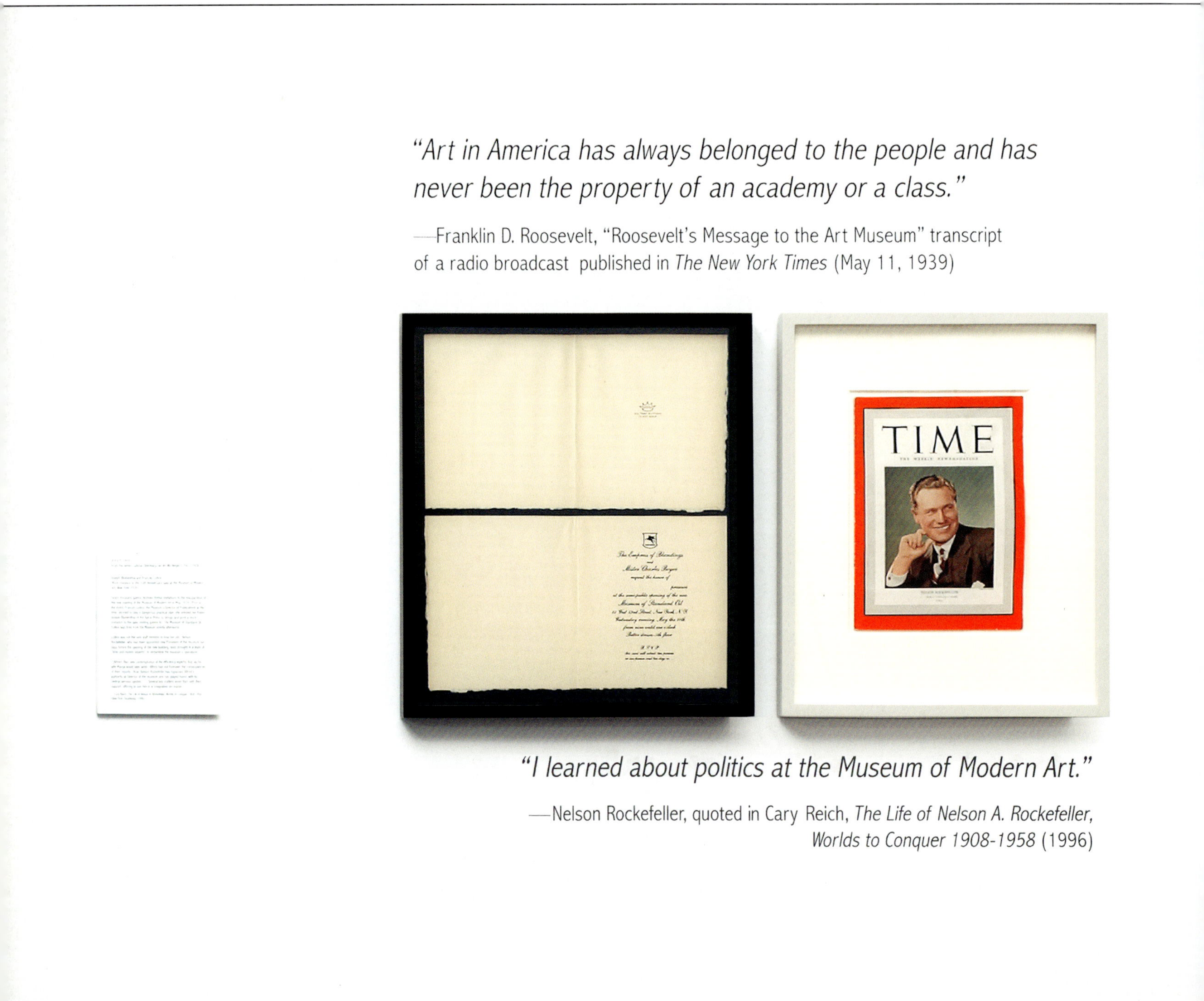

Alessandro Balteo-Yazbeck in collaboration with Media Farzin, *R.S.V.P., 1939* (from the series Cultural Diplomacy: An Art We Neglect), 2007–9

Detail of Alessandro Balteo-Yazbeck, *UNstabile-Mobile* (from the series Modern Entanglements, U.S. Interventions), 2006

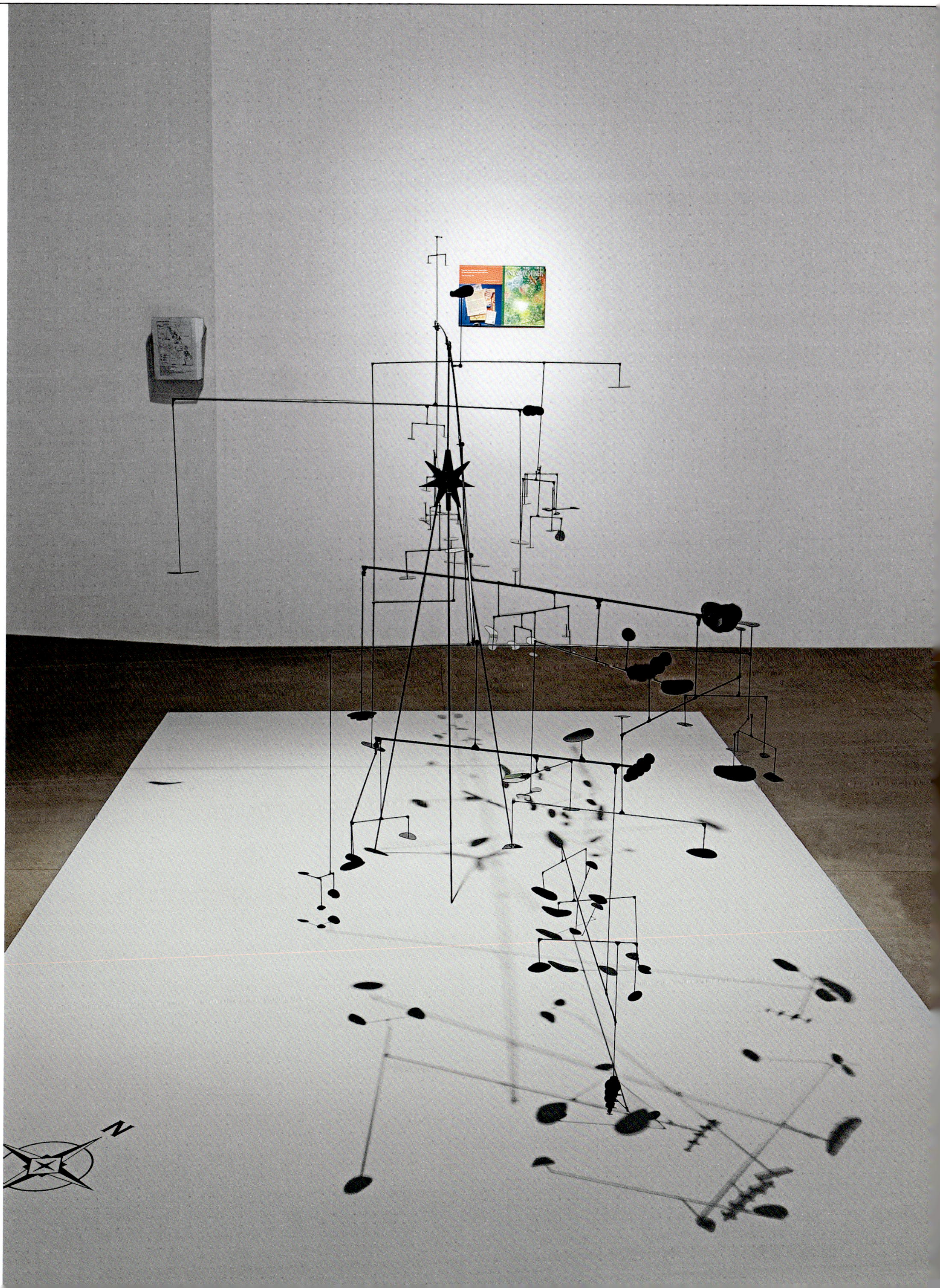

MODERN HISTORY IN AND OUT OF CONTEXT: SARAH CHARLESWORTH'S *APRIL 21, 1978*

Beth Saunders

On March 16, 1978, the left-wing terrorist group the Red Brigades (Brigate Rosse) kidnapped Aldo Moro, then president of Italy's Christian Democratic Party and former prime minister, in a dramatic gun battle that left five armed police escorts dead. After fifty-five days of captivity in the so-called people's prison, the Red Brigades executed the politician and dumped his body in the trunk of a car, which was discovered on May 9 in Rome's via Caetani (fig. 48). The events of Moro's abduction and murder played out in real time in the media; Italian newspapers, radio, and television all reported the status of ongoing investigations and relayed to the public messages (known as communiqués) issued by the Red Brigades along with personal correspondence Moro penned during his imprisonment. Ultimately, the media spectacle surrounding this event implicated not only the Red Brigades but also the press itself, the politicians from right and left who refused to negotiate with the terrorists, and the public who watched the events unfold in rapt horror.

The iconic image that has come to represent this chilling historical episode is a hostage photograph made by the Red Brigades to counter false reports of Moro's death that circulated in the press. In it, Moro slouches in front of a flag identifying the terrorist organization and holds up the previous day's newspaper, bearing the headline "Moro assasinato?" (fig. 49). Sarah Charlesworth's landmark Conceptual artwork *April 21, 1978* (1978; pp. 62–63), from the series Modern History (1977–79), consists of forty-five chromogenic prints that trace the appearance of the infamous Moro hostage photograph across the front pages of newspapers from Italy and around the world on April 21, 1978, with all text eliminated save for each publication's masthead.[1] This succinct gesture effectively exposes the way the media shapes an individual's perception of world events and reinforces the dominant political order along national lines.

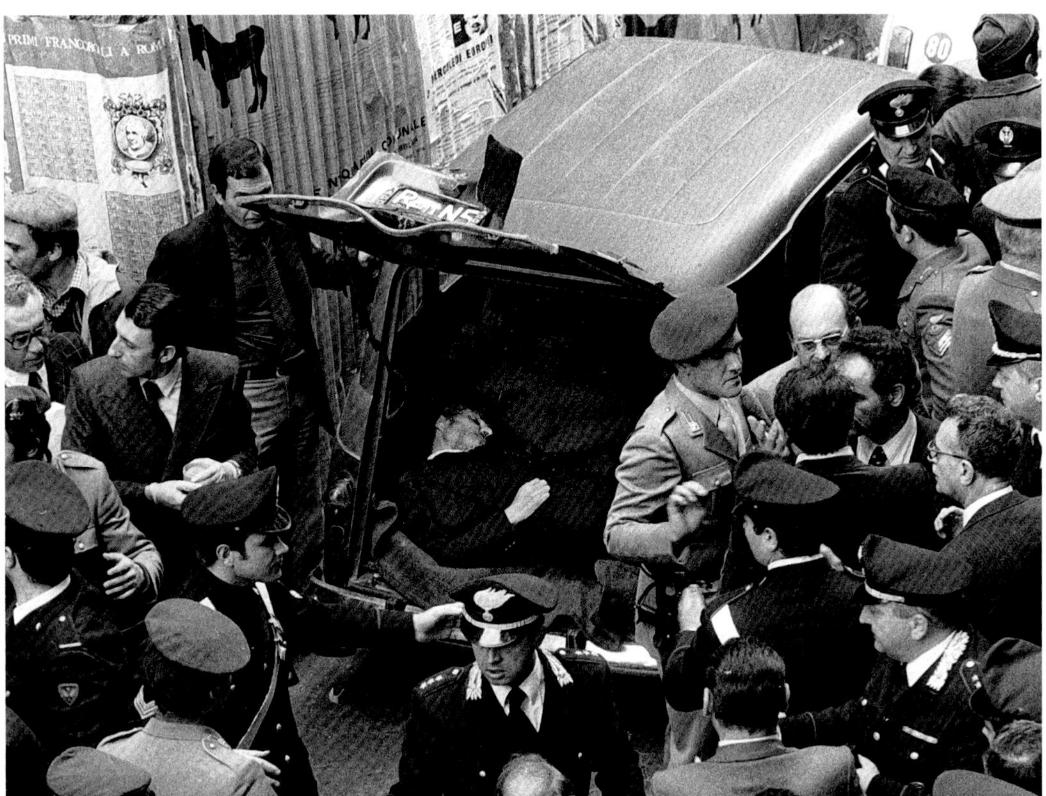

Fig. 48. Body of Aldo Moro discovered in via Caetani, Rome, May 9, 1978. Photograph by Rolando Fava

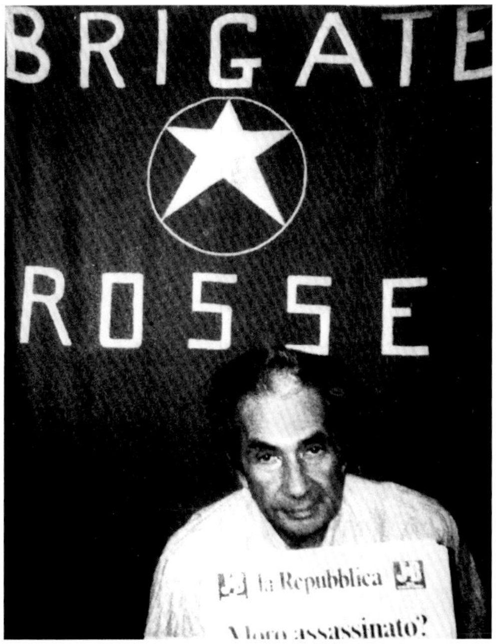

Fig. 49. Hostage Polaroid of Moro taken by the Red Brigades, published April 21, 1978

Although Charlesworth first exhibited *April 21, 1978* in Rome that year, the specific Italian context of the image it deploys has not been fully articulated.[2] Perhaps this is because, in a sense, such recuperation is antithetical to the artist's method. In 1979, she described the process behind the Modern History series as one of "unwriting," stating, "Only through systematic selection and deletion, the shifting of the plane of focus, are original texts re-animated, characters resurrected and called upon to tell another tale."[3] For Charlesworth, the process of "unwriting" history exposes the underlying systems of power that give structure to experience and articulates the way mediation at once creates and overwhelms content. Charlesworth's selection of the Moro case for this action was strategic. It appears to have been driven, on the one hand, by the opportunity for the artist to exhibit in solo shows in Rome and Florence in the fall of 1978, and on the other, by the unique media spectacle surrounding the Moro case, in which both the state and a radical fringe group manipulated control of the press for their own conflicting ends. By restoring the specificity of the Italian situation—in which the first audience for *April 21, 1978* was immersed—the impact of Charlesworth's formal and conceptual strategies can be fully recognized.

The kidnapping and murder of Aldo Moro were a climactic episode in a decadelong period of political turmoil within Italy, known as the *anni di piombo* (Lead Years).[4] In Italy, as in much of Western Europe, the year 1968 marked a flash point in the rise of activist movements, a response to the social and economic inequities of liberal democracy that had only exacerbated under the Marshall Plan largesse of the postwar period. On December 12, 1969, neo-Fascist terrorists planted a bomb in Milan's Piazza Fontana, killing fifteen and wounding another forty-five citizens (fig. 50). The attack was intended to cast blame on the ascendant political left and thus to suppress working-class revolts in northern factories that took place during the so-called Hot Autumn of that year. The Piazza Fontana bombing ushered in a period of political violence from both right and left, which resulted in no less than 153 deaths between 1969 and 1977.[5] It also held significant implications for the public interpretation of the Moro case because, as historian Robert Lumley notes, it "was the first of a long series of cases involving conspiracy and corruption in high places for which no one was found guilty and punished."[6] The revelations that the attack had aimed at undermining the momentum of left-wing protest movements and that this goal was apparently backed by high-ranking officials of the judicial and political establishment (including, it has been suggested, the CIA) bred deep disillusionment among the '68 generation and a turn to armed struggle. The Red Brigades timed Moro's kidnapping to a symbolically resonant moment in this conflict, when Moro's conservative Christian Democratic Party (Democrazia Cristiana, or DC) and the Communist Party (Partito Comunista Italiano, or PCI) were poised to make a "historic compromise" by forming, for the first time, a coalition government intended to quell the ongoing political violence. By kidnapping Moro, who was

Fig. 50. Hall of the Banca Nazionale dell'Agricoltura in the Piazza Fontana, Milan, after the bombing, December 12, 1969

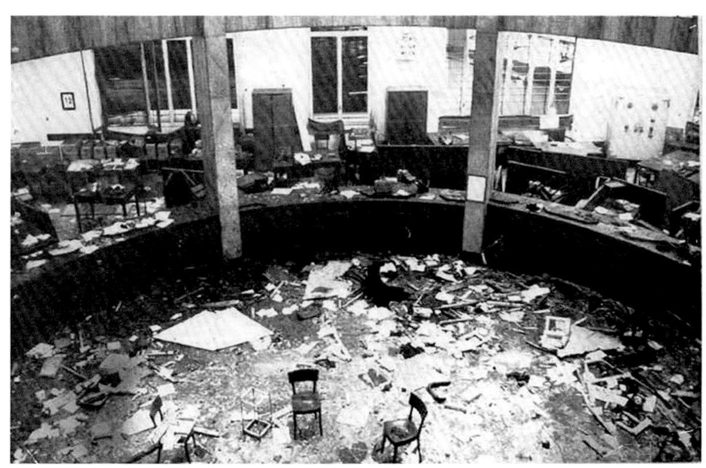

considered the architect of the policy, the radical group launched an attack on the state and registered their distaste for a Communist Party they viewed as ideologically corrupted.

The Red Brigades espoused that, in the face of state violence, the proletariat had to fight back, creating its own standards of justice to which the government would be held accountable. By publicizing their actions through textual communiqués, the group sought to legitimize their activities, counter the secrecy of state power, and gain support among the militant left. The violence they caused—and their communication strategy—escalated in 1972 with the kidnapping of Idalgo Macchiarini, the manager of the telecommunications company SIT-Siemens. The Red Brigades held Macchiarini for only twenty minutes, long enough to produce a photograph of him with a gun pressed to his cheek and a placard around his neck reading "Red Brigades—Hit and run—No one will go unpunished—Strike one and educate one hundred—All power to the armed people" (fig. 51).[7] As the historian David Moss has noted, "lead" in the phrase *anni di piombo* has a double meaning, signifying not only bullets but also printing type.[8] The 1970s saw an expansion of the press and the rise of televised news among competitive local networks, especially after the breakdown of state monopolies between 1974 and 1976.[9] In this heightened climate, the Red Brigades took advantage of new technologies—the Photostat, the Polaroid, and the video camera—to circulate their messages, which were then reproduced in the mainstream media. The dissemination of the hostage Polaroid of Macchiarini, who was the first victim in a series of highly publicized kidnappings and murders of industrial managers and judges, was a precursor to the media spectacle generated around Moro's death.

The subject of the Moro kidnapping and murder attracted Charlesworth not only because of the heavily mediated nature of the case but also owing to her personal connections to Italy. Beginning in 1973, she spent summers in Tuscany with the artist Joseph Kosuth, who owned a house there. During the 1970s, she and Kosuth traveled extensively through Europe, participating in exhibitions and forging artistic networks.[10] In a group portrait made at this time, the two artists pose informally alongside the gallerists Pio Monti (wielding a Polaroid camera), Gian Enzo Sperone, and Liliana Maniero, who were major proponents of the development of Conceptual art in Italy (fig. 52). Monti invited Charlesworth to exhibit new work in his gallery in Rome's via Principessa Clotilde in September 1978,[11] and she and Kosuth also had consecutive shows at the nonprofit artist's space Zona in Florence that month. The latter exhibition arose from a previous collaboration with a circle of Tuscan artists on a project for the 1976 Venice Biennale.[12] Like many artists working in Italy at the time, Charlesworth was preoccupied with the volatile political situation. She thus chose the Moro case as her subject for both exhibitions. Between April and September 1978, she produced three finished works and one study for the Modern History series that dealt with various aspects of the press's presentation of the events of Moro's kidnapping and murder.[13]

The series began with the work *Herald Tribune*, for which she removed the text from every front page of that paper for a month.[14] Her implementation of a commercial but widely available copying technology, the Photostat, to create the seamless textual extractions gave the series the same mass-produced aesthetic of its source material, while also referencing the proliferation of self-published pamphlets, newspapers, and flyers distributed by radical groups—such as the Red Brigades—during the same period. One of the front pages shown in *Herald Tribune*, which she first exhibited in Belgium in 1977, includes a hostage photograph of the industrialist Hanns Martin Schleyer (fig. 53). The German terrorist organization the Red Army Faction (RAF) kidnapped Schleyer and held him in exchange for the release from prison of one of the group's members. Charlesworth was interested in the way that RAF had utilized mainstream media to promulgate its message, and the image

Fig. 51. Polaroid of Idalgo Macchiarini taken by the Red Brigades, March 3, 1972

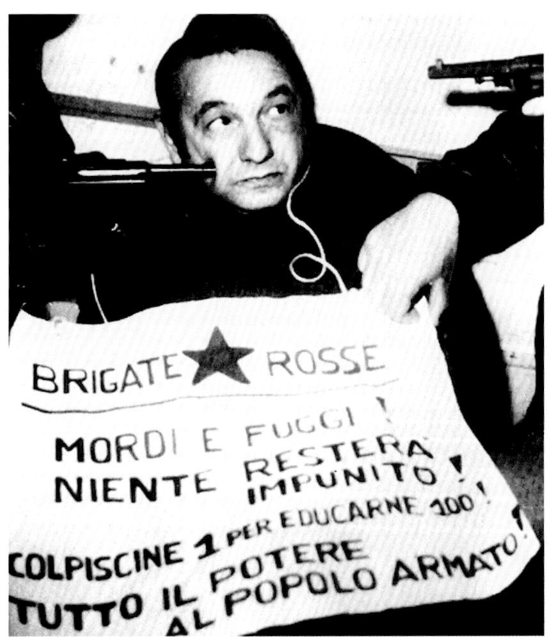

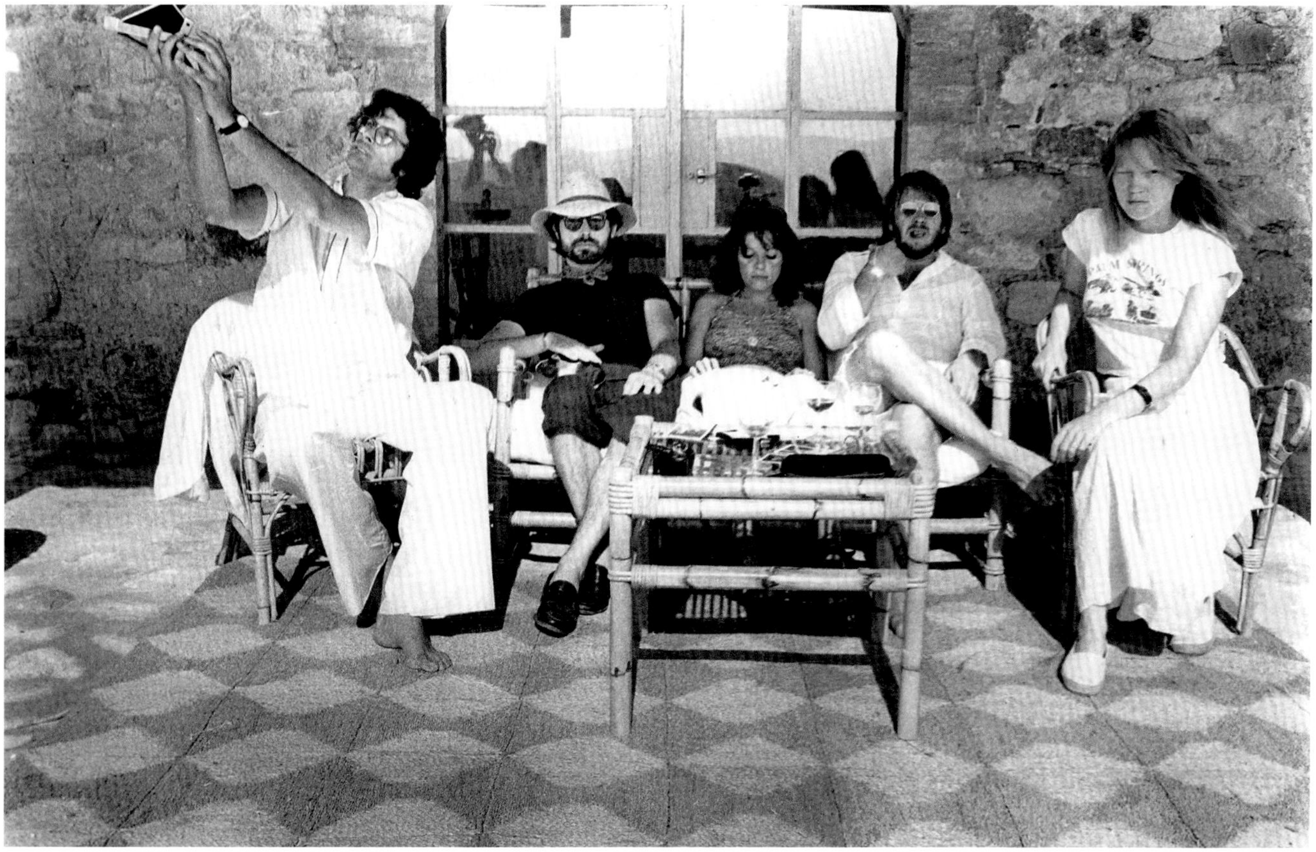

Fig. 52. Pio Monti, Gian Enzo Sperone, Liliana Maniero, Joseph Kosuth, and Sarah Charlesworth at Kosuth's home in San Casciano, Italy, 1974

compelled her deeper investigation into the press coverage of the events surrounding the Red Brigades' kidnapping and murder of Moro. The artist reflected: "By kidnapping a prime minister . . . the Red Brigades were effectively kidnapping public attention. So that meant that the newspaper itself, the front page of the paper, became almost like a battleground."[15]

In preparation for the Italian shows, the artist gathered newspapers from as many different countries as possible that featured front-page images related to the Moro case. Her sources were the United Nations bookstore in New York, the stamp of which can be seen on the masthead of several papers in the finished work, and Hotalings, a Times Square newsstand specializing in foreign press.[16] In her early installations of the Modern History series, including that of *April 21, 1978* at Pio Monti gallery, she presented the actual newspapers that constituted the source material alongside the work, thus placing her research-based methodology on full view.[17] Visitors could fill in the blank spaces left by her extractions of text by perusing the original articles in situ. Soon thereafter, Charlesworth abandoned this approach in favor of exhibiting only the finished work. In doing so, she drew attention away from the didactic content and focused it on the patterns that emerge through choices of cropping, placement, and scale across publications, allowing the viewer to draw inferences about the various political and geographic biases represented by the different newspapers.

Charlesworth's Modern History series makes visible the process by which newspapers establish "imagined communities" of like-minded readers and shore up the identities and values of modern nation-states.[18] *April 21, 1978* includes front pages from Europe, North and South America, and Japan, organized in order of geographical proximity to Italy. As one might expect, the Italian newspapers feature the Moro image most prominently, though variances in scale and placement signify subtle ideological differences even without the benefit of text. The cover of *L'Unità*, the Communist Party organ, and *Il Tempo*, a conservative Roman newspaper, both give the Moro Polaroid equal weight to an image of police

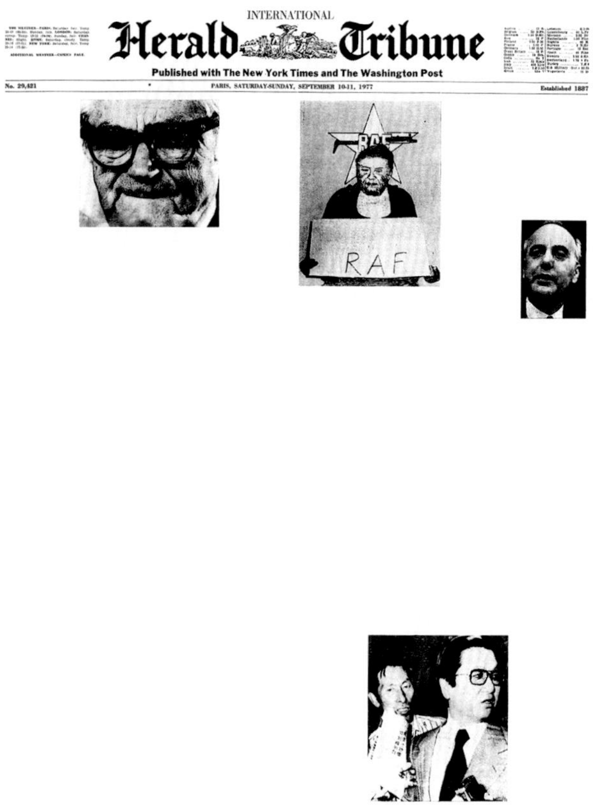

INTERNATIONAL
Herald Tribune
Published with The New York Times and The Washington Post

RAF

Fig. 53. Detail of Sarah Charlesworth (American, 1947–2013), *Herald Tribune, September 1977*, 1977. One of twenty-six black-and-white prints reproduced same size as original newspapers, 23 × 16 in. (58.4 × 40.6 cm) each

investigating the Red Brigades murder of a Milanese prison guard, a reminder from both left- and right-leaning sources that Moro was not the only victim of the group's violence at this time (p 62). Other papers suggest political disquiet happening contemporaneously across the globe. On the cover of the *New York Times*, Moro appears below the fold, while printed above is a picture of L. Patrick Gray III, the former acting director of the FBI. Gray is seen arriving at court, where he faced felony charges for ordering unlawful break-ins at the homes of relatives of fugitives from the radical left-wing Weather Underground Organization, which had carried out a series of bombings on United States government buildings and banks during the 1970s (p. 63).[19] Without text to anchor these images, their meaning becomes opaque—and only more so with the passage of time.

Charlesworth's study of semiotics—including Roland Barthes's writings on photography, which were first published in English at this time—informed her examination of the underlying structures that frame the presentation of the news.[20] She and Kosuth were affiliated with the British Conceptual group Art & Language and cofounders of the short-lived art and critical theory journal *The Fox* (1975–76).[21] For Charlesworth, the publication marked a turning point from a text-based artistic practice to one focused on the investigation of visual language by means of visual language.[22] Her new approach was manifested in the Modern History series, which examines how sequences of images carry meaning without language. In *April 21, 1978,* text nevertheless persists in the form of mastheads that situate the viewer linguistically and, thus, geographically. And yet, fluency in the various languages represented is not necessary to understand the symbolic declarations represented by the titles: "The Times," "The Sun," "The Morning," "The Evening," "The Nation," "The World," "The Universe." As in Charlesworth's organization of the work, the titles denote how local concerns quickly telescope into national and global political networks. In several instances advertisements—for Seiko and Casio electronics, J&B Scotch, and Persian carpets—appear as reminders that newspapers are driven by economic concerns, are shaped by the influence of special interests, and are often part of transnational media conglomerates. For Charlesworth, the relationship between local and international perspectives was a critical element of the Modern History series, which was motivated in part by her desire to produce artwork for a specific context.[23]

Charlesworth applied a controlled organizational structure, which she referred to as a "game plan," to each work in the Modern History series.[24] The game plan for *April 21, 1978* was to include the front page of any newspaper from the given date that featured the Moro hostage photograph. Similarly, *Second Reading (Lago Duchessa, April 20, 1978)* (now known as *April 20, 1978*), which Charlesworth exhibited in Florence in September 1978, comprises front pages from twenty-five newspapers with text removed, each documenting in a photograph the search for Moro's body in Lago Duchessa (fig. 54). In this bizarre episode, a communiqué—later proved false—claiming that Moro had been assassinated and his body dumped in a remote lake was delivered to the Roman newspaper *Il Messagero* on April 19. The press followed this development closely, and the next day, news cameras captured police detonating explosives to search the ice-capped water. Devoid of text, Charlewsworth's *April 20, 1978* reflects the surreal nature of the scene, conveyed in images of police on skis standing around a gaping hole in the ice, surrounded by the sheer white expanse of the unprinted page. As one critic wrote at the time, “The news is presumably a pretext, for the artist it is important not so much to verify how an episode is transformed into a photojournalistic image, but to identify the characteristics that pictures of the same event assume in the various national contexts of information given by the newspapers.”[25] Here, the empty media spectacle takes center stage.

In response to the events of April 20 and the fruitless search in Lago Duchessa, the Red Brigades released the infamous hostage photograph of Moro, proving that he was alive and captive. It is still not known precisely who directed the false communiqué, and this unsolved aspect of the case has spawned the theory that it was an attempt by the political establishment, both the DC and PCI alike, to gauge the potential public response to Moro’s death if they continued their hard-line position against negotiating with the terrorists.[26] In Charlesworth’s study *April 19, 20, 21, 1978* (1978; fig. 55), the unfolding in the media of this sequence of events—the false communiqué, the hunt for Moro’s body, and the revelation that he was alive—is scrutinized through a game plan in which each newspaper contains an image of the front page from the preceding day. The resulting *mise en abyme* articulates not only the process through which history is written but also the extent to which Moro ceased to be the subject of his own news story.

The lack of regard for Moro the man is an element of the case that continues to haunt its telling. In his essay “L’Affaire Moro,” published in September 1978,

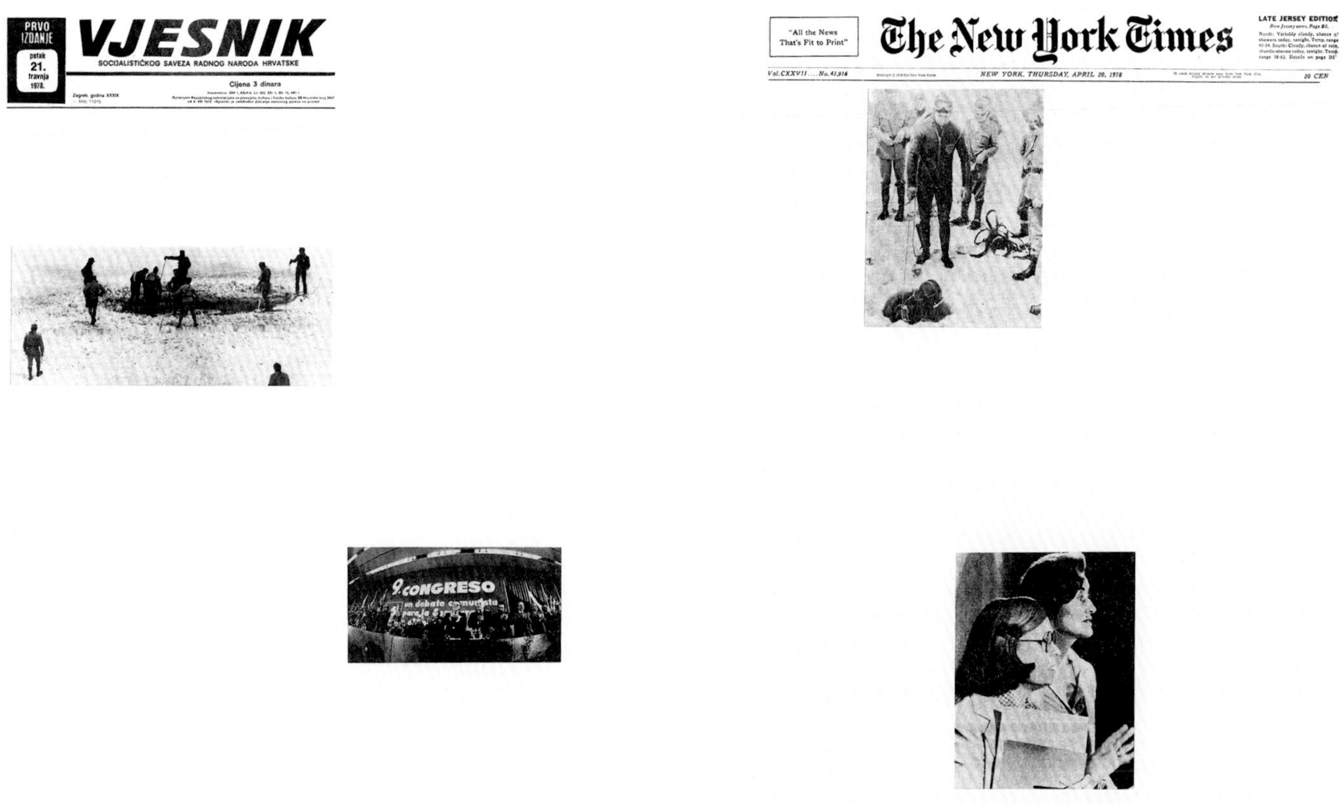

Fig. 54. Details of Sarah Charlesworth, *April 20, 1978*, 1978. Two of twenty-five black-and-white prints reproduced same size as original newspapers, varying sizes, approx. 22 × 16 in. (55.9 × 40.6 cm) each

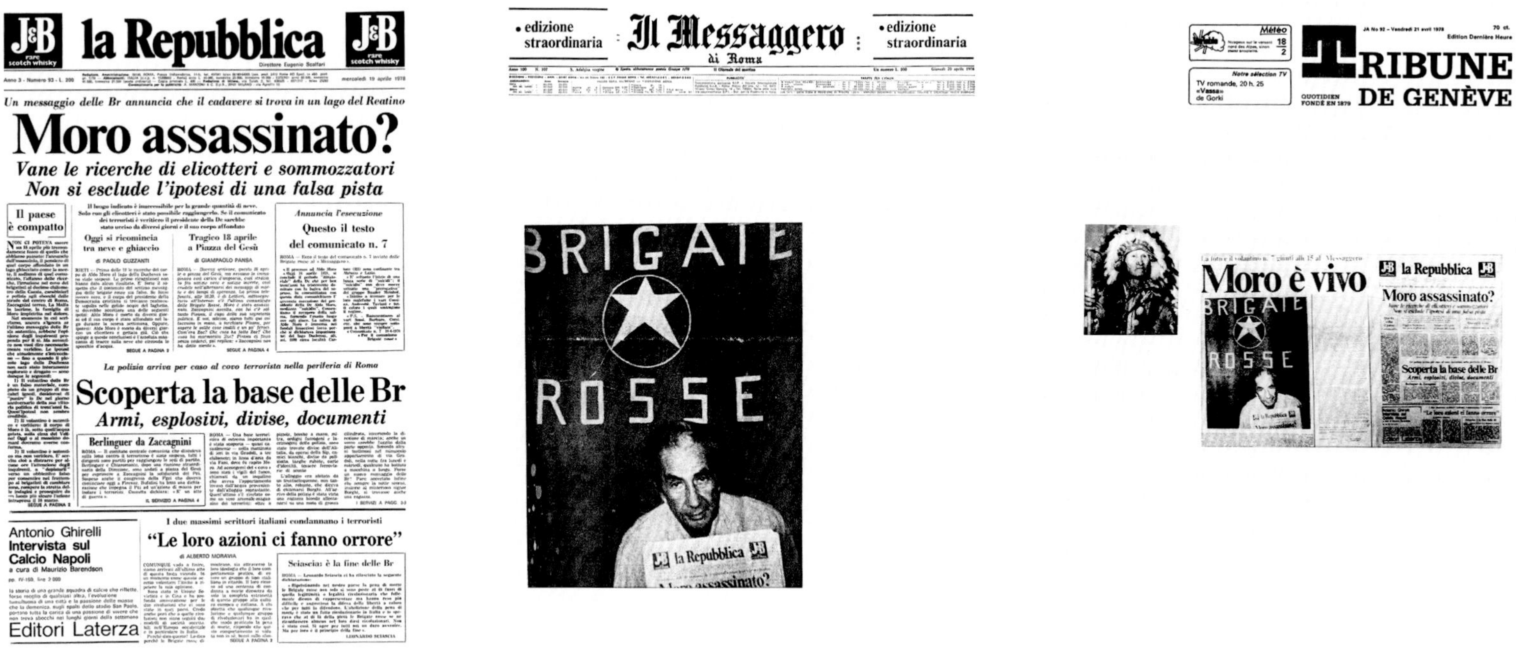

la Repubblica

Un messaggio delle Br annuncia che il cadavere si trova in un lago del Reatino

Moro assassinato?

Vane le ricerche di elicotteri e sommozzatori
Non si esclude l'ipotesi di una falsa pista

Il paese è compatto

Oggi si ricomincia tra neve e ghiaccio

Tragico 18 aprile a Piazza del Gesù

Annuncia l'esecuzione

Questo il testo del comunicato n. 7

La polizia arriva per caso al covo terrorista nella periferia di Roma

Scoperta la base delle Br

Armi, esplosivi, divise, documenti

Berlinguer da Zaccagnini

Antonio Ghirelli Intervista sul Calcio Napoli

Editori Laterza

I due massimi scrittori italiani condannano i terroristi

"Le loro azioni ci fanno orrore"

• edizione straordinaria

Il Messaggero di Roma

• edizione straordinaria

BRIGATE ROSSE

la Repubblica

TRIBUNE DE GENÈVE

Moro è vivo

la Repubblica

Moro assassinato?

Scoperta la base delle Br

Fig. 55. Sarah Charlesworth, *April 19, 20, 21, 1978*, 1978. Three black-and-white prints reproduced same size as original newspapers, varying sizes, approx. 22 × 16 in. (55.9 × 40.6 cm) each

the Radical Party parliamentarian and author Leonardo Sciascia regards Moro's disavowal by members of his own party as particularly "monstrous."[27] During his captivity, Moro wrote some ninety-seven letters and texts, twenty-six of which were delivered to their recipients. In these letters, Moro pleaded with colleagues to negotiate with the Red Brigades in order to save his life. Ironically, the DC used the letters as evidence to justify refusing to negotiate, arguing that either they were forged or Moro was not in his right mind to have written them. Inspired by Emile Zola's account of the Dreyfus affair, which helped to exonerate a Jewish captain in the French army who had been falsely convicted of giving secrets to the Germans, Sciascia's "L'Affaire Moro" casts the ultimate blame for Moro's death on the political establishment. Realizing that he would not be saved, on April 19, Moro invoked biblical judgment, writing, "If you do not intervene, a chilling page in the history of Italy will be written. My blood will fall on you, on the Party, on the country."[28] For Sciascia, whose essay became a classic of conspiracy literature about the case, Moro's words indicted his own party as complicit in his murder.

Charlesworth's *Osservatore Romano, March 17–May 10, 1978* (1978; fig. 56) visualizes the refusal of a greater power to intercede on Moro's behalf by the apparent absence of reporting on the events in the Vatican newspaper *L'Osservatore Romano*. The work includes twenty-seven front pages published between Moro's kidnapping and the recovery of his body, with text removed. What remains is a series of images seemingly detached from history; Pope Paul VI appears repeatedly—arms outstretched, blessing the faithful masses—bookended on March 17 and May 10 by the same stock portrait of Moro. Viewed in relationship to the overriding visual schema of *L'Osservatore Romano*, Moro and the entire political drama surrounding his murder barely register, as if to suggest that the continuity of the Catholic Church enfolds and supersedes all earthly matters. It should be noted, however, that the pope did attempt to intercede on Moro's behalf, going so far as offering to pay the ransom demanded by the Red Brigades. The group refused, and Prime Minister Giulio Andreotti reminded the pope of the official resolution against negotiating with terrorists. On April 21, the pontiff's final appeal to spare Moro's life was read aloud on Vatican radio and printed in a special edition of the paper.[29]

The betrayal of Moro by his party and his subsequent demise made him a political martyr in the eyes of many.

The infamous hostage Polaroid that is the focus of *April 21, 1978* has become a symbol of the entire violent chapter of the Lead Years.[30] As the photography historian Ando Gilardi presciently wrote of the image, "Two indisputably 'historic' markers have manifested the maximum level of communication that has perhaps ever been reached by a photograph: the Polaroid of Aldo Moro and the shroud of Christ."[31] The iconic image is enshrined in both Italian pop culture and works by other artists, such as Mimmo Rotella's *Il martire* (*The Martyr*) (1980; fig. 57). Like Charlesworth, the Nouveau Réaliste produced a series of works (1978–80) based on media images related to the *anni di piombo*.[32] For *Il martire* Rotella reproduced in photo emulsion on canvas a detail of the famous Moro Polaroid culled from the pages of an English-language news source. Rotella's visual clipping of the image, which recalls the *décollage* technique that he had applied to movie posters during the immediate postwar period, reinforces the blunt iconicity of the image. Charlesworth's *April 21, 1978* relies on this same iconicity—exposing the way such an image is easily digested into a martyrdom narrative that sweeps aside nuance and culpability (as Rotella's title suggests)—and also lays bare the icon's status as a "message without a code."[33] Whereas the Red Brigades and the newspapers that published the hostage photograph of Moro deployed photography as a means of visual proof, Charlesworth "unwrites" the martyrdom narrative by exposing how photography functions as a visual language. In other words, *April 21, 1978* explicates how we read photographs.

The Italian audience that first viewed *April 21, 1978* could not consider the work without Moro's kidnapping and murder fresh in their minds. The events marked a watershed moment in Italian political life that instantiated an already deep mistrust in the country's government. Many questions about the case still remain unanswered or unsatisfactorily resolved. In 2008, to commemorate the thirtieth anniversary of Moro's death, the Italian newspaper *La Repubblica* issued a special supplement.[34] A thick, glossy magazine filled with excerpted documents and hundreds of images, this pop-cultural artifact serves as a kind of amateur investigative dossier containing an exhaustive account of the case, the investigations and trials that followed, and the scandals that it revealed. Readers could peruse for themselves the Red Brigades' communiqués, peer into the confines of the "people's prison," and puzzle over an elaborate diagram mapping the dramatic moments of Moro's capture in Rome's via Fani (fig. 58). The lurid tabloid aesthetic of the magazine exemplifies one way in which the media participates in the manufacture of political spectacle. Charlesworth's Modern History series demands reflection on whom such spectacle serves.

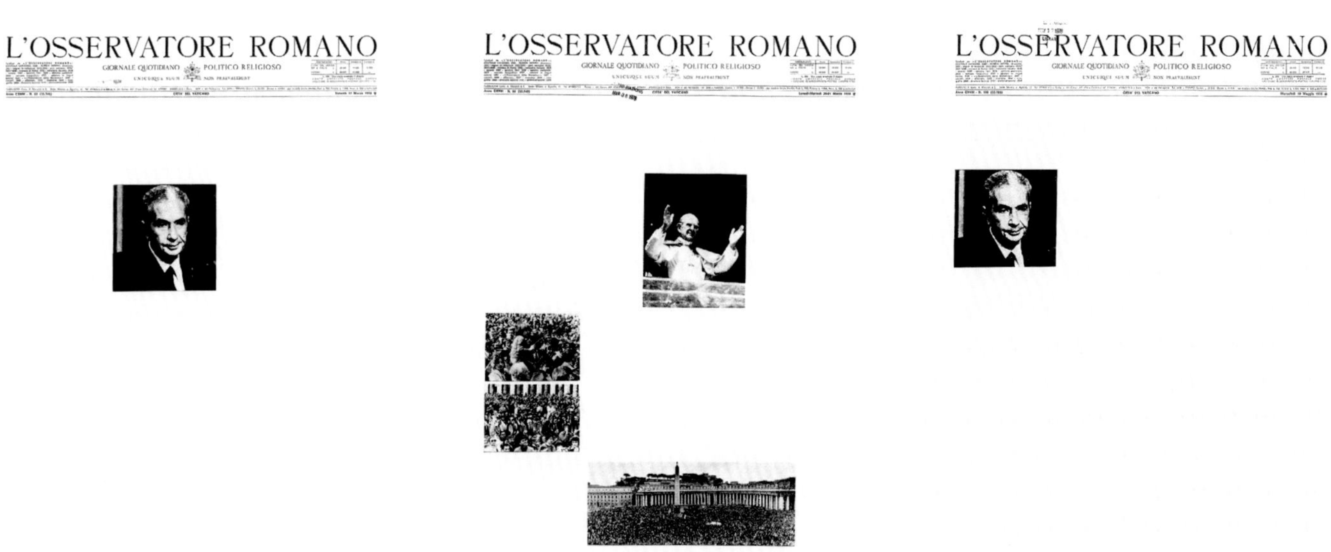

Fig. 56. Details of Sarah Charlesworth, *Osservatore Romano, March 17–May 10, 1978*, 1978. Three of twenty-seven black-and-white prints reproduced same size as original newspapers, 23½ × 16½ in. (59.7 × 41.9 cm) each

Fig. 57. Mimmo Rotella (Italian, 1918–2006), *Il martire*, 1980. Photo emulsion on canvas, 41⅝ × 29⅝ in. (105.5 × 75.1 cm). Private collection, Milan

Fig. 58. "La Strage di via Fani," *Atlante de la Repubblica: I Giorni di Moro*, March 6, 2008, pp. 14–15

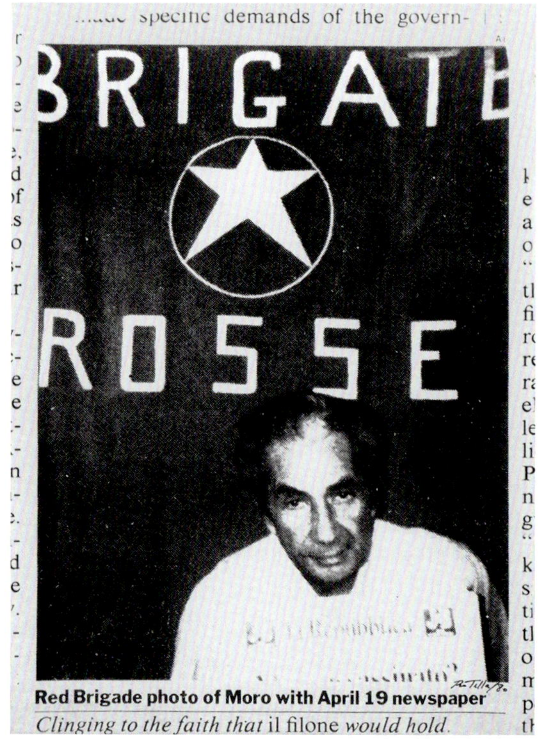

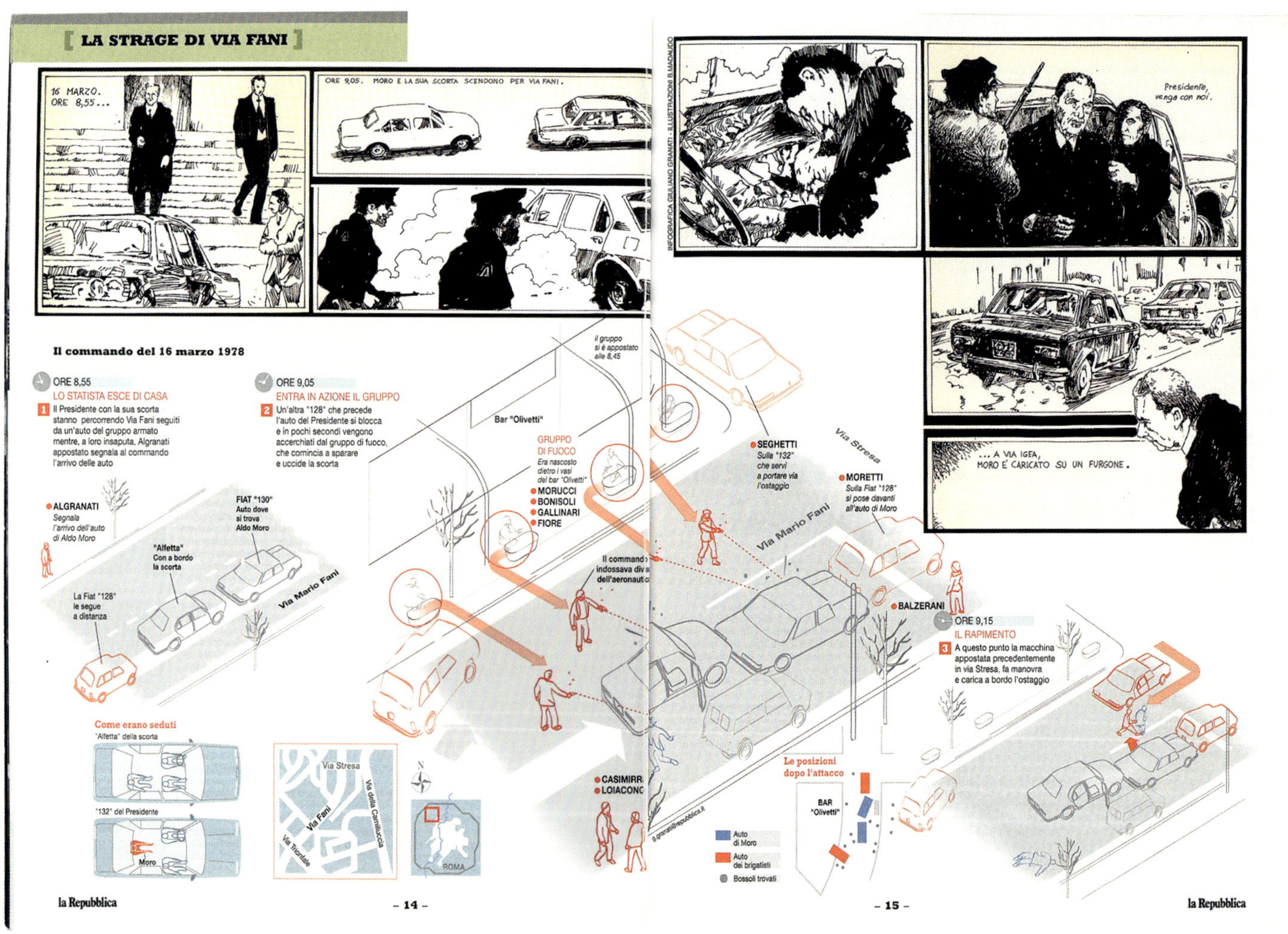

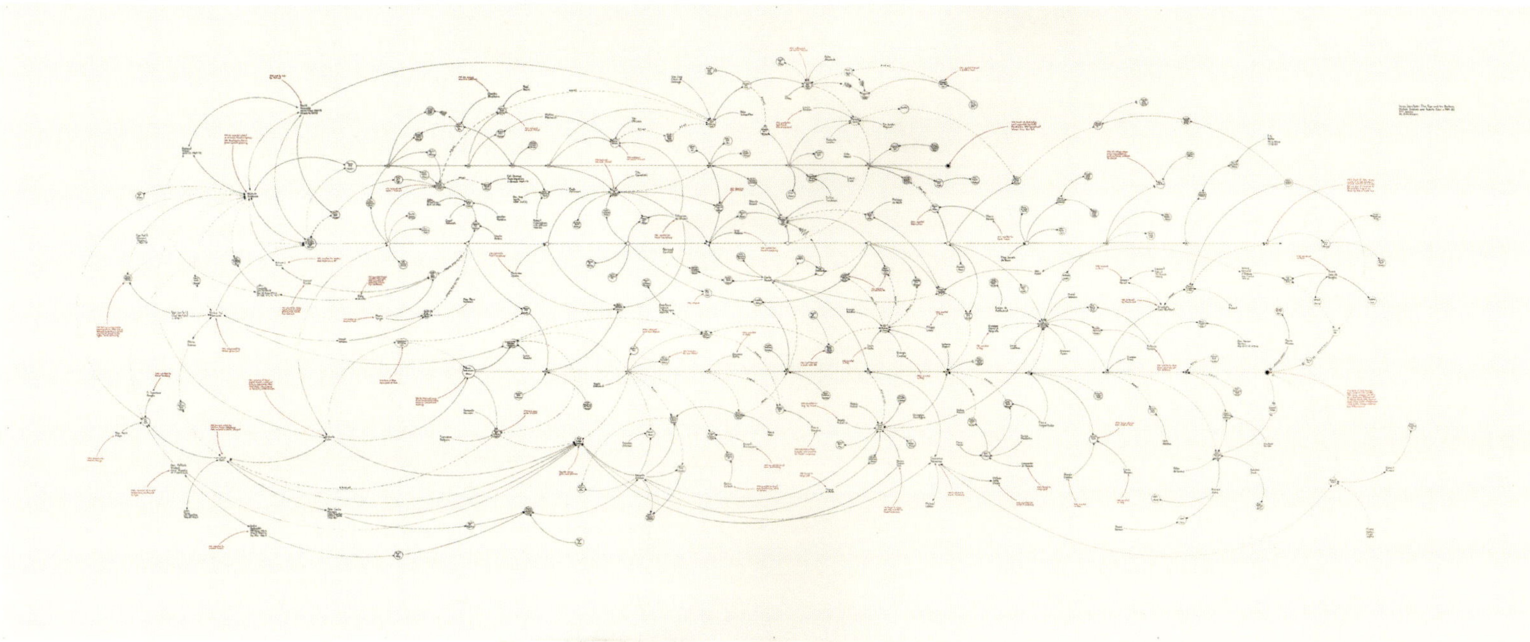

Fig. 59. Mark Lombardi (American, 1951–2000), *Inner Sanctum: The Pope and His Bankers Michele Sindona and Roberto Calvi, ca. 1959–82 (5th Version)*, 1998. Colored pencil and graphite on paper, 56½ × 126¼ in. (143.5 × 320.7 cm). Smithsonian American Art Museum, Washington, D.C.

To many, it seemed implausible that the police investigation into Moro's death could have failed so spectacularly; there had to be a larger power at play. Theories included the possibility that the Red Brigades received clandestine support from the KGB or CIA, or that a wider terror network in Europe shared financial resources and weapons with the radical organization.[35] Some speculated that the political violence of the Lead Years was a cover for foreign governments to carry out missions against Italy through Gladio (the sword), an alleged surreptitious anti-Communist army backed by the CIA. Conspiracies about United States meddling in the Italian political system proliferated after the Church Committee reports disclosed that the CIA's initial action on foreign soil was its intervention into Italy's first elections in 1947–48 in support of the DC. Among the most notorious discoveries to emerge in the wake of the Moro case was the existence of a secret masonic lodge, Propaganda Due (P2), which directly linked leading figures from the highest echelons of Italian business and government to organized crime through the Banco Ambrosiano, a bank with ties to the Vatican that laundered Mafia money and provided financial backing for right-wing terrorist attacks during the Lead Years.[36] These revelations culminated in the collapse of Italy's First Republic in 1992.

Mark Lombardi's epic drawing *Inner Sanctum: The Pope and His Bankers Michele Sindona and Roberto Calvi, ca. 1959–82 (5th Version)* (1998; fig. 59) untangles this Gordian knot of fraud and collusion, illuminating through its exhaustive research and formal intricacy the extent of political corruption within Italy and its international ties going back to the immediate postwar period. The drawing is an eloquent foil for Charlesworth's *April 21, 1978*. Her minimalism, which crystalizes the events of the Moro affair and the press's handling of it into a repetition of the same image across the expanse of forty-five blank rectangles, exposes the systems that shape one's understanding of exceedingly complex historical moments. Lombardi's maximalism offers a code with which to decipher Charlesworth's unmoored images, but one that, intentionally, is too oppressively complicated to navigate much less comprehend. With its brilliant economy, *Charlesworth's April 21, 1978* is able to absorb, and disavow, all context.

EXTRATERRESTRIALS UNDERGROUND AND OTHER ARTISTIC SUBLEVELS IN CALIFORNIA

Ian Alteveer

The End Is Here, Jim Shaw's title for his 1978 MFA thesis exhibition at California Institute of the Arts (CalArts), is an apt and evocative statement for a kaleidoscopic group of works that channeled government conspiracy theories, apocalyptic religious fervor, and alien lifeforms. Notwithstanding its historical moment, one deeply fraught with political and social instability, Shaw's exhibition title also appropriately signaled the end of his days as a student at CalArts (fig. 60)—a time perhaps already replete with its own anxiety. As the artist later explained to his good friend and classmate Mike Kelley, part of the impetus for the project was that he "had been informed by some other students that Richard Artschwager was almost ready to flunk me, so I thought that I'd better do something dramatic."[1]

The birth of Los Angeles as an international art center is intrinsically tied to the rise of CalArts as an interdisciplinary, cutting-edge place to study art-making, however implausible that insitution's beginnings may have been. The school's roots lie in the Chouinard Art Institute, a traditional fine-arts academy founded by World War I widow Nelbert Chouinard in 1921. In the school's early years, Chouinard entered an informal relationship with Walt Disney, who was searching out inexpensive evening courses for his movie animators.[2] Disney eventually joined the board in 1955, and, two years later, he secured full control during a financial crisis.[3] His fantasy for a "university of the arts," a place where anyone who worked on his films could study, from animators to set designers to musical composers, was put in place before his death in 1966. He granted land on his former ranch in Valencia, high in the foothills north of the city, and named the school California Institute of the Arts.[4] The new campus opened there in 1972, and, under the direction of a group of avant-garde educators, the school quickly pivoted its orientation away from Disney's plans for a traditional arts program, disposing of what critic Peter Plagens called "the stifling of visionary artists by conservative curricula" and declaring "that 'art' means the use of new media and technical procedures."[5]

That CalArts then morphed into a radical place for art education mere years after Disney's death is the stuff of legend. As Douglas Eklund has explained elsewhere, the academically liberal atmosphere at CalArts was partly engendered by its first dean, Paul Brach, who recruited John Baldessari, Allan Kaprow, and other artists with nontraditional views on pedagogy to form the school's first faculty.[6] Baldessari advocated a "post-studio" model that leveled the distinction between teacher and student and got rid of the life-drawing classes that made up the core of most first-year programs in art, while other faculty came from backgrounds in public theater and performance.[7] Herbert Blau, for example, served as provost in the early years and, based in part on his experiences at Black Mountain College in the 1940s and 1950s, seems to have had a strong hand in the loose curriculum and experimental atmosphere.[8] (Blau's Actor's Workshop, which he cofounded in San Francisco in 1952, was legendary for staging Samuel Beckett's *Waiting for Godot* for inmates at San Quentin Prison in 1957.[9]) The ground at CalArts was thus fertile for artists like Shaw who were eager to move beyond the traditions of studio practice into other realms.

The End Is Here represents not only a summation of Shaw's varied interests at the beginning of his career but also the first of many large-scale, deeply researched bodies of work that he produced in the following decades. For the show, he manufactured a faux religious cult that was based, in part, upon the California-kitsch Universal World Church, an evangelical group founded in the early 1950s in Los Angeles by Orval Lee Jaggers and his wife (and first cousin), Miss Velma.[10] Their ministry preached

Fig. 60. Main building of California Institute of the Arts (CalArts), Valencia, California, 1970

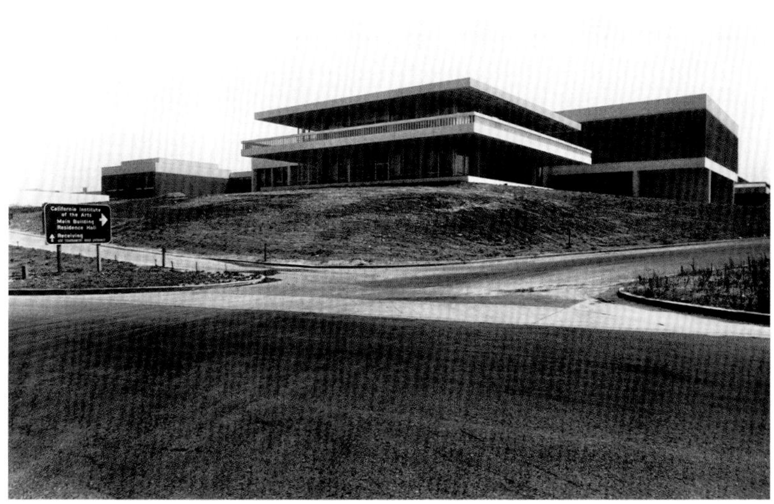

both the gospel and the study of UFOs; among O. L. Jaggers's many publications are *Flying Saucers* (1952) and *The Atomic and Hydrogen Bombs in Bible Prophecy* (1953).[11] As Shaw later said, "Miss Velma and Dr. Jaggers had a regular TV show on channel 13 . . . one time they had a feature where he was doing spermatozoa in outer space, and he would say, 'As a doctor of genetics I can prove without a doubt that Jesus was 100% the DNA of God and not at all human!'"[12] The Jaggerses' flamboyant, campy evangelism was amplified by the large, golden altar they eventually installed at their headquarters on North Lake Street near Beverly Boulevard. Regular newspaper ads throughout the 1970s joyfully proclaimed that the altar cost a million dollars (fig. 61).[13] Shaw included a golden altar of his own in the installation of *The End Is Here*.[14]

Shaw layered the work with references to UFOism. Inspired by the amusingly clumsy reportage in supermarket tabloid photography and the then-burgeoning theory that a race of lizards disguised as humans secretly rule the planet, Shaw altered snapshots of his friends to create his *Martian Portraits* (1978; p. 121 top and bottom),[15] retouching the portraits with an airbrush to reveal the monsters that supposedly lurked underneath their otherwise placid countenances. Though he rephotographed the doctored images in order to diminish the visibility of his alterations, his incursions remained in his words "ridiculously obvious." Shaw wanted to emphasize that they were "overtly faked."[16] Similarly, he forged photographs of UFO sightings in which lights or spaceships hover over either innocuous landscapes (1977–78; p. 120) or John F. Kennedy's Dallas motorcade, the latter captured in stills from Abraham Zapruder's infamous home movie of the 1963 assassination (p. 119 bottom).

Shaw's implication that some might think extraterrestrials lurk all around—whether in the humdrum sprawl of Southern California suburbs or behind some of the most trenchant events of our time—aligned with a certain overall paranoia in the 1970s zeitgeist. Fantasies of the End of Days and of worlds beyond our own have inspired bizarre beliefs for centuries, but nowhere did they seem to collide with such fervor or hold such sway as in California after the social and cultural revolutions of the 1960s, a decade convulsed by the assassinations of the Kennedys and Civil Rights leaders, by the Watts Rebellion and other uprisings, and by the escalation of the Vietnam War. Following the summer of 1969, when Charles Manson's Family carried out the Tate-LaBianca murders in an attempt to spur race warfare, Los Angeles and, indeed, the world may have seemed at a tipping point. Although Manson's

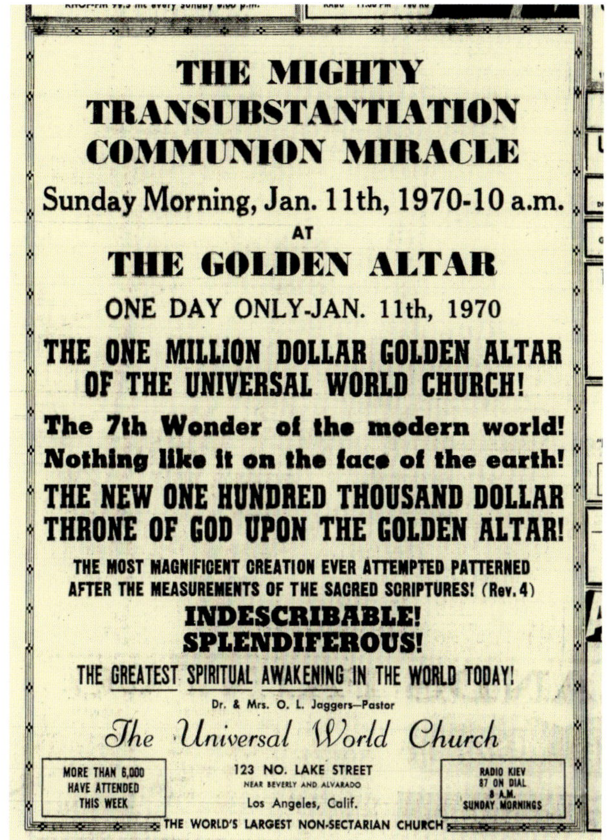

Fig. 61. Universal World Church advertisement, *Los Angeles Times,* January 10, 1970

Helter Skelter may not have explicitly arrived (however much the FBI was already at work on that effort by deliberately undermining various movements aligned with Black Power; see Douglas Eklund's essay "Wake Up!" in this volume, pp. 21–31), the public's definitive distrust of what they saw as a secretive and conspiratorial government only intensified following the release of the Pentagon Papers in 1971 and Nixon's subsequent counterconspiracies, including the Watergate scandal—the president's "White House horrors."[17]

In retrospect, one can see why a book such as John Gribbin and Stephen Plagemann's 1974 best-selling astronomical invective, *The Jupiter Effect*, also had Angelenos terrified that an astral alignment of planets behind the sun in 1982 would result in a major earthquake.[18] Meanwhile, science-fiction and disaster movies made in the Golden State—everything from Steven Spielberg's *Close Encounters of the Third Kind* and George Lucas's *Star Wars* to American International Pictures' H. G. Wells–inspired B-movies *Empire of the Ants* and *The Island of Dr. Moreau* (all 1977)—fueled the feeling that, according to Shaw, "people, at that

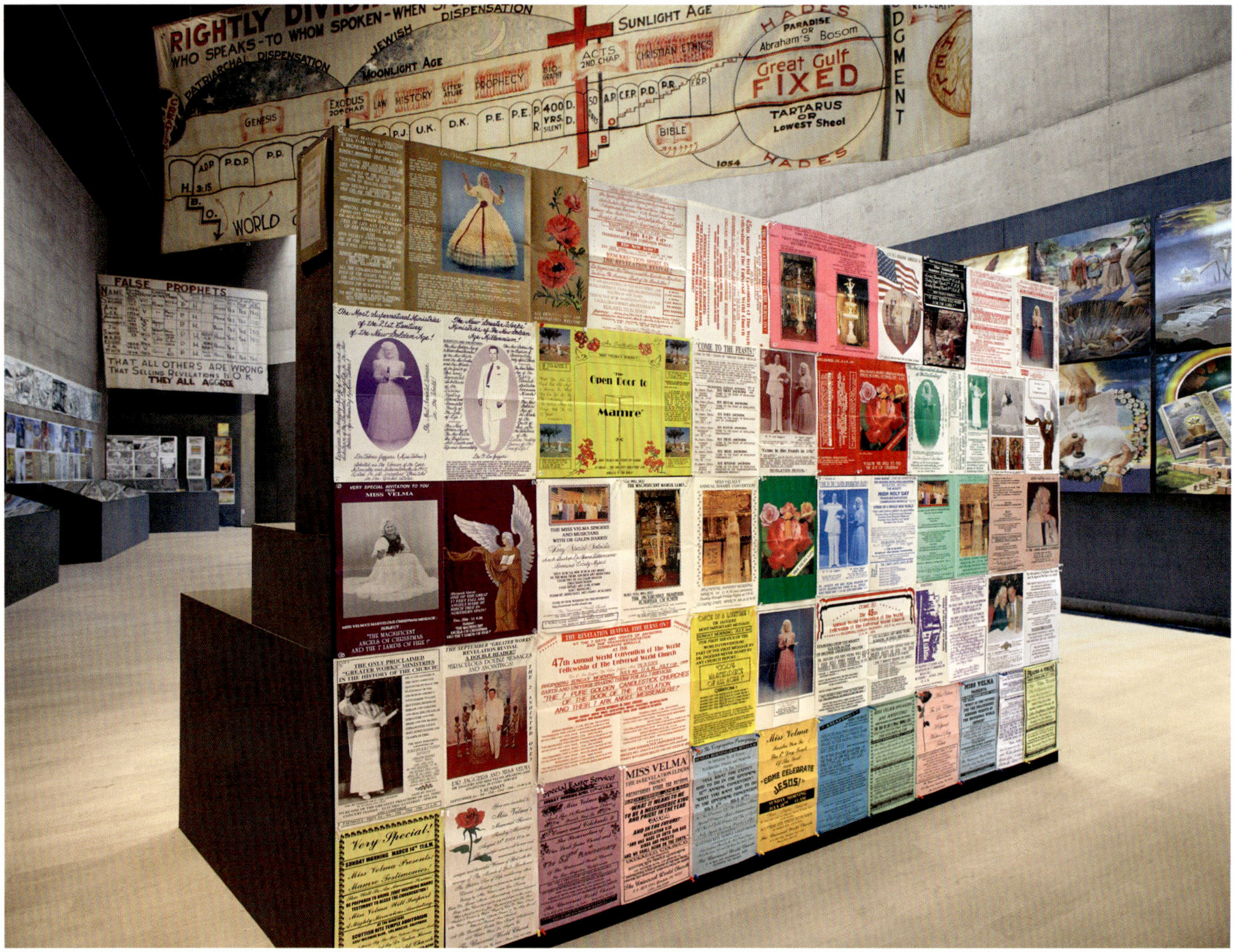

Fig. 62. Installation view of "*The Hidden World*–Jim Shaw Didactic Art Collection with Jean-Frédéric Schnyder and Friedrich Dürrenmatt" at the Centre Dürrenmatt Neuchâtel, Switzerland, 2014

moment, would rather just have everything over with than look forward to an eternity spent in drudgery."[19] For the artist it was all too clear that fantasies—as much as he, too, warily admired their alternately kitschy or sophisticated aesthetics—were potent distractions from what was truly at hand.

To this end, Shaw accompanied his exhibition with a pamphlet (pp. 118–19, 161) done in the distinctive style of the Jehovah's Witness magazine *Awake!*, one of the publications distributed by an arm of the Watch Tower Bible and Tract Society to propagandize that group's focus on the Last Judgment and Satan's omnipresence in the actions of the secular world. The artist had collected issues of *Awake!* for years, just as he had painstakingly gathered leaflets and flyers from the Universal World Church in the 1970s (an overwhelming, yet fractional, part of these vast holdings has been displayed more recently in Shaw's installations of religious ephemera such as *The Hidden World* [2014; fig. 62]).[20] Indeed, while an undergraduate at the University of Michigan he had already amassed all manner of salvage, from records, pulp fiction, and thrift-store paintings to toys and sci-fi collectibles, in a dilapidated Victorian at 741 Packard Street in Ann Arbor.[21] Mike Kelley, Shaw's classmate (and fellow bandmate, with Cary Loren and Niagara, in Destroy All Monsters), who moved into the basement of the Ann Arbor house, called it, affectionately or not, a "garbage dump with a path running through it." [22] To Shaw, it was "God's Oasis Drive-In Church."[23] On Kelley's suggestion, Shaw also applied to CalArts for graduate school, and they both enrolled in the fall of 1976, bringing their love of secondhand merchandise and bibliomania with them to Valencia.[24]

Included among Shaw's deep holdings of ephemera is an issue of the early, pulp science-fiction magazine *Amazing Stories*, featuring Richard Sharpe Shaver's 1948 story "Gods of Venus" (fig. 63), one of an immensely popular series published in the magazine in the immediate post–World War II years, from 1945 to 1953.[25] As curator Brian Tucker writes, Shaver "insisted that his tales were fundamentally true; they were presented in the guise of fiction only because the underlying reality he described was too outlandish to be published as fact by the mainstream press."[26] Indeed, according to Shaver, humankind was being manipulated by the Dero, corrupted descendants of ancient and noble creatures who inhabited the antediluvian world and built resplendent subterranean metropolises. The Dero did not escape the planet alongside their kin and now used the powerful ray guns and other devices left behind to manipulate and brainwash those unfortunate enough to live above ground. As Jim Shaw tells it, this seemingly delusional fantasy was in part brought on by a potential occupational hazard: "In the beginning Shaver was working in an auto assembly plant in Detroit, and a welding gun would be swung to him, and he started having these visions from the arcs and sparks."[27]

Fig. 63. *Amazing Stories* issue featuring the 1948 science-fiction story "Gods of Venus" by Richard Sharpe Shaver

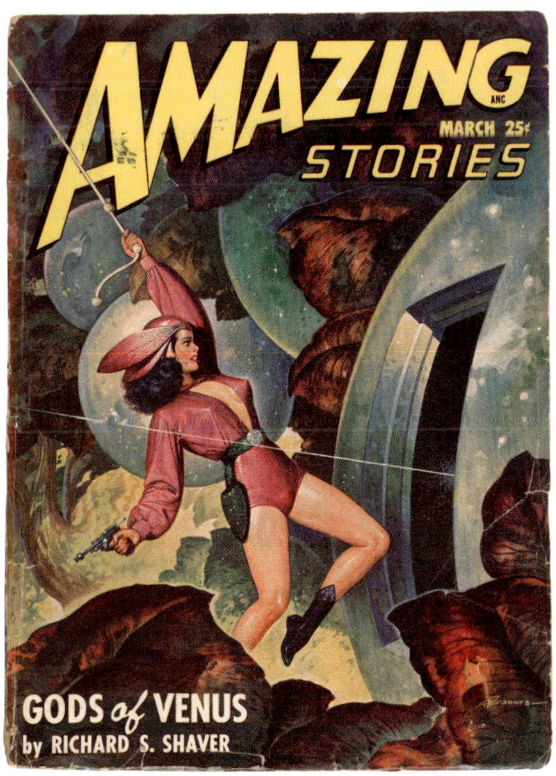

After more mainstream media began to cover the "Shaver Mystery," and a number of his fans also claimed to have been influenced by the evil rays of the Dero, *Amazing Stories* canceled the series and Shaver was left to his own devices.[28] In his eventual exile in rural Arkansas, he became convinced that he could uncover the culture of these ancient civilizations by carefully examining the geological formations where they had embedded images and stories with their strangely powerful machinery. He first interpreted the signs and symbols he found in these so-called Rock Books in the medium of paint. He then spent the remaining decade of his life slicing into the stones themselves and photographing their surfaces, often picking out the imagery he saw therein with paint and other media in order to further reveal their complex symbology. His resulting works (pp. 124–25) read as earnest and impassioned finding aids for the viewer that ape the language of anthropology, archaeology, and mysticism in equal and engaging parts.

While Shaver believed that there were malignant forces lurking below the Earth's crust, the sense that subterranean or extraterrestrial beings might be influencing what occurs in the human sphere could be seen as a more widespread and symptomatic response to things such as government secrecy and its machinations. In his lifetime, Shaver, alongside many other Americans, witnessed the revelation of an expanding series of government cover-ups, both suspected and real, from warnings about Pearl Harbor to the JFK assassination, the Pentagon Papers, and Watergate. As historian Kathryn Olmsted so convincingly writes, for example, "conspiracy theories are endemic to American democracy" precisely because government actions have increasingly allowed them to thrive.[29] She describes vividly, both in this volume (see pp. 158–65) and elsewhere, how, in reaction to the exposure of governmental scandals in the 1970s—particularly Watergate and the reopening by the Church Committee of investigations into covert CIA operations—amateur investigators began to look back to find evidence of past government cover-ups, such as the crash of a supposed UFO in Roswell, New Mexico, in 1947.[30]

In the bleak light of this burgeoning paranoia, Tony Oursler, who had befriended Shaw and Kelley while an undergraduate at CalArts in the late 1970s, began to address government lies and corruption through multimedia installations incorporating video, sound, sculptural objects, and visual effects. *Son of Oil* (1982/1999; p. 126), one of the first works Oursler produced upon his return to New York after graduation, moved beyond the single-channel videos he had made in California toward something "more and more elaborate," with full-scale painted sets as backdrops for his increasingly baroque and politically nuanced narratives.[31] The artist based his amorphously connected stories on solid bodies of research—in this case, on the oil embargo of the prior decade—through which he linked everything from monster movies, Howard Hughes, and the 1970s serial killer David Berkowitz (Son of Sam) to "petro-politics and paranoid personal perception."[32] At P.S.1 in Long Island City, Oursler built a "graveyard gas station" set for the work, filmed a scene against that backdrop, and then showed the full video on a monitor embedded in one of the set's cardboard gravestones-cum-gasoline pumps.[33] The video itself "is a cautionary tale about the decline of Western civilization, as only Oursler could envision it," wrote video art expert Lori Zippay. In the installation as a whole "[o]il is the central metaphor around which he constructs a burlesque critique of the cults of money and power that fuel economic and sexual systems, social pathology, and cultural mythologies."[34]

Artist and writer John Miller was also part of the CalArts cohort, one year behind Kelley and Shaw in the graduate program (see his essay in this volume, pp. 166–69). Among the works he has made in the decades since graduating in 1979 is a group of paintings from the mid- to late 1990s based on American television game shows. In these Game Show Paintings, Miller rendered stills from popular programs such as *The Price Is Right* and *Wheel of Fortune*, emphasizing their lurid banality by removing key elements from the scenes. For the artist, these tableau are "the obverse of southwest American landscapes," a reference to those compositions that generally "pertain to an idealized national image: pioneer spirit, rugged individualism, God's country, the sublime" and embody, in essence, all of the triumphalist tropes of Manifest Destiny still present in the American psyche (and typified by places like Roswell and Valencia, the high-desert ranching and golfing locale of CalArts).[35] In Miller's words, the Game Show Paintings manifest a darker side of American life and, notwithstanding their aspirational glitz, "exemplify values most would disavow: disillusion, passive consumption, conformity, and degradation."[36] Perhaps the most trenchant example is *ZOG* (1998; p. 127), to which Miller added a layer of conspiratorial paranoia. Here, while host Pat Sajak looks on gleefully, longtime hostess Vanna White reveals three letters that spell the nickname used by right-wing anti-Semitic radicals to represent their belief that Washington is a "Zionist occupied government," an acronym they use in place of "USA" in hate-filled screeds.[37]

In a similar fashion, Miller's friend Jim Shaw continued to build on his decades-long study of conspiracies, American religion, and the occult as he began a new series of installations in the early 2000s, naming it Left Behind. At the time, he described being "wrapped up in the build-up to the 2004 U.S. election, the Iraq invasion, and thinking a lot about the societal change begun by Reagan and Thatcher, and cemented by Bush Jr., from the ethos and mythos of the New Deal to the fever dream of the neoliberal present."[38] Shaw noted that *Left Behind* is the title of a series of Christian apocalyptic fantasy novels about the End of Days. With his usual piercing insight, he also inferred that it referenced the state of the U.S. labor force, one the artist saw as deserted "by globalism, with a weak labor movement and little support from the Democrats. Many have turned to born-again Christianity in lieu of any other hope for the future, which has in turn been exploited heavily by the right wing."[39]

Shaw's accidental discovery of a cache of worn theatrical backdrops in Los Angeles had inspired the series. The backdrop for *The Miracle of Compound Interest* (2006; pp. 122–23), for example, perfectly illustrates the paradoxes inherent in the complex American economic dream he describes—an implicit phantom in so many Hollywood films of his youth. The original backdrop's scene of a small-town gasoline station reminded Shaw of the rural California pumping station in the 1947 film *Out of the Past*, where Robert Mitchum's character, Jeff, has taken refuge from the ghosts of his career as a big-city private investigator and tried to begin anew. When his wealthy—and corrupt—foil and former employer Whit, an inveterate gambler played by Kirk Douglas, finally catches up with him, Jeff delivers a lecture: "It's very simple," he says, having reported to Whit's estate near Reno. "I sell gasoline. I make a small profit. With that I buy groceries, the grocer makes a profit. They call it earning a living. Maybe you've heard of it."[40] For many, Jeff's short lesson on small-town economics—placed in high relief to Whit's debauchery and excesses—belies an underlying specter of economic insecurity that haunts the American century. In the film's frequent contrast between the so-called good life of the idyllic American countryside and the dark forces of the city, as Sean McCann writes, there is "an intense anxiety about the vast extension and unpredictability of a capitalist economy."[41] For Shaw, he "felt [Jeff's statement] was a fitting evocation of the switch from the mythology of The New Deal to the roll of dice version of neoliberal

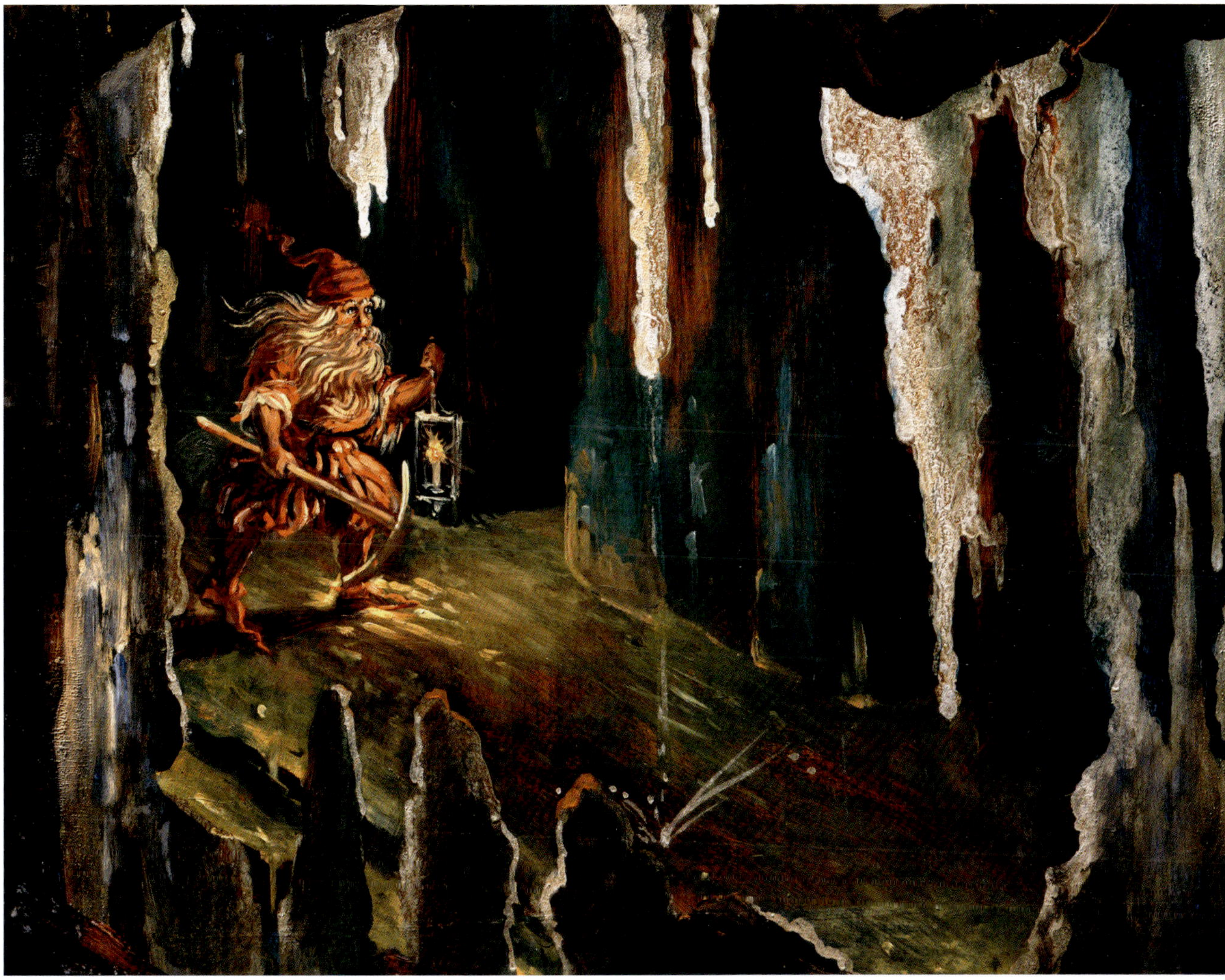

Fig. 64. Detail of a painted wood door with fantastic scenes evoking the kabbalah and Masonic symbols, including a gnome searching for diamonds in a cave, 1905. Museo Stibbert, Florence

capitalism espoused during the Reagan era, where lotteries replaced taxes as the preferred method of revenue gathering, and a high stakes gambler was the leading intellectual force in the . . . administration."[42]

Shaw differentiates this direct economy of simple necessities from what lies beyond the doorway of the station, where, behind the backdrop, he installed a checkerboard floor based on the decor of a Scottish-Rite Masonic temple. Inside, gnomes huddle around a glowing dollar sign (detail, p. 123; fig. 64 shows a historical example of these motifs). According to Shaw, "The references are to the archetype of dwarves-caves-jewels à la Snow White as well as Wagner, and the anti-Semitic side of conspiracy theory combining bankers and the 'international Jewish Conspiracy' and the dark side of Masonry."[43]

As Olmsted writes in her introduction to *Real Enemies*, "Americans have worried that their country is especially open—and vulnerable—to alien subversion. Over the past two hundred years, frightened Americans have targeted Catholics, Masons, Mormons, and Jews because these native groups were allegedly guided by the instructions of an alien power."[44] It is just this type of conspiracy thinking that formed the basis for Shaw's 1978 MFA thesis exhibition twenty-five years before. Indeed, the lizard people and Richard Sharpe Shaver's theories return in spirit through Shaw's direct allusion, in his notes on the work, to Zecharia Sitchin, an author who believed that his "translations" of Sumerian tablets "tell the creation story of Genesis as an alien conspiracy fomented by seemingly immortal aliens from the 10th

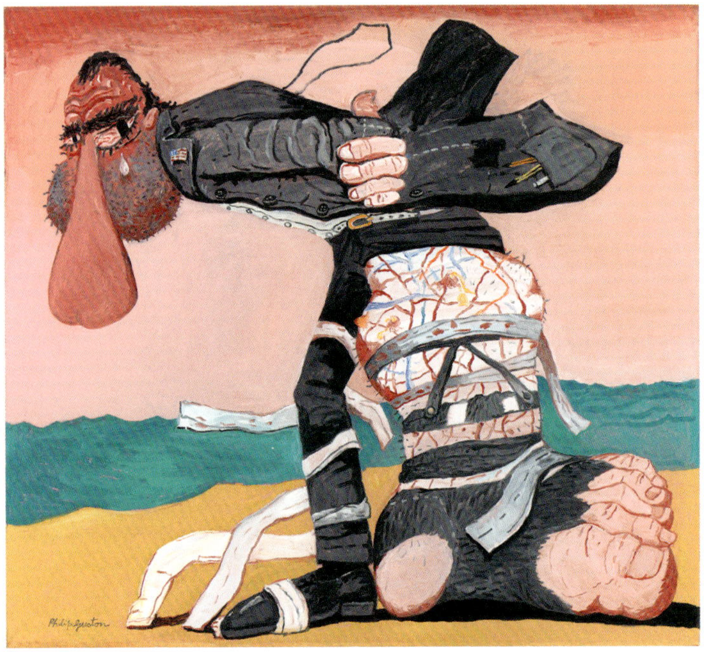

Fig. 65. Philip Guston (American, born Canada, 1913–1980), *San Clemente,* 1975. Oil on canvas, 68 × 73¼ in. (172.7 × 186.1 cm). Glenstone Museum, Potomac, Maryland

planet Nibiru."[45] These aliens "created hybrid ape/ Nibirunian slaves to mine gold and other minerals for their planet . . . then created Adam and Eve . . . and have somehow controlled our actions as well as royal families and leading individuals through some nefarious alien DNA bloodline superiority, some of which makes its way into the Da Vinci Code."[46]

Raymond Pettibon, another Los Angeles artist, confronts the crises and conflicts of American postwar culture through raw drawings often replete with verbose texts.[47] Pettibon's work speaks to the many layers of Southern California subcultures of the 1970s and 1980s, and it uses a distinct, cartoonlike style to address all manner of dark histories, cults, and conspiracy theories, such as the Manson Family and the indoctrination of Patty Hearst by the Symbionese Liberation Army—as well as the literature of Saint Augustine, James Joyce, Lord Byron, and beyond—in a disarming and often scatological fashion.[48] Pettibon is also a great admirer of Philip Guston's late, satirical paintings of the 1970s, which focus on, among other things, "Tricky Dick" throughout Watergate and its aftermath.[49] In *San Clemente* (1975; fig. 65), for example, Guston portrays the tarnished former president in exile, mourning at his seaside estate in Southern California and trailing his engorged, phlebitic leg (various reports claimed that Nixon's leg had swollen to twice its size following the stress of the impeachment proceedings and that Gerald Ford's subsequent pardon had not helped either this or his depression).[50]

In works from the mid-1980s, such as *No Title (Coup d'etats were . . .)* and *No Title (I've prayed . . .)* (both 1984; pp. 128 top left and bottom), Pettibon sets single, graphic figures against stark, unpopulated backgrounds. Brief, pithy lines of handwritten text in his characteristic block lettering refer to the gloom of past events with acid tongue in cheek. As critic Peter Schjeldahl writes, each "Pettibon phrasing sounds like a quotation from someone else, often in the formal, slightly stilted tones of a Victorian wordsmith."[51] In later works, such as *No Title (Who but Hoover . . .)* (1991; p. 128 top right), text fills more of the sheet around the inky black figures, the words full of an uncertain rage against the hypocrisies and paradoxes of the government and its intelligence apparatus.

In a recent suite of drawings on the subject of the Kennedys—long a locus of fascination for the artist—Pettibon revisits these themes with laser focus (pp. 130–31). As the artist writes on one recent drawing, which depicts JFK's head and upper torso as he lay dead at Parkland Memorial Hospital in Dallas, "Cause of death: unknown but still pondered over." With their layered texts, these works continue Pettibon's now decades-long engagement with the darker side of American life in the twentieth century in order to highlight its ongoing presence in our national psyche. The sometimes lacerating language with which the artist takes on our most revered figures—see, for example, *No Title (When It Came . . .)*, (2002–17; p. 130)—is at once disconcerting and liberating, especially in a moment of deep distrust of the government.

Sue Williams, a painter known for her frank, scatological depictions of sex and bodily functions, graduated from CalArts in 1976, the year Kelley and Shaw entered. Her works made in the decades that followed move increasingly toward abstraction, combining gestural marks with crude vignettes of sometimes violent interactions. Following September 11, 2001, her paintings approached a near-neon palette applied in virtuoso curvaceous loops and coils whose exuberance is haunted by ghosts of trauma (see Meredith A. Brown's essay in this volume, pp. 136–43). Their offhand, yet often ominous, titles reflect Williams's knowledge of conspiracy theory, while their effusion of bodily viscera looks back to Kelley's works on paper from the early 1990s, such as *Low Definition Presidency* (1993; p. 86) and *Untitled (Government and Business)* (1991; p. 87), in which he used the medium of drawing to work out ideas about the corrupt interconnectedness of neoliberal U.S.

administrations and the corporations that supported them.[52] Some of Williams's most trenchant critiques of power come in the form of collage, a medium whose use for political messages dates back to the last century. At first, works such as *Five Collages* (2016–17) seem innocent in their domestic trappings, which include scraps of wallpaper and drawings of bathroom fixtures. On closer look, however, one notices that the wallpaper sample in one panel (p. 155) is cut away to reveal the smirking faces of Ronald Reagan and his CIA director William J. Casey, who died in 1987 before the extent of his involvement in the Iran-Contra scandal could be fully revealed.[53] That these politicians—who directly took part in the flourishing shadow governments initiated in earlier administrations—lurk beneath the seeming innocence of sprigged drapery is exactly the kind of disclosure Williams's incisive work means to enact.

Among these artists who developed their careers in Los Angeles in the 1970s, Mike Kelley spoke most explicitly in his work about the (often-traumatic) period of adolescence. He also specifically referenced the American educational apparatus, especially with regard to art school and, in particular, to CalArts. In the late 1980s Kelley initiated a body of work that incorporated stuffed animals and knitted or crocheted blankets culled from thrift stores. In *More Love Hours Than Can Ever Be Repaid and the Wages of Sin* (1987, Whitney Museum of American Art), for example, the artist sewed together such found objects into a large tableau. The result is half altar and half allover abstraction, an assemblage of soft, corporeal totems that someone had once loved, that maybe had been gifted by a loved one, and that carry with them the traces of past "love hours." As such, the work comments on both abandonment and the passage into a new world of adulthood.

Kelley's interest in the personal and psychological residue inherent in his selected materials continued into the following decade. His *Arenas* (fig. 66), shown at Metro Pictures in New York in 1990, incorporated more abandoned stuffed toys and afghans arranged in careful combinations. Some were stitched together in chains

Fig. 66. Mike Kelley (American, 1954–2012), *Arena #7 (Bears)*, 1990. Found stuffed animals, blanket, 11½ × 53 × 49 in. (29.2 × 134.6 × 124.5 cm). Private collection

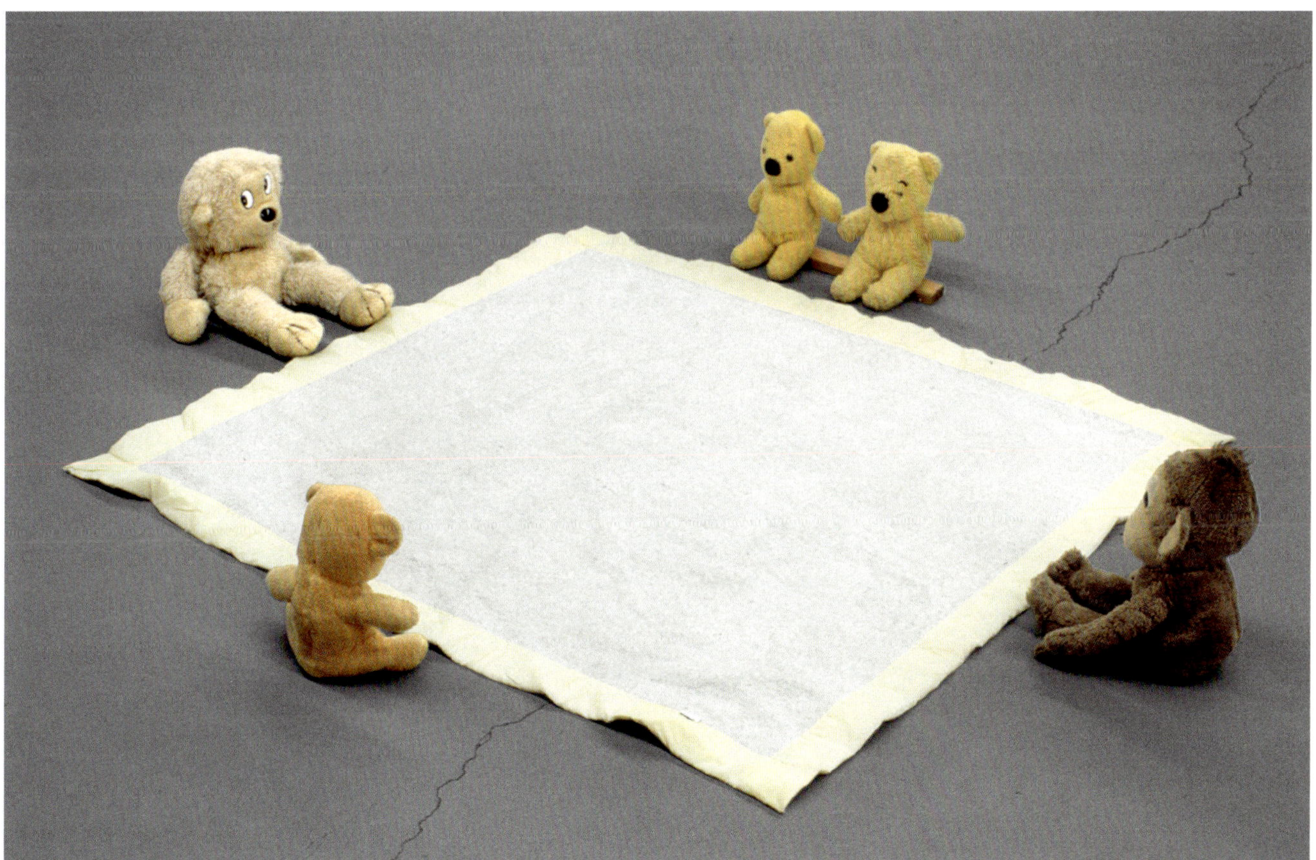

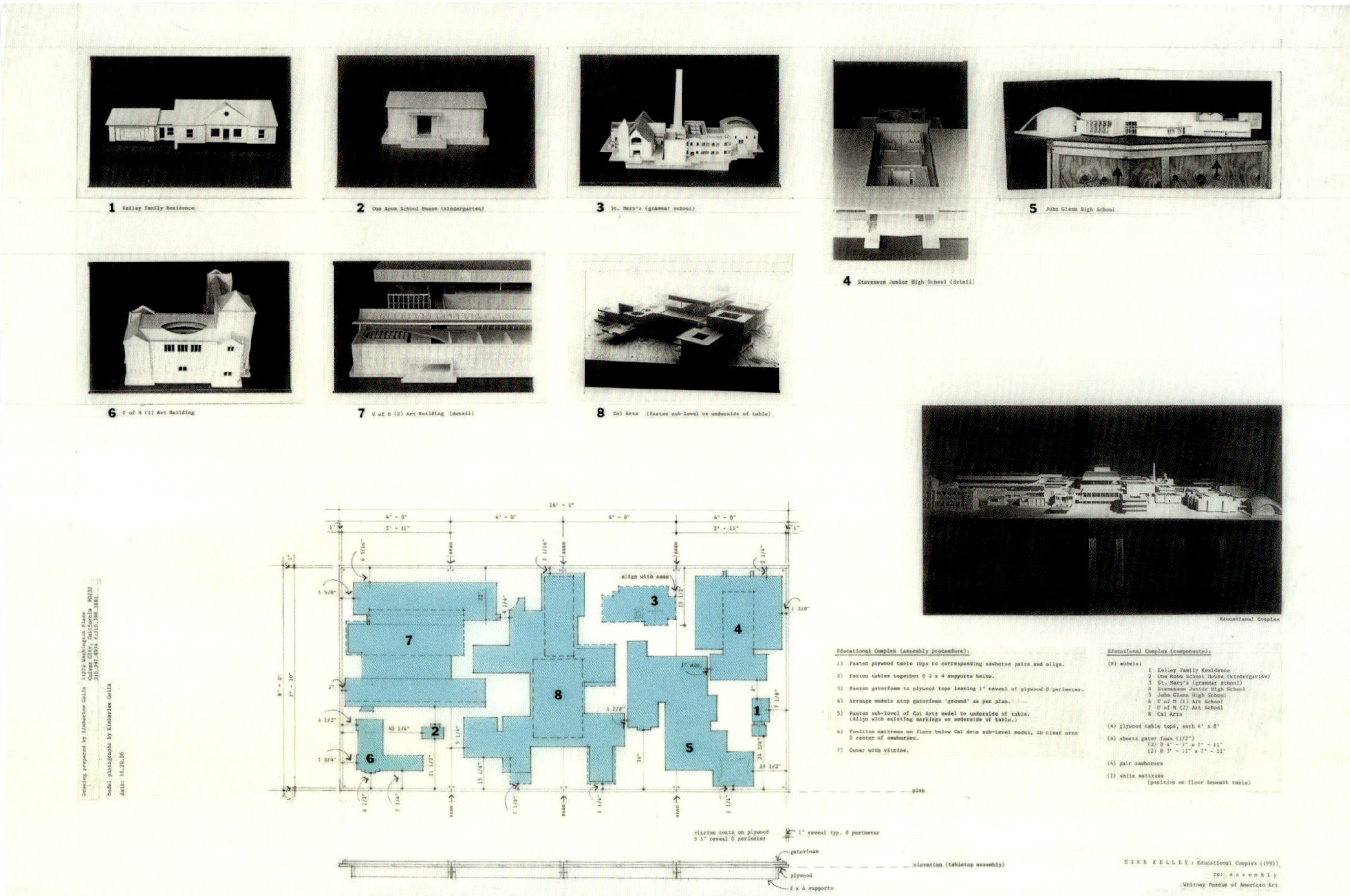

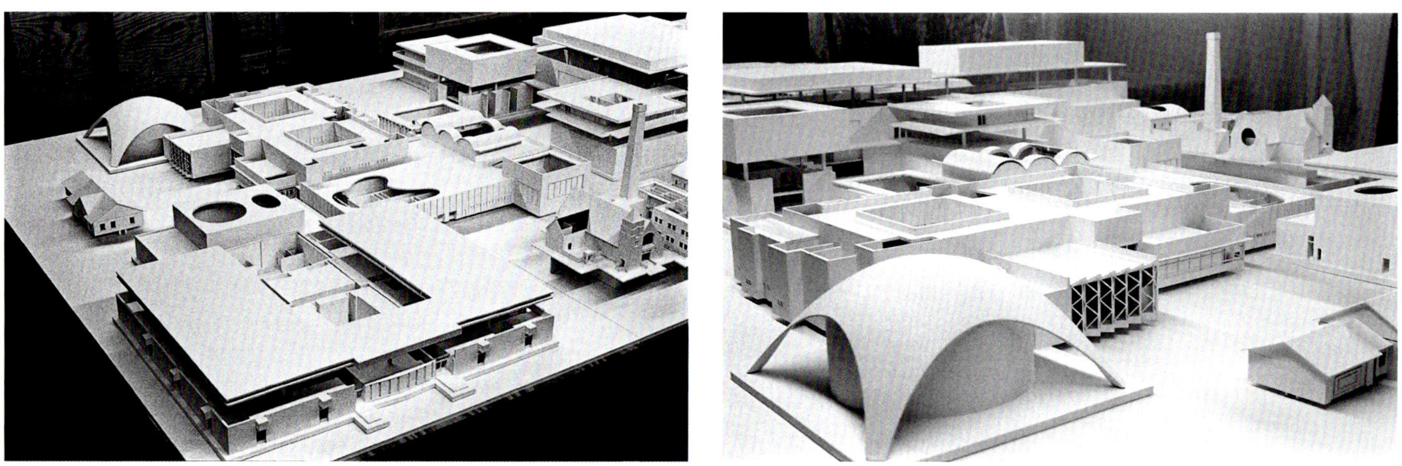

Fig. 67. Mike Kelley, installation plan for *Educational Complex* (1995; pp. 132–34)

Fig. 68. *Educational Complex* (1995; pp. 132–34) in progress: (top) John Glenn High School in foreground; (bottom) Stevenson Junior High School in foreground

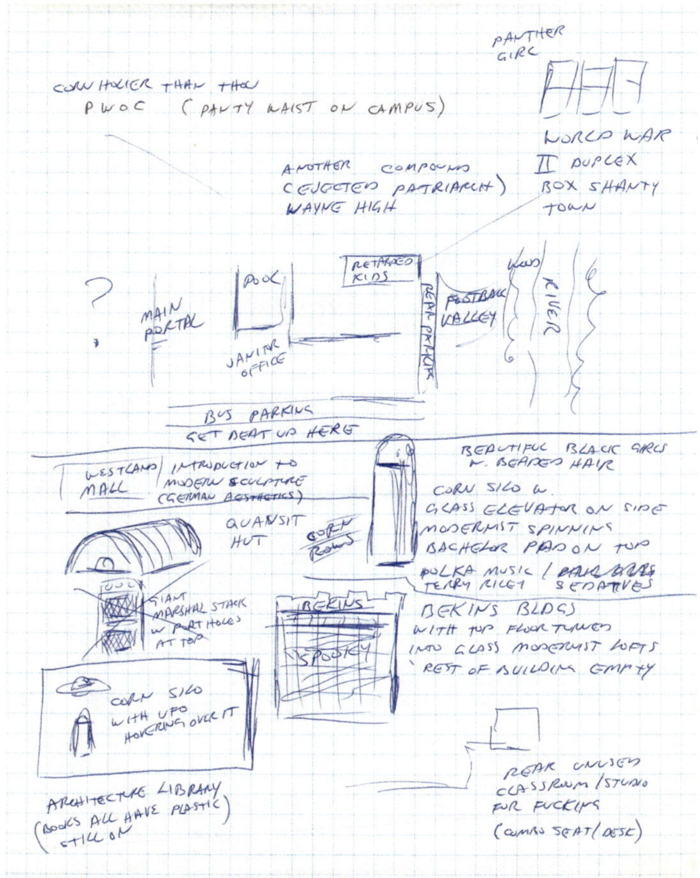

Fig. 69. Mike Kelley, *Architectural Site Drawing from Memory (Wayne High School; Studies for Fantasy Architecture)*, 1994. Ink on paper, 12 × 9½ in. (30.5 × 24.1 cm)

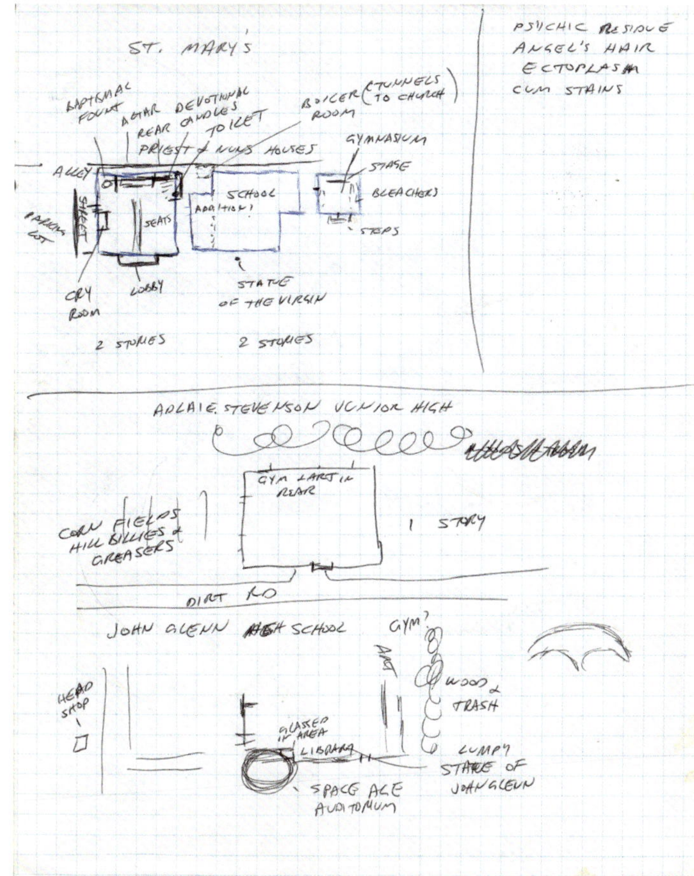

Fig. 70. Mike Kelley, *Architectural Site Drawing from Memory (University of Michigan School of Art, Old and New Buildings; CalArts)*, 1994. Ink on paper, 12 × 9½ in. (30.5 × 24.1 cm)

that cascaded from the wall; most faced off across square knit blankets placed directly on the floor. For the artist, these slightly worn but well-loved relics were not just something that their previous youthful owners used to "weave fantasies around like a doll," but rather each was "primarily a tactile object that promotes great physical pleasure."[54] In his review of the exhibition for *Artforum* that September, critic David Rimanelli wrote that Kelley's "disarmingly casual arrays of soiled stuffed animals on pilled blankets suggest a demonic McMartin Preschool phantasmagoria."[55] This reference to the purportedly rampant abuse at nurseries and preschools around the country—primarily at the McMartin Preschool in Manhattan Beach, California, but also in Maplewood, New Jersey, and Edentown, North Carolina, for example—reveals the extent to which those accusations pervaded the cultural imaginary at the time. "McMartin unleashed nationwide hysteria about child abuse and Satanism in schools. One report after another told of horrific practices, with the Devil often literally in the details," reported the *New York Times* in a recent review of the episode.[56]

Despite the fact that none of these cases ever resulted in permanent convictions—indeed, in the case of Margaret Kelly Michaels in New Jersey, convictions were thrown out after investigations proved, among other things, that the supposed child victims were all too often asked leading questions by psychiatrists and prosecutors, thus tainting their testimonies—the continued malaise and moral panic of the late 1980s and early 1990s seemed to aggravate viewers' responses to Kelley's sculptures.[57] For the artist, this imposed an unwelcome interpretation: "In past works," he has said, "especially the ones utilizing stuffed toys, many viewers had projected scenarios of a disturbed childhood upon them. That had not been my intention, yet I found the works could not escape this reading. . . . I thought I should deal with the issues these works raised."[58]

In the mid-1990s Kelley brilliantly faced this issue of supposed trauma—both sexual and educational—through

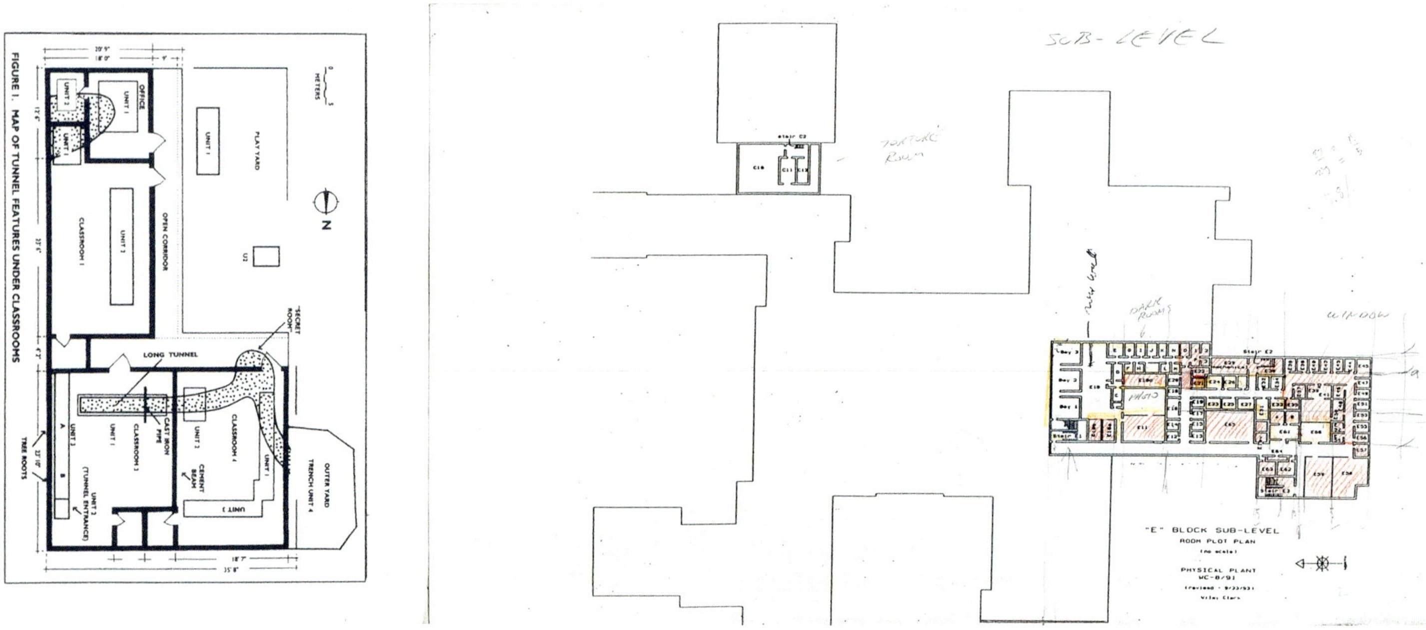

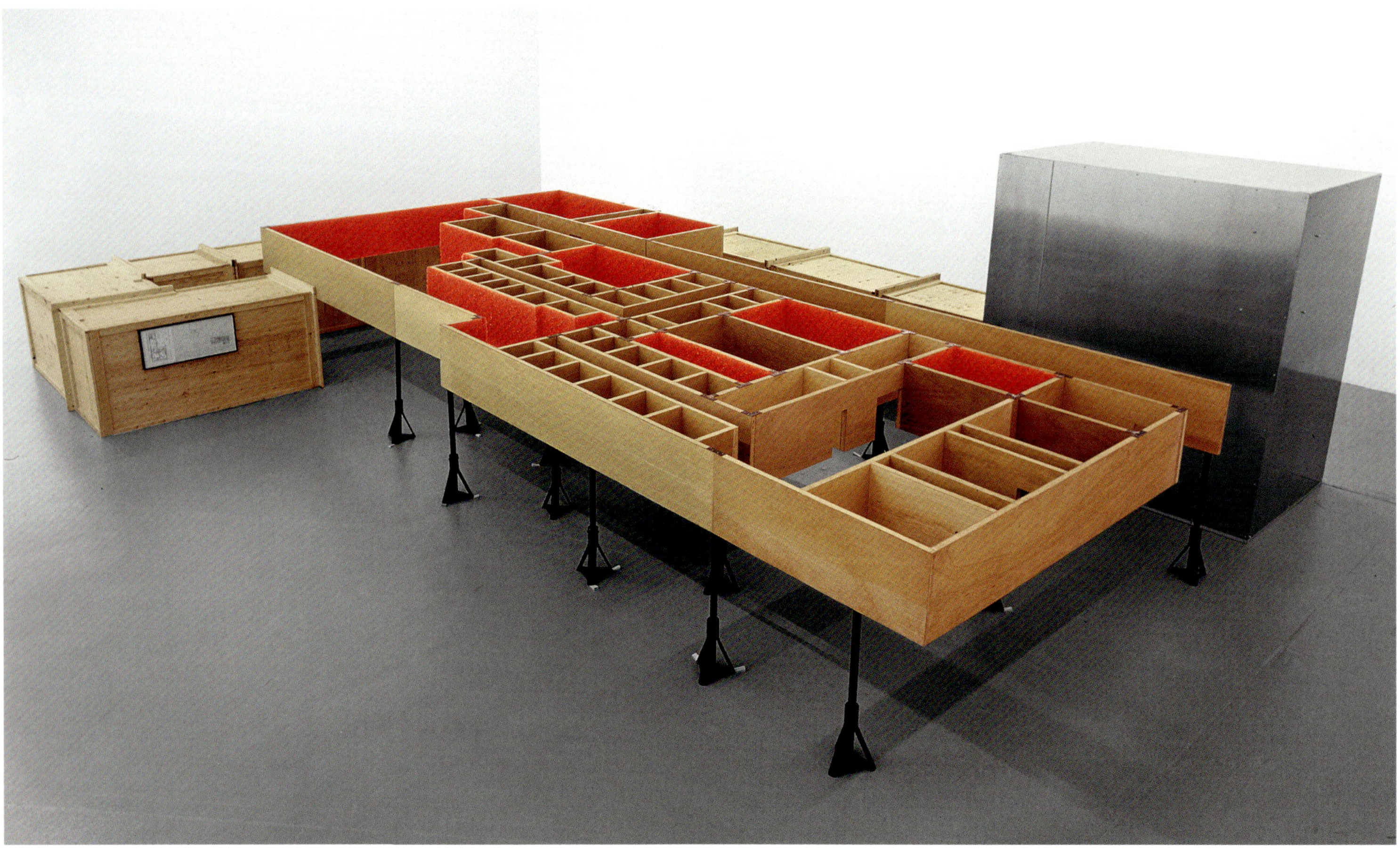

Fig. 71. Mike Kelley, *Sublevel*, 1998, detail of collage showing the McMartin Preschool floor plan incorporating a map of the suspected tunnels underneath, and the layout of the CalArts sublevel

Fig. 72. Mike Kelley, *Sublevel,* 1998. Plywood, resin, car jacks, and steel, 84⅝ × 324¼ × 233 in. (215 × 824 × 592 cm)

the lens of architecture. "Toward a Utopian Arts Complex," his 1995 exhibition at Metro Pictures, was centered around *Educational Complex* (1995; pp. 132–34 and figs. 67, 68), a large, tabletop array of ghostly white architectural models constructed of foam board that represents the seven sites, including his childhood home, where he received his training—both educational and sentimental. Kelley at first planned to construct the models entirely from memory but could not reconcile the interiors he barely recalled with their exteriors (1994; figs. 69, 70).

> It soon became apparent that my memories of the structures were so poor that it was impossible to generate three-dimensional models. My attempts at drawing floor plans resulted in incomprehensible sketches of disconnected rooms with no information about their spatial relationships. I was also incapable of placing them, roughly, within the approximate shapes of the building exteriors that I could recall. These thumbnail sketches were so formless that they defied architectural realization.[59]

Realizing that his complicated process of reconstituting spatial recollections was in some part a metonym for memory suppression, he decided to source images and architectural elevations of the various buildings but leave his modeled interiors more or less unresolved. In his words, these absences would represent those spaces that had been lost to memory suppression, lacunae "supposedly the result of some 'trauma' that occurred in those spots, which has caused me to repress them."[60]

Dominating the center of *Educational Complex* is the hulking, modernist structure of CalArts' main building, whose basement level falls below the table's surface and is visible only by peering underneath the installation (p. 134). By many accounts, this was a haunting space of labyrinthine, dimly lit corridors that, for Kelley, seemed the perfect analogy for the depths of psychic repression, not to mention a sinister parallel to the supposed caverns and subterranean tunnels where the McMartin Preschool employees supposedly enacted Satanic acts on their pupils. Kelley's later *Sublevel* (1998; fig. 71) makes this linkage literal by overlaying a basement floorplan of CalArts with a schematic drawing of the purported tunnels dug under the kindergarten for nefarious purposes. He also constructed a plywood maze installation that leads to a literal tunnel through which the visitor eventually emerges into a confining chamber full of dildos and other phallic implements (figs. 72, 73).

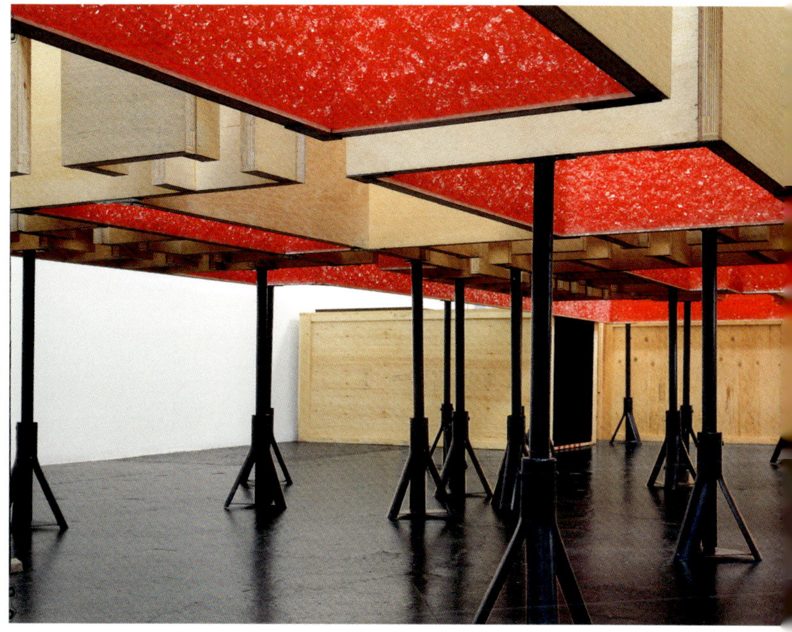

Fig. 73. Installation view of the tunnel entrance of Mike Kelley's *Sublevel*, Jablonka Galerie, Cologne, 1998

Kelley's work from the late 1990s, like that of many of the artists discussed in this book, plays a brilliant double-game. A case in point is his *Abuse Report* (1995; p. 135), a blown-up copy of a California Department of Justice form used to report suspected child abuse, wherein the abused is the artist and the abuser is painter and educator Hans Hofmann, whom Kelley explicitly condemns for his theory of "Push-Pull," one of the founding justifications for abstraction's dominance over figurative painting. Like so many related projects in the exhibition by Kelley and his cohort, *Abuse Report* aims to document purported traumas, both real and imaginary (art education, the justice system, childhood abuse), using institutional language or governmental mechanisms. These are some of the very mechanisms, however, through which the actual reportage of real abuses becomes unwieldy (or perhaps entirely unmanageable), especially as it enters the public eye through the media or government intervention. In response to these mechanisms—shadow governments, the economic inequities of capitalism, the use of evangelical religious fervor or the so-called moral majority as cover for true injustices and disenfranchisement—these artists uncover all the kitschy ghosts, zombies, and aliens hidden in plain sight in the spirit of speaking truth to power.

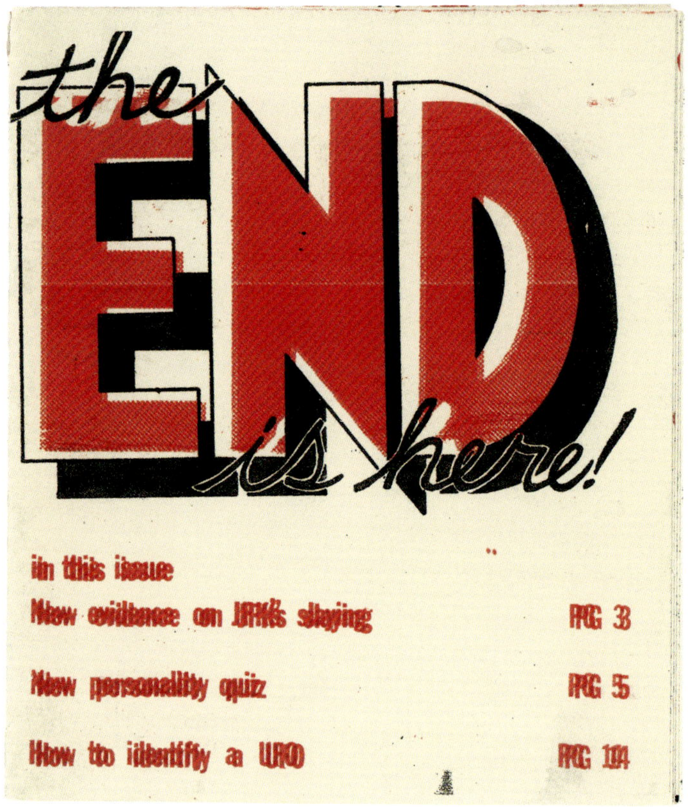

the END is here!

in this issue

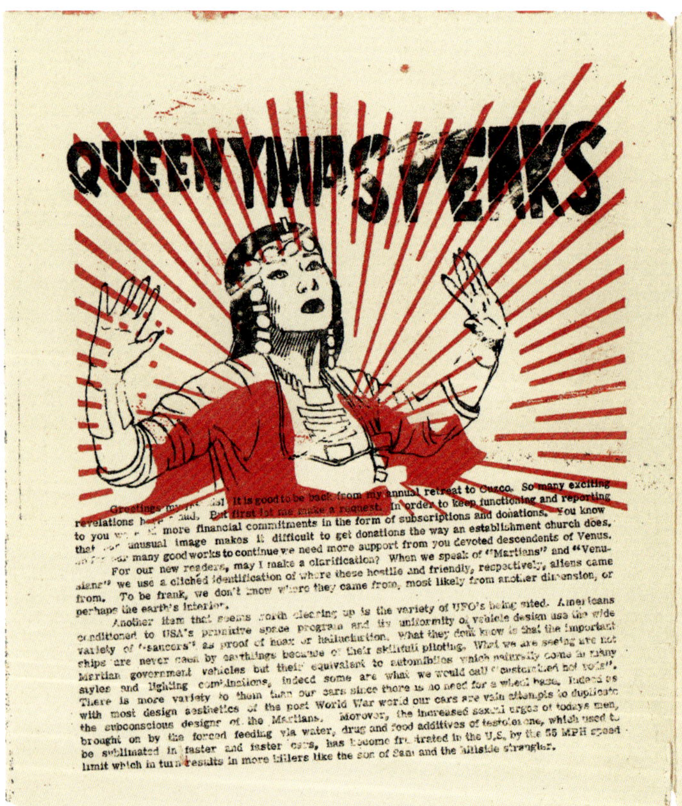

QUEEN YMP'S PERKS

Greetings my [illegible] It is good to be back from my annual retreat to Cuzco. So many exciting revelations [illegible] But first let me make a request. In order to keep functioning and reporting to you [illegible] more financial commitments in the form of subscriptions and donations. You know that [illegible] unusual image makes it difficult to get donations the way an establishment church does. [illegible] many good works to continue we need more support from you devoted descendents of Venus.

For our new readers, may I make a clarification? When we speak of "Martians" and "Venusians" we use a clichéd identification of where these hostile and friendly, respectively, aliens came from. To be frank, we don't know where they came from, most likely from another dimension, or perhaps the earth's interior.

Another item that seems worth clearing up is the variety of UFO's being sited. Americans conditioned to USA's primitive space program and the uniformity of vehicle design use the wide variety of "saucers" as proof of hoax or hallucination. What they don't know is that the important ships are never seen by earthlings because of their skillful piloting. What we are seeing are not Martian government vehicles but their equivalent to automobiles which naturally come in many styles and lighting combinations, indeed some are what we would call "customized hot rods". There is more variety to them than our cars since there is no need for a wheel base. Indeed as with most design aesthetics of the post World War world our cars are vain attempts to duplicate the subconscious designs of the Martians. Morover, the increased sexual urges of todays men, brought on by the forced feeding via water, drug and food additives of testosterone, which used to be sublimated in faster and faster cars, has become frustrated in the U.S. by the 55 MPH speed limit which in turn results in more killers like the son of Sam and the hillside strangler.

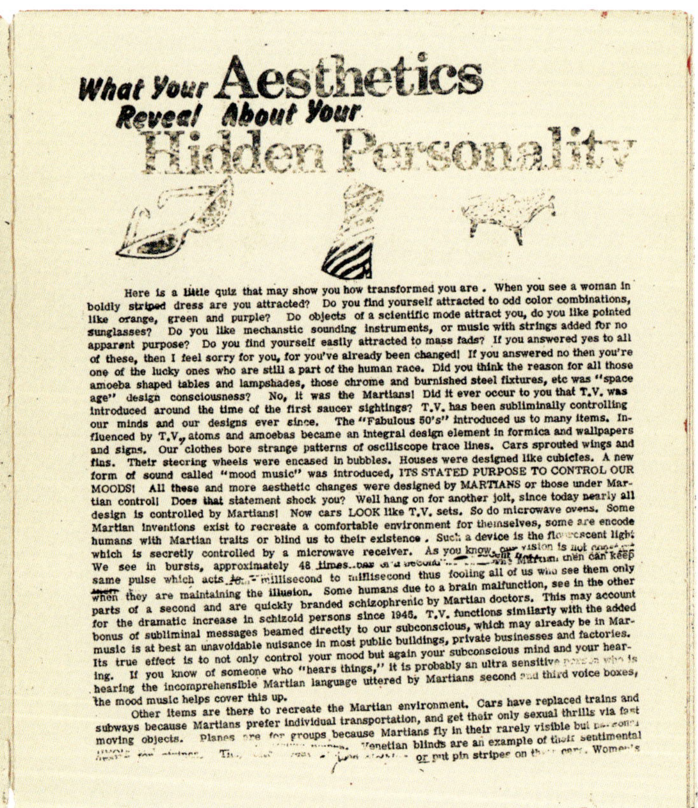

What Your Aesthetics Reveal About Your Hidden Personality

Here is a little quiz that may show you how transformed you are . When you see a woman in boldly striped dress are you attracted? Do you find yourself attracted to odd color combinations, like orange, green and purple? Do objects of a scientific mode attract you, do you like pointed sunglasses? Do you like mechanstic sounding instruments, or music with strings added for no apparent purpose? Do you find yourself easily attracted to mass fads? If you answered yes to all of these, then I feel sorry for you, for you've already been changed! If you answered no then you're one of the lucky ones who are still a part of the human race. Did you think the reason for all those amoeba shaped tables and lampshades, those chrome and burnished steel fixtures, etc was "space age" design consciousness? No, it was the Martians! Did it ever occur to you that T.V. was introduced around the time of the first saucer sightings? T.V. has been subliminally controlling our minds and our designs ever since. The "Fabulous 50's" introduced us to many items. Influenced by T.V., atoms and amoebas became an integral design element in formica and wallpapers and signs. Our clothes bore strange patterns of oscilliscope trace lines. Cars sprouted wings and fins. Their steering wheels were encased in bubbles. Houses were designed like cubicles. A new form of sound called "mood music" was introduced, ITS STATED PURPOSE TO CONTROL OUR MOODS! All these and more aesthetic changes were designed by MARTIANS or those under Martian control! Does that statement shock you? Well hang on for another jolt, since today nearly all design is controlled by Martians! Now cars LOOK like T.V. sets. So do microwave ovens. Some Martian inventions exist to recreate a comfortable environment for themselves, some are encode humans with Martian traits or blind us to their existence . Such a device is the flourescent light which is secretly controlled by a microwave receiver. As you know, our vision is not [illegible] We see in bursts, approximately 48 times [illegible] Martians then can keep same pulse which acts [illegible] millisecond to millisecond thus fooling all of us who see them only when they are maintaining the illusion. Some humans due to a brain malfunction, see in the other parts of a second and are quickly branded schizophrenic by Martian doctors. This may account for the dramatic increase in schizoid persons since 1946. T.V. functions similarly with the added bonus of subliminal messages beamed directly to our subconscious, which may already be in Martian control. Mood music is at best an unavoidable nuisance in most public buildings, private businesses and factories. Its true effect is to not only control your mood but again your subconscious mind and your hearing. If you know of someone who "hears things," it is probably an ultra sensitive person who is hearing the incomprehensible Martian language uttered by Martians second and third voice boxes, the mood music helps cover this up.

Other items are there to recreate the Martian environment. Cars have replaced trains and subways because Martians prefer individual transportation, and get their only sexual thrills via fast moving objects. Planes are for groups because Martians fly in their rarely visible but [illegible] Venetian blinds are an example of their sentimental [illegible] or put pin stripes on their cars. Women's

Details of Jim Shaw, *The End Is Here*, 1978

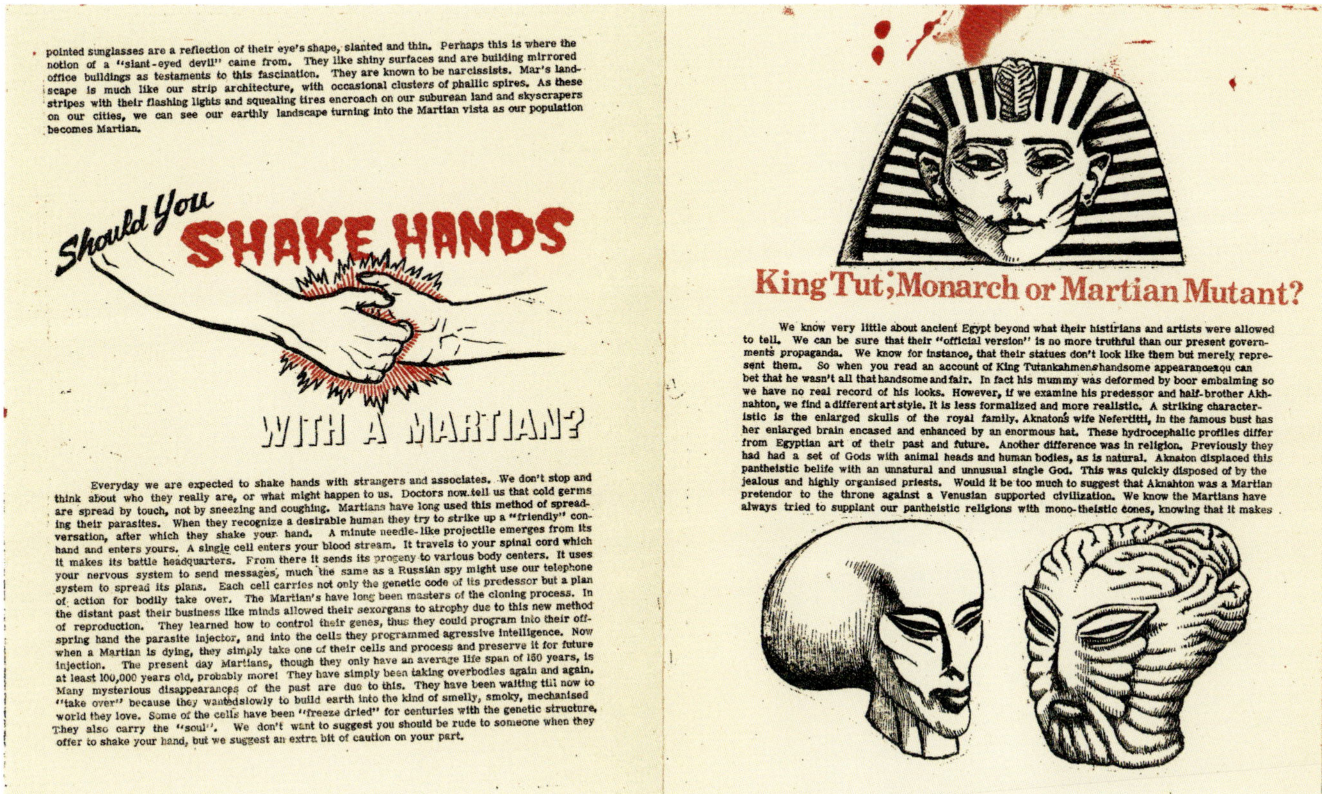

pointed sunglasses are a reflection of their eye's shape, slanted and thin. Perhaps this is where the notion of a "slant-eyed devil" came from. They like shiny surfaces and are building mirrored office buildings as testaments to this fascination. They are known to be narcissists. Mar's landscape is much like our strip architecture, with occasional clusters of phallic spires. As these stripes with their flashing lights and squealing tires encroach on our suburean land and skyscrapers on our cities, we can see our earthly landscape turning into the Martian vista as our population becomes Martian.

Should You SHAKE HANDS WITH A MARTIAN?

Everyday we are expected to shake hands with strangers and associates. We don't stop and think about who they really are, or what might happen to us. Doctors now tell us that cold germs are spread by touch, not by sneezing and coughing. Martians have long used this method of spreading their parasites. When they recognize a desirable human they try to strike up a "friendly" conversation, after which they shake your hand. A minute needle-like projectile emerges from its hand and enters yours. A single cell enters your blood stream. It travels to your spinal cord which it makes its battle headquarters. From there it sends its progeny to various body centers. It uses your nervous system to send messages, much the same as a Russian spy might use our telephone system to spread its plans. Each cell carries not only the genetic code of its predessor but a plan of action for bodily take over. The Martian's have long been masters of the cloning process. In the distant past their business like minds allowed their sexorgans to atrophy due to this new method of reproduction. They learned how to control their genes, thus they could program into their offspring hand the parasite injector, and into the cells they programmed agressive intelligence. Now when a Martian is dying, they simply take one of their cells and process and preserve it for future injection. The present day Martians, though they only have an average life span of 150 years, is at least 100,000 years old, probably more! They have simply been taking overbodies again and again. Many mysterious disappearances of the past are due to this. They have been waiting till now to "take over" because they wanted slowly to build earth into the kind of smelly, smoky, mechanised world they love. Some of the cells have been "freeze dried" for centuries with the genetic structure. They also carry the "soul". We don't want to suggest you should be rude to someone when they offer to shake your hand, but we suggest an extra bit of caution on your part.

King Tut; Monarch or Martian Mutant?

We know very little about ancient Egypt beyond what their histirians and artists were allowed to tell. We can be sure that their "official version" is no more truthful than our present governments propaganda. We know for instance, that their statues don't look like them but merely represent them. So when you read an account of King Tutankahmens handsome appearance you can bet that he wasn't all that handsome and fair. In fact his mummy was deformed by boor embalming so we have no real record of his looks. However, if we examine his predessor and half-brother Akhnahton, we find a different art style. It is less formalized and more realistic. A striking characteristic is the enlarged skulls of the royal family. Aknaton's wife Nefertitti, in the famous bust has her enlarged brain encased and enhanced by an enormous hat. These hydrocephalic profiles differ from Egyptian art of their past and future. Another difference was in religion. Previously they had had a set of Gods with animal heads and human bodies, as is natural. Aknaton displaced this pantheistic belife with an unnatural and unnusual single God. This was quickly disposed of by the jealous and highly organised priests. Would it be too much to suggest that Aknahton was a Martian pretendor to the throne against a Venusian supported civilization. We know the Martians have always tried to supplant our pantheistic religions with mono-theistic cones, knowing that it makes

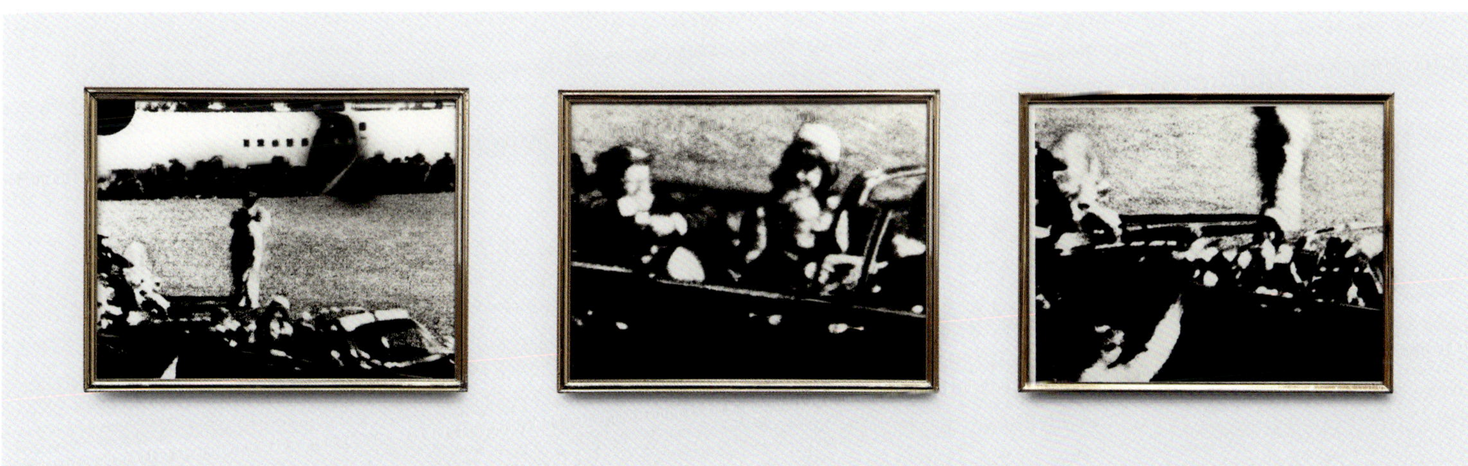

Jim Shaw, *UFO Photos: Zapruder Film*, 1978–92

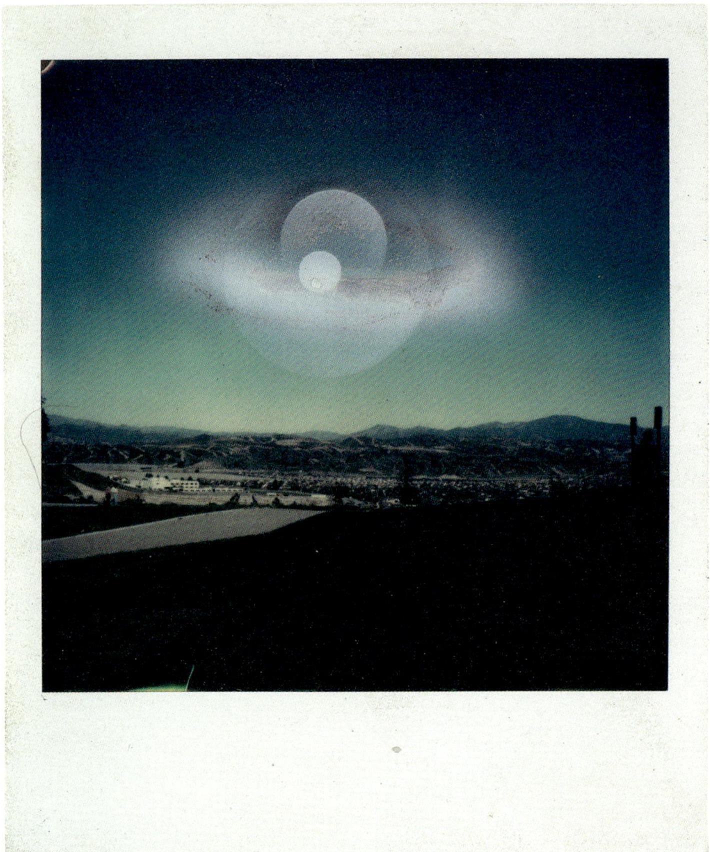

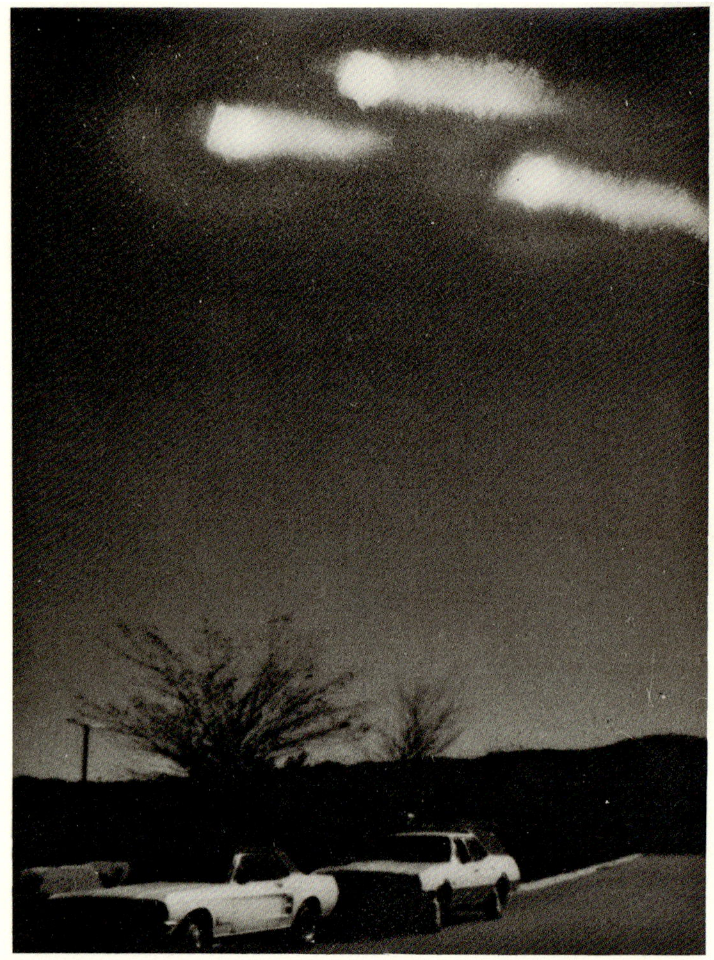

Jim Shaw, *UFO Polaroid* (from the UFO Photos Series), 1977

Jim Shaw, *UFO Photo* (from the UFO Photos Series), 1978

Jim Shaw, *Martian Portraits*, 1978

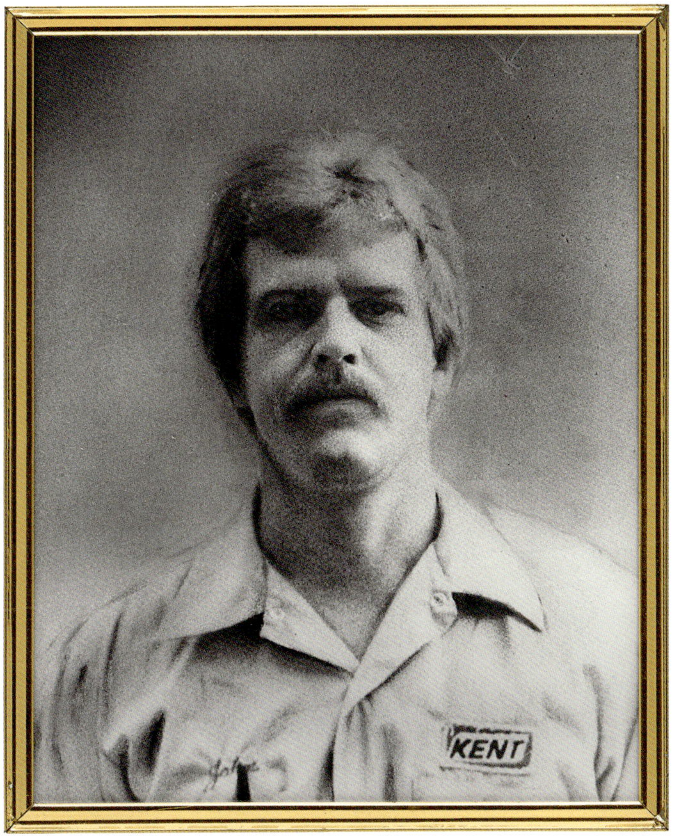
KENT

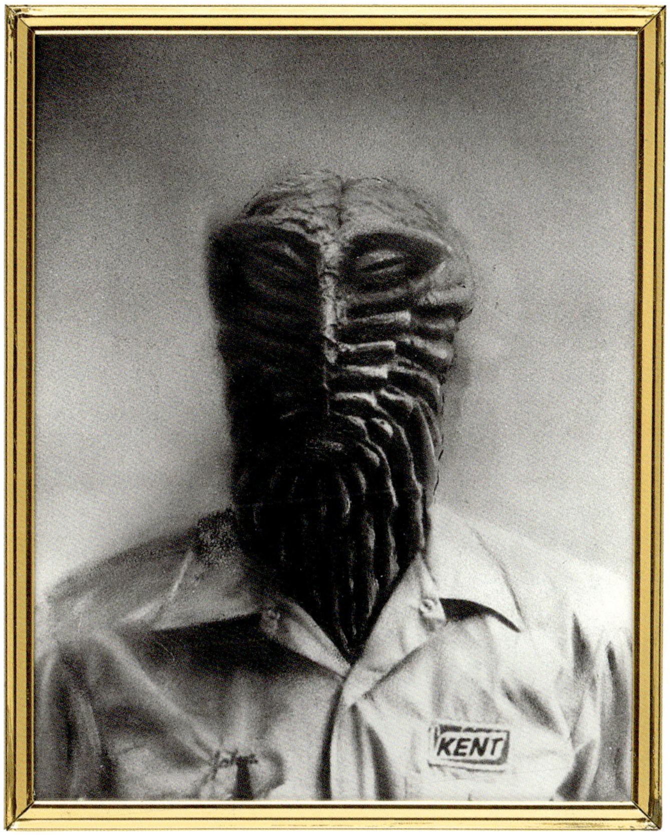
KENT

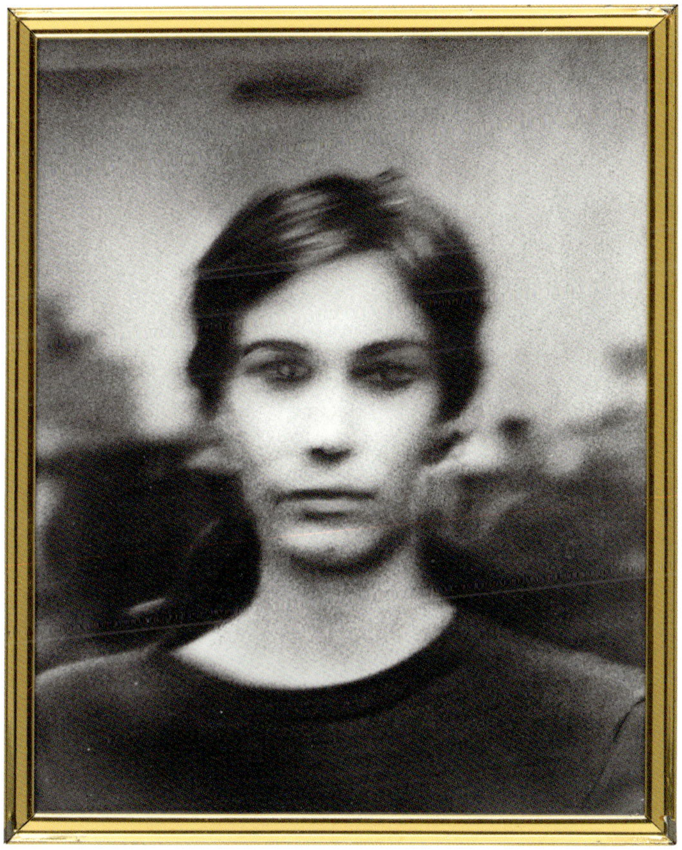

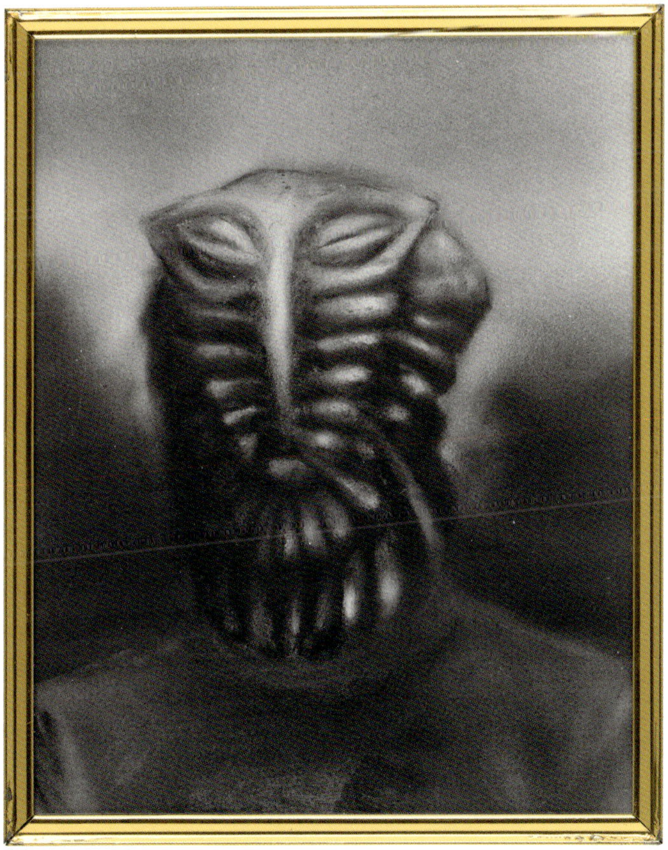

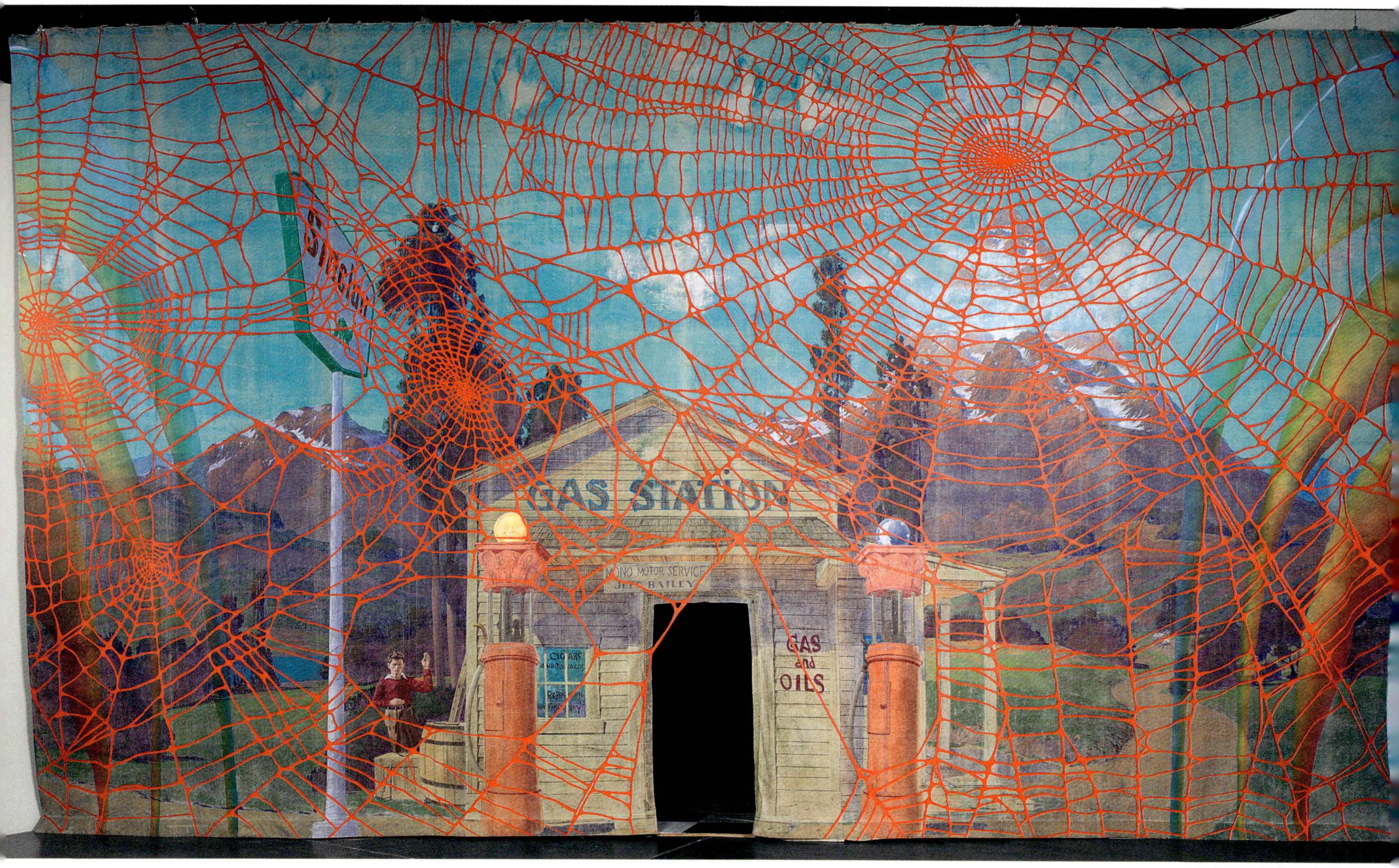

Jim Shaw, *The Miracle of Compound Interest*
(from the series Left Behind), 2006.
Installation view and details

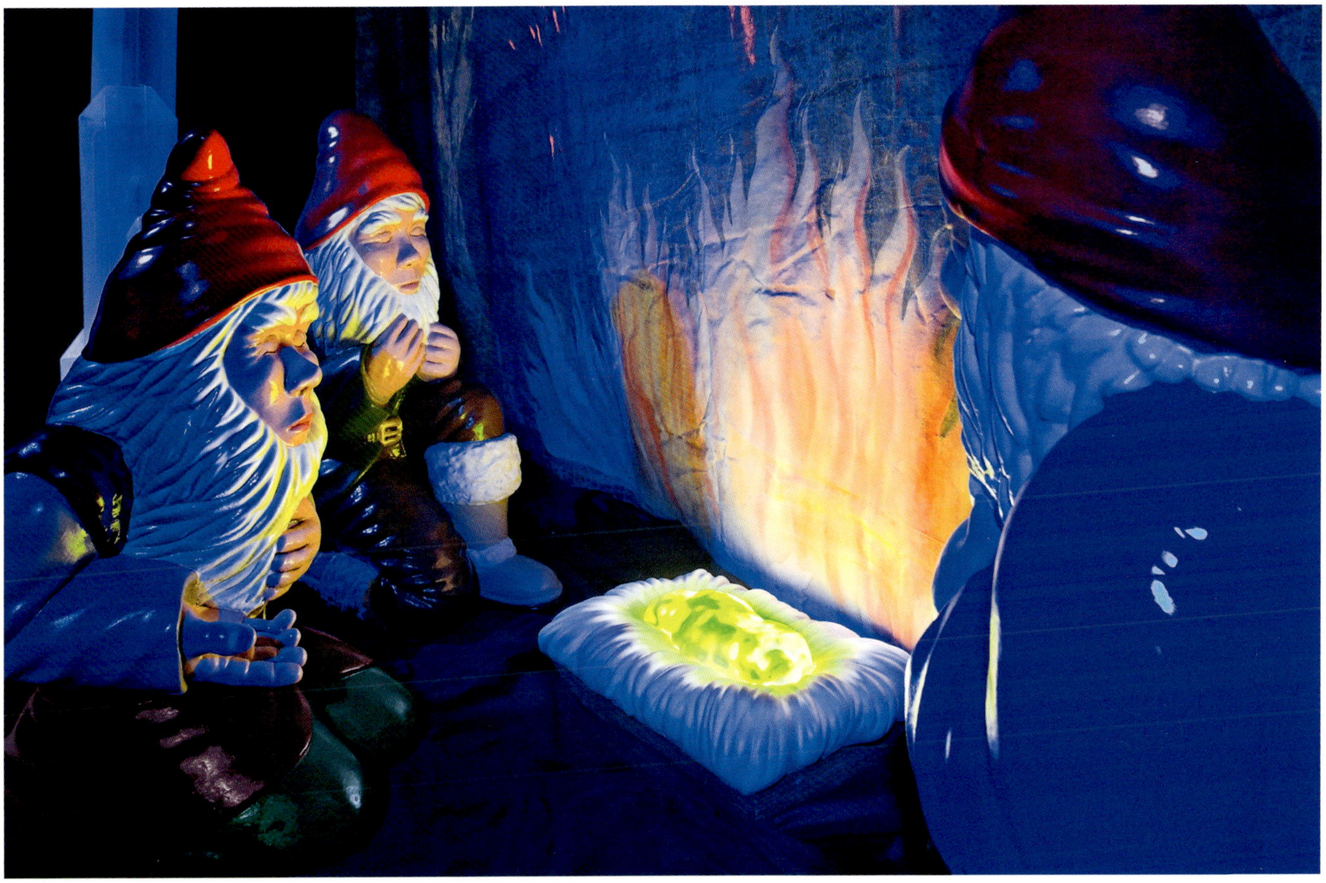

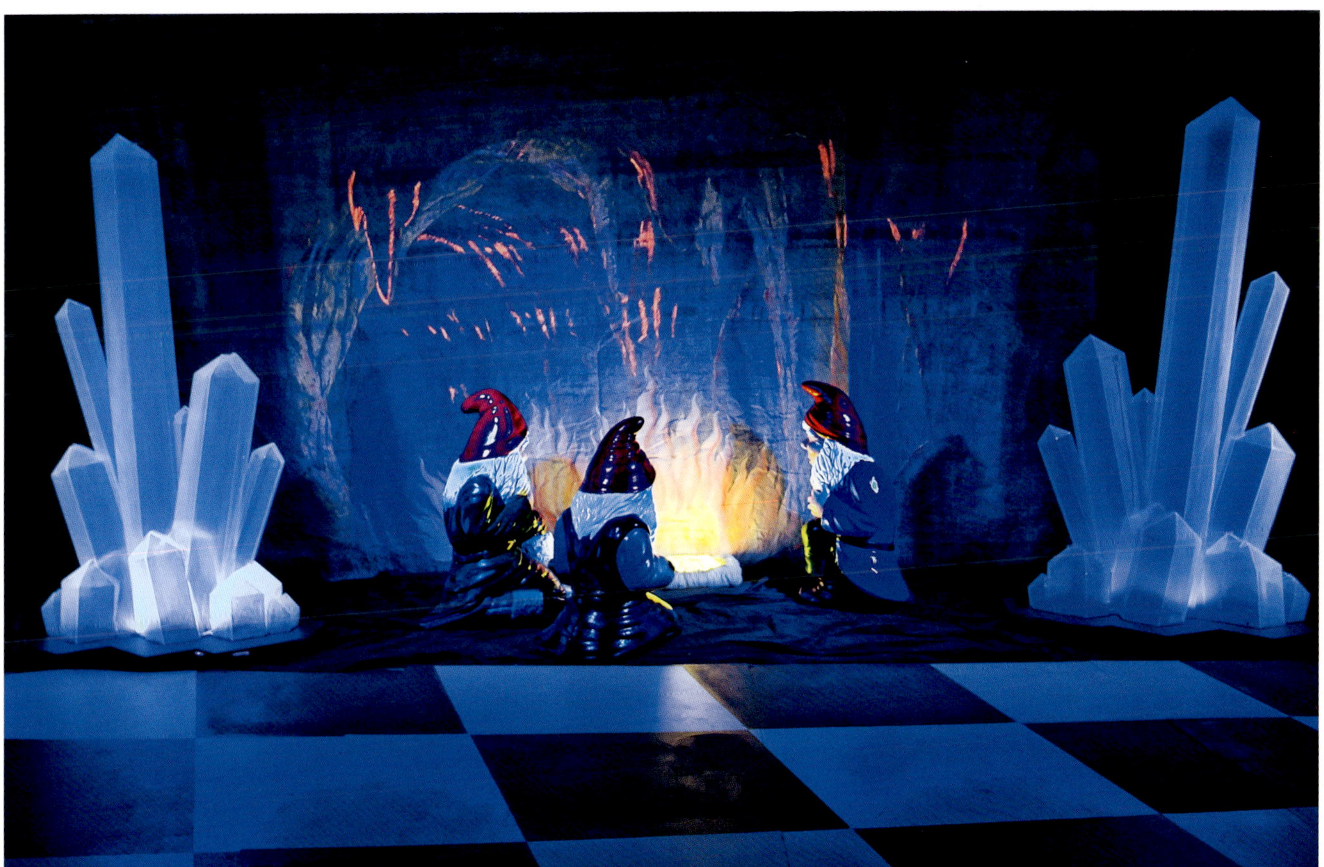

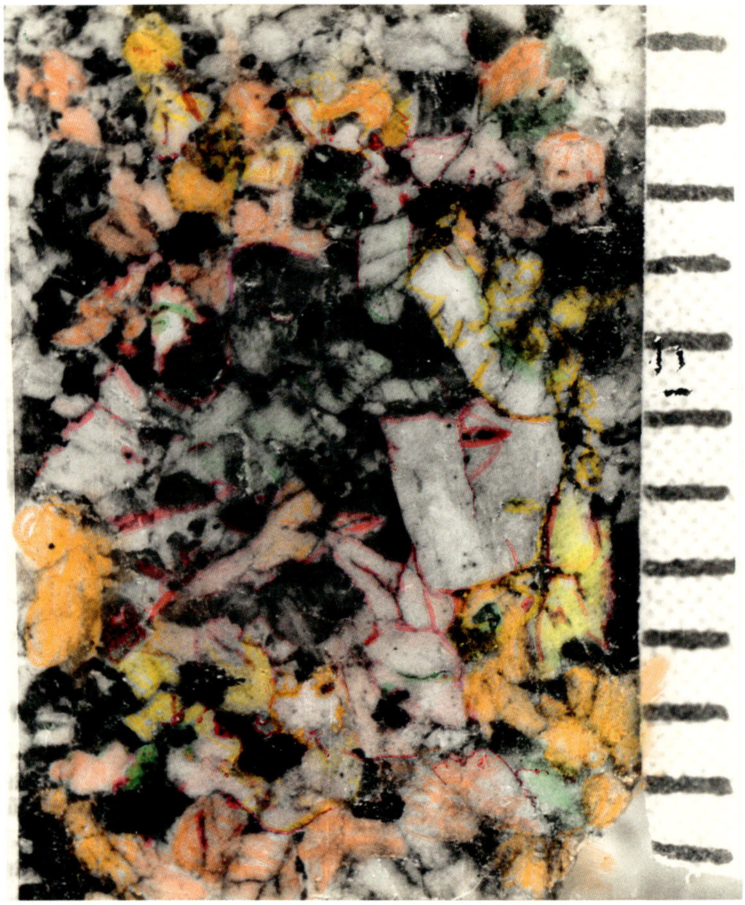

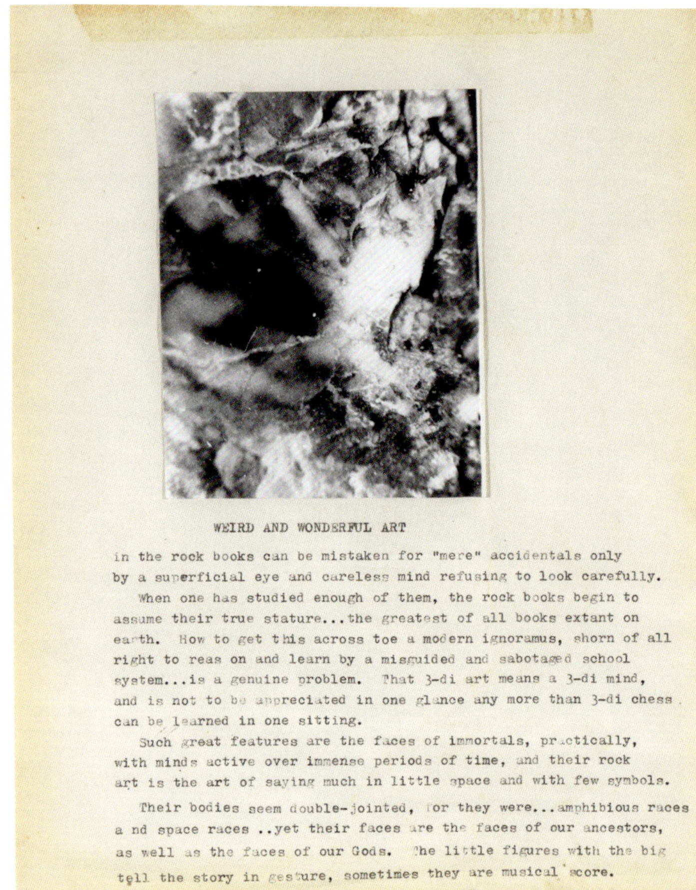

WEIRD AND WONDERFUL ART

in the rock books can be mistaken for "mere" accidentals only by a superficial eye and careless mind refusing to look carefully.

When one has studied enough of them, the rock books begin to assume their true stature...the greatest of all books extant on earth. How to get this across toe a modern ignoramus, shorn of all right to reas on and learn by a misguided and sabotaged school system...is a genuine problem. That 3-di art means a 3-di mind, and is not to be appreciated in one glance any more than 3-di chess can be learned in one sitting.

Such great features are the faces of immortals, practically, with minds active over immense periods of time, and their rock art is the art of saying much in little space and with few symbols.

Their bodies seem double-jointed, for they were...amphibious races a nd space races ..yet their faces are the faces of our ancestors, as well as the faces of our Gods. The little figures with the big tell the story in gesture, sometimes they are musical score.

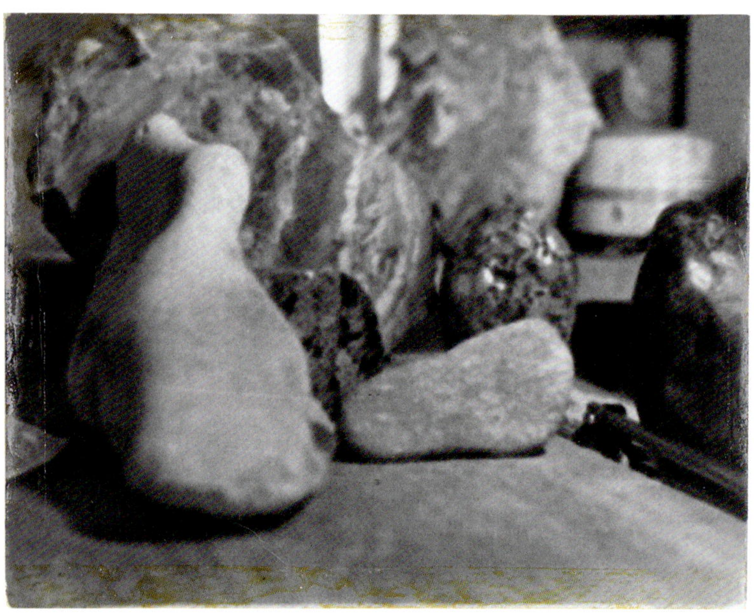

Richard Sharpe Shaver, *"Accenting a B&W print with colored pens gives you faces . . . ,"* ca. 1972

Richard Sharpe Shaver, *WEIRD AND WONDERFUL ART*, ca. 1970

Richard Sharpe Shaver, *Mer feet: "Mermaid show form for when they began to emerge onto land . . . ,"* date unknown

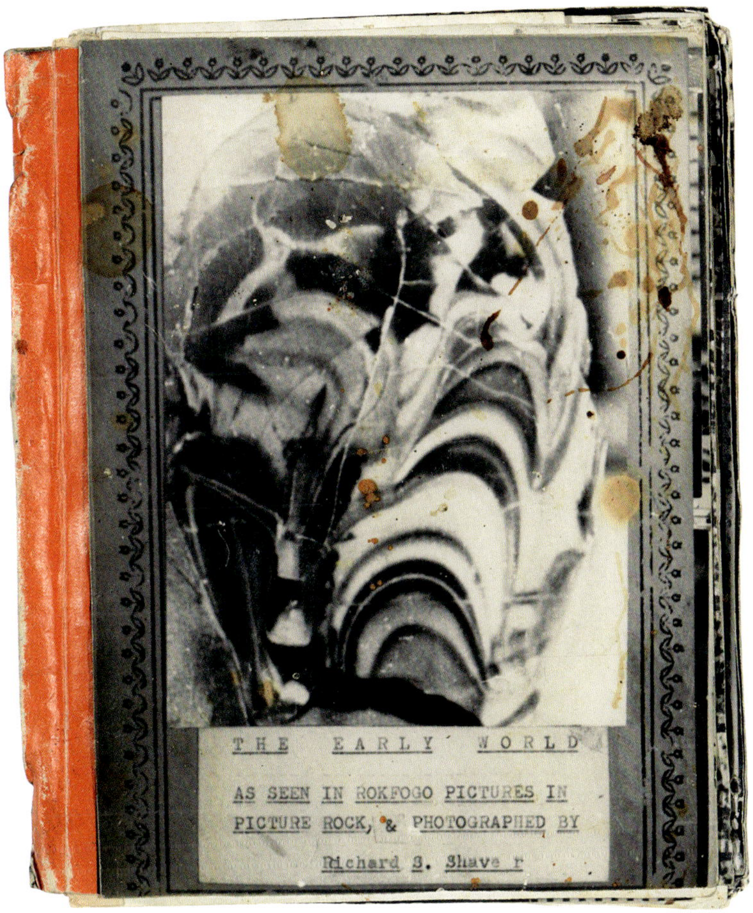

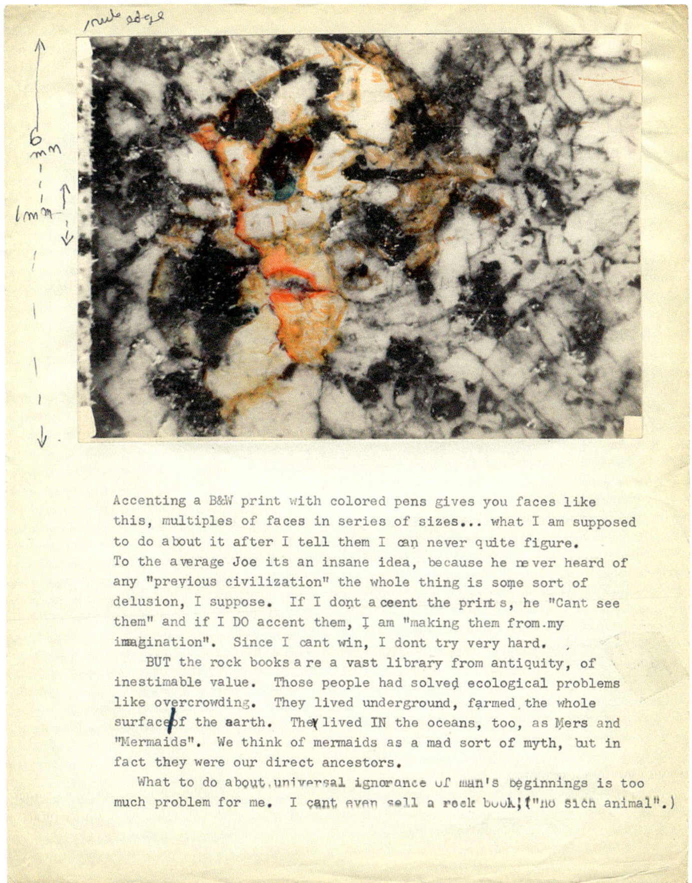

Accenting a B&W print with colored pens gives you faces like this, multiples of faces in series of sizes... what I am supposed to do about it after I tell them I can never quite figure.
To the average Joe its an insane idea, because he never heard of any "previous civilization" the whole thing is some sort of delusion, I suppose. If I dont accent the prints, he "Cant see them" and if I DO accent them, I am "making them from my imagination". Since I cant win, I dont try very hard.

BUT the rock books are a vast library from antiquity, of inestimable value. Those people had solved ecological problems like overcrowding. They lived underground, farmed the whole surface of the aarth. They lived IN the oceans, too, as Mers and "Mermaids". We think of mermaids as a mad sort of myth, but in fact they were our direct ancestors.

What to do about universal ignorance of man's beginnings is too much problem for me. I cant even sell a rock book! ("no such animal".)

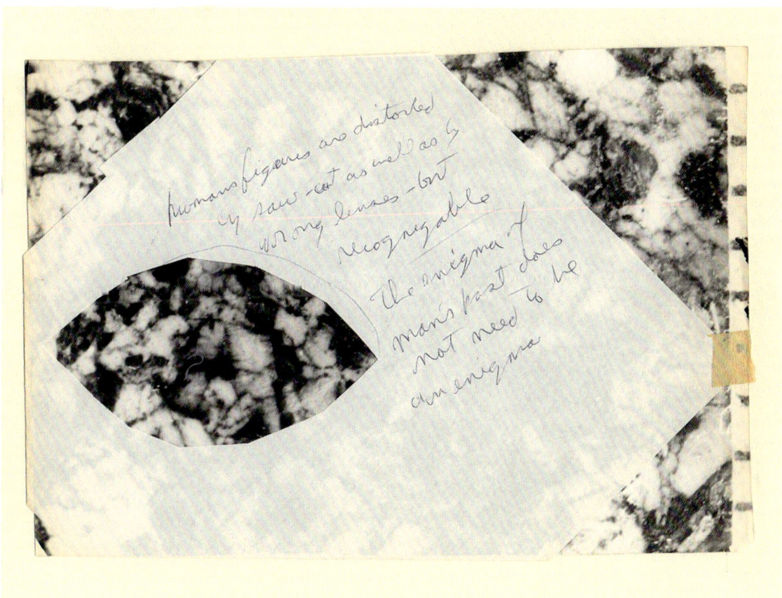

Richard Sharpe Shaver, *The Early World*, ca. 1970

Richard Sharpe Shaver, hand-colored *Rock Book* photo, ca. 1972

Richard Sharpe Shaver, *Human Figures Are Distorted . . .*, ca. 1972

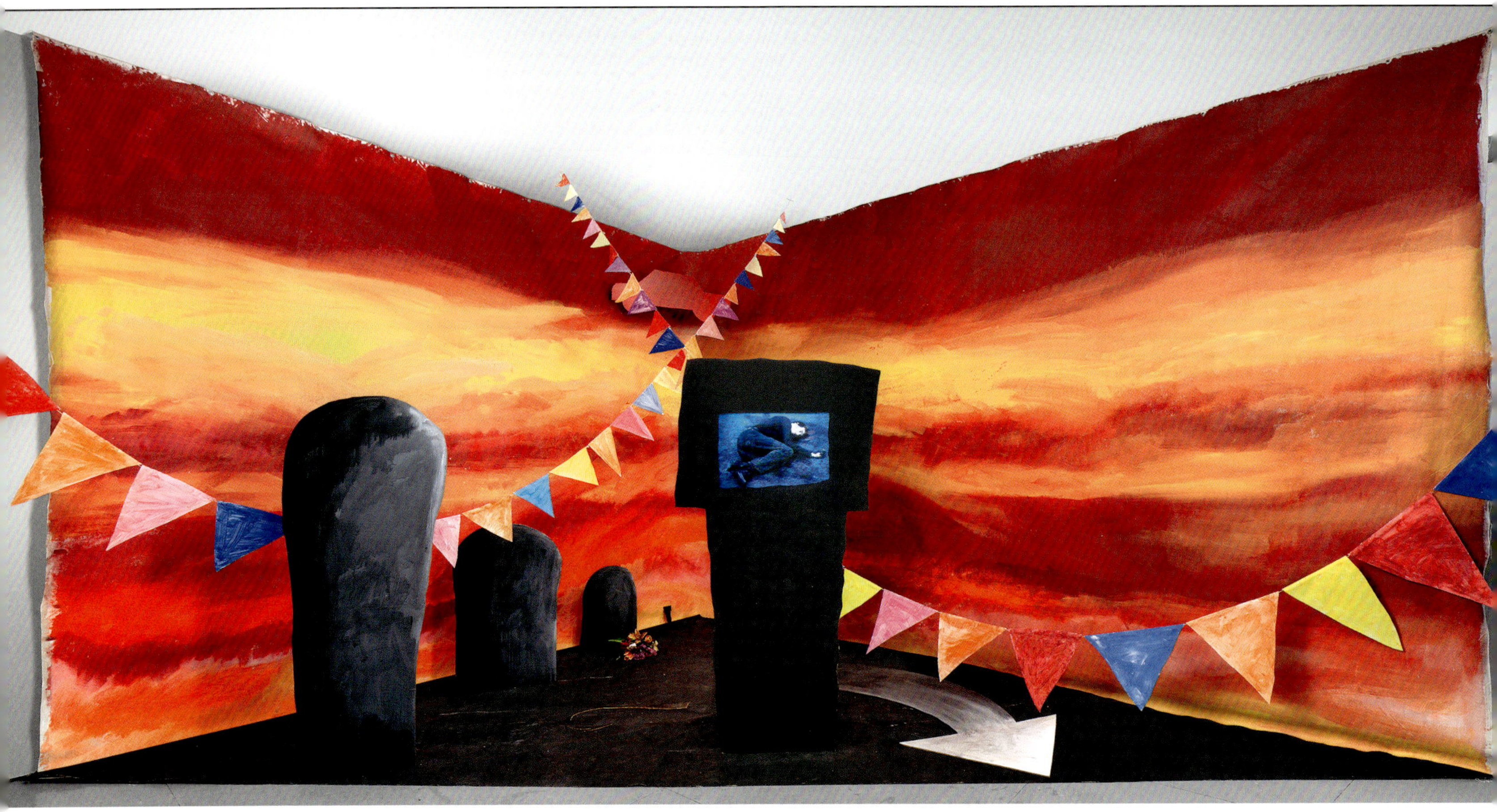

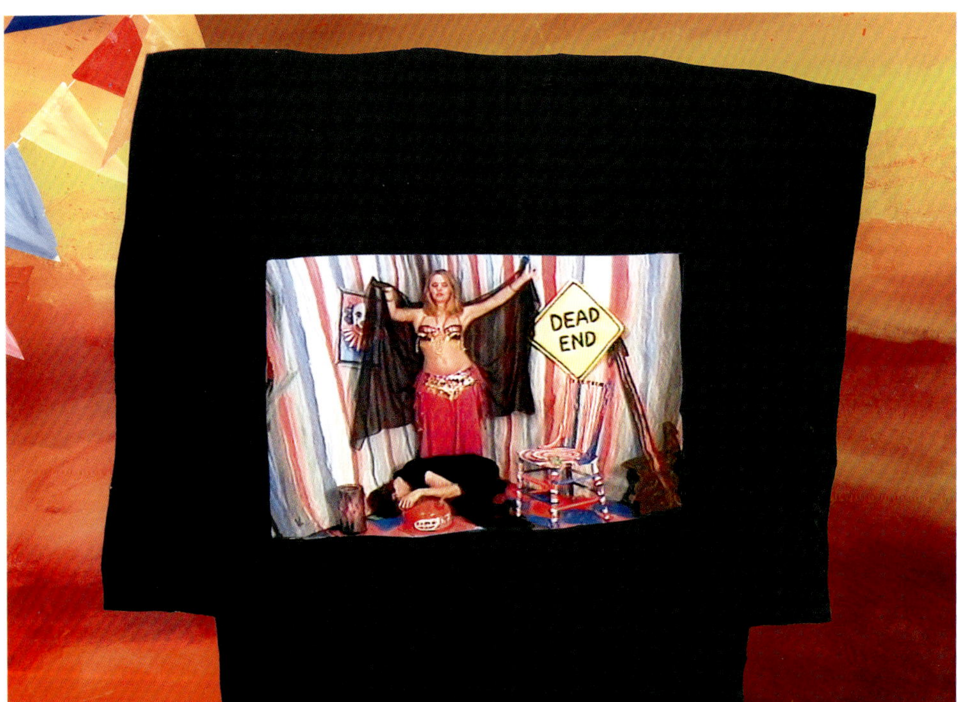

Tony Oursler, *Son of Oil*, 1982 (re-created 1999)

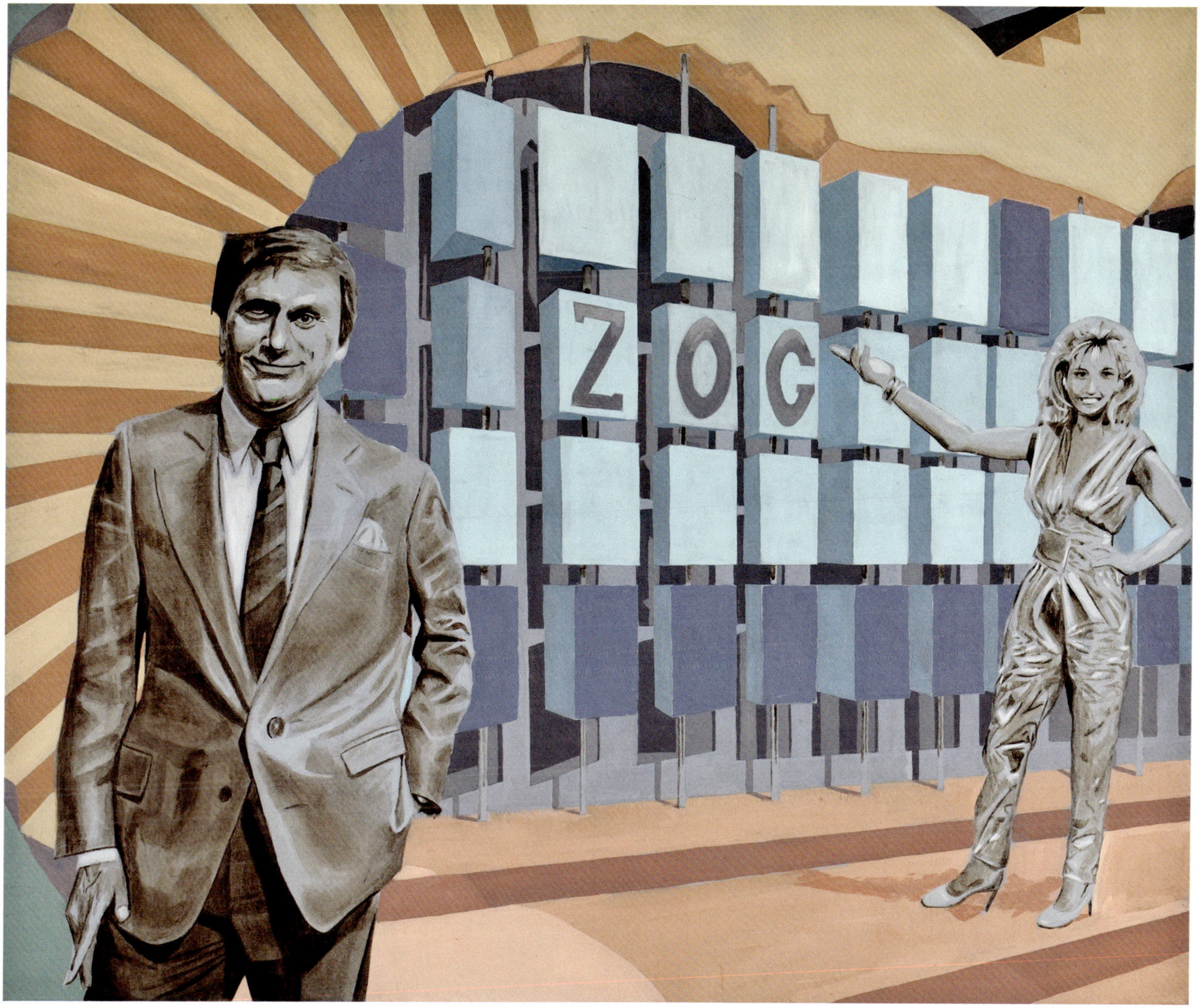

John Miller, *ZOG*, 1998

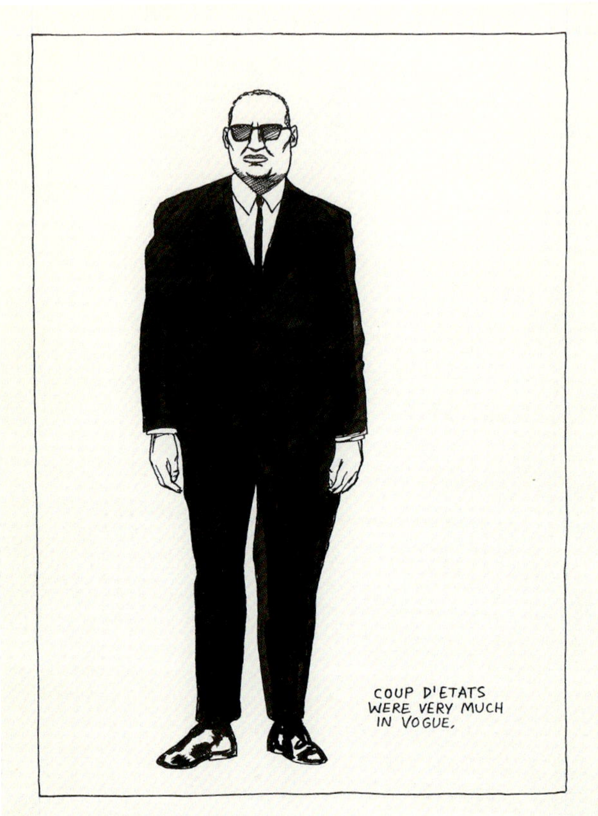

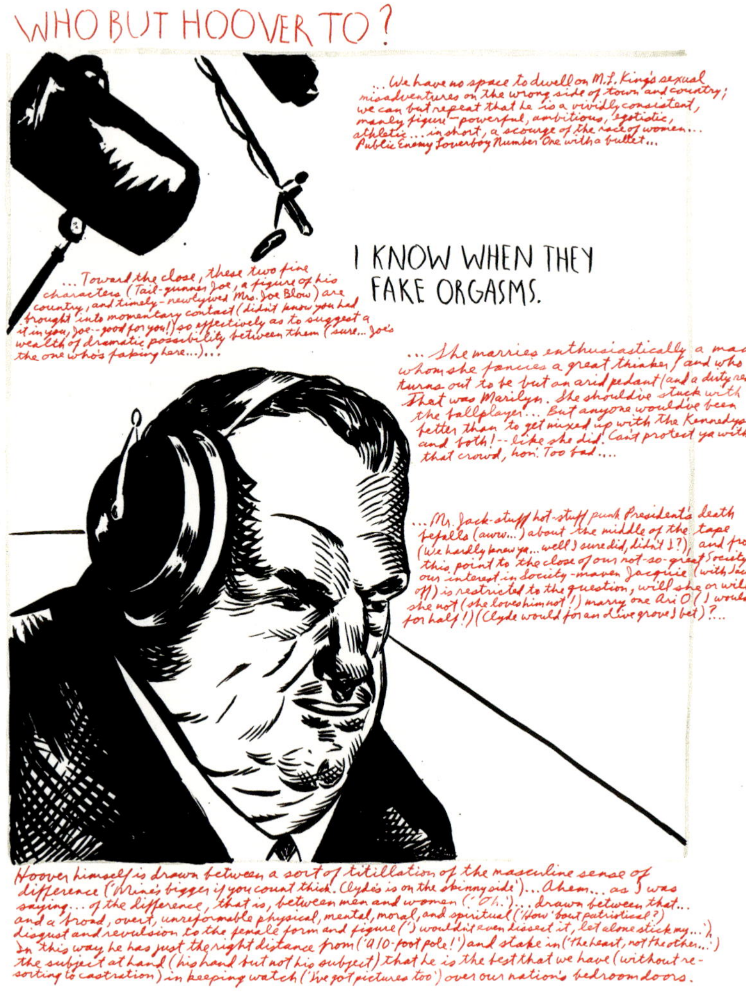

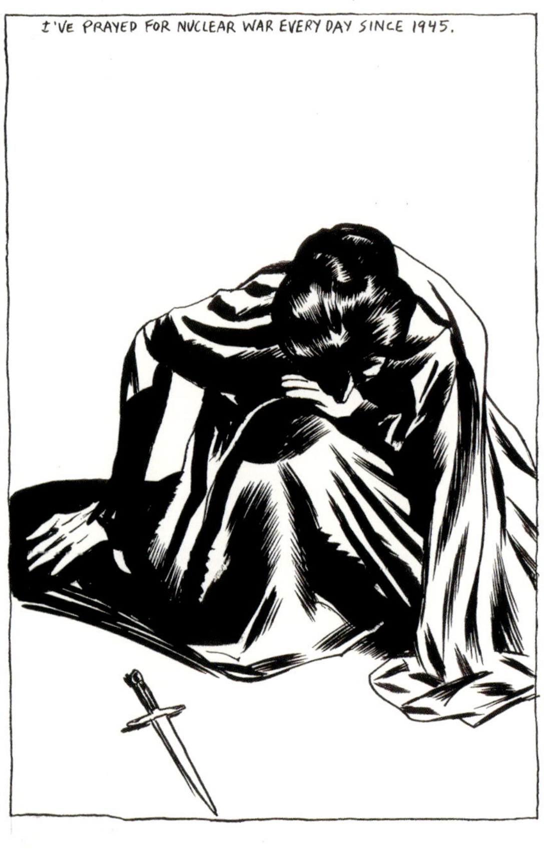

Raymond Pettibon, *No Title (Coup d'etats were . . .)*, 1984

Raymond Pettibon, *No Title (Who but Hoover . . .)*, 1991

Raymond Pettibon, *No Title (I've prayed . . .)*, 1984

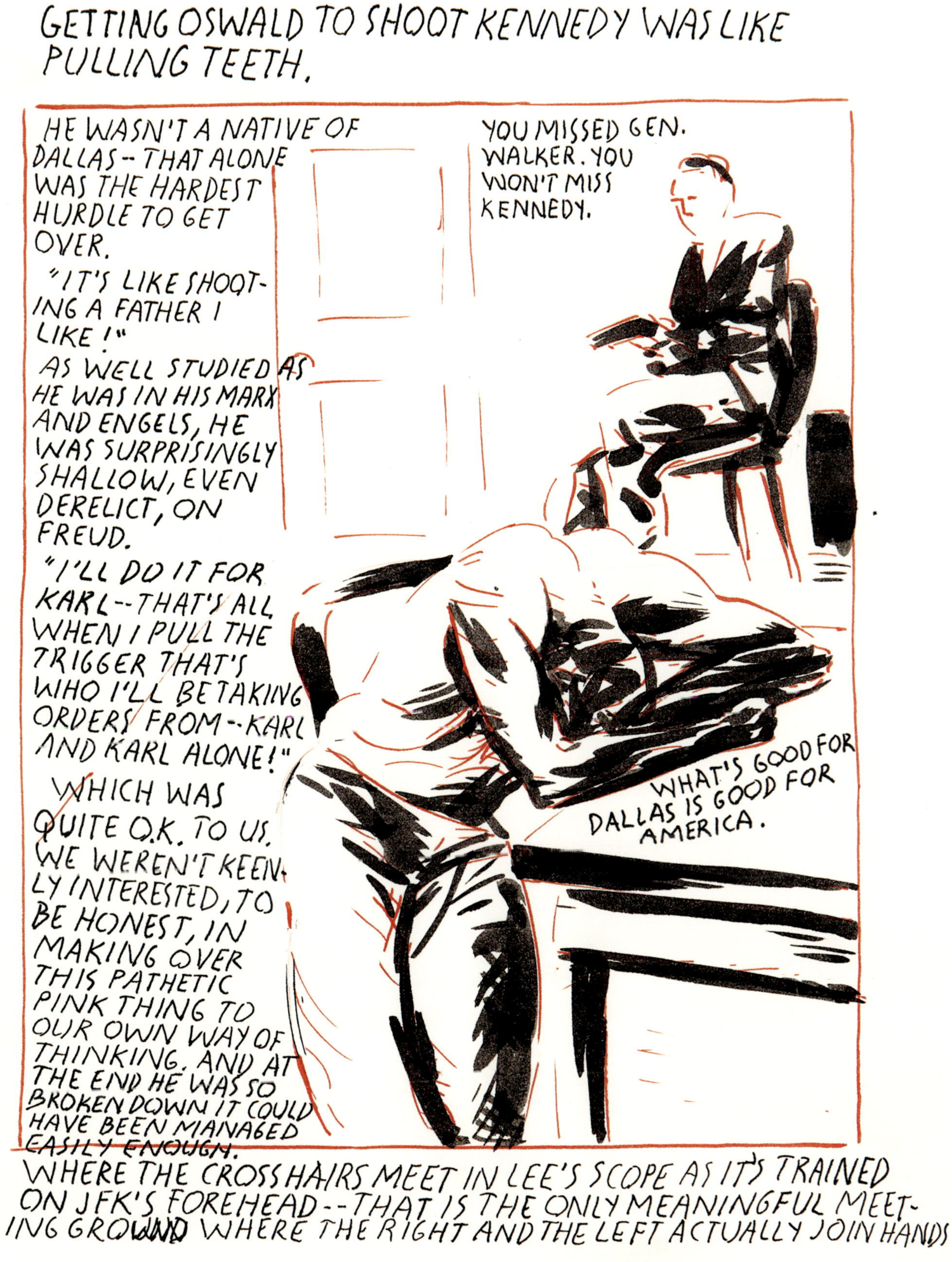

Raymond Pettibon, *Untitled (Getting Oswald To . . .)*, 1992

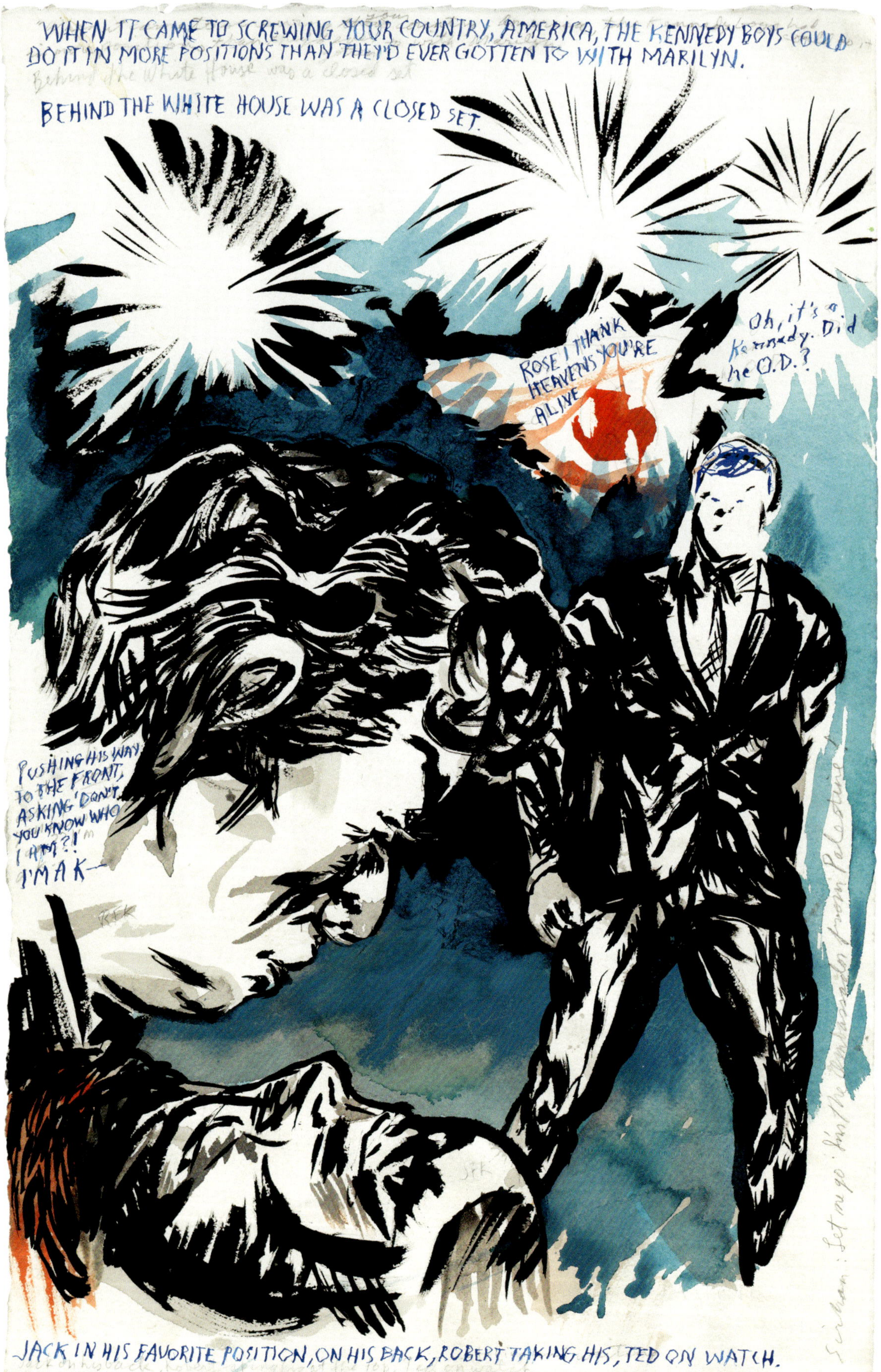
WHEN IT CAME TO SCREWING YOUR COUNTRY, AMERICA, THE KENNEDY BOYS COULD DO IT IN MORE POSITIONS THAN THEY'D EVER GOTTEN TO WITH MARILYN.
BEHIND THE WHITE HOUSE WAS A CLOSED SET.
ROSE I THINK HEAVENS YOU'RE ALIVE
Oh, it's a Kennedy. Did he O.D.?
PUSHING HIS WAY TO THE FRONT, ASKING 'DON'T YOU KNOW WHO I AM?!' I'M A K—
JACK IN HIS FAVORITE POSITION, ON HIS BACK, ROBERT TAKING HIS, TED ON WATCH.

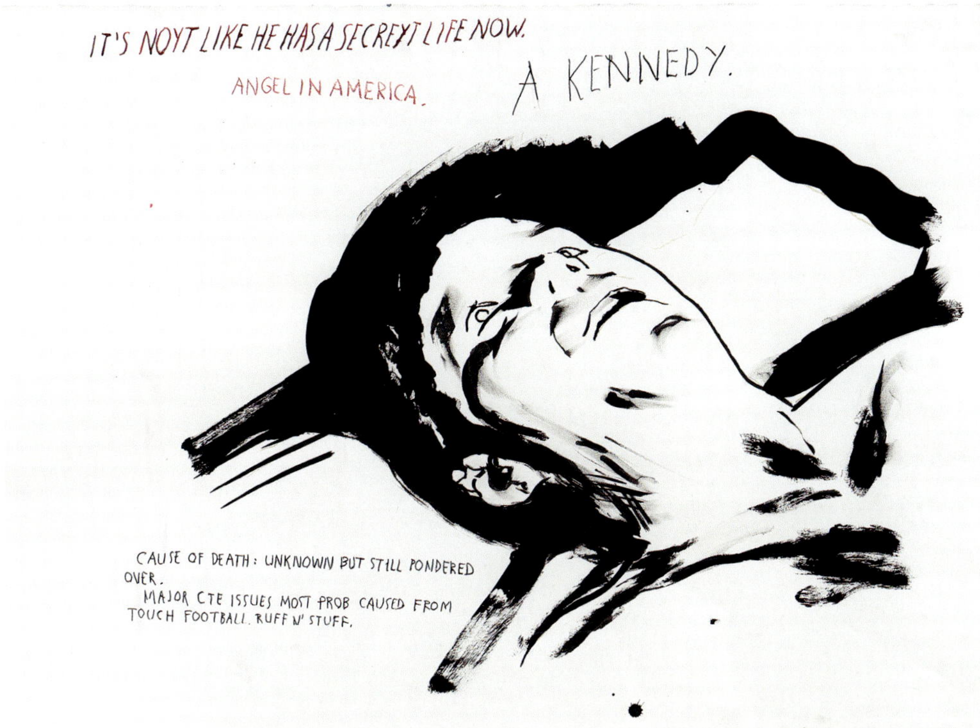

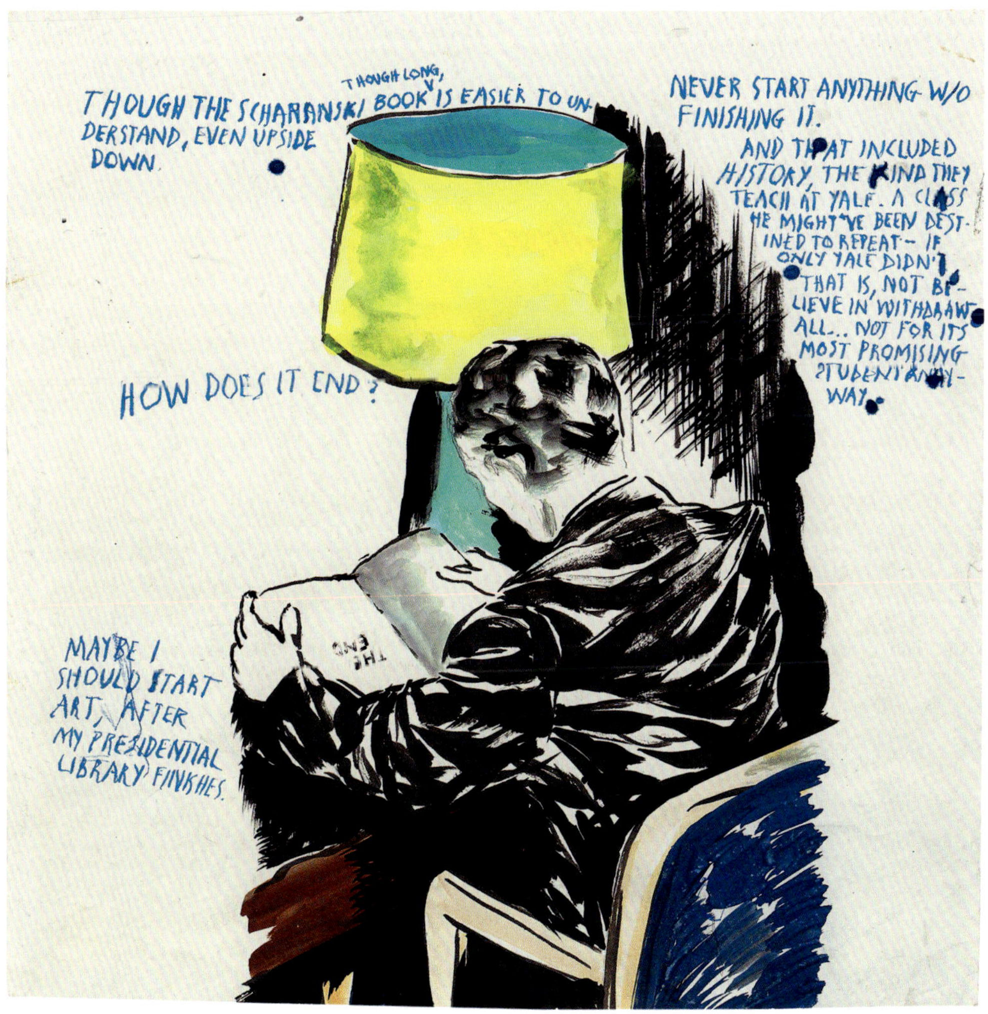

Raymond Pettibon, *No Title (When It Came . . .)*, 2002–17

Raymond Pettibon, *No Title (It's Noyt Like . . .)*, 2017

Raymond Pettibon, *No Title (Though the Scharanski . . .)*, 2017

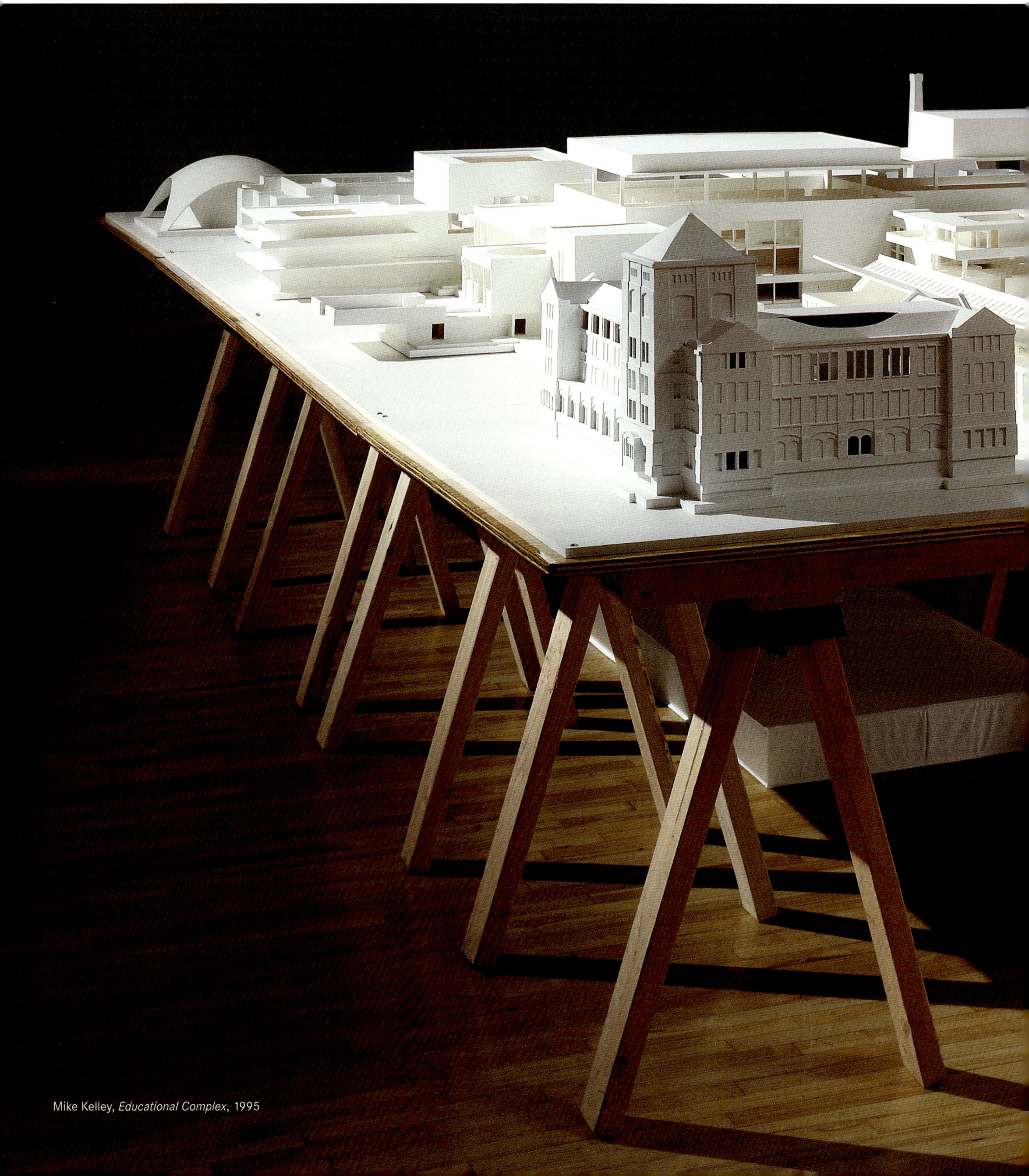

Mike Kelley, *Educational Complex*, 1995

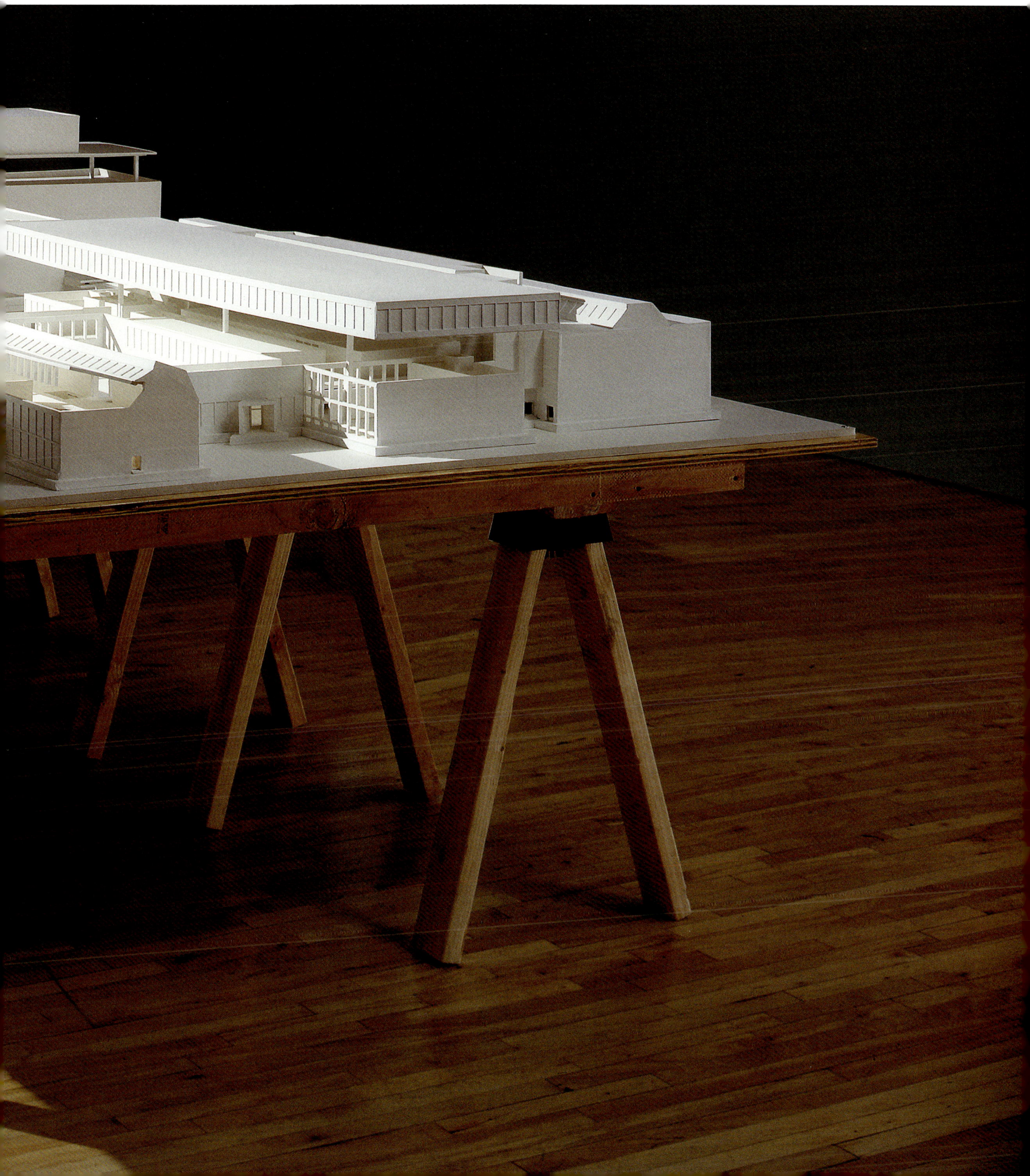

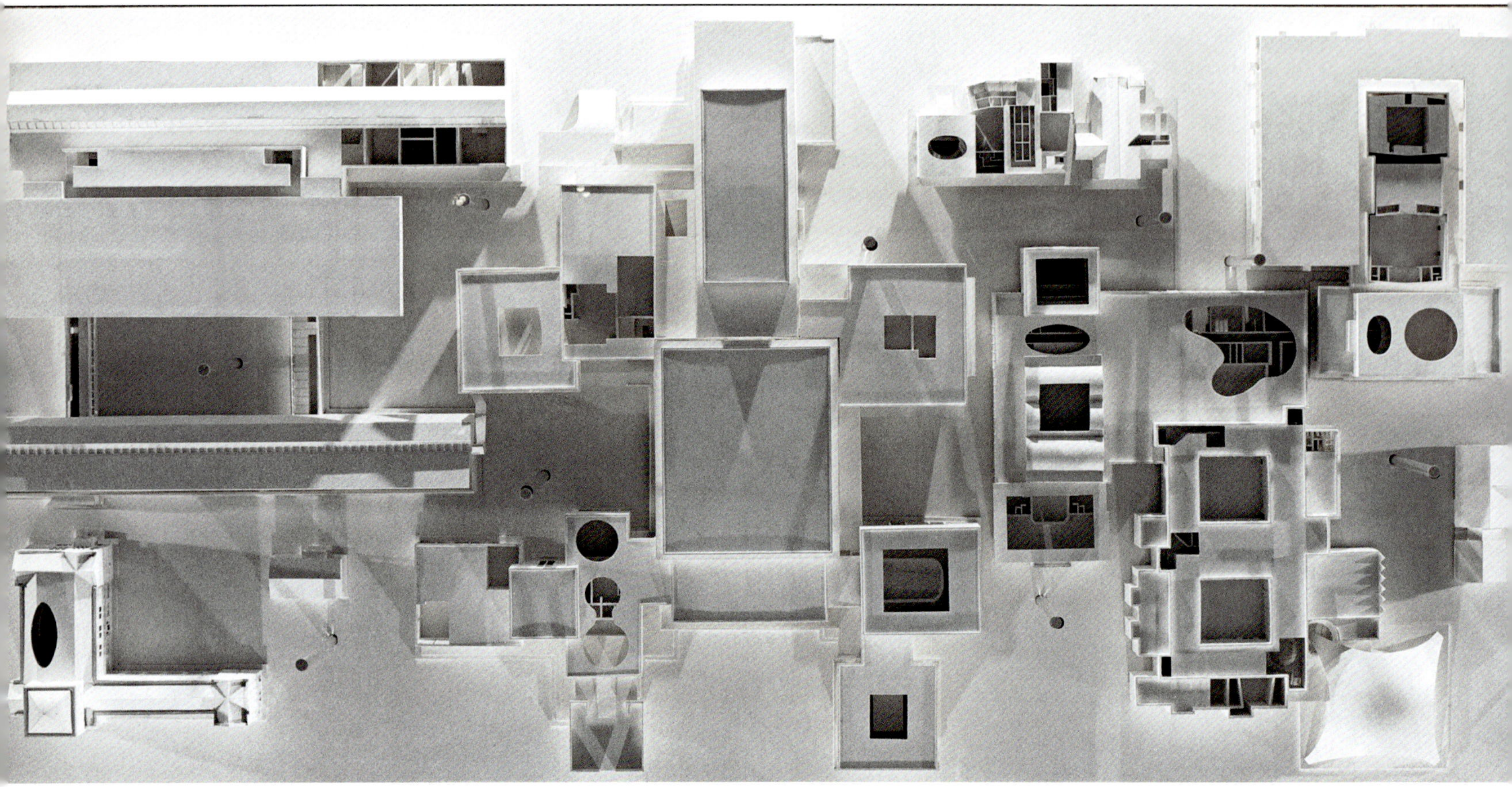

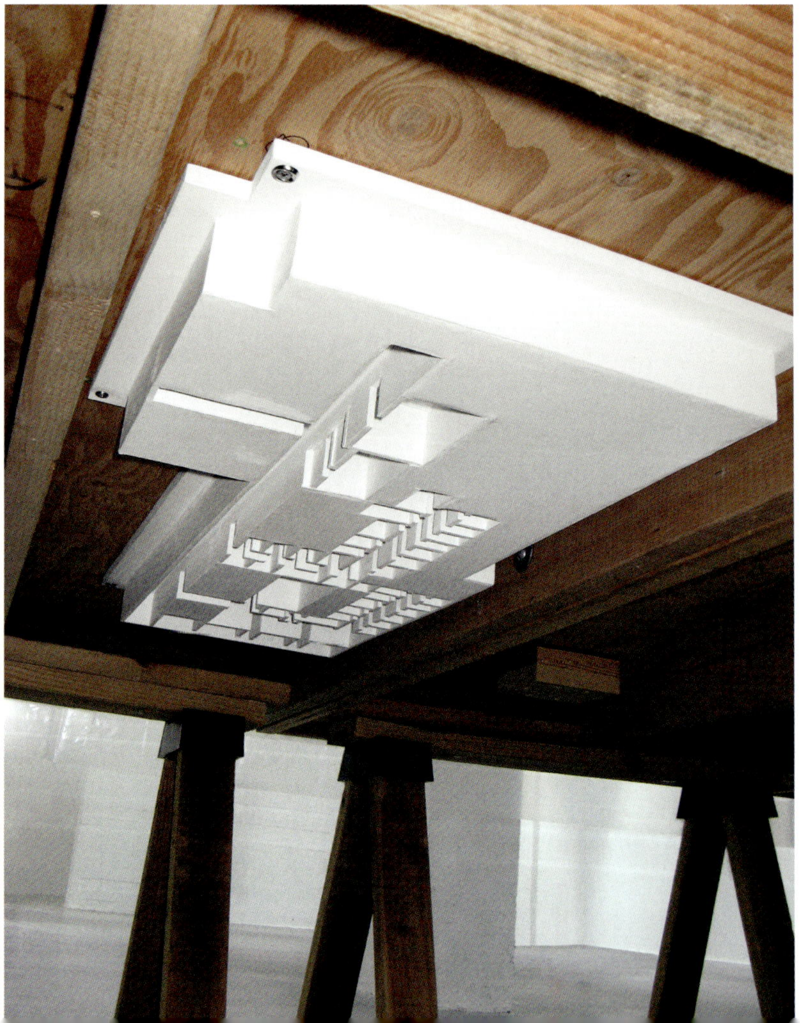

Details from Mike Kelley, *Educational Complex*, 1995

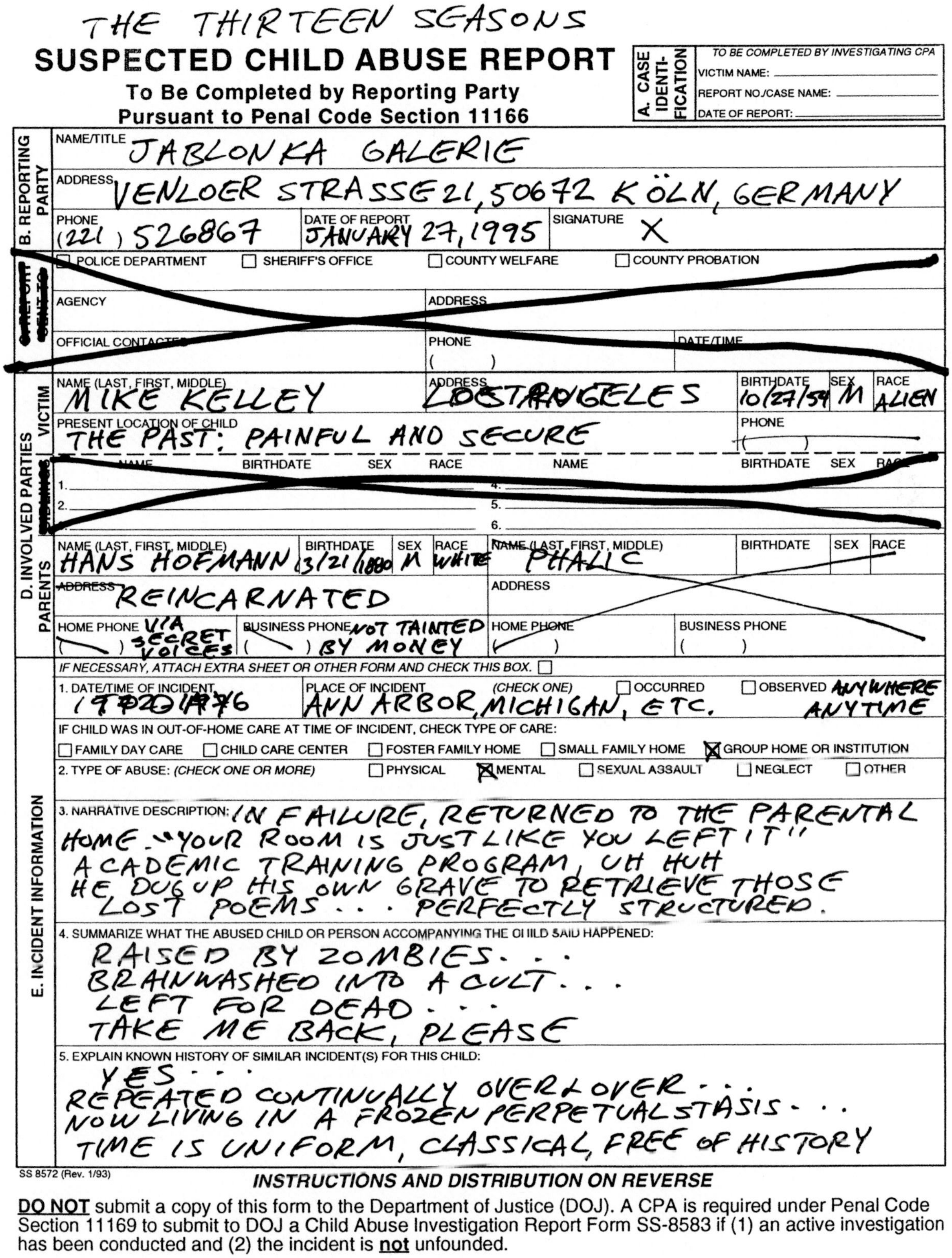

THE THIRTEEN SEASONS

SUSPECTED CHILD ABUSE REPORT

To Be Completed by Reporting Party
Pursuant to Penal Code Section 11166

A. CASE IDENTIFICATION — TO BE COMPLETED BY INVESTIGATING CPA
VICTIM NAME:
REPORT NO./CASE NAME:
DATE OF REPORT:

B. REPORTING PARTY
NAME/TITLE: JABLONKA GALERIE
ADDRESS: VENLOER STRASSE 21, 50672 KÖLN, GERMANY
PHONE: (221) 526867 — DATE OF REPORT: JANUARY 27, 1995 — SIGNATURE: X

~~C. REPORT SENT TO~~
~~POLICE DEPARTMENT / SHERIFF'S OFFICE / COUNTY WELFARE / COUNTY PROBATION~~
~~AGENCY / ADDRESS~~
~~OFFICIAL CONTACTED / PHONE ( ) / DATE/TIME~~

D. INVOLVED PARTIES
VICTIM — NAME (LAST, FIRST, MIDDLE): MIKE KELLEY — ADDRESS: ~~LOS~~ ANGELES — BIRTHDATE: 10/27/54 — SEX: M — RACE: ALIEN
PRESENT LOCATION OF CHILD: THE PAST: PAINFUL AND SECURE — PHONE: ( )

~~SIBLINGS — NAME / BIRTHDATE / SEX / RACE / NAME / BIRTHDATE / SEX / RACE~~
~~1. 2. 3. 4. 5. 6.~~

PARENTS — NAME (LAST, FIRST, MIDDLE): HANS HOFMANN — BIRTHDATE: 3/21/1880 — SEX: M — RACE: WHITE
~~NAME (LAST, FIRST, MIDDLE)~~: PHALLIC
~~ADDRESS~~: REINCARNATED — ADDRESS:
HOME PHONE: ( ) VIA SECRET VOICES — BUSINESS PHONE: ( ) NOT TAINTED BY MONEY — ~~HOME PHONE ( )~~ — BUSINESS PHONE ( )

E. INCIDENT INFORMATION
IF NECESSARY, ATTACH EXTRA SHEET OR OTHER FORM AND CHECK THIS BOX. ☐
1. DATE/TIME OF INCIDENT: 19~~20~~ 1976 — PLACE OF INCIDENT: ANN ARBOR, MICHIGAN, ETC. — (CHECK ONE) ☐ OCCURRED ☐ OBSERVED — ANYWHERE ANYTIME
IF CHILD WAS IN OUT-OF-HOME CARE AT TIME OF INCIDENT, CHECK TYPE OF CARE:
☐ FAMILY DAY CARE ☐ CHILD CARE CENTER ☐ FOSTER FAMILY HOME ☐ SMALL FAMILY HOME ☒ GROUP HOME OR INSTITUTION
2. TYPE OF ABUSE: *(CHECK ONE OR MORE)* ☐ PHYSICAL ☒ MENTAL ☐ SEXUAL ASSAULT ☐ NEGLECT ☐ OTHER
3. NARRATIVE DESCRIPTION: IN FAILURE, RETURNED TO THE PARENTAL HOME. "YOUR ROOM IS JUST LIKE YOU LEFT IT" ACADEMIC TRAINING PROGRAM, UH HUH HE DUG UP HIS OWN GRAVE TO RETRIEVE THOSE LOST POEMS . . . . PERFECTLY STRUCTURED.
4. SUMMARIZE WHAT THE ABUSED CHILD OR PERSON ACCOMPANYING THE CHILD SAID HAPPENED:
RAISED BY ZOMBIES . . .
BRAINWASHED INTO A CULT . . .
LEFT FOR DEAD . . .
TAKE ME BACK, PLEASE
5. EXPLAIN KNOWN HISTORY OF SIMILAR INCIDENT(S) FOR THIS CHILD:
YES . . .
REPEATED CONTINUALLY OVER & OVER . . .
NOW LIVING IN A FROZEN PERPETUAL STASIS . . .
TIME IS UNIFORM, CLASSICAL, FREE OF HISTORY

SS 8572 (Rev. 1/93)

INSTRUCTIONS AND DISTRIBUTION ON REVERSE

DO NOT submit a copy of this form to the Department of Justice (DOJ). A CPA is required under Penal Code Section 11169 to submit to DOJ a Child Abuse Investigation Report Form SS-8583 if (1) an active investigation has been conducted and (2) the incident is **not** unfounded.

Police or Sheriff-WHITE Copy; County Welfare or Probation-BLUE Copy; District Attorney-GREEN Copy; Reporting Party-YELLOW Copy

Mike Kelley, *Abuse Report*, 1995, printed 2007

DISCONSOLATE TONGUES: THE VISUAL LANGUAGE OF TRAUMA AND SURVIVAL

Meredith A. Brown

In the title essay of *The White Album* (1979), Joan Didion describes a nervous breakdown of sorts that she experienced in the late 1960s and early 1970s, writing, "I found it necessary to revise the circuitry of my mind."[1] She chronicles this crisis in deft, seemingly straightforward language, weaving together facts and impressions from her personal biography with atrocities that took place near her home in Hollywood—murders, suicides, overdoses, child abuse—and many disturbing events that have become part of the era's turbulent history: the assassination of the Kennedys, the Vietnam War, the intensifying violence by and toward the Black Panthers, the drug-fueled paranoia of posthippie counterculture, student protests, and, significantly, the Manson murders. To Didion, this time of psychic disjuncture was paradoxically also one of connection:

> In this light all connections were equally meaningful, and equally senseless. Try these: on the morning of John Kennedy's death in 1963 I was buying, at Ransohoff's in San Francisco, a short silk dress in which to be married. A few years later this dress of mine was ruined when, at a dinner party in Bel-Air, Roman Polanski accidentally spilled a glass of red wine on it. Sharon Tate was also a guest at this party, although she and Roman Polanski were not yet married. On July 27, 1970, I went to the Magnin-Hi Shop on the third floor of I. Magnin in Beverly Hills and picked out, at Linda Kasabian's request, the dress in which she began her testimony about the murders at Sharon Tate Polanski's house on Cielo Drive. . . . I believe this to be an authentically senseless chain of correspondences, but in the jingle-jangle morning of that summer it made as much sense as anything else did.[2]

Didion's conflation of personal, quotidian moments of dress shopping and socializing with catastrophic national events speaks to the experience of trauma, to the disjointed reality that results from surviving a pain, a shock, or an ordeal so acute that it is felt not merely as distress but as a rupture ("I found it necessary to revise the circuitry of my mind").

According to psychoanalyst and feminist scholar Juliet Mitchell, trauma "must create a breach in a protective covering of such severity that it cannot be coped with by the usual mechanisms by which we deal with pain or loss. . . . In trauma we are ultimately ripped."[3] She asserts that trauma is often expressed verbally as either a non-recognition of people or events or its opposite, too much recognition. Reflecting on the traumatic events of the late 1960s and her own psychic condition, Didion uses uncomplicated language to describe a convoluted kind of misrecognition in which all connections are as meaningful as they are senseless. In related yet individuated ways, visual artists Jenny Holzer, Sue Williams, and Sarah Anne Johnson each deal with trauma—physical, psychical, personal, political—through the creation or appropriation of verbal and visual language, making work that occludes, conflates, and exposes the inexpressible while revealing the complex ways in which trauma (mis)shapes our reality.

The vicissitudes of language have occupied Jenny Holzer for four decades. Although she trained as a painter, she first received notice for her Truisms, a series of works in various formats that turn the verbal into the visual. In 1977 Holzer began composing short, pithy statements, maxims of a sort, and exhibiting them publicly, first on commercially produced, typeset broadsides circulated around New York City and then in other formats such as T-shirts, billboards, LED signs, bronze plaques, and marble benches (fig. 74). These declarative one-liners—"Money creates taste," "Protect me from what I want," "Abuse of power comes as no surprise," "Bad intentions can yield good results"—take on a subversive quality by delivering confusing, sometimes contradictory messages, and this ambiguity, perhaps even ambivalence, is what gives the work its potency, allowing for a multiplicity of readings. As Holzer explained, "I wanted a lot simultaneously: to leave art outside for the public . . . to be explicit but not didactic, to find the right subjects, to transform spaces, to disorient and transfix people, to offer up beauty, to be funny and never lie. . . . I focused on what traditional painting couldn't do in public spaces and used language to carry the greater part of my content."[4]

By using language as an aesthetic tool, Holzer's Truisms harness the force of the written word, situating it not as literature, poetry, or journalism but rather in the realm of Conceptual sculpture or "material intervention" in the public domain.[5] In the late 1970s and 1980s other artists similarly engaged with language as a means to explore socially and politically charged ideas,

A LITTLE KNOWLEDGE CAN GO A LONG WAY
A LOT OF PROFESSIONALS ARE CRACKPOTS
A MAN CAN'T KNOW WHAT IT'S LIKE TO BE A MOTHER
A NAME MEANS A LOT JUST BY ITSELF
A POSITIVE ATTITUDE MAKES ALL THE DIFFERENCE IN THE WORLD
A RELAXED MAN IS NOT NECESSARILY A BETTER MAN
A SENSE OF TIMING IS THE MARK OF GENIUS
A SINCERE EFFORT IS ALL YOU CAN ASK
A SINGLE EVENT CAN HAVE INFINITELY MANY INTERPRETATIONS
A SOLID HOME BASE BUILDS A SENSE OF SELF
A STRONG SENSE OF DUTY IMPRISONS YOU
ABSOLUTE SUBMISSION CAN BE A FORM OF FREEDOM
ABSTRACTION IS A TYPE OF DECADENCE
ABUSE OF POWER SHOULD COME AS NO SURPRISE
ACTION CAUSES MORE TROUBLE THAN THOUGHT
ALIENATION PRODUCES ECCENTRICS OR REVOLUTIONARIES
ALL THINGS ARE DELICATELY INTERCONNECTED
AMBITION IS JUST AS DANGEROUS AS COMPLACENCY
AMBIVALENCE CAN RUIN YOUR LIFE
AN ELITE IS INEVITABLE
ANGER OR HATE CAN BE A USEFUL MOTIVATING FORCE
ANIMALISM IS PERFECTLY HEALTHY
ANY SURPLUS IS IMMORAL
ANYTHING IS A LEGITIMATE AREA OF INVESTIGATION
ARTIFICIAL DESIRES ARE DESPOILING THE EARTH
AT TIMES INACTIVITY IS PREFERABLE TO MINDLESS FUNCTIONING
AT TIMES YOUR UNCONSCIOUS IS TRUER THAN YOUR CONSCIOUS MIND
AUTOMATION IS DEADLY
AWFUL PUNISHMENT AWAITS REALLY BAD PEOPLE
BAD INTENTIONS CAN YIELD GOOD RESULTS
BEING ALONE WITH YOURSELF IS INCREASINGLY UNPOPULAR
BEING HAPPY IS MORE IMPORTANT THAN ANYTHING ELSE
BEING HONEST IS NOT ALWAYS THE KINDEST WAY
BEING JUDGMENTAL IS A SIGN OF LIFE
BEING SURE OF YOURSELF MEANS YOU'RE A FOOL
BELIEVING IN REBIRTH IS THE SAME AS ADMITTING DEFEAT
BOREDOM MAKES YOU DO CRAZY THINGS
CALM IS MORE CONDUCIVE TO CREATIVITY THAN IS ANXIETY
CATEGORIZING FEAR IS CALMING
CHANGE IS VALUABLE BECAUSE IT LETS THE OPPRESSED BE TYRANTS
CHASING THE NEW IS DANGEROUS TO SOCIETY
CHILDREN ARE THE CRUELEST OF ALL
CHILDREN ARE THE HOPE OF THE FUTURE
CLASS ACTION IS A NICE IDEA WITH NO SUBSTANCE
CLASS STRUCTURE IS AS ARTIFICIAL AS PLASTIC
CONFUSING YOURSELF IS A WAY TO STAY HONEST
CRIME AGAINST PROPERTY IS RELATIVELY UNIMPORTANT
DECADENCE CAN BE AN END IN ITSELF
DECENCY IS A RELATIVE THING
DEPENDENCE CAN BE A MEAL TICKET
DESCRIPTION IS MORE VALUABLE THAN METAPHOR
DEVIANTS ARE SACRIFICED TO INCREASE GROUP SOLIDARITY
DISGUST IS THE APPROPRIATE RESPONSE TO MOST SITUATIONS
DISORGANIZATION IS A KIND OF ANESTHESIA
DON'T PLACE TOO MUCH TRUST IN EXPERTS
DON'T RUN PEOPLE'S LIVES FOR THEM
DRAMA OFTEN OBSCURES THE REAL ISSUES
DREAMING WHILE AWAKE IS A FRIGHTENING CONTRADICTION
DYING AND COMING BACK GIVES YOU CONSIDERABLE PERSPECTIVE
DYING SHOULD BE AS EASY AS FALLING OFF A LOG
EATING TOO MUCH IS CRIMINAL
ELABORATION IS A FORM OF POLLUTION
EMOTIONAL RESPONSES ARE AS VALUABLE AS INTELLECTUAL RESPONSES
ENJOY YOURSELF BECAUSE YOU CAN'T CHANGE ANYTHING ANYWAY
EVEN YOUR FAMILY CAN BETRAY YOU
EVERY ACHIEVEMENT REQUIRES A SACRIFICE
EVERYONE'S WORK IS EQUALLY IMPORTANT
EVERYTHING THAT'S INTERESTING IS NEW
EXCEPTIONAL PEOPLE DESERVE SPECIAL CONCESSIONS
EXPIRING FOR LOVE IS BEAUTIFUL BUT STUPID
EXPRESSING ANGER IS NECESSARY
EXTREME BEHAVIOR HAS ITS BASIS IN PATHOLOGICAL PSYCHOLOGY
EXTREME SELF-CONSCIOUSNESS LEADS TO PERVERSION
FAITHFULNESS IS A SOCIAL NOT A BIOLOGICAL LAW
FAKE OR REAL INDIFFERENCE IS A POWERFUL PERSONAL WEAPON
FATHERS OFTEN USE TOO MUCH FORCE
FEAR IS THE GREATEST INCAPACITATOR
FREEDOM IS A LUXURY NOT A NECESSITY
GIVING FREE REIN TO YOUR EMOTIONS IS AN HONEST WAY TO LIVE
GOING WITH THE FLOW IS SOOTHING BUT RISKY
GOOD DEEDS EVENTUALLY ARE REWARDED
GOVERNMENT IS A BURDEN ON THE PEOPLE
GRASS ROOTS AGITATION IS THE ONLY HOPE
GUILT AND SELF-LACERATION ARE INDULGENCES
HABITUAL CONTEMPT DOESN'T REFLECT A FINER SENSIBILITY
HIDING YOUR MOTIVES IS DESPICABLE

Fig. 74. Jenny Holzer (American, born 1950), *Truisms*, 1978–87. Photostat, 8 ft. × 40 in. (243.9 × 101.6 cm). The Museum of Modern Art, New York, Gift of the artist (177.1988)

notably Barbara Kruger, who adopted and subverted the visual format of advertising by overlaying found black-and-white photographs with directive slogans in bold typeface and circulating the results in public spaces (fig. 75). In Kruger's work, unlike Holzer's, the photographic image and the language carry equal weight. Kruger's combined visual-verbal mode of address makes the viewer conscious of the ways in which images are produced to promote ideologies, particularly stereotypes of women. Or, as Craig Owens described it in 1984, she "proposes the *mobilization* of the spectator."[6] Holzer's Truisms, too, use language to mobilize and provoke, although their mechanism is a proliferation of inscrutable words in the absence of images. In 1978, someone vandalized a poster of the Truisms by throwing a bolt through the street-level window of Franklin Furnace, an alternative art space in downtown Manhattan, appropriately hitting the phrase "Boredom makes you do crazy things" (fig. 76).[7] As Lucy Lippard wrote of Holzer's early language-based work: "The message seems to be *think for yourself*."[8]

Following her enigmatic Truisms, Holzer continued to address the politics of postmodern discourse in text-based works. "From a political standpoint," she has said, "I was drawn to writing because it was possible to be very explicit about things."[9] In recent years she has turned to the language of war—and its resulting traumas—as the subject of her art. In response to the launch of the so-called War on Terror and the United States' invasions of Iraq and Afghanistan, Holzer began to use the bureaucratic language of declassified, often heavily redacted government documents related to U.S. policy in the Middle East: inquiries into al Qaeda, CIA abuses, torture at Abu Ghraib, prisoner maltreatment at Guantanamo Bay, covert military operations. Unlike the Truisms, for which she composed the text, these works reproduce actual documents. Ranging from memos and forms to maps and letters, the source material has been redacted by government censors to remove names and other information deemed too sensitive for public release, creating stranded phrases, confusing sentences, and gaps that can leave the text nearly incomprehensible.

That Holzer appropriates real documents (which, despite being part of the public record, are largely unknown) and that through their redacted logic these documents take on a strange visual poetry render her art both profoundly affective and deeply disquieting. In *Red Yellow Looming* (2004; pp. 144, 164), thirteen double-sided horizontal LED displays span the space between two parallel walls, creating a kind of staircase of words that emits an eerie red and yellow glow. Text pulled from State Department memos of the George

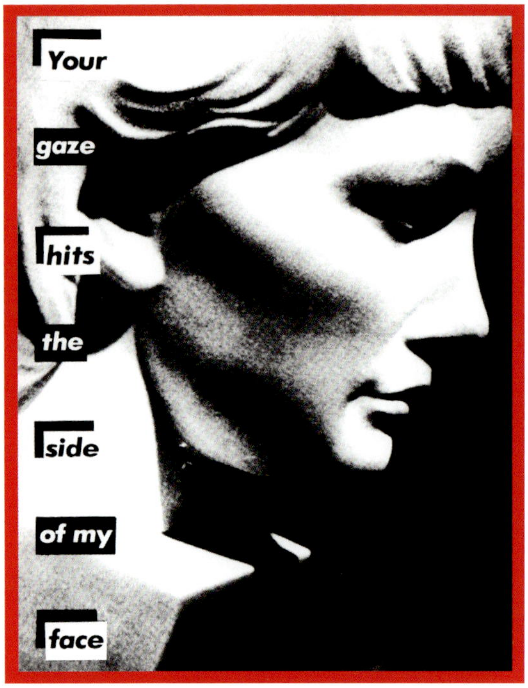

Fig. 75. Barbara Kruger (American, born 1945), *Untitled (Your gaze hits the side of my face)*, 1981. Photograph, 55 × 41 in. (140 × 104 cm)

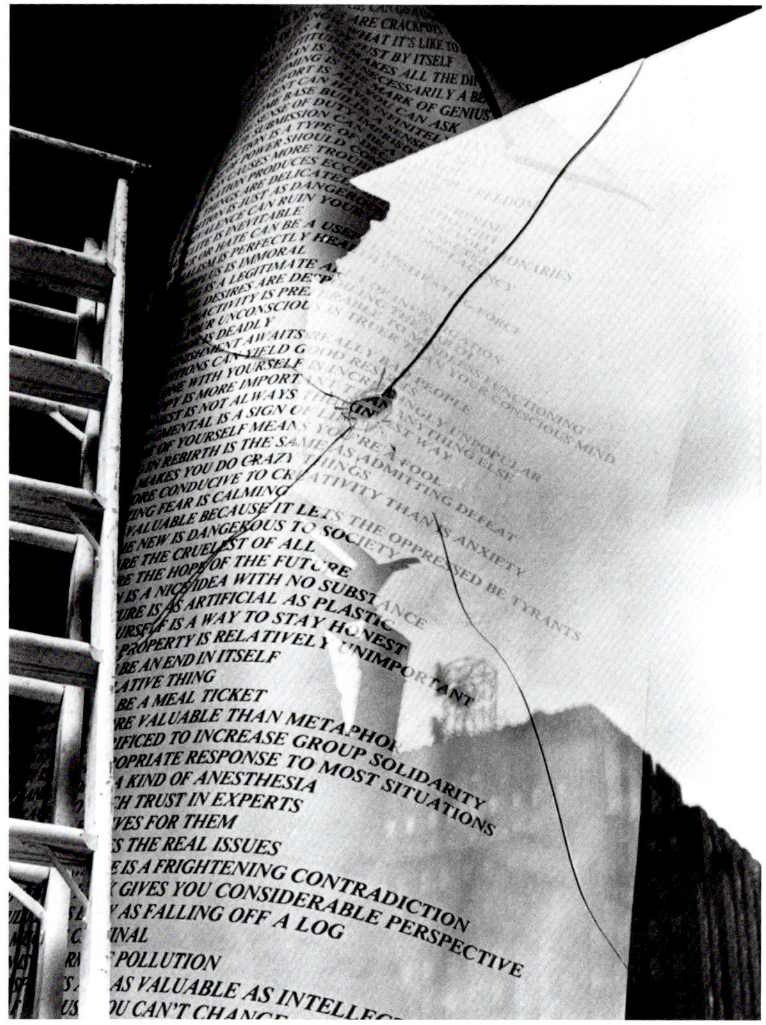

Fig. 76. Jenny Holzer's *Truisms* viewed through the window at Franklin Furnace, New York, 1978

H. W. Bush administration related to the First Gulf War and relevant language from documents produced by the Clinton and Reagan administrations create a linguistically and visually complex pattern that scrolls up, down, and across the LED screens. The light-emitting diodes appear to move endlessly to and fro, forming a dizzying dance of numbers, codes, and words—the bureaucratic speak designed to disguise the human costs of torture and war. This anxiety-inducing installation mimics, in a way, the anxious state of war itself. Writing in the mid-1960s in the midst of the Cold War, with its ever-present threat of nuclear destruction, Italian psychoanalyst Franco Fornari made the case that war operates as the externalization of "illusory internal danger," or, as art historian Mignon Nixon succinctly explains, "war projects internal anxiety onto others."[10] Masked by the coded language of governmental memos, this anxiety looms from Holzer's work, emerging imminent and threatening. The *New York Times* described the experience of seeing *Red Yellow Looming* as traumatic: "Reading even a little of it is like watching something start to go down the drain while being strangled in red tape."[11]

These works unveil the human presence behind the rhetoric, the actions taken by individuals to further the policies of violence perpetrated by the state. In paintings such as *Secretary of Defense* (2006; p. 145 bottom) and *The White House, 2002* (2006; p. 145 top), Holzer reproduced, at nearly four times their actual size, documents from 2002 related to the so-called torture memos and policy statements on detainee abuse. Although their enlarged scale makes them unfamiliar, the documents are silkscreened in black paint on white ground to underscore that they are real.[12] They use the language of official policy to erase the role of the policy maker, creating a distance between the individual and the torture he has authorized. For each painting, Holzer selected a memo that combines what Nixon calls the "typographic rhetoric of the document" with the singular handwriting of its recipient or sender.[13] In

Fig. 77. Jenny Holzer, *Accordingly*, 2012. Oil on linen, 102¼ × 79 in. (259.7 × 200.7 cm). The Metropolitan Museum of Art, New York, Gift of the artist, 2013 (2013.969)

Secretary of Defense, for example, the contrast between the impersonal, coded language ("RECOMMENDATION: That SECDEF approve USSOUTHCOM Commander's use of those counter-resistance techniques") and the personal scrawl of Donald Rumsfeld (questioning the recommendation to limit detainee standing to four hours when he chooses to stand "for 8–10 hours a day") exposes the pitiless, secretive behavior of the U.S. government after 9/11. The effect on the viewer is chilling.

Holzer's redaction paintings not only magnify the secret policies, shocking behaviors, and traumatic events that the government has attempted to suppress, forcing a public memory where a blind spot has been created, but also signify the psychic toll of trauma. In most of the documents released to the public through the Freedom of Information Act, large portions of the text are blacked out, leaving partial phrases or a handful of scattered words from which the reader can attempt to glean information. The significance of these blacked-out rectangles, when transferred to canvas, is seemingly amplified. In *Accordingly* (2012; fig. 77), for example, sections of obscured text, which are rendered in gray, blue, and cream-colored paint, dominate the enormous linen canvas, creating an abstract composition that emphasizes the lacunae. The message of these works is delivered not by the text's legibility but by its suppression, which becomes a visual metaphor for the repression often caused by a traumatic event. When a physical or psychic trauma occurs, it is common for the immediate effect to be a linguistic blind spot, an inability to speak, an "uncertainty about words"—in other words, an unconscious redaction.[14] As journalist and writer Joshua Craze argues, the redaction paintings "have a content that is not reducible to information: she is letting the absences exist, and insisting that we look at them."[15] In essence, by making visible the absence of language, Holzer forces us to confront trauma and its psychic effects.

Whereas Holzer focuses on the politics of language, using words as content, Sue Williams and Sarah Anne Johnson harness visual and verbal language to address both personal and political traumas. Like Holzer, these artists are informed by feminism and deploy their art to expose abuses of power. In the late 1980s Williams began to make cartoonish drawings on canvas that deal explicitly with misogyny, often in its most gruesome form as acts of sexual violence and emotional cruelty. These scribbled sketches on paper mounted to canvas depict grotesque and darkly comic scenes of sexual assault accompanied by sardonic or ambiguous captions scrawled near the figures. For example, the text above the face of a woman whose mouth, eyes, ears, and nose are being forcefully penetrated by penises reads "try to be more accommodating." The meaning behind Williams's combinations of image and text can be difficult to decipher. As one critic wondered, "There was violent mockery in those early paintings, but it was not always easy to tell who was being mocked. Men or women? Humanity in general or the artist herself in particular?"[16] This dark social satire, expressed through the convergence of voracious corporeality and provocative, sarcastic language, comes from the artist's own history of trauma. "I've had so many really bad things happen to me and it just seems absurd," she explained. "Yeah, I was raped and sodomized and there is so much autobiographical stuff in the paintings."[17] By mining her experience as a victim, Williams provides a language for other victims. As she put it in 1993, "Sometimes victims don't have voices and it's not a good way to be. . . . A lot of my work has been about being angry and communicating things I need to communicate."[18]

Williams operates in a feminist, even activist, mode, giving voice to the silenced while exposing the broader social conditions that sustain misogyny and propagate violence. The inequalities she addresses in her practice not only exist in interpersonal relationships but are built into the culture. In her painting *Spiritual America* (1992; fig. 78), Williams repurposes sexually explicit cartoons of doctors fondling female patients, a man penetrating a woman from behind while holding a pistol to her head, and a pert naked woman with a paper bag over her head. These shocking depictions of women as objects repeat across the canvas, partially masked by washes of white, while a fractured joke about male impotence stutters beneath them. Perhaps a comment on the ubiquity in popular culture of flippant images of violence toward women, *Spiritual America* also mocks the masculinity of the art world. Williams borrowed her title from Richard Prince's controversial 1983 re-photograph of a prepubescent nude Brooke Shields, drawing a parallel between pornographic cartoons and male artists' exploitations of female sexuality.[19] Her inclusion of a hackneyed joke, too, may be an aggressive feminist send-up of Prince's paintings from the 1980s featuring jokes about the psychological and sexual anxieties and fantasies of white, straight, middle-class American men (fig. 79).[20]

Williams's insistence that her cartoons and text-based works are paintings rather than drawings further critiques the male-dominated art world. She has said, "People seem to want to see me as someone who has contempt for painting and doesn't really paint. 'Painter' is immediately perceived as a male word."[21] As curator Dan Cameron argues, Williams's feminism comes through in these early paintings in her depictions of "both personal and cultural rage over sexism in the art world and daily life" that "[twist] the victimization of women into a form of comedic bludgeon." He continues, "By acting the role of transgressor in her violation of existing taboos concerning the acceptability of certain subjects, Williams was able to simultaneously parody the machismo of most painterly archetypes while breaking through a few formal barriers of her own."[22]

In the latter half of the 1990s, Williams embarked on a formal shift, developing a visual language of bright, brash, acid-hued paint and fragmented, almost graffiti-like forms that extend all over the canvas, each seemingly abstract line or shape suggestive of a sexualized body part. With this new iconography of obscene corporeality, she also pivoted away from the notion that, as second-wave feminism would have it, the personal is political, and moved toward making art in which the political is made intimately personal. Referring to the terror attacks of 9/11 and America's military involvement in the Middle East, as well as earlier disturbing government policies, Williams explained in 2010, "I wanted to put something in my art that was related to all this stuff going on in the world that I was so passionate about in my thinking and my activities. *Why isn't this all connected*—you know?"[23] In the years following the attacks on the World Trade Center and Pentagon, Williams's treatment of the abuses of power moved from the strictly sexual into the realm of the explicitly political. Further, as text disappeared from the paintings, the titles of the works took on greater significance. For example, in a large square painting from 2008, acrid green and red shapes resembling entrails, testicles, anuses, nipples, and jagged, comic explosions twist and extend abstractly across the canvas (fig. 80). Through its enigmatic title, *Golfing at*

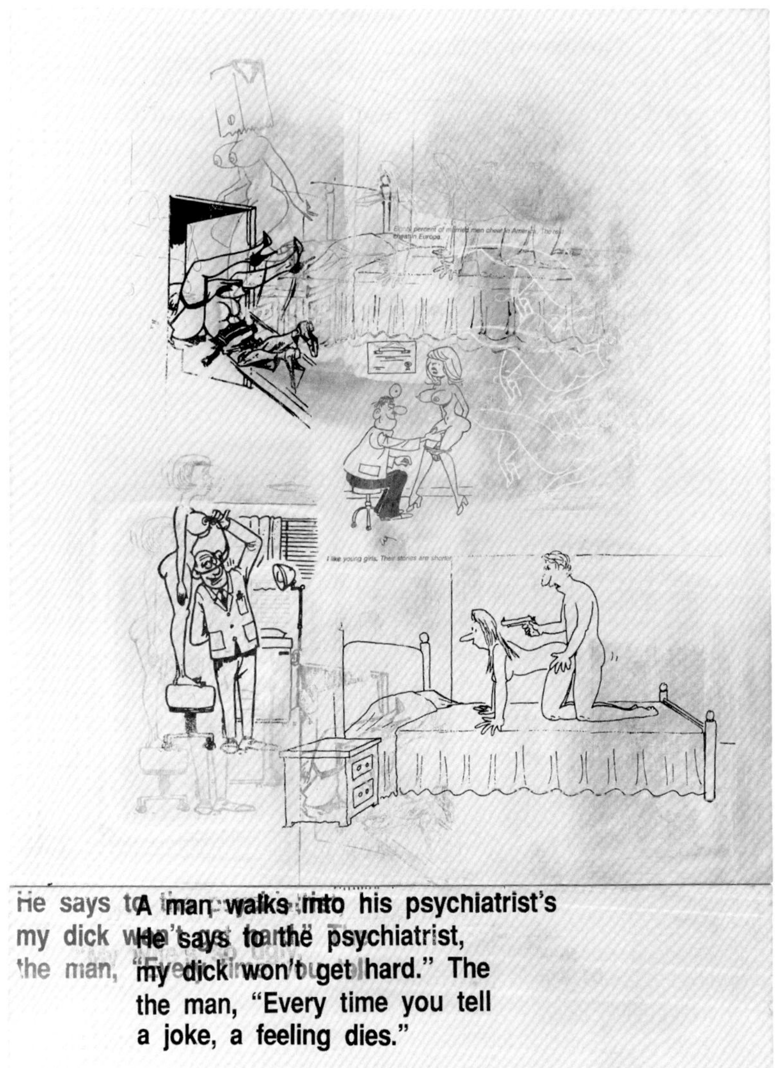

Fig. 78. Sue Williams (American, born 1954), *Spiritual America*, 1992. Acrylic on canvas, two panels, 56 × 48 in. (142.2 × 121.9 cm); 12 × 48 in. (30.5 × 121.9 cm)

Fig. 79. Richard Prince (American, born 1949), *Tell Me Everything*, 1987. Acrylic and silkscreen on canvas, 56 × 48 in. (142.2 × 121.9 cm). The Museum of Modern Art, New York, Gift of Steven and Alexandra Cohen (1343.2016)

Northwoods, the painting further reveals itself; the shapes of golf clubs, tees, and holes (some of which are exploding), as well as the plaid patterns of golf attire become apparent, indicating the leisure activity of the privileged and powerful who make their (secret) deals on the golf course.[24] "Northwoods" refers to Operation Northwoods, a covert plan proposed in 1962 by the Department of Defense for the CIA to stage terrorist attacks on American soil and blame them on the Cuban government in an attempt to gain support for a war with Cuba.[25] A shocking proposition, Operation Northwoods received renewed attention in the wake of 9/11 as theories developed that the attacks had been an inside job. Rather than depict the frightening Northwoods plot, Williams instead uses her visual language of explosive, biomorphic shapes and the verbal clues of the title to expose the disturbing actions of the CIA and indict the American government.

Conspiratorial questions, particularly around war and terrorism, have continued to occupy Williams. Indeed, in the 2010 gallery retrospective "Al-Qaeda Is the CIA," she showed work related to 9/11 and the conspiracy theories it spawned (see pp. 154–55). Her most recent paintings address the attacks on the World Trade Center and the government's so-called War on Terror in obscure and ambiguous ways. With a cacophony of electric, tropical colors and loose brushwork, paintings such as *Hill and Dale, Black-Ops* (2013; p. 153 top) and *All Roads Lead to Langley* (2016; p. 153 bottom) appear lyrically expressionistic; it takes a moment to notice the twisting, bending shapes of the Twin Towers (those architectural phalluses), the falling bodylike forms, and the blood-red blotches that hint at a more traumatic, insidious subject. In *Mike and Zbigniew* (2012; p. 152), Williams conflates the history of the American policy that led to the 9/11 attacks with personal tragedy. Painted shortly after the artist Mike Kelley committed suicide, Williams titled the work for Kelley and Zbigniew Brzezinski, who was Jimmy Carter's hawkish national security adviser and the architect of the CIA's covert action supporting Islamic militants in Afghanistan against invading Soviet troops, a policy that contributed to the rise of al Qaeda and the Taliban. In the center of the canvas stands a turquoise-headed stork—a spirit animal of sorts for Kelley—and the ghostly white outlines of the Twin Towers.[26] The painting is both excessively beautiful and obscene; clouds of smoke, entrails, phalluses, bubbles, blotches, orifices, tendrils, and a small sketch of the Pentagon in flames, all rendered in vivacious neon colors, explode across the canvas. Text reappears in this work, in words and letters scattered around the composition: Mike, Help, No, Lump, NSC, Everything, Zbigniew, Nanothermite.[27] The abject shapes and words painted in capital letters, as if they are being shouted, together suggest the inner rage and destruction of the death drive, an anxiety directed outward in the case of war or inward in the case of suicide. A painterly depiction of the combined traumas of Kelley's death and 9/11, *Mike and Zbigniew* operates in the visual language of dreams, in which, as Mitchell asserts, words and images "become expressions of feeling rather than of meaning."[28]

Sarah Anne Johnson's multipart project *House on Fire* similarly communicates through phantasmagorical language. Generally known for her photographs and sculptures dealing with the environment, Johnson produced a highly personal series of sculptures and works on paper that chronicle her own family's nightmarish history. In the late 1950s Johnson's maternal grandmother, Velma Orlikow, suffering from what is now called postpartum depression, entered treatment at Montreal's Allan Memorial Institute of Psychiatry at McGill University, under the care of renowned psychiatrist Dr. D. Ewen Cameron (fig. 81). While she entered therapy willingly, she and her family were unaware for nearly three decades that her treatment

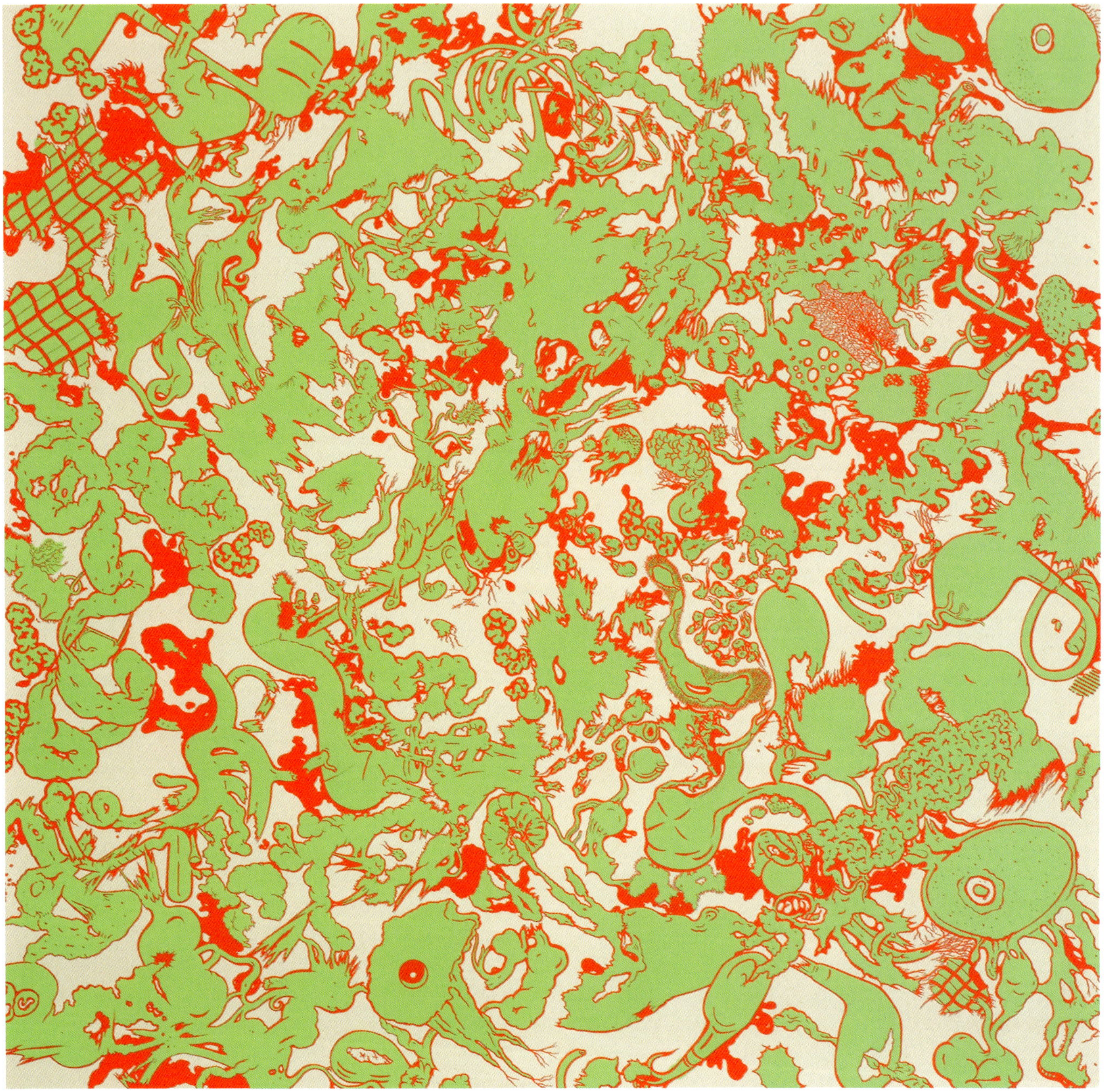

Fig. 80. Sue Williams, *Golfing at Northwoods*, 2008. Oil and acrylic on canvas, 70 × 70 in. (177.8 × 177.8 cm)

was part of Subproject 68 of the CIA-sponsored MK-ULTRA mind-control program.[29] For several years, under Cameron's supervision, Orlikow was involuntarily subjected to mind-altering brainwashing experiments that involved extreme electroshock therapy, sleep deprivation, LSD and other experimental psychochemicals, and radiation. Although she survived the torturous experience, Orlikow was never the same, prone to periods of depression and bouts of rage. "Before the hospital," Johnson recalled, "she had been a huge reader, but now she just was sitting there in the middle of her own failure."[30] Johnson lived with the residual pain of her grandmother's abuse and her mother's difficult memories for years before she took on the subject in her art.

In the body of work that constitutes *House on Fire*, Johnson creates a visual language to reflect, and perhaps expunge, three generations of trauma. She

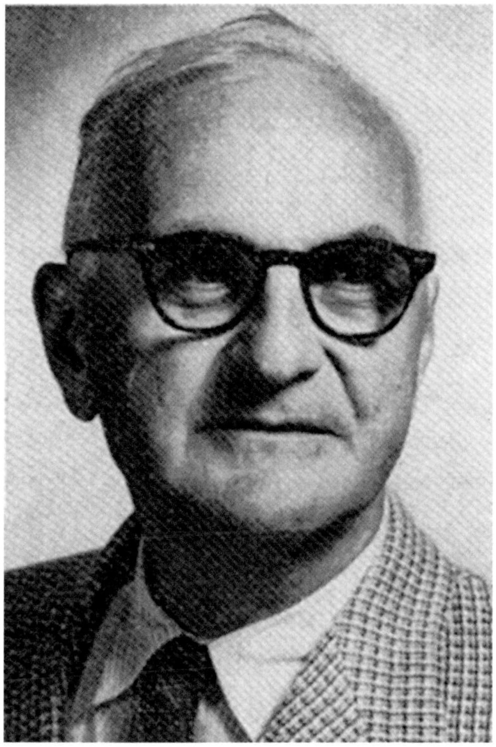

Fig. 81. Dr. D. Ewen Cameron, May 6, 1981

explained, "In this work I'm trying to make my internal world a better one."[31] Loops and lines snake across the works on paper like vines, cables, or strands of DNA. Some of these Johnson did atop newspaper articles about Cameron, MK-ULTRA, and her grandmother's treatment. In *Brain Drain* (2008; p. 150 top right), a chain of drawings of Cameron's face—so many sinister eyes—coils across a feature article about his CIA-sponsored experiments, mimicking the paper's illustration of a snake slithering through patients' brains. Similarly, in *House of Horrors* (2008; p. 150 top left) vines unfurl and a ropelike tongue extends from Cameron's mouth in one photograph to wrap around Orlikow's shoulders in another photograph on the newspaper spread, eerily ending in her mouth and eyes. The drawings render the articles beneath them nearly impossible to read, covering the reporters' factual language with the disturbing visual metaphors of binding, slithering, and seemingly infinite replication. Johnson also uses this hallucinatory visual language on two photographs of her grandmother, turning family snapshots into psychedelic portraits. In one, *Lysergic Acid Diethylamide* (2008; p. 151), across the surface of a black-and-white headshot of Orlikow the artist drew an effusion of circles and dots to create a kaleidoscopic pattern. In the other, a picture of her grandmother in the kitchen, she obliterated the figure's head by submerging it in a black cloud, as the pattern of her dress floats into the space around her (*Black Cloud*, 2008; p. 150 bottom).

Yet it is in a dollhouse—the house on fire—that Johnson most elaborately narrates the familial psychic suffering (2008; pp. 146–49, 162). Flames erupt through the attic roof as lights inside allow the viewer to peer through the windows, some of which are set sideways or upside down, and glimpse the horrors within: staircases lead nowhere; the kitchen is covered in white ooze; stumps of trees sprout from the dining-room floor as a bonfire blazes on the table; the library vibrates with white spirals spinning out of control across the walls, floor, and furnishings; the empty bed in the bedroom is appointed with two restraining belts; an "observation room" with a two-way mirror is piled floor to ceiling with stacks of documents; and in a curious sort of snow cave two figures dance—a white-haired man in glasses, shirt, and tie and a heavyset naked woman with a black bag over her head. Each unnerving room "tells its own tale of maltreatment, distortion and abuse, a domestic mise-en-scène unimaginable if it weren't true."[32] Johnson's dollhouse discloses the shocking details of Orlikow's story, using hallucinatory, frightening imagery to speak to the ways in which the torture inflicted by the psychiatric institution invaded the family home. As writer Andrew Berardini put it, "There are no words for her suffering. . . . The tragedy echoes through generations."[33] In the traumatic loss of language, Johnson has substituted images for words, purging her grandmother's unspeakable memories in flames.

Holzer, Williams, and Johnson—each in her own way through the use of verbal and visual language—reveal the psychic rips of personal and political trauma, attempting to make sense of the horrific and unexplainable while uncovering broader structural power imbalances in the process. Their art depicts how traumatic events shape the lives of individuals, nations, and generations, altering histories large and small. "We tell ourselves stories in order to live," Didion writes at the beginning of *The White Album*. What Holzer, Williams, and Johnson lay bare are stories of survival.

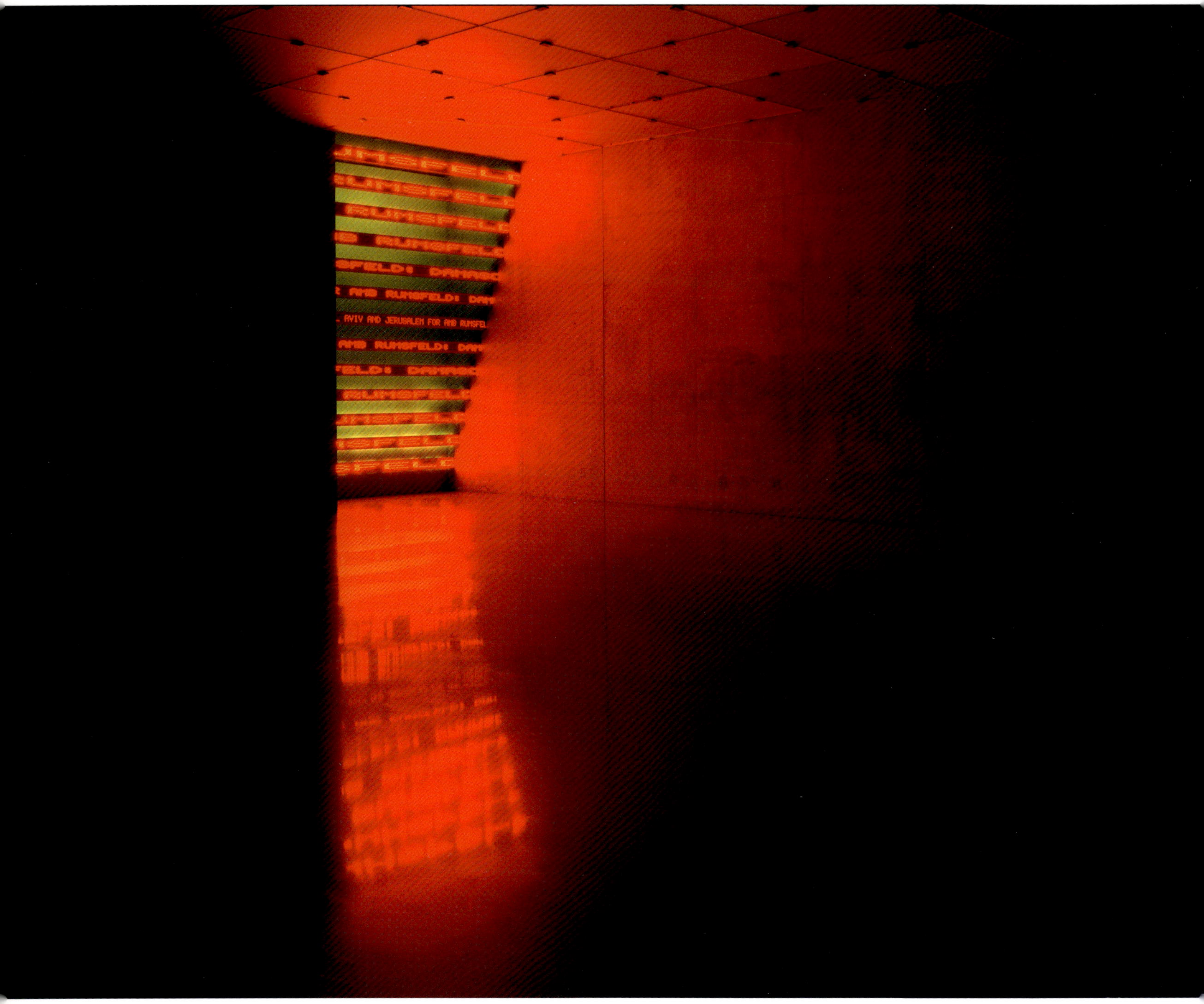

Jenny Holzer, *Red Yellow Looming*, 2004

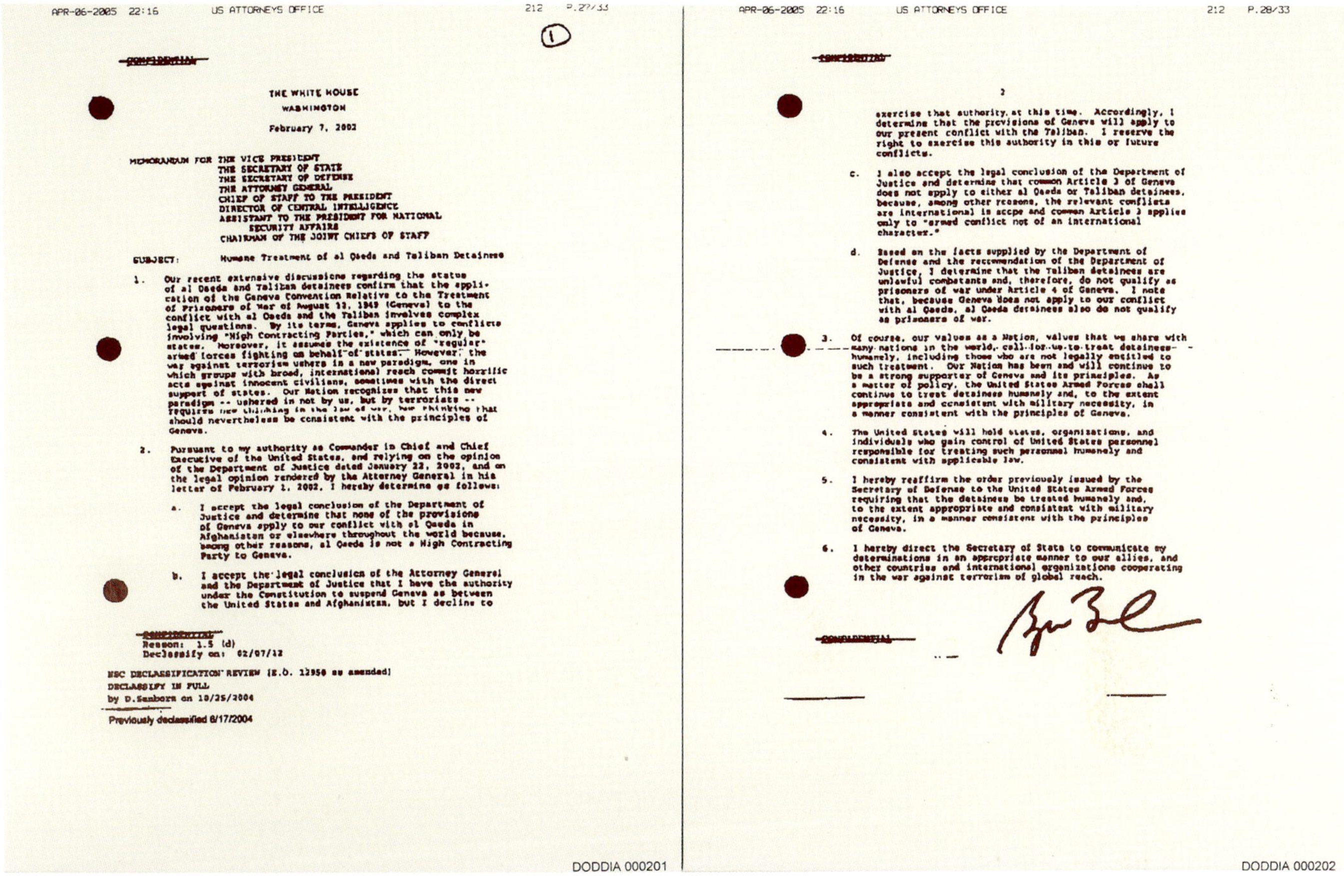

APR-06-2005 22:16 US ATTORNEYS OFFICE 212 P.27/33

①

~~CONFIDENTIAL~~

THE WHITE HOUSE

WASHINGTON

February 7, 2002

MEMORANDUM FOR THE VICE PRESIDENT
THE SECRETARY OF STATE
THE SECRETARY OF DEFENSE
THE ATTORNEY GENERAL
CHIEF OF STAFF TO THE PRESIDENT
DIRECTOR OF CENTRAL INTELLIGENCE
ASSISTANT TO THE PRESIDENT FOR NATIONAL SECURITY AFFAIRS
CHAIRMAN OF THE JOINT CHIEFS OF STAFF

SUBJECT: Humane Treatment of al Qaeda and Taliban Detainees

1. Our recent extensive discussions regarding the status of al Qaeda and Taliban detainees confirm that the application of the Geneva Convention Relative to the Treatment of Prisoners of War of August 12, 1949 (Geneva) to the conflict with al Qaeda and the Taliban involves complex legal questions. By its terms, Geneva applies to conflicts involving "High Contracting Parties," which can only be states. Moreover, it assumes the existence of "regular" armed forces fighting on behalf of states. However, the war against terrorism ushers in a new paradigm, one in which groups with broad, international reach commit horrific acts against innocent civilians, sometimes with the direct support of states. Our Nation recognizes that this new paradigm -- ushered in not by us, but by terrorists -- requires new thinking in the law of war, but thinking that should nevertheless be consistent with the principles of Geneva.

2. Pursuant to my authority as Commander in Chief and Chief Executive of the United States, and relying on the opinion of the Department of Justice dated January 22, 2002, and on the legal opinion rendered by the Attorney General in his letter of February 1, 2002, I hereby determine as follows:

a. I accept the legal conclusion of the Department of Justice and determine that none of the provisions of Geneva apply to our conflict with al Qaeda in Afghanistan or elsewhere throughout the world because, among other reasons, al Qaeda is not a High Contracting Party to Geneva.

b. I accept the legal conclusion of the Attorney General and the Department of Justice that I have the authority under the Constitution to suspend Geneva as between the United States and Afghanistan, but I decline to

~~CONFIDENTIAL~~
Reason: 1.5 (d)
Declassify on: 02/07/12

NSC DECLASSIFICATION REVIEW [E.O. 12958 as amended]
DECLASSIFY IN FULL
by D.Sanborn on 10/25/2004

Previously declassified 6/17/2004

DODDIA 000201

APR-06-2005 22:16 US ATTORNEYS OFFICE 212 P.28/33

~~CONFIDENTIAL~~

2

exercise that authority at this time. Accordingly, I determine that the provisions of Geneva will apply to our present conflict with the Taliban. I reserve the right to exercise this authority in this or future conflicts.

c. I also accept the legal conclusion of the Department of Justice and determine that common Article 3 of Geneva does not apply to either al Qaeda or Taliban detainees, because, among other reasons, the relevant conflicts are international in scope and common Article 3 applies only to "armed conflict not of an international character."

d. Based on the facts supplied by the Department of Defense and the recommendation of the Department of Justice, I determine that the Taliban detainees are unlawful combatants and, therefore, do not qualify as prisoners of war under Article 4 of Geneva. I note that, because Geneva does not apply to our conflict with al Qaeda, al Qaeda detainees also do not qualify as prisoners of war.

3. Of course, our values as a Nation, values that we share with many nations in the world, call for us to treat detainees humanely, including those who are not legally entitled to such treatment. Our Nation has been and will continue to be a strong supporter of Geneva and its principles. As a matter of policy, the United States Armed Forces shall continue to treat detainees humanely and, to the extent appropriate and consistent with military necessity, in a manner consistent with the principles of Geneva.

4. The United States will hold states, organizations, and individuals who gain control of United States personnel responsible for treating such personnel humanely and consistent with applicable law.

5. I hereby reaffirm the order previously issued by the Secretary of Defense to the United States Armed Forces requiring that the detainees be treated humanely and, to the extent appropriate and consistent with military necessity, in a manner consistent with the principles of Geneva.

6. I hereby direct the Secretary of State to communicate my determinations in an appropriate manner to our allies, and other countries and international organizations cooperating in the war against terrorism of global reach.

~~CONFIDENTIAL~~

DODDIA 000202

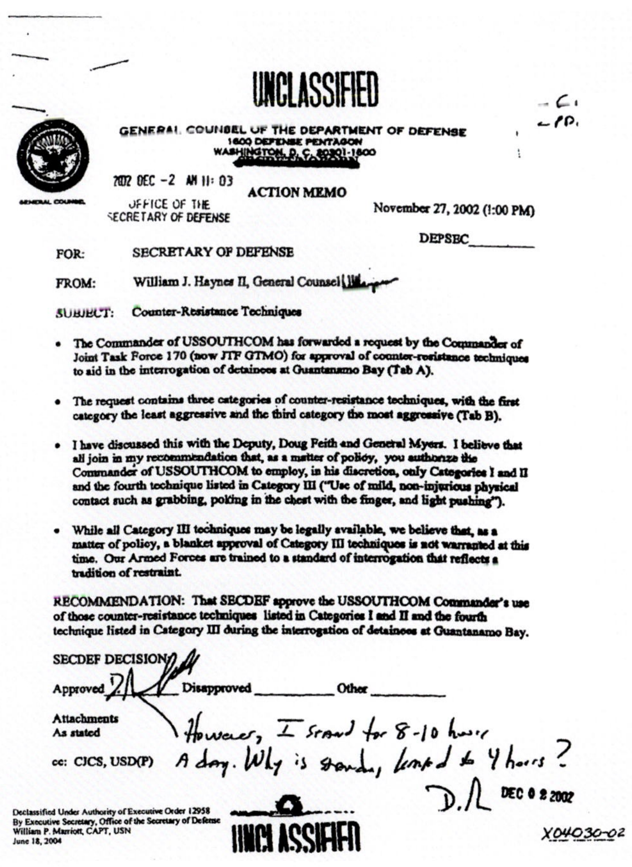

UNCLASSIFIED

GENERAL COUNSEL OF THE DEPARTMENT OF DEFENSE
1600 DEFENSE PENTAGON
WASHINGTON, D. C. 20301-1600

GENERAL COUNSEL

2002 DEC -2 AM 11: 03

OFFICE OF THE SECRETARY OF DEFENSE

ACTION MEMO

November 27, 2002 (1:00 PM)

DEPSEC________

FOR: SECRETARY OF DEFENSE

FROM: William J. Haynes II, General Counsel

SUBJECT: Counter-Resistance Techniques

- The Commander of USSOUTHCOM has forwarded a request by the Commander of Joint Task Force 170 (now JTF GTMO) for approval of counter-resistance techniques to aid in the interrogation of detainees at Guantanamo Bay (Tab A).
- The request contains three categories of counter-resistance techniques, with the first category the least aggressive and the third category the most aggressive (Tab B).
- I have discussed this with the Deputy, Doug Feith and General Myers. I believe that all join in my recommendation that, as a matter of policy, you authorize the Commander of USSOUTHCOM to employ, in his discretion, only Categories I and II and the fourth technique listed in Category III ("Use of mild, non-injurious physical contact such as grabbing, poking in the chest with the finger, and light pushing").
- While all Category III techniques may be legally available, we believe that, as a matter of policy, a blanket approval of Category III techniques is not warranted at this time. Our Armed Forces are trained to a standard of interrogation that reflects a tradition of restraint.

RECOMMENDATION: That SECDEF approve the USSOUTHCOM Commander's use of those counter-resistance techniques listed in Categories I and II and the fourth technique listed in Category III during the interrogation of detainees at Guantanamo Bay.

SECDEF DECISION

Approved D.R. Disapproved __________ Other __________

Attachments
As stated

However, I stand for 8-10 hours a day. Why is standing limited to 4 hours?

cc: CJCS, USD(P)

D.R. DEC 0 2 2002

Declassified Under Authority of Executive Order 12958
By Executive Secretary, Office of the Secretary of Defense
William P. Marriott, CAPT, USN
June 18, 2004

UNCLASSIFIED

X04030-02

Jenny Holzer, *The White House 2002*, 2006

Jenny Holzer, *Secretary of Defense*, 2006

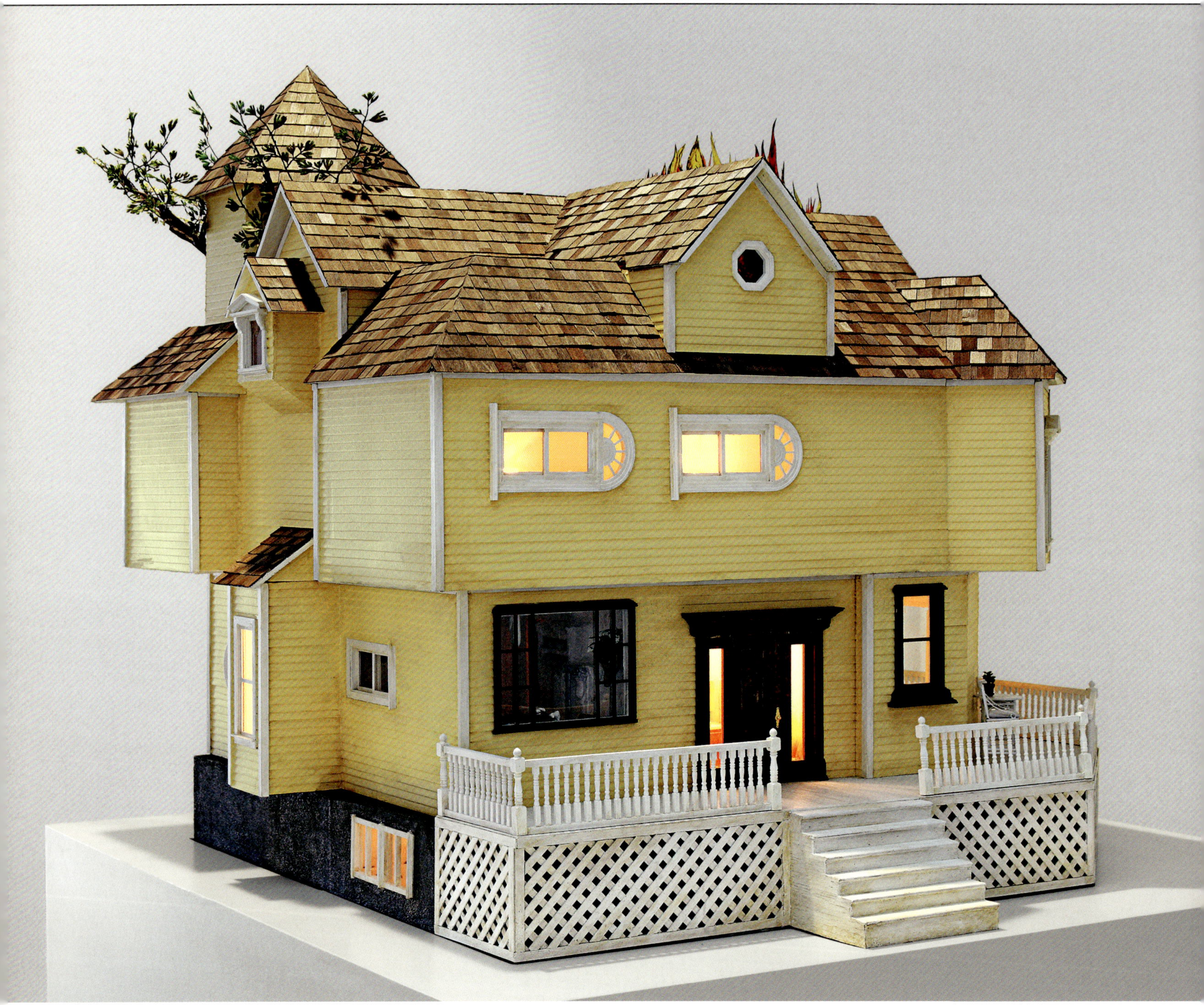

Sarah Anne Johnson, *House on Fire*, 2008

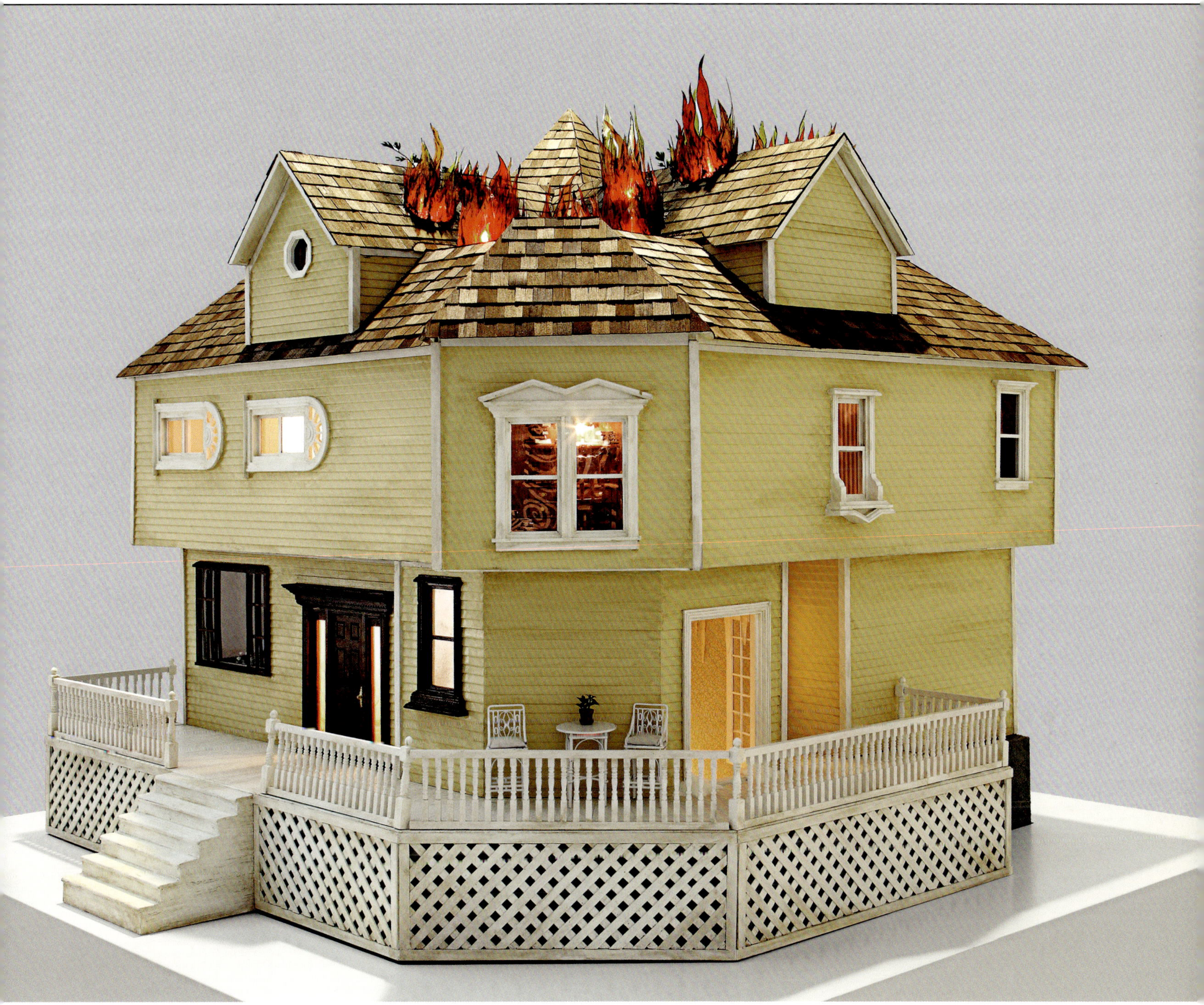

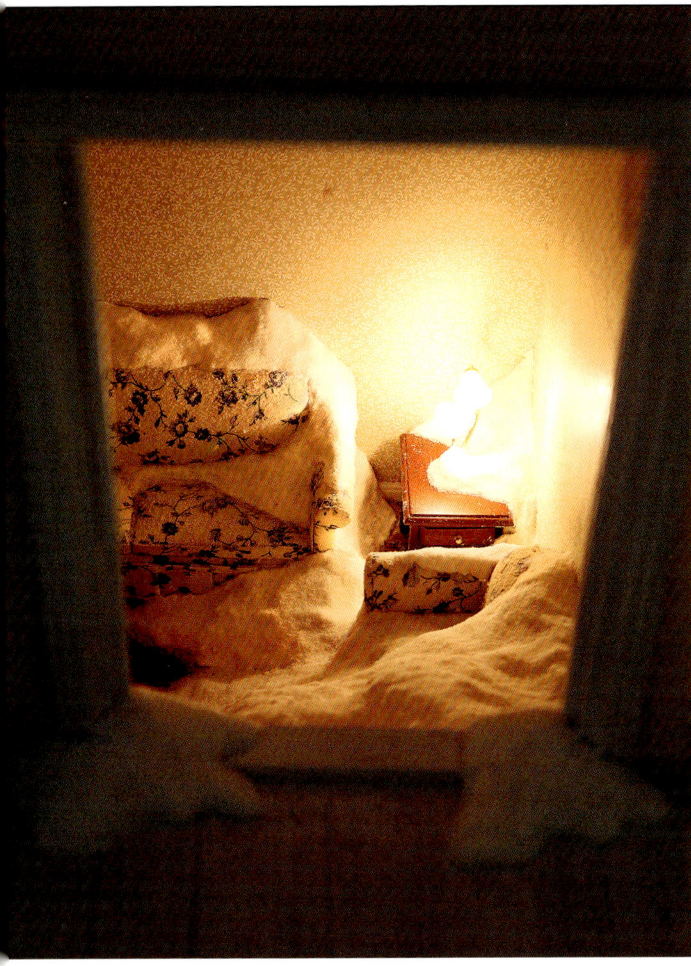

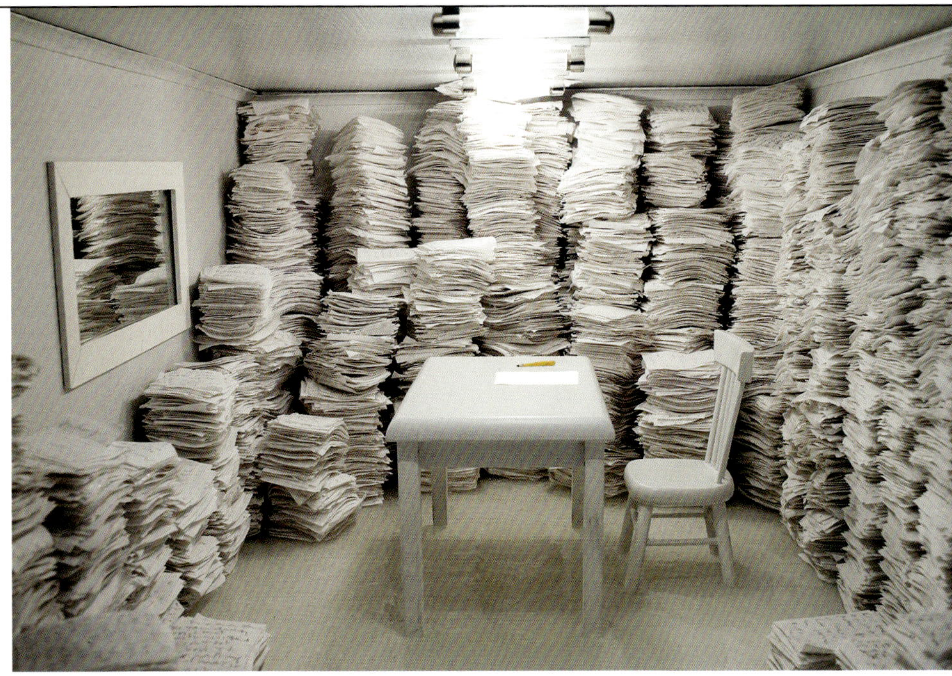

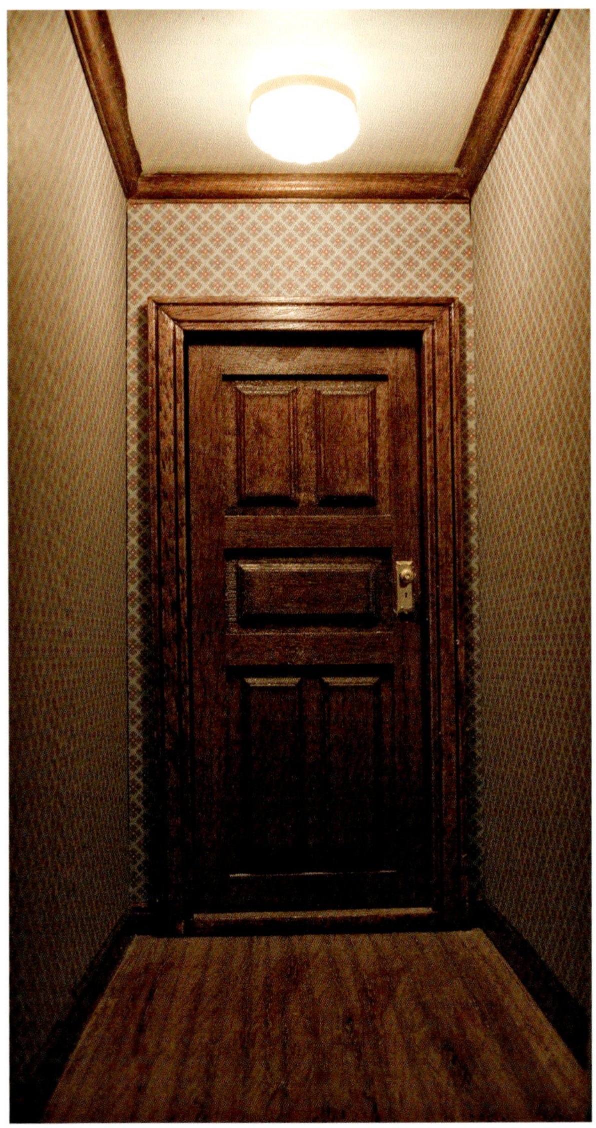

Details of Sarah Anne Johnson, *House on Fire*, 2008

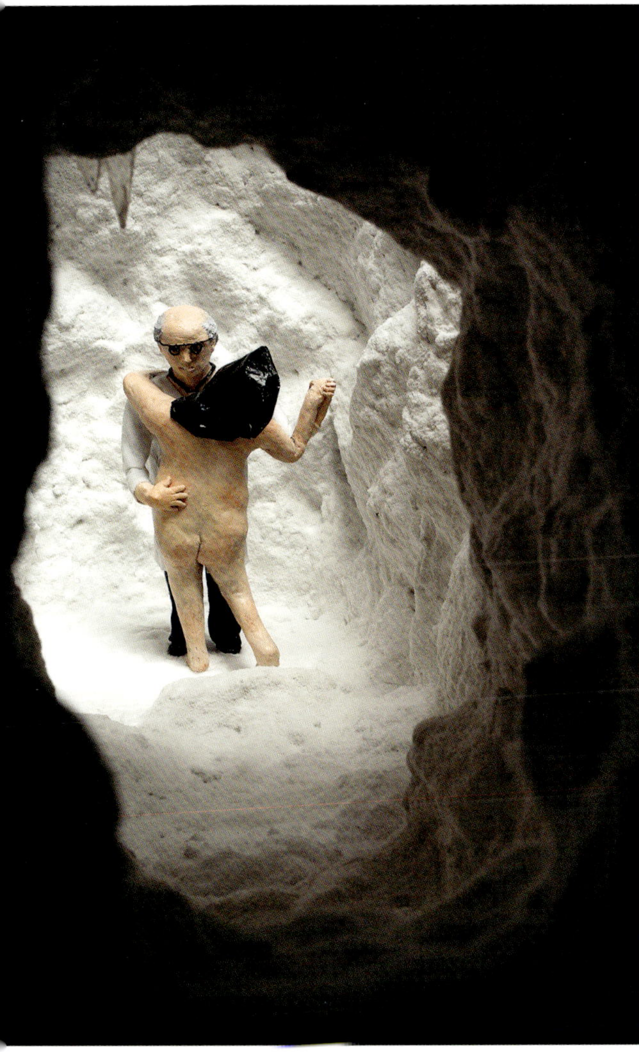

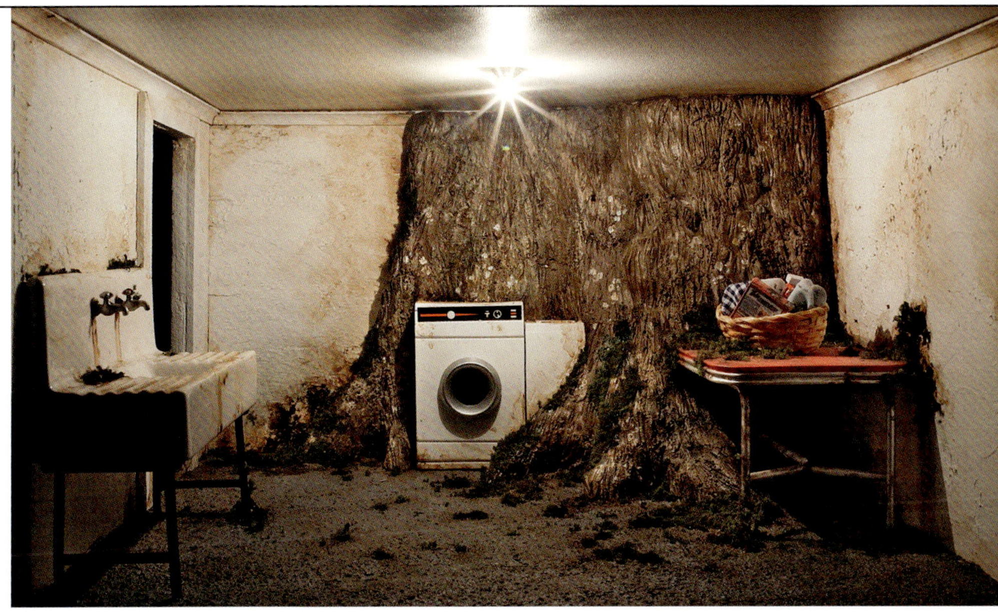

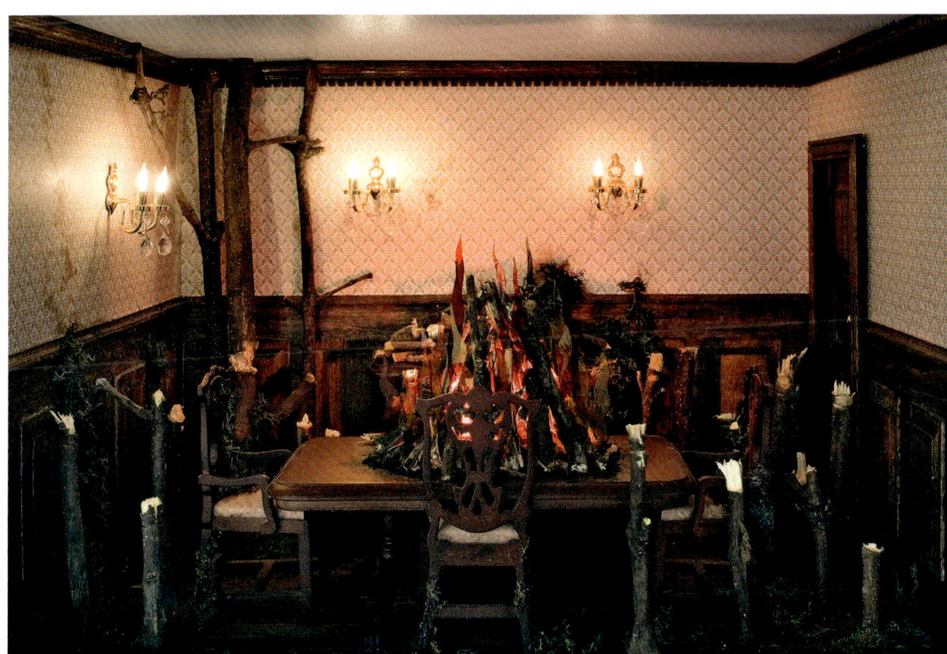

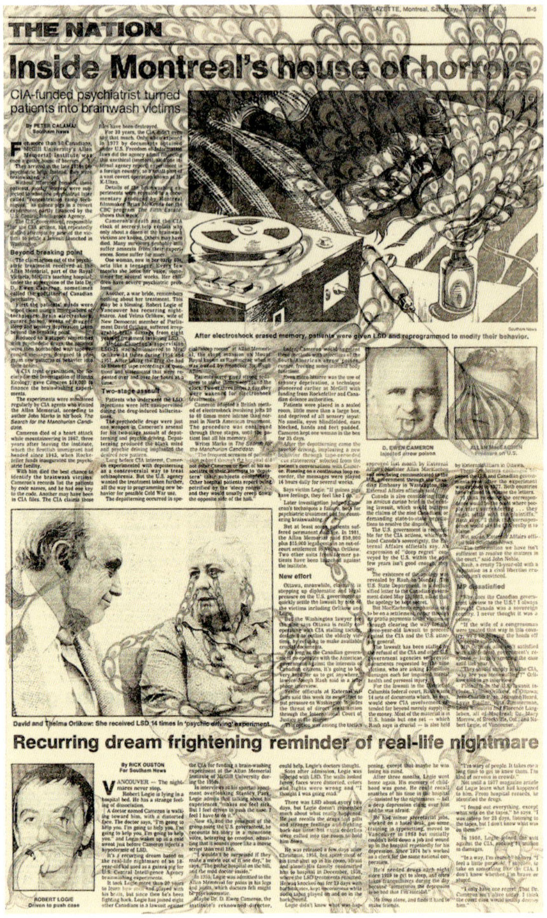

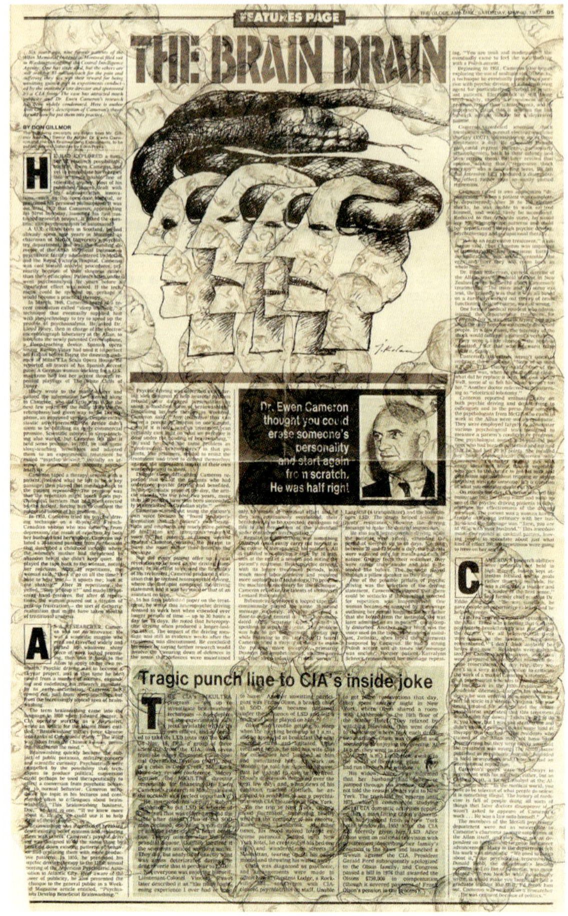

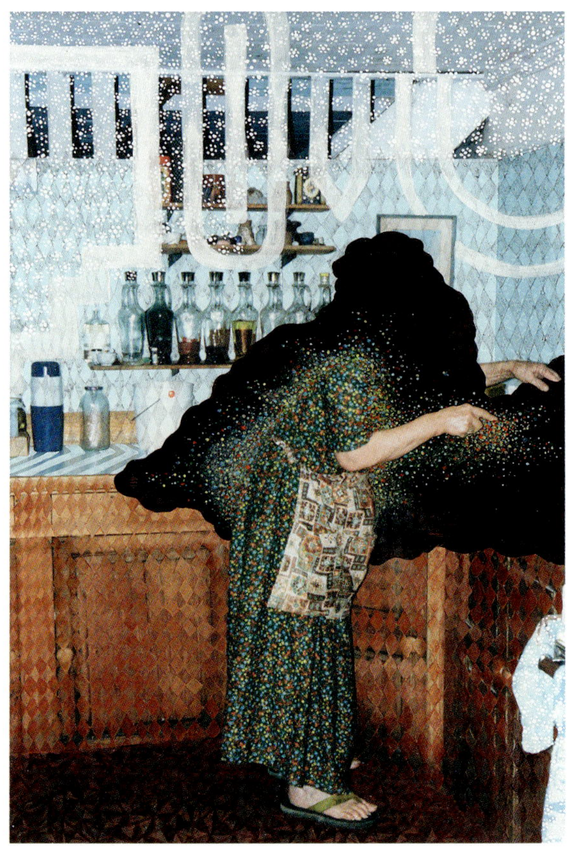

Sarah Anne Johnson, *House of Horrors*, 2008

Sarah Anne Johnson, *Brain Drain*, 2008

Sarah Anne Johnson, *Black Cloud*, 2008

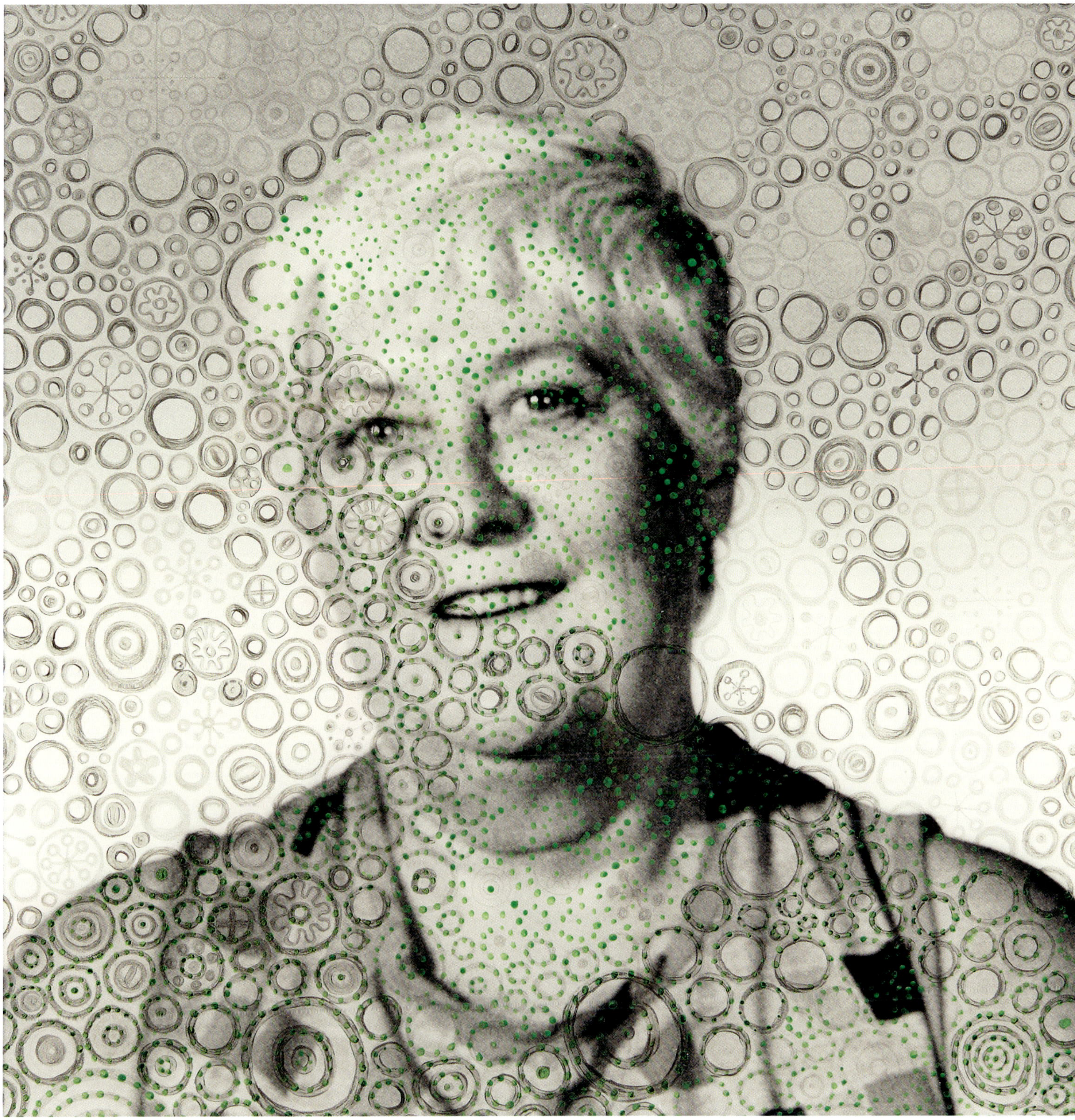

Sarah Anne Johnson, *Lysergic Acid Diethylamide*, 2008

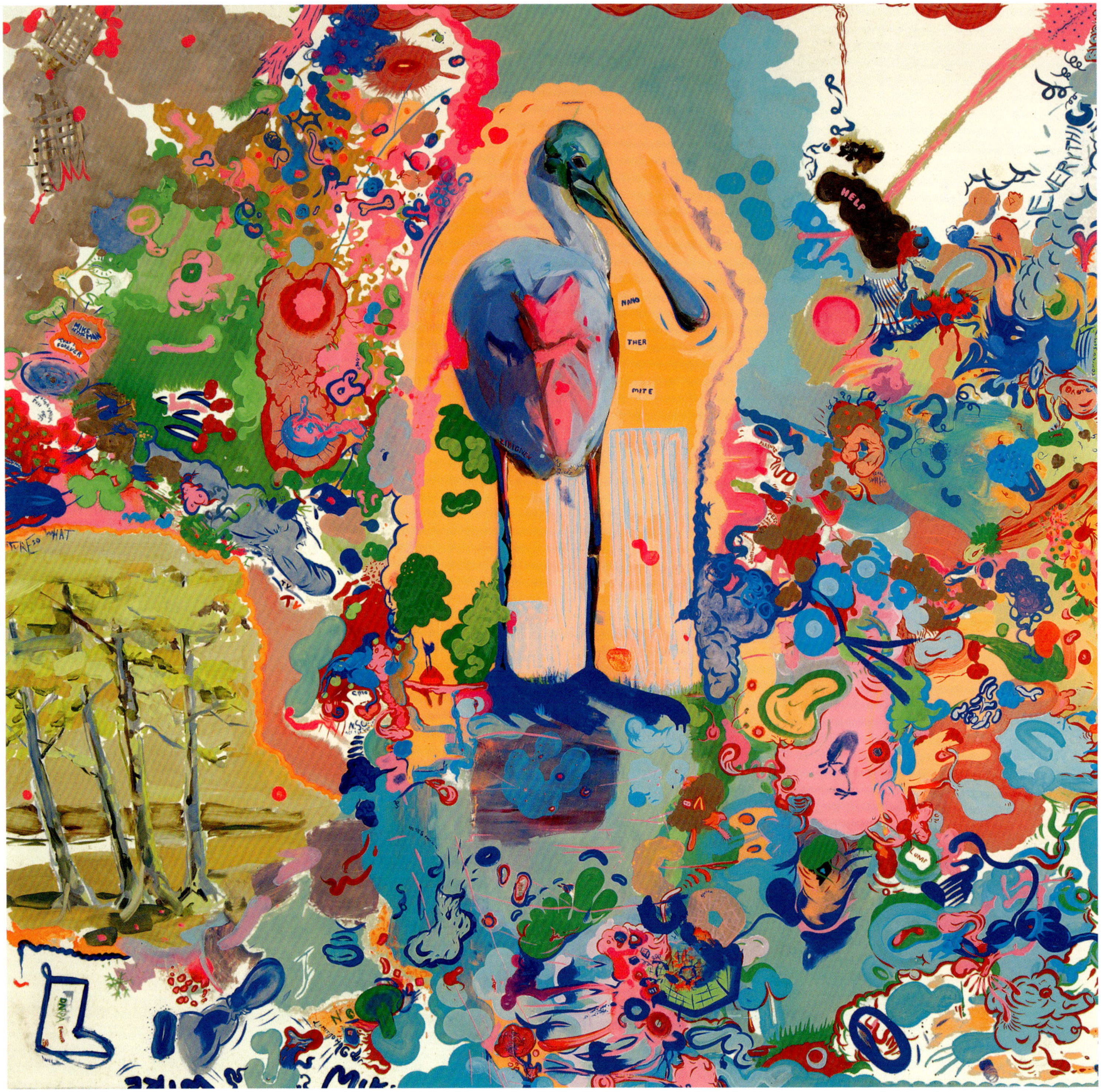

Sue Williams, *Hill and Dale, Black-Ops*, 2013

Sue Williams, *Mike and Zbigniew*, 2012

Sue Williams, *All Roads Lead to Langley*, 2016

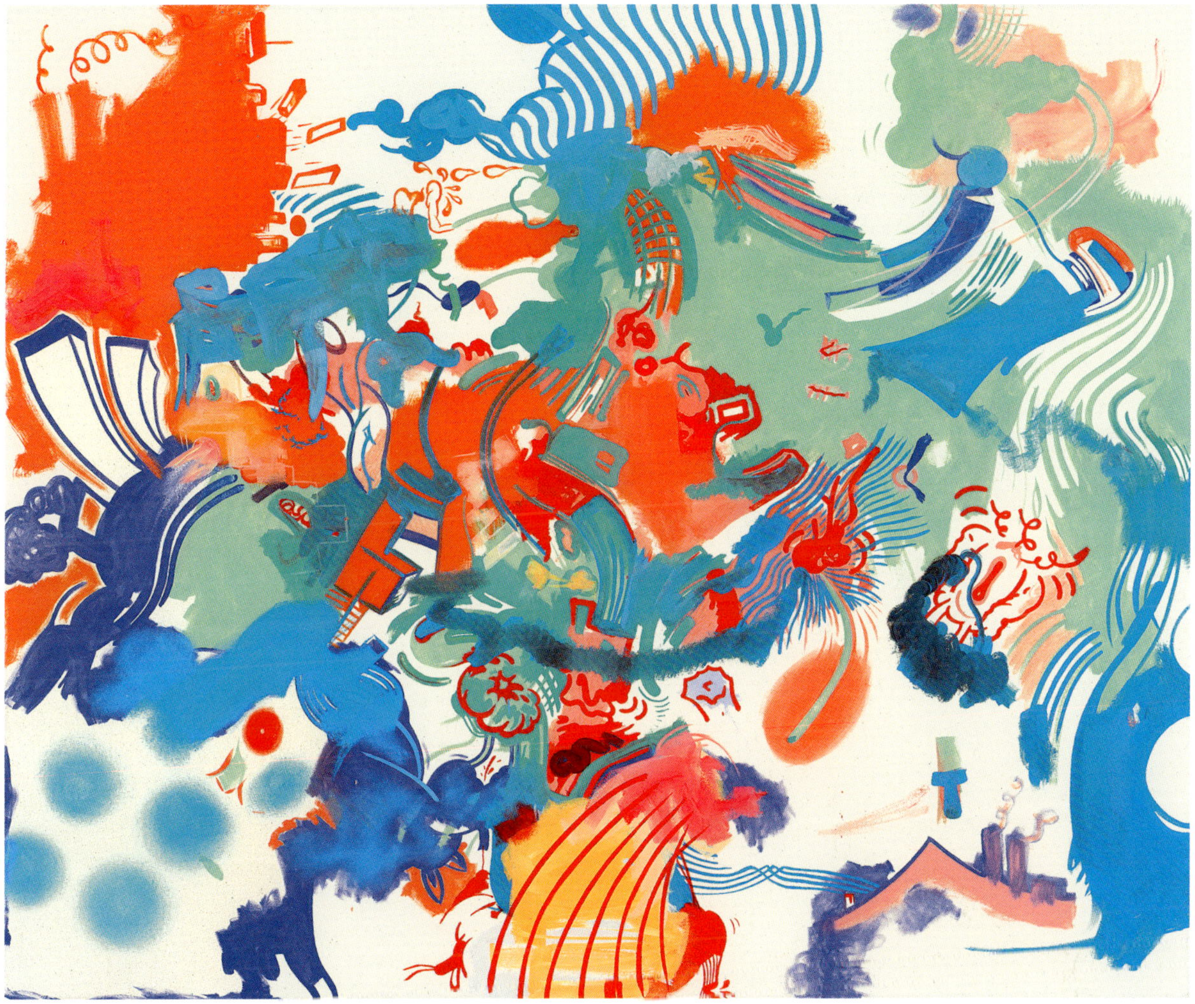

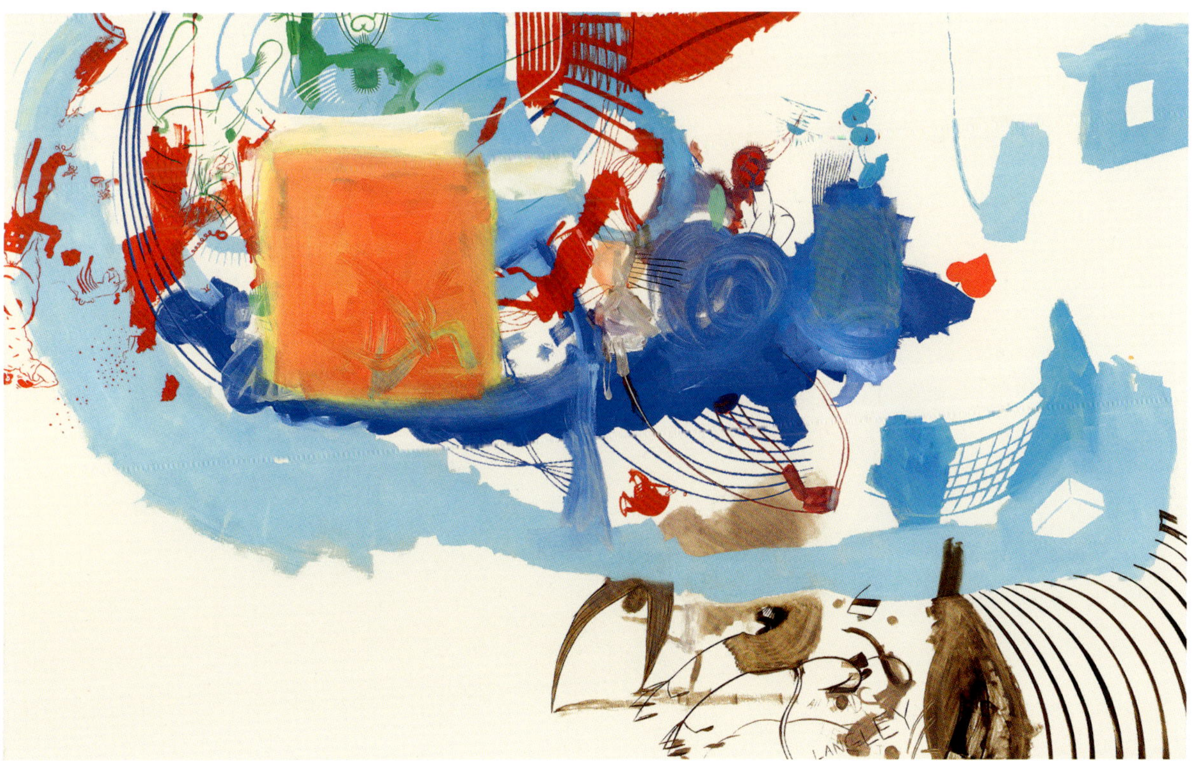

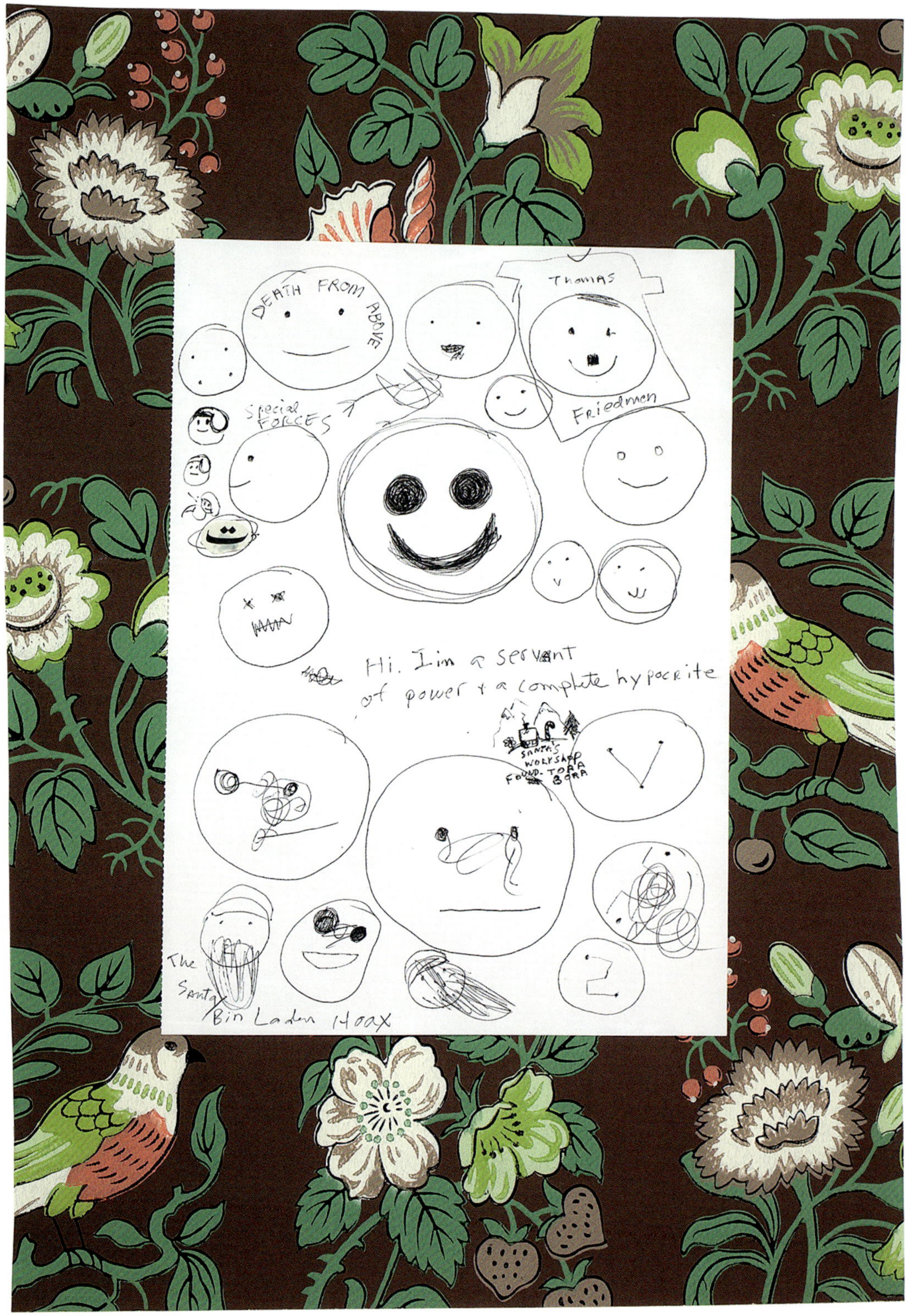

Sue Williams, *Gaudy Dutch/Happy Face*, 2010

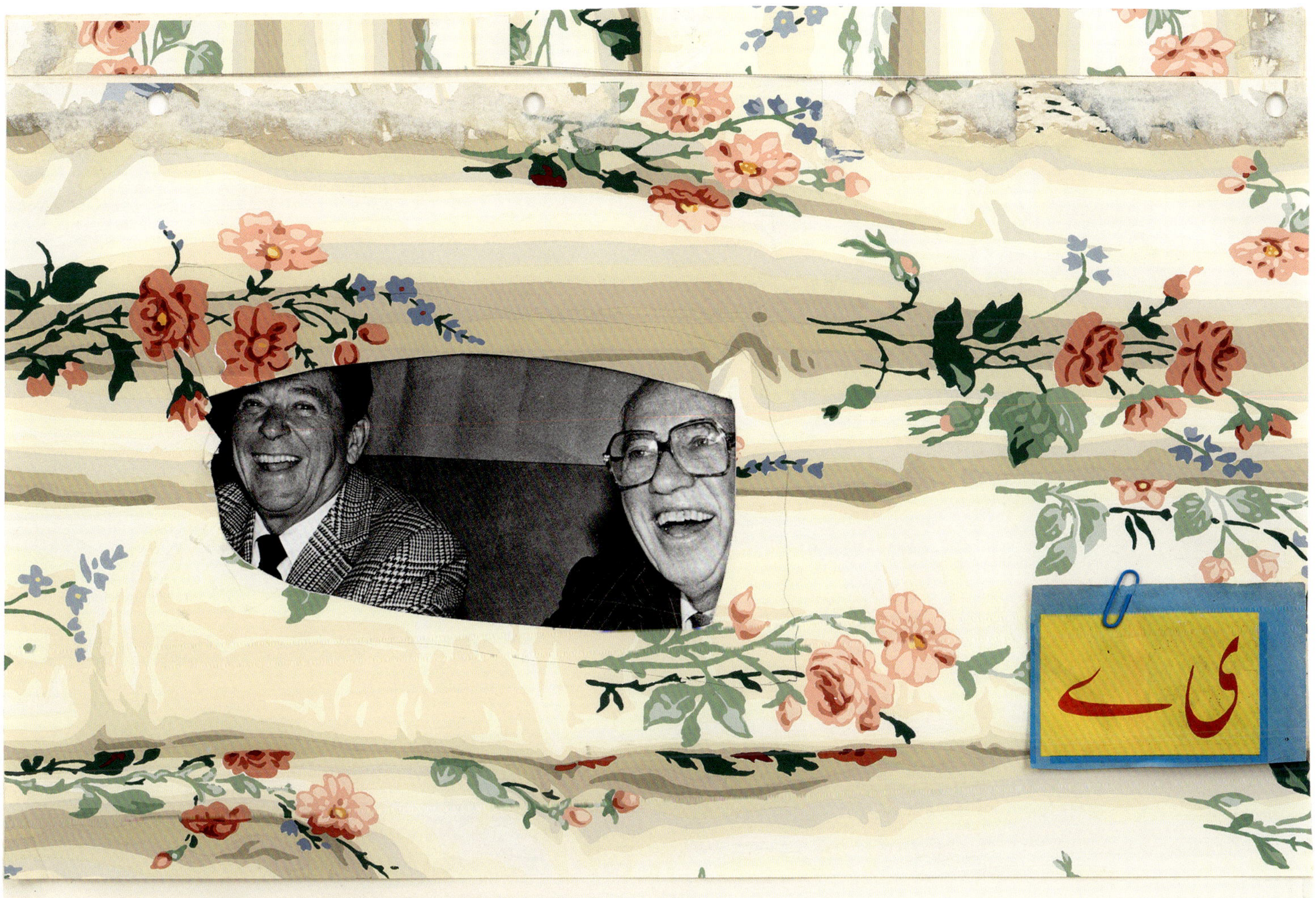

Sue Williams, *Ronald Reagan & William Casey*, 2016, detail from *Five Collages (i. Revere, ii. 2 Horses, iii. Curtain, iv. Ronald Reagan & William Casey, v. . . . Sat There Weeping, Weeping . . .)*, 2016–17

C O N S P I R A C Y

I N

C O N T E X T

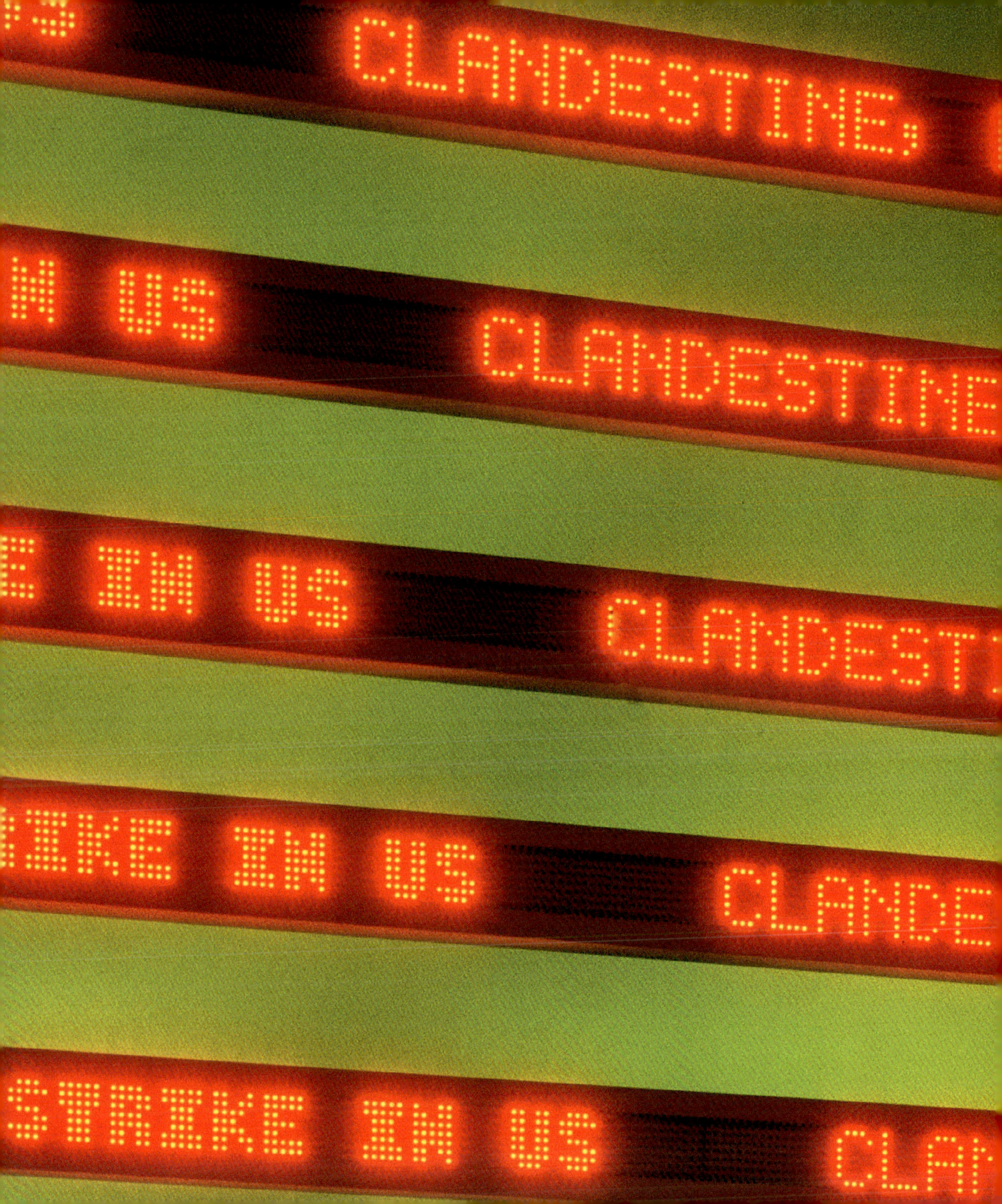
CLANDESTINE,
US CLANDESTINE
IN US
IN US
STRIKE IN US

HISTORY AND CONSPIRACY

Kathryn Olmsted

In 1993, President Bill Clinton asked a high-level appointee at the Justice Department to find out the answers to two questions: "One, who killed JFK? And two, are there UFOs?"[1] Clinton's questions reflected the changing status of conspiracy and conspiracy theory in late twentieth-century culture. As trust in government plunged, conspiracy theories were no longer isolated on the fringes of American politics. Even the president and others at the very heart of government could plausibly wonder if agencies were withholding information that was central to understanding our nation's recent history.

The works by the artists in this exhibition grapple with the important themes of trust and distrust, secrets and transparency, connections and gaps. During the Watergate hearings, congressional investigators repeatedly asked of the president's men: What did you know, and when did you know it? These artists ask: What did "they" know? And what do we make of their answers and of the things they have chosen to keep hidden?

The increase in Americans' distrust in their government is a relatively recent development. In the 1960s, at the height of the New Deal order and the Cold War consensus, more than three-quarters of Americans said that they trusted the federal government to do the right thing all or most of the time. About the same number trusted the media to tell the truth.[2] And then came a series of disasters, disappointments, and revelations of real government conspiracies.

One of the first shocks arrived on November 22, 1963, with the assassination of President John F. Kennedy in Dealey Plaza in Dallas. Two days later his alleged killer, Lee Harvey Oswald, was gunned down on live television. U.S. government officials tried to maintain public trust in the wake of these killings, but their attempts to control the narrative of Kennedy's death failed spectacularly. President Lyndon Johnson worried that the American people might push him into nuclear war with the Soviets if they believed, as he did, that a Communist-led conspiracy had plotted Kennedy's death. To reassure Americans that Oswald had acted alone, Johnson appointed a blue-ribbon commission to investigate the assassination. Chief Justice Earl Warren, one of the most respected figures in the nation, headed the formal inquest. Over nine months, the Warren Commission members and their staff heard ninety-four witnesses, read the depositions of hundreds more, and analyzed thousands of exhibits. In the end, they published twenty-six volumes of hearings and exhibits and came to a definitive conclusion: the prime suspect, Oswald, a twenty-four-year-old warehouse worker, had shot the president and had done so alone.[3] The report seemed to satisfy most Americans. After its release, polls showed that a majority shared the commission's lone-gunman theory.[4]

Then, starting in 1966, several books came out that questioned the Warren Commission report.[5] These conspiracy theories highlighted the bizarre circumstances surrounding the assassination and Oswald's murder. First was Oswald's complicated and confusing personal history: he had joined the Marines, then defected to the Soviet Union, and then re-defected to the United States. In New Orleans, he had set up a one-man chapter of an organization that supported the leader of Communist Cuba, Fidel Castro; but, at the same time, he had tried to infiltrate an anti-Castro group.[6] Most mysteriously, he was killed forty-eight hours after the assassination, as he was being moved from the Dallas jail. The shooter was a Dallas strip-club owner named Jack Ruby, who, depending on which account you believed, may or may not have been associated with Mafia figures.

The mysteries of the Kennedy assassination—and the Warren Commission's apparent failure to solve them—inspired a national, grassroots effort to find the "real killer." Groups of assassination researchers, as they called themselves, sprang up in cities, suburbs, and rural areas around the nation. Some of the most dedicated researchers traveled to Dallas to interview eyewitnesses and "earwitnesses" for themselves. They installed photo blow-ups of Dealey Plaza in their living rooms and scanned them for ominous shadows that might hide second shooters. Above all, they read, reread, and sometimes committed to memory parts of the same document that they denounced as part of a government whitewash: the Warren Report. Some of the photographs in the report, especially the pictures of Oswald standing in his backyard holding a rifle and copies of radical newspapers, generated many conspiracy theories. Just where had the sun been in the sky at that moment, and did those shadows under his nose prove that the photo was faked?

The most prominent public official to promote conspiracy theories about the assassination was New Orleans district attorney Jim Garrison. Later immortalized in Oliver Stone's movie *JFK* (1991), Garrison was the only prosecutor to put someone on trial for Kennedy's murder.[7] Garrison alleged that a New Orleans businessman had worked with the Central Intelligence Agency (CIA) to kill Kennedy because the president wanted to withdraw American forces from Vietnam. A jury took less than an hour to find the businessman innocent of the charges. Nonetheless, Garrison's theory that a right-wing cabal killed the president began to take hold of the public imagination. At the same time, Russian spies started planting similar stories about a right-wing military coup against the president. In a move that might seem familiar to present-day Americans, the Russians spread "fake news" in hopes of undermining the credibility of the U.S. government and destabilizing American democracy.[8]

But Americans really didn't need Russian propagandists to convince them that their government was lying: many official U.S. government investigators accomplished that task all by themselves. In 1974, with the Watergate scandal, Oval Office audiotapes revealed that President Richard Nixon had obstructed justice when Congress and the Justice Department tried to probe the many cases of bribery, blackmail, illegal surveillance, and burglaries committed by his re-election campaign. When Nixon resigned, trust in government briefly rebounded—only to plunge again when his successor, Gerald Ford, granted him a full pardon.

Conspiracy theories and their adherents increased in number during the 1970s, along with the percentage of Americans who distrusted their government. After Watergate, several congressional committees and one presidential commission began to investigate possible abuses and crimes by government officials. The most significant of these committees was headed by Senator Frank Church of Idaho. Over the course of an eighteen-month inquiry, the Church Committee revealed an array of U.S. government secrets, including plots by the CIA (whose motto is "The Truth Shall Make You Free") to overthrow the democratically elected government of Chile. In their inquiries into crimes committed against citizens in the United States, the Church investigators uncovered illegal surveillance of protesters by the CIA, interception of phone calls and telegrams by the National Security Agency (NSA), and harassment by the FBI of civil-rights leaders, including Martin Luther King Jr.[9] The FBI had even tried to blackmail King by sending him an audiotape that allegedly recorded his extramarital affairs, along with a letter urging him to commit suicide: "King, there is only one thing left for you to do. You know what it is. . . . You are done. There is but one way out for you."[10]

The Church Committee also revealed that the CIA had hidden critical information from the Warren Commission: it had failed to tell the investigators that, at the same time that Kennedy was killed, Kennedy was trying to kill Castro. On at least eight different occasions, the committee documented, American agents had made attempts on Castro's life. It was not only the existence of the plots that astonished many citizens but also their bizarre details, which combined elements of James Bond with the Keystone Kops. The CIA experimented with poisoned coffee, poisoned cigars, and poison-filled syringes concealed in ballpoint pens. It had contaminated the breathing tubes in a skin-diving suit and attempted to deliver it to Castro; it had developed an exploding seashell with the goal of placing it near Castro's favorite diving spot. It had even engaged the Mafia to help with some of its plots because American mobsters were angry that Castro had shut down their casinos in Havana. The agency had also tried to destroy Castro's credibility, most notably by plotting to coat the inside of his boots with a depilatory (so that his beard would fall out and he'd lose his macho authority) and trying to lace his cigars with a hallucinogen (so that he would sound crazy during his speeches).[11] The poisoned cigars and the exploding seashell were often conflated in the public's mind; years later, political cartoons continued to depict the Cuban leader with a CIA-supplied cigar exploding in his face.

The Church Committee revelations inspired a raft of books that set out all sorts of conspiracy theories about Kennedy's death.[12] Polls showed that more Americans than ever believed in a Kennedy assassination conspiracy. Right after the release of the Warren Commission report in 1964, 31 percent of Americans said they thought there was a broader plot to kill Kennedy. In 1976, after the Church Committee investigation, that number surged to 81 percent.[13]

As the dramatic Church Committee hearings unfolded throughout 1975, Americans had their first chance to see the sole video record of the Kennedy assassination. Abraham Zapruder, a Dallas dressmaker, had filmed the president's death on his home movie camera. *Life* magazine had bought a copy of the film from Zapruder and had printed some of its frames soon after the assassination, but had never released the movie itself. In March 1975, Robert Groden, an optics technician, showed a bootleg print of the Zapruder film on a television talk show.[14] For the first time, Americans saw the assassination for themselves. Indeed, they watched it over and over again, as TV producers aired the film on an endless loop. They could see how the assassin's bullet had forced the president's head back and to the left—which to some seemed to indicate that he was shot from the front rather than from behind, as the Warren Commission had concluded. The commission's experts insisted that the head movement shown in the Zapruder film was consistent with a shot from behind, but to no avail. The combination of the public release of the film and the Church Committee's revelations about the Castro plots convinced Congress to reopen the case.

In September 1976, the House of Representatives voted to set up a select committee to launch a new investigation of John Kennedy's murder (as well as those of Robert Kennedy and Martin Luther King Jr.). The inquiry, which lasted almost three years, employed 250 staff members and tried to chase down every possible theory. The committee compelled testimony from everyone still alive who knew something about the assassination or who had been accused of taking part in it. Even the so-called Umbrella Man—a Dealey Plaza bystander whose mysterious opening and closing of an umbrella had been caught on the Zapruder film—traveled to Washington to testify under oath.

The House investigation did not satisfy the skeptics. New leads unearthed by the investigators either turned out to support the conclusions of the Warren Commission or proved to be dead ends. The committee's photography experts concluded that the backyard photos of Oswald were genuine. The Umbrella Man, it turned out, was not signaling a confederate but making an obscure point about the president's father, Joseph Kennedy, supporting British Prime Minister Neville Chamberlain's policy of appeasement toward the Nazis before World War II. Significantly, forensics experts agreed with the Warren Commission's finding that Oswald had shot and killed the president. At first the committee concluded that there had been a second shooter in Dallas that day—a shooter who missed his target —but then audio experts quickly proved that they had misinterpreted a key piece of evidence. The new Kennedy assassination investigation, in short, was a complete disaster. Instead of finding "the truth," the investigators persuaded most Americans that they still did not—and never would—know who killed the president.[15]

In the wake of distrust following the Watergate scandal, the Church Committee, the House Select Committee on Assassinations, and their associated investigations had all tried to restore faith in the government's credibility. Here's what we've done, Frank Church and the others said: here are the skeletons in our national closet. Now you can really trust us. But the inquiries had the opposite effect. By the end of the 1970s, Americans not only mistrusted their government but also believed it was guilty of conspiracy.

Several works in this exhibition reflect Americans' fascination with the Kennedy assassination and with the clandestine government programs revealed by the Church Committee and other congressional investigations. Lutz Bacher's eighteen-part collage piece, *The Lee Harvey Oswald Interview* (pp. 60–61), was created in 1976, the year that the Church Committee issued its final reports. That same year, the House of Representatives set up its special inquiry. Bacher's use of a photocopier not only chimes with how subcultures of conspiracy theorists circulated their theories but also makes a broader claim that the "original" truth can never be discovered. "What it means is that it's something you can't ever know," Bacher says in the transcript of her discussion with an imaginary interviewer. "People will never be able to know for sure."

Jim Shaw's photocopied booklet *The End Is Here* (pp. 118–19, fig. 82) appeared in 1978, two years after Bacher's collages and at the peak moment of public distrust of the official explanation of the Kennedy assassination, a time when conspiracy theories proliferated. The variety of the theories would later inspire a famous *Onion* headline: "Kennedy Slain by CIA, Mafia, Castro, LBJ, Teamsters, Freemasons: President Shot 129 Times from 43 Different Angles."[16] Shaw concocts his own theory in his underground newspaper story containing "proof" that Kennedy was a "partially transubstantiated Martian" who turned against his alien overlords. The artist's fake conspiratorial account reports that the Martians were feeding Kennedy a cocktail of "cocaine, methedrine, barbituates, and testosterone," a wild gloss on rumors of the president's addiction to painkillers for his ailing back. Besides needing to silence the Martian/president, the aliens hoped that the assassination would lead to "massive nationwide drug taking." The artist manages to link Martians, "General Walker's crack assassination squad," Watergate conspirators G. Gordon Liddy and E. Howard Hunt, and Jackie Kennedy and her second husband, Greek tycoon Aristotle Onassis, in a monumental plot to kill the president and facilitate (and hide) the Martian invasion.

Shaw's absurd allegations of Martian mind control echo another set of real government conspiracies uncovered in the 1970s: secret brainwashing experiments. In 1975, in an unsuccessful attempt to head off a comprehensive congressional investigation of the intelligence community, President Gerald Ford appointed a blue-ribbon commission headed by Vice President Nelson Rockefeller and ordered its members

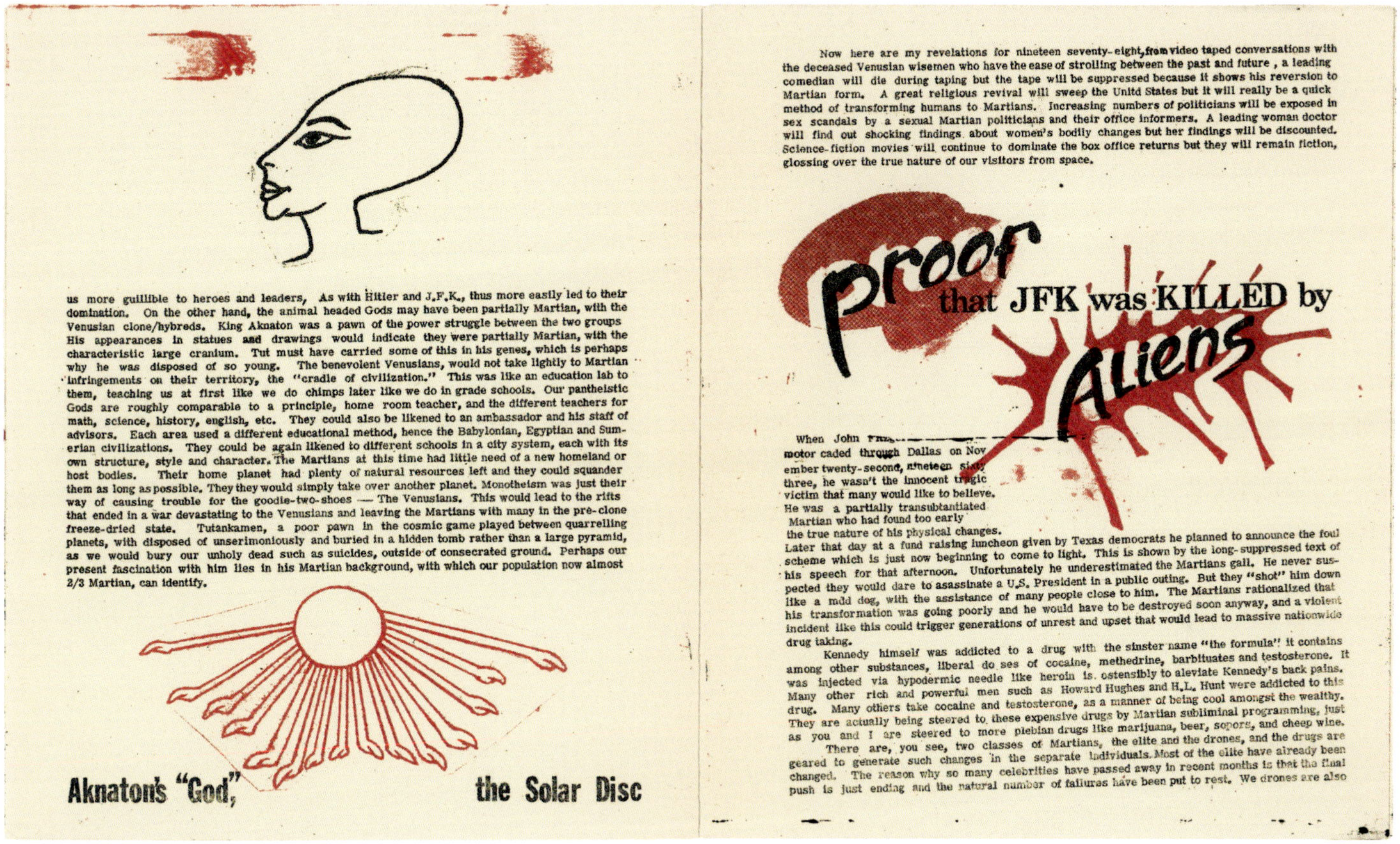

Fig. 82. Detail of Jim Shaw, *The End Is Here*, 1978

to examine CIA activities within the United States. The Rockefeller Commission disclosed that an unnamed Army scientist, later revealed to be Fort Detrick's Frank Olson, leaped to his death from a New York hotel room after his colleagues spiked his Cointreau with LSD at a CIA party. The section on Olson's death included two mysterious sentences: "The drug program was part of a much larger CIA program to study possible means for controlling human behavior. Other studies explored the effects of radiation, electric-shock, psychology, psychiatry, sociology, and harassment substances."[17] These revelations not only fed the public's appetite for evidence of conspiracy but also prompted investigative reporter John Marks to file a Freedom of Information Act request for more clues about the CIA program. Marks, along with congressional investigators, pried loose documents that outlined CIA mind-control experiments from the 1950s and 1960s.

In all, some 185 researchers at eighty different universities, foundations, hospitals, and prisons participated in the CIA's mind-control research. In one operation, spies hired prostitutes to slip LSD into unsuspecting Americans' drinks so the government could study the targets' reactions. The agency did not follow up on their experiments or even record the names of these involuntary subjects, so no one knows if they suffered long-term consequences from their unwitting ingestion of hallucinogenic drugs. Presumably, many of them believed that they had lost their minds.[18]

Among the most horrifying of the government's secret abuses exposed by the congressional investigators involved psychiatric experiments. At the height of the Cold War, the CIA supported the research of D. Ewen Cameron, a world-renowned psychiatrist at the Allan Memorial Institute in Montreal, who attempted to wipe out his patients' memories through what he called "depatterning" experiments and "reprogrammed" them, allegedly for the public good. Cameron dosed his unknowing patients with strange drug cocktails, stashed them in sensory-deprivation chambers, subjected them to electroshocks far beyond the usual voltage, and forced them to listen to reprogramming messages that played on audio loops for up to sixteen hours a day. The doctor believed that these experimental treatments could change so-called deviant personalities and improve society; the CIA saw depatterning and reprogramming people's minds as potentially useful weapons in the Cold War.

Sarah Anne Johnson has a personal connection to this story of covert abuse: her maternal grandmother was a victim. In the late 1950s, Velma Orlikow, a Canadian woman who suffered from postpartum depression, entered the care of Dr. Cameron with no knowledge that she would be a guinea pig in a U.S. government-funded project. Under Cameron's care, Orlikow was medicated with LSD and powerful sedatives and depressants. For up to six hours a day, the doctor bombarded her with repetitive verbal messages that debased and degraded her; then, after he decided she had been sufficiently broken, he played an endless loop of audio messages urging her to change her ways. Other patients were deprived of sound or sight for days, drugged into unconsciousness for weeks, and shocked so badly that they never fully recovered. Once they learned about the CIA's role in the research, Orlikow and several other victims sued the Montreal psychiatric hospital and the CIA. By the time the group won a settlement in 1988, numerous print and broadcast journalists had covered the shocking story—and, in the process, inspired more conspiracy theories.[19]

In *House on Fire* (2008; pp. 146–49, fig. 83), Johnson depicts her grandmother's victimization at the hands of the CIA by filling a dollhouse with scenes that evoke the hallucinations and mental torture she underwent. Hardly a stereotypical haven from a heartless world, the surreal, nightmarish home represents the horrors that Velma Orlikow endured as a brainwashing patient. Johnson's other artworks reinforce the sense of the pain and trauma that this real government conspiracy inflicted upon one woman.

Fig. 83. Detail of Sarah Anne Johnson, *House on Fire*, 2008

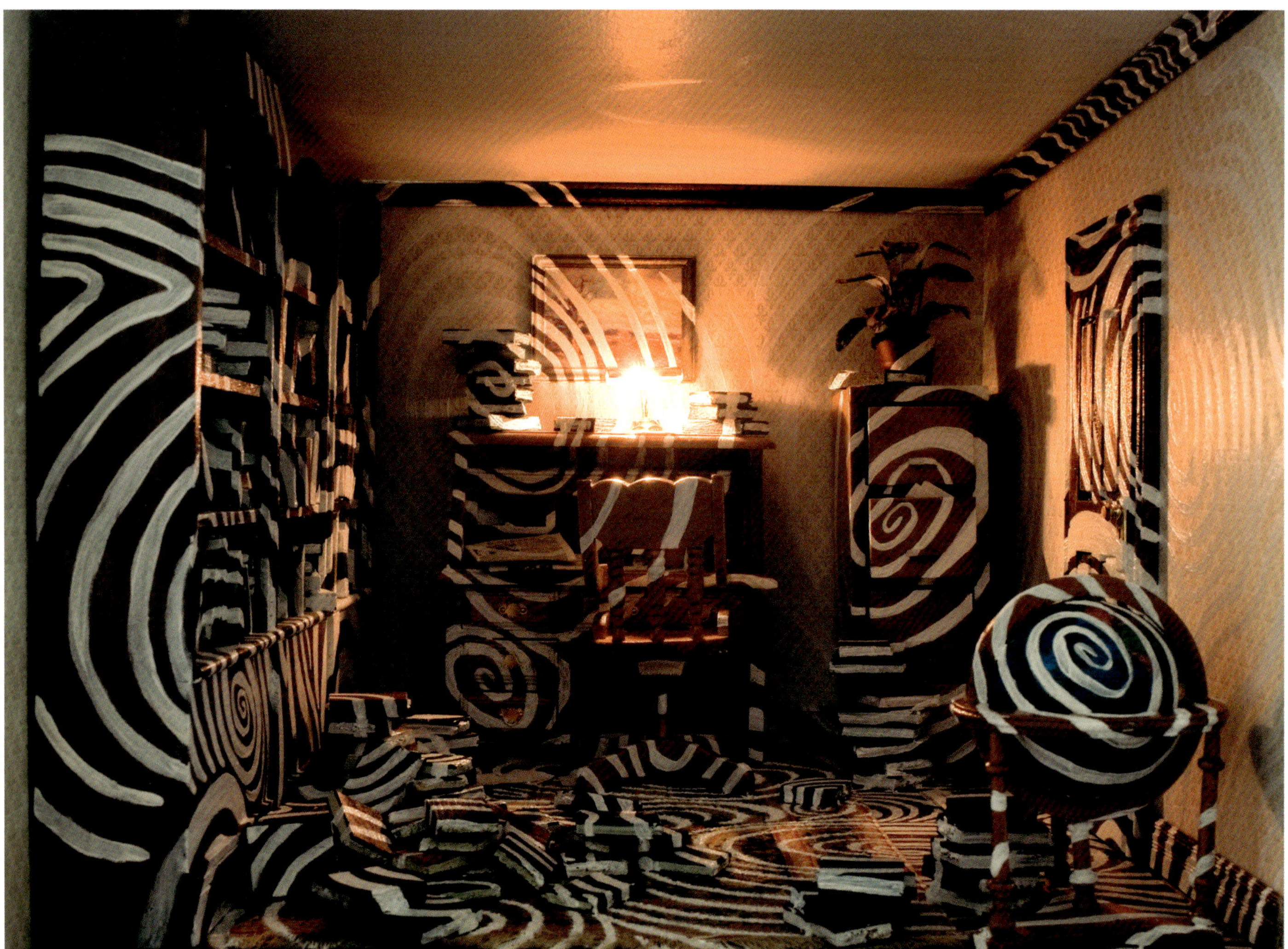

The continuing revelation of actual government plots in the 1980s stimulated new conspiracy theories. In 1986, the media began to report that officials in Ronald Reagan's administration secretly funneled money to the Contras, a counterrevolutionary army in Nicaragua, after Congress had specifically prohibited the use of U.S. funds for that purpose. At the same time, Reagan advisers arranged to covertly sell arms to the government of Iran in return for Iran's help in securing the release of American hostages in Lebanon. National Security Council officials then diverted the profits from the arms sales to the Contras.

The Iran-Contra scandal's complexities were hard to grasp, but the underlying significance was clear: the president and his advisers had repeatedly lied to Congress, the press, and the American people, and many involved had committed crimes. Although Reagan escaped impeachment, largely because investigators could not prove that he had known about the diversion of funds, several of his advisers were convicted of felonies. None of them spent time in prison, however, thanks to appellate rulings and to pardons by Reagan's successor, George H. W. Bush. As Bush left office, Americans' faith in their government continued to decline: in 1993, just one-quarter of Americans said that they trusted the government all or most of the time, compared to three-quarters in the early 1960s.[20]

Like the Kennedy assassination and the Watergate scandal, the Iran-Contra affair gave birth to a vast array of antigovernment conspiracy theories. After all, conspiracy theorists reasoned, if U.S. government officials publicly assailed terrorists, yet privately made deals with them, how could Americans trust anything they said?

As Bill Clinton's first question to his friend at the Justice Department shows, many of these suspicions continued to center on the assassination of John Kennedy. Some thirty years later, the percentage of Americans who rejected the conclusions of the Warren Commission was still growing. More specifically, 55 percent of those who believed in a "broader plot" accused the CIA of killing the president, as opposed to 40 percent who blamed Communists. In other words, more Americans suspected people in agencies within their own government than they did foreign enemies. These beliefs were not unique to the left or the right but instead united activists on both ends of the political spectrum, in what journalist Michael Kelly called "fusion paranoia."[21]

Oswald, in particular, became a subject of fascination for historians, novelists, and artists alike. Who was he, really? Communist or anti-Communist? Psychopathic loner, patsy, or master spy? In *Peach Oswald* (2001; p. 73), Wayne Gonzales—a New Orleans native who counted one of Garrison's investigators as a family friend—depicts a canny Oswald, his eyes signaling that only he knows the secret: did he, or didn't he? Cady Noland's iconic *Bluewald* (1989–90; fig. 30) is not about the Kennedy assassination per se but rather comments on our prurient interest in an individual's death. Noland uses the famous, Pulitzer-prizewinning photograph of the moment of Oswald's murder to force the viewer to confront the cruelty and horror of the media feeding frenzy. At the same time, the holes in Oswald's body might refer to newspaper editors' old practice of perforating negatives that they chose not to use—or, in this case, to the media punching holes in alternative theories of the assassination and stuffing a flag in Oswald's mouth to prevent him from ever telling us what he knew. Raymond Pettibon's *Untitled (Getting Oswald To . . .)* (1992; p. 129), rather than critique the media, suggests a conspiracy between far right and far left in the assassination, capturing the fusion paranoia at the heart of the conspiracy theories: "Where the crosshairs meet in Lee's scope as it's trained on JFK's forehead—that is the only meaningful meeting ground where right and left actually join hands."

American conspiracism—once fringe, now mainstream—has continued to spread in the twenty-first century. Given the recent history of distrust of government, it is not surprising that the 9/11 terrorist attacks on the World Trade Center and the Pentagon prompted even more suspicion. Many Americans already believed that their government had been guilty in the past of perpetrating, and then concealing, heinous crimes. Add to that background the George W. Bush administration's willingness to deceive and manipulate the public, and you have a recipe for new antigovernment conspiracy theories.

Some skeptics began proposing possible scenarios about 9/11 immediately after the attacks. Theorists on the far right were quick to blame the Jews, or the Communists, or various big businesses (airlines and insurance companies) that could have, they argued, profited from the attacks. But Americans on the left soon became the leaders of the 9/11 truth movement. Many were deeply suspicious of President Bush because the Supreme Court "selected" him as president in 2000 after he had lost the popular vote to Al Gore. By 2003, as Bush and his vice president, Dick Cheney, pushed for an invasion of Iraq, this distrust soared. Bush administration officials argued that Saddam Hussein was building weapons of mass destruction and that the Iraqis could pass them to terrorists. "We don't

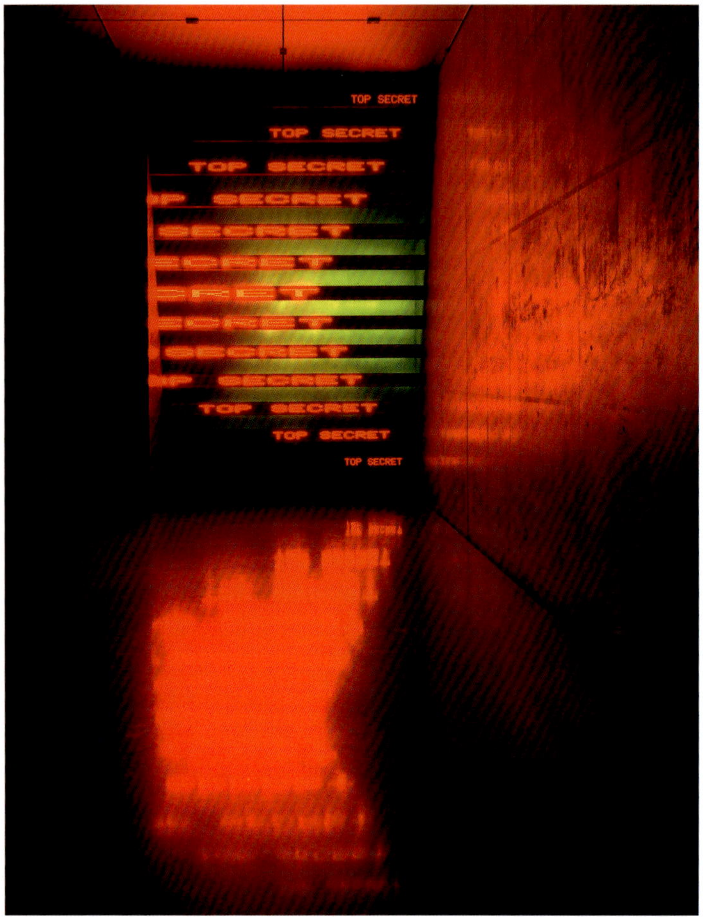

Fig. 84. Jenny Holzer, *Red Yellow Looming*, 2004

want the smoking gun to be a mushroom cloud," National Security Adviser Condoleezza Rice warned.[22] But when U.S. forces invaded Iraq, they found no evidence of a functioning nuclear, chemical, or biological weapons program.

Bush and Cheney themselves had proposed a kind of conspiracy theory: that Iraq might have conspired with the 9/11 hijackers. However, several independent investigations found no link at all between Hussein and the terrorists. In response, conspiracy theorists drew their own connections between Iraq and 9/11, but their conclusions were the mirror image of those presented by administration officials. Yes, they said, the 9/11 attack was the result of a conspiracy—but one perpetrated by Washington, not Baghdad. To the 9/11 truth movement, Bush and Cheney appeared to get everything they wanted from the incident: the concentration of power in the executive branch, the opportunity to spy on and harass their critics, and the chance to invade Iraq and control its oil supply.

The 9/11 truthers, as they became known, found a historical precedent for their theories in an unlikely place: the official U.S. government records on the Kennedy assassination. In 1962, just before the Cuban Missile Crisis, the U.S. Joint Chiefs of Staff had proposed that the military stage fake terrorist attacks—including shooting down a civilian airliner—and then blame the terrorism on the Cuban government. Kennedy apparently vetoed the plan, which had the code name "Operation Northwoods." The government quietly declassified the document in 1997, and the National Security Archive, a nonprofit research group, posted it on the Internet in 1998. Forty years after it was written, the Northwoods plan became central to 9/11 conspiracy theories. In the view of 9/11 truthers, Bush-Cheney officials were like the joint chiefs who drew up the Northwoods plan, devising their own version of the Reichstag fire. Only this time there was no President Kennedy to stop them.

Sue Williams's work comments on the cost of U.S. imperialism and the links among the members of the global elite who profit from it. For example, the title of *Golfing at Northwoods* (2008; fig. 80) refers to both the Northwoods plan and the Northwood Golf Club in Monte Rio, California. The club is across the Russian River from the Bohemian Grove, a luxurious private camp whose members have included several presidents, generals, businessmen, and other world leaders. The painting depicts fragments of the plaid outfits worn by the golfers who arrange the invasions of foreign lands.

And how does the U.S. government justify these invasions? Jenny Holzer's paintings and LED installations show the secrecy, deception, and horror at the heart of the Bush administration's Iraq policies, especially its embrace of so-called enhanced interrogation techniques. Holzer uses declassified government documents to highlight the arrogance and hypocrisy of the officials' attempt to find legal cover for torture. These documents, wrested from the government by Freedom of Information Act lawsuits brought by groups such as the American Civil Liberties Union, show the president and the secretary of defense using dull, legalistic arguments to legitimize inherently barbaric, primitive practices. In an ironic gesture, Holzer figures that making paintings and installations of these documents magnifies their words and increases our chances of not forgetting them amid today's tsunami of information.

In Holzer's *The White House, 2002* (2006; p. 145 top), President Bush uses impenetrable bureaucratic language to insist that while al Qaeda is not covered by the Geneva Convention, the Taliban is; however, Taliban detainees are unlawful combatants and therefore *not* legally protected by Geneva. Yet, the text explains, the U.S. military is an inherently moral institution, so it nevertheless "shall continue to treat detainees humanely and, *to the extent appropriate and consistent with military necessity*, in a manner consistent with the principles of Geneva" (emphasis added). There are no redactions in this document, and the banality of evil, to use Hannah Arendt's phrase, leaps out at the reader. Holzer's *Secretary of Defense* (2006; p. 145 bottom) also horrifies the viewer. In the 2002 memo, a Defense Department lawyer recommends that Defense Secretary Donald Rumsfeld authorize U.S. interrogators at Guantanamo to use some of the "counter-resistance" techniques listed in an unseen attachment. The techniques are classified according to their degree of aggressiveness, and the lawyer advises Rumsfeld to approve the first two categories, but only one technique in the most aggressive category ("Use of mild, non-injurious physical contact such as grabbing, poking in the chest with the finger, and light pushing"). The approved techniques also apparently include forcing the detainees to stand for four hours at a stretch. While Rumsfeld agrees with the recommendations, he can't help adding a handwritten protest: "I stand for 8–10 hours a day. Why is standing limited to 4 hours?"

Rumsfeld was the Bush administration's most profound epistemologist. As he famously said: "There are known knowns. There are things we know we know. . . . There are known unknowns. That is to say, we know there are some things we do not know. But there are also unknown unknowns—the ones we don't know we don't know."[23] In other works in this exhibition, Holzer uses the government's redactions to highlight the unknowns. In *Red Yellow Looming* (2004; p. 144, fig. 84), lines from Rumsfeld's torture memos are lit with red LEDs and alternate with yellow strips that denote the redactions. The viewer sees the words anew as they form a ladder to hell. *Accordingly* (2012; fig. 77) presents a document in which the letterhead and lead paragraphs have been completely obliterated. Yet the anonymous author of the memo uses what we cannot see or know to conclude that torture is necessary: "Accordingly, in view of the grave danger to the United States and its citizens, [redacted] have approved the implementation of the enhanced interrogation techniques described above."

The authors of these documents, the men who insisted that the use of torture by the U.S. military was necessary and legal, never intended us to see any of their memos. Their words terrify us, and so do the empty spaces that continue to hide their words. Holzer captures the contradictions inherent in the discovery process. There are the known knowns, in the revealed text, and the known unknowns, in the redactions. The redactor actively removed the information from the knowledge base; it's not only that we don't know, but also that we've been prevented from knowing.

Ultimately, as Holzer's paintings remind us, it is the real conspiracies by the government—plots to ignore the Geneva Conventions or, in earlier days, to conspire with the Mafia to kill a foreign leader—that prompt Americans to believe in antigovernment conspiracy theories. The redactions in the official documents cause conspiracy thinking, but so does the information that is released. More information does not bring knowledge or understanding. Indeed, Lutz Bacher reaches this conclusion in *The Lee Harvey Oswald Interview*: "I could have a thousand pictures and I would still be going nowhere. It should be that more pictures would tell you more but what happens is they tell you less and less." As Frank Church would argue, the truth doesn't set you free. It just inspires more questions.

POLITICS OF HATE IN THE U.S.A.: ANTI-SEMITISM AND CONSPIRACY THEORY

John Miller

Modern conspiracy theory traces its roots to the late eighteenth century. In 1797 the French cleric Abbé Barruel wrote an account of the French Revolution focused on the Jacobins, behind whom he saw a conspiracy of three secret societies: the Order of Templars, the Order of Freemasons, and the Illuminati.[1] In a letter to Barruel the retired army officer J. B. Simonini later praised the cleric's analysis but pointed out the "omission" that Jews had founded both the Freemasons and the Illuminati in order to gain world domination.[2] The Scotsman John Robison likewise argued in his 1797 book *Proofs of a Conspiracy: Against All the Religions and Governments of Europe*, "Nothing is more clear than that the design of the Illuminati was to abolish Christianity."[3] Many in the United States, clergymen especially, took this polemic to heart and greeted the French Revolution with suspicion. In May 1798, for example, the Reverend Jedidiah Morse warned of a Jacobin-derived plot against American political and religious institutions. Soon after, journalists exposed the Robison book as fraudulent, and by the end of 1799 the Illuminati affair was, for the time being, over.[4] Nonetheless, a virulent strain of anti-Semitism remained.

Around 1881 the novel *Biarritz* (1868), written by Prussian postal worker Hermann Goedsche under the pen name Sir John Retcliffe, gained notoriety throughout Europe. What captivated many of its readers was a sensationalistic chapter titled "In the Jewish Cemetery in Prague." In it, elders from the twelve tribes of Israel gather at the grave of the most venerable rabbi to discuss the progress of their plot to take over the world. This text was reprinted in various forms as "The Rabbi's Speech" and distributed throughout Russia and France. In time, readers came to accept this story as fact, and it became the basis for the *Protocols of the Elders of Zion*, which purports to be a transcript of lectures given by leading Jews at an 1840 world congress in Kraców, Poland.[5] The texts were pieced together between 1872 and 1895 from various sources: the writings of Barruel, Simonini, and Goedsche, as well as books by Maurice Joly and Roger Gougenot des Mousseaux.[6] According to James Ridgeway:

> The *Protocols* argue that people are incapable of governing themselves, and only a despot using armed force can govern effectively. . . . .[The Jews have plotted their] rise to power by pitting the Gentiles against one another until, eventually . . . [they] will be able to enlist the masses in overthrowing their indolent gentile leaders. Thereafter the masses will be kept under firm control through an efficient government that will banish unemployment, apply taxation in proportion to wealth, and promote education. During this messianic age the Jewish masters will shrewdly promise, but never deliver, liberty.[7]

Although *London Times* correspondent Philip Graves showed that parts of Joly's satirical book *The Dialogue in Hell between Machiavelli and Montesquieu* (1864) had been plagiarized in the *Protocols*, the content of these bogus lectures too became accepted as fact. Shortly before the October Revolution of 1917, the czar's secret police published another version in an attempt to smear its opponents.[8]

In the 1920s Henry Ford widely distributed the *Protocols* in the United States. His weekly newspaper, the *Dearborn Independent*, included excerpts of the book as part of a series on "the Jewish international conspiracy" (fig. 85). According to the *Independent*, Jewish influence was everywhere. Jews forced William Howard Taft to break a commercial treaty with Russia, thereby weakening the czar. They controlled Woodrow Wilson's administration, particularly through Bernard Baruch, chair of the War Industries Board. (Wilson initiated the League of Nations, forerunner to the far right's much-hated United Nations.) Communism itself was a Jewish plot. The *Independent* also charged that Paul Warburg intended to control the U.S. financial system with the Federal Reserve. Ford later anthologized the entire series as *The International Jew* and distributed the four-volume book worldwide. Half a million copies circulated in the United States alone. In Germany, it became a cornerstone of fascist propaganda.

In 1927 Aaron Sapiro sued the *Independent* for libel in its series "Jewish Exploitation of Farmer Organizations." Although the lawsuit ended in a mistrial, Ford closed the newspaper.[9] During this highly publicized case, the *Independent's* editor, William J. Cameron, took full blame for the newspaper's policies. Wilson and the Warburg family also challenged Ford's accusations. Ford retracted them, claiming his employees had published the material without his consent. Yet, in 1938, Ford accepted the Grand Cross of the German Eagle, becoming the first American to be decorated with that medal.[10]

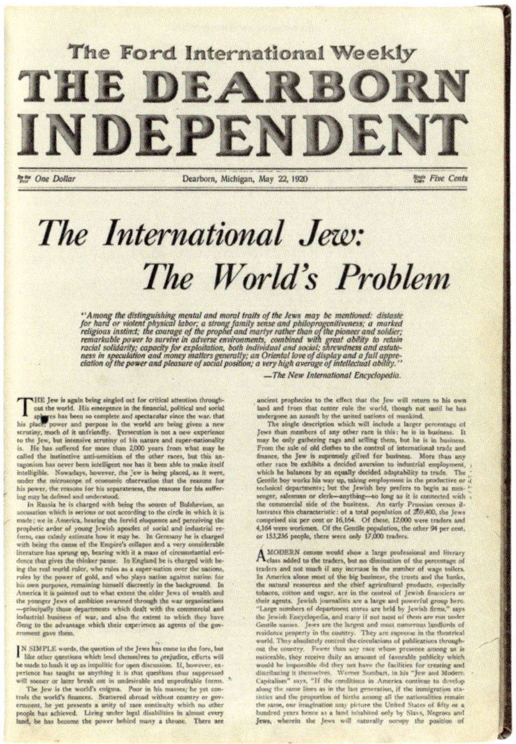

The Ford International Weekly

THE DEARBORN INDEPENDENT

One Dollar — Dearborn, Michigan, May 22, 1920 — Five Cents

The International Jew: The World's Problem

"Among the distinguishing mental and moral traits of the Jews may be mentioned: distaste for hard or violent physical labor; a strong family sense and philoprogenitiveness; a marked religious instinct; the courage of the prophet and martyr rather than of the pioneer and soldier; remarkable power to survive in adverse environments, combined with great ability to retain racial solidarity; capacity for exploitation, both individual and social; shrewdness and astuteness in speculation and money matters generally; an Oriental love of display and a full appreciation of the power and pleasure of social position; a very high average of intellectual ability."

—The New International Encyclopedia.

THE Jew is again being singled out for critical attention throughout the world. His emergence in the financial, political and social spheres has been so complete and spectacular since the war, that his place, power and purpose in the world are being given a new scrutiny, much of it unfriendly. Persecution is not a new experience to the Jew, but intensive scrutiny of his nature and super-nationality is. He has suffered for more than 2,000 years from what may be called the instinctive anti-semitism of the other races, but this antagonism has never been intelligent nor has it been able to make itself intelligible. Nowadays, however, the Jew is being placed, as it were, under the microscope of economic observation that the reasons for his power, the reasons for his separateness, the reasons for his suffering may be defined and understood.

In Russia he is charged with being the source of Bolshevism, an accusation which is serious or not according to the circle in which it is made; we in America, hearing the fervid eloquence and perceiving the prophetic ardor of young Jewish apostles of social and industrial reform, can calmly estimate how it may be. In Germany he is charged with being the cause of the Empire's collapse and a very considerable literature has sprung up, bearing with it a mass of circumstantial evidence that gives the thinker pause. In England he is charged with being the real world ruler, who rules as a super-nation over the nations, rules by the power of gold, and who plays nation against nation for his own purposes, remaining himself discreetly in the background. In America it is pointed out to what extent the elder Jews of wealth and the younger Jews of ambition swarmed through the war organizations—principally those departments which dealt with the commercial and industrial business of war, and also the extent to which they have clung to the advantage which their experience as agents of the government gave them.

IN SIMPLE words, the question of the Jews has come to the fore, but like other questions which lend themselves to prejudice, efforts will be made to hush it up as impolitic for open discussion. If, however, experience has taught us anything it is that questions thus suppressed will sooner or later break out in undesirable and unprofitable forms.

The Jew is the world's enigma. Poor in his masses, he yet controls the world's finances. Scattered abroad without country or government, he yet presents a unity of race continuity which no other people has achieved. Living under legal disabilities in almost every land, he has become the power behind many a throne. There are ancient prophecies to the effect that the Jew will return to his own land and from that center rule the world, though not until he has undergone an assault by the united nations of mankind.

The single description which will include a larger percentage of Jews than members of any other race is this: he is in business. It may be only gathering rags and selling them, but he is in business. From the sale of old clothes to the control of international trade and finance, the Jew is supremely gifted for business. More than any other race he exhibits a decided aversion to industrial employment, which he balances by an equally decided adaptability to trade. The Gentile boy works his way up, taking employment in the productive or technical departments; but the Jewish boy prefers to begin as messenger, salesman or clerk—anything—so long as it is connected with the commercial side of the business. An early Prussian census illustrates this characteristic: of a total population of [illegible], the Jews comprised six per cent or 16,164. Of these, 12,000 were traders and 4,164 were workmen. Of the Gentile population, the other 94 per cent, or 153,236 people, there were only 17,000 traders.

A MODERN census would show a large professional and literary class added to the traders, but no diminution of the percentage of traders and not much if any increase in the number of wage toilers. In America alone most of the big business, the trusts and the banks, the natural resources and the chief agricultural products, especially tobacco, cotton and sugar, are in the control of Jewish financiers or their agents. Jewish journalists are a large and powerful group here. "Large numbers of department stores are held by Jewish firms," says the Jewish Encyclopedia, and many if not most of them are run under Gentile names. Jews are the largest and most numerous landlords of residence property in the country. They are supreme in the theatrical world. They absolutely control the circulations of publications throughout the country. Fewer than any race whose presence among us is noticeable, they receive daily an amount of favorable publicity which would be impossible did they not have the facilities for creating and distributing it themselves. Werner Sombart, in his "Jew and Modern Capitalism" says, "If the conditions in America continue to develop along the same lines as in the last generation, if the immigration statistics and the proportion of births among all the nationalities remain the same, our imagination may picture the United States of fifty or a hundred years hence as a land inhabited only by Slavs, Negroes and Jews, wherein the Jews will naturally occupy the position of

Fig. 85. "The International Jew: The World's Problem," *The Dearborn Independent*, May 22, 1920

Michael Barkun, an expert on the Christian Identity movement, which provides a religious and ideological foundation for many recent hate groups, has noted the irony of Ford's anti-Semitism:

> The so-called "pseudo-agrarian" movements . . . beginning in the 1890s . . . sought to blame rural and small-town social dislocations on an urban, plutocratic conspiracy. More often than not, this cabal was identified as explicitly Jewish, and it became a convenient scapegoat for those troubled by departures from traditional social values. It was ironical that Henry Ford, himself an agent of some of these changes . . . became . . . one of the principal voices for an anti-Semitic politics of resentment.[11]

The precursor of the Christian Identity movement was, oddly enough, a nineteenth-century philo-Semitic theology: British-Israelism, which construed Anglo-Saxons to be descendants of the lost tribes of Israel who belonged to God's chosen people.[12] As the highly decentralized Zionist movement came to the fore in Britain, aspects of the belief took on a low-key, anti-Semitic inflection. Because Anglo-Israelites believed that both the House of Israel (the Anglo-Saxons) and the House of Judah (the Jews) must return to the Promised Land before the Second Coming, Zionist exclusivity presented an obstacle to their redemption.[13]

When British-Israelism came to the United States in the late 1870s, it mutated into outright anti-Semitism by focusing on a combination of Victorian-era pseudoscience and specious scholarship that progressively denigrated Jews. In the 1930s Howard B. Rand emerged as a key popularizer of the ideology, founding the influential Anglo-Saxon Federation of America. Rand's group embraced James Larratt Battersby's *The Holy Book of Adolf Hitler*, which portrays *der Führer* as a religious saint. Among other things, it advocates polygamy to better propagate the Aryan race.[14] Rand made Detroit the Federation headquarters, and it was there he met a fellow believer: William J. Cameron, the former editor of Henry Ford's *Dearborn Independent*, who aided in spreading the belief as vehement anti-Semitism.[15]

In the 1930s a new religious groundswell swept across the United States, reviving, among other things, the anti-Semitism Ford had espoused earlier. Just as a convulsive modernization left Germany open to Nazism, so economic turmoil and rapid urbanization drove many Americans to fundamentalist religion. With fire-and-brimstone preachers grimly warning of the coming apocalypse, paranoia and racism were overlaid on these beliefs. Three figures dominated the fundamentalist movement: Gerald B. Winrod, William Pelley, and Gerald K. Smith.[16]

Gerald B. Winrod preached that Christ would soon return for the Battle of Armageddon. He believed that while anti-Semitism is founded in biblical prophecies, only a "certain element" of world Jewry advocates subversion. The widow of Christian Identity minister Wesley Swift believes that it was Winrod who introduced her husband to British-Israelism.[17] What distinguished Winrod from other preachers was his 1938 bid for the U.S. Senate in Kansas. He finished third in the Republican primary elections with considerable support from Mennonite communities and the Ku Klux Klan.[18]

At the outset of his career, William Pelley had been a supporter of Woodrow Wilson and the League of Nations. In 1927, he underwent a sudden mystical transformation, withdrawing from society and experiencing a reported rebirth, during which he claimed to have heard voices from other worlds. He came back to public life believing in reincarnation—particularly in the reappearance of "demon souls" as Jews. Later, Pelley embraced the work of pyramidologist David Davidson, who was a follower of British-Israelism. By integrating Davidson's work with anti-Semitism, Pelley helped lay the groundwork for Christian Identity.[19] After Hitler came to power in Germany, Pelley founded the Silver Legion—or Silver Shirts as Pelley sometimes called them, after the Brown Shirts. Pelley even claimed that Christ himself had accepted his offer to become an honorary Silver Shirt. In 1942, trying to quash nativist reactionaries, the Roosevelt administration charged both Pelley and Winrod with sedition. Pelley served eight years of a fifteen-year prison sentence and was paroled in 1950.[20]

Like Winrod, Gerald K. Smith was a fundamentalist who entered politics. In 1933 he joined Pelley's Silver Shirts, then went on to help manage Huey Long's presidential campaign. After Long's assassination in 1935, Smith unsuccessfully ran for office. He then formed the Union Party with Father Charles Coughlin and Francis Townsend. The Union Party ran William Lemke against Franklin D. Roosevelt in the 1936 election but received fewer than a million votes. Smith next moved to Detroit and met Henry Ford, who sponsored his radio broadcasts and furnished him with investigators for compiling the "Ford Company Red File," a list of known or suspected Communists. This work inspired feverish visions of Jewish conspiracy in Smith's mind. He proclaimed, "Communism is Jewish," and speculated that Roosevelt never died, but rather that Jews had hidden him to later bring him back as "President of the World."[21] Even after World War II, Smith maintained that people had misunderstood Hitler and that the Holocaust was a hoax. Despite his bizarre speculations, Smith was a commanding speaker who could rally large audiences. During the war he had met with Christian Identity theologian Wesley Swift and converted to his obscure sect.[22] As an agitator, Smith helped politicize the Identity cause; using key Identity figures to forward his own political agenda, he lent coherence to an otherwise fragmented movement.[23]

More than any other, Wesley Swift was the figure around whom a fully formed Christian Identity belief—with no remaining ties to Britain—coalesced. Swift founded his church in Lancaster, California, in 1946 and later changed its name from the Anglo-Saxon Christian Congregation to Church of Jesus Christ Christian (as opposed to Jesus Christ, King of the Jews). He had also been involved in an attempt to revive the California Ku Klux Klan in the 1920s and later headed the California Anti-Communist League. During the 1960s he was reputed to have formed links with paramilitary groups: the California Rangers and the Christian Defense League.[24]

A friend of Gerald K. Smith's, Swift successfully popularized Identity in right-wing circles through a combination of extremist religious, racial, and political platforms. As its name implies, the psychological basis of its ideology concerns identity formation and reinforcement. This process typically requires the construct of otherness to fortify a sense of self. Swift's theology embraced a Manichaean worldview that merged religion and politics. It reinterpreted the book of Genesis, postulating a "two-seed theory," according to which both Adam and the Devil, as the serpent, impregnated Eve. It construed the name "Adam" to mean "showing blood in the face." This ability to show shame or embarrassment is what supposedly distinguishes the Aryan race from others.[25] Anglo-Saxons are therefore the "Adamic race," while Jews are "spawn of the Devil" and thus absolutely demonized. Yet, this portrayal creates an obvious contradiction. On the one hand, Identity warns of an overwhelming Jewish threat; on the other, it claims that Aryan supremacy is inevitable. Other races, or "mud people," are "pre-Adamic," i.e., created by God before he perfected the first full-fledged human beings. Because Christian Identity churches view the United States as "God's Country"—or more specifically as New Israel, Jews no longer play any part in the End Days. The return of the True Israelites to the Promised Land presages Armageddon, the ultimate battle between good and evil prophesied in the book of Revelation. Identity followers believe they had already reached this stage during the Revolutionary War. Barkun clarifies the radicalization and separatism that arises from this twisted logic:

> Since the essence of conspiracy theories is their claim to parsimony—explaining all evil through single causes—the incorporation of satanic paternity into already existing theories of a world Jewish conspiracy gave to the theory ultimate parsimony: everything that was or is undesirable in the world has come from a single source. If that source is destroyed, the world will be perfected and the millennium will begin. Further, as with all conspiracy theories, this one defies falsification. A plot of such cunning is presumed to be able to mislead those who would try to detect it, so that any evidence that appears to contradict the theory must necessarily have been fabricated by the conspirators themselves. . . . Thus the theory becomes a closed system of self-referential ideas, from which all contradictory information has been excluded.[26]

Kenneth Goff, a Christian Identity minister and protegé of Minuteman founder Robert DePugh, preached that the conspirators had infiltrated and controlled international politics throughout the twentieth century. According to him, Benito Mussolini, Vladimir Lenin, and "Colonel" Edward Mandell House (a chief aide to Wilson) laid the plans for World War I at a conference in Belgium during the early 1900s. After House convinced Czar Nicholas II to abdicate his throne, Jacob Schiff, through the financial firm of Kuhn, Loeb & Co., engineered Lenin's rise to power. To cover their tracks, Zionists launched a "disinformation campaign" portraying their allies, the Russian Communists, as anti-Semitic.[27] Goff claimed that the international Jewish banking cabal further consolidated its hold on the world economy through marriages between the Loeb, Rothschild, and Warburg families. To win sympathy, they fabricated accounts of the Holocaust in Nazi Germany and used the charge "anti-Semitic" to disable their critics. Alger Hiss, whom Goff and other conspiracy theorists considered a "Jewish agent," served on the U.S. delegation to the Yalta Conference and helped arrange to grant the Soviet Union veto power in the United Nations (he was later accused of spying for Russia).[28] From Goff's perspective, a secret cabal controlled mainstream television, radio, and newspapers as well: the so-called Jews' media. Those who subscribe to anti-Semitic conspiracy theories have come to call the federal government the Zionist Occupied Government—or ZOG, for short.

In 1991, Pat Robertson's book *The New World Order* became a *New York Times* bestseller with almost a half million copies in print. It effectively legitimated the bizarre ideas of the patriot movement within a broader evangelical Christian community. Although his book simply updates well-established conspiracy themes, Robertson, then unofficially heading the Christian Coalition, disavowed that approach.[29] Nonetheless, he claimed to have traced "an invisible cord" of influence connecting "[Woodrow] Wilson . . . to the JP Morgan bank, to the Rockefellers and the Council on Foreign Relations . . . to the powerful Carnegie, Rockefeller and Ford Foundations, to the United Nations, to Henry Kissinger . . . , to the Trilateral Commission, to Jimmy Carter, to George Bush."[30] Critic Michael Lind attacked Robertson's implicit racism in the February 1995 *New York Review of Books*:

> Not since Father Coughlin or Henry Ford has a prominent white American so boldly and unapologetically blamed the disasters of modern world history on the machinations of international high finance in general and on a few international Jews in particular.[31]

Robertson responded, "I deeply regret that anyone in the Jewish community believes that my description of international bankers and use of the phrase 'European bankers' in my book refers to Jews."[32] Even so, Robertson quoted the work of well-known anti-Semites Nesta Webster and Eustace Mullins in support of his theories.[33] Defenders of the book dismissed its anti-Semitism by pointing out Robertson's support for Israel. For a dispensational premillennialist such as Robertson, backing Israel does not necessarily preclude anti-Semitism. According to this belief, the Jews must return to Israel before the Second Coming.

Michael Barkun has described how conspiracy theory relies on an inverse logic of credibility: one that stigmatizes ideas bearing the approval of prestigious institutions and that legitimizes, by default, those not associated with such institutions. He links this inversion to British sociologist Colin Campbell's notion of the "cultic milieu":

> [First, the term] refers to a society's "rejected knowledge," beliefs considered unacceptable by such authoritative institutions as conventional religion, universities, the state, and the mass media. Second, the cultic milieu refers not simply to this body of rejected knowledge but to its expression in the form of a "cultural underground," a "network of individuals, groups, practices, institutions, [and] means of communication."[34]

Clearly, this inverse logic is a compensatory rationalization of otherwise unacceptable social changes. It pertains not so much to active cultural dissent itself as it does to withdrawal from status-quo adversity. A disaffected person is always the most susceptible to this form of belief. One can always more easily scapegoat another than confront one's own failings. Consensus within a cult, moreover, can intensify and seemingly objectify almost any belief. Laird Wilcox, a critic of the radical right, points out that once people enter conspiracy discourse, they become "insulated from outside forces, they listen to themselves and no one criticizes them. . . . You have an internal myth built up by this incestuous feedback."[35] Political analyst Chip Berlet further observes that once a group establishes this insularity, "instead of engaging in a political struggle based on debate, compromise, and informed consent . . . [conspiracy theorists only] want to expose and neutralize the bad actors."[36] The emergence of the Internet has reinforced this kind of thinking. There, when verification for these ideas is lacking, predisposition—that is, a *fervent need to believe*—sanctions them anyway.

BEYOND THE GRASSY KNOLL

Douglas Eklund

Someone once said that beneath or behind all political and cultural warfare lies a struggle between secret societies.
—Ishmael Reed, *Mumbo Jumbo*

In early 2018, a diagram of conspiracy theories—as intricate looking as any presented here—went viral (fig. 86).[1] It first spread in chat rooms devoted to QAnon (or just Q), another recent viral sensation, which claims to be perched high up in the ranks of military intelligence. About once a week QAnon posts elliptical missives that are so cryptic as to be humorous, readers interpret and debate them with the solemnity of Talmudic scholarship. This example, taken at random, relates to a recent school shooting: "Who do you think is leaking the info? // Take a wild guess. // Analyze shooter (pawn). // Voices in his head? // We know. // We are taking action behind the scenes. // CNN was set up. // STUPID // Q." Of course, whether Q is "real" or a diversionary "psyop" is much debated online. But to the silent majority clustered around the ideological center of American politics, the pronouncements of Q are as ridiculous as those of the members of the John Birch Society who first warned of fluoride in the drinking water half a century ago.

The QAnon posts and the related diagram (as well as the countless YouTube channels featuring gonzo amateurs of varying degrees of seriousness) seem like they could have come from the minds of Robert Anton Wilson and Robert Shea, whose trilogy *The Illuminatus!* was published in 1975. Unlike Ishmael Reed's *Mumbo Jumbo* (1972) and Thomas Pynchon's *Gravity's Rainbow* (1973), *The Illuminatus!* is not a highbrow masterwork of conspiracy literature but rather a set of turgid potboilers that wed the loopy what-ifs of science fiction with the aspirational fantasies of young men for sex, drugs, and rock and roll, what Pynchon termed "mindless pleasures" (its slightly nerdy reputation is epitomized by the role-playing card game it spawned). The trilogy's most notable feature is the head-spinning way in which every page introduces a new conspiracy theory. While working as editors at *Playboy* magazine (conspiracy theory unsurprisingly grew roots in men's magazines in the 1960s), Wilson and Shea got the idea for the trilogy from the crackpot letters that deluged the magazine's Forum section, which they collected as a kind of anonymous folk art. These letters, from the fringe of the fringe, reported accounts of UFOs and Hitler's postwar life in South America that were more florid and fantastical than any case of reasoned paranoia experienced by radicals and minorities in the 1960s and 1970s. (That paranoia, however, largely drives the ham-fisted plot.)

The various characters in *The Illuminatus!* pursue a conspiracy so grand that it connects every conspiracy theory together. As they pass from novices to adepts, they finally attain a Zen-like enlightenment based on a nonjudgmental acceptance of absurdity, as when one character tells another, "You are well on your way to paranoia. . . . Just remember: *it's not true unless it makes you laugh*."[2] Pioneers of "fusion paranoia," Wilson and Shea saw the final stage of conspiracy thinking as a benighted skepticism that nevertheless did not foreclose the ultimate truth or fiction of any given conspiracy. It was crucial for the adept to reach a plateau of cosmic irony beyond the illusory ideological distinctions between left and right (although, as countercultural figures, the authors definitely leaned left). Wilson later described their aim as "'guerrilla ontology,' an attempt to so mix the elements of each book that the reader must decide on each page, 'How much of this is real and how much is a put-on?'"[3]

Wilson's trickster persona, espousing conspiracy theory as pure play, resonates in our own confused time. In including himself in the cosmic con of conspiracy theorizing, Wilson is an emblematic figure for the nerdish obsessives of the Twitterverse, who, while they take real historical figures and events as their subjects, ultimately express a detachment from whatever is "actually" happening. As legal scholar Mark Fenster commented, "Play has transformed the manically depressive pessimism of conspiracy theory into a recreational outing through an ironic, cynical detachment from its dystopian implications."[4]

In the end, conspiracy theory circa 2018 may be just another self-regulating bubble of the kind we all live in now. Even many of those who rely on a steady diet of CNN and the *New York Times* understand the idea of living in a bubble, which syncs up perfectly with the constantly churning, though barely acknowledged, imagination of pending disaster or apocalypse that defines how we structure our government and society. What one might term *bubble paranoia*, the lurking fear that you may be wrong and are avoiding an impending reckoning with reality, is getting to be a thing. Philip K. Dick described it as the sneaking suspicion that "reality is that which, when you stop believing in it, doesn't go away."[5]

In his 2016 documentary *HyperNormalisation*, filmmaker Adam Curtis compares the West during the early twenty-first century to the Soviet Union in its final decades. The way the Internet seduces us into a second life, Curtis claims, is akin to how the Potemkin Village of appearances seeped into the subjective experience of daily life in the Soviet Union. Hypernormalization represents the constant normalization of ever-worsening conditions by simply refusing to acknowledge that they are happening. And when the contradictions between ideological pseudo-realities and Dick's "reality . . . that doesn't go away" are exacerbated exponentially, as they seem to be today, then conspiracy theory (or analysis or research, depending on your perspective) goes from being a quest for transparency to another form of diversion.

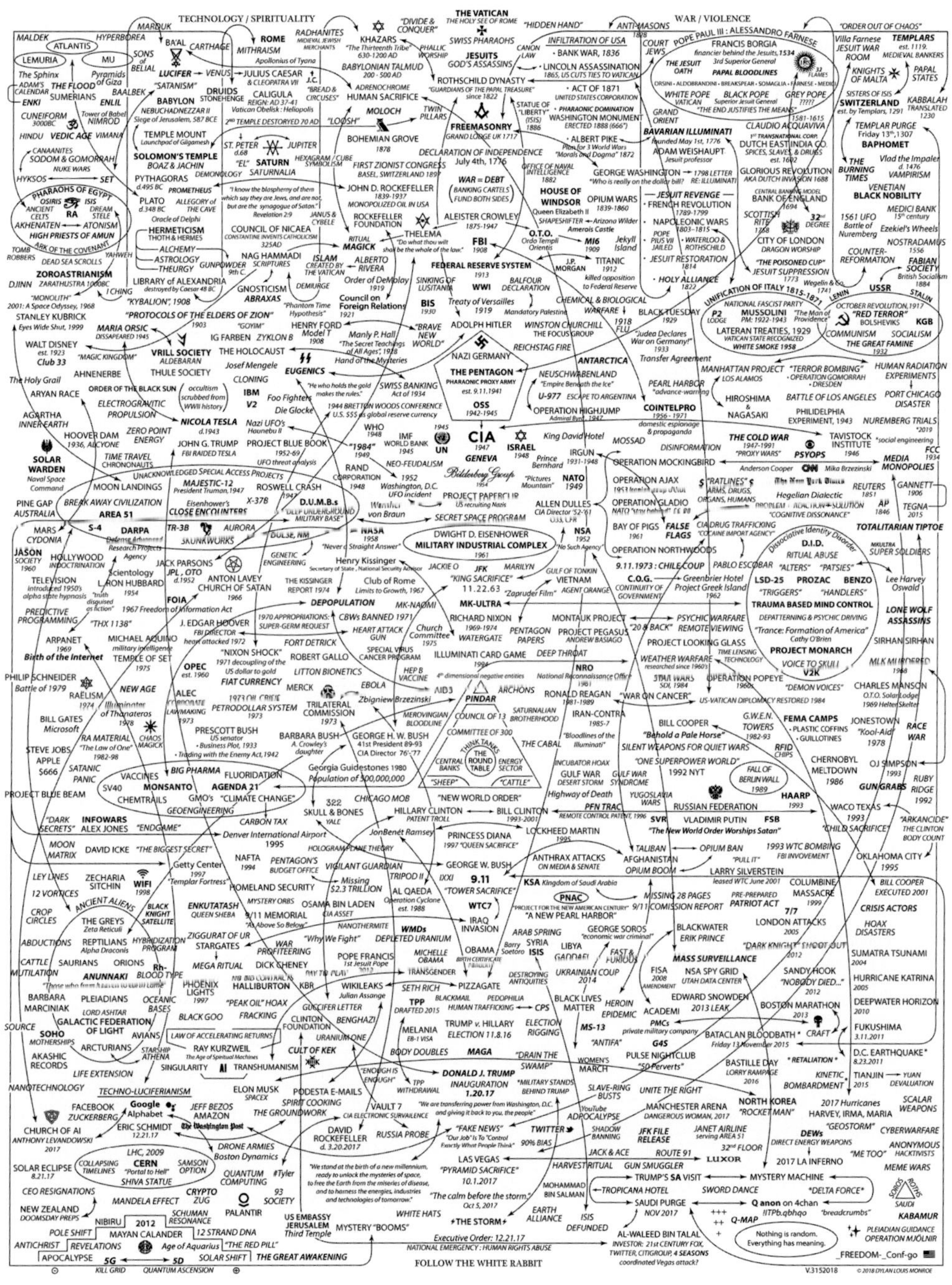

Fig. 86. Dylan Louis Monroe (American, born 1985), *Q Web*, 2017. Mixed media on paper

the END is here!

in this issue

WORKS IN THE EXHIBITION

Lutz Bacher (American, born 1943)
The Lee Harvey Oswald Interview, 1976
Photocopies, typescript, tape, and ink on paper
11 × 8½ in. (27.9 × 21.6 cm) each
The Metropolitan Museum of Art, New York, Purchase, The Horace W. Goldsmith Foundation Gift, through Joyce and Robert Menschel and Anonymous Gift, 1999 (1999.387a–r)
Pages 60–61, front endpapers

Alessandro Balteo-Yazbeck (Venezuelan, born Caracas 1972)
UNstabile-Mobile (from the series Modern Entanglements, U.S. Interventions), 2006
Carbon fiber, Plexiglas, polypropylene, nylon, brass, lead, vinyl, photocopies, and offset lithographs
8 ft. × 11 ft. 6 in. × 13 ft. (243.8 × 350.5 × 396.2 cm) minimum
El Museo del Barrio, New York. Acquired through "PROARTISTA: Sustaining the Work of Living Contemporary Artists," a fund from the Jacques and Natasha Gelman Trust
Page 95

Alessandro Balteo-Yazbeck (Venezuelan, born Caracas 1972)
Media Farzin (American and Iranian, born 1979)
R.S.V.P., 1939 (from the series Cultural Diplomacy: An Art We Neglect), 2007–9
Chromogenic print, offset lithograph, vinyl, and inkjet print on paperboard
35⁷⁄₁₆ × 47¼ in. (90 × 120 cm)
Courtesy the artist and Henrique Faria, New York
Page 94

Jeremy Blake (American, Fort Sill, Oklahoma 1971–2007 New York)
Winchester, 2002
Digital animation with sound; 12 min.
The Metropolitan Museum of Art, New York, Gift of the Estate of Jeremy Aaron Blake and the Estate of Lance Kinz, 2017 (2017.668)
Page 75 top

Jeremy Blake (American, Fort Sill, Oklahoma 1971–2007 New York)
1906, 2003
Digital animation with sound; 21 min.
The Metropolitan Museum of Art, New York, Purchase, Henry Nias Foundation Inc. Gift, 2017 (2017.669)
Page 75 middle

Jeremy Blake (American, Fort Sill, Oklahoma 1971–2007 New York)
Century 21, 2004
Digital animation with sound; 12 min.
The Metropolitan Museum of Art, New York, Purchase, Vital Projects Fund Inc. Gift, through Joyce and Robert Menschel, 2017 (2017.670)
Page 75 bottom

Sarah Charlesworth (American, East Orange, New Jersey 1947–2013 Falls Village, Connecticut)
April 21, 1978, 1978
Chromogenic prints
Frames: approx. 24 × 17 in. (61 × 40.6 cm) each
The Metropolitan Museum of Art, New York, Purchase, Vital Projects Fund Inc. Gift, through Joyce and Robert Menschel, and Charlotte and Bill Ford Gift, 2010 (2010.554a–ss)
Pages 62–63

Emory Douglas (American, born Grand Rapids, Michigan 1943)
The Black Panther (front cover), September 27, 1969
Offset lithograph
17½ × 11½ in. (44.5 × 29.2 cm)
Center for the Study of Political Graphics, Culver City, California
Page 32 top left

Emory Douglas (American, born Grand Rapids, Michigan 1943)
The Black Panther (back cover), July 25, 1970
Offset lithograph
17½ × 11½ in. (44.5 × 29.2 cm)
The Metropolitan Museum of Art, New York, Joyce F. Menschel Photography Library
Page 32 top right

Emory Douglas (American, born Grand Rapids, Michigan 1943)
The Black Panther (back cover), December 5, 1970
Offset lithograph
17½ × 11½ in. (44.5 × 29.2 cm)
Center for the Study of Political Graphics, Culver City, California
Not illustrated

Emory Douglas (American, born Grand Rapids, Michigan 1943)
The Black Panther (back cover), February 17, 1973
Offset lithograph
17½ × 11½ in. (44.5 × 29.2 cm)
The Metropolitan Museum of Art, New York, Joyce F. Menschel Photography Library
Page 32 bottom right

Emory Douglas (American, born Grand Rapids, Michigan 1943)
The Black Panther (back cover), March 16, 1974
Offset lithograph
15½ × 11½ in. (38.7 × 29.2 cm)
The Metropolitan Museum of Art, New York, Joyce F. Menschel Photography Library
Page 32 bottom left

Emory Douglas (American, born Grand Rapids, Michigan 1943)
The Black Panther (back cover), September 21, 1974
Offset lithograph
15 × 11½ in. (38.1 × 29.2 cm)
The Metropolitan Museum of Art, New York, Joyce F. Menschel Photography Library
Page 33

Öyvind Fahlström (Swedish, São Paulo, Brazil 1928–1976 Stockholm)
World Map, 1972
Acrylic and India ink on vinyl mounted on wood
36 × 72 in. (91.4 × 182.9 cm)
Private collection
Pages 40–41

Avram Finkelstein (American, born Brooklyn, New York 1952)
Donald Moffett (American, born San Antonio, Texas 1955)
Fact or Fiction, 1989
Offset lithograph
8½ × 17 in. (21.6 × 43.2 cm)
The Metropolitan Museum of Art, New York, Purchase, Stanley Posthorn Gift, 2018 (2018.225)
Page 39 bottom

Avram Finkelstein (American, born Brooklyn, New York 1952)
Vince Gagliostro (American, born 1954)
Enjoy AZT, 1990
Offset lithograph
13½ × 11 in. (34.3 × 27.9 cm)
The Metropolitan Museum of Art, New York, Purchase, Stanley Posthorn Gift, 2018 (2018.226)
Page 39 top left

Wayne Gonzales (American, born New Orleans, Louisiana 1957)
Dallas Police 36398, 1999
Acrylic on canvas
94⁵⁄₁₆ × 80⅛ in. (239.5 × 203.5 cm)
Collezione Maramotti, Reggio Emilia, Italy
Page 72

Wayne Gonzales (American, born New Orleans, Louisiana 1957)
Peach Oswald, 2001
Acrylic on canvas
8 ft. 4 in. × 75 in. (254 × 190.5 cm)
Collection of the artist and Stephen Friedman Gallery, London
Page 73

Gran Fury (active 1988–95)
AIDS: 1 in 61, 1988
Offset lithograph
22 × 17 in. (55.9 × 43.2 cm)
The Metropolitan Museum of Art, New York, Purchase, Stanley Posthorn Gift, 2018 (2018.224)
Page 38 right

Hans Haacke (German, born Cologne, 1936)
Sol Goldman and Alex DiLorenzo Manhattan Real Estate Holdings, A Real-Time Social System, as of May 1, 1971, 1971
Gelatin silver prints, typescript, and offset lithographs
6 frames: 22¼ × 24⅜ × 1¼ in. (56.5 × 61.9 × 3.2 cm)
10 frames: 48⅝ × 12¹¹⁄₁₆ × 1¼ in. (123.5 × 32.5 × 3.2 cm)
1 frame: 46¾ × 12¹¹⁄₁₆ × 1¼ in. (118.7 × 32.5 × 3.2 cm)
1 frame: 42⅝ × 12¹¹⁄₁₆ × 1¼ in. (108.3 × 32.5 × 3.2 cm)
LeWitt Collection, Chester, Connecticut
Pages 42–43

Rachel Harrison (American, born New York 1966)
Snake in the Grass, 1997
Aluminum, drywall, wood, latex, acrylic, garbage bags, rope, chromogenic prints, inkjet print, FEGS chart, lamp, polystyrene, tape deck, bottled water, snakeskin, shovel, baking sheet, olive pits, cigar, and hunting traps
11 ft. 6 in. × 24 ft. × 41 ft. 6 in. (350.5 × 731.5 × 1,264.9 cm)
Courtesy the artist and Greene Naftali, New York
Pages 68–71

Jenny Holzer (American, born Gallipolis, Ohio 1950)
Red Yellow Looming, 2004
LED displays
11 ft. 11 in. × 9 ft. 1 in. × 52 in. (363.2 × 276.9 × 132.1 cm)
Private collection, courtesy The Heller Group
Pages 144, 164

Jenny Holzer (American, born Gallipolis, Ohio 1950)
Secretary of Defense, 2006
Oil on linen
33 × 25½ in. (83.8 × 64.8 cm)
Courtesy the artist
Page 145 bottom

Jenny Holzer (American, born Gallipolis, Ohio 1950)
The White House 2002, 2006
Oil on linen
Two panels, overall dimensions: 33 × 51 in. (83.8 × 129.5 cm)
Courtesy the artist
Page 145 top

Alfredo Jaar (Chilean, born Santiago de Chile 1956)
11.09.73.12.10, 1974
Letraset on paperboard
Board: 12 × 28½ in. (30.5 × 72.4 cm)
Courtesy the artist and Galerie Lelong, New York
Page 65 bottom

Alfredo Jaar (Chilean, born Santiago de Chile 1956)
September 11, 1973, 1974
Letraset and graphite on offset lithograph (commercially printed calendar)
8¹⁄₁₆ × 10¼ in. (20.4 × 26 cm)
Courtesy the artist and Galerie Lelong, New York
Not illustrated

Alfredo Jaar (Chilean, born Santiago de Chile 1956)
Dear Mr. Jaar, 1976
Inkjet prints
9¾ × 7½ in. (24.8 × 19.1 cm) each
Courtesy the artist and Galerie Lelong, New York
Page 65 top

Alfredo Jaar (Chilean, born Santiago de Chile 1956)
Searching for K, 1984
Offset lithographs and inkjet print
Dimensions variable
Courtesy the artist and Galerie Lelong, New York
Page 64

Alfredo Jaar (Chilean, born Santiago de Chile 1956)
Kissinger, Allende, Kissinger, Kissinger, Allende, 1985
Inkjet print
15 × 50 in. (38.1 × 127 cm)
Courtesy the artist and Galerie Lelong, New York
Not illustrated

Alfredo Jaar (Chilean, born Santiago de Chile 1956)
Nothing of very great consequence, 2008
Chromogenic transparency in light box
12½ × 18½ in. (31.8 × 47 cm)
Courtesy the artist and Galerie Lelong, New York
Not illustrated

Sarah Anne Johnson (Canadian, born Winnipeg 1976)
Black Cloud, 2008
Acrylic on inkjet print
27¾ × 21¾ in. (70.5 × 55.3 cm)
Art Gallery of Ontario, Toronto, Purchased with the assistance of Michael F. B. Nesbitt, 2009 (2009/75)
Page 150 bottom

Sarah Anne Johnson (Canadian, born Winnipeg 1976)
Brain Drain, 2008
Graphite on offset lithograph
32½ × 23¼ in. (82.6 × 59.1 cm)
Art Gallery of Ontario, Toronto, Purchased with the assistance of Michael F. B. Nesbitt, 2009 (2009/76)
Page 150 top right

Sarah Anne Johnson (Canadian, born Winnipeg 1976)
House of Horrors, 2008
Graphite on offset lithograph
32½ × 23¼ in. (82.6 × 59.1 cm)
Art Gallery of Ontario, Toronto, Purchased with the assistance of Michael F. B. Nesbitt, 2009 (2009/71)
Page 150 top left

Sarah Anne Johnson (Canadian, born Winnipeg 1976)
House on Fire, 2008
Balsa wood, paper, epoxy sculpt, acrylic paint, fabric, electrical components, plastic gels, plastic leaves, motor, metal, light bulbs
31 × 33 × 45 in. (78.7 × 83.8 × 114.3 cm)
Art Gallery of Ontario, Toronto, Purchased with the assistance of Michael F. B. Nesbitt, 2009 (2009/77)
Pages 146–49, 162

Sarah Anne Johnson (Canadian, born Winnipeg 1976)
Lysergic Acid Diethylamide, 2008
Graphite on inkjet print
22¼ × 21¾ in. (56.5 × 55.2 cm)
Art Gallery of Ontario, Toronto, Purchased with the assistance of Michael F. B. Nesbitt, 2009 (2009/69)
Page 151

Mike Kelley (American, Wayne, Michigan 1954–2012 South Pasadena, California)
Untitled (Government and Business), 1991
Acrylic on paper
60 × 83¾ in. (152.4 × 212.7 cm)
Collection of Jason N. Pritzker
Page 87

Mike Kelley (American, Wayne, Michigan 1954–2012 South Pasadena, California)
Low Definition Presidency, 1993
Acrylic on paper
34½ × 22⁷⁄₁₆ in. (87.6 × 57 cm)
Museum of Contemporary Art Chicago, Gift of Howard and Donna Stone (1997.128)
Page 86

Mike Kelley (American, Wayne, Michigan 1954–2012 South Pasadena, California)
Educational Complex, 1995
Acrylic, latex, foam core, fiberglass, plywood, and wood
57¾ × 192³⁄₁₆ × 96⅛ in. (146.7 × 488.2 × 244.2 cm)
Whitney Museum of American Art, New York, Purchase, with funds from the Contemporary Painting and Sculpture Committee (96.50)
Pages 132–34

Mike Kelley (American, Wayne, Michigan 1954–2012 South Pasadena, California)
Abuse Report, 1995/2007
Inkjet print mounted on Plexiglas
42 × 32½ in. (106.7 × 82.6 cm)
Mike Kelley Foundation for the Arts
Page 135

Mark Lombardi (American, Syracuse, New York 1951–2000 New York)
Bill Clinton, the Lippo Group, and Jackson Stephens of Little Rock, Arkansas (5th Version), 1999
Graphite and colored pencil on paper
57¾ × 78 in. (146.7 × 198.1 cm)
Collection of Mickey Cartin
Page 90

Mark Lombardi (American, Syracuse, New York 1951–2000 New York)
BCCI-ICIC & FAB, 1972–91 (4th Version), 1996–2000
Graphite and colored pencil on paper
51⅛ in. × 11 ft. 5¾ in. (129.9 × 349.9 cm)
Whitney Museum of American Art, New York, Purchase, with funds from the Drawing Committee and the Contemporary Painting and Sculpture Committee (2000.250.1)
Pages 88–89

Julia Meltzer (American, born Hollywood, California 1968)
David Thorne (American, born Boston 1960)
"It's Not My Memory of It": three recollected documents, 2003
Single-channel video; color; sound; 25 min.
The Metropolitan Museum of Art, New York, Purchase, Henry Nias Foundation Inc. Gift, 2018 (2018.217)
Page 91; exhibited at The Met Fifth Avenue

John Miller (American, born Cleveland, Ohio 1954)
ZOG, 1998
Acrylic on canvas
54 × 64 in. (137.2 × 162.6 cm)
Collection of Ed Ruscha
Page 127

Peter Nagy (American, born Bridgeport, Connecticut 1959)
est Graduate, 1984
Inkjet print
40 × 30 in. (101.6 × 76.2 cm)
Courtesy the artist and Magenta Plains, New York
Page 66 bottom

Peter Nagy (American, born Bridgeport, Connecticut 1959)
International Survey Condominiums, 1985
Inkjet print
30 × 40 in. (76.2 × 101.6 cm)
Courtesy the artist and Magenta Plains, New York
Page 66 top

Cady Noland (American, born Washington, D.C. 1956)
Untitled (Vince Foster), 1992–93
Silkscreen on aluminum
Ringier Collection, Switzerland
Page 67

Tony Oursler (American, born New York 1957)
Son of Oil, 1982/1999
Acrylic on paper and cardboard and single-channel video; color; sound; 18 min.
Dimensions variable
Courtesy the artist; Lehmann Maupin, New York, Hong Kong, and Seoul; and Video Data Bank
Page 126

Trevor Paglen (American, born Camp Springs, Maryland 1974)
Black Site, Kabul, Afghanistan, 2006, 2006
Dye sublimation metal print
24 × 36 in. (61 × 91.4 cm)
Courtesy the artist, Metro Pictures, New York, and Altman Siegel Gallery, San Francisco
Page 92

Trevor Paglen (American, born Camp Springs, Maryland 1974)
The Salt Pit, Northeast of Kabul, Afghanistan, 2006
Dye sublimation metal print
24 × 36 in. (61 × 91.4 cm)
Courtesy the artist, Metro Pictures, New York, and Altman Siegel Gallery, San Francisco
Page 93

Raymond Pettibon (American, born Tucson, Arizona 1957)
No Title (Coup d'etats were . . .), 1984
Ink and colored pencil on paper
14⅛ × 10⁵⁄₁₆ in. (35.9 × 26.2 cm)
Collection of Bridgitt and Bruce Evans
Page 128 top left

Raymond Pettibon (American, born Tucson, Arizona 1957)
No Title (I've prayed . . .), 1984
Ink on paper
13¾ × 11 in. (35 × 28 cm)
Private collection, courtesy Sadie Coles HQ, London
Page 128 bottom

Raymond Pettibon (American, born Tucson, Arizona 1957)
No Title (Who but Hoover . . .), 1991
Ink on paper
22 × 17 in. (55.9 × 43.2 cm)
Courtesy the artist and David Zwirner, New York, London, and Hong Kong
Page 128 top right

Raymond Pettibon (American, born Tucson, Arizona 1957)
Untitled (Getting Oswald To . . .), 1992
Ink on paper
14 × 11 in. (35.6 × 27.9 cm)
Courtesy the artist and David Zwirner, New York, London, and Hong Kong
Page 129

Raymond Pettibon (American, born Tucson, Arizona 1957)
No Title (When It Came . . .), 2002–17
Graphite, watercolor, and ink on paper
22¼ × 14⅛ in. (56.5 × 35.9 cm)
Courtesy the artist and David Zwirner, New York, London, and Hong Kong
Page 130

Raymond Pettibon (American, born Tucson, Arizona 1957)
No Title (It's Noyt Like . . .), 2017
Ink and colored pencil on paper
22⅜ × 29⅞ in. (56.8 × 75.9 cm)
Courtesy the artist and David Zwirner, New York, London, and Hong Kong
Page 131 top

Raymond Pettibon (American, born Tucson, Arizona 1957)
No Title (Though the Scharanski . . .), 2017
Graphite, watercolor, and ink on paper
18⅜ × 17⅞ in. (46.7 × 45.4 cm)
Courtesy the artist and David Zwirner, New York, London, and Hong Kong
Page 131 bottom

Peter Saul (American, born San Francisco 1934)
Government of California, 1969
Acrylic on canvas
68 × 96 in. (172.7 × 243.8 cm)
Collection of KAWS
Page 36

Peter Saul (American, born San Francisco 1934)
Untitled (Hitler's Brain Is Alive), 2006
Acrylic and colored pencil on paper
49½ × 41¼ in. (125.7 × 104.8 cm)
Courtesy David Nolan Gallery, New York
Page 37

Richard Sharpe Shaver (American, Berwick, Pennsylvania 1907–1975 Summit, Arizona)
Amazing Stories, June 1947
Offset lithograph
11 × 8½ in. (27.9 × 21.6 cm)
Collection of Christine Burgin
Not illustrated

Richard Sharpe Shaver (American, Berwick, Pennsylvania 1907–1975 Summit, Arizona)
"Once you get accustomed to high contrast rock-photo prints . . . ," ca. 1970
Typescript and gelatin silver print
11 × 8½ in. (27.9 × 21.6 cm)
The Morgan Library & Museum, New York, Purchased as the gift of Peter J. Cohen (2015.125)
Not illustrated

Richard Sharpe Shaver (American, Berwick, Pennsylvania 1907–1975 Summit, Arizona)
WEIRD AND WONDERFUL ART, ca. 1970
Typescript and gelatin silver print
11 × 8½ in. (27.9 × 21.6 cm)
Collection of Christine Burgin
Page 124 top right

Richard Sharpe Shaver (American, Berwick, Pennsylvania 1907–1975 Summit, Arizona)
The Early World, ca. 1970
Typescript and gelatin silver prints
Approx. 7 × 5 in. (17.8 × 12.7 cm)
Collection of Christine Burgin
Page 125 top left

Richard Sharpe Shaver (American, Berwick, Pennsylvania 1907–1975 Summit, Arizona)
"Accenting a B&W print with colored pens gives you faces . . . ," ca. 1972
Typescript and gelatin silver print with applied color
11 × 8½ in. (27.9 × 21.6 cm)
Collection of Brian Tucker
Page 124 top left

Richard Sharpe Shaver (American, Berwick, Pennsylvania 1907–1975 Summit, Arizona)
Human Figures are Distorted . . . , ca. 1972
Gelatin silver print with cut and pasted paper, ink, and tape
11 × 8½ in. (27.9 × 21.6 cm)
Collection of Brian Tucker
Page 125 bottom

Richard Sharpe Shaver (American, Berwick, Pennsylvania 1907–1975 Summit, Arizona)
Hand-colored *Rock Book* photo, ca. 1972
Gelatin silver print with applied color
7¹¹⁄₁₆ × 9⅜ in. (19.5 × 23.8 cm)
The Morgan Library & Museum, New York, Purchased as the gift of Peter J. Cohen (2015.126)
Page 125 top right

Richard Sharpe Shaver (American, Berwick, Pennsylvania 1907–1975 Summit, Arizona)
Mer feet: "Mermaid show form for when they began to emerge onto land . . . ," date unknown
Gelatin silver print
4 × 5 in. (10.2 × 12.7 cm)
Collection of Christine Burgin
Page 124 bottom

Jim Shaw (American, born Midland, Michigan 1952)
UFO Polaroid (from the UFO Photos Series), 1977
Instant color print with airbrush paint
3⅛ × 3¹⁄₁₆ in. (7.9 × 7.8 cm)
The Metropolitan Museum of Art, New York, Purchase, Vital Projects Fund Inc. Gift, through Joyce and Robert Menschel, 2015 (2015.461)
Page 120 left

Jim Shaw (American, born Midland, Michigan 1952)
The End Is Here, 1978
Mimeograph pamphlet
8½ × 7¼ in. (21.6 × 18.4 cm)
Copy 1: Courtesy the artist; Blum & Poe, Los Angeles/New York/Tokyo; and Metro Pictures, New York
Copy 2: The Metropolitan Museum of Art, New York, Joyce F. Menschel Photography Library Fund, 2012
Pages 118–19, 161

Jim Shaw (American, born Midland, Michigan 1952)
Martian Portraits, 1978
Gelatin silver prints
14 × 11 in. (35.6 × 27.9 cm) each
The Metropolitan Museum of Art, New York, Purchase, Vital Projects Fund Inc. Gift, through Joyce and Robert Menschel, 2016 (2016.132a, b)
Page 121 top

Jim Shaw (American, born Midland, Michigan 1952)
Martian Portraits, 1978
Gelatin silver prints
14 × 11 in. (35.6 × 27.9 cm) each
The Metropolitan Museum of Art, New York, Purchase, Vital Projects Fund Inc. Gift, through Joyce and Robert Menschel, 2016 (2016.133a, b)
Page 121 bottom

Jim Shaw (American, born Midland, Michigan 1952)
UFO Photo (from the UFO Photos Series), 1978
Gelatin silver print
6⁹⁄₁₆ × 4¾ in. (16.7 × 12.1 cm)
The Metropolitan Museum of Art, New York, Purchase, Vital Projects Fund Inc. Gift, through Joyce and Robert Menschel, 2015 (2015.462)
Page 120 right

Jim Shaw (American, born Midland, Michigan 1952)
UFO Photos: Zapruder Film, 1978–92
Gelatin silver prints
8 × 10 in. (20.3 × 25.4 cm) each
Courtesy the artist; Blum & Poe, Los Angeles/New York/Tokyo; and Metro Pictures, New York
Page 119 bottom

Jim Shaw (American, born Midland, Michigan 1952)
The Miracle of Compound Interest (from the series Left Behind), 2006
Acrylic on muslin, board, Plexiglas, wood, plastic, and foam
Crystal sculptures: 82 × 18 × 38 in. (208.3 × 45.7 × 96.5 cm) each
Backdrop: 23 ft. × 39 ft. (7 × 11.9 m)
Courtesy the artist; Blum & Poe, Los Angeles/New York/Tokyo; and Metro Pictures, New York
Pages 122–23

Silence = Death Project (American, founded 1987)
Silence = Death poster, 1986
Offset lithograph
34 × 24 in. (86.4 × 61 cm)
Avram Finkelstein Archive, Fales Library, New York University
Page 39 top right

Silence = Death Project (American, founded 1987)
AIDSGATE, 1987
Offset lithograph
33¾ × 22⅛ in. (85.7 × 56.2 cm)
The Metropolitan Museum of Art, New York, Gift of Avram Finkelstein, 2013 (2013.973)
Page 38 left

Videofreex (American, active 1969–78)
Fred Hampton: Black Panthers in Chicago, 1969
Single-channel video; black and white; sound; 24 min.
Dimensions variable
The Metropolitan Museum of Art, New York, Purchase, Henry Nias Foundation Inc. Gift, 2018
Page 34

Gerald Williams (American, born Chicago 1941)
Wake Up, 1969
Acrylic and offset lithograph on canvas
48 × 36 in. (121.9 × 91.4 cm)
The David and Alfred Smart Museum of Art, The University of Chicago; Purchase, The Paul and Miriam Kirkley Fund for Acquisitions
Page 35

Sue Williams (American, born Chicago 1954)
Gaudy Dutch/Happy Face, 2010
Ink on cut and pasted paper and wallpaper
17 × 11 in. (43.2 × 27.9 cm)
Courtesy the artist and 303 Gallery, New York
Page 154

Sue Williams (American, born Chicago 1954)
Mike and Zbigniew, 2012
Oil and acrylic on canvas
70 × 70 in. (177.8 × 177.8 cm)
Courtesy the artist and 303 Gallery, New York
Page 152

Sue Williams (American, born Chicago 1954)
Hill and Dale, Black-Ops, 2013
Oil and acrylic on canvas
54 × 64 in. (137.2 × 162.6 cm)
Private collection, New York
Page 153 top

Sue Williams (American, born Chicago 1954)
All Roads Lead to Langley, 2016
Oil and acrylic on canvas
50¼ × 78 in. (127.6 × 198.1 cm)
Courtesy the artist and 303 Gallery, New York
Page 153 bottom

Sue Williams (American, born Chicago 1954)
Ronald Reagan & William Casey, 2016, detail from *Five Collages (i. Revere, ii. 2 Horses, iii. Curtain, iv. Ronald Reagan & William Casey, v. . . . Sat There Weeping, Weeping. . .)*, 2016–17
Cut and pasted offset lithographs and paper, plastic-coated metal paperclip, and wallpaper
12 × 17½ in. (30.5 × 44.5 cm)
Ringier Collection, Switzerland
Page 155

Jane and Louise Wilson (British, born Newcastle-upon-Tyne 1967)
Stasi City, 1997
Four-channel digital video, transferred from Super 16mm film; color; sound; 4 min., 50 sec.
Projection: 11 ft. 5 13/16 in. × 15 ft. 7 in. (3.5 × 4.75 m), each channel
The Metropolitan Museum of Art, New York, Purchase, Harvey Sawikin and Andrea Krantz Gift and Vital Projects Fund Inc. Gift, through Joyce and Robert Menschel, 2016 (2016.17)
Page 74

NOTES

INTRODUCTION

1. Chris Cillizza, "We Are All Conspiracy Theorists Now," *Washington Post*, March 9, 2017, https://www.washingtonpost.com/news/the-fix/wp/2017/03/09/we-are-all-conspiracy-theorists-now/(accessed January 3, 2018).
2. Lance DeHaven-Smith, *Conspiracy Theory in America* (Austin: University of Texas Press, 2013), p. 107. Dispatch 1035-960 was released in response to a 1976 Freedom of Information Act request by the *New York Times*; see p. 107.
3. Ibid.
4. In late 2016, President Barack Obama signed the 2017 National Defense Authorization Act into law, nullifying the Smith-Mundt Act's 1948 prohibition against the American government propagandizing its own citizens. See Michael B. Kelley, "The NDAA Legalizes the Use of Propaganda on the US Public," May 22, 2012, http://www.businessinsider.com/ndaa-legalizes-propaganda-2012-5. It is interesting to note that Obama's head of the Office of Information and Regulatory Affairs from 2008 to 2012 was legal scholar Cass Sunstein, who in 2009 published a symposium paper titled "Conspiracy Theories: Causes and Cures," which recommended a strategy of infiltrating online communities reminiscent of COINTELPRO (COunter INTELigence PROgram) actions by the FBI's secret police; see Cass R. Sunstein and Adrian Vermule, "Conspiracy Theories: Causes and Cures," *The Journal of Political Philosophy* 17, no. 2 (2009), pp. 202–27.
5. Richard Hofstadter, "The Paranoid Style in American Politics," *Harper's* (November 1964), https://harpers.org/archive/1964/11/the-paranoid-style-in-american-politics (accessed November 6, 2017).
6. Peter Knight, *Conspiracy Culture: From the Kennedy Assassination to The X-Files* (London: Routledge, 2000), p. 5.
7. In a 1967 *New Yorker* article about amateur researchers of the Kennedy assassination, Calvin Trillin quotes his main subject, an assistant professor of philosophy at Haverford College: "'This is an obsession,' Thompson says. 'And happy, typical Americans aren't obsessed. Jack Armstrong isn't obsessed. There's a fantastic way in which the assassination becomes a religious event. There are relics, and scriptures, and even a holy scene—the killing ground. People make pilgrimages to it. And, as in any religious event, what happened there isn't clear, it's ambiguous, surrounded by mystery, uncertain, dubious.'" Calvin Trillin, "A Reporter at Large: The Buffs," *New Yorker*, June 10, 1967, pp. 41–71.
8. "About the paranoia often noted under the drug, there is nothing remarkable. Like other sorts of paranoia, it is nothing less the onset, the leading edge, of the discovery that *everything is connected*, everything in the Creation, a secondary illumination—not yet blindingly One, but at least connected, and perhaps a route In for those like Tchitcherine who are held at the edge." Thomas Pynchon, *Gravity's Rainbow* (New York: Penguin, 1973), p. 703.
9. Strangelove's dialogue is a parodic take on the ideas of Cold War military strategists, such as the game theory of the RAND Corporation's Herman Kahn and John von Neumann's theory of Mutually Assured Destruction. Upon seeing the film, Daniel Ellsberg, leaker of the Pentagon Papers and past employee of the RAND Corporation, is reported to have exclaimed, "that was a documentary!"; see Fred Kaplan, "Truth Stranger Than 'Strangelove,'" *New York Times*, October 10, 2004, http://www.nytimes.com/2004/10/10/movies/truth-stranger-than-strangelove.html (accessed January 4, 2018). Sellers's accent for his character is thought to be based on the photographer Weegee's; see https://dangerousminds.net/comments/weegees_photos_from_the_set_of_dr._strangelove (accessed January 4, 2018).
10. Kenneth E. Boulding, *The Organizational Revolution: A Study in the Ethics of Economic Organization* (New York: Harper & Bros., 1953), quoted in Clarissa Terranova, "Systems and Automatisms: Jack Burnham, Stanley Cavell, and the Evolution of a Neoliberal Aesthetic," *Leonardo* 47, no. 1 (2014), p. 57.
11. For those skeptical of the idea of a shadow government operating behind the scenes of the official one, it is important to note that David Wise and Thomas Ross wrote in 1964 of an "invisible government" composed of an "interlocking, hidden machinery," observing that the average reader might "come to suspect that the foreign policy of the United States often works publicly in one direction and through the Invisible Government in just the opposite direction." David Wise and Thomas Ross, *Invisible Government* (New York: Random House, 1964), pp. 1–2, quoted in Knight, *Conspiracy Culture*, p. 28.
12. Conner told this to his late assistant Michelle Silva, per the author's conversation with Steve Henry of Paula Cooper Gallery, February 22, 2018.
13. Robert Storr, *Gerhard Richter: Forty Years of Painting*, exh. cat. (New York: Museum of Modern Art, 2002), pp. 74–77.
14. Mike Kelley and John Miller, "Mike Kelley interviewed by John Miller in Los Angeles, March 26, 1991," in *Mike Kelley*, edited by William S. Bartman and Miyoshi Barosh (New York: A.R.T. Press, 1992), p. 45.

WAKE UP! ART AND CITIZEN JOURNALISM

Epigraph: James Baldwin, "An Open Letter to My Sister, Angela Davis," November 19, 1970, published in *New York Review of Books*, January 7, 1971, http://www.nybooks.com/articles/1971/01/07/an-open-letter-to-my-sister-miss-angela-davis/ (accessed September 18, 2017).
1. Rebecca Zorach, "'Dig the Diversity in Unity': AfriCOBRA's Black Family," *Afterall* 28 (Autumn–Winter 2011), p. 103.
2. Barbara Jones-Hogu, "The History, Philosophy, and Aesthetics of AfriCOBRA," in *Afri-Cobra III*, exh. cat. (Amherst: University of Massachusetts, 1973), author's 2008 revised version available at http://areachicago.org/the_history_phil_and_aesth_of_africobra (accessed April 23, 2018).
3. Rebecca Zorach, "Interview with Gerald Williams," November 2011, https://never-the-same.org/interviews/gerald-williams/ (accessed January 8, 2018).
4. In an October 1971 segment of Tony Brown's *Black Journal* (on National Education Television), Williams appeared with *Newsweek* correspondent Samuel Yette, author of *The Choice: The Issue of Black Survival in America* (New York: G. P. Putnam, 1971), to discuss what Williams termed the "final solution to the Black question—vaporization." It may be tempting to relegate these fears to the same neurosis of right-wing conspiracy theorists who talk of FEMA camps, but the black population had to wonder, why exactly were Japanese Americans and not German Americans put into camps in the United States during World War II? And wouldn't those fears be confirmed the following July when the *Washington Post* and *New York Times* "broke" news of the infamous Tuskegee experiments in Alabama, from 1932 to 1972, which involved injecting poor black men with syphilis under the guise of free health care? In 2007, a newly declassified document dated July 7, 1950—twelve days after the beginning of the Korean War—from FBI chief J. Edgar Hoover to President Truman outlined the former's plan to suspend habeas corpus and imprison 12,000 Americans deemed potential subversives. Tim Weiner, "Hoover Planned Mass Jailing in 1950," *New York Times*, December 23, 2007, https://www.nytimes.com/2007/12/23/washington/23habeas.html (accessed March 3, 2017).
5. Ayana Baltrip-Balagás, "The Art of Self-Defense," *Print* 60 (March–April 2006), p. 87.
6. Colette Gaiter, "What Revolutions Look Like: The Work of Black Panther Artist Emory

Douglas," in *Black Panther: The Revolutionary Art of Emory Douglas*, edited by Sam Duran (New York: Rizzoli, 2007), p. 98.

7. The Oakland, California, chapter of the Black Panthers initiated the Free Breakfast program, which quickly became mandatory for all chapters nationwide. In May 1969, FBI head J. Edgar Hoover told his agents: "The program has met with some success and has resulted in a favorable light and clouds the violent nature of the group and its ultimate aim of insurrection"; https://genius.com/Federal-bureau-of-investigation-hoover-memo-on-black-panthers-breakfast-for-children-program-annotated.

8. The existence of COINTELPRO was first revealed when a group of antiwar activists, aiming to destroy draft cards, broke into a Selective Service office in Media, Pennsylvania, that also housed a secret FBI office. The activists took the COINTELPRO papers and distributed them to reporters.

9. Huey P. Newton, "The Minister of Defense and Supreme Commander of the Black Panther Party, Huey P. Newton's Message at Boston College—November 18, 1970," transcript, http://www.itsabouttimebpp.com/Huey_P_Newton/pdf/Huey.pdf (accessed August 29, 2017).

10. Öyvind Fahlström, "Historical Painting," *Flash Art* 43 (December 1973), quoted in Jean-François Chevrier, *Öyvind Fahlström: Another Space for Painting*, exh. cat. (Barcelona: Museu d'Art Contemporani de Barcelona, 2000), p. 262.

11. Öyvind Fahlström, "Take Care of the World," in *Öyvind Fahlström*, exh. cat. (New York: Solomon R. Guggenheim Museum, 1982), p. 58.

12. Newton, "The Minister of Defense."

13. Judith Richards, "Interview with Peter Saul, November 3–4, 2009," Archives of American Art, Smithsonian Institution, Washington, D.C.

14. Peter Saul, quoted in Richard Leydier, "Saul's Stupid Painting," *Art Press* 275 (January 2002), pp. 9–25.

15. John Ehrlichman, interviewed in 1994 by Dan Baum and quoted in his article, "Legalize It All: How to Win the War on Drugs," *Harper's* (April 2016), https://harpers.org/archive/2016/04/legalize-it-all/ (accessed January 8, 2018).

16. Lucy Lippard, "The Art Workers' Coalition: Not a History," originally published in *Studio International* (November 1970), reprinted in Lucy Lippard, *Get the Message? A Decade of Art for Social Change* (New York: E. P. Dutton, 1984), pp. 10–19.

17. Thomas Messer, quoted in Brian Wallis, ed., *Hans Haacke: Unfinished Business*, exh. cat. (New York: New Museum of Contemporary Art, 1986), p. 96.

18. Rosalyn Deutsche, "Property Values: Hans Haacke, Real Estate, and the Museum," in *Evictions: Art and Spatial Politics* (Chicago: Graham Foundation for Advanced Studies in the Fine Arts; Cambridge, Mass.: MIT Press, 1996), p. 162.

19. Louis Althusser, "Ideology and Ideological State Apparatuses (Notes towards an Investigation)," originally published in *La Pensée* (1970), in *Lenin and Philosophy and Other Essays* (New York: Monthly Review Press, 1971); https://www.marxists.org/reference/archive/althusser/1970/ideology.htm (accessed September 3, 2017). For a discussion of Althusser in relation to Haacke, see Frederic Jameson, "Hans Haacke and the Cultural Logic of Late Capitalism," in Wallis, *Hans Haacke: Unfinished Business*, p. 47.

20. Althusser, "Ideology and Ideological State Apparatuses."

21. See Avram Finkelstein, *After Silence: A History of AIDS through Its Images* (Oakland: University of California Press, 2017).

22. Douglas Crimp with Adam Rolston, *AIDS Demo Graphics* (Seattle: Bay Press, 1990), pp. 33–34, 36 (illus. in color), 37. For a general discussion of the conspiracy theories surrounding the genesis of the AIDS virus, see Karen Grigsby Gates, "Is It Genocide?" *Essence* (September 1990), pp. 76–78, 116, 118; and John S. James, "AIDS Conspiracy—Just a Theory," *SF Sentinel*, September 12, 1986.

23. Crimp, *AIDS Demo Graphics*, pp. 33–34.

"A WILDERNESS OF MIRRORS": CONSPIRACY AND IDENTITY

Epigraph: Don DeLillo, *Libra* (New York: Penguin, 1988), p. 215.

1. Donald Fagen, liner notes for *The Nightfly Trilogy* (Rhino Entertainment Company/Reprise Records, 2007).

2. This is not to say that there wasn't a vibrant, if small, community of researchers into the assassination during the 1960s. Mark Lane's book *Rush to Judgment: A Critique of the Warren Commission's Inquiry into the Murders of President John F. Kennedy, Officer J. D. Tippit and Lee Harvey Oswald* was published in 1966, and Emile de Antonio's documentary of the same title came out in the following year. James G. Hepburn's *Farewell America* was first published in France in 1968 with the title *L'Amerique Brule (America is Burning)*.

3. Jefferson Morley, *The Ghost: The Secret Life of CIA Spymaster James Jesus Angleton* (New York: St. Martin's Press, 2017), p. 8.

4. Jefferson Morley, "Wilderness of Mirrors," *The Intercept,* January 1, 2018, https://theintercept.com/2018/01/01/the-complex-legacy-of-cia-counterintelligence-chief-james-angleton/ (accessed January 1, 2018).

5. Seymour Hersh, "Huge CIA Operation Reported in U.S. Against Antiwar Forces, Other Dissidents in Nixon Years," *New York Times*, December 22, 1974, quoted in Morley, *The Ghost*, pp. 233–34. For a discussion of Angleton and Oswald, see "Oswald Again," ibid., pp. 136–41. See also Ian Shapira and Michael E. Miller, "New Batch of JFK Assassination Files: Oswald in Mexico City and the Watergate Burglars," *Washington Post*, November 4, 2017, https://www.washingtonpost.com/news/retropolis/wp/2017/11/03/new-batch-of-jfk-assassination-files-oswald-in-mexico-city-and-watergate-burglars/ (accessed March 6, 2018).

6. Jean-François Chevrier, *Öyvind Fahlström: Another Space for Painting*, exh. cat. (Barcelona: Museu d'Art Contemporani de Barcelona, 2000), p. 350.

7. Andreas Killen, *1973 Nervous Breakdown: Watergate, Warhol, and the Birth of Post-Sixties America* (New York: Bloomsbury, 2006), p. 282.

8. Sidney Blumenthal and Harvey Yazijian, *Government by Gunplay: Conspiracy Theories from Dallas to Today* (New York: New American Library, 1976), ix, quoted in ibid., p. 241.

9. Richard Warren Lewis, *The Scavengers and Critics of the Warren Report—The Endless Paradox, Based on an Investigation by Lawrence Schiller* (New York: Delacorte Press, 1967).

10. Mae Brussell, KLRB interview, June 30, 1971, from *The Mae Brussell Radio Archive Collection 1971–1988.*

11. Adam Parfrey, "Preface: Brussell Sprouts," in *The Essential Mae Brussell: Investigations of Fascism in America*, edited by Alex Constantine (Port Townsend, Wash.: Feral Press, 2014), ix.

12. Quoted in Ryszard Kapuściński, "Vidal Salon," *The Guardian*, May 5, 2007, https://www.theguardian.com/books/2007/may/05/featuresreviews.guardianreview14 (accessed January 21, 2018).

13. Matt Lewis, "Meet the Woman Who Was Nixon Era's Alex Jones," *Daily Beast*, January 20, 2018, https://www.thedailybeast.com/meet-the-woman-who-was-alex-jones-before-alex-jones-existed (accessed March 5, 2018).

14. Mae Brussell, March 28, 1981, broadcast, https://www.youtube.com/watch?v=s24uG5hpbpg (accessed March 5, 2018).

15. Stephen Greer reported on the planned meeting in a segment of "ABC News" on March 31, 1981; https://www.youtube.com/watch?v=BIJ0AfuE97I (accessed on March 15, 2018).

16. Charles Hollander, "Pynchon, JFK, and the CIA: Magic Eye Views of *The Crying of Lot 49*,"

Pynchon Notes, nos. 40–41 (Spring–Fall 1997), pp. 61–106, http://www.ottosell.de/pynchon/magiceye.htm.
17. See Red Marriott, "How the Allied Multinationals Supplied Nazi Germany throughout World War II," libcom.org, December 13, 2006, https://libcom.org/library/allied-multinationals-supply-nazi-germany-world-war-2 (accessed March 9, 2018). For information on Reinhard Gehlen, see David Talbot, *The Devil's Chessboard: Allen Dulles, the CIA, and the Rise of America's Secret Government* (New York: Harper Perennial, 2016), pp. 268–86.
18. Annie Jacobsen, *Operation Paperclip: The Secret Intelligence Program That Brought Nazi Scientists to America* (New York: Little, Brown, 2014). Mae Brussell discussed Operation Paperclip on her broadcast of January 10, 1977, https://www.youtube.com/watch?v=zgcGWPiad6M (accessed February 18, 2018).
19. Andrew Berandini, "Lutz Bacher: In Pieces and All at Once," *Art in America* (March 2012), p. 127.
20. *Sarah Charlesworth: Modern History*, exh. cat. (Edinburgh: New 57 Gallery, 1979), p. 1.
21. Geoffrey Batchen, "Response," in issue "Exit Theory: Thinking Photography and Thinking History from One Crisis to Another," *British Art Studies* 4 (Autumn 2016), http://www.britishartstudies.ac.uk/issues/issue-index/issue-4/exit-theory-photography (accessed September 28, 2017).
22. John Tagg, "The Currency of the Photograph: New Deal Reformism and Documentary Rhetoric," in *The Burden of Representation: Essays on Photographies and Histories* (Amherst: University of Massachusetts Press, 1988), p. 166. First published in *Screen Education* 28 (Autumn 1978), xii. Not coincidentally, the journal *October* published a special issue on photography in 1978.
23. See Art Simon, *Dangerous Knowledge: The JFK Assassination in Art and Film* (Philadelphia: Temple University Press, 2013). First published in 1996, Simon's book features case studies of works of art dealing with this subject, but its great strength is an astonishing narrative dealing specifically with how this contestation of power between researchers on one side and the government and mass media on the other unfolded in different historical moments.
24. Conversation with Christopher Williams, February 28, 2018.
25. Interview with Matt Mullican, who attended est meetings but was not one of its hardcore acolytes. See Douglas Eklund, *The Pictures Generation, 1974–1984*, exh. cat. (New York: The Metropolitan Museum of Art, 2009), p. 57.
26. Killen, *1973 Nervous Breakdown*, p. 238.
27. Kirkpatrick Sale, quoted in ibid., p. 241.
28. For a biographical account of Jaar in Chile, see Caille Millner, "Alfredo Jaar and the Happiness of Chile," *Los Angeles Review of Books*, December 8, 2013, https://lareviewofbooks.org/article/alfredo-jaar-and-the-happiness-of-chile/.
29. The journalists Seymour Hersh and Christopher Hitchens have been the two most dogged pursuers of Kissinger. See, in particular, Hersh, *The Price of Power: Kissinger in the Nixon White House* (New York: Summit Books, 1983); and Hitchens, *The Trial of Henry Kissinger* (London: Atlantic Books, 2012). For a summary review of Hersh's book, see Stanley Hoffman, "The Kissinger Antimemoirs," *New York Times Book Review*, July 3, 1983, http://www.nytimes.com/1983/07/03/books/the-kissinger-antimemoirs.html (accessed February 17, 2018).
30. Kathleen MacQueen, "The Strength to See: A Portrait of Alfredo Jaar as a Young Seer in Search of Ways to Bridge the Divides between Perception, Representation and Recovery," *Flash Art* 290 (May–June 2013), pp. 122–26.
31. Cady Noland, "Towards a Metalanguage of Evil," *Balcon* 4 (1989), pp. 70–85, reproduced in Rhea Anastas and Michael Brenson, eds., *Witness to Her Art: Art and Writings by Adrian Piper, Mona Hatoum, Cady Noland, Jenny Holzer, Kara Walker, Daniela Rossell, and Eau de Cologne* (Annandale-on-Hudson, N.Y.: Center for Curatorial Studies, Bard College, 2006).
32. The October 13, 1971, episode of Mae Brussell's radio show "Dialogue: Conspiracy" was devoted to the Manson trial; https://www.youtube.com/watch?v=fdjk9e1H_to (accessed February 8, 2018).
33. Neil Sanders, *Now Is the Only Thing That's Real: A Reexamination of the Manson Murders, Motives, and Mythos* (Nottingham, U.K.: Number Six Dance Publishing, 2017), p. 9.
34. While the Whitewater investigation of the mid-1990s is considered by Democratic loyalists to be a political witch hunt against Bill and Hillary Clinton, the death of Vince Foster has consumed right-wing conspiracy theorists to this day, when it is the best known of what is called the "Clinton Body Count."
35. Cady Noland, in conversation with James Rondeau, May 20, 1996. See Note 2 in James Rondeau and Andrea Miller-Keller, *Cady Noland / MATRIX 130*, exh. cat. (Hartford, Conn.: Wadsworth Atheneum, 1996), p. 11.
36. Eric Banks and Sarah Valdez, eds., *Rachel Harrison: Museum with Walls*, exh. cat. (Annandale-on-Hudson, N.Y.: Center for Curatorial Studies, Bard College, 2010), p. 42. Pier Paolo Pasolini et al., "Observations on the Long Take,"*October* 13 (Summer 1980), pp. 3–6.
37. Email correspondence from Rachel Harrison to the author, February 15, 2018.
38. Devon Dikeou, "Rachel Harrison: The Look of Dress-Separates; Greene Naftali, New York, New York," *zingmagazine* 4 (1997), p. 244.
39. Banks and Valdez, *Rachel Harrison*, p. 12.
40. John Kelsey, "Sculpture in an Abandoned Field," in *Rachel Harrison: If I Did It*, edited by Heike Munder and Ellen Seifermann (Zurich: JRP Ringier, 2007), p. 120.
41. Robert Scheer, "Oliver Stone Builds His Own Myths," *Los Angeles Times*, December, 15, 1991, http://articles.latimes.com/1991-12-15/entertainment/ca-926_1_oliver-stone-builds (accessed February 19, 2018).
42. Peter Knight, *Conspiracy Culture: From the Kennedy Assassination to The X-Files* (London: Routledge, 2000), p. 28.
43. Ibid., p. 218.
44. This biographical sketch is indebted to an interview by Steel Stillman, "In the Studio: Wayne Gonzales," *Art in America* (December 2009), https://www.artinamericamagazine.com/news-features/magazines/wayne-gonzales/ (accessed February 18, 2018).
45. Wayne Gonzales, quoted in ibid.
46. Ibid.
47. Robert Darnton, "The Stasi Files," in *Ctrl [Space]: Rhetorics of Surveillance from Bentham to Big Brother*, edited by Thomas Y. Levin (Karlsruhe, Germany: ZKM Center for Art and Media; Cambridge, Mass.: MIT Press, 2002), p. 172.
48. Lisa Corrin and Peter Schjeldahl, *Jane and Louise Wilson*, exh. cat. (London: Serpentine Gallery, 1999), p. 8.
49. "The Eye of Power: A Conversation with Jean-Pierre Barou and Michelle Perrot," in Michel Foucault, *Power / Knowledge: Selected Interviews and Other Writings 1972–1977* (New York: Pantheon, 1980), p. 152.
50. In a talk at the Guggenheim Museum (April 9, 2004), the Wilsons noted the correspondence between the tonal range of the teak wood in different offices from dark to light and the bureaucratic hierarchy of the Staatssicherheit, exemplifying their extremely sensitive and perceptive attention to historical detail. While this semiotic distinction is not evoked explicitly in the film, its pretensions are wittily deflated when the wood is used as a backdrop for the improbable fakery of the tree stump.
51. In his essay in the catalogue of the Hannover exhibition of *Stasi City*, sculptor Raimund Kummer rehearses the central principle of this early visual technology: "Besides the obvious references to the fact that they are twins, this duality also may be seen as an allusion to the double image of the stereoscope, which in fusing two similar yet

imperceptibly different images, brings them to a single point in another dimension." *Jane and Louise Wilson: Stasi City*, exh. cat. (Hannover: Hannover Kunstverein, 1997), p. V.

52. Kummer interview, in ibid., p. IX.

53. Rachel Teagle, "Cerca Series: Jeremy Blake," exh. brochure (San Diego: Museum of Contemporary Art, 2002).

54. Jeremy Blake, quoted in Holly Willis, "Gunslinging Psychedelia: The Moving Paintings of Jeremy Blake," *res magazine* (January–February 2005), pp. 60–61.

55. Philip Monk, *Spirit Hunter: The Haunting of American Culture by Myths of Violence; Speculations on Jeremy Blake's Winchester Trilogy*, exh. cat. (Toronto: Art Gallery of York University, 2005).

56. Jeremy Blake, quoted in "SFMOMA Presents U.S. Premiere of Blake's Recently Completed Winchester Series," press release, September 27, 2004.

THE ARTIST AS RESEARCHER

1. Margaret Thatcher, interview by Douglas Kay, September 23, 1987, https://www.margaretthatcher.org/document/106689.

2. Dan Rottenberg, "About That Urban Renaissance . . . There'll Be a Slight Delay," *Chicago Magazine*, May 1, 1980, http://www.chicagomag.com/Chicago-Magazine/May-1980/Yuppie/ (accessed November 7, 2017).

3. A sign of the continued currency of *They Live* is Jonathan Lethem's monographic study *They Live* (Berkeley: Soft Skull Press, 2010).

4. Neil Postman, *Amusing Ourselves to Death: Public Discourse in the Age of Show Business* (New York: Viking Penguin, 1985), p. 13.

5. Ibid., pp. 155–56.

6. See Jonathan Lethem, "Knitting the Monster's Socks" in this volume, pp. 10–11.

7. Guy Debord, quoted in Anselm Jappe, *Guy Debord* (Berkeley: University of California Press, 1999), p. 117.

8. The phrase is Fredric Jameson's, from one of two statements he made on conspiracy theory; see Ian Alteveer's essay in this volume, pp. 106–17.

9. Roberta Smith, "Art: 'Interpretive Link': View of Pivotal Moment," *New York Times*, November 14, 1986, https://www.nytimes.com/1986/11/14/arts/art-interpretive-link-view-of-pivotal-movement.html (accessed March 15, 2018).

10. Mike Kelley and John Miller, "Mike Kelley interviewed by John Miller in Los Angeles, March 26, 1991," *Mike Kelley* (New York: A.R.T. Press, 1992), p. 45.

11. Mike Kelley, "Foul Perfection: Thoughts on Caricature" (1989), quoted in *Mike Kelley*, edited by Eva Meyer-Hermann and Lisa Gabrielle Mark, exh. cat. (Munich and New York: Delmonico Books/Prestel, 2013), p. 173.

12. James Ridgeway, "It's All One Big Conspiracy: Suddenly the Left Is Interested in the Right's Favorite Bugaboos–Secret Plots and the Jews," *Village Voice*, November 5, 1991, p. 19.

13. James Ridgeway and Doug Vaughan, "The Last Days of Danny Casolaro. Murder or Suicide: However You Look at It, the Story Killed Him," *Village Voice*, October 15, 1991. See also Mark Fenster, "Danny Casolaro and the Collective True Crime Narrative," in *Conspiracy Theories: Secrecy and Power in American Culture* (Minneapolis: University of Minnesota Press, 2008), pp. 182–94.

14. Talk of a shadow government did not appear out of the blue in 1991. In 1986, *The Nation* covered a lawsuit brought by the Christic Institute (dismissed by the time the article ran); "Is There Really a 'Secret Team,'" *The Nation*, July 2–9, 1988, p. 10. See also Peter Dale Scott, *The Iran-Contra Connection: Secret Teams and Covert Operations in Reagan Era* (Boston: South End Press, 1987).

15. Kelley and Miller, "Mike Kelley interviewed by John Miller."

16. Greg Stone, quoted in Frances Richard, "Toward a Diagram of Mark Lombardi," 2001, http://www.whale.to/c/mark_lombard3.html (accessed April 24, 2008).

17. Robert Hobbs, *Mark Lombardi: Global Networks*, exh. cat. (New York: Independent Curators International, 2003), p. 30.

18. Ibid., p. 32.

19. Ibid., p. 66.

20. Deven Golden, "Mark Lombardi," *Bomb* (Fall 2003), pp. 102–3.

21. Hobbs, *Mark Lombardi*, p. 66.

22. Ibid., p. 107. See also Susan Schmidt and Michael Weisskopf, "Indonesian Family Forged Arkansas Links More Than a Decade Ago," *Washington Post*, October 20, 1996, A27, https://www.washingtonpost.com/wp-srv/national/longterm/campaign/ (accessed June 4, 2018).

23. Mark Lombardi, "BCCI, ICIC & FAB c. 1972–91," first published in *Gulf Coast* 8, no. 2 (Summer–Fall 1996), reproduced in Hobbs, *Mark Lombardi*, pp. 96–97.

24. Patricia Goldstone, *Interlock: Art, Conspiracy, and the Shadow Worlds of Mark Lombardi* (Berkeley, Calif.: Counterpoint, 2015), p. 14.

25. See Fenster, "A Failure of Imagination: Competing Narratives of 9/11 Truth," *Conspiracy Theories*, pp. 233–78.

26. John Menick, "The Art of Forgetting: Speculative Archive's *It's Not My Memory of It*," *Parachute* 118 (July–August 2005), p. 119.

27. In 2008, the Whitney Museum's Independent Studies Program organized a survey of contemporary art called "For Reasons of State," which dealt with "how governments can act through corporations (and vice versa), which removes transparency of who authors and implements often contentious regulations that relinquish social obligations." The exhibition included Trevor Paglen, Mark Lombardi, Speculative Archive, and Jenny Holzer, among others. See Angelique Campens, Erica Cooke, and Steven Lam, *For Reasons of State*, exh. cat. (New York: Whitney Museum of American Art, 2008), p. 5.

28. See Hélène Chouteau-Matikian, "War, There, Over There," In Walid Raad, *I Might Die Before I Get a Rifle: Hasselblad Award 2011* (Göttingen, Germany: Steidl, 2011), p. 105.

29. Julian Stallabrass, "Negative Dialectics in the Google Era: A Conversation with Trevor Paglen," *October* 138 (Fall 2011), p. 7.

30. Giorgio Agamben, "The Paradox of Sovereignty," in *Homo Sacer: Sovereign Power and Bare Life* (Stanford: Stanford University Press, 1995), pp. 15–29.

31. See Franco Ordoñez, "Venezuela Accuses Rubio, CIA of Plotting to Topple Caracas Government," *Miami Herald*, July 25, 2017, http://www.miamiherald.com/news/politics-government/article163540068.html; and The Aspen Institute, "The View from Langley," Aspen Security Forum 2017, http://aspensecurityforum.org/wp-content/uploads/2017/07/The-View-from-Langley.pdf.

32. Aleca Le Blanc, "Alessandro Balteo-Yazbeck: Christopher Grimes Gallery," *ArtNexus* 8, no. 74 (September–November 2009), p. 116.

33. Lisa Ann Favero, "Miami: Alessandro Balteo-Yazbeck," *Sculpture* 26, no. 8 (October 2007), pp. 75–76.

34. Alex J. Taylor, "Unstable Motives: Propaganda, Politics, and the Late Work of Alexander Calder," *American Art* 26, no. 1 (Spring 2012), pp. 25–47.

35. The extent to which programs such as MoMA's "colluded" with USIA is disputed; see note 5 in Taylor, "Unstable Motives," p. 45.

36. Serge Guilbaut, *How New York Stole the Idea of Modern Art: Abstract Expressionism, Freedom, and the Cold War* (Chicago: University of Chicago Press, 1983).

37. Then gallerist and now critic Christian Viveros-Fauné coined the sobriquet "Pop Conceptualism" to describe the work of Lombardi, Beth Campbell, and Danica Phelps, stating, "It's not eye candy . . . but at a certain level, it is." Quoted in Richard, "Toward a Diagram of Mark Lombardi."

38. Philip K. Dick, "How To Build a Universe That Doesn't Fall Apart Two Days Later," a 1978 speech anthologized in Lawrence Sutin, ed.,

The Shifting Realities of Philip K. Dick: Selected Literary and Philosophical Writings, quoted in Maria Popova, "How to Build a Universe: Philip K. Dick on Reality, Media Manipulation, and Human Heroism," https://www.brainpickings.org/2013/09/06/how-to-build-a-universe-philip-k-dick/ (accessed February 24, 2018).
39. Ibid.
40. Examples of this influence include the CIA's Operation Mockingbird and the agency's current $600 million Cloud Services contract with Amazon, owned by the owner of the *Washington Post*. Norman Solomon, "Jeff Bezos is Doing Huge Business with the CIA, While Leaving His Washington Post Readers in the Dark," *Alternet*, December 18, 2013. For information on Operation Mockingbird, see Joseph J. Trento, *The Secret History of the CIA* (New York: Carroll & Graf, 2005).

MODERN HISTORY IN AND OUT OF CONTEXT: SARAH CHARLESWORTH'S *APRIL 21, 1978*

1. On *April 21, 1978* and the Modern History series, see *Sarah Charlesworth: Modern History*, exh. cat. (Edinburgh: New 57 Gallery, 1979); "Sarah Charlesworth: *April 21, 1978*," *California Museum of Photography Bulletin* 3, no. 5 (1984); Louis Grachos and Susan Fisher Sterling, *Sarah Charlesworth: A Retrospective*, exh. cat. (Santa Fe: SITE Santa Fe, 1997); Douglas Eklund, *The Pictures Generation, 1974–1984*, exh. cat. (New York: The Metropolitan Museum of Art, 2009), pp. 144–48; Mark Godfrey, "Modern History," in Rochelle Steiner et al., *Sarah Charlesworth*, exh. cat. (Munich and New York: DelMonico Books/Prestel, 2017), pp. 133–38.
2. "Sarah Charlesworth: *April 21, 1978*," unpag.; Susan Fisher Sterling, "In-Photography: The Art of Sarah Charlesworth," in Grachos and Sterling, *Sarah Charlesworth*, p. 88; Godfrey, "Modern History," p. 137.
3. Charlesworth, *Modern History*, p. 1.
4. For historical background on the Lead Years, see David Moss, *The Politics of Left-Wing Violence in Italy, 1969–85* (New York: St. Martin's Press, 1989); Robert Lumley, *States of Emergency: Cultures of Revolt in Italy from 1968 to 1978* (London: Verso, 1990); Paul Ginsborg, *A History of Contemporary Italy: Society and Politics, 1943–1988* (New York: Palgrave Macmillan, 2003); and Anna Cento Bull and Adalgisa Giorgio, eds., *Speaking Out and Silencing: Culture, Society and Politics in Italy in the 1970s* (London: Legenda, 2006).
5. Moss, *Politics of Left-Wing Violence in Italy*, p. 1.
6. Lumley, *States of Emergency*, p. 285.
7. Ibid., p. 282.
8. Moss, *Politics of Left-Wing Violence in Italy*, p. 9.
9. Ibid., p. 13.
10. Godfrey, "Modern History," p. 137.
11. Email correspondence with Pio Monti, October 19, 2017.
12. I thank Maurizio Nannucci, one of the cofounders of Zona, for sharing his recollections of Charlesworth's exhibition there. Email correspondence with Maurizio Nannucci, February 8, 2018. Charlesworth discussed the Biennale in Sarah Charlesworth and Judith Olch Richards, "Oral History Interview with Sarah Edwards Charlesworth," November 2–9, 2011, Archives of American Art, Smithsonian Institution.
13. Charlesworth, *Modern History*, p. 2.
14. *Contemporary Currents: Sarah Charlesworth, Special Project, Herald Tribune: November, 1977*, exh. cat. (New York: Queens Museum of Art, 1992).
15. Charlesworth and Richards, "Oral History Interview with Sarah Edwards Charlesworth."
16. "Sarah Charlesworth: *April 21, 1978*," unpag.
17. Email correspondence with Pio Monti, October 19, 2017.
18. The term "imagined communities" is theorized in Benedict Anderson, *Imagined Communities: Reflections on the Origin and Spread of Nationalism* (London: Verso, 1983).
19. Godfrey, "Modern History," p. 137.
20. Eklund, *Pictures Generation*, 144–45.
21. On Art & Language and *The Fox*, see Alexander Alberro, "Reconsidering Concpetual Art, 1966–1977," *Conceptual Art: A Critical Anthology*, edited by Alexander Alberro and Blake Stimson (Cambridge, Mass: MIT Press, 2000), xvii–xx.
22. Charlesworth and Roberts, "Oral History Interview with Sarah Edwards Charlesworth."
23. Ibid.
24. "Sarah Charlesworth: *April 21, 1978*," unpag.
25. Carlo Bertocci, "Firenze: Testo Contesto," *Segno: Notiziario di arte contemporanea* 9 (Summer 1978), p. 15.
26. Ruth Glynn and Giancarlo Lombardi, eds., *Remembering Aldo Moro: The Cultural Legacy of the 1978 Kidnapping and Murder* (London: Legenda, 2012), p. 2.
27. Leonardo Sciascia, *The Moro Affair; and, the Mystery of Majorana* (New York: New York Review Books, 2004), p. 56. See also Ellen Nerenberg, "Doxa, Orthodox, Paradox, Heterodox, Oxymoron: Aldo Moro's Lettere dalla prigione del popolo," in Glynn and Lombardi, *Remembering Aldo Moro*, p. 66; Jennifer Burns, "A Leaden Silence? Writers' Responses to the anni di piombo," in Bull and Giorgio, *Speaking Out and Silencing*, pp. 81–94.
28. "Se voi non intervenite, sarebbe scritta una pagina agghiacciante nella storia d'Italia. Il mio sangue ricadrà su voi, sul Partito, sul Paese. Pensateci bene, cari amici. Siate indipendenti. Non guardate al domani, ma al dopo domani." Aldo Moro, quoted in Nerenberg, "Doxa, Orthodox, Paradox, Heterodox, Oxymoron," p. 72.
29. Nerenberg, "Doxa, Orthodox, Paradox, Heterodox, Oxymoron," p. 74.
30. See Sergio Bianchi and Raffaella Perna, *Le polaroid di Moro* (Rome: Derive Approdi, 2012).
31. Ando Gilardi, quoted in Christian Uva, "Images of Violence, Violence of Images: The 'Years of Lead' and the Practice of Armed Struggle between Photography and Video," in *Stillness in Motion: Italy, Photography and the Meanings of Modernity*, edited by Sarah Patricia Hill and Giuliana Minghelli (Toronto: University of Toronto Press, 2014), p. 247.
32. See Vincenzo Trione and Pierluigi Battista, *Mimmo Rotella: Anni di Piombo* (Milan: Abscondita, 2012).
33. Roland Barthes, *Image/Music/Text* (New York: Hill and Wang, 1977), p. 336.
34. *Atlante de la Repubblica: I Giorni di Moro*, newspaper supplement, March 6, 2008 (Rome: La Repubblica, 2008).
35. Glynn and Lombardi, *Remembering Aldo Moro*, pp. 4–9.
36. Daniele Ganser, "Beyond Democratic Checks and Balances: The 'Propaganda Due' Masonic Lodge and the CIA in Italy's First Republic," in *Government of the Shadows: Parapolitics and Criminal Sovereignty*, edited by Eric Wilson (London: Pluto Press, 2009), pp. 246–75; James E. Miller, "Taking Off the Gloves: The United States and the Italian Elections of 1948," *Diplomatic History* 7, no. 1 (1983), 35–55; Lilith Mahmud, "In the Name of Transparency: Gender, Terrorism, and Masonic Conspiracies in Italy," *Anthropological Quarterly* 85, no. 4 (Fall 2012), pp. 183–88.

EXTRATERRESTRIALS UNDERGROUND AND OTHER ARTISTIC SUBLEVELS IN CALIFORNIA

1. "Here Comes Everybody: A Conversation between Jim Shaw and Mike Kelley," in *Jim Shaw, 1974–1999: Everything Must Go*, exh. cat. (Santa Monica: Smart Art Press, 1999), p. 22.
2. Robert Perine, *Chouinard: An Art Vision Betrayed* (Encinitas, Calif.: Artra Publishing, 1985), p. 25.
3. Ibid., p. 159.

4. Ibid., pp. 167–8.
5. Peter Plagens, *Sunshine Muse: Contemporary Art on the West Coast* (New York: Praeger Publishers, 1974), p. 161.
6. See Douglas Eklund, "Image Art after Conceptualism: CalArts, Hallwalls, and Artists Space," in Douglas Eklund, *The Pictures Generation, 1974–1984*, exh. cat. (New York: The Metropolitan Museum of Art, 2009), pp. 22–117. Brach accepted his position at CalArts on the condition that his wife, artist Miriam Schapiro, could also join the faculty. Adding to CalArts's radical sensibilities, she cofounded the school's groundbreaking Feminist Art Program with colleague Judy Chicago, who had first premiered such a program at Fresno State in 1970. See Sandra Sider, "WOMANHOUSE: Cradle of Feminist Art, January 30–February 28, 1972," in *Art Spaces Archives Project* (August 5, 2010), http://www.as-ap.org/content/womanhouse-cradle-feminist-art-sandra-sider-0 (accessed May 9, 2018).
7. Ibid., pp. 23–24.
8. See, for example, the March 7, 1970 KPFA Berkeley radio interview with Blau about CalArts archived by Other Minds, https://archive.org/details/AM_1970_03_07_c1 (accessed February 18, 2013).
9. David Ng, "Herbert Blau, Theater Director and Former CalArts Provost, Dies at 87," *Los Angeles Times*, May 8, 2013, http://articles.latimes.com/2013/may/08/entertainment/la-et-cm-herb-blau-theater-calarts-20130508 (accessed February 17, 2013).
10. On the Jaggerses' relationship and wedding, see "Pastor O. L. Jaggers Marries First Cousin," *Los Angeles Times*, July 22, 1957, p. A3.
11. Jaggers's beliefs may seem particularly outré in the age of televangelism and the powerful Religious Right, but some excellent recent scholarship has unpacked Christian liberalism before that advent; see in particular David R. Swartz, *Moral Minority: The Evangelical Left in an Age of Conservatism* (Philadelphia: University of Pennsylvania Press, 2014).
12. Jim Shaw, quoted in Marc-Olivier Wahler, ed., *The Hidden World: Jim Shaw, Didactic Art Collection* (London: Koenig Books, 2014), p. 330; and in Marc-Olivier Wahler, "The Hidden World," in Gary Carrion-Murayari and Massimiliano Gioni, eds., *Jim Shaw: The End Is Here,* exh. cat. (New York: New Museum and Skira Rizzoli, 2015), pp. 65; see p. 263 for the flyers' installation.
13. See, for example, the 1970 ad announcing the "THE MIGHTY TRANSUBSTANTIATION COMMUNION MIRACLE AT . . . THE ONE MILLION DOLLAR GOLDEN ALTAR OF THE UNIVERSAL WORLD CHURCH," *Los Angeles Times*, January 10, 1970, p. 20 (fig. 61); see also the ca. 1978 flyer reproduced in *Jim Shaw, 1974–1999,* p. 25 (the flyer is undated in the publication, but June 18 fell on a Sunday in 1978).
14. "Here Comes Everybody," pp. 22–24.
15. On Shaw's inspiration from tabloid photography, see "Here Comes Everybody," p. 24; on lizard people, see, for example, Jon Ronson, *Them: Adventures with Extremists* (London: Picador, 2001); on Shaw's reference to them, see also my catalogue entry in Mia Fineman, *Faking It: Manipulated Photography before Photoshop*, exh. cat. (New York: The Metropolitan Museum of Art, 2012), p. 253, cats. 191, 192 (variants titled *Before and After*).
16. "Here Comes Everybody," p. 24.
17. These are what Attorney General John Mitchell dubbed the Nixon administration's various abuses of power. Kathryn S. Olmsted, *Real Enemies: Conspiracy Theories and American Democracy, World War I to 9/11* (New York: Oxford University Press, 2009), p. 150.
18. See, for example, Walter Sullivan, "March Doomsday? Don't Plan on It," *New York Times*, February 14, 1982, http://www.nytimes.com/1982/02/14/us/march-doomsday-dont-plan-on-it.html (accessed January 30, 2018).
19. "Here Comes Everybody," p. 22.
20. Ibid., p. 21. *The Hidden World* was on view at the Châlet Society, Paris, and the Centre Dürrenmatt Neuchâtel, 2013–14. See Carrion-Murayari and Gioni, eds., *Jim Shaw,* pp. 162–63, for an installation view at the Centre Dürrenmatt (fig. 62).
21. Natalie Bell, "In-a-Gadda-Da-Vida," in Carrion-Murayari and Gioni, *Jim Shaw,* p. 220. See also Mike Kelley, "Destroy All Monsters: Liner Notes for 3 CD Box Set," in John C. Welchman, Isabelle Graw, and Anthony Vidler, *Mike Kelley* (London: Phaidon, 1999), pp. 16–17.
22. Mike Kelley, "To the Throne of Chaos: Where the Thin Flutes Pipe Mindlessly" (1993), liner notes for the album *Destroy All Monsters: 1974/1976* (Ecstatic Peace/Father Yod, 1994); quoted in Bell, "In-a-Gadda-Da-Vida," p. 230. See also Mike Kelley and Jim Shaw, eds., *Destroy All Monsters: Geisha This* (Oak Park, Mich.: Book Beat Gallery, 1995).
23. Mike Kelley, "Destroy All Monsters," pp. 16–17.
24. On the move to Valencia, see Natalie Haddad, "A Homecoming for Mike Kelley and Jim Shaw," *Hyperallergic,* February 10, 2018, https://hyperallergic.com/426051/michigan-stories-mike-kelley-and-jim-shaw-msu-broad/ (accessed March 18, 2018).
25. Wahler, *The Hidden World*, pp. 112–38.
26. Brian Tucker, "Rock Books," *Cabinet*, no. 15 (fall 2004), p. 42.
27. Jim Shaw, quoted in Cory Reynolds, "Jim Shaw: The Hidden World," *Artbook Blog* (Oct. 12, 2014), http://www.artbook.com/9783863355845.html (accessed January 22, 2017).
28. Shaver's early editor at *Amazing Stories*, Ray Palmer, eventually produced a compendium of Shaver's universe: Ray Palmer, ed., *The Secret World, Volume One, 1975: The Diary of a Lifetime of Questioning the "Facts"* (Amherst, Wis.: Amherst Press, 1975).
29. Olmsted, *Real Enemies*, p. 234.
30. The flames of the "Roswell Incident" continued to be fanned throughout the 1980s, growing particularly frenzied just at the height of (and perhaps in reaction to) the testimony in Washington on the Iran-Contra scandal of the Reagan administration. Ibid., pp. 183–85.
31. Mike Kelley, "An Endless Script: A Conversation with Tony Oursler," in *Tony Oursler*, edited by Elizabeth Janus and Gloria Moure, exh. cat. (Valencia: Instituto Valenciano de Arte Moderno; Barcelona: Ediciones Polígrafa, 2001), p. 118.
32. Tony Oursler, quoted in *Tony Oursler: Vox Vernacular, an Anthology*, edited by Denis Gielen, exh. cat. (New Haven, Conn.: Yale University Press, 2013), p. 238.
33. Kelley, "An Endless Script," p. 118.
34. Lori Zippay, quoted in Gielen, *Tony Oursler: Vox Vernacular,* p. 238.
35. "John Miller in Conversation with Beatrix Ruf," in *John Miller: A Refusal to Accept Limits*, edited by Beatrix Ruf, exh. cat. (Zurich: Kunsthalle Zürich and JRP/Ringier, 2009), p. 25.
36. Ibid.
37. See John Miller, "Politics of Hate in the U.S.A., Part II: Right-Wing Mysticism and Beliefs," *e-flux journal* 34 (April 2012), http://www.e-flux.com/journal/34/68352/politics-of-hate-in-the-usa-part-ii-right-wing-mysticism-and-beliefs/ (accessed January 10, 2018].
38. Jim Shaw, "Spoiler Alert! The Theater Backdrop Murals," in *Jim Shaw: Essays/Essais*, exh. cat. (Dijon: Les Presses du Réel; Bordeaux: CAPC-Musée d'Art Contemporain de Bordeaux, 2012), p. 10.
39. Ibid.
40. *Out of the Past* (1947), directed by Jacques Tourneur and based on the final novel by Daniel Mainwaring, *Build My Gallows High* (New York: William Morrow & Company, 1946).
41. Sean McCann, "Dark Passages: Jazz and Civil Liberty in the Postwar Crime Film," in Frank Krutnik et al., *"Un-American" Hollywood: Politics and Film in the Blacklist Era* (New Brunswick, N.J.: Rutgers University Press, 2007), p. 119.
42. Shaw, "Spoiler Alert!," pp. 25–26. Shaw

refers here to Reagan's Secretary of Education William J. Bennett (1985–88), who, after also leading the Office of National Drug Control Policy under George H. W. Bush (1989–90), had recently been exposed as an inveterate gambler at casinos in Las Vegas and Atlantic City; see Katharine Q. Seelye, "Moral Crusader Says He Will Gamble No More," *New York Times*, May 6, 2003, http://www.nytimes.com/2003/05/06/us/moral-crusader-says-he-will-gamble-no-more.html (accessed February 2, 2018).

43. Shaw, "Spoiler Alert!," p. 26. Here Shaw might be referring to several different dark takes on Freemasons: that they worship Satan, that they reject Christianity, and that, more simply, they manipulate the economy.

44. Olmsted, *Real Enemies*, p 3. An important reference here is Richard Hofstadter, *The Paranoid Style in American Politics and Other Essays* (1964; Cambridge, Mass.: Harvard University Press, 1996).

45. Shaw, "Spoiler Alert!," p. 24. See also Corey Kilgannon, "Origin of the Species, from an Alien View," *New York Times*, January 8, 2010, p. MB4.

46. Shaw, "Spoiler Alert!," p. 25.

47. Geeta Dayal, "Black Flag: A Re-Formation Gone Wrong," *The Guardian*, December 6, 2013, https://www.theguardian.com/music/musicblog/2013/dec/06/black-flag-punk-band-bad-reunion (accessed January 10, 2018); Peter Schjeldahl, "Man of Many Words: The Enigmatic Art of Raymond Pettibon," *New Yorker*, February 13–20, 2017, pp. 96–97.

48. Carey Levine, *Pay for Your Pleasures: Mike Kelley, Paul McCarthy, Raymond Pettibon* (Chicago: University of Chicago Press, 2013).

49. On Pettibon's admiration for Guston, along with Goya, William Blake, and Otto Dix, among others, see Michael Kimmelman, "The Underbelly Artist," *New York Times Magazine*, October 9, 2005, https://newyorktimes.com/2005/10/09/magazine/the-underbelly-artist.html.

50. Lawrence K. Altman, "Doctor Says Nixon Has a New Attack of Phlebitis in Leg," *New York Times*, September 14, 1974, p. 1.

51. Schjeldahl, "Man of Many Words."

52. Although a relatively diminutive drawing, *Low Definition Presidency* became an important source for Kelley's series of black-and-white Paintings in Time, shown together with the Thirteen Seasons at Jablonka Galerie, Cologne, in 1994. Eva Meyer-Hermann and Lisa Gabrielle Mark, eds., *Mike Kelley*, exh. cat. (Munich and New York: Delmonico Books/Prestel, 2013), p. 193.

53. Eric Pace, "William Casey, Ex-C.I.A. Head, Is Dead at 74," *New York Times*, May 7, 1987, http://www.nytimes.com/1987/05/07/obituaries/william-casey-ex-cia-head-is-dead-at-74.html (accessed January 30, 2018).

54. Mike Kelley, "Playing with Dead Things," in *The Uncanny* (Arnhem: Sonsbeek 93; Los Angeles: Fred Hoffman, 1993), p. 7; quoted in John Miller, *Mike Kelley: Educational Complex* (Cambridge, Mass.: MIT Press, 2015), p. 16.

55. David Rimanelli, "Mike Kelley: Arenas," *Artforum* 29, no. 1 (September 1990), p. 151; for this and additional, generally positive criticism of the show, see Miller, *Educational Complex,* p. 110 n. 9.

56. Clyde Haberman, "The Trial That Unleashed Hysteria Over Child Abuse," *New York Times Retro Report*, March 9, 2014, https://www.nytimes.com/2014/03/10/us/the-trial-that-unleashed-hysteria-over-child-abuse.html (accessed January 19, 2018).

57. Ibid., and Evelyn Nieves, "Prosecutors Drop Charges in Abuse Case from Mid-80's," *New York Times*, December 3, 1994, http://www.nytimes.com/1994/12/03/nyregion/prosecutors-drop-charges-in-abuse-case-from-mid-80-s.html (accessed January 20, 2018).

58. "Isabelle Graw in conversation with Mike Kelley," in Welchman, Graw, and Vidler, *Mike Kelley*, p. 19.

59. Mike Kelley, "Repressed Architectural Memory Replaced with Psychic Reality," *ANY: Architecture New York*, no. 15 (1996), p. 38.

60. "Isabelle Graw in conversation with Mike Kelley," in Welchman, Graw, and Vidler, *Mike Kelley*, p. 19.

DISCONSOLATE TONGUES: THE VISUAL LANGUAGE OF TRAUMA AND SURVIVAL

1. Joan Didion, *The White Album* (1979; New York: Farrar, Straus and Giroux, 2009), p. 44.

2. Ibid., pp. 44–45.

3. Juliet Mitchell, "Trauma, Recognition, and the Place of Language," *Diacritics* 28, no. 4 (Winter 1998), p. 121.

4. Jenny Holzer, quoted in Benjamin Buchloh, "To Whom It May Concern," *Modern Painters* (November 2008), p. 65.

5. Ibid., p. 66.

6. Craig Owens, "The Medusa Effect, or, the Specular Ruse," *Art in America* (January 1984), p. 104; reprinted in Craig Owens, *Beyond Recognition: Representation, Power, and Culture*, edited by Scott Bryson et al. (Berkeley: University of California Press, 1992), p. 199. Emphasis original.

7. Toni Sant, *Franklin Furnace and the Spirit of the Avant-Garde: A History of the Future* (Bristol, U.K.: Intellect, 2011), p. 95.

8. Lucy Lippard, "Hot Potatoes: Art and Politics in 1980" (1981), in *Feminism–Art–Theory: An Anthology 1968–2000*, edited by Hilary Robinson (Malden, Mass.: Blackwell, 2001), p. 115.

9. Jenny Holzer, quoted in Jeanne Siegel, "Jenny Holzer's Language Games," *Arts Magazine* 60, no. 4 (December 1995), p. 64.

10. Franco Fornari, *The Psychoanalysis of War*, translated by Alenka Pfeifer (1966; Garden City, N.Y.: Anchor Books, 1974), p. xv; Mignon Nixon, "Mary Kelly's *Minimus*: Feminism's Waves," in *Mary Kelly*, edited by Mignon Nixon (Cambridge, Mass.: MIT Press, 2016), p. 179.

11. Roberta Smith, "Sounding the Alarm, in Words and Light," *New York Times*, March 12, 2009, p. C21.

12. Jenny Holzer, quoted in Buchloh, "To Whom It May Concern," p. 69.

13. Nixon, "Mary Kelly's *Minimus*," p. 176.

14. Mitchell, "Trauma, Recognition, and the Place of Language," p. 122.

15. Joshua Craze, "In the Dead Letter Office," in *Jenny Holzer: War Paintings*, edited by Kristen Asp, exh. cat. (Cologne: Buchhandlung Walther König, 2015), p. 16.

16. Barry Schwabsky, "Abjection by Other Means," *Art in America* (January 2002), p. 93.

17. Sue Williams, quoted in Nancy Spero and Sue Williams, "Sue Williams," *Bomb* 42 (Winter 1993), p. 26.

18. Sue Williams, quoted in K. K. Kozik, "Interview with Sue Williams," *Journal of Contemporary Art* 6, no. 1 (1993), p. 101.

19. Ruth Erickson, "Sue Williams," *Digital Archive*: *Take It or Leave It: Institution, Image, Ideology*, https://hammer.ucla.edu/take-it-or-leave-it/artists/sue-williams/ (accessed December 18, 2017). Prince had taken the title *Spiritual America* from a 1923 photograph by Alfred Stieglitz of a detail of a harnessed horse's castrated genitalia.

20. Williams exhibited *Spiritual America* at 303 Gallery in 1992, and Prince had a retrospective at the Whitney Museum of American Art that same year. When Prince made his first joke painting in 1985, he was living in the back room of 303 Gallery.

21. Sue Williams, quoted in in Kozik, "Interview with Sue Williams," p. 103.

22. Dan Cameron, "Sue Williams," in *Sue Williams: Art for the Institution and the Home*, edited by Rike Frank and Matthias Herrmann, exh. cat. (Cologne: König, 2003), p. 39.

23. Sue Williams, quoted in Rachel Wolff, "Fear and Fancy: A Sue Williams Retrospective Celebrates Her Grotesquely Comical Vision," *New York Magazine*, September 5, 2010, http://nymag.com/arts/art/features/67931/ (accessed August 5, 2017).

24. For further discussion of this work, see

Kathryn Olmsted's essay in this volume, pp. 158–65.
25. The proposal was rejected by the Kennedy administration and remained a secret for forty years until the documents were released to the public. The National Security Archive has published fifteen pages of the Operation Northwoods memorandum on its website; see https://nsarchive2.gwu.edu/news/20010430/northwoods.pdf.
26. Sue Williams, in conversation with Ian Alteveer and Douglas Eklund at 303 Gallery, New York, April 28, 2017.
27. Nanothermite is a composite that can be used as an explosive. Conspiracy theories have circulated that nanothermite caused the destruction of the World Trade Center, not the force of the airplanes hitting the towers.
28. Mitchell, "Trauma, Recognition, and the Place of Language," p. 132.
29. After MK-ULTRA came to light, several victims, led by Orlikow, filed a class-action lawsuit against the CIA. In October 1988, the U.S. Justice Department settled out of court with Orlikow and eight other victims for a total of $750,000, while admitting no responsibility for Cameron's experiments. Two years after Orlokow's death in 1990, the government of Canada agreed to pay Cameron's victims up to $80,000 in compensation. For more on MK-ULTRA, see John Marks, *The Search for the "Manchurian Candidate": The CIA and Mind Control* (New York: Quadrangle, 1979). For more on Dr. Cameron's Subproject 68, see chapter 1 of Naomi Klein, *The Shock Doctrine: The Rise of Disaster Capitalism* (New York: Picador, 2007).
30. Sarah Anne Johnson, quoted in Sarah Milroy, "They Were Looking for the Ideal Manchurian Candidate," *The Globe and Mail*, July 13, 2009, https://www.theglobeandmail.com/arts/they-were-looking-for-the-ideal-manchurian-candidate/article4278968/ (accessed January 10, 2018).
31. Sarah Anne Johnson, quoted in Meeka Walsh, "Containing Intimacy: The Utopic Visions of Sarah Anne Johnson," in *Wonderland: Sarah Anne Johnson, 2002–2014*, edited by Steven Matijcio, exh. cat. (Raleigh, N.C.: CAM Raleigh, 2015), p. 14.
32. Walsh, "Containing Intimacy," p. 14.
33. Andrew Berardini, "Just a Picture," in Matijcio, *Wonderland*, p. 75.

HISTORY AND CONSPIRACY

1. Webb Hubbell, *Friends in High Places: Our Journey from Little Rock to Washington, D.C.* (New York: William Morrow, 1997), p. 282.
2. Pew Research Center, "Public Trust in Government, 1958–2017," http://www.people-press.org/2017/05/03/public-trust-in-government-1958-2017/; "Americans' Trust in Mass Media Sinks to New Low," Gallup, September 14, 2016, http://www.gallup.com/poll/195542/americans-trust-mass-media-sinks-new-low.aspx.
3. *Report of the Warren Commission on the Assassination of President Kennedy* (Washington, D.C.: U.S. Government Printing Office, 1964).
4. Sheldon Appleton, "Trends: Assassinations," *Public Opinion Quarterly* 64, no. 4 (Winter 2000), p. 501.
5. See, for example, Mark Lane, *Rush to Judgment* (New York: Holt, Rinehart & Winston, 1966); Edward Jay Epstein, *Inquest: The Warren Commission and the Establishment of Truth* (New York: Viking, 1966); and Josiah Thompson, *Six Seconds in Dallas: A Microstudy of the Kennedy Assassination* (New York: Bernard Geis Associates, 1967).
6. On Oswald, see Priscilla Johnson McMillan, *Marina and Lee* (New York: Harper & Row, 1977); Jean Davison, *Oswald's Game* (New York: Norton, 1983); and Vincent Bugliosi, *Reclaiming History: The Assassination of President John F. Kennedy* (New York: Norton, 2007), pp. 513–788.
7. The film prompted Congress to pass the President John F. Kennedy Assassination Records Collection Act of 1992, which created an independent board to review the still-secret documents. The board ordered the release of all assassination-related documents within twenty-five years of the passage of the act, unless the president decided to withhold them. In October 2017, President Trump approved the release of about 2,800 previously withheld files but delayed the release of about 250 others.
8. See Christopher Andrew and Vasili Mitrokhin, *The Sword and the Shield: The Mitrokhin Archive and the Secret History of the KGB* (New York: Basic Books, 1999), pp. 225–30; and Max Holland, "The Lie That Linked CIA to the Kennedy Assassination: The Power of Disinformation," *Studies in Intelligence*, no. 11 (Fall–Winter 2001), https://www.cia.gov/library/center-for-the-study-of-intelligence/csi-publications/csi-studies/studies/fall_winter_2001/article02.html.
9. U.S. Senate Select Committee to Study Governmental Operations with Respect to Intelligence Activities, 94th Congress, 2nd session, *Final Report* [hereafter Church Committee report] (Washington, D.C.: Government Printing Office, 1976), volume 5 ("The National Security Agency and Fourth Amendment Rights"), volume 6 ("The Federal Bureau of Investigation"), volume 7 ("Covert Action").
10. Ibid., Book 2, p. 221.
11. The Castro plots are laid out in ibid., "Interim Report: Alleged Assassination Plots Involving Foreign Leaders," pp. 71–180.
12. The most important were Robert Sam Anson, *"They've Killed the President!": The Search for the Murderers of John F. Kennedy* (New York: Bantam Books, 1975) and the paperback edition of Josiah Thompson's *Six Seconds in Dallas* (New York: Berkley Pub Group, 1976).
13. Appleton, "Assassinations," p. 514.
14. Groden had acquired a copy of the film from the photo lab where it was processed. He had shown it at conferences, but it was not shown on network television until March 1975. See David R. Wrone, *The Zapruder Film: Reframing JFK's Assassination* (Lawrence: University Press of Kansas, 2003), pp. 65, 67–69.
15. See Kathryn S. Olmsted, *Real Enemies: Conspiracy Theories and American Democracy, World War I to 9/11* (New York: Oxford University Press, 2009), pp. 169-70. For the final report, see U.S. House, Select Committee on Assassinations, *The Final Assassinations Report: Report of the Select Committee on Assassinations* (New York: Bantam Books, 1979).
16. Scott Dikkers and *Onion* editors, eds., *Our Dumb Century: The Onion Presents 100 Years of Headlines from America's Finest News Source* (New York: Crown Publishers, 1999), p. 101.
17. Commission on CIA Activities within the United States, *Report to the President* (Washington, D.C.: Government Printing Office, 1975), p. 226.
18. See U.S. Senate, Select Committee on Intelligence and the Subcommittee on Health and Scientific Research of the Committee on Human Resources, *Joint Hearings on Project MKULTRA, the CIA's Program of Research in Behavioral Modification*, 95th Congress, 1st session, August 3, 1977 (Washington, D.C.: Government Printing Office, 1977); and John D. Marks, *The Search for the "Manchurian Candidate": The CIA and Mind Control* (New York: Quadrangle, 1979).
19. On the settlement, see Harvey M. Weinstein, *Psychiatry and the CIA: Victims of Mind Control* (Washington, D.C.: American Psychiatric Press, 1990), pp. 257–82.
20. Pew Research Center, "Public Trust in Government, 1958–2017."
21. Michael Kelly, "A Reporter at Large: The Road to Paranoia," *New Yorker*, June 19, 1995, p. 62. For the survey numbers, see Appleton, "Assassinations," pp. 495–522.
22. Transcript of interview with Condoleezza Rice, "CNN with Wolf Blitzer," aired September 7, 2003, available at http://transcripts.cnn.com/TRANSCRIPTS/0309/07/le.00.html.
23. *The Unknown Known*, documentary film directed by Errol Morris (2013, The Weinstein Company).

POLITICS OF HATE IN THE U.S.A.: ANTI-SEMITISM AND CONSPIRACY THEORY

1. The Illuminati, founded by Bavarian law professor Adam Weishaupt in 1776, was a secret organization whose members studied rationalistic philosophy and the humanities to achieve "illumination." Today, some mainstream historians view the Jacobins as an offshoot of the Illuminati movement, though hardly a conspiratorial one. See James Coates, "Survival of the Fittest," *Armed and Dangerous: The Rise of the Survivalist Right* (New York: Hill and Wang, 1987), p. 238.
2. James Ridgeway, *Blood in the Face: The Ku Klux Klan, Aryan Nations, Nazi Skinheads, the Rise of a New White Culture* (New York: Thunder's Mouth Press, 1990), pp. 46–47. Some historians contend that French political police forged the Simonini letter, written in 1806, to turn Napoleon I against French Jews. See Richard Abanes, "The International Jew," *American Militias: Rebellion, Racism, and Religion* (Downers Grove, Ill.: InterVarsity Press, 1996), p. 136.
3. David H. Bennett, "Nativism in Early American History: A Colonial Heritage," in *The Party of Fear: The American Far Right from Nativism to the Militia Movement* (New York: Vintage Books, 1995), p. 24.
4. Ibid., pp. 24–25.
5. Ridgeway, *Blood in the Face*, p. 60.
6. Abanes, "The International Jew," *American Militias*, pp. 138–39.
7. Ridgeway, *Blood in the Face*, p. 50.
8. Ibid.
9. Michael Barkun, "The Emergence of Christian Identity," *Religion and the Racist Right: The Origins of the Christian Identity Movement* (Chapel Hill: University of North Carolina Press, 1994), p. 34.
10. Ridgeway, *Blood in the Face*, pp. 60–61.
11. Barkun, "The Emergence of Christian Identity," *Religion and the Racist Right*, p. 34.
12. John Wilson, the son of a radical Irish weaver, set forth this belief in an 1840 book titled *Lectures on Our Israelitish Origin*, and Edward Hine definitively reshaped it in his 1871 book *The English Nation Identified with the Lost House of Israel by Twenty-Seven Identifications*. Barkun, "Origins of British-Israelism," *Religion and the Racist Right*, pp. 6–12.
13. Barkun, "Christian Identity's Millenarian Vision of History," *Religion and the Racist Right*, pp. 112–15.
14. Coates, "Identity Christians," *Armed and Dangerous*, p. 93.
15. Barkun, "The Emergence of Christian Identity," *Religion and the Racist Right*, pp. 29–38.
16. Ridgeway, *Blood in the Face*, p. 62.
17. Barkun, "The Emergence of Christian Identity," *Religion and the Racist Right*, p. 62.
18. Ridgeway, *Blood in the Face*, p. 64–65.
19. Barkun, "Creating Christian Identity, 1937–1975," *Religion and the Racist Right*, p. 53.
20. *Blood in the Face*, pp. 62–64. See also "William Dudley Pelley, 75, Dies; Founded Fascist Silver Shirts," *New York Times*, July 2, 1965.
21. An entry titled "In Memory of Gerald L. K. Smith, a Prophet and a Patriot (1898–1976)" on the White Supremacist website *The Cross and the Flag* attributes the quote "Communism is Jewish" to Smith; http://www.thecrossandflag.com/ (accessed October 19, 2017). For Smith's theory that Roosevelt did not die, See Ridgeway, *Blood in the Face*, pp. 68–69.
22. Ridgeway, *Blood in the Face*, pp. 65–72.
23. Barkun, "Creating Christian Identity, 1937–1975," *Religion and the Racist Right*, p. 55.
24. Barkun, "The Emergence of Christian Identity," *Religion and the Racist Right*, pp. 60–65.
25. Kevin Flynn and Gary Gerhardt, "Alan Berg: the Man You Love to Hate," *The Silent Brotherhood* (New York: Signet Books, 1995), p. 229.
26. Barkun, "Demonization of the Jews," *Religion and the Racist Right*, pp. 171–72.
27. The term is Goff's. See James Coates, "Survival of the Fittest," *Armed and Dangerous*, p. 243.
28. Ibid., pp. 242–45.
29. The Christian Coalition initiated the political strategy of "flying below the radar," that is, putting local and regional elections ahead of national ones.
30. Pat Roberston, "The World Order Agenda," *A New World Order* (Dallas: World Publishing, 1991) p. 8.
31. Michael Lind, quoted in Abanes, "Infiltration of Hate," *American Militias*, p. 197.
32. Pat Robertson, quoted in Gustav Neibuhr, "Pat Robertston Says He Intended No Anti-Semitism in Book He Wrote Four Years Ago," *New York Times*, March 4, 1995, http://www.nytimes.com/1995/03/04/us/pat-robertston-says-he-intended-no-anti-semitism-in-book-he-wrote-four-years-ago.html (accessed October 19, 2017).
33. Robertson, *New World Order*, pp. 71, 180.
34. Barkun, "The Politics of Ultimacy," *Religion and the Racist Right*, p. 247.
35. Laird Wilcox, quoted in Abanes, "Anatomy of a Conspiracy," *American Militias*, p. 105.
36. Abanes, "Anatomy of a Conspiracy," *American Militias*, p. 101.

BEYOND THE GRASSY KNOLL

Epigraph: Ishmael Reed, *Mumbo Jumbo* (New York: Scribner, 1972). Robert Anton Wilson and Robert Shea unintentionally misquoted this line as the epigraph to *The Eye in the Pyramid*, the first novel in *The Illuminatus! Trilogy*.
1. The chart of conspiracies circulated without attribution for months, but in March 2018, a thirty-three-year-old artist named Dylan Louis Monroe came forward to claim its authorship.
2. Robert Shea and Robert Anton Wilson, *The Eye in the Pyramid*, in *The Illuminatus! Trilogy* (New York: Dell, 1984), p. 200, quoted in Mark Fenster, *Conspiracy Theories: Secrecy and Power in American Culture* (Minneapolis: University of Minnesota Press, 2008), p. 171.
3. Robert Anton Wilson, *The Illuminati Papers* (Berkeley, Calif.: Ronin Publishing, 1990), p. 2, quoted in Fenster, *Conspiracy Theories*, p. 168.
4. Fenster, *Conspiracy Theories*, 179.
5. Philip K. Dick, "How To Build a Universe That Doesn't Fall Apart Two Days Later," a 1978 speech anthologized in Lawrence Sutin, ed., *The Shifting Realities of Philip K. Dick: Selected Literary and Philosophical Writings*, quoted in Maria Popova, "How to Build a Universe: Philip K. Dick on Reality, Media Manipulation, and Human Heroism," https://www.brainpickings.org/2013/09/06/how-to-build-a-universe-philip-k-dick/ (accessed February 24, 2018).

SELECTED BIBLIOGRAPHY

Althusser, Louis. "Ideology and Ideological State Apparatuses (Notes towards an Investigation)." Originally published in *La Pensée* (1970). In *Lenin and Philosophy and Other Essays*. New York: Monthly Review Press, 1971.

Asp, Kristen, ed. *Jenny Holzer: War Paintings*. Exh. cat., Museo Correr, Venice. Cologne: König, 2015.

Baerwaldt, Wayne, and Tim Price. *Sarah Anne Johnson: House on Fire*. Calgary, Canada: Illingworth Kerr Gallery, 2009.

Bailey, Robert. "Unknown Knowns: Jenny Holzer's Redaction Paintings and the History of the War on Terror." *October* 142 (Fall 2012), pp. 144–61.

Baldwin, James. "An Open Letter to My Sister, Angela Davis," November 19, 1970. *The New York Review of Books*, January 7, 1971.

Baltrip-Balagás, Ayana. "The Art of Self-Defense." *Print* 60 (March–April 2006), pp. 84–89.

Banks, Eric, and Sarah Valdez, eds. *Rachel Harrison: Museum with Walls*. Exh. cat., Center for Curatorial Studies, Bard College, Annandale-on-Hudson, N.Y.; Whitechapel Gallery, London; and Portikus, Frankfurt am Main. Annandale-on-Hudson, N.Y.: Center for Curatorial Studies, Bard College, 2010.

Bartman, William S., and Miyoshi Barosh, eds. *Mike Kelley*. New York: A.R.T. Press, 1992.

Berardini, Andrew. "Lutz Bacher: In Pieces and All At Once." *Art in America* (March 2012), pp. 124–30.

Bierut, Michael. "Mark Lombardi and the Ecstasy of Conspiracy." *Design Observer* (November 24, 2003).

Blake, Nayland. *Lutz Bacher*. New York: Simon Watson, 1990.

Bovier, Lionel, ed. *Sue Williams*. Zurich: JRP Ringier, 2015.

Buchloh, Benjamin. "To Whom It May Concern." *Modern Painters* (November 2008), pp. 62–69.

Bull, Anna Cento, and Adalgisa Giorgio, eds. *Speaking Out and Silencing: Culture, Society and Politics in Italy in the 1970s*. London: Legenda, 2006.

Cameron, Dan, Michael Duncan, and Robert Storr. *Peter Saul*. Exh. cat., Orange County Museum of Art, Newport Beach, Calif., and other venues. Ostfildern, Germany: Hatje Cantz, 2008.

Campens, Angelique, Erica Cooke, and Steven Lam. *For Reasons of State*. Exh. cat. New York: Whitney Museum of American Art, 2008.

Chau, Christina. "Kinetic Systems: Jack Burnham and Hans Haacke." *Contemporaneity: Historical Presence in Visual Culture* 3, no. 1 (2014), pp. 63–75.

Chevrier, Jean-François. Öyvind *Fahlström: Another Space for Painting*. Exh. cat. Barcelona: Museu d'Art Contemporani de Barcelona, 2000.

Constantine, Alex, ed. *The Essential Mae Brussell: Investigations of Fascism in America*. Port Townsend, Wash.: Feral Press, 2014.

Corn, David. "Is There Really a 'Secret Team.'" *Nation*, July 2, 1988, p. 10.

Cornell, Lauren, Julia Bryan-Wilson, and Omar Kholeif. *Trevor Paglen*. New York: Phaidon Press, 2018.

Corrin, Lisa, and Peter Schjeldahl. *Jane and Louise Wilson*. Exh. cat. London: Serpentine Gallery, 1999.

Crimp, Douglas, with Adam Rolston. *AIDS Demo Graphics*. Seattle: Bay Press, 1990.

Darnton, Robert. "The Stasi Files." In *Ctrl [Space]: Rhetorics of Surveillance from Bentham to Big Brother*, edited by Thomas Y. Levin. Exh. cat., ZKM Center for Art and Media, Karlsruhe, Germany. Cambridge, Mass.: MIT Press, 2002.

Dean, Jodi. *Publicity's Secret: How Technocracy Capitalizes on Democracy*. Ithaca: Cornell University Press, 2002.

DeHaven-Smith, Lance. *Conspiracy Theory in America*. Austin: University of Texas Press, 2013.

Deutsche, Rosalyn. "Property Values: Hans Haacke, Real Estate, and the Museum." In *Evictions: Art and Spatial Politics*. Chicago: Graham Foundation for Advanced Studies in the Fine Arts; Cambridge, Mass.: MIT Press, 1996.

Didion, Joan. *The White Album*. 1979. New York: Farrar, Straus and Giroux, 2009.

Dikeou, Devon. "Rachel Harrison: The Look of Dress-Separates; Greene Naftali, New York, New York." *zingmagazine* 4 (1997), pp. 244–47.

Doherty, Claire, and Jeremy Millar. *Jane and Louise Wilson*. London: Ellipsis, 2000.

Donaldson, Jeff R. "AfriCOBRA Manifesto? 'Ten in Search of a Nation.'" *Nka: Journal of Contemporary African Art* 30 (Spring 2012), pp. 76–83.

Durant, Sam, ed. *Black Panther: The Revolutionary Art of Emory Douglas*. New York: Rizzoli, 2007.

Eklund, Douglas. *The Pictures Generation, 1974–1984*. Exh. cat. New York: The Metropolitan Museum of Art, 2009.

Erickson, Ruth. "Sue Williams." *Digital Archive: Take It or Leave It: Institution, Image, Ideology*. https://hammer.ucla.edu/take-it-or-leave-it/artists/sue-williams/ (accessed December 18, 2017).

Fahlström. Exh. cat. New York: Sidney Janis Gallery, 1967.

Favero, Lisa Ann. "Miami: Alessandro Balteo-Yazbeck." *Sculpture* 26, no. 8 (October 2007), pp. 75–76.

Fenster, Mark. *Conspiracy Theories: Secrecy and Power in American Culture*. Minneapolis: University of Minnesota Press, 2008.

Finkelstein, Avram. *After Silence: A History of AIDS through Its Images*. Oakland: University of California Press, 2017.

Flügge, Matthias, and Robert Fleck, eds. *Hans Haacke: For Real, Works 1959–2006*. Exh. cat., Akademie der Künste, Berlin; and Deichtorhallen, Hamburg. Düsseldorf: Richter Verlag, 2006.

Fornari, Franco. *The Psychoanalysis of War*. Translated by Alenka Pfeifer. 1966; Garden City, N.Y.: Anchor Books, 1974.

Foucault, Michel. "The Eye of Power: A Conversation with Jean-Pierre Barou and Michelle Perrot." In *Power/Knowledge:*

Selected Interviews and Other Writings 1972–1977. New York: Pantheon, 1980.

Frank, Rike, and Matthias Herrmann, eds. *Sue Williams: Art for the Institution and the Home*. Exh. cat., Secession, Vienna; and IVAM-Institut Valencià d'Art Modern, Valencia. Cologne: König, 2003.

Freedman, Carl. "Towards a Theory of Paranoia: The Science Fiction of Philip K. Dick." *Science Fiction Studies* 11, no. 1 (March 1984), pp. 15–24.

Ginsborg, Paul. *A History of Contemporary Italy: Society and Politics, 1943–1988*. New York: Palgrave Macmillan, 2003.

Godfrey, Mark, and Zoé Whitley, eds. *Soul of a Nation: Art in the Age of Black Power*. Exh. cat., Tate Modern, London, and other venues. London: Tate, 2017.

Golden, Deven. "Mark Lombardi." *Bomb* (Fall 2003), pp. 102–3.

Goldstone, Patricia. *Interlock: Art, Conspiracy, and the Shadow Worlds of Mark Lombardi*. Berkeley, Calif.: Counterpoint, 2015.

Grachos, Louis, and Susan Fisher Sterling. *Sarah Charlesworth: A Retrospective*. Exh. cat. Santa Fe: SITE Santa Fe, 1997.

Guilbaut, Serge. *How New York Stole the Idea of Modern Art: Abstract Expressionism, Freedom, and the Cold War*. Chicago: University of Chicago Press, 1983.

Haacke, Hans. *Hans Haacke. Volume II, Works 1978–1983*. Exh. cat. Eindhoven: Stedelijk Van Abbemuseum; London: Tate Gallery, 1984.

Hertz, Richard. *Jack Goldstein and the CalArts Mafia*. Ojai, Calif.: Minneola Press, 2003.

Hobbs, Robert, et al. *Mark Lombardi: Global Networks*. Exh. cat. New York: Independent Curators International, 2003.

Hobbs, Robert, and Tan Lin. *Mark Lombardi: Preparatory Drawings 1994–2000*. Exh. cat. Brooklyn, N.Y.: Pierogi, 2003.

Hofstadter, Richard. "The Paranoid Style in American Politics." In *The Paranoid Style in American Politics and Other Essays*. 1964. Cambridge, Mass.: Harvard University Press, 1996.

Hollander, Charles. "Pynchon, JFK, and the CIA: Magic Eye Views of *The Crying of Lot 49*." *Pynchon Notes*, nos. 40–41 (Spring–Fall 1997), pp. 61–106.

Holzer, Jenny. *Endgame*. Exh. cat., Skarstedt Gallery, New York; Spruth Magers, Berlin. Berlin: Distanz Verlag, 2012.

——. *Redaction Paintings*. Exh. cat. New York: Cheim & Read, 2006.

Isikoff, Michael. "Conspiracy Theories Find Foster Case Hard to Resist: Rumors Abound Despite Lack of Supporting Evidence." *Washington Post*, March 13, 1994, p. A10.

Jameson, Frederic. "Cognitive Mapping." In *Marxism and the Interpretation of Culture*, edited by Cary Nelson and Lawrence Grossberg. Urbana: University of Illinois Press, 1988, pp. 347–60.

Jappe, Anselm. *Guy Debord*. Berkeley: University of California Press, 1999.

Jeremy Blake: Winchester. Exh. cat. Madrid: Museo Nacional Centro de Arte Reina Sofía, 2003.

Jeremy Blake: Winchester Trilogy and Reading Ossie Clark. Exh. cat. Burgos, Spain: Centro de Arte Caja de Burgos, 2004.

Jones-Hogu, Barbara. "The History, Philosophy, and Aesthetics of AfriCOBRA." In *Afri-Cobra III*. Amherst: University of Massachusetts, 1973. Revised by the author in 2008. http://areachicago.org/the-history-philosophy-and-aesthetics-of-africobra/ (accessed April 23, 2018).

Kelly, Michael. "A Reporter at Large: The Road to Paranoia." *New Yorker*, June 19, 1995, pp. 60–75.

Killen, Andreas. *1973 Nervous Breakdown: Watergate, Warhol, and the Birth of Post-Sixties America*. New York: Bloomsbury, 2006.

Klein, Naomi. *The Shock Doctrine: The Rise of Disaster Capitalism*. New York: Picador, 2007.

Knight, Peter. *Conspiracy Culture: From the Kennedy Assassination to The X-Files*. London: Routledge, 2000.

——, ed. *Conspiracy Nation: The Politics of Paranoia in Postwar America*. New York: New York University Press, 2002.

Koenig, Kasper, ed. *Hans Haacke: Framing and Being Framed, 7 Works, 1970–75*. Halifax: Nova Scotia College of Art and Design; New York: New York University Press, 1975.

Kotz, Liz. "Sex with Strangers: Lutz Bacher." *Artforum* 31, no. 1 (September 1992), pp. 83–85.

Kozik, K. K. "Interview with Sue Williams." *Journal of Contemporary Art* 6, no. 1 (1993), pp. 99–108.

Le Blanc, Aleca. "Alessandro Balteo-Yazbeck: Christopher Grimes Gallery," *ArtNexus* 8, no. 74 (September–November 2009), p. 116.

Lepdor, Catherine, and Nicole Schweizer. *Alfredo Jaar: La politique des images*. Exh. cat., Musée Cantonal des Beaux-Arts, Lausanne. Zurich: JRP Ringier, 2007.

Lethem, Jonathan. *They Live*. Berkeley: Soft Skull Press, 2010.

Lewis, Richard Warren. *The Scavengers and Critics of the Warren Report—The Endless Paradox, Based on an Investigation by Lawrence Schiller*. New York: Delacorte Press, 1967.

Leydier, Richard. "Saul's Stupid Painting." *Art Press* 275 (January 2002), pp. 9–25.

Lin, Tan. "Following the Money." *Art in America* (November 2003), pp. 142–47, 177.

Lippard, Lucy. "The Art Workers' Coalition: Not a History." *Studio International* (November 1970). In Lucy Lippard. *Get the Message? A Decade of Art for Social Change*. New York: E. P. Dutton, 1984, pp. 10–19.

Lord, Catherine, ed. *CalArts: Skeptical Beliefs*. Exh. cat. Newport Beach, Calif.: Newport Harbor Art Museum; Chicago: Renaissance Society, 1988.

Lumley, Robert. *States of Emergency: Cultures of Revolt in Italy from 1968 to 1978*. London: Verso, 1990.

MacQueen, Kathleen. "The Strength to See: A Portrait of Alfredo Jaar as a Young Seer in Search of Ways to Bridge the Divides between Perception, Representation and Recovery." *Flash Art* 290 (May–June 2013), pp. 122–26.

Marks, John D. *The Search for the "Manchurian Candidate": The CIA and Mind Control*. New York: Quadrangle, 1979.

Matijcio, Steven, ed. *Wonderland: Sarah Anne Johnson, 2002–2014*. Exh. cat. Raleigh, N.C.: CAM Raleigh, 2015.

Menick, John. "The Art of Forgetting: Speculative Archive's *It's Not My Memory of It*." *Parachute* 118 (July–August 2005), p. 119.

Meyer-Hermann, Eva, and Lisa Gabrielle Mark, eds. *Mike Kelley*. Exh. cat., Stedelijk Museum, Amsterdam, and other venues. Munich and New York: Delmonico Books/Prestel, 2013.

Milazzo, Richard. *Peter Nagy: Entertainment Erases History, Works 1982 to 2004 to the Present*. Brooklyn, N.Y.: Eisbox Projects, 2014.

Miller, John. *Mike Kelley: Educational Complex*. Cambridge, Mass.: MIT Press, 2015.

——. "Politics of Hate in the U.S.A., Part I: Repressive Tolerance." *e-flux journal* 33 (March 2012).

——. "Politics of Hate in the U.S.A., Part II: Right-Wing Mysticism and Beliefs." *e-flux journal* 34 (April 2012).

——. "Politics of Hate in the U.S.A., Part III: Posse Comitatus, Grassroots Rebellion, and Secret Societies." *e-flux journal* 35 (May 2012).

Millner, Caille. "Alfredo Jaar and the Happiness of Chile." *Los Angeles Review of Books*, December 8, 2013.

Milroy, Sarah. "They Were Looking for the Ideal Manchurian Candidate." *The Globe and Mail*, July 13, 2009.

Mitchell, Juliet. "Trauma, Recognition, and the Place of Language." *Diacritics* 28, no. 4 (Winter 1998), pp. 121–33.

Monk, Philip. *Spirit Hunter: The Haunting of American Culture by Myths of Violence; Speculations on Jeremy Blake's Winchester Trilogy*. Exh. cat. Toronto: Art Gallery of York University, 2005.

Morley, Jefferson. *The Ghost: The Secret Life of CIA Spymaster James Jesus Angleton*. New York: St. Martin's Press, 2018.

——. "Wilderness of Mirrors." *The Intercept*, January 1, 2018; https://theintercept.com/2018/01/01/the-complex-legacy-of-cia-counterintelligence-chief-james-angleton/ (accessed January 1, 2018).

Moss, David. *The Politics of Left-Wing Violence in Italy, 1969–85*. New York: St. Martin's Press, 1989.

Munder, Heike, and Ellen Seifermann, eds. *Rachel Harrison: If I Did It*. Exh. cat., Migros Museum für Gegenwartskunst, Zurich; and Kunsthalle, Nuremberg. Zurich: JRP Ringier, 2007.

Newton, Huey, P. "The Minister of Defense and Supreme Commander of the Black Panther Party, Huey P. Newton's Message at Boston College—November 18, 1970." http://www.itsabouttimebpp.com/Huey_P_Newton/pdf/Huey.pdf (accessed August 29, 2017).

Öhrner, Annika. "Öyvind Fahlström: World Making." *Flash Art* 283 (March–April 2012), pp. 76–78.

Olmsted, Kathryn S. *Real Enemies: Conspiracy Theories and American Democracy, World War I to 9/11*. New York: Oxford University Press, 2009.

Ostrow, Saul. "Peter Saul." *Bomb* 104 (Summer 2008).

Owens, Craig. *Beyond Recognition: Representation, Power, and Culture*, edited by Scott Bryson et al. Berkeley: University of California Press, 1992.

Öyvind Fahlström. Exh. cat. Stockholm: Moderna Museet, 1979.

Öyvind Fahlström. Exh. cat. New York: Solomon R. Guggenheim Museum, 1982.

Paglen, Trevor. *Invisible: Covert Operations and Classified Landscapes*. New York: Aperture Foundation, 2010.

Paglen, Trevor, and A. C. Thompson. *Torture Taxi: On the Trail of the CIA's Rendition Flights*. Hoboken, N.J.: Melville House, 2008.

Pasolini, Pier Paolo, et al. "Observations on the Long Take." *October* 13 (Summer 1980), pp. 3–6.

Pécoil, Vincent. "Art's Double Agent." *Artext* 77 (Summer 2002).

Peter Saul: Fifty Years of Painting. Exh. cat. New York: Haunch of Venison, 2011.

Peter Saul: From Pop to Punk, Paintings from the '60s and '70s. Exh. cat. New York: Venus Over Manhattan, 2015.

Popova, Maria. "How to Build a Universe: Philip K. Dick on Reality, Media Manipulation, and Human Heroism." https://www.brainpickings.org/2013/09/06/how-to-build-a-universe-philip-k-dick/ (accessed February 24, 2018).

Postman, Neil. *Amusing Ourselves to Death: Public Discourse in the Age of Show Business*. New York: Viking Penguin, 1985.

Pynchon, Thomas. *The Crying of Lot 49*. New York: Penguin, 1966.

Pynchon, Thomas. *Gravity's Rainbow*. New York: Penguin, 1973.

Richard, Frances. "'Obsessive-Generous': Toward a Diagram of Mark Lombardi." Originally published on Williamsburg Quarterly website (www.wburg.com). http://www.whale.to/c/mark_lombard3.html.

Richards, Judith. "Interview with Peter Saul, November 3–4, 2009." Archives of American Art, Smithsonian Institution, Washington, D.C.

Ridgeway, James. "It's All One Big Conspiracy: Suddenly the Left Is Interested in the Right's Favorite Bugaboos—Secret Plots and the Jews." *Village Voice*, November 5, 1991, p. 19.

Ridgeway, James, and Doug Vaughan. "The Last Days of Danny Casolaro. Murder or Suicide: However You Look at It, the Story Killed Him." *Village Voice*, October 15, 1991.

Robertson, Darryl. "The Black Panther Party and the Free Breakfast for Children Program." *Black Perspectives*, February 26, 2016. https://www.aaihs.org/the-black-panther-party/ (accessed April 11, 2018).

Robinson, Hilary, ed. *Feminism—Art—Theory: An Anthology 1968–2000*. Malden, Mass.: Blackwell, 2001.

Rondeau, James, and Andrea Miller-Keller. *Cady Noland / MATRIX 130*. Exh. cat. Hartford, Conn.: Wadsworth Atheneum, 1996.

Ruf, Beatrix, ed. *Blasted Allegories: Works from the Ringier Collection*. Exh. cat., Kunstmuseum, Lucerne. Zurich: JRP Ringier, 2008.

Sanders, Neil. *Now Is the Only Thing That's Real: A Reexamination of the Manson Murders, Motives, and Mythos*. Nottingham, U.K.: Number Six Dance Publishing, 2017.

Sant, Toni. *Franklin Furnace and the Spirit of the Avant-Garde: A History of the Future*. Bristol, U.K.: Intellect, 2011.

Sarah Charlesworth: Modern History. Exh. cat. Edinburgh: New 57 Gallery, 1979.

Schimmel, Paul. *Helter Skelter: L.A. Art in the 1990s*. Exh. cat. Los Angeles: Museum of Contemporary Art, 1992.

Schneider, Eckhard, ed. *Jenny Holzer: Truth before Power*. Exh. cat. Bregenz, Austria: Kunsthaus Bregenz, 2004.

Schwabsky, Barry. "Abjection by Other Means." *Art in America* (January 2002), pp. 92–95.

Sciascia, Leonardo. *The Moro Affair; and, the Mystery of Majorana*. New York: New York Review Books, 2004.

Scott, Andrea K. "Rachel Harrison." *4 Columns* (June 7, 2017). http://www.4columns.org/scott-andrea-k/rachel-harrison (accessed April 11, 2018).

Sedgwick, Eve Kosofsky. *Touching Feeling: Affect, Pedagogy, Performativity*. Durham, N.C.: Duke University Press, 2003.

Shapira, Ian, and Michael E. Miller. "New Batch of JFK Assassination Files: Oswald in Mexico City and the Watergate Burglars." *Washington Post*, November 4, 2017.

Shea, Robert, and Robert Anton Wilson. *The Illuminatus! Trilogy: The Eye in the Pyramid, The Golden Apple, Leviathan*. New York: Dell, 1984.

Siegel, Jeanne. "Jenny Holzer's Language Games." *Arts Magazine* 60, no. 4 (December 1995), pp. 64–68.

Simon, Art. *Dangerous Knowledge: The JFK Assassination in Art and Film*. Philadelphia: Temple University Press, 2013.

Skrebowkski, Luke. "All Systems Go: Recovering Hans Haacke's Systems Art." *Grey Room* 30 (Winter 2008), pp. 54–83.

Smith, Elizabeth A. T., et al. *Jenny Holzer: Protect Protect*. Exh. cat., Museum of Contemporary Art, Chicago; and Beyeler Museum, Riehen/Basel. Ostfildern, Germany: Hatje Cantz, 2008.

Smith, Richard Cándida. *Utopia and Dissent: Art, Poetry, and Politics in California.* Berkeley: University of California Press, 1995.

Smith, Roberta. "Review: 'Peter Saul: from Pop to Punk,' a Firebrand Willing to Offend." *New York Times*, March 12, 2015, p. C23.

——. "Sounding the Alarm, in Words and Light." *New York Times*, March 12, 2009, p. C21.

Spero, Nancy, and Sue Williams. "Sue Williams." *Bomb* 42 (Winter 1993), pp. 22–27.

Stabler, Albert. "Mike Kelley and the Supermax: The Traumatic Architecture of Artificial Memory." *Third Text* 30, nos. 1–2 (December 22, 2016), pp. 27–42.

Stallabrass, Julian. "Negative Dialectics in the Google Era: A Conversation with Trevor Paglen." *October* 138 (Fall 2011), pp. 3–14.

Steiner, Rochelle, et al. *Sarah Charlesworth*. Exh. cat. Munich and New York: DelMonico Books/Prestel, 2017.

Stillman, Steel. "In the Studio: Wayne Gonzales." *Art in America* (December 2009).

Storr, Robert. "An Interview with Mike Kelley." *Art in America* (June 1994), pp. 90–93.

Sunstein, Cass R., and Adrian Vermule. "Conspiracy Theories: Causes and Cures." *Journal of Political Philosophy* 17, no. 2 (2009), pp. 202–27.

Sussman, Elizabeth. "Rachel Harrison: Hessel Museum of Art and CCS Galleries at Bard College, Annandale-on-Hudson, New York." *Artforum* 48, no. 3 (November 2009), pp. 222–23.

Talbot, David. *The Devil's Chessboard: Allen Dulles, the CIA, and the Rise of America's Secret Government.* New York: Harper Perennial, 2016.

Taylor, Alex J. "Unstable Motives: Propaganda, Politics, and the Late Work of Alexander Calder." *American Art* 26, no. 1 (Spring 2012), pp. 25–47.

Taylor, Paul. "Interview with Hans Haacke." *Flash Art* 126 (February–March 1986), pp. 39–41.

Teagle, Rachel. "Cerca Series: Jeremy Blake." Exh. brochure. San Diego: Museum of Contemporary Art, 2002.

Teasdale, Parry D. *Videofreex: America's First Pirate TV Station and the Catskills Collective That Turned It On*. Hensonville, N.Y.: Black Dome, 1999.

Terranova, Clarissa. "Systems and Automatisms: Jack Burnham, Stanley Cavell, and the Evolution of a Neoliberal Aesthetic." *Leonardo* 47, no. 1 (2014), pp. 57–62.

Trillin, Calvin. "A Reporter at Large: The Buffs." *New Yorker*, June 10, 1967, pp. 41–71.

Valdez, Sarah. "Political Graphics: The Revolution Will Be Visualized." *Art in America* (June–July 2008), pp. 106–8.

Walker, Jesse. *The United States of Paranoia: A Conspiracy Theory*. New York: HarperCollins, 2013.

Wallis, Brian, ed. *Hans Haacke: Unfinished Business*. Exh. cat. New York: New Museum of Contemporary Art, 1986.

Watson, Elizabeth K. "London Seen." *International Review of African-American Art* 22, no. 3 (2009), pp. 38–39.

Wayne Gonzales. Exh. cat. Málaga, Spain: Centro de Arte Contemporáneo de Málaga, 2011.

Wayne Gonzales: Light to Dark / Dark to Light. Exh. cat. New Orleans: New Orleans Museum of Art, 2011.

Weil, Benjamin, and Mitchell Schwarzer. *Jeremy Blake: Winchester*. Exh. cat. San Francisco: San Francisco Museum of Modern Art, 2005.

Willman, Skip. "Traversing the Fantasies of the JFK Assassination: Conspiracy and Contingency in Don DeLillo's *Libra*." *Contemporary Literature* 39, no. 3 (Autumn 1998), pp. 405–33.

Wilson, Robert Anton, and Miriam John Hill. *Everything Is Under Control: Conspiracies, Cults, and Cover-Ups*. New York: William Morrow Paperbacks, 1998.

Wolff, Rachel. "Fear and Fancy: A Sue Williams Retrospective Celebrates Her Grotesquely Comical Vision." *New York Magazine*, September 5, 2010.

Zorach, Rebecca. "'Dig the Diversity in Unity': AfriCOBRA's Black Family." *Afterall* 28 (Autumn–Winter 2011), pp. 102–11.

——. "Interview with Gerald Williams." https://never-the-same.org/interviews/gerald-williams/ (accessed January 8, 2018).

INDEX

Page numbers in *italics* refer to illustrations.

PHOTOGRAPH CREDITS

Front cover: © Peter Saul. Courtesy Mary Boone Gallery, New York; **back cover:** © 2018 Wayne Gonzales. Courtesy Stephen Friedman Gallery, London; **endpapers:** Courtesy Lutz Bacher and Greene Naftali, New York. Image © Metropolitan Museum of Art; **p. 3:** © Sue Williams. Courtesy 303 Gallery, New York; **p. 13:** Art © Mike Kelley Foundation for the Arts. All Rights Reserved / Licensed by VAGA, New York, NY, photo by Michael Tropea

Introduction
Fig. 1: © The Estate of Garry Winogrand. Courtesy Fraenkel Gallery, San Francisco; **fig. 2:** Courtesy John W. Knott, Jr., Bookseller; **fig. 3:** Lorne Bair Rare Books; **fig. 4:** Columbia Picture / Photofest © Columbia Pictures; **fig. 5:** © The Estate of Jacques Lowe, All Rights Reserved; **fig. 6:** Burton Constable Foundation; **fig. 7:** © 2018 Banco de México Diego Rivera Frida Kahlo Museums Trust, Mexico, D.F. / Artists Rights Society (ARS), New York; **fig. 8:** Artwork © 2018 The Andy Warhol Foundation for the Visual Arts, Inc. / Licensed by ARS. Image © Metropolitan Museum of Art; **fig. 9:** © Conner Family Trust; **fig. 10:** © Gerhard Richter 2018 (0001)

Wake Up! Art and Citizen Journalism
Fig. 11: Image © Metropolitan Museum of Art; **figs. 12, 13:** © 2018 Emory Douglas / Artists Rights Society (ARS), New York. Photo courtesy Emory Douglas / Art Resource, NY; **fig. 14:** Courtesy the Center for the Study of Political Graphics; **fig. 15:** Courtesy Special Collections, University Library, University of California Santa Cruz. Pirkle Jones Photographs; **fig. 16:** © 2018 Emory Douglas / Artists Rights Society (ARS), New York; **fig. 17:** Image © Metropolitan Museum of Art, photo by Heather Johnson; **fig. 18:** Private Collection / Bridgeman Images; **figs. 19–21:** © Hans Haacke / Artists Rights Society (ARS), New York. Courtesy Hans Haacke and Paula Cooper Gallery, New York; **fig. 22:** Image and Artwork © 2018 The Andy Warhol Foundation for the Visual Arts, Inc. / Licensed by ARS; **p. 32 (top left):** © 2018 Emory Douglas / Artists Rights Society (ARS), New York. Photo courtesy Emory Douglas / Art Resource, NY; **pp. 32 (top right, bottom right, bottom left), 33:** © 2018 Emory Douglas / Artists Rights Society (ARS), New York. Image © Metropolitan Museum of Art, photo by Eugenia Burnett Tinsley; **p. 34:** © Videofreex. Courtesy Video Data Bank, www.vdb.org, School of the Art Institute of Chicago; **p. 35:** Photograph © 2018 courtesy The David and Alfred Smart Museum of Art, The University of Chicago, Gerald Williams, and Kavi Gupta, Chicago; **p. 36:** © Peter Saul. Courtesy Mary Boone Gallery, New York; **p. 37:** © Peter Saul. Courtesy David Nolan Gallery, New York; **p. 38 (left):** Image © Metropolitan Museum of Art; **pp. 40–41:** © 2018 Sharon Avery-Fahlström. Image © Metropolitan Museum of Art, photo by Peter Zeray; **pp. 42–43:** © Hans Haacke / Artists Rights Society (ARS), New York. Courtesy Hans Haacke and Paula Cooper Gallery, New York

"A Wilderness of Mirrors": Conspiracy and Identity
Fig. 23: © The Richard Avedon Foundation. Image © Metropolitan Museum of Art; **fig. 24:** Image © Metropolitan Museum of Art, photo by Heather Johnson; **fig. 25:** © 1965 Wes Wilson; **fig. 26:** © 2018 Douglas Huebler, courtesy Darcy Huebler / Artists Rights Society (ARS), New York. Image © Metropolitan Museum of Art; **fig. 27:** © 2018 Lawrence Weiner / Artists Rights Society (ARS), New York; **fig. 28:** Courtesy Photofest; **fig. 29:** Courtesy The Richard Nixon Presidential Library and Museum (National Archives and Records Administration); **fig. 30:** © 2018 Cady Noland. Photo: Allen Phillips / Wadsworth Atheneum; **fig. 31:** © 2018 Cady Noland. Digital Image © The Museum of Modern Art / Licensed by SCALA / Art Resource, NY; **fig. 32:** Courtesy Photofest; **fig. 33, 34:** © 2018 Wayne Gonzales; **fig. 35:** © 2018 Artists Rights Society (ARS), New York / VG Bild-Kunst, Bonn. Image © Metropolitan Museum of Art; **pp. 60–61:** Courtesy Lutz Bacher and Greene Naftali, New York. Image © Metropolitan Museum of Art; **pp. 62–63:** © The Estate of Sarah Charlesworth. Image © Metropolitan Museum of Art; **pp. 64–65:** Courtesy Alfredo Jaar and Galerie Lelong, New York; **p. 66 (top):** Courtesy Peter Nagy and Magenta Plains, New York. Image © Metropolitan Museum of Art, photo by Mark Morosse; **p. 66 (bottom):** Courtesy Peter Nagy and Magenta Plains, New York; **p. 67:** © 2018 Cady Noland. Photo: Ringier Collection, Switzerland, © Jessica Pooch; **pp. 68, 69 (top), 70, 71:** Courtesy Rachel Harrison and Greene Naftali, New York, photo by Oren Slor; **p. 69 (middle right, bottom right):** Courtesy Rachel Harrison and Greene Naftali, New York, photo by Rachel Harrison; **p. 69 (middle left):** Courtesy Rachel Harrison and Greene Naftali, New York; **p. 72:** © 2018 Wayne Gonzales. **p. 73:** © 2018 Wayne Gonzales. Courtesy Stephen Friedman Gallery, London; **p. 74:** © Jane and Louise Wilson. Courtesy 303 Gallery, New York; **p. 75:** © The Estate of Jeremy Aaron Blake

The Artist as Researcher
Fig. 36: Stephen Crowley / The New York Times / Redux; **figs. 37–39:** Courtesy Photofest; **fig. 40:** Courtesy Peter Nagy and Magenta Plains, New York; **fig. 41:** Image © Metropolitan Museum of Art, photo by Heather Johnson; **fig. 42:** Courtesy the Gretchen Bender Estate and OSMOS, photo by Andreas Rossetti; **fig. 43:** From United States. President's Special Review Board, Report of the President's Special Review Board, Superintendent of Documents, U.S. Government Printing Office, Washington, DC, 1987, p. C-17. Image © The Metropolitan Museum of Art, photo by Heather Johnson; **fig. 44:** Courtesy The Lombardi Family and Pierogi Gallery. Image © Metropolitan Museum of Art, photo by Oi-Cheng Lee; **fig. 45:** © Walid Raad. Courtesy Paula Cooper Gallery, New York; **fig. 46:** Courtesy Judicial Watch; **fig. 47:** Courtesy Alessandro Balteo-Yazbeck and Henrique Faria, New York; **p. 86:** Art © Mike Kelley Foundation for the Arts. All Rights Reserved / Licensed by VAGA, New York, NY. Photo by Nathan Keay, © MCA Chicago; **p. 87:** Art © Mike Kelley Foundation for the Arts. All Rights Reserved / Licensed by VAGA, New York, NY, photo by Michael Tropea; **pp. 88–89:** Courtesy The Lombardi Family and Pierogi Gallery. Image © Whitney Museum of American Art, New York; **p. 90:** Courtesy The Lombardi Family and Pierogi Gallery. Image © Metropolitan Museum of Art, photo by Bruce Schwarz; **p. 91:** © Julia Meltzer and David Thorne; **pp. 92–93:** Courtesy Trevor Paglen and Metro Pictures, New York; **p. 94:** © Alessandro Balteo-Yazbeck. Courtesy Alessandro Balteo-Yazbeck and Henrique Faria, New York. Photo by Arturo Sánchez; **p. 95:** © Alessandro Balteo-Yazbeck. Courtesy Alessandro Balteo-Yazbeck, Cisneros Fontanals Art Foundation and Henrique Faria, New York. Photo by Oriol Tarridas

Modern History In and Out of Context: Sarah Charlesworth's *April 21, 1978*
Fig. 48: © ANSA / Rolando Fava; **fig. 50:** © ANSA; **fig. 52:** Courtesy Pio Monti; **figs. 53–56:** © The Estate of Sarah Charlesworth; **fig. 57:** © 2018 Mimmo Rotella by SIAE. Photo: Alessandro Zambianchi, Simply.it srl, Milano; **fig. 58:** Image © Metropolitan Museum of Art, photo by Heather Johnson; **fig. 59:** Courtesy The Lombardi Family and Pierogi Gallery. Photo: Smithsonian American Art Museum, Washington, DC / Art Resource, NY

Extraterrestrials Underground and Other Artistic Sublevels in California
Fig. 60: Courtesy the California Institute of the Arts Institute Archives; **fig. 61:** General Research Division, The New York Public Library, Astor, Lenox and Tilden Foundations; **fig. 62:** © CDN / Swiss Confederation; **fig. 63:** Image © Metropolitan Museum of Art, photo by Heather Johnson; **fig. 64:** Alfredo Dagli Orti / Art Resource, NY; **fig. 65:** © The Estate of Philip Guston; **figs. 66–72:** Art © Mike Kelley Foundation for the Arts. All Rights Reserved / Licensed by VAGA, New York, NY; **fig. 73:** Art © Mike Kelley Foundation for the Arts. All Rights Reserved / Licensed by VAGA, New York, NY, photo by Nic Tenwiggenhorn; **pp. 118–19, 122–23:** © Jim Shaw. Courtesy Jim Shaw and Blum & Poe, Los Angeles / New York / Tokyo; **pp. 120–21:** © Jim Shaw. Courtesy Jim Shaw and Blum & Poe, Los Angeles / New York / Tokyo. Image © Metropolitan Museum of Art; **p. 124 (top left):** The Pierpont Morgan Library, New York; **pp. 124 (top right, bottom left), 125 (top left):** Courtesy the Collection of Christine Burgin; **p. 126:** © Tony Oursler. Image © Metropolitan Museum of Art, photo by Joseph Coscia; **p. 127:** Courtesy John Miller and Metro Pictures, New York; **pp. 128 (top left, top right), 129:** © Raymond Pettibon. Courtesy David Zwirner, New York / Hong Kong; **p. 128 (bottom left):** © Raymond Pettibon. Courtesy Raymond Pettibon and Sadie Coles HQ, London; **pp. 130–31:** © Raymond Pettibon. Courtesy David Zwirner, New York / Hong Kong, photo by Dan Bradica; **pp. 132–33:** Art © Mike Kelley Foundation for the Arts. All Rights Reserved / Licensed by VAGA, New York, NY. Photo courtesy Metro Pictures, New York; **pp. 134–35:** Art © Mike Kelley Foundation for the Arts. All Rights Reserved / Licensed by VAGA, New York, NY

Disconsolate Tongues: The Visual Language of Trauma and Survival
Fig. 74: © 2018 Jenny Holzer, member Artists Rights Society (ARS), New York. Digital Image © The Museum of Modern Art / Licensed by SCALA / Art Resource, NY; **fig. 75:** © Barbara Kruger. Courtesy Mary Boone Gallery, New York; **fig. 76:** © 2018 Jenny Holzer, member Artists Rights Society (ARS), New York. Courtesy Jenny Holzer / Art Resource, NY, photo by Mike Glier; **fig. 77:** © 2018 Jenny Holzer, member Artists Rights Society (ARS), New York. Image © Metropolitan Museum of Art, photo by Juan Trujillo; **fig. 78:** © Sue Williams. Courtesy 303 Gallery, New York. Photo by Farzad Owrang; **fig. 79:** © Richard Prince; **fig. 80:** © Sue Williams. Courtesy 303 Gallery, New York; **fig. 81:** Paul Fearn / Alamy Stock Photo; **p. 144:** © 2018 Jenny Holzer, member Artists Rights Society (ARS), New York. Courtesy Jenny Holzer / Art Resource, NY, photo by Attilio Maranzano; **p. 145:** © 2018 Jenny Holzer, member Artists Rights Society (ARS), New York. Courtesy Jenny Holzer / Art Resource, NY; **pp. 146–51:** © Sarah Anne Johnson; **pp. 152–55:** © Sue Williams. Courtesy 303 Gallery, New York

Conspiracy in Context
Page 157: © 2018 Jenny Holzer, member Artists Rights Society (ARS), New York. Courtesy Jenny Holzer / Art Resource, NY, photo by Attilio Maranzano; **fig. 82, p. 172:** © Jim Shaw. Courtesy Jim Shaw and Blum & Poe, Los Angeles / New York / Tokyo; **fig. 83:** © Sarah Anne Johnson; **fig. 84:** © 2018 Jenny Holzer, member Artists Rights Society (ARS), New York. Courtesy Jenny Holzer / Art Resource, NY, photo by Attilio Maranzano; **fig. 85:** General Research Division, The New York Public Library, Astor, Lenox and Tilden Foundations; **fig. 86:** © 2018 Dylan Louis Monroe

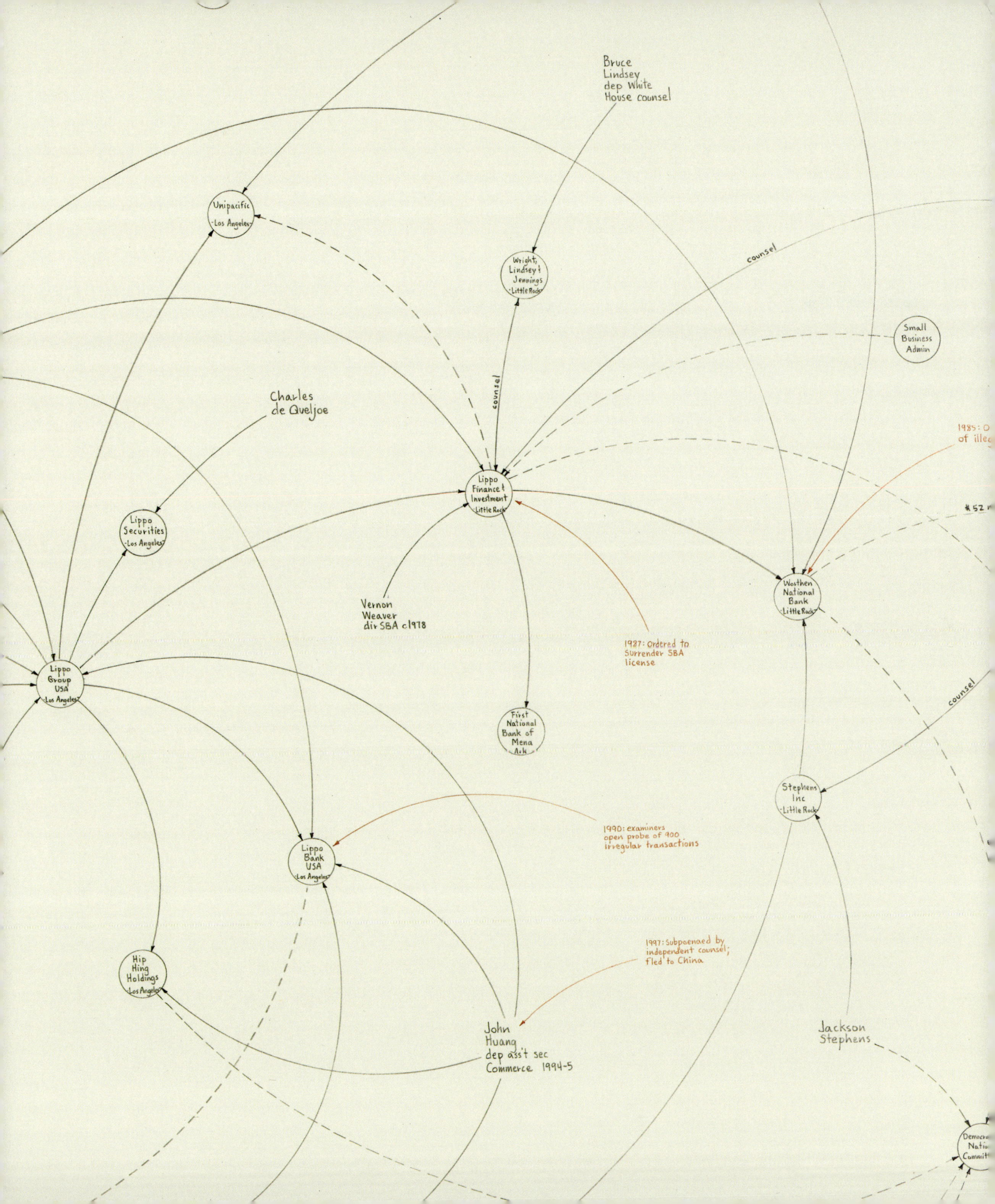

Bruce
Lindsey
dep White
House counsel
Unipacific
Los Angeles
Wright,
Lindsey &
Jennings
Little Rock
counsel
Small
Business
Admin
Charles
de Queljoe
counsel
Lippo
Finance &
Investment
Little Rock
1985: O
of illeg
Lippo
Securities
Los Angeles
#52
Vernon
Weaver
dir SBA c1978
Worthen
National
Bank
Little Rock
1987: Ordered to
surrender SBA
license
Lippo
Group
USA
Los Angeles
First
National
Bank of
Mena
Ark
counsel
Stephens
Inc
Little Rock
1990: examiners
open probe of 900
irregular transactions
Lippo
Bank
USA
Los Angeles
1997: Subpoenaed by
independent counsel;
fled to China
Hip
Hing
Holdings
Los Angeles
John
Huang
dep ass't sec
Commerce 1994-5
Jackson
Stephens

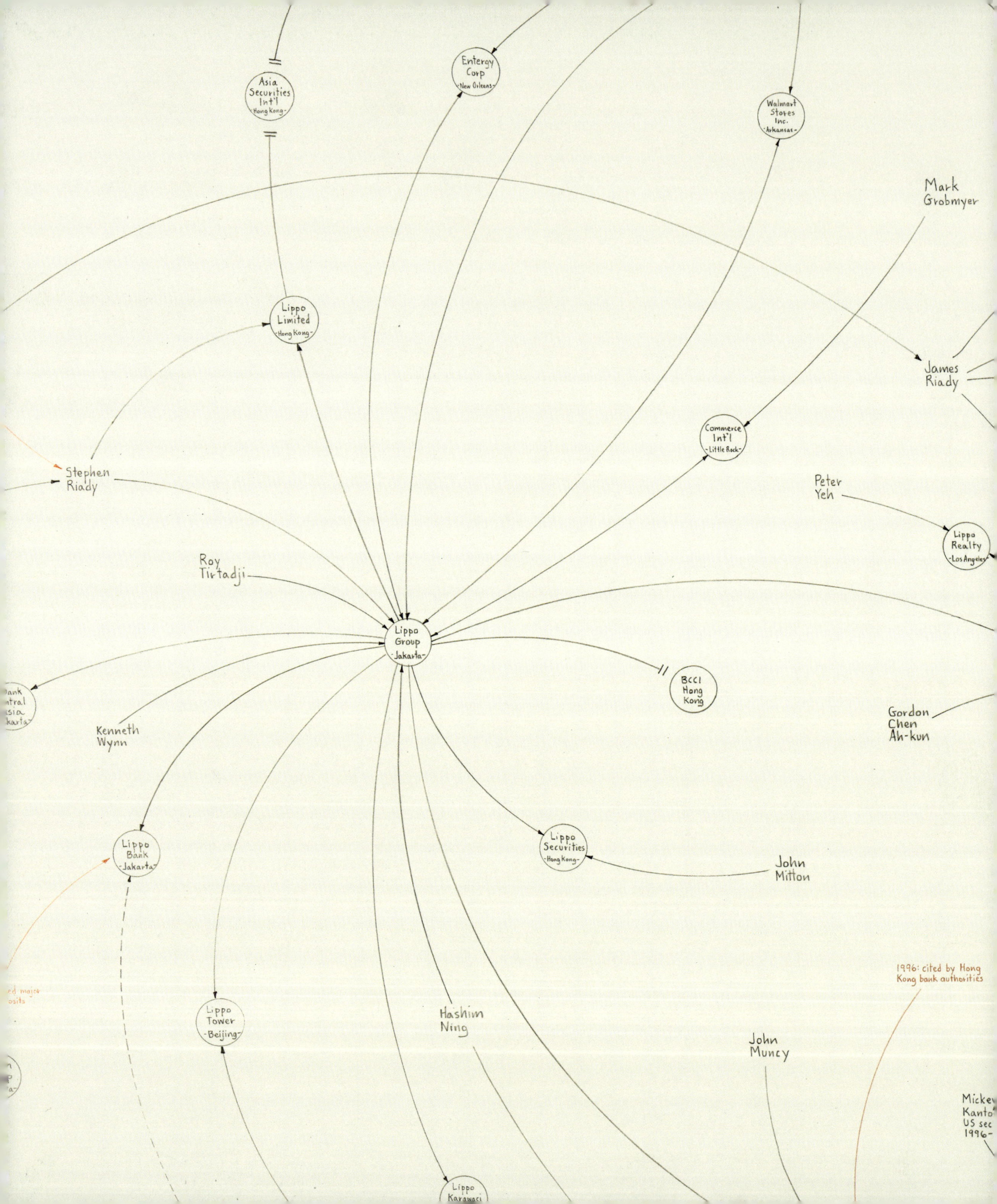
Asia Securities Int'l -Hong Kong-
Entergy Corp -New Orleans-
Walmart Stores Inc. -Arkansas-
Mark Grobmyer
Lippo Limited -Hong Kong-
James Riady
Commerce Int'l -Little Rock-
Stephen Riady
Peter Yeh
Lippo Realty -Los Angeles-
Roy Tirtadji
Lippo Group -Jakarta-
BCCI Hong Kong
Kenneth Wynn
Gordon Chen Ah-kun
Lippo Bank -Jakarta-
Lippo Securities -Hong Kong-
John Mitton
1996: cited by Hong Kong bank authorities
Lippo Tower -Beijing-
Hashim Ning
John Muncy
Lippo Karawaci